Lecture Notes in Computer Science   7060

Commenced Publication in 1973
Founding and Former Series Editors:
Gerhard Goos, Juris Hartmanis, and Jan van Leeuwen

Editorial Board

David Hutchison
  Lancaster University, UK
Takeo Kanade
  Carnegie Mellon University, Pittsburgh, PA, USA
Josef Kittler
  University of Surrey, Guildford, UK
Jon M. Kleinberg
  Cornell University, Ithaca, NY, USA
Alfred Kobsa
  University of California, Irvine, CA, USA
Friedemann Mattern
  ETH Zurich, Switzerland
John C. Mitchell
  Stanford University, CA, USA
Moni Naor
  Weizmann Institute of Science, Rehovot, Israel
Oscar Nierstrasz
  University of Bern, Switzerland
C. Pandu Rangan
  Indian Institute of Technology, Madras, India
Bernhard Steffen
  TU Dortmund University, Germany
Madhu Sudan
  Microsoft Research, Cambridge, MA, USA
Demetri Terzopoulos
  University of California, Los Angeles, CA, USA
Doug Tygar
  University of California, Berkeley, CA, USA
Gerhard Weikum
  Max Planck Institute for Informatics, Saarbruecken, Germany

Jan M. Allbeck   Petros Faloutsos (Eds.)

Motion in Games

4th International Conference, MIG 2011
Edinburgh, UK, November 13-15, 2011
Proceedings

Springer

Volume Editors

Jan M. Allbeck
George Mason University, Department of Computer Science
4400 University Drive MSN 4A5, Fairfax, VA 22030, USA
E-mail: jallbeck@gmu.edu

Petros Faloutsos
York University, Department of Computer Science and Engineering
4700 Keele Street, Toronto, ON, M3J 1P3, Canada
E-mail: pfal@cse.yorku.ca

ISSN 0302-9743   e-ISSN 1611-3349
ISBN 978-3-642-25089-7   e-ISBN 978-3-642-25090-3
DOI 10.1007/978-3-642-25090-3
Springer Heidelberg Dordrecht London New York

Library of Congress Control Number: 2011939765

CR Subject Classification (1998): I.2.1, I.2.9-11, I.6.8, H.5, I.3-4, H.3-4

LNCS Sublibrary: SL 6 – Image Processing, Computer Vision, Pattern Recognition, and Graphics

© Springer-Verlag Berlin Heidelberg 2011
This work is subject to copyright. All rights are reserved, whether the whole or part of the material is concerned, specifically the rights of translation, reprinting, re-use of illustrations, recitation, broadcasting, reproduction on microfilms or in any other way, and storage in data banks. Duplication of this publication or parts thereof is permitted only under the provisions of the German Copyright Law of September 9, 1965, in its current version, and permission for use must always be obtained from Springer. Violations are liable to prosecution under the German Copyright Law.
The use of general descriptive names, registered names, trademarks, etc. in this publication does not imply, even in the absence of a specific statement, that such names are exempt from the relevant protective laws and regulations and therefore free for general use.

Typesetting: Camera-ready by author, data conversion by Scientific Publishing Services, Chennai, India

Printed on acid-free paper

Springer is part of Springer Science+Business Media (www.springer.com)

Preface

Following the very successful Motion in Games events in 2008, 2009, and 2010, we organized the 4th International Conference on Motion in Games during November 13–15, 2011, in Edinburgh, UK.

Games have become a very important medium for both education and entertainment. Motion plays a crucial role in computer games. Characters move around, objects are manipulated or move due to physical constraints, entities are animated, and the camera moves through the scene. Even the motion of the player nowadays is used as input to games. Motion is currently studied in many different areas of research, including graphics and animation, game technology, robotics, simulation, computer vision, and also physics, psychology, and urban studies. Cross-fertilization between these communities can considerably advance the state of the art in this area. The goal of the Motion in Games conference is to bring together researchers from this variety of fields to present the most recent results and to initiate collaboration. The conference consisted of a regular paper session, a poster session, as well as presentations by a selection of internationally renowed speakers in the field of games and simulations.

November 2011

Jan M. Allbeck
Petros Faloutsos
Taku Komura

Organization

MIG2011 was organized in cooperation with ACM and ACM SIGGRAPH.

Program Chairs

Petros Faloutsos	York University, Toronto, Canada
Jan M. Allbeck	George Mason University, USA

Conference Chair

Taku Komura — University of Edinburgh, UK

Local Chair

Sethu Vijayakumar — University of Edinburgh, UK

Program Committee

Allen, Brian F.	NTU, Singapore
Badler, Norman I.	University of Pennsylvania, USA
Boulic, Ronan	EPFL, Switzerland
Cao, Yong	Virginia Tech, USA
Chrysanthou, Yiorgos	University of Cyprus, Nicosia, Cyprus
Coros, Stelian	Disney Research, Zurich, Switzerland
Courty, Nicolas	University of South Brittany, Vannes, France
Di Fiore, Fabian	University of Hasselt, Belgium
Egges, Arjan	Utrecht University, The Netherlands
Galoppo, Nico	Intel Corporation, Portland OR, USA
Geraerts, Roland	Utrecht University, The Netherlands
Kallmann, Marcelo	University of California at Merced, USA
Kapadia, Mubbasir	University of Pennsylvania, USA
Kim, HyungSeok	Konkuk University, Seoul, Korea
King, Scott	Texas A&M, Corpus Christi, USA
Lau, Manfred	Lancaster University, UK
Liu, Karen	Georgia Institute of Technology, USA
Loscos, Celine	Universitat de Girona, Spain

Manocha, Dinesh — University of North Carolina, USA
Multon, Franck — CNRS-INRIA, France
Neff, Michael — University of California, Davis, USA
Nijholt, Anton — Universiteit Twente, The Netherlands
Normoyle, Aline — University of Pennsylvania, USA
Paris, Sebastien — MAIA, Monaco
Pelachaud, Catherine — CNRS, France
Pelechano, Nuria — Universitat Politecnica de Catalunya, Spain
Pettré, Julien — IRISA, Rennes, France
Ronfard, Rémi — INRIA Rhone-Alpes, Grenoble, France
Shapiro, Ari — Institute for Creative Technologies, USC, USA
Thalmann, Daniel — Nanyang Technological University, Singapore
Yin, KangKang — National University of Singapore, Singapore
Zhang, Jian — Bournemouth University, UK
Zordan, Victor — University of California, Riverside, USA

Reviewers

Marco Ament
Robert Backman
Josh Barczak
Alejandro Beacco
Carlo Camporesi
Jian Chang
Sean Curtis
Kalin Gochev
Shihui Guo

Stephen Guy
Yazhou Huang
Dexin Jiao
Yejin Kim
Thibaut Lenaour
Pengcheng Luo
Mentar Mahmudi
Masaki Nakada
Chris Oat

Oktar Ozgen
Lin Shi
Jamie Snape
Safa Tharib
Herwin Van Welbergen
Jack Wang
James Wu
Yuting Ye
Job Zwiers

Sponsored by

Motion in Games 2011 was sponsored by the GATE project[1], the University of Edinburgh[2], and Intel[3].

---

[1] http://gate.gameresearch.nl The GATE project is funded by the Netherlands Organization for Scientific Research (NWO) and the Netherlands ICT Research and Innovation Authority (ICT Regie).
[2] http://www.ed.ac.uk/
[3] http://www.intel.com

Table of Contents

Character Animation I

Natural User Interface for Physics-Based Character Animation 1
    C. Karen Liu and Victor B. Zordan

Individualized Agent Interactions 15
    Ionut Damian, Birgit Endrass, Peter Huber, Nikolaus Bee, and Elisabeth André

A Real-Time System for Crowd Rendering: Parallel LOD and Texture-Preserving Approach on GPU 27
    Chao Peng, Seung In Park, Yong Cao, and Jie Tian

Motion Synthesis I

Feature-Based Locomotion with Inverse Branch Kinematics 39
    Mentar Mahmudi and Marcelo Kallmann

Planning Plausible Human Animation with Environment-Aware Motion Sampling 51
    Je-Ren Chen and Anthony Steed

Physically-Based Character Motion

Dynamic Balancing and Walking for Real-Time 3D Characters 63
    Ben Kenwright, Richard Davison, and Graham Morgan

Injury Assessment for Physics-Based Characters 74
    Thomas Geijtenbeek, Diana Vasilescu, and Arjan Egges

Reactive Virtual Creatures for Dexterous Physical Interactions 86
    Hironori Mitake, Shoichi Hasegawa, and Makoto Sato

Character Animation II

Building a Character Animation System 98
    Ari Shapiro

Energy-Based Pose Unfolding and Interpolation for 3D Articulated Characters 110
    He Wang and Taku Komura

Generating Avoidance Motion Using Motion Graph 120
  Masaki Oshita and Naoki Masaoka

Behavior Animation

Populations with Purpose 132
  Weizi Li and Jan M. Allbeck

Parameterizing Behavior Trees....................................... 144
  Alexander Shoulson, Francisco M. Garcia, Matthew Jones,
  Robert Mead, and Norman I. Badler

Animation Systems

Intelligent Camera Control Using Behavior Trees..................... 156
  Daniel Markowitz, Joseph T. Kider Jr., Alexander Shoulson, and
  Norman I. Badler

A Decision Theoretic Approach to Motion Saliency in Computer
Animations 168
  Sami Arpa, Abdullah Bulbul, and Tolga Capin

Many-Core Architecture Oriented Parallel Algorithm Design for
Computer Animation.. 180
  Yong Cao

Simulation of Natural Phenomena

Twisting, Tearing and Flicking Effects in String Animations 192
  Witawat Rungjiratananon, Yoshihiro Kanamori,
  Napaporn Metaaphanon, Yosuke Bando, Bing-Yu Chen, and
  Tomoyuki Nishita

Adaptive Grid Refinement Using View-Dependent Octree for
Grid-Based Smoke Simulation 204
  Rinchai Bunlutangtum and Pizzanu Kanongchaiyos

A Simple Method for Real-Time Metal Shell Simulation 216
  Zhi Dong, Shiqiu Liu, Yuntao Ou, and Yunxin Zheng

Motion Synthesis II

LocoTest: Deploying and Evaluating Physics-Based Locomotion on
Multiple Simulation Platforms 227
  Stevie Giovanni and KangKang Yin

Parametric Control of Captured Mesh Sequences for Real-Time
Animation 242
    *Dan Casas, Margara Tejera, Jean-Yves Guillemaut, and
Adrian Hilton*

Real-Time Interactive Character Animation by Parallelization of
Genetic Algorithms 254
    Min Zou

Crowd Simulation

Improved Benchmarking for Steering Algorithms 266
    *Mubbasir Kapadia, Matthew Wang, Glenn Reinman, and
Petros Faloutsos*

When a Couple Goes Together: Walk along Steering 278
    *Markéta Popelová, Michal Bída, Cyril Brom, Jakub Gemrot, and
Jakub Tomek*

Path Planning and Navigation I

Parallel Ripple Search – Scalable and Efficient Pathfinding for
Multi-core Architectures 290
    Sandy Brand and Rafael Bidarra

Hybrid Path Planning for Massive Crowd Simulation on the GPU 304
    *Aljosha Demeulemeester, Charles-Frederik Hollemeersch,
Pieter Mees, Bart Pieters, Peter Lambert, and Rik Van de Walle*

Space-Time Planning in Dynamic Environments with Unknown
Evolution 316
    Thomas Lopez, Fabrice Lamarche, and Tsai-Yen Li

Path Planning and Navigation II

Automatic Generation of Suboptimal NavMeshes 328
    Ramon Oliva and Nuria Pelechano

Roadmap-Based Level Clearing of Buildings 340
    Samuel Rodriguez and Nancy M. Amato

From Geometry to Spatial Reasoning: Automatic Structuring of 3D
Virtual Environments 353
    Carl-Johan Jorgensen and Fabrice Lamarche

Posters

Reconstructing Motion Capture Data for Human Crowd Study 365
  *Samuel Lemercier, Mathieu Moreau, Mehdi Moussaïd,
  Guy Theraulaz, Stéphane Donikian, and Julien Pettré*

A Quantitative Methodology to Evaluate Motion-Based Animation
Techniques 377
  Gutemberg Guerra-Filho, George Raphael, and Venkat Devarajan

Parallelized Incomplete Poisson Preconditioner in Cloth Simulation 389
  Costas Sideris, Mubbasir Kapadia, and Petros Faloutsos

Walk This Way: A Lightweight, Data-Driven Walking Synthesis
Algorithm... 400
  Sean Curtis, Ming Lin, and Dinesh Manocha

Long Term Real Trajectory Reuse through Region Goal Satisfaction.... 412
  *Junghyun Ahn, Stéphane Gobron, Quentin Silvestre,
  Horesh Ben Shitrit, Mirko Raca, Julien Pettré,
  Daniel Thalmann, Pascal Fua, and Ronan Boulic*

Directional Constraint Enforcement for Fast Cloth Simulation 424
  Oktar Ozgen and Marcelo Kallmann

A Comparison and Evaluation of Motion Indexing Techniques 436
  Gutemberg Guerra-Filho and Harnish Bhatia

Detecting 3D Position and Orientation of a Wii Remote Using
Webcams 448
  Jerry van den Heuvel and Jacco Bikker

Author Index.. 459

Natural User Interface for Physics-Based Character Animation

C. Karen Liu[1] and Victor B. Zordan[2]

[1] Georgia Institute of Technology
[2] University of California, Riverside
karenliu@cc.gatech.edu,
vbz@cs.ucr.edu

Abstract. Using natural user interface to interact with digital worlds is becoming commonplace in our daily life, as evidenced by the high demand for Microsoft Kinect since its launch in 2010. However, comparatively little research effort has focused in the past on harnessing these capabilities to create great applications. In this paper, we introduce unified framework for combining natural user interface and physics-based character animation. Our framework takes the form of a continuous controllable space for the combination of the two techniques. We also propose a human-in-the-loop control paradigm which allows a player or performer to sense and act for the character. With the information encapsulated in the human performance, the proposed framework accomplishes its goal in two steps: first, by recognizing and potentially modifying the performance such that it is appropriate for the given scenario; and second, by balancing interactivity and control in order to maintain both physical responsivity to the virtual world and faithfulness to the human performance.

1 Introduction

Character animation is a prevalent mechanism in media for entertainment, training, and socializing. The quality of the experience felt by the media participants often depends on the believability of the avatar's motion in the context of the virtual environment. Non-trivial interaction with the environment is a necessity to make a character appear capable and realistic as well as to allow the character to navigate an interesting world and take action to advance her own dilemma. One method for creating rich, intuitive forms of interaction is through the use of a physically simulation. In particular, a worthy goal is the generation of a physically consistent virtual world, where every aspect of the world is able to be manipulated in an interactive, physically-based manner.

To date, much research work has focused on creating virtual avatars capable of moving and manipulating in a physically simulated world. Most existing control algorithms operate at the mechanical level of the movement (e.g. compute the required joint torques) and assume that cognitive decisions (e.g. to walk or to run) are made by an external decision maker. For applications that involve real-time participants, an equally important but much less explored area is the user interface for controlling a physically simulated character. A character typically consists of more than 40 degrees of freedom (DOFs), constrained by the dynamics equations of motion and the kinematic limitations. How we design a user interface to control such a complex, high-dimensional dynamic system remains a daunting task.

Part of the problem seems to be answered by the recent development in motion input hardware, such as Microsoft Kinect. These so called *Natural User Interfaces*, in theory, are more suitable to control physically simulated characters, because they can capture higher dimensional and more expressive user's movements. However, gathering the data from the users motion only addresses the first hardware problem. The second problem, how to use the full-body motion is still very much unexplored.

Integrating real-time user performance with a physically simulated character immediately introduces two major challenges. First, due to discrepancies between the virtual and real world, the real-time performance might be unrealistic (or invalid) when directly applied to the virtual character. For example, if the performer is standing on the floor attempting to control a suspended virtual character hanging by her arms (say, to traverse a monkeybar set), the lower body motion of the performance is clearly a poor fit. Second, if the animation system is physically simulated, the character might not be able to produce the performers motion due to a lack of sophistication in control. As such, physics should only be used as necessary to capitalize on the richness of the human performance. These two challenges suggest that the control scheme must dynamically determine both the appropriate level of sensitivity to the performers motion and the level of physical responsiveness the character has to the virtual environment.

We propose a unified framework for combining natural user interface and physics-based character animation. Our framework takes the form of a continuous controllable space for the combination of the two techniques. The first challenge in this work is to devise a control method capable of combining the potentially conflicting inputs from the user's movements and physics engine. We propose to divide our control along two dimensions. On one dimension, the system can interpret the input from a human user in one of two manners, as a literal performance which is to be played through the character with little or no modification or as a symbolic motion, which is recognized and adjusted to meet the goal-based constraints of the identified behavior. Along the second dimension, the system adjusts the constraints applied to the characters motion from purely kinematic to purely dynamic. In this way, at one extreme, the character can act out the motion perfectly, ignoring internal and external influences such as balance or impacts. At the other extreme, the character will obey physical demands while attempting to accomplish the motion in a physically valid manner. To uphold flexibility, we propose to breakdown the control of the character both spatially and temporally, taking advantage of the best technique for controlling each section of the body, limb, or individual segment (body unit). That is, at any given moment, any body unit of the character is able to respond to the given situation in an appropriate manner, by following the movement symbolically or literally, dynamically or kinematically as appropriate.

2 Human-in-the-Loop Control

In Figure 1 we show our control space spanned by two axes that precisely address the two challenges mentioned in Section 1. The vertical axis reflects the first challenge on the sensitivity to the real-time user motion. At the bottom of the vertical dimension, the virtual character is extremely sensitive to the performance and literally mimics the entire pose. The control of the virtual character becomes increasingly symbolic and dissociated with the real-time performance as we move upward along the vertical axis. The second challenge defines the horizontal axis along which the responsiveness to the simulated environment varies. At the left extremity, the virtual character is completely kinematically controlled, oblivious to any physical perturbations applied upon her. At the other end of the axis, the motion of the virtual character is fully simulated under Newtonian physics. Here, the performance may be interpreted as desired input but the physics will be the overriding driver of the overall animation of the body. We denote these two dimensions as the literal/symbolic (LS) axis and the kinematic/dynamic (KD) axis.

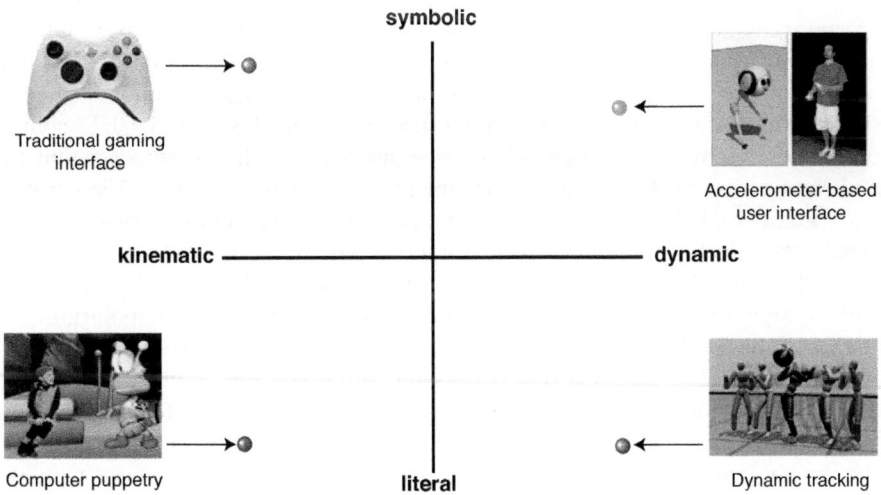

Fig. 1. Unified framework of the proposed KD/LS control space. Select applications highlight aspects of the different subspaces.

This two-dimensional space provides a systematic way to organize existing control methodologies and techniques for online character animation (examples are denoted in figure.) A typical video game controller can be represented by a point in the upper left corner of this control space, because the simple control interface maps a fully prescribed motion to a symbolic command, such as a button press. A computer puppetry system kinematically controls the virtual character through direct mapping of degrees of freedom between the performer and the virtual character. Shin and colleagues [3] provided an illustrative example of literal and kinematic control located in the bottom left corner of the control space. Researchers have also explored different control schemes on the dynamic side of the space. A dynamically tracking system can be represented as a point in the lower right corner if the input motion is an online performance [7,8]. Researchers have also developed symbolic and dynamic control on simple characters [5] as shown in the upper right corner. Our hypothesis is that all portions of this control space are indeed valuable, including the interior even though the bulk of current applications exist on the periphery.

To fully explore all possible control schemes in the domain, we propose a generic architecture which incorporates real-time user performance with physical simulation, augmented with an example motion database (Figure 2). At each time instance, a real-time pose is processed via pose composition and physical simulation steps. The architecture employs three intelligent modules to select the optimal example pose and control parameters based on the real-time performance and the state of the virtual environment. For pose composition, the system derives an intermediate pose from the input real-time posture and the optimal example pose, modulated by the control parameters in the LS dimension. The example pose is selected from a data set of pre-recorded motions or procedurally generated by inverse kinematics process. In the physics step, based on the control parameters in the KD dimension, the simulator updates the input pose, taking into account external forces and internal torques computed to track the intermediate pose. In this architecture, both the LS and the KD control parameters are determined by intelligence modules which take into account the real-time poses and the virtual environment. In particular, a recognition system matches the real-time performance with known behaviors and supervised learner aids in the selection of the control parameters based on observed training examples. The result is a final pose influenced by a combination of real-time motion and example motion, in conjunction with a modulated physical simulation.

One of the challenges of this architecture is the selection of control parameters. An important observation is that these control parameters should vary not only over time, but also across the body. In a scenario where the performer attempts to reach a virtual object with her hand, the position and orientation of the hand should be generated symbolically (e.g. using IK) in order to precisely match the objects virtual position. However, the rest of the motion can follow the performers movement literally as it provides valid joint configurations and does not interfere with the performers intention in this particular action. Likewise, if the actors arm was incidentally hit by an object, the kinematic and dynamic control could see the same divide in the body. This spatial separation is used for negotiating to produce a balanced motion which is effective but also responsive to external stimuli.

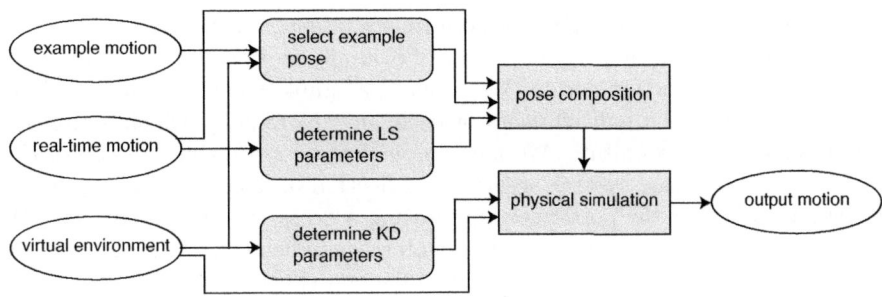

Fig. 2. Control architecture

3 Literal vs. Symbolic Mapping

To establish a mathematically meaningful domain for literal/symbolic control, we need to define a continuous function that maps the control space to the pose space. We first define a point in the control space as $\mathbf{x} \in R^n, \mathbf{0} \leq \mathbf{x} \leq \mathbf{1}$. Each component of $\mathbf{x}$ indicates the LS parameter for a particular body unit, e.g. the left hand. Any monotonic function that satisfies $f(\mathbf{0}) = \mathbf{q}_{rt}$ and $f(\mathbf{1}) = \mathbf{q}_{exp}$ can be a valid mapping between the control space and the pose space, where $\mathbf{q}_{rt}$ and $\mathbf{q}_{exp}$ denote the real-time pose and the example pose respectively. As a first step, we assume $f(\mathbf{x})$ is a simple linear function that interpolates between a real-time pose and an example, *symbolic* pose: $f(\mathbf{x}) = \mathrm{diag}(\mathbf{q}_{rt})(\mathbf{1} - \mathbf{x}) + \mathrm{diag}(\mathbf{q}_{exp})\mathbf{x}$, where $\mathrm{diag}(\mathbf{v})$ is a diagonal matrix which diagonal elements are $v_1, \cdots v_n$.

Evaluating the function f requires solving the following two problems. First, we need to determine the blending factors (LS parameters) of the interpolation for each individual body unit at each time instance. Second, we need to generate a proper example pose $\mathbf{q}_{exp}$ from a dataset instantly based on the performer's action and the current state of the environment. We solve the first problem based on the constraint state of the end-effectors. By comparing the constraint state of the end-effectors on the user against those on the virtual character, we can partition the end-effectors into constrained and unconstrained sets for the user, $\mathcal{S}_c^u$ and $\mathcal{S}_f^u$, as well as for the virtual character $\mathcal{S}_c^{vc}$ and $\mathcal{S}_f^{vc}$. Assuming a body unit is defined as a joint angle, the LS parameters are defined as follows: $x_i = 1$, if joint i is on the branch of an end-effector in $\mathcal{S}_c^u \cap \mathcal{S}_f^{vc}$. Otherwise, $x_i = 0$. For the body units where branches with different LS parameters meet, we assign x_i to an interpolated value. Intuitively, this algorithm follows the user's real-time motion unless the end-effectors of the user are constrained while those of the virtual character are free to move.

The second problem, generating an appropriate pose $\mathbf{q}_{exp}$ from the example motion, requires a recognition algorithm which selects/interpolates a proper example from the motion data base. Further, to be useful in an online setting, this recognition must be conducted in an efficient and timely manner. In particular, to be valuable, a motion example must be retrieved from the database early in a given behavior.

One simple way to recognize the performer's intention is to compare the current pose of the performer against a set of example motion clips, each of which is annotated as a certain action. We propose a simple algorithm that analyzes the correlation of the end effectors of each limb to identify which action the performer intends to imitate. We have implemented a real-time version of this for the game interface system described in Section 5. The proposed algorithm determines whether the performer is imitating a given example motion clip $\mathbf{Q}_k$ based on the performer's current unconstrained end-effectors. For example, if the performer is simply standing on the floor, the end effectors on the feet are constrained while those on the hands are unconstrained. The algorithm concludes that the performer is attempting to perform action k, if the unconstrained end effectors are mimicking the sample motion.

Our system can recognize the mimicking behavior via a simple but robust analysis in low dimensional space, invariant to users' different styles in movements or different skeletal dimensions. We use Principal Component Analysis (PCA) to project the position and the velocity of end effectors to a low dimensional space. Based on the user's current pose $\hat{\mathbf{q}}$, we first identify a set of unconstrained end effectors D. For each pose $\mathbf{q}_i^k$ in the example motion $\mathbf{Q}_k$, we compose a feature vector $\mathbf{w}_i = [\mathbf{x}_i, \mathbf{v}_i]$ which contains positions and velocities of the end effectors in D. We then apply PCA to the example motion represented by its feature matrix, $\mathbf{W} = [\mathbf{w}_1, \cdots, \mathbf{w}_n]$, where n denotes the number of frames in $\mathbf{Q}_k$. The first m principal components constitute a matrix A_k, which is defined to map a feature vector between its original and low-dimensional spaces:

$$\mathbf{u} = A_k^T \mathbf{w} \quad (1)$$
$$\mathbf{w} = A_k \mathbf{u} \quad (2)$$

To compare the similarity of the current user's pose $\hat{\mathbf{q}}$ to the example motion, we project the feature vector $\hat{\mathbf{w}}$ composed from $\hat{\mathbf{q}}$ to the low dimensional space via A_k^T, and back project into the high-dimensional space using A_k:

$$\tilde{\mathbf{w}} = A_k (A_k^T \hat{\mathbf{w}}) \quad (3)$$

Our assumption is that if action k is close to the current performance, the above operation should return a close approximation of the original features. Once the reconstruction error $e_t = ||\hat{\mathbf{w}} - \tilde{\mathbf{w}}||^2$ is obtained, we smooth e_t using a factor α as:

$$E_t = \alpha e_t + (1 - \alpha) E_{t-1} \quad (4)$$

and if E_t is smaller than the threshold value, the intention recognizer will return a positive flag indicating that the behavior has been recognized.

Once we obtain the real-time pose $\mathbf{q}_{rt}$, and determine the example pose $\mathbf{q}_{exp}$ and LS parameters $\mathbf{x}$, an interpolated pose $\hat{\mathbf{q}}$ can be trivially computed via $f(\mathbf{x})$. However, $\hat{\mathbf{q}}$ does not take into account the constraints imposed by the environment. For example, after interpolating a pose in a monkeybar motion, the hand from which the character is swinging might no longer be in contact with the bar.

To solve this issue, each example motion, in addition to joint configurations, can also store a set of kinematic constraints, such as maintaining certain contact points or facing direction while executing the example motion sequence. To compose a pose that actively interacts with the environment, we can then formulate an optimization to solve for the optimal pose that satisfies the environment constraints associated with the example motion and the internal joint limits of the character, while minimizing the difference from the interpolated pose, $\hat{\mathbf{q}}$.

4 Kinematic and Dynamic Continuum

An important concept in the proposed technique is to formalize a continuum between kinematics and dynamics approaches. Our take on this idea is that dynamics, given the proper external forces, can be forced to act like a kinematic system. We exploit this observation to create a Kinematic-Dynamic (KD) continuum between the use of physics for response and remaining faithful to the human performance. We introduce a domain for KD control defined as the continuous space that combines two distinct interpretations of the motion performance, $\hat{\mathbf{q}}$, first as a pure kinematic pose and second as a physical model following this pose as a desired setpoint. We treat the latter as a forward simulation tracking $\hat{\mathbf{q}}$ via a control routine as in [7,6,6]. By employing our KD framework, we sidestep coordinated control in lieu of two naive controllers and instead incorporate intelligence and high-level control through the interactive performance.

Formally, starting with the two interpretations of the performance, one for kinematic playback of $\hat{\mathbf{q}}$ and the other the result of a physical system tracking $\hat{\mathbf{q}}$, we must define a mathematical operation that transforms the input signals into a single KD pose. To unify the two representations, we propose to implement kinematics as a special case of the dynamics where we add additional forces, f_K, to the dynamics which override other dynamics influence of gravity and contact. The result is effectively to drive the dynamics to act kinematically by applying proper values for f_K. Next, we define a point on the KD continuum as $\mathbf{y} \in R^n, 0 \leq \mathbf{y} \leq 1$. One component of $\mathbf{y}$ indicates the KD parameter for a single body unit with n bodies. In the KD continuum, we define $\mathbf{y} = \mathbf{1}$ as pure kinematics and $\mathbf{y} = \mathbf{0}$ as pure dynamics. Within our unified framework, the influence of $\mathbf{y}$ on a single body can be interpreted simply by scaling f_K which creates a smooth continuous span between the two extremes. Finally, our choice of the weighting vector, $\mathbf{y}$, will determine the influence felt by each body for each instance in time.

4.1 Kinematic Control

Without loss of generality, we can interpret motion capture playback as a set of accelerations for each body across each timestep. Assigning dynamics parameters for the mass and inertia of each body there is an equivalence between these accelerations and a set of generalized forces which will lead to the analogous accelerations of these bodies. Effects due to gravity and external forces can also be accounted for within this framework. Indeed, this transformation is equivalent to inverse dynamics. However, rather than performing exact inverse dynamics, we pose a simpler problem which is to derive a set of forces, f_K, which will lead the character to follow the performance despite gravity and contact forces.

To compute f_K, we can propose a simple controller, for example, a Cartesian-based PD-servo as

$$f_K = k_p F(||\hat{p} - p||)(\hat{p} - p) - d_p(\dot{p}) \qquad (5)$$

where $\hat{p}$ is the body position derived from forward kinematics using $\hat{q}$ and gains k_p and d_p are manually tuned constants.

In this case, we would likely employ a modified logistic function, or another similar function, to saturate the kinematic forces so they do not go unbounded.

$$F(x) = \frac{1}{1 + e^{-sx}} - \frac{1}{2} \qquad (6)$$

where the value of the term s would control how quickly the controller saturates to the maximum. $F(x)$ would limit the bounds of the forces to avoid undesirably large influences and would help to keep the system stable. The values of k_p and d_p must be chosen such that they are large enough to become the dominant influences (overcoming gravity and contact forces) without leading to instability.

4.2 Dynamic Control

Our dynamic controller follows the performance by tracking the joint angles of the motion capture data using internal joint torques. Without the presence of disturbances, these torques would lead the character to match the joint trajectories of the performance. However, the joint tracker does not control the root body and the lack of coordination for balance would lead the character to fall over using a tracking controller alone, simply due to the influences of gravity. Rather than focusing on joint coordination using torques, we propose to employ this tracker in conjunction with f_K described and transform the character from purely dynamic to a hybrid system which combines both balance and responsivity in a simple, controllable fashion.

Specifically, the joint tracker is to compute joint torques based on the tracking error, $\hat{q} - q$, and joint velocities, $\dot{q}$, as follows

$$\tau = k_q F(||\hat{q} - q||)(\hat{q} - q) - d_q(\dot{q}) \qquad (7)$$

which follows the pose $\hat{q}$ based on the maximum value, k_q and damping d_q. As in Equation 5, $F(x)$ controls how quickly the controller saturates to k_q following Equation 6. This function allows the joint tracker to resist against deviations from the performance with a substantial torque even for small errors, but will give up stiff control when some maximum value is reached.

4.3 Integrated KD Control

The two KD controllers both guide the character to follow the human performance. However, each has its own characteristics. The forces computed in Equation 5 will maintain global Cartesian positions and will resist external forces in an unrealistic manner, in the limit ignoring them completely to follow the motion kinematically. Instead, the joint torques from Equation 7 make corrections in local joint coordinates and, therefore, will respond in a more believable manner. In contrast, the Cartesian forces provide more precise control from the perspective of the performance and can aid in balancing the full-body character, while the joint torques only provide a limited amount of control and no balance. Our proposed technique is to combine these two complementary inputs in order to get the best of both.

While there are many ways in which we can combine these two signals, we introduces a simple algorithm suitable for many free-standing behaviors. In this case, we propose to join the KD signals within the body based on the proximity of each body part to the ground plane, drawing from the assumption that the ground is the source of the reaction forces which lead to the analogous corrections that are embedded in the forces from Equation 5. In this way, we are using the f_K to make up for the under-actuation of the root seen by the joint tracker. As such, we could propose a simple, temporally changing allocation rule to combine the KD signals and incorporate the following value for **y**

$$\mathbf{y} = \alpha^{k(t)} \tag{8}$$

where α is the discount applied for each subsequent body in the shortest chain between the body and the ground. k bodies is the count of body parts from the current body and the nearest support, which can change at any instant in time. The support bodies which are in contact with the floor at a given time are assumed to have $\mathbf{y} = 1$ to be able to resist external content and follow the data kinematically. All other bodies are discounted based on α and their body count from the floor. For example if $\alpha = 1/2$ when the character is standing, then the pelvis which is the third body up from the feet feels $1/8$ of the kinematic forces computed. The result would make the character resilient to impacts which hit body parts close to support bodies while the system is also able to track well across the entire body.

5 Applications

To date, the concept of online performance animation is narrowly perceived as a real-time motion reconstruction technique that can be used in commercial applications. However, this limited definition completely ignores the most unique feature of the performance-based approach, that is, the information provided by human intelligence in real-time. In our broader view of performance animation, the performer is not only providing motion trajectories, but also revealing how humans make intelligent decisions and strategic actions based on the external situations and internal factors, such as biomechanical constraints, physiological states, or personal preferences. To ground the investigation and further discussion, we focus on two generic applications: 1) Performance capture with physical interactions, and 2) Natural user-interface for controlling avatars.

Fig. 3. Interactions from various scenarios created easily by combining motion performance and a physics-based representation of the character(s)

5.1 Performance Capture with Physical Interactions

Creating scenes with complex interaction between actors and the environment is crucial to many applications in movies and games. Although computer-generated effects enable actors to appear visually realistic in virtual worlds, producing realistic interaction between real actors and virtual objects, features, or characters remains challenging. Because actors often perform outside the context of the virtual scene, seamless integration relies heavily on manual post-processing efforts to synchronize an actor's performance with CG effects.

We introduce a technique that previsualizes final, integrated scenes at the time of performance acquisition. Our technique seeks to enforce realistic dynamic interaction in the virtual world while faithfully preserving the nuances of the actor's performance. The system combines motion capture in the form of a real-time performance with physical simulation to generate visible response to the virtual interaction. We present a hybrid approach for combining pure (kinematic) motion capture and a dynamic simulation of the character in order to create the appearance of a more immersive performance, in real time. The seamless integration of these two animation signals (kinematic and dynamic) is accomplished by transforming the kinematic signal into a dynamics representation and then balancing the influence of the original data and the physical response across the body and across time.

The description of our system architecture follows the layout diagram appearing in Figure 4. The raw performance starts with the actor and is input into a

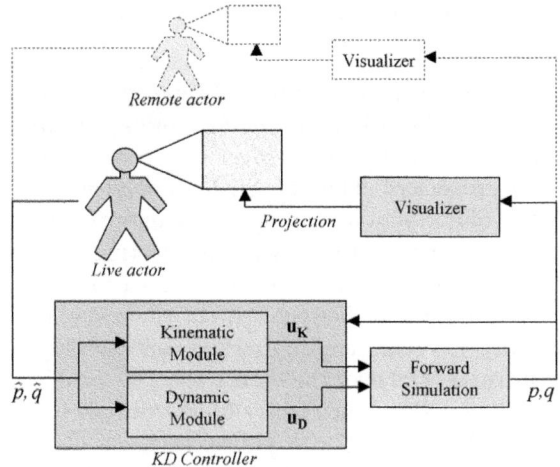

Fig. 4. The layout of the system shows the basic flow of information from the actor(s) through the motion capture system to the KD controller and the simulation. The simulation state is fed back to the control and input to the visualizer(s) which project(s) the scene for the actor(s).

combined kinematicdynamic (KD) controller. The forward simulation of the virtual world along with the physical model of the character is advanced in time based on the output of the KD control inputs. In this step, collisions are resolved by modifying the character motion and the objects in the scene. The actor gets visual feedback from the projection output and modifies the online performance appropriately.

At the core of our technique is the KD controller which seamlessly combines the (kinematic) motion performance with a physics model. The domain for our KD controller is defined as the continuous space that combines two distinct interpretations of the motion performance, first as a pure kinematic playback and second as a physical model following the performance as a desired setpoint trajectory. In our system, we implemented the latter as a forward simulation following the performance via a tracking control routine. We sidestep coordinated control in lieu of a naive tracking controller and incorporate intelligence and coordination through online performance capture.

Our system creates a single simulation within which a host of interactions are possible. For example, by adding additional simulations we can created coupled simulations like those seen in previous work [2,1,4] Also shown, with dashed lines, in Figure 4 is a networked remote actor. We extend our basic system to allow a remote performance capture and interaction between two actors in long-distant real-world locations. The networked clients remotely report the motion performance of the actors while a single local server manages the simulation that resolves interactions and generates a consistent state. This state is fed back to each remote client which uses its own visualizer that can uniquely control camera view, etc. for each actor.

5.2 Natural User-Interface for Controlling Avatars

We propose a new control interface for navigating and manipulating virtual worlds based on motion reconstructed in real-time from a human performance. Our control interface intelligently maps online motion capture data to a virtual characters action, such that the user can directly control the virtual character using her own body movement. The proposed system leverages a physical simulation, a small set of offline action examples, and an optimal integration process to synthesize the characters motion. When interacting with an object in the virtual world, the simulation ensures that the global movement of the character obeys the laws of physics, rather than directly tracking the performance. In addition, we propose a novel method for deriving active control from the performance to give intuitive control over the simulation. For local joint configurations, we integrate the online performance with offline example motions that demonstrate specific desired interactions with virtual artifacts. Recognizing when and knowing how to integrate the online and offline motion capture poses are particularly challenging because of the online nature of the input motion and real-time computation requirements. Furthermore, the identification needs to be robust against different styles of motion and different body types of users. We propose efficient algorithms to recognize the appropriate moments for integration and which body parts to include.

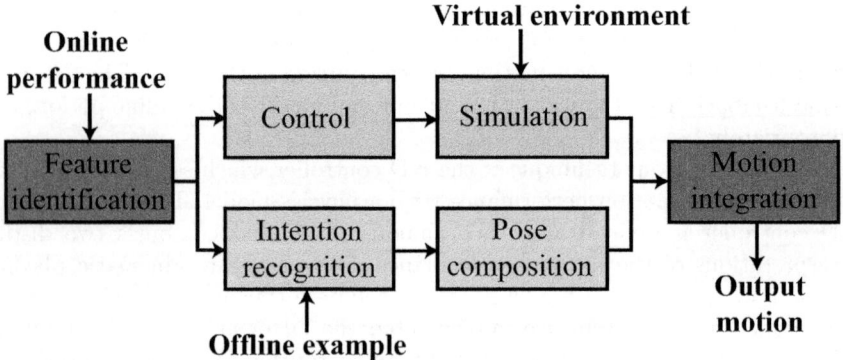

Fig. 5. Overview of the system

Our system takes as input a pose stream recorded by a motion capture device, and produces, in real time, a character animation that maps the users movements to the virtual world. To use the input motion for control of the virtual character, we need to modify the real-time input motion so that the virtual characters actions reflect the performers intention, preserve her motion style, and satisfy physical constraints in the virtual world. The designer of the virtual world plays a key role in this process by predefining the features of the world that the user can interact with and associating these features with motion sequences of possible interactions.

The overall system, shown in Figure 5, comprises both a dynamic process and a kinematic process to produce the virtual characters motion. First, we cycle through the features of the environment to check if the input motion matches their conditions for engagement. Once the interacting feature is identified, the dynamic process simulates the global motion of the virtual character by combining active control inferred from the users performance with dynamic influences from the virtual environment. In tandem, the kinematic process produces realistic context-appropriate poses by matching the users motion with the example interaction. Finally we formulate an optimization process to combine the global motion from the dynamic process and the poses from the kinematic process to produce an output motion that conforms to kinematic constraints in the virtual environment.

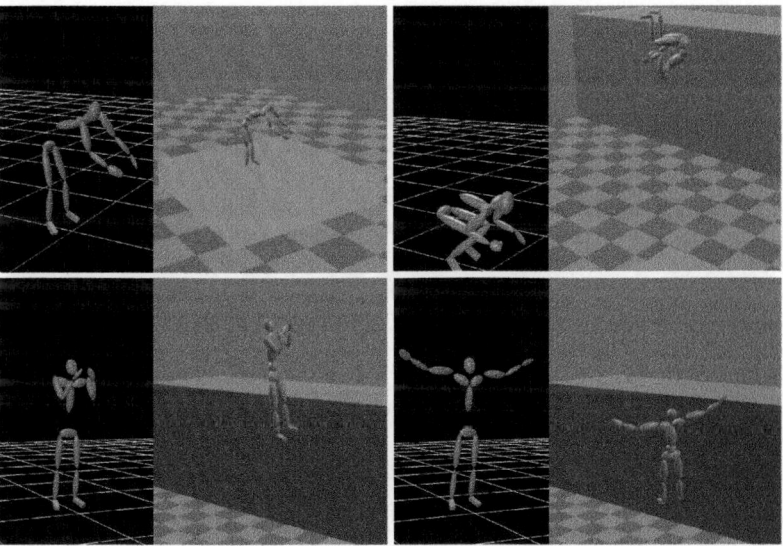

Fig. 6. The trampoline demonstrates the user's control over the dynamics of the character. Top Left: The user leans forward while jumping to generate forward angular momentum. Top Right: Tucking into a ball increases angular velocity, allowing the virtual character to flip. Bottom Row: Controlling the angular velocity by pulling in (left) and extending the arms (right).

6 Discussion

The proposed research is positioned to address the issues of generating more realistic character motion by taking advantage of online human performance, specifically recorded from full-body human motion capture, to add humanlike detail and intelligence to the animation generation process along with physical models employed for flexible, believable virtual interactions. In this research, a novel solution is proposed: a unified framework for physics and performance-based character animation. In the described method, the proposed human-in-the-loop control paradigm allows a player or performer to sense and act for the character. Specifically, a performer will: assess the situation and make a decision about the strategy that is appropriate for a given scenario; perform high-level and intermediate path planning for the character; and provide motion examples that are suitable for the current conditions. With this information encapsulated in the human performance and feedback about interaction given as the human is acting, the proposed framework accomplishes its goal in two steps: first, by recognizing and potentially modifying the performance such that it is appropriate for the given scenario; and second, by balancing interactivity and control in order to maintain both physical responsivity to the virtual world and faithfulness to the human performance.

References

1. Karen Liu, C., Hertzmann, A., Popović, Z.: Composition of complex optimal multi-character motions. In: 2006 ACM SIGGRAPH / Eurographics Symposium on Computer Animation (September 2006)
2. O'Brien, J.F., Zordan, V.B., Hodgins, J.K.: Combining active and passive simulations for secondary motion. IEEE Computer Graphics & Applications 20(4) (2000)
3. Shin, H.J., Lee, J., Gleicher, M., Shin, S.Y.: Computer puppetry: An importance-based approach. ACM Trans. on Graphics 20(2), 67–94 (2001)
4. Shinar, T., Schroeder, C., Fedkiw, R.: Two-way coupling of rigid and deformable bodies. In: 2008 ACM SIGGRAPH / Eurographics Symposium on Computer Animation (July 2008)
5. Shiratori, T., Hodgins, J.K.: Accelerometer-based user interfaces for the control of a physically simulated character. ACM Trans. on Graphics 27(5), 123:1–123:9 (2008)
6. Yin, K., Cline, M.B., Pai, D.K.: Motion perturbation based on simple neuromotor control models. In: Pacific Graphics, p. 445 (2003)
7. Zordan, V.B., Hodgins, J.K.: Motion capture-driven simulations that hit and react. In: Eurographics/SIGGRAPH Symposium on Computer Animation, pp. 89–96 (2002)
8. Zordan, V.B., Majkowska, A., Chiu, B., Fast, M.: Dynamic response for motion capture animation. ACM Trans. on Graphics (SIGGRAPH) 24(3), 697–701 (2005)

Individualized Agent Interactions

Ionut Damian, Birgit Endrass, Peter Huber,
Nikolaus Bee, and Elisabeth André

Human Centered Multimedia, Institute of Computer Science,
Augsburg University, 86159 Augsburg, Germany

Abstract. Individualized virtual agents can enhance the user's perception of a virtual scenario. However, most systems only provide customization for visual features of the characters. In this paper, we describe an approach to individualizing the non-verbal behavior of virtual agents. To this end, we present a software framework which is able to visualize individualized non-verbal behavior. For demonstration purposes, we designed four behavioral profiles that simulate prototypical behaviors for differences in personality and gender. These were then tested in an evaluation study.

1 Introduction and Motivation

Virtual simulations of social behavior can help visualize and analyze theoretical findings and assumptions in various sociological domains. However, software tools which provide such features often lack the flexibility and adaptability the researchers require. This shortcoming can also be observed in modern computer games where interactions between game characters follow a repetitive and predictable pattern which often leads to player immersion loss. For example, even though most MMORPGs (Massive Multiplayer Online Role Playing Games) allow the player to customize his or her character, this customization is only aesthetical, like clothing or hair style (Figure 1). The customization of behavioral characteristics, such as how the character gazes, how fast it gesticulates or what position and orientation it adopts during an interaction, is usually ignored.

Fig. 1. The character customization tool in CCP's computer game "EVE Online"[1]

---

[1] http://www.eveonline.com/pressreleases/default.asp?pressReleaseID=69

A solution to this problem is intelligent parametrization of the agents and the interactions. Using this approach, a designer can give each agent a set of specific parameters defining different aspects of its behavior, such as gazing techniques, positions during an interaction or gesture execution. These agents would then form realistic and diverse virtual environments.

The software framework Advanced Agent Animation (AAA) [1] is an implementation of the above mentioned approach. This framework is able to compute complex yet customizable interactions between virtual agents. This is done with the help of a powerful action parametrization system which covers all important aspects of an interaction: body location, body orientation, gestures, gazing and movement.

An evaluation study has also been conducted to offer some insight into the way people perceive differences in non-verbal behavior. The study investigated how well humans notice the individualized behavior of the virtual agents and whether they are able to recognize the different characteristics of non-verbal behavior the virtual agents simulate.

2 Related Work

There are a number of commercial software applications that can be used to simulate social behavior, however, most of them rely on explicit user input. For example, computer games, such as Second Life[2], can be used to visualize agent interaction but the positioning and orientation of the agents requires continuous user input. Pedica argues in [24] that making users think about how to coordinate their virtual bodies every time they engage in a social interaction requires too much micromanagement. These actions should happen automatically without the user having to think about it. Automated generation of nonverbal behavior during agent interaction was first proposed in BodyChat [30]. Agents reacted to world events according to a preprogrammed rule set without the need for input from the user. The automated behavior consisted of conversational cues which could then be mapped to gaze actions and facial expressions. An improvement to BodyChat was the Spark system [29] with its incorporated BEAT engine [5]. It automated not only discourse related cues but also agent interaction related cues. Another system, Demeanour, presented by Gilles [8], was able to generate reactions in form of postures. Demeanour also provided means to customize the reaction generation by allowing the user to define avatar profiles which consisted of a set of parameters that described the avatar's attitude, friendliness or situational behavior. Both Spark and Demeanour lack an automated avatar positioning and orientation system, making either the user or the designer decide what position and orientation the avatars take during an interaction.

Systems like Spark or Demeanour do not actually deal with the existence of interactions between agents, they assume that these are happening and proceed

---

[2] http://www.secondlife.com

with their computations based on this assumption. Pedica proposes, with the system CADIA Populus [24], a complex tool for simulating agent interactions. The virtual agents are able to move freely through a scene and interact with each other. The interactions in CADIA are defined as formations of virtual agents based on strong theoretical fundaments [13, 27, 10]. However, it lacks an animation system and a more realistic locomotion system, and the degree to which the generated behavior in CADIA can be customized is also unknown.

An approach to generating custom animations is presented by Neff and Kipp [21]. They describe a process in which gestures are first identified and annotated within a video corpus and are then passed to a gesture generation system. This process is able to generate unique gestures which can then be used to animate individualized virtual agents. However, the process is very complex and the annotation phase requires intensive user involvement and the availability of an appropriate video corpus. Pelachaud [25] presented a system for simulating behavior expressivity on the virtual agent *Greta*. The system uses a markup language, called APML (Affective Presentation Markup Language), to define the dialog and behavior the agents should execute. The APML also allows to control the expressivity [12] of the displayed animations.

A further notable example of animation customization is described by Chi et al. [6] in form of EMOTE. EMOTE is able to customize the execution of gestures by using the Laban [15] principles of Effort and Shape to alter the expressiveness of a gesture. This is done by varying the properties of the kinematic and spatial curve of specific keyframed actions. EMOTE can be described as a filter for animations as it can be applied to existing animations to alter their expressivity characteristics.

3 Individualizing Non-verbal Behavior

This paper focuses on the software framework for visualizing agent interactions Advanced Agent Animation (AAA) [1]. The framework automatically generates low-level behavior of virtual agents, such as moving their legs while walking or body positioning during an interaction, whereas the user or external systems are able to control the high-level behavior, such as which agent should interact with which agent or what gesture should an agent perform. The true power of the framework lies in its ability to customize most of the details of the simulation, from the stubbornness with which a virtual agent defends its personal space to the duration of the gazes the virtual agents throw each other. This is done with the help of action parametrization. Figure 2 shows a typical interaction in AAA featuring several virtual agents.

This section will describe the framework by presenting its four main features: formations, animations, gazing and movement. The focus will lie on the individualization parameters and how a designer can use them to create unique virtual agents that simulate specific characteristics of non-verbal behavior.

Fig. 2. The application Advanced Agent Animation (AAA) [1] showing an interaction between virtual agents

3.1 Formation System

The system uses F-formations [13] (Figure 3) to represent inter-agent interactions. Two or more agents can join together to form a formation. When joining a formation, a new agent automatically chooses a position inside the formation's p-space and orients itself so that its transactional segment intersects the transactional segments of the other members and the o-space of the formation. The transactional segment of an agent is the space in front of the agent where it conducts an activity, such as eating or gesticulating. Every member of a formation will try to satisfy its own preferences for interpersonal distance and orientation.

The positioning and orienting of an agent during an interaction happens automatically. This low-level behavior can be customized by altering an agent's parameters for interpersonal distances, willpower, deviation from the default orientation, and preferred formation type.

- *Interpersonal distance*: The distance between two agents is determined by the *minIPDistance* and *maxIPDistance* parameters of the two agents. Both agents will try to satisfy their two constraints on interpersonal distance during an interaction (Figure 4). For any two agents A and B which are part of the same formation, if A is closer to B then B's minIPDistance, B will move backwards until its minimal distance constraint is no longer violated. On the other hand, if A is further away from B then B's maxIPDistance, B will move towards A until the distance between them is smaller or equal its maximal distance constraint value.
- *Willpower*: If a conflict between two agents' preferences regarding interpersonal distance arises, the willpower parameter will define which agent will impose its constraints harder. The larger the willpower of an agent, the less inclined the agent will be to settle for a distance that does not satisfy its constraints.

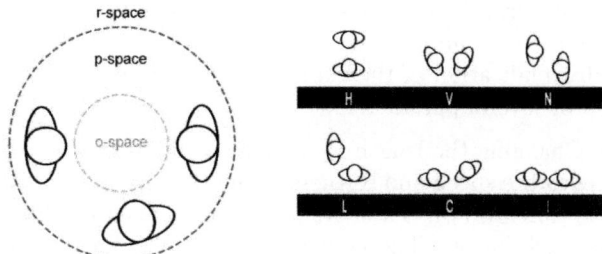

Fig. 3. The left structure represents Kendon's F-Formation [13] whereas the structures on the right represent the formation types for a pair of interlocutors described by Ciolek and Kendon [7]

– *Deviation*: This parameter will modify the body orientation of an agent during an interaction by deviating it from a normal state (Figure 4). The normal state of the body orientation is determined by the formation type. For instance, in an F-formation, the normal orientation of an agent is towards the center (o-space) of the formation. In this case, a 180 *deviation* will result in an agent that keeps its back to the formation center.

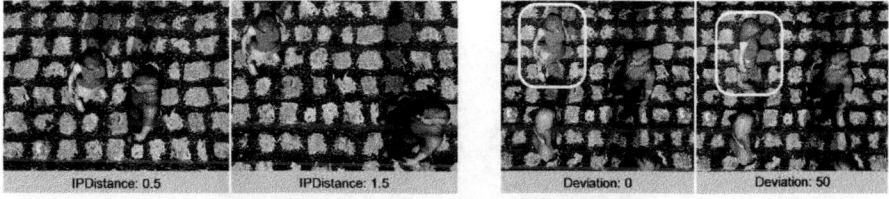

Fig. 4. The two screenshots on the left show the same agent formation but with varying interpersonal distance parameters whereas the screenshots on the right show varying deviation parameters

– *Preferred formation*: The preferred formation type controls which type of formation an agent will choose when engaging with another agent. The system uses Kendon's F-formation system [13] but can also reproduce the formation shapes described by Ciolek and Kendon [7]. Figure 3 shows illustrations for each formation type. For instance, if an agent A has a preferred formation type I, when an agent B engages in an interaction with A, they will go to an I-shaped (side-by-side) arrangement.

3.2 Animation System

The animation management system uses a powerful animation blending system which is able to realistically start the playback of an animation even if other animations are already being rendered on the agent. To achieve this, each animation is split into three phases: preparation, stroke and retraction [18]. The animation system also implements the action parametrization logic which enables the individualization of the expressivity [12] of every animation playback with the help of several parameters:

- *Fluidity*: Changing the length of the internal phases of an animation results in changes in the speed and softness of the transition from and to the animation. If an animation has a short preparation, then the blend-in phase will be shorter and sharper. The same principle applies for the retraction and the animation's blend-out phase. A short preparation and retraction also means that the stroke phase is longer and thus the phase that remains "untouched" is longer.
- *Stroke repetitions*: Each animation usually performs its stroke phase once. However, for animations such as beat gestures, it is very helpful to a designer to be able to specify how many times the stroke should be performed by the agent. This can be done with the help of the *strokeRepetition* parameter.
- *Playback speed*: Different individuals perform gestures with different speeds. This variation depends on many factors such as mood, age, gender, culture, and others. The systems allows the customization of the playback speed through the speed parameter. This controls the amount of animation frames the system performs for every application frame.

Fig. 5. Two screenshots showing the same animation playback, once with normal spatial extent and once with a lower spatial extent

- *Spatial extent*: The appearance of a gesture can vary with its spatial extent. High spatial extent means that the shape the gesture "draws" in the air will be large whereas a low spatial extent value correlates with small shapes. For instance, a "come here" gesture with a high spatial extent value would be performed with the hand at shoulder height and the arm far away from the body. However, the same gesture but with a lower spatial extent would result in the hand being lower and closer to the body (Figure 5).

3.3 Movement System

Agents are part of a virtual scene in which they are able to move freely. The agents can also orient themselves to face specific objects or coordinates. Each movement action can be customized with the help of the following parameters:

- *Walking speed*: This parameter defines the speed with which an agent will traverse the distance between its current position and the target position.
- *Movement animation*: Each movement can have an animation which the system will perform while the movement is active. For instance, a walking animation should be performed during a slow locomotion whereas a fast locomotion would require a running animation.

3.4 Gazing System

The gazing system enables virtual agents to move their heads and eyes to gaze towards specific targets such as objects or other agents. Certain events automatically trigger gazing actions. For example, when a member of a formation speaks, the other members will gaze towards it. The user or external systems can also request gazing actions. All gazing actions can be customized with the help of the following parameters:

- *Gazing speed*: The gazing speed defines how fast an agent transitions from one gaze target to another. This parameter can be used to simulate certain emotions and moods of the agents, such as boredom or stress.
- *Gaze duration*: A gaze action is not a permanent state, humans use it most often as a reflex to observing something interesting and passes as soon as the individual looses interest in the target or another point of interest appears. The duration of gazing actions of a virtual agent can be customized with the gaze duration parameter. This parameter specifies how much time it has to pass until a gaze target expires. When this happens, the agent goes back to an older valid gaze target.

3.5 Customization Examples

The customization features presented in the previous sections can be used to simulate various agent characteristics. This section will present two dimensions of non-verbal behavior variations and how a designer can use the parameters of the framework to simulate them in virtual agents. For each dimension, we will also present a parameter profile represented by a table which provides a mapping of various theoretical findings to the customization parameters of the framework. The parameter profiles only focus on the parameters for which appropriate literature has been found.

3.5.1 Personality Differences. The personality of humans has a great impact on their behavior when interacting with other people. Based on the taxonomy of personality attributes presented by Norman [22], we will now try to present some theoretical findings regarding this observation. Argyle [3] and North [23] have postulated that the spatial behavior is different for introverts and extraverts with extraverts adopting closer distances during interactions. In addition to this, several studies show that extraversion correlates with higher spatial extent values when executing gestures [14, 16, 26]. The gesture execution

Table 1. Example of parameter profiles for introversion and extraversion

Parameter	Introversion	Extraversion	Reference
minIPDistance	high	low	[3, 23]
maxIPDistance	high	low	[3, 23]
gesture speed	low	high	[16, 4]
gesture spatial extent	low	high	[14, 16, 26]
gesture fluidity	low	high	[16, 26, 28]
gaze duration	low	high	[19]

speed also tends to be higher for extraverts [16, 4] making their gestures look more powerful. Studies have also shown that introversion negatively correlates with gestural smoothness or fluidity [16, 26, 28]. In the domain of oculesics, it has been found that extraverts use more eye contact [19] which correlates with higher values for the gaze duration parameter. Table 1 shows an example of how the parameters can be used to simulate introversion and extraversion.

Table 2. Example of parameter profiles for male and female agents

Parameter	Female	Male	Reference
minIPDistance	low	high	[11]
maxIPDistance	low	high	[11]
willpower	high	low	[2]
deviation	low	normal	[9, 11]
preferred formation	F,H,V,N	all	[9, 11]
gesture spatial extent	low	high	[11]
gaze duration	high	low	[9, 11, 17, 20]

3.5.2 Gender Differences. A number of studies have shown that differences in non-verbal behavior exist between men and women. Hall [11] describes how women interact at closer distances than men. For us, this translates to smaller IPdistance values. Another interesting fact is that in mixed-sex interactions, the men also employ the close interpersonal distances that are typical for women [2]. We can simulate this with the willpower parameter. Other studies show that women are also more likely to adopt face to face orientations during an interaction [9, 11]. The way humans execute gestures has also been found to vary between genders. Studies have shown that men tend to use larger spatial extent values when executing gestures [11]. Women also tend to gaze more during interactions [9, 11, 17, 20] which we can interpret as a larger value for the gaze duration parameter. Similar to the parameter profile presented in the previous section, Table 2 shows the parameter profile for the gender differences.

4 Evaluation Study

In order to evaluate the framework's customization features, we conducted a study in which we investigated how users perceive different parameter profiles.

To this end, we implemented the previously described parameter profiles for the dimensions gender and personality into a series of scenarios which were then integrated into an evaluation study.

4.1 Study Setup

We analyzed the dimensions presented in the previous section: personality and gender. The personality dimension was featured with the values: introversion and extraversion; the gender dimension with female and male.

The study consisted of two videos for each dimension and one introduction video meant to familiarize the participant with the study. Every video showed an interaction between virtual agents. The two videos for a dimension showed identical interaction compositions and differed only through the usage of the customization parameters which were chosen based on the tables presented in Section 3. For each video, the participant had to grade the perceived behavior of the virtual agents relative to a dimension represented on a seven point scale, with the two dimension values on either side of the scale (Figure 6). Participants also had the possibility to leave a comment after each video. The study was conducted online and no restrictions for participation had been implemented.

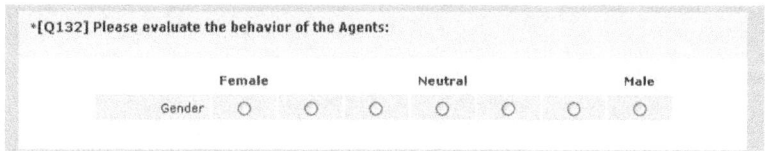

Fig. 6. A question from the online evaluation study

4.2 Results

For our analysis, we used two two sided t-tests, one for each dimension. A total of 133 participants (7 female and 126 male) took part in the study. They ranged in age from 14 to 49, with an average of 22.03. As the study was held online and offered both in German and English, the participants also varied in nationality. A total of 29 nationalities have been recorded with the majority of the participants being of western culture.

Table 3 shows the mean and median value for each video and the p-value for each dimension. The tests yielded promising results. The p value ($p < 0.001$) of the personality test suggests that the participants generally recognized the simulated personality correctly. In case of the gender dimension, the results were also significant ($p = 0.03$). Furthermore, the average values, 4.03 for the video with simulated female behavior and 4.56 for the one with simulated male behavior, show that the video with simulated female behavior was in fact perceived as more female. However, a slight tendency towards the male-end of the scale can be observed.

Table 3. Results of the survey showing the average and the p values of each dimension. The values ranged from 1 to 7, where 1 represents most introverted or female, and 7 represents most extroverted or male.

	Personality		Gender	
	Introversion	Extraversion	Female	Male
mean	2.41	5.96	4.03	4.56
median	2	6	4	5
p	<0.001		0.03	

Overall, we observed that the perception was influenced by the appearance of the virtual agents. This effect was visible in the gender test, where, due to the male appearance of the virtual agents in both videos, the results show a tendency towards the male-end of the scale. Interestingly, the personality test did not show signs of such an influence. An explanation for this is that personality is appearance independent, as all types of people are affected by personality in the same way.

The evaluation showed that individualizing the non-verbal behavior of a virtual agent does in fact result in an altered perception of the simulated interaction and that users are likely to recognize simulated characteristics of non-verbal behavior in virtual agents.

5 Conclusion

The scope of this paper was to present an approach to individualizing interactions between virtual agents. To this end, we presented a software framework which is able to compute and visualize non-verbal behavior of virtual agents. The main strength of the framework is the flexibility of the behavior generation systems which allows a high level of behavior individualization. This allows designers to generate complex scenes populated by agents that behave in an unique way.

We presented four different usages of the individualization features which simulated two dimensions of non-verbal behavior variation: personality and gender. We then proceeded to test these in a perception study which yielded positive results regarding the ability of the participants to perceive the simulated characteristics of the non-verbal behavior.

A possible topic for future work would be to investigate how other dimensions can be simulated with the individualization parameters of the framework. It would also be interesting to analyze the degree to which each parameter of a profile influences the perception of the non-verbal behavior. We can conclude that individualizing the non-verbal behavior of virtual agents can be perceived by users and, if employed, can help designers better simulate agents and agent interactions. It is also plausible that such features would support user immersion in video games by giving users the opportunity to create avatars with which they can identify themselves more easily. However, our results have also shown that individualizing the non-verbal behavior should not replace the customization of the agents' appearance, but should be rather used to complement it.

Acknowledgments. This work has been funded in part by the European Commission under the grant agreement DynaLearn (FP7-ICT-231526).

References

1. AAA: Advanced Agent Animation, http://hcm-lab.de/projects/aaa (last visited: 01.09.2011)
2. Andersen, P.R.: Nonverbal Communication: Forms and Functions. Mayfield (1998)
3. Argyle, M.: Bodily Communication, vol. 2. Methuen (1988)
4. Brebner, J.: Personality theory and movement. In: Individual Differences in Movement, pp. 27–41. MTP Press Limited (1985)
5. Cassell, J., Vilhjàlmsson, H.H., Bickmore, T.: BEAT: the behavior expression animation toolkit. In: SIGGRAPH 2001 Proceedings of the 28th Annual Conference on Computer Graphics and Interactive Techniques, pp. 477–486. ACM (2001)
6. Chi, D., Costa, M., Zhao, L., Badler, N.: The EMOTE model for effort and shape. In: Proc. Computer Graphics and Interactive Techniques, SIGGRAPH 2000, pp. 173–182. ACM Press/Addison-Wesley Publishing Co. (2000)
7. Ciolek, T.M., Kendon, A.: Environment and the spatial arrangement of conversational encounters. Sociological Inquiry 50(3-4), 237–271 (1980)
8. Gillies, M., Ballin, D.: Integrating autonomous behavior and user control for believable agents. Architecture, 336–343 (2004)
9. Guerrero, L.: Nonverbal involvement across interactions with same-sex friends, opposite-sex friends, and romantic partners: Consistency or change? Journal of Social and Personal Relationships 14, 31–59 (1997)
10. Hall, E.T.: The Hidden Dimension, vol. 6. Doubleday (1966)
11. Hall, J.A.: Nonverbal Sex Differences: Accuracy of Communication and Expressive Style. John Hopkins University Press (1984)
12. Hartmann, B., Mancini, M., Pelachaud, C.: Implementing expressive gesture synthesis for embodied conversational agents. Science 3881, 188–199 (2005)
13. Kendon, A.: Conducting Interaction: Patterns of behavior in focused encounters. Cambridge University Press (1990)
14. Knapp, M.L., Hall, J.A.: Nonverbal communication in human interaction. Holt, Rinehart and Winston New York (2009)
15. Laban, R., Lawrence, F.: Effort: Economy in Body Movement. Plays, Inc. (1974)
16. Lippa, R.: The nonverbal display and judgment of extraversion, masculinity, femininity, and gender diagnosticity: A lens model analysis. Journal of Research in Personality 32, 80–107 (1998)
17. McCormick, N., Jones, A.: Gender differences in nonverbal flirtation. Journal of Sex Education and Therapy 15, 271–282 (1989)
18. McNeill, D.: Hand and mind: What gestures reveal about thought. University of Chicago Press (1992)
19. Mehrabian, A.: Significance of posture and position in the communication of attitude and status relationships (1969)
20. Mulac, A., Studley, L.B., Wiemann, J.M., Bradac, J.J.: Male/female gaze in same-sex and mixed-sex dyads gender-linked differences and mutual influence. Human Communication Research 13(3), 323–343 (1987)
21. Neff, M., Kipp, M., Albrecht, I., Seidel, H.-P.: Gesture modeling and animation based on a probabilistic re-creation of speaker style. ACM Transactions on Graphics 27(1), 1–24 (2008)

22. Norman, W.T.: Toward an adequate taxonomy of personality attributes: Replicated factor structure in peer nomination personality ratings. Journal of Abnormal and Social Psychology 66(6), 574–583 (1963)
23. North, M.: Personality assessment through movement. Macdonald and Evans (1972)
24. Pedica, C., Vilhjálmsson, H.H.: Social Perception and Steering for Online Avatars. In: Prendinger, H., Lester, J.C., Ishizuka, M. (eds.) IVA 2008. LNCS (LNAI), vol. 5208, pp. 104–116. Springer, Heidelberg (2008)
25. Pelachaud, C.: Multimodal expressive embodied conversational agents, pp. 683–689. ACM Press (2005)
26. Riggio, R.E., Friedman, H.S.: Impression formation: the role of expressive behavior. Journal of Personality and Social Psychology 50(2), 421–427 (1986)
27. Scheflen, A.E.: Human Territories: how we behave in space-time. Prentice-Hall (1976)
28. Takala, M.: Studies of psychomotor personality tests (1953)
29. Vilhjálmsson, H.H.: Animating Conversation in Online Games. In: Rauterberg, M. (ed.) ICEC 2004. LNCS, vol. 3166, pp. 139–150. Springer, Heidelberg (2004)
30. Vilhjàlmsson, H.H., Cassell, J.: BodyChat: Autonomous communicative behaviors in avatars. In: Proceedings of the 2nd International Conference on Autonomous Agents, pp. 269–276. ACM (1998)

A Real-Time System for Crowd Rendering: Parallel LOD and Texture-Preserving Approach on GPU

Chao Peng[1,*], Seung In Park[1], Yong Cao[1], and Jie Tian[2]

[1] Computer Science Department, Virginia Tech, USA
{chaopeng,spark80,yongcao}@vt.edu
[2] Institute of Automation, Chinese Academy of Sciences, China
jie.tian@ia.ac.cn

Abstract. In modern games, rendering a massive scene with a large number of animated character is imminent and a very challenging task. In this paper, we present a real-time crowd rendering system on GPUs with a special focus on how to preserve texture appearance in progressive LOD-based mesh simplification algorithms. Our results show that the proposed parallel LOD approach can get up to 5.33 times of speedup compared with the standard pseudo-instancing approach.

Keywords: Level of detail, Crowd animation, Crowd rendering, Texture-preserving, GPGPU.

1 Introduction

Rendering large crowds of animated characters has become a common requirement in massively multi-player online games and interactive virtual environments. In many video games, human characters are the major 3D content composed of deformable meshes, where each mesh is represented with a set of triangles. In a typical massive crowd scene, one of the main challenge is how to increase rendering performance of a large number of articulated characters so that the users can have a real-time gaming experience. To do this, many Level of Detail (LOD) approaches, such as *Progressive Meshes* [7] and *Quadric Error Metrics(QEM)* [5], have been used to reduce the complexity of meshes. A LOD is a geometrically simplified representation of an original mesh without losing visual fidelity at a certain distance. In most of games, the rendering attributes, especially surface texture, are as important as geometry shapes for the realistic rendering of animated characters. And it is essential to preserve the correctness of texture appearance on different LODs.

During the past years, Graphics Processing Units (GPUs) have been significantly improved to perform general-purpose computation. By utilizing their

---

* Chao Peng is the contact author. This paper is accepted to *The Fourth International Conference on Motion in Games 2011* (MIG2011). The complemental video can be downloaded: *http://people.cs.vt.edu/chaopeng/video/MIG11Chao.mov*

highly parallel architecture, the algorithms, traditionally implemented on CPUs, can be re-designed and implemented on GPUs to increase the performance. Researchers have proposed parallel LOD algorithms on GPU to support real-time rendering [8,13]. In this paper, we extend our previous work [13], and present a GPU-based system to render crowds of animated characters while preserving their per-vertex attributes (e.g. texture coordinates). Our contribution emphasizes on a set of criteria that provide texture-preserving constraints for edge-collapsing in data preprocess. We also propose a processing pipeline that combines the NVIDIA's parallel computing architecture and OpenGL shaders to efficiently render the LOD meshes generated at runtime.

We organize the rest of the paper as follows. In Section 2, we review some previous works about LOD techniques and GPGPU computing. In Section 3, we provide a brief overview of our rendering system. In Section 4, we describe our approach of texture-preserving criteria applied in the preprocess. In Section 5, we present the pipeline for rendering animated characters. We describe our experiments and results in Section 6. Finally, we conclude our work and discuss the future works in Section 7.

2 Related Works

Mesh simplification has been well studied in the past. In this section, we review some previous approaches. We also review the works on general propose GPU computing in this area.

2.1 Mesh Simplification and LOD

LOD is a common representation for simplified meshes. It aims to reduce the complexity of 3D meshes based on some criteria, such as the distance to a camera. There are two typical types of LODs: *Discrete LOD* and *Continuous LOD*.

The concept of discrete LOD is to create a limited number of meshes offline to represent the original object. During runtime, the renderer choose a proper LOD from the already generated meshes to be the alternative for rendering. The major limitation of discrete LOD is that it can not provide smooth transitions between two LODs, and cause the "popping" artifacts. Markus Giegl and Michael Wimmer [6] presented a blending-based algorithm to avoid artifacts in image space, which is further improved by [15]. However, it requires high degree of similarities between LOD meshes in order to achieve a smooth LOD change. In addition, the noisy artifacts may occur on the silhouettes of the LODs.

Continuous LOD is supported by a data structure encoding a continuous spectrum of mesh details. A well-known algorithm of continuous LOD is progressive meshes [7], where an original mesh is simplified by collapsing edges iteratively. Then, the mesh is represented as a base mesh with a sequence of vertex splits. At runtime, a LOD mesh can be recovered by applying a prefix of splits on the base mesh. Other simplification approaches for continuous LOD include region-merging measurement [14], quadric error metrics [5], appearance-preserving method [1] and image-driven simplification [9].

2.2 GPU Computing for Mesh Simplification

With the GPU's parallel architecture, we can design and implement efficient parallel algorithm and achieve high performance. GPU-based mesh simplification has been studied in the past. In [2], the authors designed a GPU-friendly octree structure for cluster-based LOD generation. Hu et al. [8] proposed a parallel algorithm for view-dependent LOD rendering. Feng et al. [3] presented a parallel LOD approach for skinned meshes using geometry images. Peng et al. [13] presented a method of parallel progressive LOD for rendering massive and complex models interactively. Although these parallel approaches increase the performance of the LOD-based rendering, none of them are well studied on how the textures should be preserved while appearing on different LODs. Since texture is an important rendering feature for gaming-related applications, in this paper, we propose a texture-preserving criteria for the simplification of deformable mesh.

3 Overview

Our system leverages the advantages of a previous work [13], which provides an efficient and parallel LOD algorithm, and interactively renders massive and static models on GPUs. Our system includes two major stages: *Data Preprocess* and *Rendering Pipeline*. We illustrate the system overview in Fig. 1.

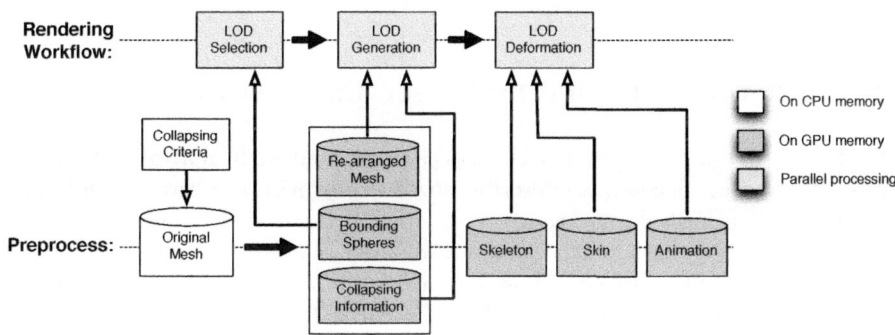

Fig. 1. The overview of preprocess and rendering pipeline

3.1 Preprocess

In preprocess stage, the vertices and triangles of the original mesh are simplified iteratively. At each iteration, one edge is chosen to be collapsed according to a collapsing criterion. We record the collapsing information into an array structure, where each element corresponds to a vertex, and the value of the element indicates the target vertex that it merges to. Then, we re-arrange the vertices and triangles of the mesh based on the order of edge-collapsing (referring to the details in [13]). We also create a Bounding Sphere(BS) for each original mesh. Note that the BS is large enough to bound the deformed mesh for any animated poses.

A BS serves two purposes at runtime. First, we determine the visibility of a character by testing the BS against the view frustum. Second, we generate a desired LOD based on the size of the projected area of the BS.

To avoid the problematic texture mapping onto the surface of each LOD, we present a texture-preserving criteria as an auxiliary control on how edges are collapsed at each iteration of simplification process. We describe our texture-preserving criteria in Section 4.

3.2 Run-Time Rendering Pipeline

At runtime, we employ the GPU parallel architecture to increase the rendering performance. Our rendering pipeline includes the following three steps to render an image frame:

1. LOD Selection. We compute the desired complexity for each character. To do this, we determine the visibilities of the characters by testing the BSes against the view frustum. If a character is visible, the LOD level is determined with the appropriate vertex and triangle counts.
2. LOD Generation. Based on the desire complexity of a character, we select a set of triangles from the original data and reform those triangles by performing the precomputed edge collapsing operations.
3. LOD Deformation. We deform the generated LODs to calculate the final positions of vertices with the skeleton, skin and motion data.

4 Mesh Simplification by Perserving Texture Appearance

We first describe how to split the vertices associated with multiple sets of texture coordinates. Second, we describe how to categorize the vertices and apply different collapsing rules to them.

An articulated character model is represented as a triangulated mesh associated with a set of texture coordinates. Thus, mesh M can be denoted as a triple, (V, U, T), where $V = \{v_1, v_2, \ldots, v_m\}$ is m vertices; $U = \{u_1, u_2, \ldots, u_r\}$ is r texture coordinates; $T = \{t_1, t_2, \ldots, t_n\}$ is n triangles. t_i is a triple of index pairs, denoted as $t_i = \{(vdx_1, udx_1), (vdx_2, udx_2), (vdx_3, udx_3)\}$, where $vdx_j (j \in [1,3])$ is a vertex index in the range of $[1, m]$, and $udx_j (j \in [1,3])$ is a texture coordinate index in the range of $[1, r]$.

4.1 Splitting Vertices According to Texture Coordinates

In OpenGL-based graphics pipeline, *Vertex Buffer Object* (VBO) is a common mechanism for storing vertex data on GPU memory. In a mesh, since multiple sets of texture coordinates may associate to a vertex, they will be indexed differently from other vertex attributes. But the OpenGL only supports one index stream used by all vertex attributes. As such, we need to duplicate the vertices which have more than one texture coordinate set so that the index pairs of a triangle, (vdx_j, udx_j), can be replaced with a single universal index, and we call this process *Vertex Splitting*. As a result, each vertex of the mesh will have only one set of texture coordinates, and the vertex count will be equal to the texture coordinate count. Then, a triangle t_i can be redefined as $\{idx_j\}(j \in 3)$, where idx_j is the universal index for all vertex attributes.

During vertex splitting, we also record the splitting information into an array, called *Adjacent Vertices*, denoted as $adjV$. The $adjV[i]$, associated to the vertex v_i, is a set of vertices that are split from the same original vertex v_i, including the original vertex v_i. For example, in Fig. 2 (a), vertex v_1 is split into v_9 and v_{10}, therefore, $adjV[1] = \{v_1, v_9, v_{10}\}$. Note that a vertex split from a boundary vertex is still treated as a boundary vertex.

4.2 Texture-Preserving Criteria

QEM [5] is a general and efficient criterion for mesh simplification. At each iteration, each edge is weighted by its cost. Then the edge with the lowest cost is chosen to be collapsed, and the triangles associated with this edge are removed. QEM considers the lengths of edges and face normals when computing the costs of edges. Thus, by using the criteria, we can avoid the mesh inversion problem and preserve the mesh boundaries so that the fidelities of the mesh approximations can be maintained. However, QEM is not sufficient to preserve the texture appearance on the surface, especially after the vertex splitting.

In order to perform a texture-preserving process of mesh simplification, we classify the vertices into three categories according to the splitting information recored in adjacent arrays. We define the categories and the rules of classification as follows (also see Fig. 2(a-b)):

Fixed Vertices. If a vertex, v_i, is a boundary vertex, or the number of vertices in adjV[i] is larger than 2, v_i is classified as a fixed vertex. The fixed vertices are non-collapsible and not involved in the iterations for collapsing edges. They constitute the simplest version of original mesh.

Companioned Vertices. If a vertex, v_i, is not a boundary vertex, and the number of vertices in adjV[i] is equal to 2, v_i is classified as a companioned vertex. If the vertex in adjV[i] is denoted as $\bar{v}_i$, $\bar{v}_i$ will be the companion of v_i during the edge-collapsing.

Regular Vertices. If a vertex v_i is not a boundary vertex, and adjV[i] is equal to 1 (did not split), v_i is classified as a regular vertex.

At each iteration, an edge, (v_a, v_b), weighted with the lowest cost is collapsed by merging v_a to v_b. We define that an edge is valid for collapsing if either of the following conditions is satisfied:

1. v_a is a regular vertex.
2. v_a is a companioned vertex; and $(\bar{v}_a, v_c)$ is an actual edge in both the world space and the texture space, where $v_c \in adjV[b]$.

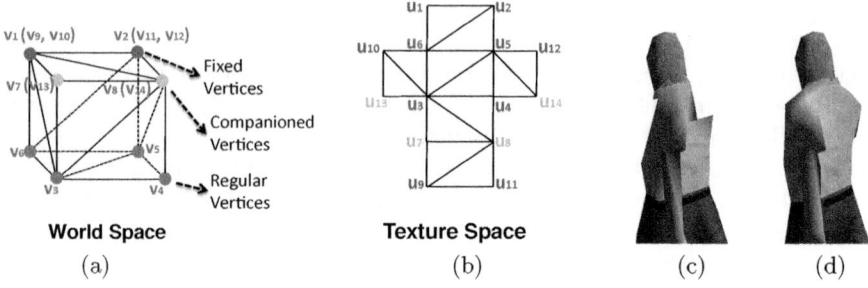

Fig. 2. (a-b) shows an example of vertex categories. (a) is the mesh after splitting vertices in world space. (b) is the texture coordinates of the mesh in texture space. The set of fixed vertices is $\{v_1, v_2, v_9, v_{10}, v_{11}, v_{12}\}$; the set of companioned vertices is $\{v_7, v_8, v_{13}, v_{14}\}$; the set of regular vertices is $\{v_3, v_4, v_5, v_6\}$. **(c-d) shows the comparison of accuracy on the deformed mesh.** (c) is the LOD based on the simplification of the static bind-pose mesh; (d) is the LOD based on the simplification considering all frames of motions. Note that both (c) and (d) are composed of 300 triangles. As a result, (d) is more accurate than (c) in visual fidelity.

When collapsing the edge (v_a, v_b), if v_a is a companioned vertex, we also collapse the edges $(\overline{v}_a, v_c)$ by merging $\overline{v}_a$ to v_c. This is because (v_a, v_b) and $(\overline{v}_a, v_c)$ are identical in 3D space, and the texture must appear continuously crossing those edges. Thus, we collapse both the edges concurrently to avoid any distorted texturing effects.

For a deformable mesh, the actual shape of the mesh changes between frames. If we perform the simplification process only on a static shape of the mesh, the LOD generated for the actual shape may not be sufficiently accurate (see Fig. 2(c-d)). This is because when a bone of the skeleton is bent, the flat region of the static shape around this joint may significantly change to a high curvature region, where more features are demanded [3]. To solve this problem, we collapse an edge by considering the actual shapes of all frames in the motions. That means that the cost to collapse an edge is the average of the costs computed from all frames. We show an example of a sequence of LODs in Fig. 3.

5 Rendering Pipeline for Animated Characters

In this section, we describe the runtime pipeline for rendering a crowd of animated characters.

5.1 LOD Selection

At runtime, we determine the complexity of each character. In our system, the complexity is represented with appropriate vertex count and triangle count. The farther a character is from the camera, the less complexity is needed to render. A common solution to compute the complexities is a distance-based method [10].

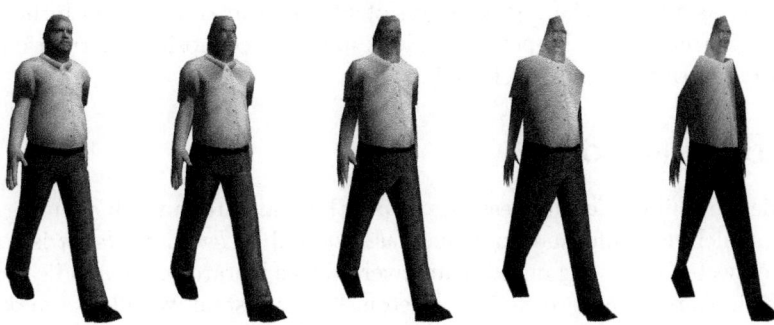

Fig. 3. A sequences of LODs generated by using texture-preserved criteria. From the left to the right, the LODs have 2620, 655, 388, 276,190 triangles respectively.

Although it is a simple and efficient method, the major disadvantage is that an arbitrary point for each character must be chosen for distance calculation, which would lead to inaccurant results. Alternatively, we use a screen-based method utilizing the projected area of BSes on the image plane. Simuliar to [13,16], we use Equation 1 to compute the complexities, and the total triangle count of all characters is smaller than a predefined maximal count.

$$k = N \frac{A_i^{\frac{1}{\alpha}}}{\sum_{i=1}^{l} A_i^{\frac{1}{\alpha}}} \qquad (1)$$

In Equation 1, k is the appropriate vertex count computed out of l characters; N is the maximal vertex count, which is predefined according to the rendering performance or quality. A_i is the projected area of BS of the ith character. $\frac{1}{\alpha}$ is a parameter determining how the model perception contributes to the selection process (Refer to [17] for the details for choosing a value of α). By mapping k to the corresponding number of triangles, we can obtain the appropriate triangle count, q, where $q \in [1, n]$.

If a character is out of the view frustum, it is invisible to users, and we set its complexity to zero. By using NVIDIA's CUDA computing framework, we first test BSes against the view frustum in parallel. Then we apply Equation 1 for all the characters inside the view frustum.

5.2 Generating LODs by Reforming Triangles

After LOD selection, for each character, we select the successive sets of vertices and triangles from the original data. The vertex and triangle data of the mesh are re-arranged according to the order of the edge collapses in preprocess. The first vertex of the mesh is the last one collapsed; and the fist triangle of the mesh is the last one removed. Thus, according to the computed complexity, we create those two sets by picking the successive vertices and triangles starting from the first. Then, the LOD of the character is generated by reforming those selected triangles. As a result, the vertex indices of a triangle are replaced with the target indices returned from the per-vertex lookup of the collapsing information. The detailed description can be referred in [13].

5.3 Deforming LODs

In order to animate a 3D mesh, we apply the standard smooth skinning algorithm, which uses information defined as *skin* and *skeleton*. *Skeleton* is a set of interconnected bones organized in an inverted tree hierarchy. *Skin* indicates how the vertices are influenced by the skeleton. In our system, we allow a maximum of 4 bones controlling one vertex, and each of 4 bones associates with a scaling factor, called *deforming weights*, to specify its strength influencing the vertex. Thus, we animate a character by deforming its LOD mesh with a *skeletal pose* defined by the movements of bones. In our system, we use the pre-captured motions, where a motion is composed of a sequence of skeletal poses. At runtime, a skeletal pose can be chosen from the motion data to deform the mesh.

To calculate the final positions of vertices, each vertex is transformed by applying the transformation matrices of its associated bones. We show the per-vertex calculation in Equation 2.

$$\vec{p}' = \sum_{i=1}^{4} w_{b_i} \cdot \bm{GT}_{b_i} \bm{B}_{b_i}^{-1} \vec{p}; \text{ where } \sum_{i=1}^{4} w_{b_i} = 1 \qquad (2)$$

where b_i is the index of the bone influencing the vertex; $\bm{G}$ is the world transformation matrix of the character having this vertex; $\bm{T}_{b_i}$ is the transformation matrix of the bone; $\bm{B}_{b_i}^{-1}$ is the inverse binding matrix of the bone defined in the initial skeleton. $\vec{p}$ is the original position of the vertex. To do this calculation efficiently, we store the skeleton, motions and skin in texture memories of GPUs, then calculate $\vec{p}'$ by reading them in the vertex shader.

6 Experiments and Results

Our system is designed to render a large number of animated characters. In this section, we show the rendering results, and evaluate the performance.

6.1 Implementation and Experiment

We have implemented our system for crowd rendering on a workstation equipped with Intel Core i7 2.67 GHz, 12GB of RAM, and a Nvidia Quadro 5000 graphics card with 2.5GB device memory. Our program uses Nvidia CUDA Toolkit v3.2. In our experiments, we use a character composed of 1642 vertices and 2620 triangles. We applied the criteria presented in Section 4 in preprocess. As shown in Fig. 3, the continuity of the texture appearing on different version of LODs is perserved. In Fig. 4, we also show a live-captured image rendering 512 characters.

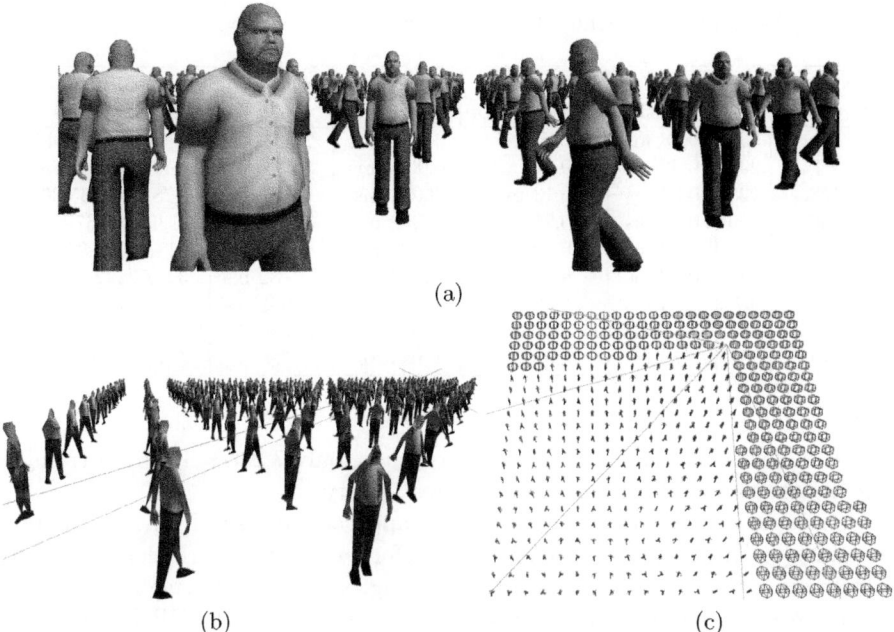

Fig. 4. An example of rendering **512 characters with 98,638 triangles in total.** (a) shows the rendering result from an user camera. (b) demonstrates the texture appearance on the LODs generated based on the camera setting in (a). In (c), we show the result of view-frustum culling of (a). The spheres indicate the characters outside the view frustum.

6.2 Performance Evaluation

We evaluate the performance of the rendering system by comparing with the OpenGL pseudo-instancing approach. Instancing technique is to render multiple instances of the same character with a single drawing call. In OpenGL graphics pipeline, pseudo-instancing has been used widely [11,12,18]. In those approaches, the crowd rendering is optimized by sharing vertex data, primitive counts and types, among all instances. It minimizes the amount of duplicated data. The technique accesses persistent vertex attributes associated in vertex shader, and per-instance data(e.g. world transforms) as textures.

We present the performance evaluation of our approach with varying counts of character instance in Table 1. Arbitrary number N is chosen to satisfy the certain base level of rendering quality. In our test case, we set such N that guarantees no over-simplification on the farthest characters from the camera. $\alpha = 3$ is configured to produce the equivalent result of Funkhouser's benefit function as in [4,17]. "Updating Animation" is the time for changing the frame index of motion, and "Rendering" is the time for the process of deformation and rasterization. "No. of triangles" represents the number of triangles used in our approach comparing to that of pseudo-instancing. Since our approach adjusts

Table 1. Performance benchmark of our approach with varying number of characters

No. of instances	FPS	LOD Selection	Triangle Reformation	Updating Animation	Rendering	No. of triangles
32	337	0.28 ms	0.084 ms	0.0004 ms	2.603 ms	40,056/83,840
64	292	0.32 ms	0.11 ms	0.0004 ms	2.994 ms	49,236/167,680
128	228	0.34 ms	0.13 ms	0.001 ms	3.915 ms	78,058/335,360
256	156	0.35 ms	0.21 ms	0.002 ms	5.848 ms	139,642/670,720
512	111	0.42 ms	0.32 ms	0.004 ms	8.265 ms	211,685/1,341,440
1,024	79	0.43 ms	0.49 ms	0.006 ms	11.732 ms	329,594/2,682,880
2,048	47	0.44 ms	0.89 ms	0.014 ms	19.933 ms	617,031/5,365,760
4,096	26	0.48 ms	1.75 ms	0.032 ms	36.200 ms	1,182,280/10,731,520
8,192	16	0.58 ms	3.08 ms	0.054 ms	58.786 ms	1,946,977/21,463,040

the complexity of character meshes at runtime, only 7.2% ∼ 47.7% of triangles are maintained while preserving the visual fidelity.

"Triangle Reformation" time shows our approach scales well with the number of triangles. The number of triangles and reformation time to render 2,048 characters are set to 1.0, and the ratios of triangles number and reformation time for the rest test cases show the linear relation in Table 2. The GPU we used has 11 stream processors in which each processor is composed of 128 computational cores. Hence, at least $11 \times 128 = 1,408$ threads need to run concurrently to prevent GPU from underutilization. In our parallel implementation, each thread performs a kernel of LOD selection and triangle reformation, therefore the test case of 2,048 instances is chosen to the base for the comparison.

Table 2. Performance and scalability

No. of Instances	No. of Triangles	Triangle Reformation	Ratio of Triangles	Ratio of Triangle Reformation
2,048	617,031	0.95 ms	1.00	1.00
4,096	1,182,280	1.75 ms	1.91	1.84
8,192	1,946,977	3.08 ms	3.15	3.24
16,384	3,103,167	5.23 ms	5.02	5.49
32,768	6,184,824	10.47 ms	10.02	11.02

Although our approach introduces additional costs on the steps of LOD selection and LOD generation, it is not the performance bottleneck of the system. As shown in Fig. 5(a), the sum of computation time spent on those two stages is 6.65% of the total time. Fig. 5(b) shows the performance comparison measured by FPS (Frames Per Second) between our approach and pseudo-instancing. The same camera setting is used for both approaches on the same number of instances. The procedure for changing the frame index of motion is also set to be identical. Our LOD-based approach achieves 1.22X to 5.33X speedup comparing to the pseudo-instancing approach.

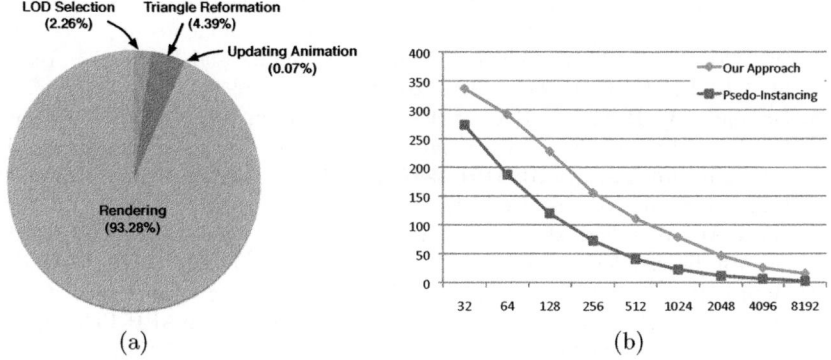

Fig. 5. (a) shows the percentages of different computation times of our approach listed in Table 1. The pie chart is generated by averaging the timing results of all nine configurations of instance counts. (b) shows the performance over different instance counts according to the FPS results in Table 1.

7 Conclusion and Future Work

We present a LOD-based real-time crowd rendering system for animated characters. Our contributions are focused on a set of texture-preserving criteria for parallel and progressive mesh simplification. In the preprocess stage, we first split the original vertices based on the layout of texture coordinates in order to preserve the continuity of texture appearing on the surface. Then, the vertices are classified into three different categories. Each category is set with different rules of how the vertices should be merged during the iterative process of edge collapsing. In our rendering pipeline, we generate the appropriate LODs on the fly, and deform them to obtain the actual shape of mesh for the current animation frame. We leverage the computing power of the parallel architecture of GPUs, and achieve the real time performance for our test cases.

In the future, we plan to apply a similar preserving criteria to other rendering attributes, such as vertex normals. We would also like to research on the parallel algorithms for occlusion culling based on frame-to-frame coherence.

References

1. Cohen, J., Olano, M., Manocha, D.: Appearance-preserving simplification. In: Proceedings of the 25th Annual Conference on Computer Graphics and Interactive Techniques, SIGGRAPH 1998, pp. 115–122. ACM, New York (1998)
2. DeCoro, C., Tatarchuk, N.: Real-time mesh simplification using the gpu. In: Proceedings of the 2007 Symposium on Interactive 3D Graphics and Games, I3D 2007, pp. 161–166. ACM, New York (2007)
3. Feng, W.W., Kim, B.U., Yu, Y., Peng, L., Hart, J.: Feature-preserving triangular geometry images for level-of-detail representation of static and skinned meshes. ACM Trans. Graph. 29, 11:1–11:13 (2010)

4. Funkhouser, T.A., Séquin, C.H.: Adaptive display algorithm for interactive frame rates during visualization of complex virtual environments. In: Proceedings of the 20th Annual Conference on Computer Graphics and Interactive Techniques, SIGGRAPH 1993, pp. 247–254. ACM, New York (1993)
5. Garland, M., Heckbert, P.S.: Surface simplification using quadric error metrics. In: Proceedings of the 24th Annual Conference on Computer Graphics and Interactive Techniques, SIGGRAPH 1997, pp. 209–216. ACM Press/Addison-Wesley Publishing Co., New York (1997)
6. Giegl, M., Wimmer, M.: Unpopping: Solving the image-space blend problem for smooth discrete lod transitions. Computer Graphics Forum 26(1), 46–49 (2007)
7. Hoppe, H.: Progressive meshes. In: Proceedings of the 23rd Annual Conference on Computer Graphics and Interactive Techniques, SIGGRAPH 1996, pp. 99–108. ACM, New York (1996)
8. Hu, L., Sander, P.V., Hoppe, H.: Parallel view-dependent refinement of progressive meshes. In: Proceedings of the 2009 Symposium on Interactive 3D Graphics and Games, I3D 2009, pp. 169–176. ACM, New York (2009)
9. Lindstrom, P., Turk, G.: Image-driven simplification. ACM Transactions on Graphics 19, 204–241 (2000)
10. Luebke, D., Watson, B., Cohen, J.D., Reddy, M., Varshney, A.: Level of Detail for 3D Graphics. Elsevier Science Inc., New York (2002)
11. Millan, E., Rudomin, I.: Impostors and pseudo-instancing for gpu crowd rendering. In: Proceedings of the 4th International Conference on Computer Graphics and Interactive Techniques in Australasia and Southeast Asia, GRAPHITE 2006, pp. 49–55. ACM, New York (2006)
12. Park, H., Han, J.: Fast Rendering of Large Crowds Using GPU. In: Stevens, S.M., Saldamarco, S.J. (eds.) ICEC 2008. LNCS, vol. 5309, pp. 197–202. Springer, Heidelberg (2008)
13. Peng, C., Cao, Y.: Gpu-based streaming for parallel level of detail on massive model rendering. Tech. Rep. TR-11-12, Computer Science, Virginia Tech. (2011), http://eprints.cs.vt.edu/archive/00001158/
14. Ronfard, R., Rossignac, J., Rossignac, J.: Full-range approximation of triangulated polyhedra. In: Rossignac, J., Sillon, F. (eds.) Proceeding of Eurographics, Computer Graphics Forum, vol. 15(3), pp. C67–C76. Eurographics, Blackwell (August 1996)
15. Scherzer, D., Wimmer, M.: Frame sequential interpolation for discrete level-of-detail rendering. Computer Graphics Forum 27(4), 1175–1181 (2008)
16. Schmalstieg, D., Fuhrmann, A.: Coarse view-dependent levels of detail for hierarchical and deformable models. Tech. rep., Vienna University of Technology, Austria (1999)
17. Wimmer, M., Schmalstieg, D.: Load balancing for smooth levels of detail. Tech. Rep. TR-186-2-98-31, Vienna University of Technology (1998)
18. Zelsnack, J.: Glsl pseudo-instancing. Tech. rep., NVIDIA Corporation (2004)

Feature-Based Locomotion with Inverse Branch Kinematics

Mentar Mahmudi and Marcelo Kallmann

University of California, Merced
Merced, CA, 95343, USA
{mmahmudi,mkallmann}@ucmerced.edu
http://graphics.ucmerced.edu

Abstract. We propose a novel Inverse Kinematics based deformation method that introduces flexibility and parameterization to motion graphs without degrading the quality of the synthesized motions. Our method deforms the transitions of a motion graph-like structure by first assigning to each transition a continuous rotational range that guarantees not to exceed the predefined global transition cost threshold. The deformation procedure improves the reachability of motion graphs to precise locations and consequently reduces the time spent during search. Furthermore, our method includes a new motion graph construction method based on geometrical segmentation features, and employs a fast triangulation based search pruning technique that confines the search to a free channel and avoids expensive collision checking. The results obtained by the proposed methods were evaluated and quantified, and they demonstrate significant improvements in comparison with traditional motion graph approaches.[1]

Keywords: Character Animation, Locomotion, Motion Capture.

1 Introduction

The realistic animation of virtual characters remains a challenging problem in computer animation. Successful approaches are mostly data-driven, using motion capture data, and often involving motion blending and search. While blending operations over motion segments adequately grouped are suitable to real-time performances, search techniques based on motion graphs provide minimum distortion of the captured sequences, and naturally allow the exploration of solutions in complex environments. Even if real-time performance is most often lost, techniques based on motion graphs can still be employed in off-line production phases for several purposes. For instance, the proposed deformation of locomotion sequences can be used to build blendable clips for real-time steering control. Little work has been done on developing deformation models that maintain minimum distortion to the captured motions. In this paper we present a simple and efficient Inverse Kinematics (IK) branch deformation technique to address this

---

[1] Accompanying video at http://graphics.ucmerced.edu/videos/11-mig-fmg.m4v

problem. Each branch of the search is treated as a kinematic chain of motion segments with joint limits representing the allowed rotational deformation at transitions. This technique produces motions precisely reaching given targets, and at the same time leads to an earlier successful termination of each search. These benefits do not sacrifice the quality of the motions as the error introduced in the deformed transitions does not exceed the same predefined threshold error used to construct the graph.

Our deformation method is also free of feet sliding artifacts thanks to a proposed new feature-based approach for constructing improved motion graphs. Feature-based motion graphs can be constructed significantly faster than traditional motions graphs by avoiding the pairwise comparison between all frames in the database. Instead, only suitable pairs of frames are chosen for transition evaluation. The chosen pairs are the output of feature detectors encoding relationships of interest among key joint positions of the given skeleton. Once these suitable frames are detected, transitions are evaluated with the usual threshold-based comparison metric, thus achieving the same quality of results.

Depending on the application, different feature detectors can be employed. A wide range of feature detectors have been proposed by Müller et al [14]. These feature detectors can be quickly evaluated and are based on spatial relationships between the joints of the character at any given frame. We have noticed that, for the purpose of locomotion synthesis, a very small set of feature detectors is sufficient to successfully segment various walking motions. For example, the forward walk detector checks for a crossing event at the ankle joints, leading to motion segments with one foot always planted on the floor. This is a desirable property as it eliminates the need for post-processing due foot-skating artifacts. Similar strategies were demonstrated by previous authors [20], but employing manually crafted clips.

We also present a search pruning technique based on planar channels with guaranteed clearance from obstacles. This is achieved by projecting all obstacles on the floor plane and maintaining a triangulation of the environment [7]. For any given start and goal positions, the triangulation returns a collision-free channel that is used to prune the branches unrolled by the motion graph search that lie outside of the channel. This results in improved search times, especially in environments with many obstacles.

Finally, extensive evaluations are presented for synthesizing locomotion among obstacles, and our results demonstrate significant improvements in time of computation, in finding solutions, and in the quality of results.

2 Related Work

A large body of work has been devoted to animating characters using human motion capture data. Motion graphs [9,1,12,2,6] represent a popular approach that is based on connecting similar frames in a database of motion capture examples. Once a motion graph is available, graph search is performed in order to extract motions with desired properties.

Kovar et al. [9] cast the search as an optimization problem and use a branch and bound algorithm to find motions that follow a user specified path. Arikan and Forsyth [1] build a hierarchy of graphs and use a randomized search to satisfy user constraints. Arikan et al. [2] use dynamic programming to search for motions satisfying user annotations. Lee et al. [12] construct a cluster forest of similar frames in order to improve the motion search efficiency. All these methods require quadratic construction time for comparing the similarity between all the frames in the database. Our method improves on this operation by connecting only selected frames.

Many improvements to motion graphs have already been proposed. Ren et al [16] combine motion graphs with constrained optimization. Shin and Oh [18] combine groups of parametrized edges into a fat edge for interactive control. Beaudoin et al [3] use a string-based model to organize large quantities of motion capture data in a compact manner. Our contributions focus on deforming motions without accruing additional error, improved construction and representation and can be used to improve any previous method relying on a motion graph structure.

Motion capture data has also been extensively used for locomotion planning among obstacles [5,15,11,21,19]. In particular, Lau and Kuffner [10] manually build a behaviour-based finite state machine of motions, which in later work is precomputed [11] to speed up the search for solutions. Choi et al [4] combine motion segments with probabilistic roadmaps. These methods however require the user to manually organize motion examples in suitable ways.

Other approaches [17,23,13] are based on the interpolation of two time-scaled paths or involve methods that solve a linear system of constraints [8]. Although these methods increase the solution space, they come with the expense of further distorting synthesized motions and they often increase the involved computation time and complexity.

In general, the main drawback of motion graph structures is the prohibitively large amount of data that may be needed in order to address practical applications involving obstacles and precise placements. The solutions presented in this paper address these problems.

3 Feature-Based Motion Graph

As usual, we build our motion capture database by concatenating multiple motions together. Each motion is composed of a sequence of frames. A frame $f = (p_r, q_0, q_1, ..., q_k)$ defines the pose of the character where p_r is the root position and q_i is the orientation of the i-th joint.

We start by segmenting the motions into semantically similar clips using feature detectors. For each motion type of interest, a feature detector is assigned to it. For example, for forward walking motions (straight and turning), the segmentation extracts from the motion capture database relatively small clips, each containing one walk cycle. Each frame is tested against a foot crossing binary test which looks whether the right ankle of the character is behind or in front

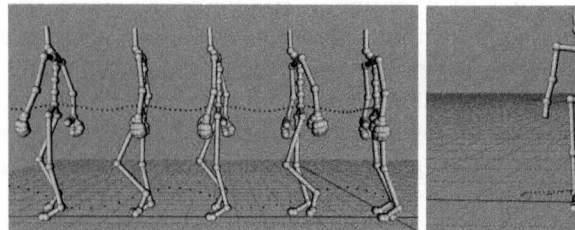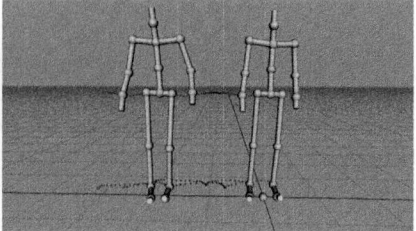

Fig. 1. Left: The alternating colors in the trajectories represent the segmentation of a walking motion into walk cycles. **Right:** Segmentation of steps similar to lateral steps. For clarity, only every second segmentation is displayed.

of the plane created by the left hip, right hip and the left ankle joint positions. This rule leads to a robust segmentation procedure as shown in Figure 1. Our motion capture database also contains lateral stepping motions. For these type of motions, we devised a feature that segments the motion when the velocity of both the left and right ankle joints is close to zero. See Figure 1 for an example.

The segmented clips start and end with frames that are very similar to the equivalent ones in the other segmented motion clips. This segmentation procedure is therefore suitable for a motion graph construction. Additional feature detectors can be designed in order to segment motions of different nature. Adding new feature detectors is straightforward and simple rules can achieve robust segmentation. For the purpose of locomotion synthesis, the two described segmentation criteria suffice to ensure that useful clips are obtained. The obtained clips are semantically similar in form and length and could potentially be categorized, parametrized or dropped if sufficient amount of motion segments have already been segmented. Another advantage of feature-based motion graphs is the automatic avoidance of foot-skating artifacts. Since blending operations are performed only at the extremities of each segmented clip, where there are only frames with one foot in contact with the floor, the skeleton can be re-parented at the contact foot before the blending operations, ensuring that the contact foot is not altered from its original position. This is done during transition generation avoiding any IK-based post-processing step for foot-skating correction. Motions extracted from a feature-based motion graph contain no foot-skating.

Our motion graph is then formed by performing a pairwise test between the initial and final frames of each segmented clip. A transition is created whenever the frame comparison metric returns a value under a threshold pre-specified by the user. We use the same distance metric and alignment transformation as in the original motion graph work [9]. In order to compute the rotation range for the transition, as will be required by our IK-based deformation model, we start with the initial transformation as returned by the metric and change the rotational component about the vertical axis in incremental steps in both clockwise and counterclockwise directions until before the transitional cost exceeds the pre-defined threshold. The achieved range is stored on each transition and defines

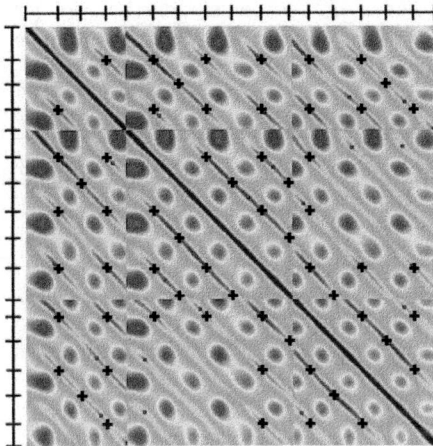

Fig. 2. 2D error image between the frames of 3 walking motion cycles containing 693 frames sampled at 60 Hz. The red regions (circular) represent highest error and the blue regions (thin and long) represent lowest error. The red points marked are the local minima and the black crosses are transitions detected by the feature segmentation. There are 57 black transitions and 42 red transitions. The bars at the top and left of the image indicate the frames that were selected during the feature segmentation phase. Black transitions are always located at intersections of segmented frames.

the allowed rotational range during motion deformation. As a final step, the largest strongly connected subgraph of the graph is selected. The remaining subgraph represents the final feature-based motion graph.

4 Analyzing Feature-Based Graphs

Figure 2 compares the transition locations selected with the standard motion graph procedure against the proposed feature segmentation. These transitions are superimposed on the 2D error image of the entire motion database. The same frame comparison threshold is used for both methods. Note that the computation of the 2D error image is required by the standard motion graph but not by the feature-based motion graph. The transitions selected by the standard motion graph are selected by detecting local minima in the 2D error image; whereas for feature-based graphs, candidate transitions are determined by the feature segmentation directly and are independent of the 2D error image.

Figure 2 shows that the feature-based transitions often occur in similar locations as the local minima ones. Since the possible transition frames are segmented by the same feature detectors, they satisfy the same geometrical constraints and thus have high chances of forming transitions. The motion capture database is also segmented at less points; moreover, our experiments show that the feature segmentation criterion will result on transition points that have higher connectivity with other transition points.

Table 1. Numerical comparison between standard motion graphs (SMG) and feature-based motion graphs (FMG). Column 'BF' illustrates the connectivity of each graph with its average branching factor, which is computed as the number of edges divided by the number of nodes.

	SMG				FMG			
Frames	Constr. time (s)	Nodes	Edges	BF	Constr. time (s)	Nodes	Edges	BF
693	208.1	42	16	1.27	1.5	51	80	1.61
1185	650.0	198	102	1.34	4.0	20	51	1.72
1660	1297.7	135	59	1.30	6.3	35	125	1.78
2329	2577.5	188	81	1.30	6.5	22	46	1.68
3347	4853.5	310	211	1.40	6.6	19	47	1.71
6887	22272.5	1245	933	1.42	27.0	100	403	1.80

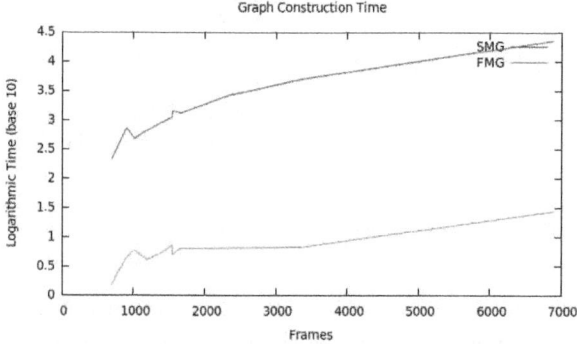

Fig. 3. Construction time spent for SMG (top line) and FMG (bottom line) as a function of the number of frames. The vertical axis represent time on a logarithmic scale (base 10). See also Table 1.

In order to evaluate our approach, we have computed both a standard motion graph (SMG) and a feature-based motion graph (FMG) from 6 different motion capture databases containing an increasing number of frames. Table 1 shows numerical comparisons between the structures, using the same transition threshold. It is possible to notice that FMGs have less nodes and more edges in most of the cases. The 'BF' column in the table shows the average branching factor obtained in each case. This column clearly indicates that FMGs exhibit higher connectivity compared to SMGs in all cases. This property makes FMGs particularly suitable for our deformation method.

FMGs are also computed much faster. The time spent for constructing a feature-based motion graph is often improved from several minutes to just a few seconds. Figure 3 depicts this comparison in logarithmic scale (with a base of 10) and shows that FMGs can be constructed 2 to 3 orders of magnitude faster than SMGs. For instance, it took 27s to create a feature-based graph from 6887 motion frames while the standard motion-graph took about 6h.

Table 2. Statistics when searching for locomotion sequences in different environments. The same threshold was used for both of the graphs. 'Size' is the number of nodes and 'BF' is the branching factor in each graph. 'Length' represents the average arc-length of the solution motions, measured with the character's root position projected to the floor. 'Exp' is the average number of node expansions during each search and 'Time' is the average time spent searching for each solution in seconds. The last three columns show the percentage improvement of FMGs over SMGs.

	SMG					FMG					Comparison		
Env.	Size	BF	Length	Exp.	Time	Size	BF	Length	Exp.	Time	Length	Exp.	Time
1	344	1.30	239.6	2391	145.3	130	1.66	219.8	1015	115.4	8.28	57.55	20.57
2	344	1.30	250.3	2903	148.1	130	1.66	229.2	1072	97.8	8.44	63.07	33.91
3	344	1.30	267.6	3745	145.6	130	1.66	243.0	1263	85.0	9.20	66.28	41.59
4	344	1.30	259.0	3671	121.9	130	1.66	234.3	1292	74.5	9.53	64.79	38.88

As showed in Table 1, FMGs contain less nodes and higher connectivity between nodes. The higher connectivity is key for improving the solutions generated from search queries. In order to quantify and evaluate the solution space of the graphs, we now present several experiments measuring and comparing the quality of our solutions in different environments with obstacles.

Table 2 summarizes the obtained statistics from 4 different environments with increasing number of obstacles. Both SMG and FMG were constructed using the same transition threshold. SMG had 344 nodes with an average branching factor of 1.30, whereas FMG had 130 nodes with an average branching factor of 1.66. Three metrics were used to compare the performance of the graphs: average optimal solution length, average expansion count and average search time (in seconds) spent during the graph search. As it can be seen on the table, FMG in average expands less nodes, spends less time searching and produces smaller errors in all of the cases. In average, FMGs show an improvement between 8-9% in length error and between 20-40% in search time in comparison to SMGs thanks to the increased solution space achieved with the higher connectivity.

5 Improving Search among Obstacles with Channels

The search procedure used in the previous section represents the standard search solution for extracting locomotion sequences from a given motion graph. We now describe our improved search for faster motion extraction, which is based on constraining the search to pre-computed channels. While the idea of pruning the search has been explored before [17], our approach employs a new technique based on fast geometrically-computed channels.

We first compute a free 2D path on the floor plane between the current position of the character and the target position using an available triangulation-based path planning technique [7]. The computed paths are obtained well under a millisecond in the presented environments. The path is computed with guaranteed clearance, therefore guaranteeing that sufficient clearance for the character

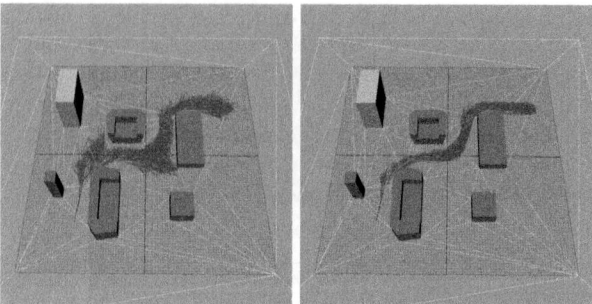

Fig. 4. Unrolled branches by a motion graph search with channel pruning disabled (left) and enabled (right)

to reach the goal is available. Once a 2D path is available, we perform a graph search by unrolling the motion graph in the environment and expanding only the nodes that remain close enough to the path. Since the path is guaranteed to be free of obstacles within its channel (i.e. within a distance r to the path), only nodes generating motion clips completely inside the free channel are expanded, and collision tests with the environment are not needed. As a result, faster searches are achieved by avoiding collision checking, which represents a major computational bottleneck when employed.

We test if a motion clip remains inside the free channel by projecting the position of key extreme joints of the character (like the hand and feet joints) to the floor, and measuring if their distances to the path are smaller than r. The projected positions are taken from the final frame and few intermediate frames of each motion clip. Collision tests are therefore reduced to point-path distance computations.

The overall search procedure starts from the node in the motion graph containing the initial character pose. This node is expanded, and every valid expansion remaining inside the free channel is inserted in a priority queue Q storing the expansion front of the search. The priority queue is sorted according to a function $f(node) = g(node) + h(node)$, where $g(node)$ is the cost-to-come value and $h(node)$ is the distance to the goal. The search stops when a node is within a distance d to the goal or when the priority queue is empty, in which case failure is reported. In our experiments d is set to 10cm. Figure 4 clearly depicts the advantage of confining the search within the computed channel.

6 IK-Based Motion Deformation

Combined with our FMG and triangulation based pruning technique, a new *Inverse Branch Kinematics* (IBK) procedure is proposed for improving the obtained solutions. As previously mentioned, section 3, we compute a lower and upper limit for the rotational component of each created transition during the graph construction step.

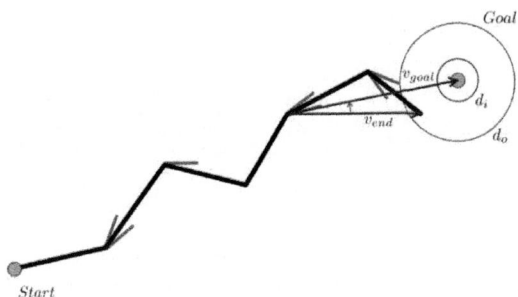

Fig. 5. A graph branch represented as a kinematic chain. Motion transitions are represented as rotational joints and the red lines represent the joint limits which are identical to the corresponding rotation limits stored in the motion graph transitions.

The search procedure is performed as previously described, stopping when a branch becomes close enough to the target in respect to a user-specified distance d_o. Then, our IBK solver is employed to iteratively optimize the solution towards the exact target location, up to a given tolerance d_i. Therefore, when $h(node) < d_o$ and $g(node) > dist(start, goal)$, $d_i < d_o$, the IBK procedure is invoked. In other words, when the distance between the node being expanded and the goal is under d_o and the length of the current path is longer than the Euclidean distance between the start and goal positions (meaning that there is room for a branch deformation), the search is then paused and the branch is deformed as a 2D kinematic chain with joint limits taken from the transition limits stored in the transitions. In our experiments we have set d_o to 50cm, d_i to 10cm. See Figure 5 for an example.

Depending on the nature of the transitions, the chain might have different joint limits. In Figure 5, the transition between the third and four node of the branch is not flexible. Thus this joint of the chain remains fixed. Also, the lower and upper joint limits do not have to be symmetric. For example, the second link has only room to move in respect to the upper limit. Once a candidate solution chain with its joints limits is obtained, the IBK solver can then evaluate rotational values at the joints in order to reach the target with the end-node of the search path. Several experiments were performed and our solver achieved best results with a Cyclic Coordinate Descent (CCD) solver [22]. We have in particular experimented with a Jacobian-based pseudo-inverse solver, however, in our highly constrained 2D kinematics chains the much simpler CCD solver was faster.

Each CCD iteration increments rotations at each joint, starting from the base joint towards the end-effector joint. At each joint two vectors v_{end} and v_{goal} are calculated. Vector v_{end} is from the current joint to the end-effector and v_{goal} is the vector from the current joint to the goal. These two vectors are shown in Figure 5 for the fifth link of the chain. The angle between the two vectors is incremented to the current joint and the result clipped against the joint limits. The last step of the CCD iteration consists of calculating the improvement from the previous iteration, which is given by how much closer the end-effector is to the target.

Fig. 6. The left image shows a typical problematic motion graph solution where an overly long motion is returned as solution to a given target. The right image shows the correct solution obtained by coupling the search with our IBK solver, which is able to deform nearby motions to the exact target without degrading the quality of the solution.

Table 3. Improvements gained when deploying IBK during search. Comparisons for both SMGs and FMGs with and without channel pruning for four different environments are shown. All values are represented as percentages. Each value is calculated as follows: if v is the value measured without deploying IBK and v_{ibk} is the value with IBK deployed then the reported percentage p is calculated a $p = -(v_{ibk} - v)/v$.

	SMG						FMG					
	Channel Prunning			Without Channel			Channel Prunning			Without Channel		
Env.	Length	Exp.	Time	Length	Exp.	Time	Length	Exp.	Time	Length	Exp.	Time
1	17.9	73.3	36.8	1.5	55.0	29.2	18.0	80.0	57.2	5.0	49.1	30.8
2	17.6	67.4	29.9	2.5	53.3	21.8	16.6	75.6	43.9	4.5	49.3	13.5
3	17.6	62.7	23.4	5.6	58.1	23.9	13.7	67.1	19.9	4.2	56.5	19.0
4	17.6	67.3	29.9	5.6	48.1	15.1	12.9	55.2	6.2	4.4	47.4	14.6

The CCD iterations stop if no improvements are detected after a number of iterations. At this point, if the distance between the end-effector and the goal is less then d_i then the solution with its new rotation values are evaluated for collisions. If no collisions occur, success is reported otherwise the search continues until another candidate branch is obtained. Figure 6 illustrates that in several cases the IK deformation is able to achieve a solution that otherwise the alternative solution without deformation would not be acceptable.

Table 3 shows the effect of employing the IBK solver for SMGs and FMGs with both the channel pruning enabled and disabled. As it can be seen from the table, IBK improves the generated solutions and reduces the search time in all the cases. The average improvement in the length of the motions when channel pruning is enabled is about 17% and 5% when pruning is disabled. The improvement on average on the search time is 31% when channel pruning is enabled and 21% when channel search is disabled. The reduced search times are a direct consequence of being able to terminate the search process early. This is possible because branches that are close to the goal can be deformed to meet the goal precisely.

7 Discussion and Conclusions

The presented evaluations demonstrate many advantages of the proposed feature segmentation, channel pruning and IBK deformation.

The first obvious advantage of the proposed FMG is that the construction time is dramatically improved in comparison to the standard motion graph procedure as our method does not need to compute a full 2D error image of the motion capture database (see Table 1). The fact that we do not search for transitions in the quadratic space of possibilities does not impose any drawbacks. On the contrary, we have shown that feature-based graphs have more connectivity and most often lead to improved results when applying search methods for locomotion synthesis around obstacles, which is always a challenging problem for discrete search structures to address. For instance, Table 2 shows up to 41% improvement on the time spent searching for all four environments.

We have also showed comparisons demonstrating the several improvements obtained by the channel pruning and the IK-based deformation technique (See Table 3). In all scenarios, these methods were able to improve both the quality of the synthesized solutions and the time taken during the search process. The IK-based procedure in particular represents a novel, simple, and effective way to optimize motions composed of motion capture segments.

In conclusion, we have presented new segmentation, search and deformation techniques for improving motion graphs. Our techniques significantly reduce the time spent for constructing the graph and at the same time lead to better solutions from search queries. We have demonstrated these benefits with several experiments in environments with obstacles, using both standard search procedures and the proposed channel pruning and IK-based motion deformation techniques. The proposed methods have showed to produce superior results in all cases.

Acknowledgments. This work was partially supported by NSF Award IIS-0915665.

References

1. Arikan, O., Forsyth, D.A.: Synthesizing constrained motions from examples. Proceedings of SIGGRAPH 21(3), 483–490 (2002)
2. Arikan, O., Forsyth, D.A., O'Brien, J.F.: Motion synthesis from annotations. Proceedings of SIGGRAPH 22(3), 402–408 (2003)
3. Beaudoin, P., Coros, S., van de Panne, M., Poulin, P.: Motion-motif graphs. In: Proceedings of the 2008 ACM SIGGRAPH/Eurographics Symposium on Computer Animation (SCA), pp. 117–126 (2008)
4. Choi, M.G., Lee, J., Shin, S.Y.: Planning biped locomotion using motion capture data and probabilistic roadmaps. Proceedings of SIGGRAPH 22(2), 182–203 (2002)
5. Esteves, C., Arechavaleta, G., Pettré, J., Laumond, J.-P.: Animation planning for virtual characters cooperation. ACM Transaction on Graphics 25(2), 319–339 (2006)

6. Gleicher, M., Shin, H.J., Kovar, L., Jepsen, A.: Snap-together motion: assembling run-time animations. In: Proceedings of the Symposium on Interactive 3D Graphics and Games (I3D), NY, USA, pp. 181–188 (2003)
7. Kallmann, M.: Shortest paths with arbitrary clearance from navigation meshes. In: Proceedings of the Eurographics / SIGGRAPH Symposium on Computer Animation (SCA) (2010)
8. Kim, M., Hyun, K., Kim, J., Lee, J.: Synchronized multi-character motion editing. ACM Trans. Graph. 28(3), 1–9 (2009)
9. Kovar, L., Gleicher, M., Pighin, F.H.: Motion graphs. Proceedings of SIGGRAPH 21(3), 473–482 (2002)
10. Lau, M., Kuffner, J.J.: Behavior planning for character animation. In: 2005 ACM SIGGRAPH / Eurographics Symposium on Computer Animation, pp. 271–280 (August 2005)
11. Lau, M., Kuffner, J.J.: Precomputed search trees: planning for interactive goal-driven animation. In: Proceedings of the ACM SIGGRAPH/Eurographics Symposium on Computer Animation (SCA), pp. 299–308 (2006)
12. Lee, J., Chai, J., Reitsma, P., Hodgins, J.K., Pollard, N.: Interactive control of avatars animated with human motion data. Proceedings of SIGGRAPH 21(3), 491–500 (2002)
13. Zhao, S.K.L., Normoyle, A., Safonova, A.: Automatic construction of a minimum size motion graph. In: Proceedings of ACM SIGGRAPH/Eurographics Symposium on Computer Animation (2009)
14. Müller, M., Röder, T., Clausen, M.: Efficient content-based retrieval of motion capture data. In: Proceedings of SIGGRAPH, pp. 677–685. ACM Press, New York (2005)
15. Pan, J., Zhang, L., Lin, M., Manocha, D.: A hybrid approach for synthesizing human motion in constrained environments. In: Conference on Computer Animation and Social Agents, CASA (2010)
16. Ren, C., Zhao, L., Safonova, A.: Human motion synthesis with optimization-based graphs. Computer Graphics Forum (In Proc. of Eurographics 2010, Sweden) 29(2) (2010)
17. Safonova, A., Hodgins, J.K.: Construction and optimal search of interpolated motion graphs. ACM Transactions on Graphics (Proceedings. of SIGGRAPH) 26(3) (2007)
18. Shin, H.J., Oh, H.S.: Fat graphs: constructing an interactive character with continuous controls. In: Proceedings of the ACM SIGGRAPH/Eurographics Symposium on Computer Animation (SCA), pp. 291–298 (2006)
19. Sung, M., Kovar, L., Gleicher, M.: Fast and accurate goal-directed motion synthesis for crowds. In: Proceedings of the Symposium on Computer Animation (SCA) (July 2005)
20. Treuille, A., Lee, Y., Popović, Z.: Near-optimal character animation with continuous control. In: Proceedings of ACM SIGGRAPH. ACM Press (2007)
21. van Basten, B.J.H., Egges, A., Geraerts, R.: Combinining path planners and motion graphs. Computer Animation and Virtual Worlds 21, 1–22 (2011)
22. Wang, L.-C.T., Chen, C.C.: A combined optimization method for solving the inverse kinematics problem of mechanical manipulators. IEEE Transactions on Robotics and Automation 7(4), 489–499 (1991)
23. Zhao, L., Safonova, A.: Achieving good connectivity in motion graphs. In: Proceedings of the 2008 ACM/Eurographics Symposium on Computer Animation (SCA), pp. 127–136 (July 2008)

Planning Plausible Human Animation with Environment-Aware Motion Sampling

Je-Ren Chen and Anthony Steed

Department of Computer Science,
University College London
{J.Chen,A.Steed}@cs.ucl.ac.uk

Abstract. The creation of plausible human animation remains a perennial problem in computer graphics. To construct long animations it is common to stitch together a sequence of motions from a motion database. Typically, this is done in two stages: planning a route and then sampling motions from the database to follow that route. We introduce an environment-aware motion sampling technique that combines the planning and sampling stages. Our observation is that in the traditional approach the route generated in the first stage over-constrains the motion sampling so that it is relatively implausible that a human would follow this animation. We combine the motion sampling and planning and show that we can find shorter and more plausible animations.

Keywords: Computer animation, motion sampling, motion planning.

1 Introduction

The creation of animations for virtual humans is an essential part of many computer graphics-based productions. One important goal is to create animations that looks plausible. By plausible we mean that the animation would be feasible for a similarly-proportioned real human and it would be likely that a real human would choose a similar motion in an analogous real-world situation. Motion capture can be used to create animations (motion clips), but it is difficult to capture all the necessary animations for a production such as a video game. Thus, the common practise is to build a database of motion clips and then construct longer animations from these shorter clips.

To construct an animation from a motion database, a query to the database must be formulated. The query is formulated as a set of constraints such as starting position, end position, specific animations to play at certain points, waypoints to travel through, etc. It is common that the query is under-constrained in that there may be many sequences of clips that achieve the goal. (e.g., "walk from the door to the chair avoiding the table"). Given that we can find a set of candidate solutions that meet the constraints, we select between these by typically choosing the one with the shortest total path length, assuming that this is the most plausible.

One way to search the motion database is to exhaustively search all possible sequences of clips, but this works only for short sequences. A typical situation involving longer sequences is when the character needs to navigate through the environment. A common strategy in this situation is to decouple the query into a path-finding stage and a path-following stage. The first stage searches for a path, i.e. a 2-D or 3-D curve, that travels through the free space between obstacles and reaches the goal. The second stage queries the motion database to find a sequence of clips that follows this curve. We can then ask two questions: can we generate an animation that follows the curve? Will the resulting animation be plausible? Our first observation is that in order to search for a path, one must make a conservative assumption about how far to stay away from the obstacle. We might thus inadvertently exclude some animations from consideration because an individual motion clip might be able to pass the obstacle more closely. Our second observation is that once a path is generated, we need to approximate it by motion clips. In doing this approximation we might need to select clips that would not be plausible from a high-level view of what sequence of motions a real human would take. Our belief is that both of these problems result from the decoupling of the path-finding stage from the path-following stage.

We propose an environment-aware motion sampler which allows us to generate plausible virtual human animations that navigate through an environment with obstacles. We propose to couple the path-finding and path-following stages in a search of a motion database. In Section 2 we discuss related work. In Section 3 we present an overview of our approach, and the new environment-aware motion sampling (EMS) algorithm. In Section 4 we explain how path-following can be achieved with explicit constraints. The main contribution is in Section 5 where we show how obstacle avoidance can be introduced as an implicit constraint. Section 6 then shows how we can find animations where the previous standard technique cannot in typical navigation problems.

2 Related Work

The purpose of motion planning is to generate motions which move a subject from one location to another without any collisions and with least effort. Commonly this is simplified as finding the shortest collision-free path to the goal. One way of finding such a path is to approximate the space by decomposing the free space into connected proximities [4] or using a grid to store discretized free space information [2]. In 2-D or 3-D it is efficient enough to search for paths connecting free cells in approximate representations, but these are inefficient when the subject has many DOFs, such as a human-like character. Thus, they are suitable for generating ground paths at a coarser level which we then can use as constraints to query a motion database to follow it.

Another approach is to take random samples of the free space and summarise it as roadmaps [11]. For example, Choi et al. [3] approximate footprints on the a roadmap and re-target biped motions on a given route, but they only evaluate the collision of the footprints rather than entire body motions. It is also possible to represent motions as sampled points with tree structures for later determination. For example, precomputed search trees [6] have been applied with motion data by plotting them into point clouds so they are intersected with obstacles to eliminate invalid branches. Our research shares a similar goal with theirs, i.e., planning animation with collision detection using motion data. However, we estimate collision errors as a soft constraint instead of using the binary decision of accepting or rejecting a solution.

Mizuguchi et al., [10], describe how motions are authored and constructed for character motion control in game production. Motions representing in-game actions and the transitions between them are hand-edited by animators such that motions are blended together to control the character at run-time. To reduce the burden of manual input, many researchers have investigated different ways of detecting and querying transitions. The term "motion graphs"([5][1][7]) are used to refer various techniques that detect motion transitions by making use of frame distance matrices. To generate an animation that satisfies user-specified goals, a motion graph defines constraints, such as desired locations and orientations, and a cost function to search for an optimal edge sequence that minimises the cost. Hence, navigation animation is typically done by identifying all necessary constraints along a feasible route obtained from a preceeding planning stage.

One way of searching for a solution that navigates through obstacles is to enumerate the states in the control-parameter space and connect these states with corresponding paths of the motion graph. Reitsma and Pollard [12] embed a motion graph into a 4-D grid space that consists of the ground position, orientation, and the motion type such that they are able to evaluate the motion graph coverage in the scene and the motion path quality of the search. Safonova and Hodgins [13] also apply an embedded motion graph but they allow the interpolation between two source motions rather than a single motion type in each state so that they are able to improve the optimality of the animation. However, the main drawback of these methods is that they need to re-embed the motion graph whenever the scene is changed.

Another way of finding a motion graph solution is using randomised search. Arikan and Forsyth [1] applied a Monte Carlo simulation on motion graph search by generating an initial random graph walk and repeatedly re-enumerating suboptimal edges with alternatives towards satisfying the constraints. We adapt their method to our motion query in this research. Whilst their method works with multiple constraints that follows a curve, we incorporate collision errors as implicit costs in the optimisation.

Reinforcement learning techniques are also applied to generate navigation animation ([14][8][9]). They do so by incorporating the obstacle configurations in the parameter space so that they can pre-compute the costs for each condition and select the best one to avoid the obstacle at run-time. However, due to limited dimensionality of the parameter space, they can only allow very few numbers of obstacle configurations to be considered. Our implicit cost function estimates the collision error directly in the work space and can be scaled with any number of obstacles.

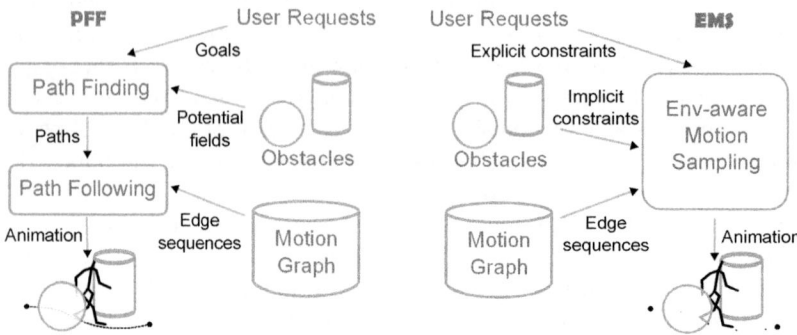

Fig. 1. The approach of decoupled search (left) and joint optimisation (right)

3 Overview

We wish to generate plausible full-body human motions for navigating a virtual environment. One typical way is to query a motion database, such as a motion graph (see Section 2), by specifying as many waypoints as needed to avoid the obstacles until we reach the goal. The waypoints are obtained by some path finding technique in a preceding stage. We propose to formulate navigation animation generation as a planning problem by jointly optimising both explicit (user-specified goals) and implicit (environmental obstacles) constraints. The aim of the optimisation is to sample a sequence of clips that minimises the explicit and implicit costs.

In this paper, we compare our joint optimisation method, called environment-aware motion sampling (EMS), with a typical decoupled search approach, called path finding and following (PFF). Figure 1 compares the two approaches. Both approaches have the same inputs: the user-requested constraints such as locations, orientations, and desired actions; the virtual environment; and a motion graph. The EMS and PFF methods both rely on a motion graph to query a motion database. They also both employ potential-field path finding [2] to select a route through the environment. Whilst PFF searches for animation that follows this route, EMS synthesises a full-body collision-free animation directly using the collision errors within the cost optimisation.

Motion Graphs. As discussed in Section 2, a motion graph is a database technique that can generate a sequence of motions from a library. To query the database, we specify certain constraints and search for a solution that minimise a cost function. We implement the Monte Carlo simulation-based motion graph search method (MCMG) [1]. This method begins a search with a random edge sequence. In each iteration, MCMG proposes the best few candidates by scoring their costs and optimises these best-so-far solutions by modifying their sub-optimal edges with their alternatives. To search the graph more efficiently, the edges are arranged as tree structures such that edge modifications, or *mutations*, only enumerate the root-level edges of the trees (hop mutations), while finer tuning of the transitions can still be made by replacing an edge with its children (demote mutations). Once an edge sequence is obtained, the animation is derived by stitching together the corresponding motion clips. Please refer to the original work for technical details [1]. This paper will focus on how we design the explicit and implicit constraints and the cost functions in order to facilitate the search algorithm for character navigation. The algorithm we describe would be applicable to types of query other than navigation.

Potential-field Path Finding. For path finding, we use potential fields [2] since it is easy to implement and is considered to be effective in low-dimensional path finding problems. The potential field method finds a path by discretising the workspace into a grid of cells and propagating a gradient of ascending distances in the free space from the goal point. The cells in this field, the potentials, are then used as a heuristic to search for a connected chain of cells from a given initial location by moving to a lower potential neighbour cell. The chain is converted into a curve (a poly-line) by connecting the centroids of consecutive cells. The curve is further straightened if any segments does not collide with an obstacle. Such property maintains the shortest path length for this route. Although we can obtain a short and collision-free path by using potential fields, we cannot query an animation to follow this path as it does not consider the volume of the character. A common workaround is to sample the animation along the curve with a safety distance to an obstacle. To achieve this in PFF, we estimate a maximum bounding cylinder from the library, and use its radius to thicken obstacles when building potential fields. We will describe how potential fields are applied to obtain the path to be followed for PFF in Section 4 and how it is used to estimate the minimal travel distance for EMS in Section 5. Note that the potential field path finding method used in this research can be replaced by other 2-D path finding techniques.

Decoupled Search versus Joint Optimisation. An animation query begins with a pair of explicit constraints: initial location, orientation and action (i.e., a specific motion clip), and goal location, orientation and action. In decoupled search, PFF first finds a poly-line that connects initial and goal locations in the path finding stage. During path following, intermediate constraints are densely planted along this path as waypoints. PFF then uses an objective function to search for a solution that strictly travels through these exact waypoints within a certain radius by minimising $Cost_{PFF} = Error_{smooth} + Error_{penalisedExplicit}$, where $Error_{penalisedExplicit}$ is the total deviation between the solution and waypoints (described in Section 4). The term $Error_{smooth}$ maintains the smoothness of the transitions and is the sum of the cost of a transition estimated by the dissimilarity between poses obtained during motion graph construction ([1]). For joint optimisation, EMS also performs path finding but does not enforce path following. Instead, EMS only considers the vertices of the poly-line as approximate waypoints to sample towards a preferable short route and to estimate the expected travel distance. Thus, EMS searches for an edge sequence that travels close to these sparse waypoints and avoid obstacles by optimising $Cost_{EMS} = Error_{smooth} + Error_{explicit} + Error_{implicit}$. We will describe how to estimate $Error_{implicit}$ in Section 5.

4 Animation Control Using Explicit Constraints

We first consider sampling motions with explicit user specifications but without the implicit constraints of collision avoidance. We begin by considering only two explicit constraints. We then describe how to sample motions with multiple constraints, and how to partially enforce constraints to allow sampling an animation along a series of constraints such as those implied by the curve generated by the PFF method.

Explicit Constraints. To animate a character moving from one spot to another, we define an explicit constraint c to be a set of triple such that $c = (act, loc, ori)$ to specify required *action*, *location*, and *orientation* constraints. Actions are labelled poses (frames) to specify a motion to be happened at a particular point. Actions are hard constraints and are obeyed by searching among the edge sequences that contain these required poses. A location constraint specifies the required position of the character's centre of mass projected on the ground (x-z plane). The orientation constraint specifies the required angle between the character's facing direction (obtained by projecting the local z-axis of the body on the ground) and the world z-axis. The location and orientation constraints are used to estimate the deviation of sampled edge sequences in the explicit objective function.

Explicit Objective Function. Let $\Omega = (e_1, ..., e_n)$ be a proposed edge sequence sampled from the motion graph with a pair of initial and goal condition as $C_{s,t} = (c_s, c_t)$ and let f be a frame of the animation derived from Ω. We define functions $locate(f)$ and $orient(f)$ to estimate the accumulated location and orientation of any f. Since we require the animation to be derived from the initial constraint c_s, the error between Ω and $C_{s,t}$ is estimated by calculating the positional and rotational deviations between the end frame f_t and the goal constraint c_t as

$$deviate(\Omega, c_t) = w_l \cdot (|locate(f_t) - loc_t|)^2 + w_o \cdot ((orient(f_t) - ori_t))^2, \quad (1)$$

where weights w_l and w_o are chosen such that the error yielded by 30cm in location is equivelent to the error of 10° in orientation, as suggested in [1].

Multiple and Partial Explicit Constraints. We may also wish to generate an animation that satisfies more than two constraints. We insert multiple constraints between c_s and c_t and accumulate the deviations raised at each constraint with Equation 1. However, to calculate the deviation, we need to determine the corresponding frame for the action of each constraint since there might exist more than one frame that satisfy the action constraint. Let $C = (c_1, ..., c_n)$

be a series of explicit constraints. We find f_i for each c_i by selecting frames in Ω that contain act_i and choose the one with the least deviation by

$$f_i = \arg\min_F deviate(\Omega, c_i), \qquad (2)$$

where F is the set of frames that are of action type act_i found in the animation that corresponds to Ω. We then chose the deviation of f_i to be the the error increased by c_i.

Occasionally, we only require the character to travel through certain locations regardless of their actions or orientations. We can partially enforce an explicit constraint by discarding its action constraint and orientation deviation in Equation 1. Thus, similar to Equation 2, for each partial explicit constraint, we find an f_i among all frames that minimises $deviate(\Omega, c_i)$ regardless the orientation. Finally, the total explicit error is

$$explicit(\Omega, C) = \sum_1^n deviate(\Omega, c_i). \qquad (3)$$

Path Following using Explicit Constraints. Once we can sample motions with multiple and partial explicit constraints, we can generate an animation that follows a curve with the motion graph. We plant intermediate partial constraints as waypoints along the curve obtained from the path-finding stage with step size d_{step}. However, as mentioned in Section 3, we cannot simply find and follow a path regardless of the volume of the body. Thus, we estimate a minimum bounding cylinder from the library and apply the radius r_{body} of the cylinder to expand the obstacles in the potential field. To ensure we sample the animation moving only inside this corridor, we penalise those frames that are far away from the intermediate partial constraints by adding

$$penalise(f_k, c_i) = (\frac{|locate(f_k) - loc_i|}{r_{body}})^{p_{follow}}, \qquad (4)$$

where $p_{follow} >= 1$ increases the penalty. Finally, we are able to generate an animation to follow the path by using $explicit(\Omega, C)$ for $Error_{penalisedExplicit}$ for $Cost_{PFF}$ in Section 3.

5 Collision Avoidance with Implicit Constraints

We now present our new approach where we introduce two implicit constraints to the search: the environmental obstacles and minimal travel distance constraints.

Implicit Constraints. We define two types of implicit constraints: one that enforces obstacle avoidance and one that selects minimal travel distance. We design the obstacle constraints using three parametric primitives (spheres, cylinders and cubes) so that collision detection can use efficient distance measurements.

Scenes can be approximated by sets of transformed primitives. For each frame, we collide a point cloud of the joint positions with the obstacles to estimate the collision error. The minimal travel distance constraint maintains a minimal cost from taking longer alternative motions to avoid obstacles. We suggest linear distances between goals as an expected travel distance and we wish to sample motions that move along these straight lines as close as possible. Hence, the minimal travel distance constraint is an error computed as the ratio of the required travel distance to the expected travel distance.

Implicit Objective Function. Let $O = (o_1, ..., o_m)$ be a set of obstacles, we define a boolean function $isInside(o_i, p)$ to determine whether a point p is inside an obstacle o_i. The collision error between the obstacle set O and each frame is estimated by

$$err_{collide}(O, f) = \sum_{i=1}^{m} \sum_{j=i}^{n} \frac{isInside(o_i, jointPos(f, j))}{n}, \quad (5)$$

where m and n are obstacle and joint numbers and $jointPos(f, j)$ is a function to obtain the world position of a joint at frame f. In practise, we perform a coarse bounding-box collision between obstacles and the point cloud to select a smaller set of O such that we do not collide with every single obstacle. The minimal travel distance error is the ratio of the required travel distance to the expected travel distance:

$$err_{travel}(\Omega, C, O) = \frac{arclength(\Omega) + |locate(f_m) - loc_n|}{arclength((c_1, ..., c_n))}. \quad (6)$$

where $arclength(\Omega)$ is the travelled distance derived from the animation and $arclength((c_1, ..., c_n))$ is the total length of the poly-line formed by the explicit constraints from initial to final goal. The distance between $locate(f_m)$ and loc_n is a penalty applied to solutions that are short but are not close to the final goal. Finally, the total cost of the implicit errors is calculated as:

$$implicit(\Omega, C, O) = (\sum_{k=1}^{n} err_{collide}(O, f_k))^2 + (w_d \cdot (err_{travel}(\Omega, C, O) - 1))^2, \quad (7)$$

where n is the number of frames of Ω and w_d is chosen by experiment given that w_l and w_o in the explicit errors (see Equation 1) are fixed.

Scene Navigation via Joint Optimisation. By introducing $implicit(\Omega, C, O)$ to $Cost_{EMS}$ described in Section 3, we are able to estimate the cost of a sampled solution. For joint optimisation, the EMS algorithm also applies potential path finding to obtain a path from the explicit constraints in the initialisation stage. Unlike path-finding in PFF, we do not expand obstacles since we require the path to be the shortest possible: the path arclength will be used to estimate the expected travel distance in Equation 6. Also, instead of strictly following the path, we only insert the vertices of this path as intermediate partial constraints to converge to a solution with a shorter route.

Table 1. Performance comparison between PFF and EMS in "Two-corner turning". Column *Average* is the mean of 10 trials while *Optimal* is the one with minimal cost among 10 trials. Column *Diff* shows the improvements by subtracting PFF from EMS.

	Average			Optimal		
	PFF	EMS	Diff	PFF	EMS	Diff
# of transitions	12.50	11.30	*1.20*	12	9	*3*
Transition costs	3.74	3.88	*-0.14*	3.97	3.23	*0.74*
# of frames	338.40	327.60	*10.80*	335	297	*38*
Location(cm)	10.10	11.16	*-1.06*	9.74	28.41	*-18.67*
Orientation(deg)	2.03	7.2	*-5.17*	0.05	0.16	*-0.11*
Travel dist.(cm)	1058.36	966.41	*91.95*	1075.70	907.89	*167.81*
Search time(sec)	106.20	39.03	*67.17*	70.43	21.34	*49.09*

6 Implementation and Results

We have implemented both methods using the C++ programming language and integrated them as a plug-in for the Maya animation software. We found $d_{cell} = 5cm$ to be a reasonable size for cells in the potential field to generate good quality paths in our experiments. For both PFF and EMS, we generate an initial random edge sequence that connects two poses of the required actions in the motion graph. During optimisation, we choose the best three candidates in each iteration. We only search in the root-level edges, i.e., the hop mutations, as we favour search speed over smoothness of the animation. The search terminates when no better mutation can be found and the optimal solution is the one that has the minimal cost among local minima. For path-following in PFF, we found $d_{step} = 30cm$ and $pow_{follow} = 2$ to be a reasonable step size and penalty to obtain an animation that follows the poly-line closely.

We have designed *two-corner turning* and *object-cluttered space* scenes to evaluate the results of both methods. We performed our experiments on an Intel P9700 2.8 GHz processor on a 64-bit Windows laptop machine with 6 GB memory. Details of our motion library are available on the project website[1]. The quality of the animation is measured by the transition numbers and costs to determine its smoothness, the location and orientation errors to the goal constraint, and the ground trajectory for travelled distance and required frames. We also compare the required motion-graph search time of both methods.

Two-corner Turning. In this experiment, we design a corridor scene that has two consecutive turns, as seen in Figure 2. The initial and goal constraints are placed at both ends of the corridor. Since the initial random edge sequence has an impact on the graph search time, we perform ten trials of searches. For each trial, we randomly choose an initial edge sequence for both methods and average their results, as shown in Table 1. For both methods, we select an optimal solution that has the lowest cost among ten trials and compare them in the *Optimal* column.

---

[1] http://www.cs.ucl.ac.uk/research/vr/Projects/EMS

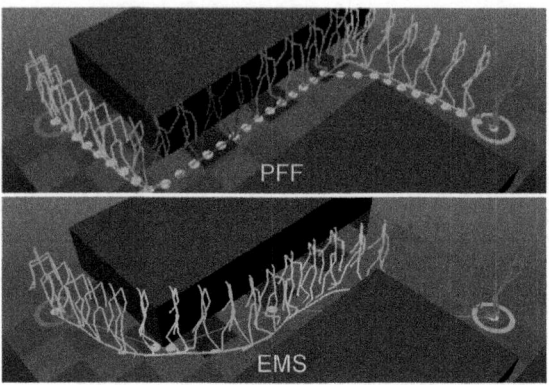

Fig. 2. Two-corner turning using PFF (top) and EMS (bottom)

In general, we found EMS can generate animation that has fewer transitions and shorter travel distance with less search time in both *Average* and *Optimal* columns. Although PFF seems to have smaller location and orientation errors, the difference between two methods is actually very small (within 20cm and 6°). Visual improvements can also be seen from the animation in Figure 2, where the result from EMS turns at the corners smoothly while PFF always makes two sharp turns in order to strictly follow the path.

Table 2. Performance comparison between PFF and EMS in "Object-cluttered space". Column *Grid* is the result before the boxes are randomly transformed.

	Average			Optimal			Grid		
	PFF	**EMS**	**Diff**	**PFF**	**EMS**	**Diff**	**PFF**	**EMS**	**Diff**
# of Transitions	22.7	11.4	*11.3*	18	5	*13*	27	6	*21*
Transition costs	6.5	3.41	*3.08*	5.63	1.60	*4.03*	5.5	1.28	*4.22*
# of frames	490.1	275	*215.1*	394	230	*164*	287	230	*57*
Location(cm)	32.88	30.13	*2.75*	20.59	8.86	*11.72*	24.45	11.67	*12.78*
Orientation(deg)	12.99	5.82	*7.17*	0.48	0.05	*0.44*	0.93	2.86	*-1.93*
Travel dist.(cm)	1481.69	831.87	*649.82*	1211.80	810.11	*401.69*	854.44	807.23	*47.21*
Search time(sec)	740.82	38.13	*702.68*	686.94	3.85	*683.09*	332.3	3.86	*328.44*

Object-cluttered Space. In the second experiment, we evaluate the performance of both methods when navigating through multiple random obstacles. First, we perform a single trial of motion search for both methods in a grid of 4×3 boxes ($40 \times 40 \times 40cm$) with a distance of $4 \times r_{body}$ between each box (see Figure 3(a)). While PFF requires more transitions to stay inside the corridor, the results of both methods are very similar. We then randomly change the size, orientation, and location of each box for ten trials, and for each random configuration, we compare the the average and optimal results generated from both methods, as shown in Table 2. Note that although this scene is more complicated

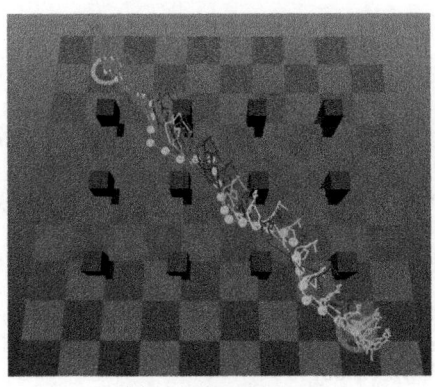
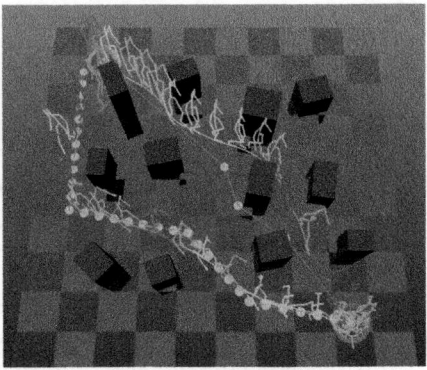

(a) A grid of boxes　　　　　　　　(b) Randomised boxes

Fig. 3. (a) Both methods generate animations that travel via a similar route. (b) While PFF can only travel through larger gaps, EMS is able to move around obstacles closely.

than the previous, the search time of EMS does not increase substantially. On the contrary, PFF requires much more search time to sample transitions as there are many turns in the paths. While PFF can only navigate through obstacles with an in-between distance larger than $2 \times r_{body}$, EMS is able to generate animations that travel through narrower gaps. Finally, unlike PFF, EMS is not over-constrained by the intermediate constraints even if it fails to find a solution that reaches all waypoints. Figure 3(b) shows an example where EMS manages to find alternative motions that reach the goal and the result is still a short route. We also provide more results in the video on our project website.

7 Conclusion

In this paper, we proposed an environment-aware motion sampling method to generate plausible human animation in a non-trivial virtual environment. The coupling of collision avoidance and motion-graph queries allows us to sample motions that reach the goals and avoid the obstacles in a more human-like way. One key reason for this is that we don't have to conservatively plan to avoid obstacles. The results show that although it is possible to apply a path finding technique to obtain explicit constraints to query a motion graph, the combination of planning and querying allows us to find more feasible solutions with fewer transitions and shorter animations to achieve the same goal.

Although we demonstrate our approach for navigation animations, the technique could be extended to other situations that involve planning motion in cluttered environments. For example, complex manipulations of objects that involve reaching into cluttered space, or planning motions that involve collision with only part of the body such as ducking or raising a hand to avoid collision with street furniture. The performance of our methode could also be improved by scoring the solutions in multiple processes or on the GPU since each simulation is independent.

References

1. Arikan, O., Forsyth, D.A.: Interactive motion generation from examples. ACM Trans. Graph. 21, 483–490 (2002)
2. Barraquand, J., Langlois, B., Latombe, J.-C.: Numerical potential field techniques for robot path planning, vol. 2, pp. 1012–1017 (June 1991)
3. Choi, M.G., Lee, J., Shin, S.Y.: Planning biped locomotion using motion capture data and probabilistic roadmaps. ACM Trans. Graph. 22(2), 182–203 (2003)
4. Choset, H., Burdick, J.: Sensor-based exploration: The hierarchical generalized voronoi graph (2000)
5. Kovar, L., Gleicher, M., Pighin, F.: Motion graphs. In: SIGGRAPH 2002: Proceedings of the 29th Annual Conference on Computer Graphics and Interactive Techniques, pp. 473–482. ACM, New York (2002)
6. Lau, M., Kuffner, J.J.: Precomputed search trees: planning for interactive goal-driven animation. In: SCA 2006: Proceedings of the 2006 ACM SIGGRAPH/Eurographics Symposium on Computer Animation, pp. 299–308. Eurographics Association, Aire-la-Ville (2006)
7. Lee, J., Chai, J., Reitsma, P.S.A., Hodgins, J.K., Pollard, N.S.: Interactive control of avatars animated with human motion data. ACM Trans. Graph. 21(3), 491–500 (2002)
8. Lee, Y., Lee, S.J., Popović, Z.: Compact character controllers. ACM Trans. Graph. 28, 169:1–169:8 (2009)
9. Lo, W.-Y., Zwicker, M.: Real-time planning for parameterized human motion. In: Proceedings of the 2008 ACM SIGGRAPH/Eurographics Symposium on Computer Animation, SCA 2008, pp. 29–38. Eurographics Association, Aire-la-Ville (2008)
10. Mizuguchi, M., Buchanan, J., Calvert, T.: Data driven motion transitions for interactive games (2001)
11. Nieuwenhuisen, D., Kamphuis, A., Overmars, M.H.: High quality navigation in computer games. Sci. Comput. Program. 67, 91–104 (2007)
12. Reitsma, P.S.A., Pollard, N.S.: Evaluating motion graphs for character animation. ACM Trans. Graph. 26(4), 18 (2007)
13. Safonova, A., Hodgins, J.K.: Construction and optimal search of interpolated motion graphs. In: SIGGRAPH 2007: ACM SIGGRAPH 2007 Papers, p. 106. ACM, New York (2007)
14. Treuille, A., Lee, Y., Popović, Z.: Near-optimal character animation with continuous control. ACM Trans. Graph, 26 (July 2007)

Dynamic Balancing and Walking for Real-Time 3D Characters

Ben Kenwright, Richard Davison, and Graham Morgan

School of Computing Science, Newcastle University, UK
{b.kenwright,richard.davison4,graham.morgan}@ncl.ac.uk

Abstract. This paper describes the real-time modeling of 3D skeletal motion with balancing properties. Our goal is to mimic human responsiveness when external forces are applied to the model. To achieve this we use an inverted pendulum as a basis for achieving a self-balancing model. We demonstrate responsiveness in stepping and posture control via a simplified biped skeletal model using our technique.

Keywords: 3D Characters, Balancing, Physics-Based Simulation, Inverted Pendulum, Virtual Pivot Point, Steering.

1 Introduction

In many immersive style games there is a need for player-controlled characters to interact with the gaming arena. Such characters provision player representation in a game and usually take human form. As a player understands how humans may act and move given certain physical environments, unexpected or restricted behavior of a player-controlled character is noticeable. Therefore, a challenging research problem is to ensure player-controlled characters are sufficiently expressive to afford the desired level of gameplay while maintaining naturally realistic movements and actions.

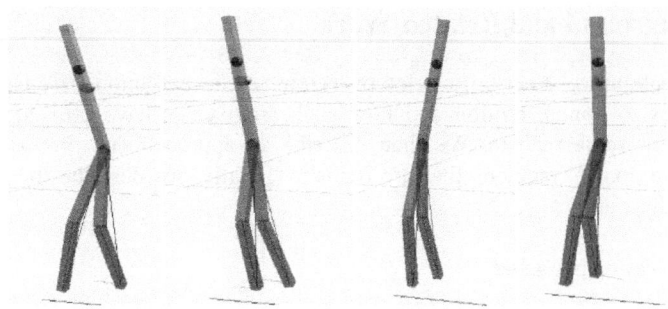

Fig. 1. Predictive stepping and posture correction due to random force disturbances being applied to the body

Data driven methods afford player-controlled characters the most natural of movements. Motion capture can ensure key-frames can be used for movement referencing or an artist could create specific animation styles. An enhanced ragdoll model can be used to blend between pre-determined animations to allow for smoothed movement (e.g., [1 – 7]). This data-driven approach looks realistic, but is restrictive in that if the animation is not pre-calculated it may not be possible to achieve. Gameplay, in essence, is restricted when reliance is placed on this technique.

The opposing technique to data driven approaches is to allow a character that is primarily controlled using physics (e.g., [8-14]) (controller approach). In this approach the physical properties of the overall character combine with feedback control principles to generate animation. The major drawback to such approaches is that they do not look as realistic as their data-driven counterparts. One major reason for this is that although the character may achieve the animation goal, it may be achieved in a manner different to that of a human. A further drawback to such methods is the level of computation required to solve non-trivial equations in real-time to calculate movement.

In many instances data driven and controller approaches are combined (e.g., [39, 40, 42]). This has the advantage that fewer pre-determined animation sequences may be required while affording a greater degree of animation. For example, a character falling over on an uneven surface (e.g., stairs) has to be achieved via physics whereas upper limb movement (e.g., reaching) could be achieved via artist directed animation. The popularity of this approach seems to indicate that the purely physics based approach may not suffice on its own (realism is lacking). However, if games are to afford complete freedom of interaction this is the only viable approach.

In this paper we consider a purely controller based approach for realistic human movement that is rendered in real-time. The key to mimicking human movement is not an attempt to recreate the appropriate physical motion alone, but to augment it with a balance controller for posture alignment. Our technique is prompted by work within theoretical robotics where an inverted pendulum is used for such purposes [28]. We demonstrate that our approach favors a human like approach to movement in terms of posture when presented with external forces. Furthermore, we extend the theoretical work described in [28] by moving our model from 2D to 3D and providing a real-time implementation.

2 Background and Related Work

In this section we describe a brief overview of the evolution of controller-based approaches to human motion and how such approaches have utilized data driven methods for more realism. We then describe an approach that provisions suitable locomotive control methods that are realistic. Finally, we describe the contribution made by this paper.

2.1 General Approaches

Achieving realistic movement of characters is an active area of research in both graphical simulation and robotics. The most basic of requirements is usually that of balance when using the controller approach, as without it few other activities are possible. Balancing in the presence of forces has been demonstrated [14, 17, 18] and more elaborate movements such as walking, running, jumping and cycling have been achieved [8, 12, 15, 16]. Further enhancements are to augment the controller with data driven approaches such as motion capture to create more stylistic motion [19, 20]. The reason for such enhancements is to bring more realism to the motions of the character. A common approach to combining data driven stylistic movement with physics is to allow a controller to maintain balance while upper body movement (which is most noticeable and more intricate) is stylized [20, 21].

A controller itself must rely on more than one physics technique if a range of transitional movements is to be accommodated (e.g., [1, 4, 10, 22]). SIMBICON [10] is a notable advancement in this area in recent years and demonstrates a biped controller that utilizes a series of poses to shape motion trajectories for flexible locomotion. Considering locomotion techniques in general, irrelevant of stylized interpretation (be it artist or motion capture inspired) a biped must place their feet in a timely manner within a particular surface area to maintain balance. This "swinging motion of legs" has been shown to be achievable via a physics technique that utilizes an inverted pendulum [23, 24].

2.2 Inverted Pendulum

The *linear inverted pendulum* (IP) may generate predictive foot placement information for balancing characters in 2D and 3D (e.g., [24, 29]). IP can be used for characters balancing while standing still or during locomotion. The IP motion is constrained to move along an elliptical path. To push the character upright a force is exerted on a character's mass from the center of the foot that is in contact with the ground. As demonstrated in [30, 31], the character's mass is concentrated into a single point (*center of mass* (CoM)) for the required calculations. To encourage a more natural motion a spring may be associated with the balancing leg [32, 33]. This makes the foot trajectory resemble a bouncing ball that mimics, to a visually convincing level, a running motion. This approach is described as a *spring loaded inverted pendulum* (SLIP).

The IP has been used as a calculation of balance to form the basis on which other aspects of human motion may be constructed [10, 19, 24, 34, 35, 36, 42]. However, as the standard IP model uses a single mass-point in its calculations there is a lack of information present to realistically represent the posture of a character. An approach to correct this issue would be to use a proportional derivative controller [16, 20, 37] to apply torque to ensure a character's body remains upright. Unfortunately, this corrective torque produces unnaturally movements due to the body not receiving feedback from the characters feet, known as the *ground reaction force* (GRF). In humans it is this force that causes people to sway and shift as they walk and change direction.

To overcome the problems of unnatural posture control in the IP approach an extended rigid body may be used to represent the trunk (enhanced IP). The hip point would be located at the base of the trunk, the CoM at the mid-point of the trunk and a *virtual pivot point* (VPP) point located parallel to the extended body and positioned above the CoM. This work was initially described in [28] and demonstrates a correlation between natural and simulated GRF. In addition, [38] describes the resultant motion demonstrated in [28] more realistic than IP without extended rigid body.

2.3 Contribution of Paper

In this paper we extend the work of the enhanced IP described in [28]. The work in [28] was 2D and only provisioned the calculated expectation of the simulation. In the field of robotics this initial investigatory stage is usual as the end goal is to actually build a robot. However, for video games we want a fully interactive 3D run-time implementation. This is what we achieved, allowing our character model to be exposed to forces and be manipulated by a player. The model itself has no data driven aspects with all foot placing's and body movements created dynamically.

The fundamental contribution of this paper is the demonstration of the enhanced 3D IP as an option for fully interactive realistic human locomotion in real-time without any data driven requirements.

3 Method

In this section we describe our method to achieving realistic motion for real-time characters. As we build directly on suggestions found in [28], we describe in more detail IP and then the enhanced version. This allows us to say quite specifically what enhancements we have made. We then describe how balancing, motion and the handling of uneven surfaces (stairs) may be achieved using our approach.

3.1 Mechanics of IP

For the purposes of balance control, we consider a human body to exhibit similar qualities to an IP. A human standing on a single leg would be equivalent to an IP assuming the body is represented by a single CoM linked to the ground contact point (*center of pressure* (CoP)). In this model we assume the legs to have no mass. This trivializes the calculation significantly while still affording the desired motion. We assume that there is no ground slippage and a single point replaces the foot.

The IP provides a simple technique for predicting where a character should place its feet to remain balanced. The diagram on the left of figure 2 shows how the different elements combine to produce a repeated motion suitable for modeling walking. The springs in the legs represent the fact that we are considering the SLIP approach to improve realism as described in [32, 33].

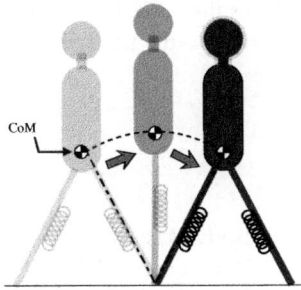 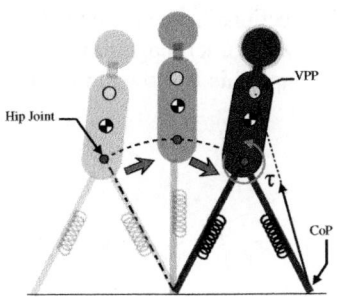

Fig. 2. (Left) Illustrates IP following a basic elliptical trajectory with no body feedback, (Right) the elongated body following a similar ellipsoid-like trajectory during locomotion, with additional torque-body feedback

3.2 Mechanics of Enhanced IP

The enhanced IP model uses all the properties of the basic SLIP model with some important additional features. The enhanced IP is shown on the right of figure 2. An elongated body is added that represents the trunk [28]. A VPP is added above the hip and parallel to the trunk.

In [28] the author provides a discussion where there is a suggestion that allowing the VPP to move outside the trunk will vary the energy in the model. Varying the energy in such a way would have the effect of speeding up or slowing down the walking motion in characters using the technique in [28]. As [28] dealt only in 2D speeding up and slowing down was all that could be accomplished. However, we realized that if this approach could be extended to 3D the VPP could ultimately be used for steering the character. Therefore, to pursue this line of research our initial technical change made to [28] was to allow the VPP to move outside the trunk to produce responsive balancing motions.

3.3 Calculations

The trunk torque is calculated by projecting the force from the leg (i.e., hip-ground spring) onto the VPP (i.e., ground-VPP) to induce a responsive self-balancing posture.

$$\hat{V}_C = \frac{(VPP - CoP)}{||VPP - CoP||} \quad (1)$$

$$\hat{V}_{TRUNK} = \frac{(VPP - CoM)}{||VPP - CoM||} \quad (2)$$

$$||GRF|| = F_L \cdot \hat{V}_C \quad (3)$$

$$GRF = ||GRF|| \cdot \hat{V}_C \quad (4)$$

$$\tau_{hip} = GRF \times \hat{V}_{TRUNK} \quad (5)$$

The directional force from the CoP to the VPP produces the GRF. Using the equations above we extract magnitude and vector to apply a torque to the trunk that feeds back to the hip. This is shown in figure 3.

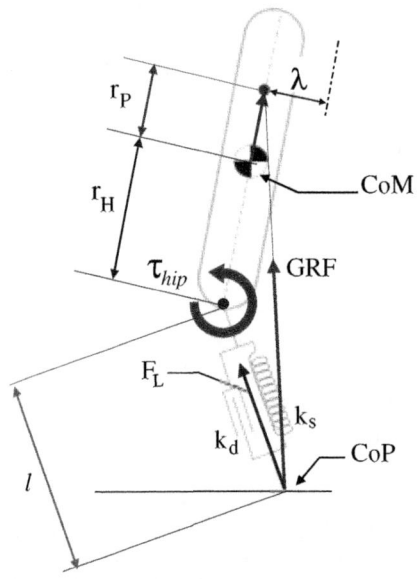

Body Mass: 75 kg
Body Length: 0.9m
Leg Length (l): 1.0m
Step Angle: ~16 deg
r_H: 0.45m
r_P: 0.18m
ks: 100000 Nm^{-1}
kd: 100 Nm^{-1}

Fig. 3. Hip torque calculated using the CoP and VPP

3.4 Managing Stairs and Slopes

Our approach can be extended to allow a character to use stairs and traverse sloping terrain by offsetting the VPP position proportional to the change in step size. In traditional approaches foot placement would be a costly exercise whereas in our approach it is a byproduct of the movement.

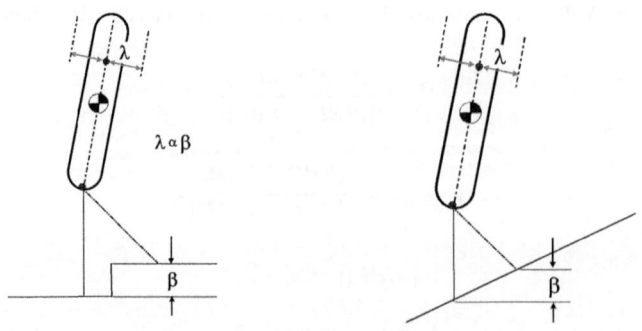

Fig. 4. Walking up stairs/steps or a gradual slope

$$\lambda \propto \beta \quad (6)$$

In (6) λ is the offset of the VPP perpendicular to the trunk and β is the change in height from the current standing foot placement.

3.5 Controllable Motion

When the VPP is shifted to the left or right, the body sways in the appropriate direction (i.e., with the VPP). If the body is moving in a specific direction, the VPP can provide small temporary offsets to maintain, speedup or slowdown a character's overall velocity.

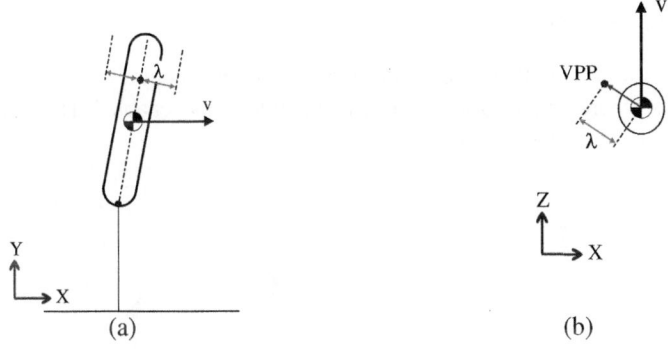

Fig. 5. Alter the direction of motion by offsetting the VPP (a) Side View (b) Top View

$$v_d \propto \lambda \quad (7)$$

We can cause a change in velocity by recognizing that the perpendicular offset relative to the trunk (λ) causes a proportional change in the desired speed (v_d).

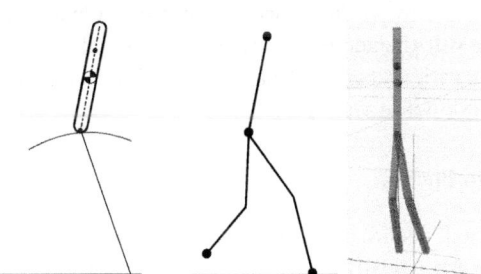

Fig. 6. The enhanced inverted pendulum generates reference motions (feet, hip positions, body orientation) that we use to control our five-link biped

Possibly the strongest reason for our approach is an ability to handle disturbances such as wind or being pushed. A character will respond naturally to the disturbing forces and attempt to take corrective steps to remain balanced. The corrective stepping automatically provides feedback to the trunk orientation to reflect these dynamic changes.

4 Results

In this section we present preliminary results for our method. Our method is used to control a five-link biped model. We consider steering, speed control and balancing in the presence of pushing. Diagrams are provided that show the different snapshots of movement over time. A YouTube video of our experiments may be viewed at [41].

4.1 Steering and Speed

A turn angle less than 10 degrees kept our locomotion natural, realistic and stable. Spline paths where created for a character to follow and enabled us to evaluate the applicability of using the VPP for steering.

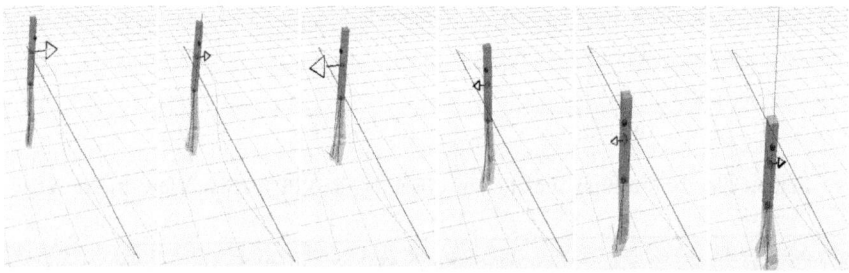

Fig. 7. Alter the VPP-offset to control the steering locomotion (Arrow in the figure indicates the desired steering direction)

The model was able to produce various types of animation and movement. These included: standing still (balancing), starting to walk, taking 2-5 steps then stopping, walking following various paths. Changing the VPP enabled us to create varying gaits dynamically (slow/fast walking).

4.2 Robustness to Pushes

We applied external disturbances to determine the robustness of our model (an ability to balance realistically). We set our model walking at a stable gait then randomly applied forces between 50N to 100N for 0.1 to 0.4 seconds at the CoM. The model passed the test if the body remained upright. Altering body mass and leg parameters affects the robustness of the model. This is a desired outcome, as eventually we would like to model a variety of human body types to gain realistic behaviors within crowds.

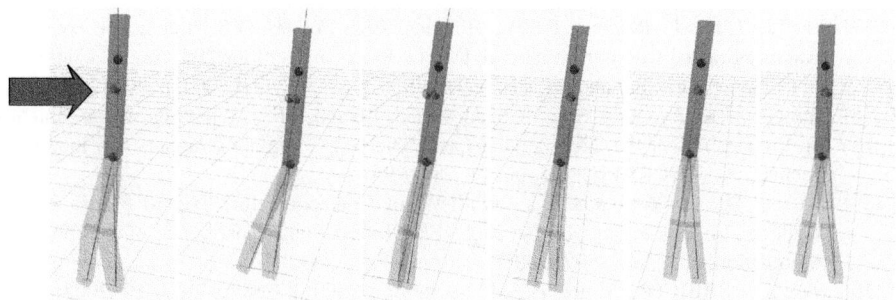

Fig. 8. Incremental screenshots of the biped model responding to a 100N push force being applied to the CoM for 0.1s

5 Conclusions and Future Work

We have described an approach for modeling mid to lower body 3D human movement in real-time. We require no data driven (e.g., key frame) elements to achieve such movement and our approach exhibits robust self–balancing properties. Furthermore, the enhanced IP used in our model also introduces movement that resembles human motion by considering the trunk of the body and hip together in posture calculations. This is the first time a real-time 3D model has made use of this technique. Significantly, we have described a technique that is not only computationally constrained, making it suitable for use in video games, but also exhibits motion that is human like without any artist or key-frame intervention.

Work will continue with the enhancement of the model to include additional body parts (e.g., arms, head, hands, feet). In addition, we will carry out comparisons to determine how well our model captures human type movement in a detailed manner as in [43]. Eventually we will create a model that exhibits sufficient realism in most instances of movement but also allows data driven approaches to superimpose desired styles. This is a must for video games as replicating realistic human movement is not the end goal because style must also be conveyed within a gaming context (e.g., angry, sad, panic).

References

[1] Sulejmanpašić, A., Popović, J.: Adaptation of performed ballistic motion. ACM Transactions on Graphics 24, 165–179 (2005)
[2] Liu, C.K., Hertzmann, A., Popović, Z.: Learning physics-based motion style with nonlinear inverse optimization. ACM Transactions on Graphics 24, 1071 (2005)
[3] Safonova, A., Hodgins, J.K., Pollard, N.S.: Synthesizing physically realistic human motion in low-dimensional, behavior-specific spaces. ACM Transactions on Graphics 23, 514 (2004)
[4] Fang, A.C., Pollard, N.S.: Efficient synthesis of physically valid human motion. ACM Transactions on Graphics 22, 417 (2003)
[5] Mandel, M.J.: Versatile and Interactive Virtual Humans: Hybrid use of Data-Driven and Dynamics-Based Motion Synthesis. Simulation (2004)
[6] Wrotek, P., Jenkins, O.C., McGuire, M.: Dynamo: Dynamic, Data-driven Character Control with Adjustable Balance. In: ACM Sandbox Symposium on Video Games (2006)

[7] Lee, J., Chai, J., Reitsma, P.S.A., Hodgins, J.K., Pollard, N.S.: Interactive control of avatars animated with human motion data. In: Proceedings of the 29th Annual Conference on Computer Graphics and Interactive Techniques, SIGGRAPH 2002, p. 491 (2002)

[8] Hodgins, J.K., Wooten, W.L., Brogan, D.C., O'Brien, J.F.: Animating human athletics. In: Proceedings of the 22nd Annual Conference on Computer Graphics and Interactive Techniques, SIGGRAPH 1995, pp. 71–78 (1995)

[9] Sharon, D., van de Panne, M.: Synthesis of Controllers for Stylized Planar Bipedal Walking. In: Proceedings of the 2005 IEEE International Conference on Robotics and Automation, pp. 2387–2392 (2005)

[10] Yin, K.: SIMBICON: Simple Biped Locomotion Control. Control 26, 1–10 (2007)

[11] Sok, K.W., Kim, M., Lee, J.: Simulating Biped Behaviors from Human Motion Data. Database 26 (2007)

[12] Wang, J.M., Fleet, D.J., Hertzmann, A.: Optimizing walking controllers. ACM Transactions on Graphics 28, 1 (2009)

[13] Lasa, M.D.: Feature-Based Locomotion Controllers. Computer Graphics Forum (2010)

[14] Adiwahono, A.H., Chew, C.-M., Huang, W., Zheng, Y.: Push recovery controller for bipedal robot walking. In: 2009 IEEE/ASME International Conference on Advanced Intelligent Mechatronics, pp. 162–167 (July 2009)

[15] Pratt, J., Pratt, G.: Exploiting natural dynamics in the control of a 3d bipedal walking simulation. In: Proceedings of the International Conference on Climbing and Walking Robots, Citeseer, pp. 797–807 (1999)

[16] Raibert, M.H.: Legged Robots That Balance. MIT Press (1986)

[17] Stephens, B.J., Atkeson, C.G.: Push Recovery by Stepping for Humanoid Robots with Force Controlled Joints. Primus

[18] Stephens, B.: Humanoid push recovery. In: 2007 7th IEEE-RAS International Conference on Humanoid Robots, pp. 589–595 (November 2007)

[19] Abe, Y., Silva, M.: Multiobjective Control with Frictional Contacts. Computing (2007)

[20] Zordan, V.B., Hodgins, J.K.: Motion capture-driven simulations that hit and react. In: Proceedings of the 2002 ACM SIGGRAPH/Eurographics Symposium on Computer Animation SCA 2002, p. 89. ACM Press, New York (2002)

[21] Nakaoka, S., Nakazawa, A., Yokoi, K., Hirukawa, H., Ikeuch, K.: Generating whole body motions for a biped humanoid robot from captured human dances. In: 2003 IEEE International Conference on Robotics and Automation (Cat. No.03CH37422), pp. 3905–3910 (2003)

[22] Faloutsos, P., van de Panne, M., Terzopoulos, D.: The virtual stuntman: dynamic characters with a repertoire of autonomous motor skills. Computers & Graphics 25, 933–953 (2001)

[23] Kim, J.-Y., Park, I.-W., Oh, J.-H.: Walking Control Algorithm of Biped Humanoid Robot on Uneven and Inclined Floor. Journal of Intelligent and Robotic Systems 48, 457–484 (2007)

[24] Tsai, Y.-Y., Lin, W.-C., Cheng, K.B., Lee, J., Lee, T.-Y.: Real-time physics-based 3D biped character animation using an inverted pendulum model. IEEE Transactions on Visualization and Computer Graphics 16, 325–337 (2010)

[25] Hodgins, J.K., Pollard, N.S.: Adapting simulated behaviors for new characters. In: Proceedings of the 24th Annual Conference on Computer Graphics and Interactive Techniques SIGGRAPH 1997, pp. 153–162 (1997)

[26] Yin, K., Coros, S., Beaudoin, P., van de Panne, M.: Continuation methods for adapting simulated skills. ACM Transactions on Graphics 27, 1 (2008)

[27] Coros, S., Beaudoin, P., Yin, K.K., van de Pann, M.: Synthesis of constrained walking skills. ACM Transactions on Graphics 27, 1 (2008)
[28] Maus, H., Rummel, J., Seyfarth, A.: Stable Upright Walking and Running using a simple Pendulum based Control Scheme, pp. 4–10 (Spring 2008)
[29] Kajita, S., Kanehiro, F., Kaneko, K., Yokoi, K., Hirukawa, H.: The 3D linear inverted pendulum mode: a simple modeling for a biped walking pattern generation. In: Proceedings 2001 IEEE/RSJ International Conference on Intelligent Robots and Systems. Expanding the Societal Role of Robotics in the the Next Millennium (Cat. No.01CH37180), pp. 239–246 (2001)
[30] Kajita, S., Tan, K.: Study of Dynamic Biped Locomotion on Rugged Terrain - Derivation and Application of the Linear Inverted Pendulum Mode. Mechanical Engineering, 1405–1411 (1991)
[31] Kajita, S., Tani, K.: Experimental study of biped dynamic walking in the linear inverted pendulum mode. In: Proceedings of 1995 IEEE International Conference on Robotics and Automation, pp. 2885–2891 (1965)
[32] Blickhan, R., Full, R.J.: Similarity in multilegged locomotion: Bouncing like a monopode. Journal of Comparative Physiology A 173 (November 1993)
[33] Full, R., Farley, C.T.: Musculoskeletal dynamics in rhythmic systems: a comparative approach to legged locomotion. In: Biomechanics and Neural Control of Posture and Movement. Springer, New York (2000)
[34] Raibert, M.H., Hodgins, J.K.: Animation of dynamic legged locomotion. ACM SIGGRAPH Computer Graphics 25, 349–358 (1991)
[35] Pratt, J.: Virtual Model Control: An Intuitive Approach for Bipedal Locomotion. The International Journal of Robotics Research 20, 129–143 (2001)
[36] Kajita, S., Kanehiro, F., Kaneko, K., Fujiwara, K., Harada, K., Yokoi, K., Hirukawa, H.: Biped walking pattern generation by using preview control of zero-moment point. In: 2003 IEEE International Conference on Robotics and Automation (Cat. No.03CH37422), pp. 1620–1626 (2003)
[37] Neville, N., Buehler, M., Sharf, I.: A bipedal running robot with one actuator per leg. In: Proceedings 2006 IEEE International Conference on Robotics and Automation, ICRA 2006, pp. 848–853 (2006)
[38] Rummel, J., Seyfarth, A.: Passive stabilization of the trunk in walking. In: Autonomous Robots, pp. 127–136 (2010)
[39] Zordan, V., Macchietto, A., Medina, J., Soriano, M., Wu, C.-C.: Interactive dynamic response for games. In: Proceedings of the 2007 ACM SIGGRAPH Symposium on Video Games (Sandbox 2007), pp. 9–14. ACM, New York (2007), doi:10.1145/1274940.1274944
[40] Zordan, V.B., Majkowska, A., Chiu, B., Fast, M.: Dynamic response for motion capture animation. In: Gross, M. (ed.) ACM SIGGRAPH 2005 Papers (SIGGRAPH 2005). ACM, New York (2005), http://doi.acm.org/10.1145/1186822.1073249, doi:10.1145/1186822.1073249
[41] http://www.youtube.com/watch?v=jLlMSD8jcBc
[42] Coros, S., Beaudoin, P., van de Panne, M.: Generalized biped walking control. ACM Transactions on Graphics 29(4), Article 130 (2010)
[43] Mordatch, I., de Lasa, M., Hertzmann, A.: Robust physics-based locomotion using low-dimensional planning. In: Hoppe, H. (ed.) ACM SIGGRAPH 2010 Papers (SIGGRAPH 2010), Article 71, 8 pages. ACM, New York (2010),
http://doi.acm.org/10.1145/1833349.1778808,
doi:10.1145/1833349.1778808

Injury Assessment for Physics-Based Characters

Thomas Geijtenbeek, Diana Vasilescu, and Arjan Egges

Games and Virtual Worlds, Utrecht University, The Netherlands

Abstract. Determining injury levels for virtual characters is an important aspect of many games. For characters that are animated using simulated physics, it is possible assess injury levels based on physical properties, such as accelerations and forces. We have constructed a model for injury assessment that relates results from research on human injury response to parameters in physics-based animation systems. We describe a set of different normalized injury measures for individual body parts, which can be combined into a single measure for total injury. Our research includes a user study in which human observers rate the injury levels of physics-based characters falling from varying heights at different orientations. Results show that the correlation between our model output and perceived injury is stronger than the correlation between perceived injury and fall height (0.603 versus 0.466, respectively, with $N = 1020$ and $p < 0.001$).

1 Introduction

Severe physical trauma is a common ordeal for many virtual game characters. In fact, many games are designed around the concept of inflicting as much injury as possible on other characters. When such games aim for high realism, it is important that the assessment of injury is accurate.

In games that use kinematic animation systems, the possibilities for assessment are limited, because there exists no direct relation to knowledge on human injury. An example indicator could be the initial height of a character that is falling to the ground, but such a measure ignores the specific forces acting on the character during impact. In physics-based animation systems, all animation is the result of simulated physics. Specific physics-based parameters can be used to estimate injury in a way that is in line with with physical reality.

There exist several games that model physical injury of physics-based characters. An example is *Stair Dismount*, a game in which the goal is to inflict as much damage as possible on a character by pushing it from a staircase. However, there exist no publications that explain what parameters and thresholds are used as a basis for these models, nor are there any published studies that show if and how such models correlate with perceived injury levels.

We propose an injury assessment model for physics-based virtual characters that is based on a comprehensive set of publications on human injury response levels. Our model produces a set of normalized measures that represent injury levels for several individual body parts. No tuning is required, as all parameters are directly derived from publications on injury research. Normalization enables straightforward combination of individual measures into a single measure representing total injury. Our research includes a user study in which the output of our injury assessment model is compared to injury levels as perceived by human observers.

We believe there are several uses for our model. First, it can be used to measure injury of in-game physics-based characters; either to keep track of the overall health of the character, or to monitor the condition of specific body parts. Furthermore, we feel our measure can also be used for the development of motion controllers for physics-based characters. More specifically, our measure can be used as an optimization criterion for controllers that need to minimize physical injury, for instance while falling or blocking obstacles.

Our physics-based character model consists of rigid bodies and does not constitute tissue damage. As a result, our model is not suitable for measuring injuries such as gunshots wounds or cuts. The use of our model is limited to injuries from to collisions with large, blunt objects. Examples of such injuries are a character falling to the ground or from a staircase, a character in a vehicle hitting a wall, or a character being hit by a rock with the shape and size of a football.

The remainder of this paper is organized as follows. We start by describing related work on physics-based character animation, injury measurement, and animation perception. We then describe in detail our injury assessment model, including sources for various model parameters. Next, we present methodology and results of the user study conducted to investigate the correlation with perceived injury levels. We conclude with a discussion and pointers for future research.

2 Related Work

Physics-based Character Animation. After a long period of focus on data-driven animation, the topic of physics-based character animation has recently been subject to renewed interest [1]. Many recent attempts have resulted in impressive behaviors, such as flexible and robust walking control [2], agile data-based locomotion control [3], and controllers for traversing uneven terrain [4, 5]. For an overview of relevant aspects, approaches and techniques, we refer to [6]. Physics-based animation research that explicitly deals with injury is limited, although several papers demonstrate its potential in that field [7, 8]. Parameter optimization (one possible use for our injury measure) has been shown to lead to interesting behaviors [9–11]. For example, Wang et al. [11] show how walking controllers can be made more robust by optimizing for random external perturbations.

Injury Assessment. There exists a long history of research on human injury assessment, most of which is based on statistical data from real-life injuries [12]. For the development of our measure we focus on research on injuries associated with motor-vehicle accidents. The *Abbreviated Injury Scale* (AIS) is a measure developed by the Association for Advancement of Automotive Medicine as a system for rating injuries in motor-vehicle accidents [13]. It consists of a dictionary of injury descriptions (mostly related to tissue or bone damage) and associated severity scores, and has been updated several times since its introduction. In 1984, General Motors published a set of reference values intended as guidelines for injury potential [14], based on experiments with the *Hybrid III crash test dummy* [15], which has been developed to represents the 50-th percentile male adult. Each of these *Injury Assessment Reference Values* (IARVs) refers "to a human response level below which a specific significant injury is considered unlikely to occur for a given individual," which corresponds roughly with AIS $\geq$ 3. Most of these values consist of physical measurements and have a direct equivalent in physics simulation. Several later publications contain similar values for various body parts [16–22]. Both the AIS and IARV focus on injuries to individual body parts. An adapted scale, called the *(New) Injury Severity Score* (ISS or NISS) defines how to combine IAS values from multiple traumas [23, 24].

Animation Perception. Since the perception of injury is an important aspect of our research, it is also relevant to mention research on animation perception. Most well-known is the work of the group of O'Sullivan, including recent publications on plausibility of animated group conversations [25], and on perception of animations subject to time-warping [26]. Studies on physical reality of character animation include the work of Reitsma and Pollard [27], who observe through user studies that errors in horizontal velocity and added accelerations in human jumping motions are easier observed by humans than errors in vertical velocity and added decelerations. Geijtenbeek et al. [28] develop a method to evaluate the physical realism of animations using a musculoskeletal model developed for research in biomechanics.

3 Injury Assessment Model

In this section we describe how our injury measures are computed, using values from physical simulation. We will describe the general form of each measure, how each individual measure is computed, and how the individual measures can be combined into a single measure representing total injury.

3.1 Overview

Our injury assessment model consists of a set of individual measures, all of which represent an IARV-normalized maximum of a simulated variable averaged over a specific time window. The size of this time window is important, since the maximum of simulated variables such as acceleration can become very high in rigid body simulation. Luckily, most referenced research papers mention appropriate time windows. An overview of all measures is shown in Table 1.

Table 1. Overview of injury measures for individual body regions. *Marked window sizes indicate estimates

Region	Physical Property	Unit	Window (w)	IARV (c)	Measure
Head	Linear Acceleration [16]	HIC	0.015	700	D_H
Neck	Axial Compression [14]	kN	0.030	4.0	D_{NC}
Neck	Axial Tension [14]	kN	0.035	3.3	D_{NT}
Chest	Thoracic spine acceleration [16]	G	0.003	60	D_C
Pelvis	Pelvis Acceleration [17, 18]	G	0.003	130	D_{PE}
Arms	Compressive Wrist Loading [22]	kN	0.010*	8.0	D_{W_L}, D_{W_R}
Legs	Femur Axial Force [14]	kN	0.010	9.1	D_{FA_L}, D_{FA_R}
Legs	Femur Planar Force [19]	kN	0.003	3.9	D_{FP_L}, D_{FP_R}
Legs	Tibia Axial Force [20]	kN	0.010*	8.0	D_{T_L}, D_{T_R}
Legs	Compressive Ankle Loading [14]	kN	0.010*	8.0	D_{A_L}, D_{A_R}
Feet	Foot Acceleration [21]	G	0.010*	150	D_{P_L}, D_{P_R}

Since all measures have a similar form (with the exception of the measure for head injury), we define the following function to simplify subsequent definitions:

$$D(v(t), w, c) = \left\{ \int_{t_0}^{t_0+w} \frac{1}{cw} v(t) dt \right\}_{max} \quad (1)$$

where w is the window length, c is the IARV value used for normalization, and t_0 is a starting time of a time window instance. $D(v(t), w, c) \to [0, \infty)$ represents the normalized maximum of the w-sized window-average of physical property $v(t)$. A value of 1 represents the threshold of significant injury.

3.2 Individual Injury Measures

Head. A common measure for head injury is the *Head Injury Criterion* (HIC), which is based on linear acceleration of the head [16]. This measure differs slightly in form from our previously defined $D(v(t), w, c)$, since it is based on a non-linear relationship:

$$HIC(w) = \left\{ \left[\frac{1}{w} \int_{t_0}^{t_0+w} \|a_H(t)\| dt \right]^{2.5} w \right\}_{max} \quad (2)$$

in which w is the window time and $a_H(t)$ is the acceleration of the head at time t. A common window time is 15ms (also referred to as the HIC-15 score), and corresponding IARV is 700 [16], which results in head injury measure D_H:

$$D_H = \frac{1}{700} HIC(0.015) \quad (3)$$

Neck. Our neck injury measure is based on studies evaluating neck compression and tension [14]. To measure these properties, we regard the axial constraint forces that are applied by the neck joint to the head and chest joint. If $\hat{F}_H(t)$ is the constraint force applied to head, and $\hat{F}_C(t)$ the constraint force applied to the chest, then the neck injury measures D_{NC} and D_{NT} can be acquired using the dot product of each force and the Y-axis of the neck joint, y_N (see Figure 2), all in the global coordinate frame:

$$D_{NC} = D(\max(\hat{F}_H(t) \cdot y_N, 0) - \min(\hat{F}_C(t) \cdot y_N, 0), 0.030, 4.0) \quad (4)$$
$$D_{NT} = D(\max(\hat{F}_C(t) \cdot y_N, 0) - \min(\hat{F}_H(t) \cdot y_N, 0), 0.035, 3.3) \quad (5)$$

Chest. Our chest injury measure is based on the maximum acceleration of the thoracic spine [16]. We acquire chest injury measure D_C by using the acceleration of the chest segment of our virtual character, $a_C(t)$:

$$D_C = D(\|a_C(t)\|, 0.003, 60) \quad (6)$$

Pelvis. Our pelvis injury measure is based on the maximum acceleration the pelvis during side impact, based on biomechanics research by Morgan et al. [17] and Janssen et al. [18]. We acquire our pelvis injury measure D_{PE} using the acceleration of the virtual pelvis segment, $a_{PE}(t)$:

$$D_{PE} = D(\|a_{PE}(t)\|, 0.003, 130) \quad (7)$$

Arms. Muller et al. [22] investigate maximum force that can be applied to the wrist before fracture. To acquire wrist injury D_W, we use the total magnitude of the constraint forces applied by the wrist joint to hand $\hat{F}_{HA}(t)$ and lower arm $\hat{F}_{LA}(t)$. Muller et al. mention no time window; based on averages from Mertz et al. [14] we decided upon using a 10ms window. The measure then becomes (computed separately for left wrist, D_{W_L}, and right wrist, D_{W_R}):

$$D_W = D(\|\hat{F}_{HA}(t)\| + \|\hat{F}_{LA}(t)\|, 0.010, 8.0) \quad (8)$$

Legs. There exist several different publications on IARV scores for legs. These include values for femur axial force (F_{FA}) [14], femur planar force (F_{FP}) [19] and tibia axial force (F_{TA}) [20]. We acquire these forces by taking the magnitude of the acceleration of the corresponding virtual body segment in a specific direction in the local coordinate frame, multiplied by the body segment mass. The resulting injury measures (D_{FA}, D_{FP} and D_T) then become (individually for left and right leg):

$$D_{FA} = D(\|F_{FA}(t)\|, 0.010, 9.1) \quad (9)$$
$$D_{FP} = D(\|F_{FP}(t)\|, 0.003, 3.9) \quad (10)$$
$$D_T = D(\|F_{TA}(t)\|, 0.010, 8.0) \quad (11)$$

Ankles. Mertz [14] has published data on maximum ankle load. We compute the corresponding ankle damage score, D_A, similar to wrist damage, using constraint forces on lower leg, $\hat{F}_{TA}(t)$, and foot, $\hat{F}_P(t)$ (individually for left and right):

$$D_A = D(\|\hat{F}_{TA}(t)\| + \|\hat{F}_P(t)\|, 0.010, 8.0) \tag{12}$$

Feet. Zeidler [21] has suggested the IARV score for foot acceleration, $a_P(t)$, to be $150G$. We again use an estimated window size of 10ms to compute our foot injury measure D_P (individually for left and right foot):

$$D_P = D(\|a_P(t)\|, 0.010, 150) \tag{13}$$

3.3 Combining Individual Measures

We have so far defined a set $\mathcal{D}$ of individual injury measures, each describing the amount of injury of a specific body part (see Table 1). Since each value is normalized to represent overall severity (with a value of 1 representing the threshold of serious injury), we can meaningfully combine the individual measures by using the average, D_{AVG}:

$$D_{AVG} = \sum_{D \in \mathcal{D}} \frac{1}{\|\mathcal{D}\|} D \tag{14}$$

Alternatively, one can choose to only use the three highest scores for this average, inspired by the *New Injury Severity Score* (NISS) [24], or to use a quadratic relation, as suggested by [23]. However, our later results do not support the idea this will lead to better estimates of perceived total injury.

4 Experimentation

To evaluate our injury assessment model, we have conducted a user study to investigate if the output of our model correlates with injury levels of virtual characters as perceived by human observers. This section describes the experiment setup and results.

4.1 Trial Data

Our trial data consisted of 30 short (4 second) video clips of a virtual character falling in a physically simulated environment. In each trial, the virtual character falls down from a random initial orientation and height. The initial orientation was generated by applying random rotations around the X and Z axis, while the initial height of the center of mass (COM) was varied between $1.5m$ and $4.5m$. An example fragment of a trial video clip is shown in Figure 1.

Fig. 1. Example fragment of animation sequence shown as part of the survey

We used the *Open Dynamics Engine* (ODE) [29] to perform the physics simulation that generated the animation, using an integration time step of 0.0003s. We utilized ODE's *Error Reduction Parameter* (ERP) and *Constraint Force Mixing* parameter (CFM) to emulate the effect of shock absorption due to soft tissues, joint compliance and ligaments (ERP = 0.5, CFM = 0.001; see [29] for details). The hierarchy and degrees-of-freedom (DOFs) of our virtual character are shown in Figure 2. Low-gain PD-controllers were used to drive the character joints towards their initial T-stance position ($k_p = 10$, $k_d = 2$), with torque maximum set to 1000Nm for each joint.

Body	Body part	Shape	Position (X, Z, Y)	Dimensions
PE	Pelvis	box	(1.20, 0.00, 1.00)	X=0.30, Z=0.25, Y=0.20
CH	Torso	box	(1.20, 0.00, 1.30)	X=0.25, Z=0.20, Y=0.50
H	Head	sphere	(1.20, 0.00, 1.75)	R=0.10
T_R	Upper leg	capsule	(1.29, 0.00, 0.68)	R=0.06, L=0.35
T_L	Upper leg	capsule	(1.11, 0.00, 0.68)	R=0.06, L=0.35
F_R	Lower leg	capsule	(1.29, 0.00, 0.25)	R=0.06, L=0.30
F_L	Lower leg	capsule	(1.11, 0.00, 0.25)	R=0.06, L=0.30
P_L	Foot	box	(1.11, -0.07, 0.03)	X=0.10, Z=0.35, Y=0.05
P_R	Foot	box	(1.29, -0.07, 0.03)	X=0.10, Z=0.35, Y=0.05
UA_L	Upper arm	capsule	(0.88, 0.00, 1.50)	R=0.05, L=0.35
UA_R	Upper arm	capsule	(1.52, 0.00, 1.50)	R=0.05, L=0.35
LA_L	Lower arm	capsule	(0.50, 0.00, 1.50)	R=0.05, L=0.30
LA_R	Lower arm	capsule	(1.90, 0.00, 1.50)	R=0.05, L=0.30
HA_L	Hand	box	(0.25, 0.00, 1.50)	X=0.15, Z=0.08, Y=0.03
HA_R	Hand	box	(2.15, 0.00, 1.50)	X=0.15, Z=0.08, Y=0.03

Fig. 2. Character DOFs, body segments, and corresponding dimensions

4.2 User Study

The trial data was presented to 34 individuals (21 male, 13 female), with ages between 23 and 35 years. Each individual was shown all clips in random order; they were instructed to assign each clip a value between 1 (minimum) and 7 (maximum), based on how much total physical damage they felt was inflicted upon the virtual character. Furthermore, they were informed that a score of 4 represents the threshold of significant injury. This resulted in a total of $N = 34 \times 30 = 1020$ evaluations.

4.3 Results

We have found a significant correlation between injury measure D_{AVG} and the corresponding user score S: corr(D_{AVG}, S) = 0.603, with $N = 1020$ and $p < 0.001$. Figure 3 displays a scatter plot of the computed D_{avg} for each trial, and the corresponding averages of user score S. In comparison, the correlation between initial COM height H and user score S is corr(H, S) = 0.466, with $N = 1020$ and $p < 0.001$. This supports the hypothesis that our measure is a more accurate representation of perceived injury than falling height, when regarding characters falling. An overview of the average of D_{AVG} for each individual user score is shown in Figure 4, affirming the correlation between the two.

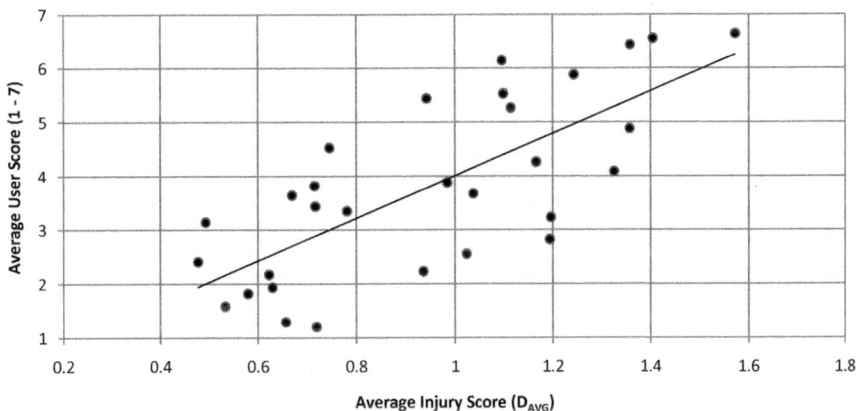

Fig. 3. Scatter plot of injury measure D_{AVG} for each trial (horizontal) and the average of user score S (vertical). corr(D_{AVG}, S) = 0.603, $N = 1020$, $p < 0.001$

If we only regarded the top 3 most occurring injuries (similar to the NISS scoring system), the correlation decreases to 0.522 ($p < 0.001$). The use of quadratic terms (as in the NISS scoring) only further decreases the correlation. This means our results do not support the use of NISS-related methods for computing overall injury.

Figure 5 shows the average value for each of the individual measures. It can be seen that neck compression injury D_{NC} is the measure with the highest average score. This is mostly due to the fact that some trials consisting of head-first landing animations had extremely high neck compression. This also explains the high standard deviation of D_{NC} in Figure 4.

Results on correlation studies for individual injury measures show that most measures have a significant positive correlation with perceived injury, while some demonstrate a stronger correlation than others. Measures for ankle compression (D_{AL} and D_{AR}) show a negative correlation. This can be explained by the fact that ankle compression is highest when a character lands on his feet, while observers generally assigned relatively low injury scores to such animations.

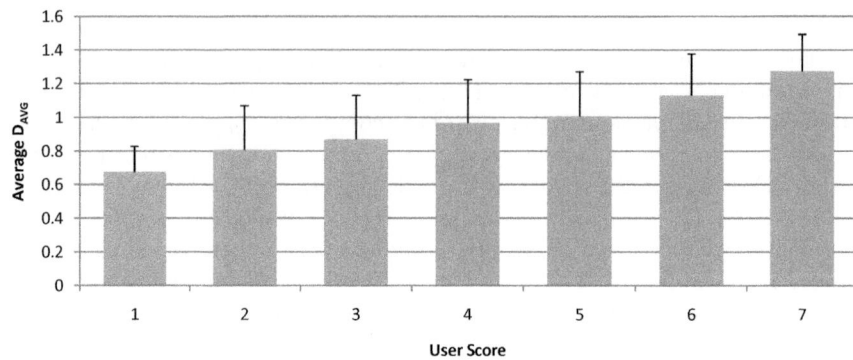

Fig. 4. Average of injury measure D_{AVG} for each user score

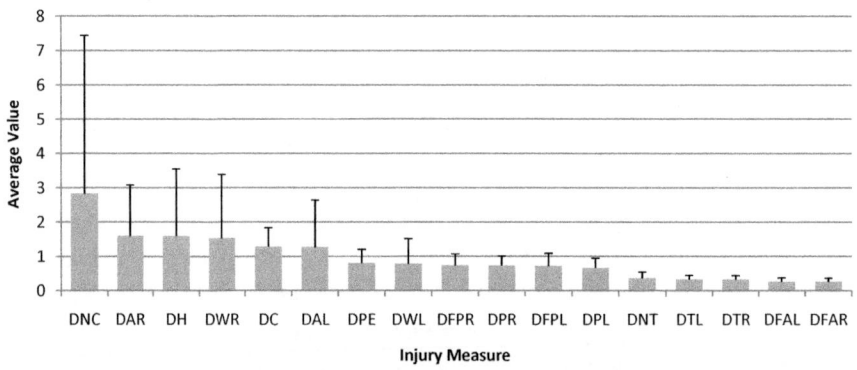

Fig. 5. Average value for each individual injury measure. A value of 1 represents the threshold of serious injury for a specific body part.

5 Conclusion, Discussion and Future Work

5.1 Conclusion

We have presented a model for computing injury measures for physics-based characters, based on research on human injury response levels. We have validated this model by demonstrating a significant correlation between the average injury measure and the total injury level as perceived by human observers. This correlation is stronger than the correlation between perceived injury and fall height (0.603 versus 0.466, respectively, with $N = 1020$ and $p < 0.001$).

5.2 Discussion

There are several limitations to our injury assessment model. Key body parts such as knees, elbows and shoulders are currently missing, because we could not

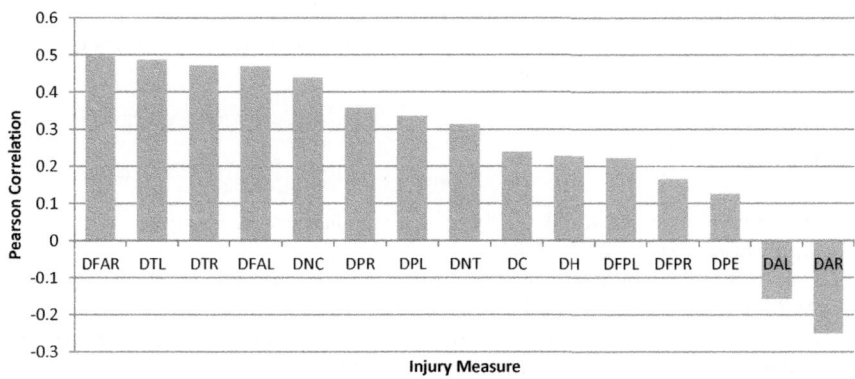

Fig. 6. An overview of the correlations between individual injury measures and perceived injury by human observers. All correlations are significant ($p < 0.001$) except the correlations for wrist injury (D_{W_L} and D_{W_R}), which are excluded from the figure.

locate any suitable data. However, we do not believe that these omissions have disrupted our research too much, since relevant trials had significant injury in neighboring body parts. If desired, proper estimates may be generated based on other measures, without the need for published data. It may be possible to assess specific facial injuries by using location-aware impact measures.

In order to measure injury types such as shot wounds or cuts, we suggest to use different approach than physical modeling. Even though it may be possible to create a model for tissue damage, it is questionable whether this is worth the effort for gaming applications.

Perception studies often leave room for debate, and ours is no different. First, we used a very basic looking character model; a more detailed model may have triggered different responses. Second, we have only tested for straight falling motions; other motions (falling from stairs, colliding with objects, etc.) may also have triggered different responses.

Several of our test subjects reported that some animations appeared unrealistic, because characters bounced where they normally would break (we did not allow any joint dislocation in our simulation). There are many additional appearance factors that complicate our perception study, such as viewing angle, playback speed, character model, background color, etc. However, test results indicate our test material was at least partly representative.

5.3 Future Work

The work presented in this paper is an initial attempt at injury assessment for physics-based virtual characters. There is much room for improvement, while additional user studies can create better insights on how injury of animated characters is perceived. As mentioned in our introduction, injury is an important aspect of gaming, which validates further research in this area.

Acknowledgments. This research has been supported by the GATE project, funded by the Netherlands Organization for Scientific Research (NWO), as well as the Dinu Patriciu Foundation.

References

1. Hertzmann, A., Zordan, V.: Physics-Based Characters. Computer Graphics and Applications 31(4), 20–21 (2011)
2. Coros, S., Beaudoin, P., van de Panne, M.: Generalized biped walking control. ACM Transactions on Graphics (SIGGRAPH) 29, 1–9 (2010)
3. Muico, U., Lee, Y., Popović, J., Popović, Z.: Contact-aware nonlinear control of dynamic characters. ACM Transactions on Graphics (SIGGRAPH) 28(3), 1–9 (2009)
4. Wu, J.-c., Popovic, Z.: Terrain-Adaptive Bipedal Locomotion Control. ACM Transactions on Graphics (SIGGRAPH) 29(4), 1–10 (2010)
5. Mordatch, I., de Lasa, M., Hertzmann, A.: Robust Physics-Based Locomotion Using Low-Dimensional Planning. ACM Transactions on Graphics (SIGGRAPH) 29(4), 1–8 (2010)
6. Geijtenbeek, T., Pronost, N., Egges, A., Overmars, M.H.: Interactive Character Animation using Simulated Physics. In: Eurographics (State-of-the-Art Reports) (2011)
7. Faloutsos, P.: The virtual stuntman: dynamic characters with a repertoire of autonomous motor skills. Computers & Graphics 25(6), 933–953 (2001)
8. Abe, Y., da Silva, M., Popović, J.: Multiobjective control with frictional contacts. In: ACM SIGGRAPH/Eurographics Symposium on Computer Animation, pp. 249–258 (2007)
9. Sims, K.: Evolving virtual creatures. In: Proc. of the 21st Annual Conf. on Computer Graphics and Interactive Techniques SIGGRAPH 1994, pp. 15–22 (1994)
10. Wang, J.M., Fleet, D.J., Hertzmann, A.: Optimizing walking controllers. ACM Transactions on Graphics (TOG), 168 (2009)
11. Wang, J.M., Fleet, D.J., Hertzmann, A.: Optimizing Walking Controllers for Uncertain Inputs and Environments. ACM Transactions on Graphics (SIGGRAPH) 29(4), 1–8 (2010)
12. Petrucelli, E.: The abbreviated injury scale: Evolution, usage and future adaptability. Accident Analysis & Prevention 13(1), 29–35 (1981)
13. The Abbreviated Injury Scale, 1990 Revision. Technical report, Association for the Advancement of Automotive Medicine, Morton Grove, Illinois (1990)
14. Mertz, H.J.: Injury assessment values used to evaluate Hybrid III response measurements. NHTSA Docket 74, 14 (1984)
15. Foster, J.K., Kortge, J.O., Wolanin, M.J.: Hybrid III-a biomechanically-based crash test dummy. Technical report, Society of Automotive Engineers, 400 Commonwealth Dr, Warrendale, PA, 15096, USA (1977)
16. Mertz, H.J., Prasad, P., Irwin, A.L.: Injury risk curves for children and adults in frontal and rear collisions. Technical report, Soc. of Automotive Engineers (1997)
17. Morgan, R.M., Marcus, J., Eppinger, R.: Side impact-the biofidelity of NHTSA's proposed ATD and efficacy of TTI. SAE Tech. Pap. Ser. (1986)
18. Janssen, E.G., Wismans, J., de Coo, P.J.A.: Comparison of Eurosid and Cadaver Responses in Side Impact. In: Twelfth International Technical Conference on Experimental Safety Vehicles (1989)

19. Kerrigan, J.R., Bhalla, K.S., Funk, J.R., Madeley, N.J., Bose, D.: Experiments for Establishing Pedestrian-Impact Lower Limb Injury Criteria. SAE Technical Paper (2003)
20. Crandall, J.R., Kuppa, S.M., Klopp, G.S., Hall, G.W., Pilkey, W.D., Hurwitz, S.R.: Injury mechanisms and criteria for the human foot and ankle under axial impacts to the foot. International Journal of Crashworthiness 3(2), 147–162 (1998)
21. Zeidler, F.: The significance of lower limb injuries of belted drivers. Journal of Orthopedics (1984)
22. Muller, M.E., Webber, C.E., Bouxsein, M.L.: Predicting the failure load of the distal radius. Osteoporosis International 14(4), 345–352 (2003)
23. Baker, S.P., O'Neill, B., Haddon Jr, W., Long, W.B.: The injury severity score: a method for describing patients with multiple injuries and evaluating emergency care. The Journal of Trauma 14(3), 187 (1974)
24. Stevenson, M., Segui-Gomez, M., Lescohier, I., Di Scala, C., McDonald-Smith, G.: An overview of the injury severity score and the new injury severity score. Injury Prevention 7(1), 3–10 (2001)
25. Ennis, C., McDonnell, R., O'Sullivan, C.: Seeing is believing: Body motion dominates in multisensory conversations. ACM Transactions on Graphics (TOG) 29(4), 1–9 (2010)
26. Prazák, M., McDonnell, R.: Perceptual Evaluation of Human Animation Timewarping. ACM SIGGRAPH Asia Sketches and Applications, 2–3 (2010)
27. Reitsma, P.S.A., Pollard, N.S.: Perceptual metrics for character animation: sensitivity to errors in ballistic motion. ACM TOG 22(3), 537–542 (2003)
28. Geijtenbeek, T., van den Bogert, A.J., van Basten, B.J.H., Egges, A.: Evaluating the Physical Realism of Character Animations Using Musculoskeletal Models. In: Boulic, R., Chrysanthou, Y., Komura, T. (eds.) MIG 2010. LNCS, vol. 6459, pp. 11–22. Springer, Heidelberg (2010), http://www.springerlink.com/index/L341N4W3X484M003.pdf
29. Smith, R.: Open Dynamics Engine User Guide v0.5 (2006)

Reactive Virtual Creatures
for Dexterous Physical Interactions

Hironori Mitake[1], Shoichi Hasegawa[1,2], and Makoto Sato[1]

[1] P&I Lab., Tokyo Institute of Technology, Kanagawa, Japan
[2] PRESTO JST, Tokyo, Japan
{mitake,hase,msato}@pi.titech.ac.jp

Abstract. Dexterous physical interactions with virtual creatures are important to bring the fun of playing with animals into arts and entertainment. For reality of interaction, virtual creatures need to react to highly varied user inputs in a variety of ways according to physical and psychological laws. We propose constructing virtual creatures using a physical simulator, sensor/attention models, and physical motion controllers. The physical simulator and motion controllers generate highly varied physically real reactions, while sensor/attention models provide psychologically feasible target selection for motion controllers. Having constructed a virtual creature prototype, we realize communicative physical interactions such as guessing and attracting attention by touching it via a haptic device. We have confirmed the prototype's effectiveness experimentally.

Keywords: Virtual Creature, Attention, Sensorimotor System, Motion Generation, Physical Interaction.

1 Introduction

Characters in games play important roles expressing personalities and stories. They interact with players and other characters, act expressively, and evoke players' empathy. Such roles are required for attractive game experiences and are similar to those of creatures (humans/animals) in the real world. Therefore, we call such characters **virtual creatures**.

Improving enjoyment of games is possible by introducing touch interaction with the virtual creatures as if they were living creatures. Because recent game devices using motion trackers or touch panels allow physical interaction between virtual worlds, there are increased expectations of real-time reaction generation methods with physical effects. Several games [9,13] already implement physical interaction between animals, albeit with reactions occurring in limited prepared ways.

Touching real creatures gives us a sense of life. Dexterous interaction by exchanging force between the parties and reacting with various expressive motions

http://haselab.net/~mitake/en/research/VirtualCreature.html

showing situational thinking (e.g., paying attention by moving their gaze) is possible. Reactions showing what is on their mind create empathy and enable us to deal with a creature's mentality.

However, dexterous physical interactions and empathetic expressions are difficult to combine. Expressive motions should be created to satisfy the nature of the human mind. Currently, this requires intervention by animators. However, dexterous physical interactions require that virtual creatures respond with highly varied reactions according to continuous player input.

This research aims to implement a method to construct virtual creatures for dexterous physical interactions with lifelike expressive reactions that depend on the interaction.

2 Related Works

Motion generation methods for characters have been widely researched to realize physical interaction. Physically simulated articulated body models are often employed [11,2,5], while prepared motion databases have been included in recent studies [15,14].

To ensure that characters' expressive behaviors happen automatically, eye-movement generation to display attention has also been studied. A psychological model for human attention [10,7] or a statistical model [6] is typically used for offline animation generation or dialogue interaction.

Psychological models are more commonly used in research on cognitive robots [3,8]. To make human-shaped robots that behave naturally and physically in the real world, sensor devices, information processing, and motor controls are constructed to mimic the psychological function of humans or animals. However, cognitive processes such as finding objects in real-world sensor data, are complicated and real robots are limited by their driving mechanism.

Our approach is a combination of real-time articulated body simulation and psychological models. Full physical simulation based motion generation ensures a variety of reactions in dexterous physical simulation. In addition, cognitive models to emulate higher functions of human mind are much simpler in virtual world, because they can obtain cognitive information directly from the simulator as the virtual world itself.

3 Approach and Proposal

We focus on several aspects of the nature of real creatures.

Sense and action cycle is a common characteristic of creatures. Real creatures use sensory organs to understand the environment and then decide what action to take. When we observe the creatures' surroundings and their reactions, we can guess what they have sensed and thought in choosing the action. Reacting without sensing appears unnatural. Limitations in the range of sense (e.g., field of view) necessitate paying attention to important targets. Motion of sensory organs in the direction of the most important target highlights the focus.

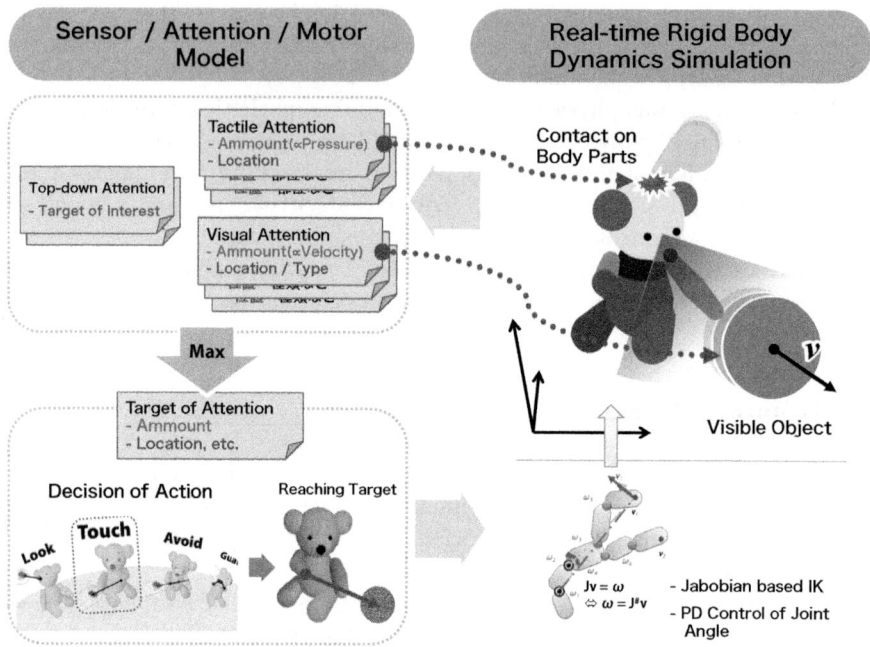

Fig. 1. Overview of the implementation of the proposed virtual creature system

Therefore, we propose constructing virtual creatures as follows. First, the system should be based on sensor models similar to real creatures to make decisions regarding actions. Second, they should also express the focus of their attention and interest in other virtual creatures using motion. Finally, these movements should be generated using a physical simulator to ensure variety of reactions.

4 Realization

In this section, we give an example of the realization of a virtual creature from the proposal. The system consists of 4 parts: a real-time physical simulator, physical motion controllers, sensor/attention models, and character AI. We describe how the proposal should be applied in the virtual creature system.

Fig. 1 shows an overview of the example system, while Fig. 2 gives a definition of the symbols used in following sections.

4.1 Physical Simulator

The virtual creature's motion is generated using a physical simulator and a simulation model of the virtual creature's body. The physical simulator generates various physically realistic motions capable of physical interaction.

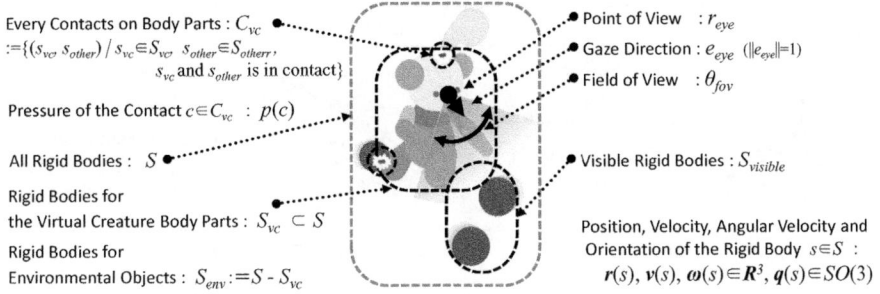

Fig. 2. Definition of symbols

We employed a real-time rigid-body dynamics simulator. Such a simulator calculates translational/rotational movements of a rigid-body object and collisions/friction between multiple objects. Virtual creature is modeled as an articulated body model, constructed with several rigid-bodies and joints. Each joint of the model is actuated by joint torque control. Not only virtual creature, but also interacting environmental objects including players' hands, are modeled as rigid-body/joint models.

The simulator calculates effect on motions or poses by forces applied to virtual creature's body parts from player's hands and fingers. This is the basis of dexterous physical interaction. The simulator also calculates forces applied to player's virtual hands from the virtual creature according to the interaction. The player can feel accurate force feedback if a haptic device is available. This enables certain interactions such as feeling movement of the virtual creature from the force feedback, or disrupting the character's movement by pushing moving body part of the character. In addition, the simulator automatically generates physically realistic action by the virtual creature depending on the situation. For example, speed of motion or position of the center of gravity will change in a carrying motion if the weight of the object changes.

4.2 Physical Motion Controller

Several motion controllers actuate physically simulated articulated body model by controlling torque of each joint. Each controller is prepared to implement particular type of motion (e.g., gaze motion or hand reaching motion).

Nevertheless, each controller must generate variety of motions. For example, changing the creature's gaze implies different motion according to the direction of the target. Generally, each controller must actuate the body to realize particular motion for any selected target. We realized such motion controller with 3 steps: calculation of target position, inverse kinematics, PD-control of the joint angle.

First, rigid body object comprising the virtual creature $s_{vc} \in S_{vc}$ (Fig. 2) is selected as an 'end effector' depending on the type of motion (e.g., a hand should be end effector of reaching motion). Then, target location for the end effector is calculated according to the location, orientation, and motion of the target.

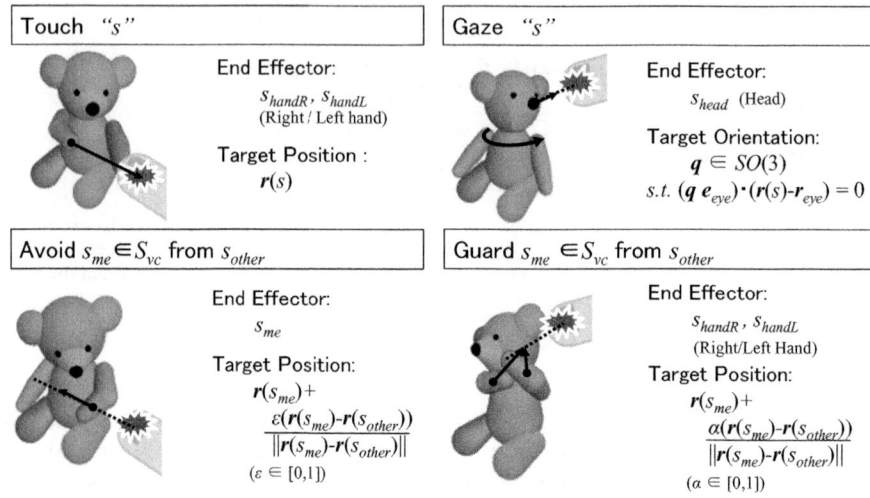

Fig. 3. Physical motion controllers

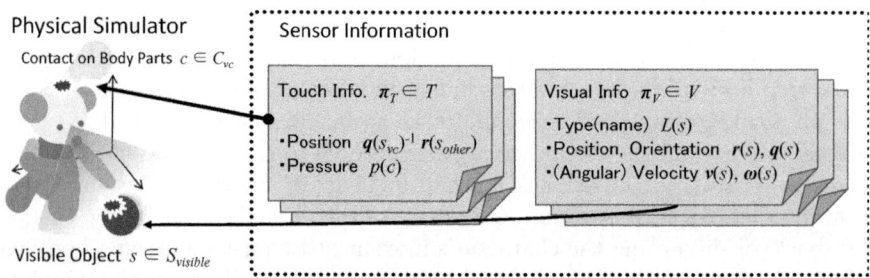

Fig. 4. Sensor information

Several types of motions can be done at the same time, such as hand reaching while looking at the target. We employed inverse kinematics (IK) based on a pseudo inverse of the Jacobian. The IK calculates target angular velocity of each joint to make each end effector approximate target position. Then, torque of each joint is determined with PD-control to realize calculated angular velocity.

In this implementation, we constructed 4 types of motion controllers. Fig. 3 shows details of each controller.

4.3 Sensor Models

Sensor model mimics a real creature's senses, thereby contributing to realizing lifelike actions such as reacting to objects entering the field of view. We focused particularly on visual and touch senses, because vision gives the greatest amount of information on the environment for most real creatures, while physical interaction including direct touch to the virtual creatures causes them to react to tactile sensation. This sense information is recreated from the information on the physical simulator.

In our implementation, visual sense is defined as information on type, location and movement of the object. Since minimum unit of an object in the rigid-body simulator is a single rigid body, the visual information is calculated for each rigid body object in the virtual creature's field of view.

As for touch sense, location and pressure of contact on virtual creature's body surface should be sensed, because players can touch each part of the virtual creature's body in various ways through physical interaction. Contact and contact forces of rigid bodies are calculated by the simulator for every pair of rigid bodies. Therefore, tactile information is created for contact on each rigid body comprising the virtual creature's body.

Definition of visual/tactile information is shown in Fig. 4 and given by Eqs. (1) and (2). Each symbol is defined in Fig. 2.

$$V := \{(s, r(s), q(s), v(s), \omega(s), L(s)) | s \in S_{visible}\} \quad (1)$$

$$T := \{(c, p(c), q(s_{vc})^{-1} r(s_{other})) | c := (s_{vc}, s_{other}) \in C_{vc}\} \quad (2)$$

Here, $S_{visible}$ is a rigid body in the field of view, defined as Eq. (3).

$$S_{visible} := \{s \in S_{env} | \left(\frac{r(s) - r_{eye}}{\|r(s) - r_{eye}\|} \cdot e_{eye} \right) \geq \cos(\theta_{fov}/2)\} \quad (3)$$

$L(s)$ is the type of the object (e.g., "right hand", "head", "apple"). The third element of tactile information $q(s_{vc})^{-1} r(s_{other})$ is the relative position of the touching object in the body centered coordinates.

4.4 Attention Model

Selective attention is a common psychological mechanism for higher animals. The mechanism causes motion of sensor organs towards the object with highest priority. This motion, typified by eye movements, reflects which target has the greater interest. Furthermore, this behavior is a strong clue in guessing creature's intention for us as the observer.

In our implementation, we mimicked the mechanism of selective attention. Real animals have 2 types of attention mechanisms: bottom-up attention caused by salient sensation stimuli and top-down attention, which is intentional. To reproduce these, we implemented attention model as follows. First, amount of bottom-up attention $A_{bot}(\pi)$ is calculated for each piece of sense information π. Next, top-down attention $A_{top}(\pi)$ is calculated according to the decision of character AI, which is a mechanism for making decisions. Finally, sensor information with maximum amount of attention for bottom-up/top-down attention is selected as focus of attention.

The model is described by Eq. (4), which selects one aspect of the sensor information $\pi_{attention}$ as the focus of attention.

$$\pi_{attention} := \arg\max_{\pi} (A_{bot}(\pi) + A_{top}(\pi)) \quad (4)$$

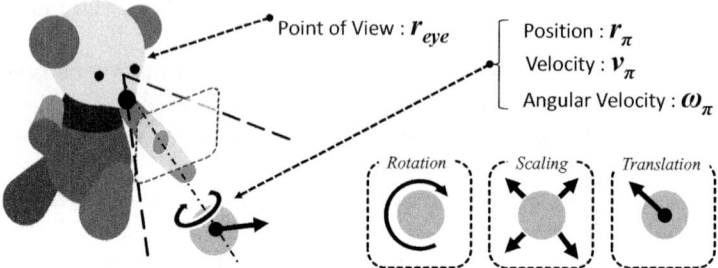

Fig. 5. Bottom-up visual attention for motion

Here,

$$\pi(\in V \cup T) = \begin{cases} (s_\pi, r_\pi, q_\pi, v_\pi, \omega_\pi, L_\pi) \\ \qquad if \ \pi \in V \\ (c_\pi, p_\pi, r_\pi) \\ \qquad if \ \pi \in T(c_\pi = (s_{vc_\pi}, s_{other_\pi})) \end{cases}$$

Calculating amount of bottom-up attention is described in detail below. As for visual attention, bottom-up attention for motion of visual stimuli is important, because motion of the player's hands and objects is important in physical interaction. In our model, amount of visual attention corresponds to motion in a retinal image of the virtual creature. In the retinal image, a moving rigid body causes 3 types of optical flow: translational, rotational, and scaling flow. Therefore, the amount of visual attention is defined by Eq. (5). According to this definition, objects moving faster attract greater attention.

$$A_{visual}(\pi) := k_T \| v_\pi - d_\pi (d_\pi \cdot v_\pi) \| + k_S \| d_\pi \cdot v_\pi \| + k_R \| d_\pi \cdot \omega_\pi \| \qquad (5)$$

Here,

$$d_\pi = \frac{r_\pi - r_{eye}}{\| r_\pi - r_{eye} \|}$$

Also, k_T, k_S, k_R are parameters to adjust each type of optical flow to affect the amount of attention.

Tactile attention is defined similarly to visual attention. The amount of tactile attention corresponds to contact pressure for each contact on the rigid bodies comprising the virtual creature (Eq. (6)). Since the definition is based on contact pressure, greater attention follows when touched with sharp edge, and not just when touched with a strong force.

$$A_{touch}(\pi) := k_P p_\pi \qquad (6)$$

Here, k_P is a parameter to adjust the correspondence between the pressure and the amount of attention.

Then, sum of visual/tactile attention gives the total amount of bottom-up attention (Eq. (7)).

$$A_{bot}(\pi) := A_{visual}(\pi) + A_{touch}(\pi) \qquad (7)$$

With the attention model, virtual creatures can behave in such a way as to express paying attention. As the definition shows, when different targets attract bottom-up/top-down attention, attention conflicts may occur. In such situations, the virtual creature acts as if it is trying to concentrate on target of interest, but being distracted by any other moving objects in sight.

The definition includes various parameters, k_T, k_S, k_R, k_P. These parameters or amounts of top-down attention for each object can be manually adjusted to change behavior of the virtual creature. The parameters should be tuned to realize expected behavior that is derived from settings of the virtual creature. It is easy to guess effects of the parameters, and adjustment can be made smoothly by observing resulting behavior.

4.5 Character AI

Character AI is a conventional mechanism to make current characters behave according to the situation, such as if-then rules or state machines. Our implementation employs character AI to make action decisions.

The character AI for the proposed method needs to make decisions according to the nature of real creatures, and is required to be used in combination with sensor/attention models and physical motion controller. To satisfy this, conditions of rules or state machines are based on the sensor information. This prevents virtual creatures from making unnatural decisions using a super sense. Then, character AI determines amount of top-down attention for each piece of sense information and selects the relevant motion controller to be used. In this way, virtual creature acts and pays attention as determined by the AI.

Our implementation uses a simple character AI with the following 2 rules, which can be activated at the same time, in which case, 2 motion controllers would run simultaneously. t_{look}, t_{touch} are thresholds for the amount of attention to activate the rules and should be adjusted manually.

- Rule 1 :
  if $A_{bot}(\pi_{attention}) + A_{top}(\pi_{attention}) > t_{look}$
  use controller Eye Movement
- Rule 2 :
  if $A_{top}(\pi_{attention}) > t_{touch}$
  use controller Reaching Movement (Hand)

5 Evaluation

We evaluated effectiveness of the method in realizing various physical interactions between the virtual creatures with lifelike expressions of attention. Experiments were carried out with the implemented virtual creature system described in Section 4.

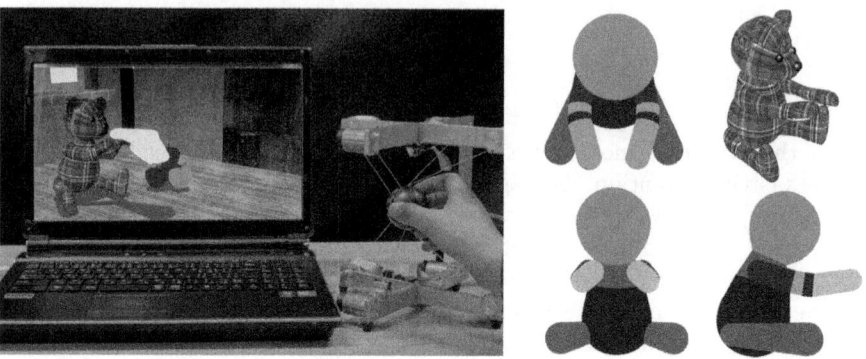

Fig. 6. Experimental environment and the rigid body model of a virtual creature

Table 1. Parameter settings for the experiment

Paramter	Value	Parameter	Value
$L(s_{pointer})$	"pointer"	$A_{top}(s_{pointer})$	0.5
$L(s_{greenapple})$	"greenapple"	$A_{top}(s_{greenapple})$	0.0
$L(s_{redapple})$	"redapple"	$A_{top}(s_{redapple})$	1.0
k_T	0.03	t_{look}	0.05
k_S	0.03	t_{touch}	0.2
k_R	0.03	k_p	2.0

5.1 Environment and Configuration of Virtual Creatures

We set up an environment to enable physical interaction with a virtual creature using a 6-DOF haptic device SPIDAR [12] (Fig. 6). Users can touch and drag both the virtual creature and environmental objects around the virtual creature.

Springhead2 [4], a real-time rigid-body dynamics simulator that runs on commonly used PCs, is employed as the physical simulator. The virtual world in the physical simulator contains the virtual creature and several different objects (apples) as targets for the attention of the virtual creature.

The implemented articulated body model of the virtual creature is shown in Fig. 6. The model has 17 rigid bodies, 16 joints, and 44 DOFs. Parameter settings for the virtual creature are given in Table 1. These values were adjusted manually to achieve appropriate behavior in the constructed environment.

5.2 Experiments and Results

In the experiments, subjects were required to interact freely with a virtual creature for 10 minutes. All interactions were recorded on video. The virtual creature's top-down attention for the apple was increased every minute, in an attempt

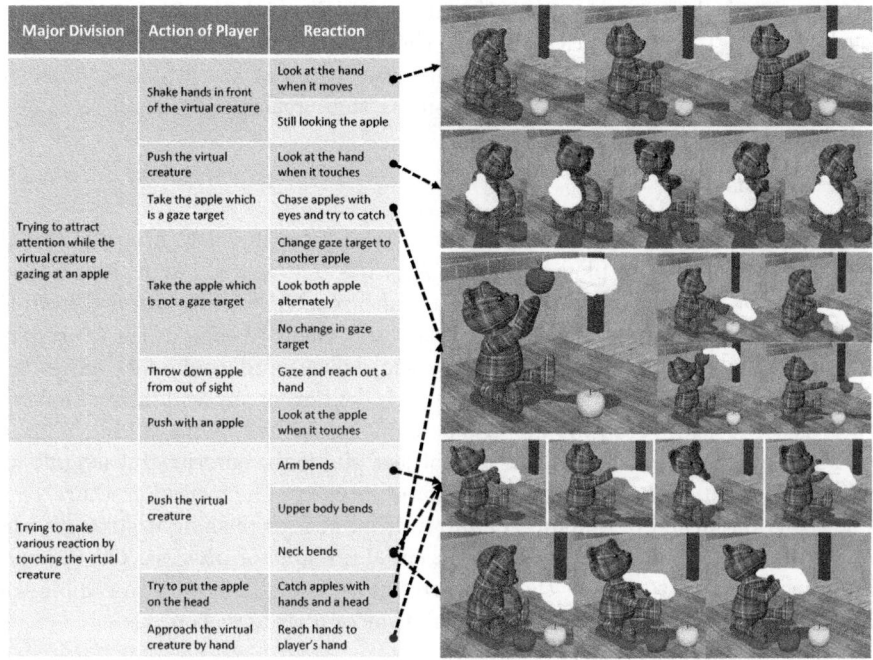

Fig. 7. Patterns and examples of resulting interaction

to change the subject's experience with the virtual creature in terms of a different top-down/bottom-up ratio. On conclusion of the experiments, we extracted patterns of interaction from the recorded video images. The subjects were 7 male adults.

The results are shown in Fig. 7. Sixteen patterns were extracted, roughly divided into 2 types: trying to invoke various reactions from the virtual creature, and trying to attract the attention of the virtual creature. Actually, reactions all differ in terms of the detail even for reactions classified as same pattern.

5.3 Exhibition

We also demonstrated the virtual creature as an interactive exhibit [1]. Over 1000 people participated, and the attendees' interactions and voices were recorded. After the exhibition, we analyzed the recorded video.

Three suggestions came out of the analysis. First, participants seemed to recognize the virtual creature's attention and interests. Several attendees tried to find out what the virtual creature was interested in, by placing apples one by one in front of the virtual creature. Second, the virtual creature seemed to be regarded as a living creature. Most of the attendees tried to feed the virtual creature an apple. Third, certain words spoken by the attendees included observation of aspects of the virtual creature's emotion. When the virtual creature was pushed strongly by a participant and the virtual creature pushed back, some comments were that the virtual creature was scared of the attendee. This suggests that attendees empathized with the virtual creature.

5.4 Discussion

In the experiments, the virtual creature reacted continuously according to the position and motion of players' hands, showing that it was paying attention to the hands or apples. The virtual creature also reacted to force applied from the haptic interface. Players could disrupt the movement of each of the body parts of the virtual creature through the haptic device, and could feel movements through accurate force feedback. In this way, dexterous physical interaction with the virtual creature reacting in various lifelike motions was realized.

The virtual creature gazed at any object suddenly entering into sight, and tried to take an apple, which was a target of interest. The virtual creature's gaze was easily disturbed by shaking a hand in front of it or pushing it strongly when it was looking at an apple with only a small amount of interest. On the other hand, it was hard to deflect the creature's gaze when directed at an apple with high interest. This behavior is similar to that of a real creature.

6 Conclusion

We proposed the construction of a virtual creature using a physical simulator and sensor/attention models. The prototype implementation shows the effectiveness of the approach experimentally.

The proposed method can be used in combination with current action determination systems for game characters. The method also has high affinity to recent motion input devices for games, or open-world games with physical simulators. Using our methods, virtual creatures can behave with various empathizing actions depending on the situation or interaction.

Sensor/attention models and motion controllers form the basis of the virtual creature system to enable creatures to behave naturally and autonomously. The next step will be the reproduction of higher functions of real creatures. In particular, memory and prediction are basic functions that determine actions. These are also important for attention models, in that memorized or expected objects attract less attention than unknown and unexpected ones.

In the future, using such virtual creature systems, designers will be able to describe higher level instruction for character AI, and virtual creatures will act automatically in indicated ways.

Acknowledgement. This work was partially supported by the International Communications Foundation Research Promotion Program.

References

1. Interactive tokyo 2010 (2010), http://interactivetokyo.jp/2010/
2. Abe, Y., Liu, C.K., Popović, Z.: Momentum-based parameterization of dynamic character motion. In: SCA 2004: Proc. of the 2004 ACM SIGGRAPH/Eurographics Symp. on Computer Animation, pp. 173–182. Eurographics Association, Aire-la-Ville (2004)
3. Brooks, R.A., Stein, L.A.: Building brains for bodies. Auton. Robots 1(1), 7–25 (1994)
4. Hasegawa, S., Sato, M.: Real-time Rigid Body Simulation for Haptic Interactions Based on Contact Volume of Polygonal Objects. Computer Graphics Forum 23(3), 529–538 (2004), http://springhead.info/
5. Hasegawa, S., Toshiaki, I., Hashimoto, N.: Human scale haptic interaction with a reactive virtual human in a realtime physics simulator. In: ACE 2005: Proc. of the 2005 ACM SIGCHI Intl. Conf. on Advances in Computer Entertainment Technology, pp. 149–155. ACM, New York (2005)
6. Lee, S.P., Badler, J.B., Badler, N.I.: Eyes alive. ACM Trans. Graph. 21(3), 637–644 (2002)
7. Itti, L., Dhavale, N., Pighin, F.: Realistic avatar eye and head animation using a neurobiological model of visual attention. In: Proc. SPIE Intl. Symp. on Optical Science and Technology, vol. 5200, pp. 64–78 (August 2003)
8. Mitsunaga, N., Miyashita, T., Yoshikawa, Y., Ishiguro, H., Kogure, K., Hagita, N.: Robovie-iv: An every day communication robot. Technical report of IEICE. PRMU 105(534), 47–52 (2006), http://ci.nii.ac.jp/naid/10017302543/en/
9. NINTENDO: nintendogs (2005), http://www.nintendo.co.jp/ds/adgj/
10. Peters, C., Sullivan, C.O.: Bottom-up visual attention for virtual human animation. In: Proc. of Computer Animation for Social Agents (2003)
11. Rose, C., Guenter, B., Bodenheimer, B., Cohen, M.F.: Efficient generation of motion transitions using spacetime constraints. In: SIGGRAPH 1996: Proc. of the 23rd Annual Conf. on Computer Graphics and Interactive Techniques, pp. 147–154. ACM Press, New York (1996)
12. Sato, M., Hirata, Y., Kawarada, H.: Space interface device for artificial reality. Journal of Robotics and Mechatronics 9(3), 177–184 (1997)
13. SCEE: Eyepet (2009), http://www.eyepet.com/
14. da Silva, M., Abe, Y., Popović, J.: Interactive simulation of stylized human locomotion. ACM Trans. Graph. 27(3), 1–10 (2008)
15. Zordan, V.B., Majkowska, A., Chiu, B., Fast, M.: Dynamic response for motion capture animation. ACM Trans. Graph. 24(3), 697–701 (2005)

Building a Character Animation System

Ari Shapiro

Institute for Creative Technologies
shapiro@ict.usc.edu
http://www.ict.usc.edu

Abstract. We describe a system for animating virtual characters that encompasses many important aspects of character modeling for simulations and games. These include locomotion, facial animation, speech synthesis, reaching/grabbing, and various automated non-verbal behaviors, such as nodding, gesturing and eye saccades. Our system implements aspects of character animation from the research community that yield high levels of realism and control.

Keywords: animation, character, graphics, system.

1 Motivation

Animating virtual humans is a complex task. Many different aspects of human behavior needs to be modeled in order to generate a convincing result. The behavior and appearance of a virtual characters needs to be recognizably human in expression, although photorealism is not necessary. People are adept at recognizing movement and human-like behavior, so the actions and appearance of a virtual character must match the expectations of the human viewer. This means that not only must the character's movements be natural, but they must be contextually appropriate, such as responding with the appropriate reaction and in the proper time frame to stimuli. Research has been done on various aspects of character animation, such as locomotion and facial animation. However, the integration of all these aspects leads to complexities. For example, coordinating locomotion with path finding, or coordinating reaching with gazing. At first glance, it appears that modeling an entire animated character can be achieved by combining individual areas, and then reassembling the final character as a combination of each individual part. For example, locomotion can be combined with a lip sync animation. This combination works since there is little relationship between locomotion and the movement of a character's lips and face. Serious problems arrive when the areas overlap and directory or indirectly impact each other. For example, performing a manipulation with your hands while simultaneously looking at another object in the virtual world. The looking behavior might engage parts of the character's body that disrupt the manipulation. Thus, although manipulation and gazing are distinct problem areas in animation research, they can interact with each other in unexpected ways.

1.1 Goals

We aim to synthesize a highly realistic, interactive character, which will likely require high-quality and possibly expensive methods. Many game engines provide robust solutions to many real time simulation problems such as mesh rendering, lighting, particle effects and so forth. However, game engines generally do not handle complex character animation. They often provide a general framework for replaying animations on a hierarchical skeleton, as well as a providing mechanism for blending between animations or looping an animation. However, the intricate and specific motion commonly associated with humans must be constructed by the game engine programmer and designer. One of the goals of this project is to develop a character animation system allows the realization of common behaviors that are used in real time games and simulations. These behaviors include: synthesizing speech, responding to speech, moving, touching, grabbing, gesturing, gazing, breathing, emotional expression and other non-verbal behavior.

The system is not intended to be a framework for the development of character animation via a well-defined interface or with pluggable animation blocks. Such well-defined interfaces are effective for well-defined and understood problems. However, animating a virtual character to a high level of realism has a number of complexities that are not well understood, and thus don't benefit greatly from such simple architectures. Such designs can either under specify the interface, leaving too much work to the game designers and programmers, or overly simplifying the system, restricting it's capabilities.

2 System Summary

The animation system is designed around a hierarchical, controller-based architecture [3]. The state of the character is manipulated by series of controllers, with the output of one passed as the input to another. Each controller can either override, modify or ignore the state of the virtual character. The controllers know the state of the character during the last step, as well as the state of the character during the evaluation phase. The controller stack, which controls the state data flow, is listed in Table 1 in the order of execution.

2.1 Problems with Generalization/Specialization Hierarchy

Some controllers can hide the impact of earlier controllers by overriding the state values. For example, the face controllers (13) overwrites the face state originally generated by the idle motion controller (2). This scheme will work for these two controllers, since the face control can be thought of as a specialization of the more generic idle pose. However, the locomotion controller (3) must entirely replace the effects of the idle motion controller (2) during a certain behaviors, such as walking. Thus, while the hierarchy implies a generalization-specialization scheme, in practice, many controllers have effects that overlaps, extend or replace the effects of earlier one. As another example, the gaze controller can engage

Table 1.

Order	Controller	Comments
1	World offset	Global orientation and position
2	Idle motion	Underlying idle pose
3	Locomotion	Overrides idle pose during locomotion phases, ignored during idle states
4	Animation	Non-locomotive animations, can encompass entire body or just upper body during locomotion.
5	Reach	Allows reaching and pointing using arms
6	Grab	Hand control for touching, grabbing, and picking up objects
7	Gaze	Looking with eyes, head, shoulders and waist
8	Breathing	Chest and diaphragm control, mostly independent from rest of skeleton hierarchy
9	Constraint	Allows constraints that may have been violated due to impact of preceding controllers (i.e. keeping character's hands on a table while turning to look at another object
10	Eye saccades	Fast movements for eyes, blended with results from gaze
11	Blink	Periodic blinking control
12	Head	Controls head movements; nods, shakes, tilts, backchanneling
13	Face	Determines activation for blend shapes or bone activations when using joint-driven faces, excluding eyes
14	General parameters	Generic controller for transferring non-skeleton data to the rendering engine, such as blushing, tears, GPU shader values, etc.
15	Override	Allows overriding of state values. Useful when taking control of character from other input devices, such as the Kinect

the entire spine during a gaze behavior when orienting a character's entire body towards a gaze target. However, this will disrupt an animation of, say, a character whose hands have been placed on a table by the animation controller (4). To restore these implicit constraints, the constraint controller (9) is activated to reposition the character's hands according to the constraints.

This controller scheme for managing character state requires many additional rules to effectively control the entire character. Also, certain controllers, such as the blink and saccade controllers (10 and 11) can work independently from the face (13), thus strict ordering is not necessary. Better models need to be developed for controlling character state that more closely match the interaction of different character behaviors with each other.

2.2 Platforms

The system is written almost entirely in C++, and has been ported to run on both Linux, OsX. At the time of this writing, we are in the process of porting to the mobile platforms, Android and iOs. The system is licensed under LGPL and is available for download at: http://sourceforge.net/projects/smartbody/

2.3 Locomotion

We have implemented and experimented with two different locomotion systems; a semi-procedural system based on [2], and an example-based system.

The semi-procedural locomotion algorithm uses two example motions; a forward walk and a strafe (sideways walk). The procedural nature of the algorithm allows the use of inverse kinematics to place the feet at the desired position as well as control the angle of the foot on uneven terrain. Since only two example motions are used algorithm, the motion can be parameterized along two axes, each representing either forward or sideways movement. Turning is controlled by setting step targets and orienting the body in line with the footsteps.

The drawbacks to using such this semi-procedural system is the lack of ability of the algorithm to allow for differing styles of movement. Because the foot placement is established by using inverse kinematics, the nuances of the leg movement from the animation data are replaced with the results from the IK algorithm. Thus, many different styles of walking on different characters tend to look very similar below the character's waist. In addition, the use of foot steps makes the motion appear to be clomping, or hard stepping, as compared with motion captured or hand-animated motion.

The example-based locomotion shown in Figure 2 includes 19 different animations to control forward, turning and lateral movement. This locomotion engine does not use IK, and relies almost entirely on blending the motion data, notwithstanding the offset of the character in world space. The example-based locomotion currently uses 5 animations for different speeds of forward movement, 5 different animations for turning left at various speeds, 5 animations for turning right at different speeds. The forward movement animations consist of two walking or running cycles, and the turning animations consist of a character turning around at various speeds; turning in place, turning in a tight circle while walking, turning in a tight circle while running and so forth. The size of the turning circle limits the amount that a character can turn while moving at a given velocity. The animations are parameterized in three dimensions; forward velocity, turning angle, and sideways velocity. Thus, it is possible to emulate any number of foot positions through a combination the various parametric animations. The parameter space of these dimensions can be modeled using tetrahedrons. The parameter values are automatically extracted from the example motions, such as determining the average forward velocity of a motion.

We have found that the example-based animation produces a more realistic result, although this method can be susceptible to foot skating if the motion data is not consistent.

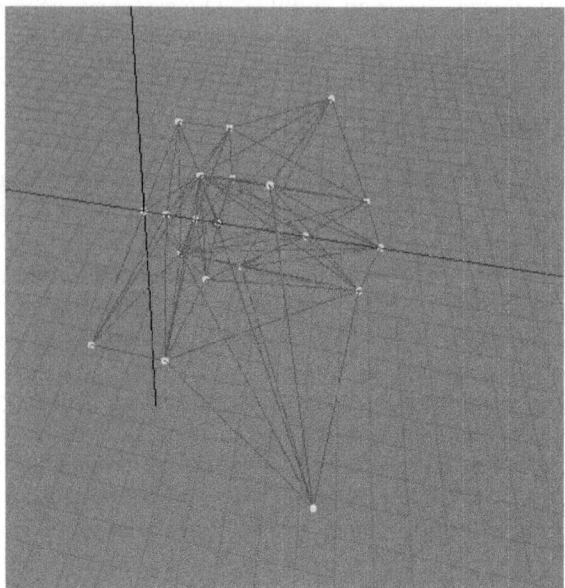

Fig. 1. Visualization of the example-based locomotion. Yellow dots on the red axis indicate moving forward (walking, jogging, running, etc.) Yellow dots along the green axis indicate turning motions. Yellow dots along the blue axis represent strafing, or sideways movement.

2.4 Path Finding

The system uses SteerSuite [8] to handle path finding. The separation of locomotion from path finding allows for the development of each area separately. For example, we have connected the SteerSuite path finding to one of three locomotion engines; the semi-procedural and example-based system as described in the section above, as well as to a simple offset engine that alters the global position of the character without changing it's pose. The simple engine is used to test the viability of the path planning engine. The more complex engines produce more realistic-looking motion.

The benefits of separating the two problem areas has a consequence; without knowing the limits of locomotion capabilities, the path planner sometimes requires movements that are sometimes unrealistically fast, and sometimes visually unappealing. For example, the path planner might decide to suddenly switch direction to avoid an obstacle faster than the locomotion system can realistically move the character, thus causing a discrepancy between the planned path and the actual path.

We noticed that many path planners handle large scale movement, such as traversing long distances are large objects, and very few path planners handle intricate movement in small areas and indoors.

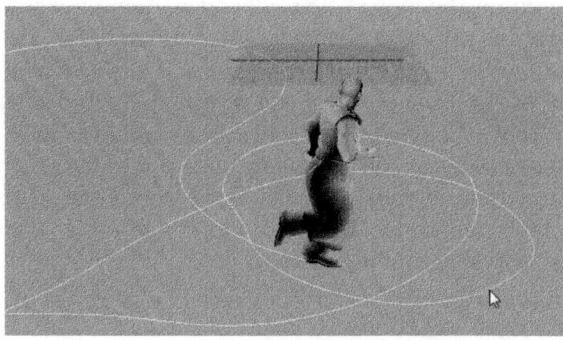

Fig. 2. Example-based locomotion and path

2.5 Reaching and Grabbing

Our system utilizes an example-based approach for reaching. From a standing position, we use 32 different reaching motions to allow a character to most objects within arms-length. Each arm uses 16 example motions from four elevations (high, mid-high, mid-low, low). Motions created for one hand can be mirrored to the other hand in order to reduce the number of examples needed. We interpolate the reach examples to generate pseudo-examples [4], as shown in Figure 3. Our reaching algorithm first finds closest sets of examples, and interpolates and time warps the motion to produce the final motion. Inverse kinematics is then used to achieve the exact desired location, similar to [1].

Because of this reaching technique is based on examples, a different example set is required for each type of reaching motion. For example, a series of reaching tasks performed while sitting requires a different set than the standing reaching set, as in Figure 3. Reaching during walking or running would require another example set. Although it is also possible to overlay the reaching examples on the upper body while animating the lower body, this will cause a loss of realism, since the body will not preserve its movement dynamics. Currently, this reaching system does not handle collisions; it assumes a clear path of movement for the reaching. In addition, the reaching examples are synthesized from the starting position, to the target, then back to the original position. The ability to reach one target, then switch to another without returning to the original pose is outside of the capabilities of the original examples. For such cases, we blend between the pose targets, resulting in passable, but not high quality, reaching animation between targets.

For grabbing, we use heuristic that determines the orientation of the hand that is needed to grab an object. For example, the grab controller will rotate the hand in order to reach around the thinnest axis of the target object. A long, narrow object will cause the hand to reorient so that the long axis is parallel to the palm, allowing the fingers and thumb to close around the object. Near end of reach behavior, the hand will blend between the current hand pose and a specific grabbing pose, which can be modified for larger or smaller objects. Collision spheres are placed on the fingers that allow detection of contact between them and the target object. Individual fingers are represented as IK chains, and will stop blending between the original hand pose and the grabbing hand pose once contact is detected with the object. Each finger IK chain reacts to the collisions independently. Thus, the hand can be seen to wrap around the target object.

The synthesize reaching and grabbing motion produces a more convincing result when appropriately timed gazing is added to the motion. The virtual character can be timed to look at the object before reaching is started, and maintained through the grabbing motion.

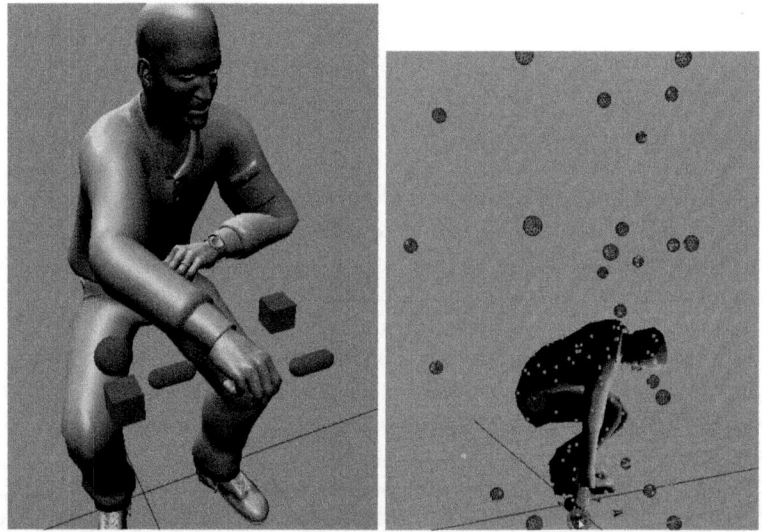

Fig. 3. (Left) Reaching and grabbing during sitting. Notice that the pinky of the right hand did not collide with the target object, and thus was allowed to blend into the grabbing pose, whereas the other fingers collided with the target object, and remain at the collision surface. (Right) Example-based reaching for right side of body. The blue spheres represent the original examples, while the green dots are examples interpolated from the original examples. Note that the character engages his entire body during the reaching motion.

2.6 Facial Animation and Speech Synthesis

The focus of our animation system is to develop autonomous characters that can think, react and perform various tasks in a dynamically changing environment. If the characters needed only to duplicate an actor's performance, the greatest amount of realism would come from performance capture coupled with prerecorded audio. However, since the dialogue of our characters is not always known in advance, nor is the content, it is important to generate a model that can produce arbitrary utterances with reasonable-looking facial movements. Our system uses a set of visemes that are activated by a text-to-speech engine (TTS).

The TTS engine translates an utterance in text format into a series of phonemes (word sounds) and time markers. These phonemes and then mapped to a smaller set of visemes (a facial movement that matches a word sound) which are used to drive the facial animation. Originally, our system used a simple scheme by creating a one-to-one mapping between phonemes and visemes. Each phoneme would trigger its corresponding viseme, and be phased-in and phased-out by overlapping the phase-out period of one viseme with the phase-in period of a second viseme. However, the visual result of many phonemes can be overpowered by the visual result of other phonemes, such as the combining an 'r' with an 'o'. Thus, many phonemes can effectively be ignored when animating the face. In addition, many phonemes produce similar-looking visemes, so those duplicates can be represented by a single viseme. In addition, the system incorporates a set of the Facial Action Coding System (FACS) units, which can be used to express emotion and display facial movements unrelated to speech.

Speech synthesis is implemented using a number of text-to-speech systems. The system can also replay prerecorded audio, when first preprocessed with viseme and timing information.

2.7 Modeling Eye Movements and Saccades

Eye movement is an important part of conveying emotion and intent when animating digital characters. Humans frequently shift their focus of attention among and between objects in the environment, as well as performing eye saccade motions to reduce cognitive load. However, many simulations involving characters ignore eye movements, yielding a virtual character that stares blankly for long periods of time, a behavior not seen in healthy humans.

The eyelid controller regulates the position of the upper and lower eyelids in relation to the pitch of the eyeball. Thus causing the eyelid to move up or down relative to the character's eye gaze direction. The system adds a small delay to the eyelid tracking speed, in order to visually separate the effect of the different physical structures of the eyeball and the eyelid. The impact can be seen in Figure 4.

Fig. 4. Lowering the lid to the level of the eye. This is achieved by activating the upper lids in combination with the eye pitch. Although the amount of this effect is small, the impact on the viewer is large, as the character appears to be in a completely different emotional state in the two images.

For eye movement, we implement an eye saccade model based on [7], which uses a statistical eye movement model for listening and speaking. In many cases, the effect of using the saccade model is effective, as it simulates the more complex cognitive processes of the character. However, these statistical models do not account for the differing context of the speech that is being heard, nor of the content of the speech being uttered. This can sometimes cause a discrepancy between the speech being uttered and eye movements associated with that speech, which can lead to a loss of realism, or even propel the characters into the Uncanny Valley. In addition, these statistical models do not consider the factors that drive the eye movements, such as objects of interest to the character, or movements in the visual field that would cause a spark of attention.

To develop a greater sense of realism, we seek to develop an eye movement model for animated characters based on a study of humans interacting with an animated character Figure 5. Participants listen to a digital character speak and respond to simple questions about personal information, as well as perform and mental tasks, such as counting backwards. An eye tracker captures the location of the eye fixation on the screen containing the animated character. In addition, a video of the participant responding to the questions is synchronized with the eye tracker data for reference. The eye fixation data is then analyzed separately according to whether the participent is listening to, speaking to or reacting to the animated character. The questions are designed to elicit different kinds of emotional reactions: boredom, surprise, mental load, recall of simple information, and so forth. With this model, we hope to generate a more complex and contextually appropriate set of eye saccade behaviors.

Fig. 5. Visualization of eye movement during listening. The size of the bubble indicates the length of time spent fixated on the point or area, while the lines indicate the path travelled. Note that the listener briefly looked at the animated character's left hand during a gesture, while remaining mostly fixated on the mouth.

2.8 Head Nods, Head Shakes, and Gazing

Our system has full control of head movements, which can reflect nodding, shaking and various other head movements. Gazing can occur from a hierarchy of joints, including the eyes, neck, shoulders and waist [9]. A number of parameters can be used to alter the gazing as well as head nodding and shaking styles, such as speed, offset, timing and so forth. In practice, most users of these capabilities tend to vary the default movements only slightly with timing, and generally do not alter the movement style. This is likely due to the complexity of the parameters, and that realistic human head and gazing movement cannot easily be specified using such parameters. In the future, we would like to pursue an example-based approach to head movements and gazing.

2.9 Breathing

Breathing is controlled my retiming and looping a breathing animation cycle that functions on a set of joints that model the chest and abdomen of the virtual character. Although more complex physical models exist [10], such effects can be simulated kinematically since the effects are often hidden underneath clothing. The breathing controller can also activate certain facial animations, such as the flaring of nostrils and the opening of the mouth.

2.10 BML Realizer

The system uses the Behavioral Markup Language (BML) [5] as an interface for controlling and synchronization speech, gesturing and other aspects of conversational modeling. Since the Vienna Draft of BML was originally designed for conversational agents, it heavily emphasizes such behaviors, with little or no support for aspects of character animation such as locomotion, reaching and so forth. Thus, our system enhances the BML with a number of extensions to support this functionality.

2.11 Non-verbal Behavior

Designing a character animation system requires the development of a number of different capabilities for a virtual character. However, the decision to use those capabilities much be left to the simulation designer, game designer, or agent (AI) developer. For example, deciding to walk towards a particular object resides in the domain of the agent, whereas navigating around obstacles should clearly be part of the motion engine. Some character capabilities fall in between the clearly defined areas of motion and intention. Aspects such as gesturing during an utterance or head movement to model awareness of the environment are such examples. They should be configurable by a designer, but represent unconscious, natural or repetitive behavior that lies close to the motion-level behavior.

Our solution to this problem is to employ a separate component that handles non-verbal behavior such as gesturing, head nodding, idle gaze behavior and facial expression, based on [6]. This component enhances or changes instructions from the agent before sending them to the motion engine. Thus, a complex motion that engages many different behaviors at once, such as head nodding while blinking, speaking and emoting, can be hidden from the agent designer. This intermediate component will extract syntactical and semantic information from an utterance, and add additional gestures, head nods, or blinks to the motion instruction. In addition, this component can trigger idle behaviors, such as consulting a saliency map that dictates an attention model to allow natural idle behavior during lull periods of a simulation.

3 Conclusion

One of the goals of our research is to locate, implement and improve techniques that can produce high quality animation. To that end, we have experimented with example-based techniques for both locomotion and reaching that yield high-quality results. We intend to replace other aspects of our system, such as head nods, shakes and gazing with a similar example-based approach. The tradeoff for achieving this level of quality comes at the expense of generating a large number of example motions for differing scenarios, which can be both slow and expensive, and remains an obstacle to development.

Acknowledgments. The SmartBody software is a combined effort of dozens of people over many years. Thanks to the current and past SmartBody team members, including Marcus Thiebaux, Yuyu Xu and Wei-Wen Feng for their hard work on developing and maintaining the system. Also thanks to the Integrated Virtual Humans team including Ed Fast, Arno Hartholt, Shridhar Ravikumar, Apar Suri, Adam Reilly and Matt Liewer for their integration, testing and development efforts.

References

1. Camporesi, C., Huang, Y., Kallmann, M.: Interactive Motion Modeling and Parameterization by Direct Demonstration. In: Safonova, A. (ed.) IVA 2010. LNCS, vol. 6356, pp. 77–90. Springer, Heidelberg (2010)
2. Johansen, R.S.: Automated Semi-Procedural Animation for Character Locomotion. Master's thesis, Aarhus University, the Netherlands (2009)
3. Kallmann, M., Marsella, S.C.: Hierarchical Motion Controllers for Real-Time Autonomous Virtual Humans. In: Panayiotopoulos, T., Gratch, J., Aylett, R.S., Ballin, D., Olivier, P., Rist, T. (eds.) IVA 2005. LNCS (LNAI), vol. 3661, pp. 253–265. Springer, Heidelberg (2005)
4. Kovar, L., Gleicher, M.: Automated extraction and parameterization of motions in large data sets. In: ACM SIGGRAPH 2004 Papers, SIGGRAPH 2004, pp. 559–568. ACM, New York (2004), http://doi.acm.org/10.1145/1186562.1015760
5. Kopp, S., Krenn, B., Marsella, S.C., Marshall, A.N., Pelachaud, C., Pirker, H., Thórisson, K.R., Vilhjálmsson, H.H.: Towards a Common Framework for Multimodal Generation: The Behavior Markup Language. In: Gratch, J., Young, M., Aylett, R.S., Ballin, D., Olivier, P. (eds.) IVA 2006. LNCS (LNAI), vol. 4133, pp. 205–217. Springer, Heidelberg (2006)
6. Lee, J., Wang, Z., Marsella, S.: Evaluating models of speaker head nods for virtual agents. In: Proceedings of the 9th International Conference on Autonomous Agents and Multiagent Systems, AAMAS 2010, International Foundation for Autonomous Agents and Multiagent Systems, Richland, SC, vol. 1, pp. 1257–1264 (2010), http://dl.acm.org/citation.cfm?id=1838206.1838370

7. Lee, S.P., Badler, J.B., Badler, N.I.: Eyes alive. ACM Trans. Graph. 21, 637–644 (2002), http://doi.acm.org/10.1145/566654.566629
8. Singh, S., Kapadia, M., Faloutsos, P., Reinman, G.: An Open Framework for Developing, Evaluating, and Sharing Steering Algorithms. In: Egges, A., Geraerts, R., Overmars, M. (eds.) MIG 2009. LNCS, vol. 5884, pp. 158–169. Springer, Heidelberg (2009), http://dx.doi.org/10.1007/978-3-642-10347-6_15
9. Thiebaux, M., Lance, B., Marsella, S.: Real-time expressive gaze animation for virtual humans. In: Proceedings of The 8th International Conference on Autonomous Agents and Multiagent Systems, AAMAS 2009, International Foundation for Autonomous Agents and Multiagent Systems, Richland, SC, vol. 1, pp. 321–328 (2009), http://dl.acm.org/citation.cfm?id=1558013.1558057
10. Zordan, V.B., Celly, B., Chiu, B., DiLorenzo, P.C.: Breathe easy: model and control of human respiration for computer animation. Graph. Models 68, 113–132 (2006), http://dl.acm.org/citation.cfm?id=1140961.1140965

Energy-Based Pose Unfolding and Interpolation for 3D Articulated Characters

He Wang and Taku Komura

Edinburgh University, 10 Crichton Street, EH8 9AB, United Kingdom

Abstract. In this paper, we show results of controlling a 3D articulated human body model by using a repulsive energy function. The idea is based on the energy-based unfolding and interpolation, which are guaranteed to produce intersection-free movements for closed 2D linkages. Here, we apply those approaches for articulated characters in 3D space. We present the results of two experiments. In the initial experiment, starting from a posture that the body limbs are tangled with each other, the body is controlled to unfold tangles and straighten the limbs by moving the body in the gradient direction of an energy function based on the distance between two arbitrary linkages. In the second experiment, two different postures of limbs being tangled are interpolated by guiding the body using the energy function. We show that intersection free movements can be synthesized even when starting from complex postures that the limbs are intertwined with each other. At the end of the paper, we discuss about the limitations of the method and future possibilities of this approach.

Keywords: Character animation, Motion planning, Pose interpolation.

1 Introduction

Controlling characters that are closely interacting with its own body, other characters and the environment is a difficult problem. As the joint angle representation, which is the most prevalent way to express the posture of characters, does not consider the spatial relationship of the body limbs, the resultant movements suffer from collisions and penetrations.

In this paper, we present the results of controlling a character by using a repulsive energy function that has been successfully applied to control 2D linkages for unfolding [3] and interpolating [12] different configurations. We define a similar energy function used in [3, 12] that is based on the Euclidian distance of the linkages of character skeletons in 3 dimensional space.

We show the results of two experiments, which are the 3D and open linkage versions of what are done in [3] and [12]. In the first experiment, starting from a posture in which the limbs of the body are tangled with each other, the character is controlled in the gradient direction of the energy function and the limbs are successfully unfolded (see Figure 3). Next, we interpolate two different postures in which the limbs are tangled with each other. For several pair of postures, we can successfully interpolate them without any collisions or penetrations of the limbs (see Figure 4). These preliminary results hint the possibility to use the repulsive energy function for path planning and motion synthesis.

The rest of the paper is composed as follows. In section 2, we review some related work of motion synthesis. In section 3, we describe about the energy function that we define to control the character. In section 4, we show the experimental results of unfolding postures in which the limbs are closely interacting with one another. In section 5, we describe the algorithm and experimental results of interpolating different postures by using this energy function. In section 6, we discuss about the problems of the method and the possible approaches for coping with the problem, and conclude the paper.

2 Related Works

Simulating the close interactions of multiple characters is an interest of many researchers in character animation. We first review some work in the field. We then review path-planning methods for synthesizing movements of close interactions. Finally, we give a brief review of some work in computational geometry that handles problems of unfolding and interpolation.

2.1 Character Interaction

The simulation of interactions between multiple characters has many applications such as computer games, virtual environments and films. Liu et al.[16] simulate the close dense interactions of two characters by repetitively updating the motion of each character by spacetime constraints. Lee and Lee [15] simulate the boxing match by using reinforcement learning. Treuille et al [20] use reinforcement learning to simulate the pedestrians avoiding each other. Shum et al [17, 19] use min-max search to find the optimal action in a competitive environment. They also propose a real-time approach based on an automatically produced finite state machine [18]. These researches do not handle very close interactions such as holding or wrestling. Ho and Komura [9] propose to evaluate the similarity of character postures based on the topological relationships. When equivalent postures are found, the postures are linearly interpolated at the level of generalized coordinates. In [8], Ho and Komura define a new coordinate system called Topology Coordinates to synthesize and interpolate keyframes in which the characters tangle their limbs with each other. The method is applied for a prototype of a wrestling game in [10]. The postures are restricted to those involve tangling and it is not very suitable when there is no tangle between the characters.

2.2 Path-Planning Movements of Close Interactions

Up to now, if we want to generate scenes of close contacts such as one character holds, carries or wrestles with another, it is necessary to plan the motions by

Fig. 1. An example of a locked 5 link chain

global path planning / collision avoidance approaches, such as Rapidly-exploring Random Trees (RRT) [14] or Probabilistic Road Maps (PRM) [13]. Yamane et al. [21] simulate motions to move luggage from one place to another by combining IK and RRT. Hirano et al [6] and Berenson et al. [1] propose to use RRT to search the state space for grasping objects. Ho and Komura [7] use RRT to plan motions such as holding and piggybacking. The problems of global planning methods are (1) they require a huge amount of computation to find collision free paths, (2) as the paths are randomly searched, they are not consistent, and (3) the resulting motion requires further refinement such as smoothing due to its jaggyness. Therefore, these approaches are not practical from the viewpoint of interactive character motion synthesis and editing.

2.3 Linkage Unfolding in Computational Geometry

In computational geometry, a number of researchers have been motivated by the question about locked chains. The main question is which types of linkages always have connected configuration spaces [5]. If the configuration is connected, it is called unlocked, and any two configurations can be interpolated. On the contrary, if there are disconnected configurations, it is called locked. In 3D, a locked open chain of five links was found by Cantarella and Johnson [2] (see Figure 1). In [4], Connelly et al. prove that there are no locked 2D chains. Upon this discovery, Cantarella et al. [3] propose an energy-driven approach to unfold linkages, and Iben et al. [12] propose an extended approach to interpolate arbitrary configurations. We apply these approaches for unfolding and interpolating postures of 3D articulated characters. Although it is proven that there can be locked configurations for 3D articulated characters, we show that this approach works well for various complex postures which we observe in daily life.

3 Unfolding the Body by Repulsive Energy

In this section, we first explain about the repulsive energy function that we use for the experiments in this paper. Next we show experimental results of unfolding a folded body posture by moving the body in the gradient direction of this energy function.

3.1 Repulsive Energy

The repulsive energy move each body segment away from each other. We design the energy such that it converges to infinity when the distance between two segments decrease to zero:

$$G = \sum_{i,j, i \neq j} E(q_i, q_j) = \frac{1}{D(q_i, q_j)} \quad (1)$$

where q_i, q_j are the configurations of the two body segments, and $D(q_i, q_j)$ is the shortest distance between the two body segments. We use this function to guide the character to either unfold from a folded posture and interpolate two different postures. The energy becomes larger when the body is folded and will be smaller when all the limbs are stretched out, as shown in Figure 2.

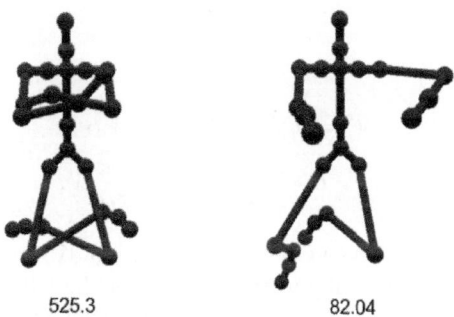

525.3 82.04

Fig. 2. A folded posture (left) and an unfolded posture (right), and their repulsive energies shown at the bottom of each posture

3.2 Unfolding Folded Postures

We use the energy function defined in Eq.1 to unfold the postures. Starting from various folded postures in which the limbs are tangled with one another, the Jacobian of the repulsive energy is computed, and the body posture is updated by moving the joint angles in the gradient direction. The updates of the body joint angles are computed by the following equation:

$$\Delta q = (-I + JJ^T) \frac{J}{\|J\|} \quad (2)$$

where q is the vector of joint angles and J is the Jacobian of the repulsive energy G: $J = \frac{\partial G}{\partial q}$. After solving Δq, it can be normalized and used to update q: $q := q + \Delta q$. However, we also need to consider other constraints, such as positional constraints and joint limits. Here we linearize the nonlinear constraints and turn inequality constraints into equality constraints by imposing them only when the original inequality constraints are violated [11]. Let us represent all the linear constraints by

$$K \Delta q = C. \tag{3}$$

Then, we project the original Δq onto the null space of these constraints by:

$$\Delta q' = \Delta q - K^T l \tag{4}$$

where

$$l = (KK^T)^{-1}(K\Delta q + \alpha \epsilon), \tag{5}$$

α is constant whose value is set to 0.01 in our experiments and $\epsilon = K\Delta q - C$. Sometimes, after projection, $\Delta q'$ might be facing the gradient direction, i.e., $J \cdot \Delta q' > 0$. In such a case, we need to update $\Delta q'$ by a further projection:

$$\Delta q'' = \Delta q' - D^T l' \tag{6}$$

where

$$l' = (DD^T)^{-1}(D\Delta q' + \alpha \gamma) \tag{7}$$

$$D = \begin{bmatrix} K \\ G \end{bmatrix}, \gamma = \begin{bmatrix} \epsilon \\ \sigma/\alpha \end{bmatrix}, \tag{8}$$

and σ is a small negative value which is set to -0.01 in our experiments.

Starting from various configurations shown in the left-most column in Figure 3, the body can be unfolded into postures shown in the right-most column. It can be observed that the body can succesfully unfold the limbs in these examples.

Although the unfolding is known to always converge for 2D linkages [3], this is not always the case in 3D. This is simply because simply moving the body in the gradient of a repulsive energy can fall into local minima especially when the limbs are making knots with each other. However, we have not faced such situations in our experiments, even for a very complex yoga pose shown in the bottom of Figure 3.

4 Interpolating Postures by the Repulsive Energy

In this section, we present the method and the experimental results of interpolating different postures using the repulsive energy defined in section 3.1. We are applying the algorithm of interpolating arbitrary configurations by 2D linkages [12] to 3 dimensional tree structures.

4.1 Methodology

Assume we are interpolating two different postures represented by q_1 and q_2. The algorithm proceeds by iteratively updating the two postures such that they approach towards each other. Again we assume there are linear constraints imposed

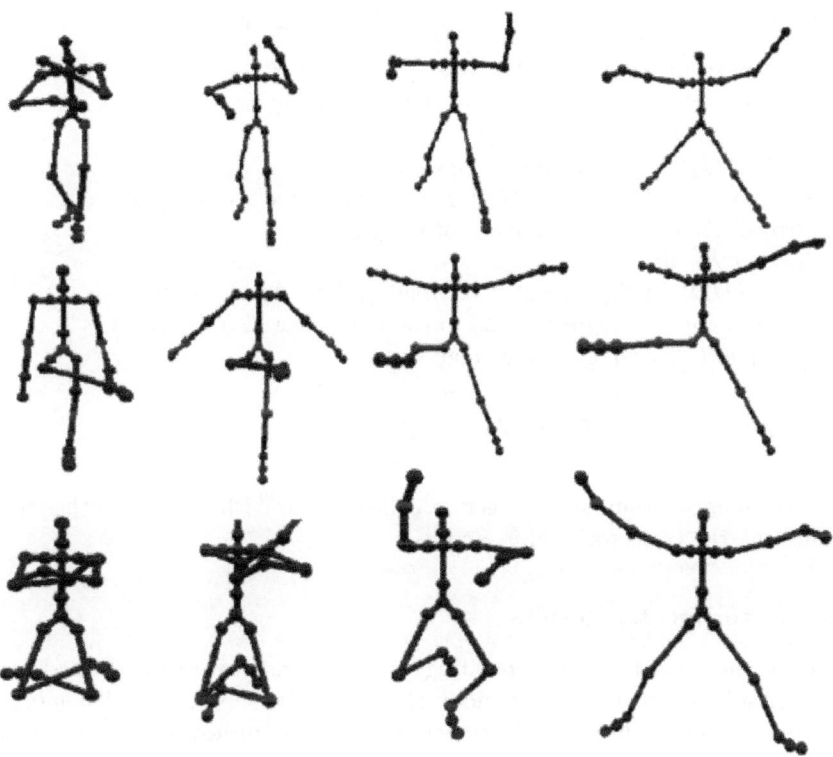

Fig. 3. Examples of unfolding movements starting from postures in the left

to the system represented by Eq.3. In each iteration, we first examine the energy of two postures, then move the posture with the higher energy, say q_h, towards the lower one, say q_l. We first calculate the update vector: $\Delta q = q_l - q_h$. Since moving along this direction could violate some linear constraints, we project the vector to the null space of the constraints by Eq. 4. Because moving in this direction might increase the repulsive energy, we apply another projection by Eq. 6. If such a direction cannot be found (if DD^T in Eq.7 is not invertible), we project the gradient-descent direction vector of the energy to the null space of the linear constraints. Once the update vector is calculated, we move q_h along this direction by a small amount.

Below is the pseudo code of the interpolation algorithm:

1. Initialization: $q_1 \leftarrow q_1^0$ and $q_2 \leftarrow q_2^0$.
2. Compute the energy G_1 and G_2 at q_1 and q_2 by Eq.1
3. $\Delta q \leftarrow sign(G_2 - G_1)(q_1 - q_2)$
4. if$(G_1 > G_2)$ $q \leftarrow q_1$ else $q \leftarrow q_2$
5. Compute the Jacobian of G by partial difference : $J = \frac{\partial G}{\partial q}(q)$
6. Project Δq onto the null space of K by Eq. 4
7. if $(\Delta q \cdot J > 0)$
   if $(DD^T$ in Eq.7 is not invertible) update Δq by Eq. 6
   else $\Delta q \leftarrow -J$, project Δq to the null space of K by Eq. 4
8. $q \leftarrow q + \beta \frac{\Delta q}{\|\Delta q\|}$ where β is a small constant.
9. if $(G_1 > G_2)$ $q_1 \leftarrow q$ else $q_2 \leftarrow q$
10. If q_1 and q_2 are close enough, terminate.
11. Go to step 2.

Once the algorithm is converged, a collision free path can be synthesized by connecting the trajectories of q_1 and q_2.

4.2 Experimental Results

Here we show results of interpolating two different postures explained in the previous subsection. The initial and final postures are shown in the left-most and right-most columns in Figure 4, respectively. The snapshots of the interpolated motions are shown in the middle columns. It can be observed that the postures can be interpolated without any collisions or penetrations. In our experiments, all different combinations of interpolations succeeded without getting stuck at local minima. It is to be noted that the interpolation of these postures using joint angles or joint positions can easily result in penetrations of the limbs in these examples.

5 Discussions and Conclusion

In this paper, we have shown experimental results of unfolding and interpolating tangled body postures using a repulsive energy function. Although intersection-free movements are assured for linkages in 2D, this is not the case for 3D skeletons

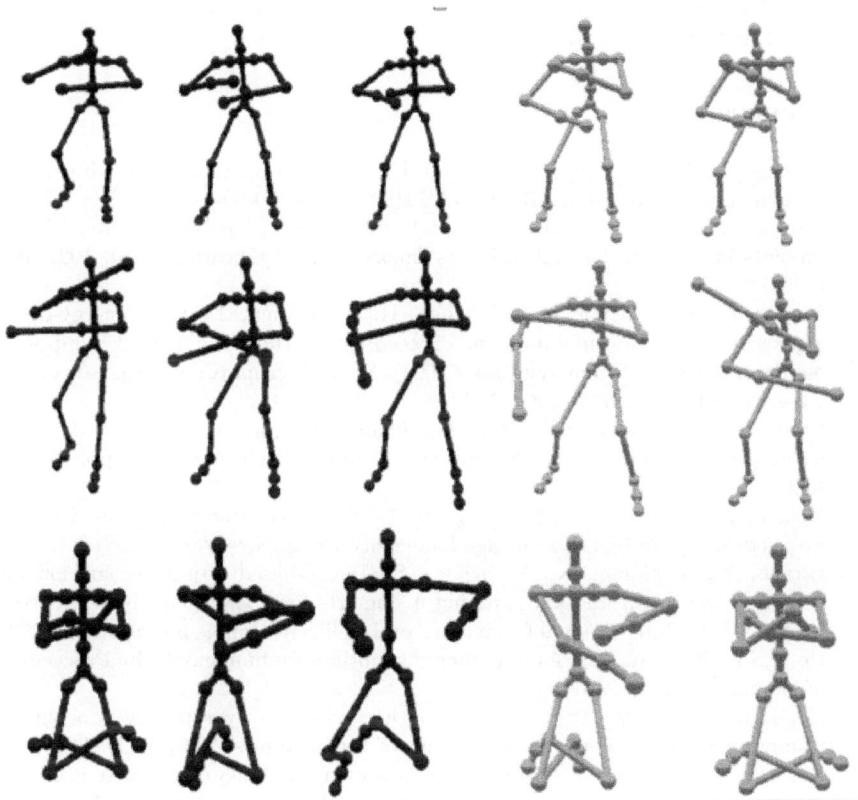

Fig. 4. Examples of interpolating two different poses

due to locks and possible knotted postures. Despite the concern, valid movements can be synthesized in most of our experiments. This can be because the body limbs are only composed of three to four short linkages, which is not enough to compose complex knots. In order to unfold or interpolate configurations with complex knots, it will be necessary to analyze the postures and find out the knots, and control the limbs to desolve them.

One problem of the energy-based approach is that even the postures can be unfolded / interpolated in most of the cases, the motion synthesized is usually very dynamic and not realistic in terms of human movements. Producing natural smooth motions using the repulsive energy function can be an interesting research direction to follow.

References

[1] Berenso, D., Diankovage, R., Nishiwaki, K., Agami, S.K., Kuffner, J.: Grasp planning in complex scenes. In: IEEE/RAS Humanoids (2007)
[2] Cantarella, J., Johnson, H.: Nontrivial embeddings of polygonal intervals and unknots in 3-space. Journal of Knot Theory and Ramifications 7(8), 1027–1039 (1998)
[3] Cantarella, J.H., Demaine, E.D., Iben, H.N., O'Brien, J.F.: An energy-driven approach to linkage unfolding. In: Proceedings of the 20th Annual Symposium on Computational Geometry (June 2004), http://graphics.cs.berkeley.edu/papers/Cantarella-AED-2004-06/
[4] Connelly, R., Demaine, E.D., Rote, G.: Straightening polygonal arcs and convexifying polygonal cycles. In: Discrete and Computational Geometry pp. 432–442 (2000)
[5] Demaine, E.D., O'Rourke, J.: Geometric Folding Algorithms: Linkages, Origami, Polyhedra, reprint edn. Cambridge University Press, New York (2008)
[6] Hirano, Y., Kitahama, K., Yoshizawa, S.: Image-based object recognition and dexterous hand/arm motion planning u sing rrts for grasping in cluttered scene. In: IEEE/RSJ International Conference on Intelligent Robots and Systems (2005)
[7] Ho, E.S.L., Komura, T.: Planning tangling motions for humanoids. In: Proceedings of Humanoids 2007 (2007)
[8] Ho, E.S.L., Komura, T.: Character motion synthesis by topology coordinates. Computer Graphics Forum (Proceedings of Eurographics 2009) 28(2) (2009)
[9] Ho, E.S.L., Komura, T.: Indexing and retrieving motions of characters in close contact. IEEE Transactions on Visualization and Computer Graphics 15(3), 481–492 (2009)
[10] Ho, E.S.L., Komura, T.: A finite state machine based on topology coordinates for wrestling games. In: Computer Animation and Virtual Worlds pp. n/a–n/a (2011), http://dx.doi.org/10.1002/cav.376
[11] Ho, E.S.L., Komura, T., Tai, C.L.: Spatial relationship preserving character motion adaptation. ACM Trans. Graph. 29(4) (2010)
[12] Iben, H.N., O'Brien, J.F., Demaine, E.D.: Refolding planar polygons. Discrete and Computational Geometry 41(3), 444–460 (2009), http://graphics.cs.berkeley.edu/papers/Iben-RPP-2009-04/
[13] Kavraki, L., Svestka, P., Latombe, J., Overmars, M.: Probabilistic roadmaps for path planning in high-dimensional configuration spaces. Tech. rep., Stanford, CA, USA (1994)

[14] LaValle, S., Kuffner, J.: Rapidly-exploring random trees: Progress and prospects. Robotics: The Algorithmic Perspective. In: 4th Int'l Workshop on the Algorithmic Foundations of Robotics (2001)
[15] Lee, J., Lee, K.H.: Precomputing avatar behavior from human motion data. In: Proceedings of 2004 ACM SIGGRAPH/Eurographics Symposium on Computer Animation, pp. 79–87 (2004)
[16] Liu, C.K., Hertzmann, A., Popovic, Z.: Composition of complex optimal multi-character motions. In: ACM SIGGRAPH / Eurographics Symposium on Computer Animation, pp. 215–222 (2006)
[17] Shum, H.P.H., Komura, T., Yamazaki, S.: Simulating competitive interactions using singly captured motions. In: Proceedings of ACM Virtual Reality Software Technology 2007, pp. 65–72 (2007)
[18] Shum, H.P.H., Komura, T., Yamazaki, S.: Simulating interactions of avatars in high dimensional state space. In: ACM SIGGRAPH Symposium on Interactive 3D Graphics (i3D) 2008, pp. 131–138 (2008)
[19] Shum, H.P.H., Komura, T., Yamazaki, S.: Simulating multiple character interactions with collaborative and adversarial goals. IEEE Transactions on Visualization and Graphics (2011)
[20] Treuille, A., Lee, Y., Popović, Z.: Near-optimal character animation with continuous control. ACM Transactions on Graphics 26(3), 1–7 (2007)
[21] Yamane, K., Kuffner, J., Hodgins, J.K.: Synthesizing animations of human manipulation tasks. ACM Transactions on Graphics 23(3), 532–539 (2004)

Generating Avoidance Motion Using Motion Graph

Masaki Oshita and Naoki Masaoka

Kyushu Institute of Technology
680-4 Kawazu, Iizuka, Fukuoka 820-8502, Japan
oshita@ces.kyutech.ac.jp, masaoka@cg.ces.kyutech.ac.jp

Abstract. We propose a method of generating avoidance motions. We use a motion graph to generate continuous motions, including both avoidance and other kinds of motions. In the combat of real humans, trained fighters avoid an attack with minimal movement. To realize such avoidance motion, we developed criteria to find an appropriate path (series of edges) in the motion graph. The characters are expected to move their body by only a minimal distance to avoid an attack. We introduced attack, body and avoidance space–time volumes to evaluate this criterion. Each candidate path is evaluated according to the distance between attack and body volumes and the overlap between attack and avoidance volumes. We also introduced a method to control the execution speeds of edges, and thus adjust the timing of avoidance motions. Moreover, to find a path in real time, we developed methods to facilitate the searching process such as the use of grid-based indices to look up candidate paths and GPU-based quick collision detection to cull candidate paths. We tested our approach on an application in which a character avoids incoming balls controlled by a user and demonstrated the effectiveness of our approach.

Keywords: avoidance motion, motion graph, space–time volume.

1 Introduction

Generating the realistic animation of combating characters, especially the generation of avoidance motions, is a challenge in the field of computer animation, because a character's motion must vary dynamically in response to the opponent's motion. Currently, many computer games that involve combat between characters generate character motions by selecting a suitable motion from a set of a limited number of precreated motions and playing that motion. In the combat of real humans, trained fighters avoid an attack with minimal movement. However, this kind of avoidance motion cannot be realized in computer animation when taking the current approach. The characters in computer games instead avoid an attack by taking a large step or making a large leap. To realize good avoidance motions as real fighters do, the system requires methods for organizing many avoidance motions and executing an appropriate motion acceding to an incoming attack at an interactive speed.

In this paper, we propose a method to generate avoidance motions in real time by solving the abovementioned problems. We use a motion graph [2] to generate continuous motions, including both avoidance and other kinds of motion.

A motion graph is a set of connected short motion segments (edges). It is constructed from a set of long motion sequences by finding similar postures in the input motions and converting the similar postures into nodes of the motion graph and converting the motion segments into directional edges. Once a motion graph is constructed, a continuous motion is generated by traversing edges in the motion graph while playing them. However, to generate meaningful motion, the system needs rules for choosing an appropriate next edge or a path (series of edges) from the edge currently being played. Many kinds of rules have been proposed, such as those relating to walking [2,8], interactive control by the user [11], and reactions to impacts [1]. However, generating avoidance motion has been a difficult challenge.

In this research, we developed criteria to find an appropriate path (series of edges) in the motion graph to generate motion to avoid an incoming attack in a way similar to that employed by human fighters. The characters are expected to move their bodies only a minimal distance to avoid an attack. We introduced attack, body and avoidance space–time volumes to evaluate this criterion. Each candidate path (motion) is evaluated according to the distance between the attack and body volumes and the overlap between the attack and avoidance volumes. In addition, we also introduced a method to control execution speeds of edges, and thus adjust the timings of avoidance motions. Moreover, to find a path in real time, we developed methods to facilitate the searching process such as using grid-based indices to look up candidate paths and graphics processing unit (GPU)-based quick collision detection to cull candidate paths. We tested our approach on an application in which a character avoids incoming balls controlled by a user and demonstrated the effectiveness of our approach.

The rest of this paper is organized as follows. In Section 2, we review related works. In Section 3, we present the flow of our method. Section 4 explains the criteria for evaluating candidate paths. Section 5 explains the methods employed for computational efficiency. Finally, Section 6 presents experimental results.

2 Related Work

Motion graphs [2,3,6] have been widely used in recent research. To generate motions using a motion graph, criteria that determine appropriate edges and an efficient algorithm to search for a path (series of edges) that satisfies the criteria are necessary. Various criteria have been proposed depending on the types of motions, as mentioned in Section 1. To find a path, general algorithms such as the branch and bound algorithm [2], reinforcement learning [4], Markov decision process control [11,5], and the min-max algorithm [9] are used. However, these approaches cannot be simply applied to our problem, because a path cannot be evaluated until it reaches the avoidance motion part. It is thus difficult to search for avoidance motions efficiently.

Several research works have addressed the generation of combat or avoidance motion. Zordan et al. [13] employed a support vector machine, which is a pattern recognition technique, to select an avoidance motion according to feature vectors containing the position, direction and speed of an incoming attack. However, since the approach does not evaluate space–time conditions between the attack and avoidance motions, it is difficult to generate proper avoidance motion. In fact, a character prepares for an incoming attack but then was hit by the attack. Lee and Lee [4] generated attack motions based on a given target position using a motion graph. However, to generate avoidance motions, not only a point in space and time but also space–time volumes must be considered. Therefore, generating avoidance motions is a more difficult problem. Shum et al. [9] selected combat motions including avoidance, but did not consider the criteria for natural-looking avoidance motions. Shum et al. [10] also generated combat motions using combined attack and avoidance motions. However, taking this approach, each avoidance motion is coupled with a corresponding attack motion and avoidance motions cannot be generated for any incoming attack. The patterns of avoidance and attack motions are limited. Wampler et al. [12] proposed a framework for planning two characters' continuous motions in real time. Their method also requires that the attacker's motion be generated using the same method, and avoidance motion for any attack is not realized. We propose novel criteria to select avoidance motions from a motion graph using space–time volumes.

3 Overview

Our system generates a character's avoidance motions using a motion graph that contains avoidance and other kinds of motions that are necessary for the application. Overall runtime processes are shown in Fig. 1 (a). When there is no incoming attack, any rules to select edges can be applied. When information of an incoming attack (its space–time volume) is given, our method searches for a path (series of edges in the motion graph) starting from the edge currently being executed to realize an avoidance motion. The system then executes the selected path to generate a resulting animation.

The details of the data representation of attack volumes are explained in Section 4.2. The space–time volume of an incoming attack can be generated in various ways depending on the application. In our experiment, we develop an application in which a user throws a ball at a character by clicking a point on the screen. In this case, an attack volume is generated from the half line in the virtual world corresponding to the clicked point on the screen. If a developer wants to generate an animation of fighting characters, he/she can generate the motion of an attacker using the motion graph or other dynamic motion-generation techniques. In this case, an attack volume can be generated from motion data with some additional information such as the body part used for the attack and the time at which the attack is supposed to hit.

In general, a large number of possible motions can be generated from a starting edge. For computational efficiency, a conventional search algorithm [2,3,4,5,9,11] attempts to cut less promising paths as early as possible and to develop promising paths by evaluating the incomplete candidate paths. However, we cannot apply the same approach for avoidance motion because a candidate path generally cannot be evaluated until it reaches the avoidance motion part. Therefore, our system enumerates possible candidate paths that include an avoidance motion first. The avoidance part of each candidate path is then evaluated to select the best among all candidate paths. This approach requires some computational time to enumerate and evaluate many possible candidate paths. For computational efficiency, we developed several methods that are explained in Section 5.

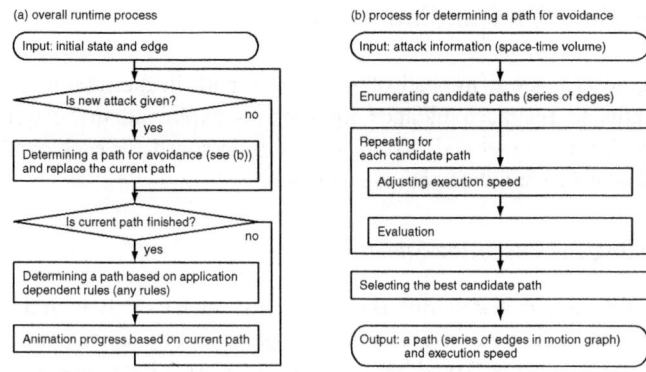

Fig. 1. System flow

The process for determining a path to be executed is shown in Fig. 1 (b). When attack information is given, the system enumerates possible candidate paths starting from the current edge that have avoidance motion within a certain time window. Although we adjust the execution speed of each candidate path later, the timing of the avoidance motion is expected to be within a certain time window T_{window} from the timing of the attack. The interval from the beginning of the path to the center of the avoidance part t_{avoid} must satisfy the following condition.

$$t_{attack} - T_{window}/2 < t_{avoid} < t_{attack} + T_{window}/2, \qquad (1)$$

where t_{attack} is the interval from the beginning of the path to the center of the attack time. In our implementation, we use $T_{window} = 1.0$. By traversing all edges from the current edge, all possible candidate paths are enumerated. The evaluation of candidate paths including calculation of the execution speed of them is explained in Section 4.

3.1 Constructing a Motion Graph Including Avoidance Motions

To construct and represent motion graphs, we use methods similar to those used in previous works [1,2,3,8,9]. A motion graph consists of nodes and edges. Each directional edge represents a short segment of motion. Each node represents a posture connecting adjacent edges. By traversing edges, continuous motions can be generated. A motion graph is constructed from a number of motion clips by analyzing them and identifying similar parts in them and generating edges from the similar parts.

To realize avoidance motions, we label avoidance parts on edges in the motion graph. We specify avoidance parts (time intervals) in the original motion clips manually before constructing the motion graph; the information is inherited by the edges in the constructed motion graphs. During construction of the motion graph, each avoidance part is preserved and not divided into more than one edge.

In addition, some information is computed automatically. Body and avoidance volumes and speed adjustment condition are computed for each edge. A grid-based index is constructed for each node.

4 Evaluation of a Candidate Path

This section describes our method of selecting a path in the motion graph from the candidate paths to realize avoidance motion. As explained in Section 3, possible candidate paths are enumerated first. The execution speed for each candidate path is adjusted before each candidate path is evaluated.

4.1 Adjusting the Execution Speed

The timing of the avoidance motion is expected to match exactly with the timing of an incoming attack. However, in general, such paths hardly exist among the limited number of candidate paths. To address this problem, we adjust the execution speed of each candidate path so that the generated motion meets the timing constraint. For each candidate path, the execution speeds of edges in the candidate path are determined.

Our key insight for this process is that we change the execution speed for the part of the motion (edges in the motion graph) for which the change does not cause a noticeable problem. If part of the original motion is fast, it is considered that that part can be slowed down a little. On the other hand, if part of the original motion is slow, it is considered that that part can be sped up a little. If part of the original motion is still or almost still, it can be either slowed down or sped up, because neither greatly affects the original movement.

When the motion graph is constructed, the system analyzes each edge and determines if the edge can be sped up, slowed down, both, or neither on the basis of the velocities of the end effectors. The velocities of four end effectors (hands and feet) $v_{r\_hand}^t, v_{l\_hand}^t, v_{r\_foot}^t, v_{l\_foot}^t$ are calculated for each frame, and the maximum velocity among all frames and end effectors is denoted v_{max}. If $v_{max} > V_{fast}$, the movement of the edge is determined to be fast and allowed to slow down. If $V_{slow} > v_{max} > V_{still}$, the movement of the edge is determined to be slow and allowed to speed up. If $v_{max} < V_{still}$, the movement of the edge is determined to be still and allowed to either speed up or slow down. $V_{fast}, V_{slow}, V_{still}$ are thresholds. In our implementation, we set $V_{fast}, V_{slow}, V_{still}$ as 0.3, 0.1, and 0.0 m/s, respectively.

Each candidate path is adjusted so that its avoidance time and the attack time in the given attack information match. First, the overall scale of the speed change is calculated from the avoidance and attack times. Next, the speeds of edges that can be adjusted are scaled as shown in Fig. 2. For example, if the path must be sped up, the speed of all edges that are allowed to be sped up (dashed edges in Fig. 2) is scaled at the same ratio. We let t_{avoid} be the interval from the beginning of the path to the center of the avoidance part and t_{attack} be the interval to the center of the attack time window. The candidate path consists of adjustable edges and non-adjustable edges.

$$t_{avoid} = t_{avoid\_adjustable} + t_{avoid\_nonadjustable} \qquad (2)$$

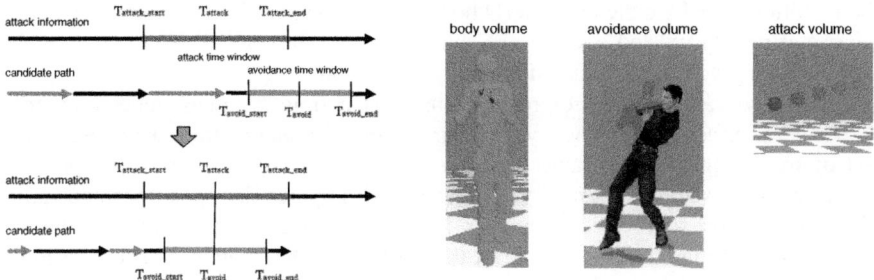

Fig. 2. Speed control   **Fig. 3.** Example of volumes

The time scaling parameter s_{time} for all the adjustable edges is computed as

$$s_{time} = \left(t_{attack} - t_{avoid\_nonadjustable}\right) / t_{avoid\_adjustable}. \quad (3)$$

If there is no edge that can be adjusted in a candidate path, the path is removed from the set of candidate paths. To avoid too much speed adjustment that may cause unnatural movement, we also evaluate the adjustment ratio of speed s_{time} as explained later. Our approach may result in discontinuity at transitions between scaled and non-scaled edges. To address this problem, smooth time warping between the edges or dynamic filtering ensuring continuous motion may be further applied.

4.2 Evaluation of a Candidate Path

This subsection describes our method of evaluating candidate paths. Even when the opponent character performs the same attack motion, appropriate avoidance motions in response to the attack vary depending on the relative positions and orientations of the characters and the defending character's current state. An appropriate candidate must be chosen on the fly. As explained in Section 1, human fighters attempt to avoid an attack with minimal movement. We developed criteria to find such candidates. A character is expected to move his/her body only a minimal distance to avoid an attack.

To realize such avoidance motion, obviously the character's body should not be touched by the attack. In addition, the character should move his/her body away from where an incoming attack passes through immediately before the attack would hit the body. To evaluate these factors, we introduce attack, body and avoidance space–time volumes. The factors are evaluated by computing the overlap or distance between volumes. The attack volume is given as the input to the system. The body and avoidance volumes are computed from the motion graph.

Human fighters sometimes shield or parry attacks by intentionally intercepting attacks with a body part. Our method does not consider such non-avoidance reactions to attacks and focuses on avoidance motions.

Definition of Attack, Body and Avoidance Volumes. Figure 3 shows an example of attack, body and avoidance volumes. These volumes are space–time (four-dimensional) volumes. The attack volume is the volume affected by the attack. The body volume is where the character's body exists. The avoidance volume is where the character's body existed a while ago, but not now. The specific definitions of these volumes are given in the remainder of this subsection.

There are various ways of representing space–time volumes depending on the expected accuracy and efficiency. For our current implementation, we chose to use a set of spheres in discrete frames (1/10 seconds). We assign a number of spheres on the character's skeleton manually in advance with appropriate positions and radii so that the spheres cover the character's body. Using these preset spheres, the body volume in a frame is computed from the posture of the character. The positions of spheres between discrete frames are computed by interpolating two adjacent frames. During evaluation, overlap and distance between volumes are evaluated in discrete frames (1/20 seconds). The intervals between frames for volume representation and evaluation can be changed or be adaptive depending on the application. Especially when attacks are fast, smaller intervals may be necessary. The avoidance volume in each frame is defined as a difference between the body volume when the avoidance motion began and the body volume at the current time. An attack volume is given as an input. How to calculate attack volumes depends on the application.

Evaluation of the Overlap between Attack and Avoidance Volumes. The first criterion is the overlap between the attack volume and the avoidance volume of the candidate path. The penetration of the attack volume into the avoidance volume during avoidance motion is computed. Since we use a set of spheres to represent the volumes, we compute the sum of overlaps between each pair of spheres.

$$e'_{avoidance} = \sum_{t,i,j} \begin{cases} 0 & \text{if } D(S_{attack}^{t,i}, S_{avoidance}^{t,j}) \geq 0 \\ -D(S_{attack}^{t,i}, S_{avoidance}^{t,j}) \Delta t & \text{if } D(S_{attack}^{t,i}, S_{avoidance}^{t,j}) < 0 \end{cases} \quad (4)$$

for the i-th sphere of the attack volume and j-th sphere of the avoidance volume in frame t (interval of 1/20 seconds). $D(S_1, S_2)$ calculates the distance between/overlap of two spheres. If the value is positive, the spheres do not overlap and the value represents the distance between them. If the value is negative, the spheres overlap and the value represents the depth of penetration. Because the avoidance volume is defined as the difference between body volumes as explained above, the penetration depth in equation (4) is computed as follows, where t_0 is the time when the avoidance part starts.

$$D(S_{attack}^{t,i}, S_{avoidance}^{t,j}) = D(S_{attack}^{t,i}, S_{body}^{t_0,j}) - D(S_{attack}^{t,i}, S_{body}^{t,j}) \quad (5)$$

Finally, we scale this value from 0.0 to 1.0 using a scaling parameter $E_{avoidance}$.

$$e_{avoidance} = \sum_{t,i,j} \begin{cases} 1 - e'_{avoidance} / E_{avoidance} & \text{if } e'_{avoidance} > E_{avoidance} \\ 0 & \text{if } e'_{avoidance} \geq E_{avoidance} \end{cases} \quad (6)$$

In experiments, it appears that the character avoids the attack when $e'_{avoidance}$ is greater than 0.5. Therefore, we use $E_{avoidance} = 0.5$

Evaluation of the Distance between Attack and Body Volumes. The second criterion is the minimal distance between the attack volume and the body volume. It is computed as follows, where t is repeated for each frame of the candidate path.

$$d = \min_{t,i,j} \{ D(S_{attack}^{t,i}, S_{body}^{t,j}) \} \quad (7)$$

If $d < 0$, the attack and body volumes overlap and the character fails to avoid the attack. On the other hand, if $d > 0$, they do not overlap. In this case, the shorter the distance is, the better the avoidance motion looks. However, if we simply give high evaluation to shorter distances, the character tries to approach the attack, even when the character does not have to move to avoid the attack. Therefore, we decided to give a high evaluation to the shorter distance when the distance is greater than that when the motion starts d_0, where D_{body} is a scaling parameter.

$$e_{body} = \begin{cases} 1 & \text{if } d \leq d_0 \\ (d - d_0)/D_{body} & \text{if } d_0 < d < d_0 + D_{body} \\ 1 & \text{if } d \geq d_0 + D_{body} \end{cases} \quad (8)$$

Evaluation of the Rate of Adjustment of the Execution Speed. In addition to the two criteria above, the rate of adjustment of the execution speed is evaluated because it may cause unnatural motions. Although the allowable speed change depends on the motion, through our experiments, we determined that it is acceptable if the speed rate change is within a factor of 4 $(E_{time} = 4)$.

$$e_{timescale} = \begin{cases} |s_{time}|/E_{time} & \text{if } |s_{time}| > 1 \\ 1/(|s_{time}|E_{time}) & \text{if } |s_{time}| < 1 \end{cases} \quad (9)$$

Total Evaluation. Each candidate path is evaluated according to

$$e = w_a e_{avoidance} + w_b e_{body} + w_t e_{timescale}, \quad (10)$$

where w_a, w_b, w_t are weights that control the contributions of these factors, while $E_{avoidance}$, D_{body}, and E_{time} in equations (6)–(9) are determined considering each factor independently. In our implementation, we set all weights w_a, w_b, w_t as 1.0. As explained in Section 3, among all candidate paths, the candidate path whose evaluation value is smallest is chosen and used to generate avoidance motion.

5 Methods Employed for Computational Efficiency

Because the number of candidate paths can be large, enumerating and evaluating all candidate paths is time consuming. Therefore, we introduce a grid-based index and GPU-based collision detection. These are popular approaches to achieve computation efficiency. This section describes how we employ these approaches in our system.

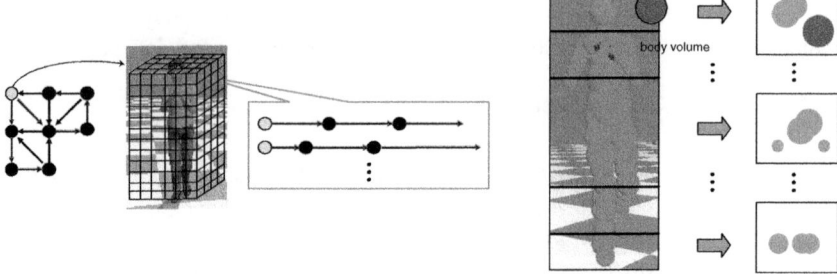

Fig. 4. Grid-based index   **Fig. 5.** GPU-based collision detection

5.1 Grid-Based Index for Candidate Paths

The most important criterion for selecting candidate paths is the overlap between attack and avoidance volumes. The number of candidate paths having overlap is limited compared with the total number of possible candidate paths. Therefore, we index such candidate paths using a grid-based index for each node in the motion graph. Without traversing the motion graph from the current edge, the candidate paths can be retrieved from the index of the current node according to the attack volume. If there is no candidate path for which the avoidance volume in the index, candidate paths are enumerated by traversing the motion graph as explained in Section 3.

The grid-based index is constructed in advance for each node in the motion graph. The space around the character at the node is divided into a grid as shown in Fig. 4. In our implementation, the size of each cell in the grid is 10 cm. First, possible paths that start from the node and contain avoidance motion within a certain time window are enumerated by traversing the motion graph. Then, for each cell, all paths for which the avoidance volume overlaps the cell are recorded.

During runtime, the attack volume is rotated and transformed into the local coordinates of the current node. Corresponding cells in the grid of the current edge are then determined according to the attack volume. The number of corresponding cells can be more than one since the attack volume is a space–time volume.

5.2 GPU-Based Collision Detection for Culling

Another important criterion for selecting candidate paths is the overlap between attack and body volumes. If they overlap on a candidate path, it means that the attack hits the character and the candidate paths should be removed. However, detecting the overlap between two volumes is time consuming. Therefore, we introduce GPU-based quick collision detection to cull candidates.

We divide the space into several horizontal segments as shown in Fig. 5. For each segment, collision detection between volumes is computed on a two-dimensional space by drawing volumes. In our implementation, we divide the space into nine horizontal segments. For each segment of each edge in the motion graph, the place where the body volume exists during for entire edge is drawn on a texture in the local coordinates in advance. During runtime, the attack volume is first drawn on a texture for each segment. The body-volume texture of each segment is then drawn on the same texture by applying rotation and translation according to the character's position and orientation when the edge is executed. The number of pixels of the overlap between attack and body volumes is counted using the GPU. When the number is greater than a threshold, it is expected that the attack hits the body.

Since we discretize the space and time, this is an approximation method for collision detection. However, it is considered to be sufficient for quick culling.

6 Experiments

We implemented the proposed methods and developed an application in which a user throws balls at a character by clicking on the screen and the character performs an avoidance motion. Although our method can be used to generate animations of multiple characters combating each other, we developed this application of generating the animation of a single character avoiding given attacks so that we can test our methods with various inputs of attacks. When there is no attack coming, the next edge is determined randomly. When an attack is given by the user, an attack volume is created from the trajectory as explained in Section 3. Only the part of the trajectory of the ball that is close to the character is used to create the attack volume. An avoidance motion is then generated according to the attack volume. When there no valid candidate path is found, the character may be hit by the ball.

For our experiments, a motion graph was constructed from motion clips of 2 minutes and 40 seconds including 16 avoidance motions such as twisting the upper body, ducking, swinging at the waist, and jumping. The experiments were done on a standard PC with a Pentium 4 CPU, 2.5 GB RAM, and GeForce FX5700 256M GPU.

We also implemented multi-threading to execute and search motions. When an attack is given, the process of finding a path for avoidance motions begins on the background thread. Until the path is found, the next edge is randomly selected when the current edge has finished being executed. The candidate paths that do not contain the next edge are removed from the candidates. When a path is determined, the background thread stops and the path is used in the thread for motion execution.

Table 1. Average time for selecting a candidate path

Condition		Time (milliseconds)
With GPU-based culling	Candidate paths in the grid	14
	No candidate path in the grid	225
Without GPU-based culling	Candidate paths in the grid	18
	No candidate path in the grid	496

6.1 Computational Time for Path Selection

We measured the computational times from the time of an attack given by the user until the time that a path for avoidance motion is selected. In this experiment, we did not employ multi-threading. The measured time is that for enumerating and evaluating candidate paths.

The results are presented in Table 1. As explained in Section 5.2, when there are candidate paths in the grid-based index, these paths are evaluated. On the other hand, when there is no candidate path, candidate paths are enumerated. It was about 20 times faster to use the grid-based index, because it does not require the enumerating of candidates and there are fewer candidates. The average number of candidate paths was 5 when the grid-based index was used, while the number was 100 when the grid-based index was not used. This explains the difference in results for the two cases.

In our experiments, in 90% of cases, the grid-based index was used. This is probably because the user attempted to attack the character and clicked a point on or near the character. If an attack volume is away from the character, it is likely that no candidate is found in the grid-based index. However, in general, it is expected that attacks occur near a character. Employing GPU-based collision detection for culling, the computation was about twice as fast on average. This was effective especially when there was no candidate path in the grid-based index.

The overall computational was approximately 20 to 200 milliseconds. Our method can be used in real-time applications employing multi-threading even when the index is not used. When we activate multi-threading, in 50% of cases, a path was found before the current edge was finished being executed.

6.2 Evaluation of Avoidance Motions

We also evaluated the quality of generated avoidance motions. In general, it is difficult to evaluate the naturalness of motion. In our experiment, we asked a subject who is a graduate student majoring in computer animation to observe all candidate paths and to select the one that generates the most natural-looking avoidance motion. We then compared whether the path selected by the subject matched the path selected using our method. In 90% of 40 trials, the paths matched. When they did not match, the major reason was that there were no good avoidance motions in the candidate paths and selecting the best path was difficult even for us. This is because the number of reachable avoidance motions in the motion graph within the time window was limited even though it seemed that a sufficient number of avoidance motions were used. We could use a wider time window. However, that may increase the computational time and require large speed adjustments. We constructed a standard motion graph in this research. We may need to develop a method to construct a sophisticated motion graph with which various avoidance motions can be easily reached from any node. This is one of our future works. Conducting extended evaluation including subjective evaluation by many subjects, comparison with a ground truth (motion capture data of combating people), and measuring the rate of successful avoidance are other future work.

7 Conclusion

We presented a method of generating avoidance motions using a motion graph. We proposed new criteria based on attack, avoidance and body space–time volumes. We also introduced methods to achieve computational efficiency. In addition to the method of constructing a sophisticated motion graph as mentioned in Section 6, development of data structures and algorithms that are more efficient such as [5] is future work. In general, it is difficult to select a perfect avoidance motion for any attack. We may need a method of modifying a selected motion according to an attack such as [1]. As explained in Section 4.2, human fighters sometimes shield or parry attacks by intentionally intercepting attacks with a body part instead of avoiding them. Generating these kinds of motions is also a future work.

References

1. Arikan, O., Forsyth, D.A., O'Brien, J.F.: Pushing People Around. In: ACM SIGGRAPH/Eurographics Symposium on Computer Animation 2005, pp. 59–66 (2005)
2. Kovar, L., Gleicher, M., Pighin, F.H.: Motion Graphs. ACM Transactions on Graphics (SIGGRAPH 2002) 21(3), 473–482 (2002)
3. Lee, J., Chai, J., Reitsma, P., Hodgins, J., Pollard, N.: Interactive Control of Avatars Animated with Human Motion Data. ACM Transactions on Graphics (SIGGRAPH 2002) 21(3), 491–500 (2002)
4. Lee, J., Lee, K.H.: Precomputing Avatar Behavior from Human Motion Data. In: ACM SIGGRAPH/Eurographics Symposium on Computer Animation, pp. 79–87 (2004)
5. Lee, Y., Wampler, K., Bernstein, G., Popović, J., Popović, Z.: Motion Fields for Interactive Character Locomotion. ACM Transactions on Graphics (SIGGRAPH Asia 2010) 29(6), Article No. 138 (2007)
6. Li, Y., Wang, T., Shum, H.-Y.: Motion Texture: A Two-Level Statistical Model for Character Motion Synthesis. ACM Transactions on Graphics (SIGGRAPH 2002) 21(3), 465–472 (2002)
7. McCann, J., Pollard, N.S.: Responsive Characters from Motion Fragments. ACM Transactions on Graphics (SIGGRAPH 2007) 26(3), Article No. 6 (2007)
8. Reitsma, P.S.A., Pollard, N.S.: Evaluating Motion Graphs for Character Navigation. In: ACM SIGGRAPH/Eurographcis Symposium on Computer Animation, pp. 89–98 (2004)
9. Shum, H.P.H., Komura, T., Yamazaki, S.: Simulating Competitive Interactions Using Singly Captured Motions. In: ACM Virtual Reality Software and Technology 2007, pp. 65–72 (2007)
10. Shum, H., Komura, T., Shiraishi, M., Yamazaki, S.: Interaction Patches for Multi-Character Animation. ACM Transactions on Graphics (SIGGRAPH Asia 2008) 26(3), Article No. 114 (2008)
11. Treuille, A., Lee, Y., Popović, Z.: Near-optimal Character Animation with Continuous Control. ACM Transactions on Graphics 26(3), Article No. 7 (2007)
12. Wampler, K., Andersen, E., Herbst, E., Lee, Y., Popović, Z.: Character Animation in Two-Player Adversarial games. ACM Transactions on Graphics (SIGGRAPH 2011) 29(3), Article No. 26 (2010)
13. Zordan, V., Macchietto, A., Medin, J., Soriano, M., Wu, C.-C., Metoyer, R., Rose, R.: Anticpation from Example. In: ACM Virtual Reality Software and Technology 2007, pp. 81–84 (2007)

Populations with Purpose

Weizi Li and Jan M. Allbeck

Laboratory for Games and Intelligent Animation
George Mason University
4400 University Drive, MSN 4A5
Fairfax, VA 22030
http://cs.gmu.edu/~gaia/

Abstract. There are currently a number of animation researchers that focus on simulating virtual crowds, but few are attempting to simulate virtual populations. Virtual crowd simulations tend to depict a large number of agents walking from one location to another as realistically as possible. The virtual humans in these crowds lack higher purpose. They have a virtual existence, but not a virtual life and as such do not reasonably depict a human population. In this paper, we present an agent-based simulation framework for creating virtual populations endowed with social roles. These roles help establish reasons for the existence of each of the virtual humans. They can be used to create a virtual population embodied with purpose.

Keywords: Crowd Simulation, Social Roles.

1 Introduction

Military training and other applications desire simulations that establish normal human behavior for an area. Once normalcy is established, observers can be trained to recognize abnormal and possibly dangerous behaviors. This requires the simulation of longer periods of time including different times of day. The problem is how to select reasonable, purposeful behaviors for a population for such periods of time. Roles are, in part, expected patterns of behavior and therefore seem like an intuitive feature for authoring these scenarios. Furthermore, role switching would enable plausible variations in behaviors throughout a day, but requires mechanisms to initiate the switching. While admittedly not comprehensive, role switching based on schedules, reactions, and needs, seems like a good starting point.

This paper describes an agent-based simulation framework for creating virtual populations endowed with various social-psychological factors including social roles. These roles help establish reasons for the existence of the virtual humans and can be used to create a virtual population embodied with purpose. Human decisions and the behaviors that result, stem from a complex interplay of many factors. The aim of this work is not to try to replicate all of these factors. We have focused on social roles because they are so heavily linked to meaningful behaviors.

From this starting point we have included other factors that are linked to role and that can add reasonable variability to behaviors while still maintaining a framework where scenarios can be feasibly authored, modified, and controlled.

In addition, our framework focuses on higher level control mechanisms as opposed to lower level animation implementations. It also links roles and role switching to different action types such as reactions, scheduled actions, and need-based actions. As such the authoring of roles is largely just associating a set of these actions with a role. The techniques and methodologies used are adopted from a number of research disciplines including multi-agent systems, social psychology, ontologies, and knowledge representations, as well as computer animation.

2 Related Work

Crowd simulation research has been approached from several different perspectives. Some research groups are addressing how to simulate large crowds mainly through focusing on global path planning and local collision avoidance [18,17,19]. The behaviors in these simulations are for the most part limited to locomotion maneuvers.

Work has also been done on adding contextual behavioral variations through spatial patches [26,11,23]. The common theme in these works is defining regions in the virtual world and associating these regions with certain behaviors and interactions. The computer game, *The Sims*, might also be considered to incorporate spatially dependent behavior [25]. For example, if an agent is hungry and near a refrigerator, even if not being explicitly directed by the player, he would eat. While these certainly add richness to the virtual world, they still fall short of embodying consistent reasonable behaviors with purpose.

Most of the works described so far included few or no social psychology factors. There have, however, been some that do. The work of Pelechano et al. included the concept of role and other psychological factors, but the roles were limited to leaders and followers which along with the other factors influence only the navigation behavior of agents [20]. In [16], Musse and Thalmann describe a crowd simulation framework that includes sociological factors such as relationships, groups, and emotion, but again the behaviors are centered around locomotion actions.

In [21] Shao and Terzopoulos describe a virtual train station. Here they classified their autonomous pedestrians into a few categories, including commuters, tourists, performers, and officers. Each type of character is then linked to hand coded action selection mechanisms. Similarly in [27] the authors introduce a decision network which addresses agent social interaction based on probabilities and graph theory, however action selection is still manually coded.

Some research groups have worked directly on incorporating roles into virtual humans. Hayes-Roth and her collaborators were one of the first research groups to develop virtual roles [8]. Their interactive intelligent agent was instilled with the role of bartender and a set of actions were defined such that the user's expectations would be met. There was, however, no switching of roles for this character and the behaviors were only related to communication acts.

Most recently work by Stocker et al. introduced the concept of priming for a virtual agent [22]. Here agents are primed for certain actions based on the other agents and events around them. While they do not address roles specifically, this concept of priming is somewhat similar to the role switching behaviors we will describe in this paper.

3 Approach Overview

In this section, we provide an overview of our approach and describe the social psychological models on which it is founded, including a definition of roles, factors affecting role switching, and action types.

3.1 Definition of Role

A role is *the rights, obligations, and expected behavior patterns associated with a particular social status* [1]. Ellenson's work [6] notes that each person plays a number of roles. Taking into consideration these descriptions as well as discussions from other social psychologists [13,4], we conclude that roles are patterns of behaviors for given situations or circumstances. Roles can demand certain physical, intellectual, or knowledge prerequisites, and many roles are associated with social relationships.

3.2 Role Switching

People's priorities are set by a number of interplaying factors, including emotions, mood, personality, culture, roles, status, needs, perceptions, goals, relationships, gender, intelligence, and history, just to name a few. In this work, we have chosen a few factors that are related to roles and role switching that we believe will help endow virtual humans with meaningful, purposeful behaviors.

Switching from one role to another can be linked to time, location, relationships, mental status, and needs (See Figure 1). For example, one can imagine someone switching to a *businessman* role as the start of the work day approaches or as he enters his office or when he encounters his boss. Also, someone may need to shop for groceries to provide for his family. The *shopping* behavior would stem from a need and cause a switch in role to *shopper*. Elements of mental status, such as personality traits, can impact the selection and performance of these roles. For example, a non-conscientious person might not shop for groceries even if the need exists.

Action and role selection is further affected by a filtration of proposed actions according to an agent's *Conventional Practice* and *World Knowledge* [10,4,3]. *Conventional Practice* is a set of regulations and norms that each individual in the society should obey. *World Knowledge* indicates that certain physical, intellectual, and knowledge elements are required for specific roles.

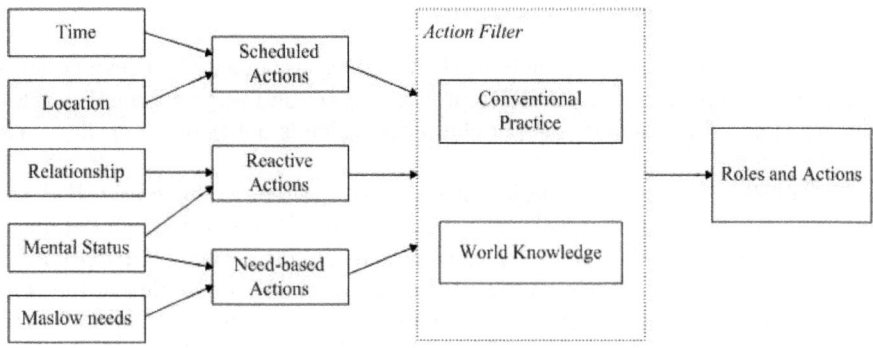

Fig. 1. System Diagram

Another perspective from which to consider selection is to examine what triggers various behaviors. Some actions are planned for such as going to work or attending a meeting. These actions, called *Scheduled* actions, tend to establish a person's daily routine and are often heavily coupled with their roles. Other actions are not so predetermined. Some actions arise to fulfill needs. Among these needs might be those depicted in *Maslow's Hierarchy of Needs*, including, food, water, excretion, friendship, family, employment, and creativity [12]. These type of actions, called *Need-based* actions, can also be linked to roles. For example, in order to maintain employment safety, a businessman might need to contact his clients are on regular basis. Still other actions, *Reactive actions*, are responses to agents, objects, or events in the world. Who and what we react to is at least partially determined by our roles. If we see a friend or co-worker as we are walking to work, we are likely to stop and greet them.

While we cannot claim that these three types of actions make a complete categorization of all behaviors, we believe that they can encompass a wide range of behaviors and provide strong ties to roles and purposeful behaviors. Another key factor is the ability to easily author or initiate these behaviors. Each requires a finite, straightforward amount of data:

Scheduled actions: $Sch = \langle P, A, L, T \rangle$, where P is the performer (an individual or group), A is the action to be performed (simple or complex), L is the location where the action is to be performed (based on an object or a location), and T is an indication of the time (i.e. start time and duration).

Reactive actions: $Rea = \langle P, S, A \rangle$, where P is the performer (an individual or group), S is the stimulus (an object, type of object, person, location, event, etc) and A is the action to be performed (simple or complex).

Need-based actions: $Nee = \langle P, N, D, C \rangle$, where P is the performer (an individual or group), N is the name of the need, D is the decay rate, and C is a set of tuples $\langle A, O, F \rangle$, where A is the action to be performed (simple or complex), O is a set of object types, and F is the fulfillment rate.

4 Implementation

The work presented here extends work previously reported [2]. Previous work included an implementation of different action types and very rudimentary roles, but was limited to a single role per character which is not realistic for day scale simulations.

To continue to ensure scenario authoring is feasible, we have extended our data-driven approach where all of the vital scenario data is stored in a database. This includes information about each agent such as conventional practices, mental status, world knowledge, and role sets. We also store a mapping of the relationships between agents. Information about the world, objects in the world, and actions are also stored in the database. This includes the specification of schedules, needs, and reactions. As such, scenarios can be authored entirely through the database and without any coding. In addition, our framework is built on an existing crowd simulator that provides navigation and collision avoidance for the agents [19].

We have extend the previous implementation including now a much richer definition of role. The most important component of a role is a set of actions [13]. This action set corresponds to the conventional practices associated with the role. These actions may be scheduled, need-based, or reactive actions as mentioned in the previous section. Furthermore, these actions may also be linked to parameters such as location, object participants, start-times, and durations. Interpersonal roles are also associated with relationships, which are a simple named linking of agents. Among agent parameters is a set of capabilities corresponding to actions that they can perform. These capabilities form the foundation of an agent's world knowledge.

As described in the previous section, factors influencing role selection include, time, location, relationships, mental status, and needs. In this section, we will describe the implementation of each of these factors and how they have been incorporated into the three action types. We will also discuss how actions and roles are further filtered by conventional practice and an agent's world knowledge (See Figure 1).

4.1 Action Types

A large part of the definition of a role includes a pattern of behaviors. Our framework associates each role with a set of actions. These actions can be of any of the three types of actions described earlier, namely *Scheduled*, *Reactive*, or *Need-based*.

Scheduled Actions. Scheduled actions include time and location parameters [2] and can be used to establish an agenda for a day. Some roles are directly associated with scheduled actions. For example, a businessman may be scheduled to work in his office from 9am to 5pm. As 9am approaches, the framework will initiate processing of the scheduled work in office action and send the character to his office and the businessman role.

However, if an agent does not have a scheduled action to perform, they will perform a default action that is associated with their current role. Generally default actions are the actions most often performed by that role. For example, a businessman or administrator might work in an office. A shopkeeper might attend to the cash register. Just as in real life, scheduled actions can be suspended by higher priority need-based and reactive actions.

Need-based Actions. Need-based actions are merely database entries associating a decay rate, actions, objects, and a fulfillment quotient. The examples described in this paper are based on *Maslow's Hierarchy of Needs* [12]. Conceptually, there is a reservoir that corresponds to each need for each agent. Currently the initial level of each reservoir is set randomly at the beginning of the simulation. At regular intervals, the reservoirs are decreased by the specified decay rates. When the level of a reservoir hits a predetermined threshold, the fulfilling action is added to the agent's queue of actions. Its priority will increase as the reservoir continue decreases eventually its priority will greater than all actions on the queue. Then the agent will perform the action, raising the level of the reservoir.

We have chosen to use *Mental Status* as an influence on needs (and reactions), because social scientists have linked it to roles and we feel it adds plausible variability. It includes several factors, but we focus on personality as it addresses an individual's long-term behavior. There are several psychological models of personality. One of the most popular is the Five-Factor or OCEAN model [24]. The five factors are: *Openness* (i.e. curious, alert, informed, perceptive), *Conscientiousness* (i.e. persistent, orderly, predictable, dependable, prompt), *Extroversion* (i.e. social adventurous, active, assertive, dominant, energetic), *Agreeableness* (i.e. cooperative, tolerant, patient, kind), and *Neuroticism* (i.e. oversensitive, fearful, unadventurous, dependent, submissive, unconfident).

We have based our implementation of personality on the work of Durupinar et al. [5]. An agent's personality π is a five-dimension vector, where each is represented by a personalty factor Ψ_i. The distribution of the personality factors in a populations of individuals is modeled by a Gaussian distribution function with mean μ_i and standard deviation σ_i:

$$\pi = \langle \Psi^O, \Psi^C, \Psi^E, \Psi^A, \Psi^N \rangle$$
$$\Psi^i = N(\mu_i, \sigma_i^2), for\ i \in O, C, E, A, N$$
$$\text{where}\quad \mu \in [-10, 10],\ \sigma \in [-2, 2]$$

Since each factor is bipolar, Ψ can take both positive and negative values. For instance, a positive for *Extroversion*, E+, means that the individual has extroverted character; whereas a negative value means that the individual is introverted. In Section 4.1, we will describe how personality dimensions affect the decay rates of need reservoirs, creating reasonable variations in behaviors from person to person.

Needs and priorities differ from person to person. We represent this variation by linking the personality traits just described with needs. This is, of course, a massive oversimplification, but one that leads to plausible variations. Table 1 shows our mapping from Maslow needs to OCEAN personality dimensions. It should be noted that just the personality dimension is represented, not the valence of the dimension. For example, neuroticism is negatively correlated with needs for security of employment and family. This mapping was formulated by examining the adjectives associated with the personality dimensions and the descriptions of the Maslow needs.

Table 1. Mapping between Maslow need reservoirs and personality dimensions

Reservoir Descriptions	Personality Traits
problem solving, creativity, lack of prejudice	O, A
achievement, respect for others	O, A
friendship, family	E
security of employment, security of family	C, N
water, food, excretion	

In this work, we represent the decay rate as β. For example, $\beta^{friendship}$ indicates the decay rate of the *friendship* reservoir. For Maslow based needs, we also apply a correlation coefficient r which ranges from (0,1] to represent the relationship between decay rate and personality traits. More precisely, $r_{E,friendship}$ represents how strongly the *Extroversion* trait and *friendship*'s decay rate correlated. The closer r gets to 1 the faster reservoir empties (i.e. the decay rate is high indicating the agents strong need for friendship). Since a need can be affected by more than one personality trait, for those needs marked with multiple personality traits we assign weights to each one: $\omega_{E,friendship}$ meaning the impact of *Extroversion* on *friendship*. If a need has more than one trait's influence, its summation of ω should be equal to one and for simplicity in this work we assume each personality trait contributes the same weight.

Consequently, for ith agent the decay rates and their relationship with personality traits are shown below (here we list two examples):

security of employment (se):
$\beta_i^{se} = (\omega_{C,se}|r_{C,se} \times \Psi_i^C| + \omega_{N,se}|r_{N,se} \times \Psi_i^N|) \times 0.1$
where $\omega_{C,se} + \omega_{N,se} = 1$, $\beta_i^{se} \propto C, N$ and $\beta_i^{se} \in [0, 10]$

friendship (fr):
$\beta_i^{fr} = (\omega_{E,fr}|r_{E,fr} \times \Psi_i^E|) \times 0.1$
where $\omega_{E,fr} = 1$, $\beta_i^{fr} \propto E$ and $\beta_i^{fr} \in [0, 10]$

Reactive Actions. As a simulation progresses, agents make their way through the virtual world, attempting to adhere to their schedules and meet their needs. In doing so, agents encounter many stimuli to which a reaction might be warranted. Reactions play an important part in our implementation of roles. In [7],

Merton states that a person might switch roles as a response to those around him. Relationships are a major impetus for reactive role switching. For example, if two agents encounter each other and are linked by a relationship such as friendship, they will switch to the friend role.

Since reactive actions must be performed soon after the stimulus is encountered, they are given a higher priority and generally result in the suspension of whatever other action might be being performed, though this is not always the case. For example, if an agent is fulfilling a high priority need, then they might not react to the people and things around him.

The duration of responses can vary according to the activity and characteristics of the agents. For example, an agent that is hurrying off to work or who is introverted, may not linger as long on the street to greet a friend, as someone strolling home from work or an extrovert would.

4.2 Action Filter

Once a set of actions and roles have been purposed, some may be eliminated due to conventional practice constraints or an agent's lack of necessary world knowledge.

Conventional Practice. Social science researchers believe that when an agent plays a role in a given organizational (or social) setting, he must obey *Conventional Practices*, meaning *behavioral constraints* and *social conventions* (e.g. the businessman must obey the regulations that his company stipulates) [15,14]. To be more specific, behavioral constraints are associated with the following factors: responsibilities, rights, duties, prohibitions and possibilities [15]. Role hierarchies include conventional roles (e.g. *citizen, businessman, mailman*) and interpersonal roles (e.g. *friends, lovers, enemies*). Figure 2 shows part of the conventional role hierarchy that we designed according to the taxonomy presented in [9]. We have linked each conventional practice norm with an impact factor (range [0, 1]) which reflects how strongly these norms are imposed on certain roles. Having 1 as an impact factor would indicate that it is the most powerful norm. For convenience, we have set all impact factors in our current simulations to be high enough to indicate that every agent would obey not only the conventional practice of current professions but also those inherited from upper levels of the hierarchy. However, users could choose whatever impact factors they would like according to the behaviors that they desire.

World Knowledge. Some roles have physical or intellectual requirements and these requirements may be difficult to obtain. Also some people are just naturally more physically or intellectually gifted or have more talent in an area than others. These factors can put limitations on what roles a person can take on [4]. We represent world knowledge as capabilities. Agent capabilities are the set of actions that the agent can perform. Actions are categorized and placed in a hierarchy to lessen the work of assigning capabilities to agents and also checking to ensure that agents meet the capability conditions before performing an action.

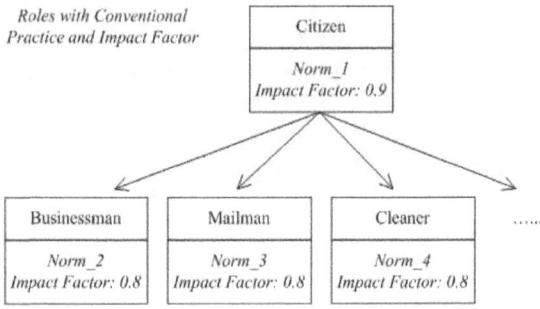

Fig. 2. Role Hierarchy with Conventional Practice and Impact Factor

5 Examples

To explore the effects of roles and more precisely role switching on virtual human behaviors, we have authored a typical day in a neighborhood. As with real humans, each virtual human is assigned a set of roles. Figure 3 demonstrates one agent taking on the role of *businessman* as he enters his office building (i.e. location-based role switching). Two other agents react to seeing each other by switching to *friend* roles (i.e. relationship-based role switching). Another agent reacts to trash in the street by starting her *cleaner* role (i.e. behavior selection-based role switching).

These first examples of agents going to work demonstrate how time, location, and behavior selection impact role switching. They focus on role transitions caused by scheduled and reactive actions. The following office examples concentrate more on need-based actions. The top image of Figure 4a shows that the businessman's *creativity* reservoir is approaching the critical threshold (i.e. 2). When it reaches the threshold, he suspends his current action and starts a conversation with his co-worker. This exchange of ideas causes the *creativity* reservoirs of both men to refill.

Fig. 3. Locations, relationships and behavior selection affect role switching

Fig. 4. (a) The businessman's *creativity* need prompts him to speak to a co-worker, causing both to switch to *collaborator* roles and replenish their creativity reservoirs. (b) The businessman's role remains while eating to refill his hunger reservoir.

Figure 4b shows that not all need-based actions cause role switching. The hunger need is associated with the role of being human, because *businessman* is a descendant of this role in the role hierarchy there is no need to switch. The final scene depicts a late afternoon in our neighborhood. Figure 5a shows a *businesswoman* becoming a *parent* when playing with her children. In Figure 5b, a man was headed home from work, but before he could reach his door, the *security of family* need prompted him to switch his role and instead he go to the grocery store.

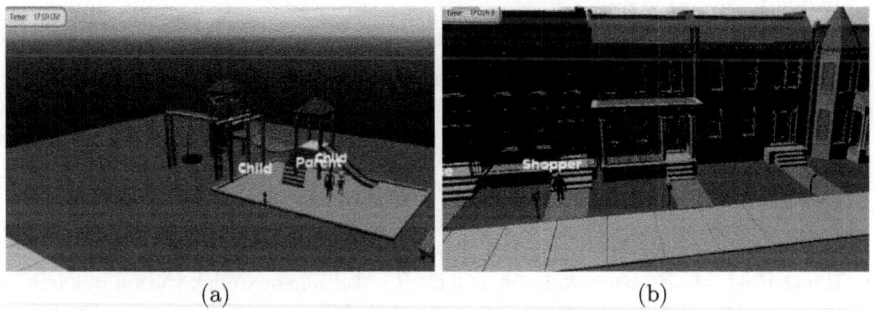

Fig. 5. (a) A businesswoman switches her role to parent when she spends time with her children. (b) A businessman is heading home after work, when his *security of family* need preempts this action and switches his role to *shopper*.

6 Discussion

In this paper, we have presented a framework for instilling virtual humans with roles and role switching to produce more typical virtual worlds where people's behaviors are purposeful. The methods presented are based on social psychology models and focus on approaches that facilitate authoring and modifications. As people's complicated lives rarely allow them to embody just a single role during the course of a day, role switching is important to creating reasonable virtual human behaviors. The framework presented can also be used to include abnormal behaviors. For example, one could author a subversive role for a character that includes reacting to pedestrians by robbing them or includes a strong need for drugs and alcohol.

There are numerous possible extensions to this work. First, we could illustrate the dynamics that stem from status hierarchies by experimenting with the concepts of power scale and social distance. We might also address situations where multiple roles could be adopted. For example, a man being approached by both his boss and his child. Here, social power scales and social distance might result in different social threats which would cause one role to be favored over the other. Finally, we could focus on agents that learn role definitions by observing the behaviors of others, enabling each agent to have customized definitions based on their own experiences.

Acknowledgments. Partial support for this effort is gratefully acknowledged from the U.S. Army SUBTLE MURI W911NF-07-1-0216. We also appreciate donations from Autodesk.

References

1. Webster's College Dictionary. Random House (1991)
2. Allbeck, J.M.: CAROSA: A tool for authoring NPCs. Motion in Games, 182–193 (2010)
3. Barker, R.G.: Ecological Psychology: Concepts and methods for studying the environment of human behavior. Stanford University Press (1968)
4. Biddle, B.J.: Role Theory: Concepts and Research. Krieger Pub. Co. (1979)
5. Durupinar, F., Pelechano, N., Allbeck, J.M., Gudukbay, U., Badler, N.I.: How the OCEAN personality model affects the perception of crowds. IEEE Computer Graphics and Applications 31(3), 22–31 (2011)
6. Ellenson, A.: Human Relations, 2nd edn. Prentice Hall College Div. (1982)
7. Fan, J., Barker, K., Porter, B., Clark, P.: Representing roles and purpose. In: International Conference on Knowledge Capture (K-CAP), pp. 38–43. ACM (2001)
8. Hayes-Roth, B., Brownston, L., van Gent, R.: Multiagent Collaboration in Directed Improvisation. In: Readings in Agents, pp. 141–147. Morgan Kaufmann Publishers Inc., San Francisco (1998)
9. Hewitt, J.P.: Self and society: A symbolic interactionist social psychology, Oxford, England (1976)
10. Ickes, W., Knowles, E.: Personality, Roles, and Social Behavior, 1st edn. Springer, Heidelberg (1982)
11. Lee, K.H., Choi, M.G., Lee, J.: Motion patches: Building blocks for virtual environments annotated with motion data. In: Proceedings of the 2006 ACM SIGGRAPH Conference, pp. 898–906. ACM, New York (2006)
12. Maslow, A.: A theory of human motivation. Psychological Review 50, 370–396 (1943)
13. McGinnies, E.: Perspectives on Social Behavior. Gardner Press, Inc. (1994)
14. Merton, R.K.: Social Theory and Social Structure. Free Press (1998)

15. Moulin, B.: The social dimension of interactions in multiagent systems. Agents and Multi-agent Systems, Formalisms, Methodologies, and Applications 1441/1998 (1998)
16. Musse, S.R., Thalmann, D.: A model of human crowd behavior: Group interrelationship and collision detection analysis. In: Workshop Computer Animation and Simulation of Eurographics, pp. 39–52 (1997)
17. Narain, R., Golas, A., Curtis, S., Lin, M.C.: Aggregate dynamics for dense crowd simulation. In: Proceedings of the 2009 ACM SIGGRAPH Asia Conference, pp. 122:1–122:8. ACM, New York (2009)
18. Ondřej, J., Pettré, J., Olivier, A.H., Donikian, S.: A synthetic-vision based steering approach for crowd simulation. In: Proceedings of the 2010 ACM SIGGRAPH 2010 Conference, pp. 123:1–123:9. ACM, New York (2010)
19. Pelechano, N., Allbeck, J.M., Badler, N.I.: Controlling individual agents in high-density crowd simulation. In: Proceedings of the 2007 ACM SIGGRAPH/ Eurographics Symposium on Computer Animation, pp. 99–108. Eurographics Association (2007)
20. Pelechano, N., O'Brien, K., Silverman, B., Badler, N.I.: Crowd simulation incorporating agent psychological models, roles and communication. In: First International Workshop on Crowd Simulation, pp. 21–30 (2005)
21. Shao, W., Terzopoulos, D.: Autonomous pedestrians. In: Proceedings of the 2005 ACM SIGGRAPH/Eurographics Symposium on Computer Animation, pp. 19–28. ACM, New York (2005)
22. Stocker, C., Sun, L., Huang, P., Qin, W., Allbeck, J.M., Badler, N.I.: Smart Events and Primed Agents. In: Safonova, A. (ed.) IVA 2010. LNCS, vol. 6356, pp. 15–27. Springer, Heidelberg (2010)
23. Sung, M., Gleicher, M., Chenney, S.: Scalable behaviors for crowd simulation. Computer Graphics Forum 23(3), 519–528 (2004)
24. Wiggins, J.: The Five-Factor Model of Personality: Theoretical Perspectives. The Guilford Press, New York (1996)
25. Wright, W.: The Sims (2000)
26. Yersin, B., Maïm, J., Pettré, J., Thalmann, D.: Crowd patches: Populating large-scale virtual environments for real-time applications. In: Proceedings of the 2009 Symposium on Interactive 3D Graphics and Games, pp. 207–214. ACM, New York (2009)
27. Yu, Q., Terzopoulos, D.: A decision network framework for the behavioral animation of virtual humans. In: Proceedings of the 2007 ACM SIGGRAPH/ Eurographics Symposium on Computer Animation, pp. 119–128. Eurographics Association (2007)

Parameterizing Behavior Trees

Alexander Shoulson, Francisco M. Garcia, Matthew Jones,
Robert Mead, and Norman I. Badler

Department of Computer and Information Science
University of Pennsylvania
Philadelphia, PA 19104-6389, USA
{shoulson,fgarcia,majo,robmead,badler}@seas.upenn.edu

Abstract. This paper introduces and motivates the application of parameterization to behavior trees. As a framework, behavior trees are becoming more commonly used for agent controllers in interactive game environments. We describe a way by which behavior trees can be authored for acting upon functions with arguments, as opposed to being limited to nonparametric tasks. We expand upon this idea to provide a method by which a subtree itself can be encapsulated with an exposed parameter interface through a lookup node, which enables code reuse in a manner already exploited by object oriented programming languages. Parameterization also allows us to recast Smart Events (a mechanism for co-opting agents to perform a desired activity) as behavior trees that can act generically upon groups of typed agents. Finally, we introduce a tool called Topiary, which enables the graphically-oriented authoring of behavior trees with this functionality as part of a broader testbed for agent simulation.

Keywords: Behavior Trees, Smart Events, Behavioral AI, Agents.

1 Introduction

While traditionally known for use in industrial and commercial environments for describing large-scale projects [4], behavior trees are garnering attention in the computer gaming industry for use in designing the artificial intelligence logic for environmental agents. In particular, they have been applied in sophisticated, popular games requiring intelligent teammates and adversaries such as Spore [2], Halo 2 [5], and Halo 3 [6], among others. This formalism is a natural choice for game AI, as behavior trees lend themselves well to behavior-oriented design for complex systems [3]. The paradigm enables sophisticated sequences of actions and contingencies to be represented as a concise graphical structure following a set of very simple rules with equivalent representations as Communicating Sequential Processes (CSPs). The notation allows task requirements and specifications, normally conceptualized in natural language, to be captured and expressed in an actionable format [12] that can be converted to code or data streams [7].

One of the most appealing aspects of behavior trees is their simplicity. As part of this, we recognize that Millington and Funge [9, p. 361] insist, "We certainly don't want to pass data into tasks as parameters to their run method" when a leaf node calls a subroutine. This follows a guideline of building behavior trees that can invoke tasks solely as if they were functions with no explicit parameters. However, lexicalized parameter sequences are a powerful feature of object-oriented programming languages [8], and avoiding them results in opaque and confusing data flow. Making each node aware of the parameters of its associated agent member function is a simple task given a description of that agent, and streamlines the way in which these functions are invoked. With the parameters of functions exposed to the nodes that use them, an author has the power to directly modulate the way in which an agent performs a certain action using just that node on the behavior tree itself.

For communication between nodes and with invoked functions, behavior trees traditionally rely on a *blackboard*, which is a centralized, flat repository of data to which all interested parties have access [9]. This approach does not lend itself well to encapsulation and, as a result, frustrates subtree reuse. The behavior tree structure itself can make it difficult to track what and where data is stored where in the blackboard. For example, two encapsulated subtrees may both use the same fields of the blackboard several layers down in their hierarchy, and could overwrite each other in a manner difficult to trace.

We also would like to allow external parameterization, such as a subtree where an agent sleeps for N hours. This is possible with a blackboard; one could first write N somewhere on the blackboard and then build the subtree to read that field. However, this paradigm is clumsy and unintuitive – there is no explicitly visualized causality in the tree between setting a value for N and executing the "sleep" subtree, especially if that sleep subtree is buried under layers of hierarchy. This approach is also made difficult by the common "parallel" node construct for cooperative multithreading in trees, where each subtree is executed in an interwoven fashion. If two independent subtrees read and write the same parameter fields on the blackboard, race conditions can occur, and so we would require decorators to lock nodes all for the sake of parameterizing subtrees. All of this machinery directly contradicts the simplicity that makes behavior trees desirable.

To help alleviate this problem, we propose a system designed to intuitively reduce behavior tree reliance on blackboard fields. We not only expose the parameters of the functions invoked by tree leaves, but parameterize subtrees themselves – encapsulating them as nodes with their own allocated parameter scope that is exposed to the parent tree as an interface. Parameters are now given to these wrapped subtree nodes without a blackboard, and can be clearly represented in the tree. We draw this idea from Parameterized Action Representations (PARs) [1], but generalize it further into any behavior tree that provides a parameter interface at its topmost level.

Introducing the notion of parameterization to the structure of behavior trees enables new opportunities for code flexibility. We gain the ability to parameterize not only the way in which tasks are executed, but also which agents are executing the tasks, which also allows us to revisit the Smart Event [11] formalism from a behavior tree perspective. In the remainder of this paper we discuss the various methods we employ to recast PARs and Smart Events within a behavior tree framework that exploits a new, reasoned approach to subtree encapsulation and parameterization. We also describe a tool currently in development, called Topiary, that enables the graphical construction of parameterized behavior trees and behavior tree-based Smart Events for use in the Agent Development and Prototyping Testbed (ADAPT), a simulation platform built on the Unity game engine.

2 Parameterizing Subtrees

2.1 The Agent Model

Before building a behavior tree for an agent, we must have some description of that agent with respect to the data it stores and the actions it can perform. We refer to these two sets of qualities as *traits* and *capabilities*. In an object-oriented environment, we define an agent as an object class, where traits are specially tagged member variables, and capabilities are similarly tagged member functions. We use a tagging system to differentiate them from internal data and helper functions that we do not wish to expose to the behavior tree. Traits comprise the key components of an agent's state – any information that may be necessary for the agent to make a decision about its next action in a behavior tree. Capabilities contain all of the mechanics needed to perform the atomic tasks with which they are associated. An agent may have a "yawn" capability, which plays an animation and a sound. A capability may act on data, either that of its parameters or that stored in or perceived by the agent. For instance, the "yawn" capability may take a parameter for the volume of the played sound, which would be specified upon invocation of the capability function. The "yawn" capability may also consider a "rudeness" quality inherent to the agent, to determine whether or not to display the agent covering its mouth according to social norms.

Traits and capabilities have parallel representations as behavior tree leaf nodes. Traits are manifested as *assertion* leaf nodes, which compare the given trait's value to another expression when ticked, and succeed if and only if the comparison evaluates to true. Capabilities are utilized by *action* nodes that, when started, invoke the underlying capability function and return its status result (success, failure, or still running) after each tick. Trees are built for an agent after the interface of the agent model is defined, and so the lexicon of nodes available to the behavior tree designer follows directly from reading that interface.

Assertions take parameters comprising the expression to which they are compared, and actions take as many parameters as the underlying capability function in the agent model interface. The values for these parameters can come from three sources. First, they can be hardcoded literals embedded in the tree by the author. Second, parameters can be taken from the traits of the world or agent itself, so the volume parameter to the example "yawn" capability could be drawn from the time of day in the environment or the agent's "tiredness" trait. Finally, parameter values can be satisfied with what we call a *PAR argument*.

2.2 Subtrees with Arguments

PAR arguments serve as parameters to the scope of specific subtree. They can be created as needed by the tree designer and can be reused in multiple places for the parameters to multiple tree leaf nodes. For example, we can designate an *arg_tiredness* PAR argument, and pass that same argument with respect to both the volume for a yawning sound, and the speed at which an agent should walk for two distinct nodes in a single behavior tree.

The key value of PAR arguments arises when we revisit behavior tree abstraction and encapsulation. Recall that in behavior trees, distinct trees can be designed and stored, and then used in other trees by means of a "lookup" node. Wherever that "lookup" node appears in a tree, it is treated as if root of that subtree stood in its place. When we design and store a behavior tree with PAR arguments and then reference that tree in a larger tree by means of a lookup node, the PAR arguments of that referenced tree are exposed as parameters to the lookup node itself. These operates the same was as action nodes that take parameters for agent capabilities.

PAR arguments can traverse nested layers of scope and change names in each. That is, a behavior tree can invoke a subtree with parameters, for which it uses another PAR argument as a value. If that parent tree is encapsulated in another lookup node reference, the value of that top-level PAR argument is propagated down to the internal lookup node's parameter, which then populates the internal subtree's PAR argument. This is directly analogous to the way function calls can be nested in the body of another function.

With this technique, we can build libraries of parameterized behavior trees (to which we refer as PAR trees) that take various parameters and reuse their logic in places throughout the larger tree without the need for storing and retrieving parameter data from the blackboard. Because the entire parent-child message passing system is encoded in the structure of the tree itself, it can be handled programmatically without the use of an external data structure. This eases subtree encapsulation (hierarchy-based abstraction already being a key benefit of behavior trees) and exposes it to the designer of the tree in an intuitive fashion that is already paradigmatically ubiquitous in familiar programming languages.

3 Smart Events as Behavior Trees

Smart Events provide an event-centric behavior authoring approach in which desired or scheduled occurrences in the environment contain all of the information the agent requires in order to participate [11]. This is especially useful for behaviors requiring the simultaneous control of multiple agents. Rather than designing agents to react to one another when, say, taking turns in a conversation, the entire interplay of the interaction can be placed in a single structure dictating the actions of the appropriate agent at the appropriate position in the sequence. Authoring behavior from the perspective of the entire event gives us a clearer point of view than we are afforded when focusing individually on the behavior of each individual participating agent out of context.

Traditional Smart Events influence agents by use of a message board. Agents in the environment regularly consult an appropriate message board to determine which action they should perform at that moment based on the situation in which they are involved. From the contents of that message board, agents retrieve the appropriate action and follow the sequence of behaviors encoded within. In introducing behavior trees as the underlying control structure, we must change this process to some degree. In particular, externally changing which node is active in a behavior tree, or otherwise affecting the node execution order can yield undesired results (not unlike arbitratily jumping to or reordering lines of code in a traditional programming language). Rather than attempting to externally manipulate an active behavior tree, we find it easier to split behaviors into multiple behavior trees that can be started, stopped, and replaced with one another depending on desired activity outcome.

With this in mind, we say the following: the behavior contained within an event is represented as a behavior tree that preempts any other behaviors that the agents involved in that event would perform. In other words, agents outside of events will traverse the environment and accomplish tasks based on their own individualized behavior trees, but whenever that agent is involved in an event, that internal agent tree is stopped, the agent is temporarily stripped of all autonomy, and the tree contained in the event itself begins to act upon the agent. When the event ends, the agent restarts its own internal behavior tree and regains the autonomy to act according to it. Note that we do not *resume* the original tree – any well-designed behavior tree should always find an appropriate action to perform when started based on the agent's context.

For events involving multiple agents at once, we build one centralized tree for the event that can act upon participating agents by treating them as limbs of the same entity. In trees for these multi-agent events, all assertion and action nodes take an additional parameter identifying which agent will be performing that node. The agent in the first role may be told to perform an action, and then the agent in the second, and so on. Of course, in events with heterogenous agents, certain types of assertion and action nodes are restricted only to the agents with the appropriate traits and capabilities. In a sense, the participating agents themselves become parameters of that *event PAR tree*. For example, a conversation may be designed generically for any three agents to perform (in three different roles), and then at runtime any three appropriate agents may be selected to enact those roles in the event.

Event trees and agent-specific trees can leverage the same set of encapsulated PAR trees, provided the subject is appropriate. When a PAR tree is designed for one or more agents and stored as an encapsulated subtree, that subtree description stores the agent type(s) for which that subtree was built. If we design a subtree for a particular type of agent and wrap it as a PAR tree, it can be invoked by the agent's own internal tree, or by any event that has that agent type in one of its roles and wishes to make that particular agent role perform that PAR tree.

Events are also allocated their own variable scope, which can be instantiated with data and modified at any time by both the event's internal control PAR tree and external components of the system interested in manipulating the progression of the event. Note that because of this unique scope, the top-level PAR tree for an event cannot have PAR arguments. Instead, it can access the variables in the event scope in the same way it would access the traits of an agent, using them to fill in parameters for nodes, or evaluating them using assertion nodes. These three qualities of an event – the agents involved and their types, the fields in the event's scope, and the behavior tree dictating the actions those agents perform are all authored by a designer as a cohesive structure to be later instantiated and dispatched to groups of agents as appropriate.

4 Example

We will now present an example incorporating all of these techniques. Suppose we wish to display two human agents haggling over a large flower pot on the ground. Upon purchase, the seller will permit the buyer to pick the object up and leave. First, we define a very simple human agent model as follows:

```
class HumanAgent {
    [Traits]
    name : String
    strength : Int
    tiredness : Int

    [Capabilities]
    function perform(act_name : String) {
        // Perform the named animation and/or sound
        ...
        return Success
    }

    function Grasp(item_reference : Item) {
        // Reach out and grab the referenced item
        ...
        return Success
    }

    function WalkTo(location_name : String) {
        // Walk towards the named location in the environment
        ...
        return Success
    }

    function Wander() {
        // Wander around the environment
        ...
        return Success
    }
}
```

Obviously, problems such as locomotion and hand positioning for grasping are well beyond the scope of our discussion and would be handled in the capability functions themselves.

We will continue by building behavior trees. Like any large system, we will organize individual components, encapsulate them, and build them into the larger structure. For instance, we encapsulate a 'pick up' PAR tree for bending over and grabbing an item from the ground in Fig. 1. On the left, we create a

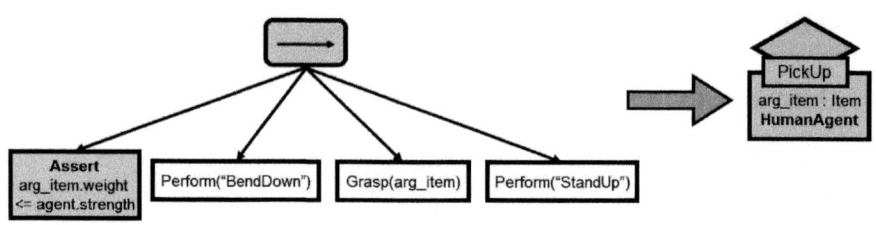

Fig. 1. An encapsulation of a parameterized subtree as a PAR tree with one argument

sequence node with four children. The leftmost child, an assertion, will succeed if and only if the weight of the item (specified as a PAR argument) is less than or equal to the strength of the agent. The next three nodes, all actions, will invoke the agent's capabilities to display the agent bending down, grasping the item, and standing up. When we store this tree as a PAR tree, we can access it later with a lookup node (on the right) called "PickUp". This lookup node takes one parameter, arg_item of type Item, and because it uses traits and capabilities from the HumanAgent agent model, it can only be invoked on agents of type HumanAgent (as indicated at the bottom of the lookup node's description). Omitted from this tree are a number of other assertions, such as the agent being close enough to the object to grasp it. We exclude these for simplicity, providing a single assertion when in fact there would be several requirements to satisfy. These preparatory specifications (as they are called in the original PAR knowledge frame) are also expressed in the behavior tree. To ensure that the agent is close enough to the object, we would use a selector node with two children: an assertion that the agent is close, and a subtree navigating the agent closer (executing only if the assertion fails).

For our simple example, we give the two agents small trees for their behavior when they are not involved in any events. These are illustrated in Fig. 2. Observe that though the two agents are of the same type, they can have two different individualized trees. Both trees have an infinite loop decorator at their root, so that they will continue to perform their behaviors unless interrupted. On the left, the buyer wanders the environment until interrupted by the transaction. On the right, the seller will randomly alternate between tapping his foot, checking his watch, or idly waiting, as he does not want to walk away and leave the flower pot unguarded (the ϕ-sequence node is a stochastic sequence, which performs its children in random order). This is a distant analogue of CAROSA's aleatoric actions [10], though here simplified to triviality for the sake of illustration. Note

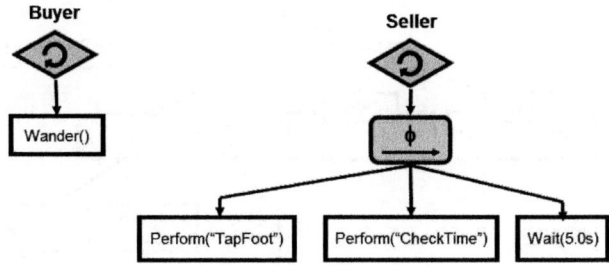

Fig. 2. The two agent trees for when each agent is not involved in an event

that the Wait(5.0s) function is not part of the agent model, but a global capability of the world itself. These trees start and receive ticks as soon as the simulation begins, so that the agents are always active.

Finally, we design the event tree for the transaction itself, which is more sophisticated, as shown in Fig. 3. The root of this tree is not a loop decorator, which means that the event can end upon completion. The first child of the root sequence node initializes a variable in the event variable scope, called price, to be equal to seven. We use this for counting the progress of the haggling transaction. We consider the goal of the buyer to reduce that value to four. The next child instructs the buyer to perform its WalkTo capability to approach the buying location, at which point the seller greets the buyer. We use a tag at the top-left of a node to indicate the subject of that action or assertion, if there is one. Next, we enter the haggling loop. The bottom sequence node, with five children, displays the sequence of events in a successful pass of the haggling action from the perspective. If the current agreed upon price is greater than four, the buyer will perform a haggling animation, we will succeed on a random chance of 50%, and then the seller will perform an agreement animation and the price will be decreased. If any of these nodes fail (mainly the assertion or the random coin toss), the failure will be propagated through that sequence node through the loop decorator (terminating it), and then through the invert decorator, which will convert the result into a success so that the root sequence node at the top of the event tree can continue on to its next child.

After the haggling sequence terminates, the root sequence node advances to its selector node child. The selector's leftmost child checks to see if the haggling loop managed to reduce the price below four. If the final price was indeed below four, that assertion will fail and so the selector node will advance to its second child, a sequence which will execute the PickUp lookup node we defined in Fig. 1 and a WalkTo command for the buyer. of the buyer. This subtree will instruct the Buyer to perform that PickUp action, filling in its arg_item parameter with with a reference to the flower pot, and then walk towards the exit. If the agreed upon price ended up being greater than or equal to 4, then the assertion will succeed, so the selector will succeed and skip over its second child (i.e., the buyer will not pick up the flower pot and leave). At this point, the event terminates. If

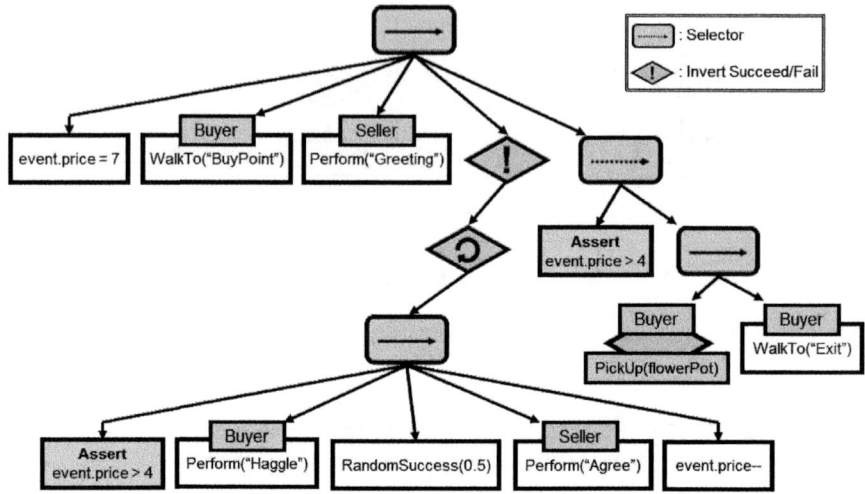

Fig. 3. The PAR tree for the haggling event

the buyer has not left with the flower pot, it will restart its individualized tree and continue wandering the environment.

Only the PickUp complex action was encapsulated as a PAR tree as a demonstration, but other subtrees within this event could have been abstracted. PAR trees can be built to accommodate multiple agents, acting in a sense like sub-events without their own variable scope. Note in our example that no external process initialized or modified the event's data, but some other structure could have changed the event.price value at any time. Finally, while Fig. 3 explicitly states "Buyer" and "Seller" as the subjects of the actions performed during the event, these are roles local to the event, not global to the environment. Any other pair of agents of type HumanAgent could be used as the Buyer or Seller, or the original two agents could have had their positions reversed.

5 Topiary and ADAPT

Topiary is a tool, currently in development, for the graphical creation of behavior trees with awareness of and support for the parameterization described in the previous sections. It is designed to work with ADAPT, our platform wrapping the components needed for agent simulation (like locomotion and pathfinding) for use with the Unity engine. We follow a short pipeline for authoring agent behavior. First, the agent model is created as a C# class, using code from Unity and ADAPT for traits and capabilities, which are tagged with C# attributes. That agent (along with any others) is then built into an agent DLL, which is then both imported into Unity and read by Topiary. Topiary extracts the tagged capabilities and attributes using C# reflection from each DLL, and uses this information to populate a list of available action and assertion nodes for that particular agent. In each PAR tree, Topiary allows the addition of one or more agents from the available types, and facilitates the assembly of trees using nodes specific to those agents (actions and assertions), along with global nodes (waits, etc.), and structural nodes available to all behavior trees (sequences, selectors, parallel nodes, etc.). Actions and assertions, gleaned from the tagged function signatures and data types in the agent model class, can be parameterized accordingly (using hardcoded values, data from agents or the world, or

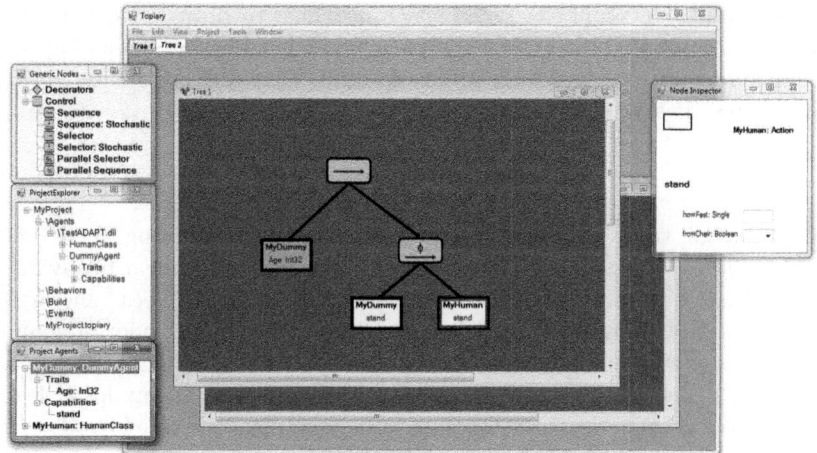

Fig. 4. Building a PAR tree in Topiary

PAR arguments), and PAR trees can be saved and used in other PAR trees, with parameters, using lookup nodes. All of this is performed in a drag-and-drop development environment designed to be familiar to users of tools like Microsoft Visual Studio and Adobe Photoshop.

Once agent and event PAR trees are built, they will be able to be built into C# scripts by Topiary, which can be imported into Unity for use in game objects. The scripts are designed to call the requisite functions and access the appropriate data in the agent models against which they have been built. Both the agent model and the behavior tree are attached to the game object in Unity, the former providing a wrapper for the functionality of that game object, and the latter responsible for its decision logic. What results is an integrated development environment for building PAR trees to control arbitrary agent models (as defined by some author for the functionality of that agent). Figure 4 displays the current Topiary interface. The center window is the canvas for arranging and connecting nodes in the PAR tree. To the left, windows display the following:

- The library of generic nodes (decorators and control structures)
- The current files in the project, including the imported agents and already authored PAR trees for both agents and events
- For the current active window, the agents that have been added to the PAR being built, along with the action and assertion nodes available to them

The Node Inspector sits at the right of the screenshot, which displays the selected node (currently the "stand" action node of the MyHuman agent), the parameters of that action (with fields to fill in their values), and space for setting comments or renaming nodes.

The Topiary canvas can be dynamically sized to accommodate large trees, but we ultimately bring into question the scalability of behavior tree design. A large, sophisticated tree for complex agent behavior cannot be visualized in its entirety without some degree of abstraction, no matter the representational system. After a certain point, we simply lack the space in which to draw the entire tree. It is far more reasonable to present compact trees that delegate to lookup nodes for managing subtrees at a finer grain of detail, for which parameterization of behavior trees is a valuable asset.

6 Conclusions

While behavior trees are already a powerful tool for authoring agent behaviors, the adding capability for encapsulated code reuse within a behavior tree framework exploits an already prominent feature of behavior trees – hierarchical abstraction. Already we can use decorators to modify the behavior of a subtree at its root, say by looping that subtree or preventing its execution, but decorators cannot penetrate that subtree to modify its behavior at any lower level in great detail. Parameterization allows us to do just that. If a tree is built around key parameters to modify its execution, the author of the tree gains the power to tweak the nature of that tree without unwrapping its abstracted components and modifying its integral structure. An entire subtree, for example, can be disabled at a very low level in the tree using an assertion on a boolean parameter. In code, it is difficult to visualize and manage this encapsulation in the context of a behavior tree structure, but a highly visual tool such as Topiary simplifies the process with its awareness of PAR tree parameterization and arguments. Without a tool like Topiary, one of the key advantages of Behavior Trees – intuitive visualization – is entirely lost.

This method does not entirely eliminate the need for information to be stored in a central location for trees to access. In particular, for passing information between distinct branches of a tree, parameterization will not help. However, this data would already likely fall under the category of information associated with the agent's state, and would have space allocated for it in the agent model itself.

The application of Smart Events as a parameterized behavior tree greatly simplifies the process of authoring events. Where agents were programmed to be reactive to messages from a central message board, agents can now be entirely co-opted by a smart event, which specifies all of the details (leveraging abstraction) of how to execute that event. This recasting of Smart Events also provides the simplifying assumption of control. In particular, the knowledge that an author for an event has complete authority over that agent for its duration (unless preempted by an event of higher priority) mitigates the set of contingencies and emergent misbehavior that arises when designing agents to participate in group activities purely from a standpoint of reacting to stimuli. This cannot be accomplished, however, in a behavior tree framework that does not accommodate the parameterization of its subjects and objects. While intentionally simplified, the merchant haggling example illustrates how idle agents in the environment can be involved in an arbitrary event, perform the requisite actions, and then return to plausible individual behavior all dictated by behavior trees. It is parameterization on the layer of encapsulating entire trees with exposed interfaces that makes this possible.

Acknowledgements. The research reported in this document/presentation was performed in connection with Contract Number W911NF-10-2-0016 with the U.S. Army Research Laboratory. The views and conclusions contained in this document/presentation are those of the authors and should not be interpreted as presenting the official policies or position, either expressed or implied, of the U.S. Army Research Laboratory, or the U.S. Government unless so designated by other authorized documents. Citation of manufacturers or trade names does not constitute an official endorsement or approval of the use thereof. The U.S. Government is authorized to reproduce and distribute reprints for Government purposes notwithstanding any copyright notation heron.

References

1. Badler, N.I., Bindiganavale, R., Allbeck, J., Schuler, W., Zhao, L., Palmer, M.: Parameterized action representation for virtual human agents. In: Embodied Conversational Agents, pp. 256–284. MIT Press, Cambridge (2000)
2. Hecker, C., McHugh, L., Argenton, M., Dyckho, M.: Three approaches to Halo-style behavior tree ai. In: Game Developers Conference (2007)
3. Colvin, R., Grunske, L., Winter, K.: Probabilistic Timed Behavior Trees. In: Davies, J., Gibbons, J. (eds.) IFM 2007. LNCS, vol. 4591, pp. 156–175. Springer, Heidelberg (2007)
4. Colvin, R.J., Hayes, I.J.: A semantics for behavior trees using csp with specification commands. Sci. Comput. Program. 76, 891–914 (2011)
5. Isla, D.: Handling complexity in the Halo 2 ai. In: Game Developers Conference (2005)
6. Isla, D.: Halo 3 - building a better battle. In: Game Developers Conference (2008)
7. Knafla, B.: Data-oriented streams spring behavior trees (April 2011), http://altdevblogaday.com/2011/04/24/data-oriented-streams-spring-behavior-trees/
8. Meyer, B.: Object-Oriented Software Construction, 2nd edn. Prentice Hall, Upper Saddle River (1997)
9. Millington, I., Funge, J.: Artificial Intelligence for Games. Morgan Kaufmann, Elsevier (2009)
10. Pelechano, N., Allbeck, J.M., Badler, N.I.: Virtual Crowds: Methods, Simulation, and Control. In: Lectures on Computer Graphics and Animation. Morgan & Claypool Publishers (2008)
11. Stocker, C., Sun, L., Huang, P., Qin, W., Allbeck, J.M., Badler, N.I.: Smart Events and Primed Agents. In: Safonova, A. (ed.) IVA 2010. LNCS, vol. 6356, pp. 15–27. Springer, Heidelberg (2010)
12. Winter, K.: Formalising Behaviour Trees with CSP. In: Boiten, E.A., Derrick, J., Smith, G.P. (eds.) IFM 2004. LNCS, vol. 2999, pp. 148–167. Springer, Heidelberg (2004)

Intelligent Camera Control Using Behavior Trees

Daniel Markowitz, Joseph T. Kider Jr., Alexander Shoulson,
and Norman I. Badler

Department of Computer and Information Science
University of Pennsylvania
Philadelphia, PA 19104-6389, USA
{idaniel,kiderj,shoulson,badler}@seas.upenn.edu

Abstract. Automatic camera systems produce very basic animations for virtual worlds. Users often view environments through two types of cameras: a camera that they control manually, or a very basic automatic camera that follows their character, minimizing occlusions. Real cinematography features much more variety producing more robust stories. Cameras shoot establishing shots, close-ups, tracking shots, and bird's eye views to enrich a narrative. Camera techniques such as zoom, focus, and depth of field contribute to framing a particular shot. We present an intelligent camera system that automatically positions, pans, tilts, zooms, and tracks events occurring in real-time while obeying traditional standards of cinematography. We design behavior trees that describe how a single intelligent camera might behave from low-level narrative elements assigned by "smart events". Camera actions are formed by hierarchically arranging behavior sub-trees encapsulating nodes that control specific camera semantics. This approach is more modular and particularly reusable for quickly creating complex camera styles and transitions rather then focusing only on visibility. Additionally, our user interface allows a director to provide further camera instructions, such as prioritizing one event over another, drawing a path for the camera to follow, and adjusting camera settings on the fly. We demonstrate our method by placing multiple intelligent cameras in a complicated world with several events and storylines, and illustrate how to produce a well-shot "documentary" of the events constructed in real-time.

Keywords: intelligent cameras, behavior trees, camera control, cinematography, smart events.

1 Introduction

Filmmaking is a complex visual medium that combines cinematography and editing to convey a story. The camera must film the right event at the right time to produce the right picture. Cinematography and editing are both complex art forms in their own right, as they involve many highly subjective stylistic decisions. Given the opportunity to shoot the same event, two different directors are likely to produce very different footage with varying shot choices, shot length, and editing techniques. Unfortunately, many games limit a user's experience to a manually controlled camera, or an automatic camera designed to minimize occlusions. This basic control does not use cinematic principles to help tell the game's narrative. Films use more shooting variety and style for capturing movies. Our system provides the user with a way to create and style complex camera transitions to provide a more engaging experience in the game.

Cinematography follows a variety of rules and principles to communicate information and story in a clear and coherent fashion. Christianson and his colleagues [6] describe some of the established cinematographic techniques, and Arijon [2] and Lukas [21] provide additional detail. Cristie and Olivier [8] and Cristie et al. [7] outline the state of the art in camera control in graphics. Some principles include the 180-degree rule: if a horizontal line is imagined to cut across the camera's field of view, the camera should not instantly rotate and cross this line in consecutive shots; if it does, subjects that originally appeared on the right side of the frame will now appear on the left, and vice versa. Similarly, the 30-degree rule states that when the camera cuts to a different view of the same subject, it should be rotated at least 30 degrees in any direction to avoid a jump cut. In the case of clear communication, editing should be essentially "invisible": breaking these rules can lead to jarring edits.

The progression of shots facilitates clear communication: when an event occurs, a so-called "establishing shot" depicts the event from a distance and gives the viewer context; next, close-ups and other shots fill in the details. In single shots, framing assists in highlighting parts of the image that draw attention, by using selective focus or keeping objects in the middle of the frame. Negative space should also be left in front of moving objects, and the actor should always lead. These techniques apply to both live-action and virtual films. These camera semantics are cast as behavior trees in our system. Using behavior trees gives a quick and modular method to create intricate camera styles.

In this paper, we introduce an intelligent camera system that automatically reacts to events that occur in a virtual world. Our camera's actions are programmed as behavior trees that react to "smart events". We capture actions in real-time while following standard principles of cinematography and editing. We provide a user interface for a "director" to control and override camera semantics such as prioritizing one event over another, drawing a path for the camera to follow, and adjusting camera settings on the fly. This allows multiple intelligent cameras to film events, and allows for a customizable approach to editing a final animation. Our test environment tracks multiple rolling balls, a crowd scene, and a conversation to demonstrate how to create a well-shot "documentary" of multiple events edited in real time. Our world is built in the Unity Game engine demonstrating the usefulness of our technique for producing videos for games.

Our system gives the game designer a more robust way to customize how he wants to portray his game. Because the cameras are intelligent, once the camera behavior is programmed, it automatically shoots the character, action, or events occurring in real-time. A designer, much like a film director, brings his own unique style to controlling the player's visual experience. Additionally, our user interface allows players to create custom "cut scenes" out of real-time gameplay, and permits a player to create cinematic replays of his gameplay to post on social media.

2 Background

Many researchers have focused on integrating cinematographic principles into automatic camera control. These approaches provide sophisticated control to a user. Christianson et al. [6] divide cinematography into simple fragments in a "Declarative Camera Control Language". They also develop a "Camera Planning System" that partitions a character's movement into individual actions. He et al. [15] encode a finite state machine that controls the camera's position and parameters. This implementation does not work in real-time and is limited to simple scenarios involving two characters. Our approach works for multiple simultaneous events, operates in real-time, and expands to more robust scenarios, such as crowds, tracking an object/character, and conversations.

The CINEMA system [9] implements a method for camera movements (pans, tilts, rolls, and dollies). This method procedurally generates camera moves based on prior user inputs. CamDroid [10] implements intelligent cameras by defining camera modules similar to Christianson et al.'s [6] approach. While they demonstrate their work on both a conversation and football match, the approach requires prespecified constraints by the user for how to implement a particular shot. Bares et al. [4] developed an interactive fiction system using a constraint-based approach. Bares et al. [3] also looked at using storyboard frames to constrain a virtual camera. Friedman and Feldman [12] used non-monotonic reasoning for their camera's behavior and other knowledge-based systems [13]. Amerson et al. [1] abstractly described cinematographic expressions to control their camera.

Portraying a narrative correctly is an important aspect in storytelling [25], and many games fail to use complex camera behaviors to provide a mood and style. Elson and Riedl [11] introduced Cambot that used an offline algorithm to automatically produce a film. Jhala [18] proposed a method to generate a narrative for events and directives.

Recent camera control work focuses on visibility planning. The camera is automatically controlled to keep the actor visible. Li and Cheng [19] used a probabilistic roadmap to update the camera's position. Halper et al. [14] used a point-based visibility method. Oskam et al. [22] demonstrated a robust global planning algorithm. They used a visibility aware roadmap to avoid occlusions. Of all of the previous camera control systems, Lino et al.'s work [20] is the most similar to our approach. They rely on "Director Volumes" to partition the space, determine visibility cells, and provide details for performing cinematic camera control. The "Director Volumes" allow a user to program his own style by ranking preferences. Our approach does not replace these systems, but complements them. Our contribution provides a dynamic and modular approach to linking various camera behaviors to "smart events". Camera behaviors are determined by the entire sequence of multiple events. A more complex visibility planner can be programmed into our system based on a user's needs. Our demonstration uses a simplified version of the Oskam et al. [22] approach.

Pereira et. al [23] presented a model to describe events stored in a table by their relationships. Their camera control merely frames the active agent, but their system does not respond to events that occur in their scenario. Stocker and her colleagues [24] programmed behaviors and responses into events. The "smart event" informed an agent how to respond to a scenario. The user does not have to plan and program how agents respond to each other, since the event provides the appropriate behaviors. We leverage this approach in our method to provide a novel control for our intelligent camera system. As new events occur, a camera is assigned to an event, and the event itself provides the necessary parameters to pick and execute a behavior tree to control the camera's semantics. This approach is more efficient for controlling multiple intelligent cameras since it does not spend time planning how to shoot the event.

Fig. 1. This figure shows the basic cinematography movement controls for our cameras: tracking, tilting, and panning. Most camera movement is broken down to these controls.

3 Cinematography Principles

Camera shots provide organization and style to a movie or game in a sequence of scenes. Moving the camera, however, is a delicate art based on some well-established principles. Researchers have outlined many complex details of spatio-temporal cinematography standards [2,21]. In a game, however, a user interacts with a virtual world in a sequence of play in real-time. Similar guidelines should be used to guide game cameras as in film. Our intelligent cameras follow similar principles of cinematography to provide a more robust visual experience. This allows a game designer to set various facets of the gameplay's setting, characters, and themes.

Camera Movement: The camera movement shapes and informs a shot's meaning. Basic camera moves include three actions: pans, tilts, and tracks. In general, most complex camera moves are simply mixtures of these basic components. A camera pans when it rotates horizontally, either from left to right or from right to left, normally establishing a scene. The camera rotates vertically to tilt, either from up to down or from down to up. In a tracking shot, the entire camera moves, rather than simply changing the direction of its focus to provide detail. These moves provide 6 degrees of freedom allowing the camera to position and orient itself and are illustrated in Figure 1.

Framing Shots: In games, framing and composition impart information to the player. The tightness of a frame provides different information to the player. If the shot is "tight," it is more personal, focused, and offers less information. This shot creates anxiety in a player. If the shot is "wide" there is more information making it easier for the player to find his objective. Changing the shot type changes the mood and provides the game with an "emotional evolution". The composition should also allow for empty space in front of the character, both when he is moving and where he is looking (Figure 2). Also, care should be taken not to cut a character off at the ankles, knees or neck.

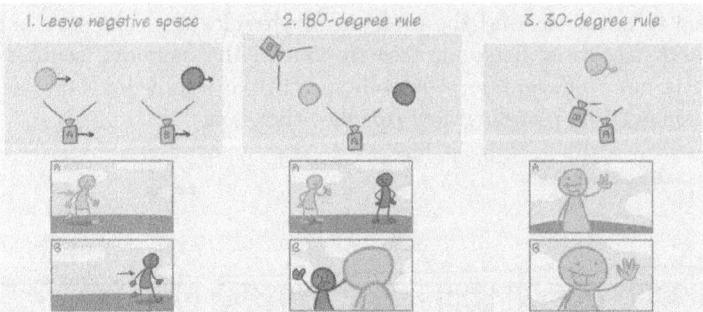

Fig. 2. This figure illustrates some advanced camera shots and editing principles. The top demonstrates how leaving some negative space allows the actor to lead. The middle shows the 180-degree rule related to the invisible line of action in a scene. The bottom displays the 30-degree rule, which shows the minimal distance a camera should move.

Basic Editing Rules: Enforcing basic editing rules provides continuity to a sequence of shots. These act as constraints that ensure that the player is not disoriented in a game. For example, the 180-degree rule is related to the invisible line of action in a scene. Once it's established that the camera is on one side of that line, abruptly cutting across it will be disorienting for viewers. The 30-degree rule ensures the camera moves enough when it cuts, otherwise a jump-cut or indecisive cut results. "Line of action" and "line of interest" are two continuity rules that should be enforced as well [20].

3.1 Intelligent Camera Representation

Using more shot types and enforcing some basic cinematography principles improve a game's narrative, visual appearance, and play. Our intelligent cameras use these three basic camera controls and take care framing shots. We set range parameters on the camera cuts to enforce basic editing rules. We define our intelligent cameras by the following parameters:

- **Position(x,y,z)** - position of the camera
- **Rotation(rx,ry,rz)** - rotation of the camera
- **Zoom(level)** - zoom level
- **DepthOfField(level)** - depth of field
- **FocusPoint(x,y,z)** - focus point if different than center point
- **Style(type)** - behavior style of the camera
- **FollowDistance(dist)** - follow distance
- **FollowHeight(height)** - follow height
- **ShotDuration(time)** - how long the shot will be held

- **Cuttingspeed(speed)** - how fast cuts take place
- **lastCutPosition(x,y,z, rx,ry,rz)** - if only one camera enforces edit rules
- **EventID(ID)** - The smart event the camera is assigned

Shot Idioms: The standard convention in previous work is to break shots up into "fragments" and stitch multiple fragments together, composing an intricate shot idiom as an element in the narrative [6,10,20]. These cinematic shot idioms are sequences of camera setups. An idiom is encoded by defining the necessary parameters in the scene (actors, times, angles). Idioms allow a game designer to bring different styles into frame sequences. The shot idiom is chosen by the "smart event" that assigns a shooting priority to the shots. The idiom's parameters are assigned at run-time for the scene by this "smart event". For example, a simple dialogue scene is handled with a "shot/reverse" shot idiom. The game designer programs these narrative idioms as behavior trees (defined in the next section). So idioms are quickly scripted by the designer and are very modular.

4 Implementation

Behavior Trees are simple data structures that provide a graphical representation and formalization for complex actions. Behavior Trees control our intelligent cameras using "AND/OR" logic with actions, assertions, and other constructions to implement various shot idioms. Behavior Trees are used in modern games to provide agents with intelligence: examples include Halo2 [16], Halo3 [17], and Spore [5]. Behavior trees are preferable to finite state machines for two reasons: goal direction and hierarchical abstraction. A behavior tree can be designed a series of actions geared towards accomplishing a single goal, with contingencies to handle any obstacles that arise. Larger trees built for accomplishing broader goals are built by combining smaller sub-goals, for which subtrees can be invoked.

Figure 3 shows an example of making our intelligent cameras behave like cinematographers. The tree describes how a single camera behaves. At the top of the tree is a "Loop" decorator followed by a "Selector"-in simpler terms, this means that the camera is in a constant loop of "selecting" which of the two subtrees (left or right) to follow. Assertions, the white rectangles in the tree, test something and then return either success or failure. A selector attempts to execute each of its children (in-order), and stops once a child return reports success at its level. If a child fails, the selector advances and tries the next. The left subtree is a behavior for when the camera is not assigned to an event, and the right subtree is behavior for when it is assigned. The Parallel box means that its children execute simultaneously. So, in the left subtree, the Assert node will constantly check to make sure that there's no event assignment, and the camera will "wander" as long as that assertion is returning success. This enforces constraints on the cameras: the parallel node has one child that is constantly enforcing some constraints on the execution of its other child. The abstracted subtree "wander" represents a "Sequence": if you think of: "Selection" acts like "OR" while "Sequence" acts like "AND". Whereas a "Selector" would try children until it finds one that returns success, a "Sequence" node attempts to execute each of its

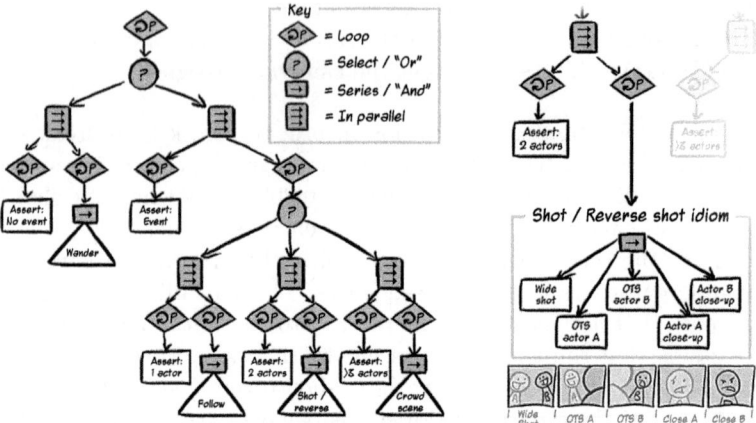

Fig. 3. On the left, this figure shows an intelligent camera's behavior tree. Initially, the camera wanders until it is assigned to an event. The camera reacts to information provided based on the type of "smart event". On the right, we show the abstracted subtree for filming a dialogue scene with a shot / reverse-shot idiom.

children, in order. If any child fails, the sequence node ceases execution (ignoring all subsequent children) and reports failure at its level. The "Sequence" succeeds only after its last child succeeds. In this case, the children of "Wander" would be different actions that cause the camera to move how the designer wishes.

The right subtree starts with another "Parallel" node, which makes sure that it will execute while the camera is still assigned to an event (once the event ends, we should revert back to wandering around). Another "Selector" decides

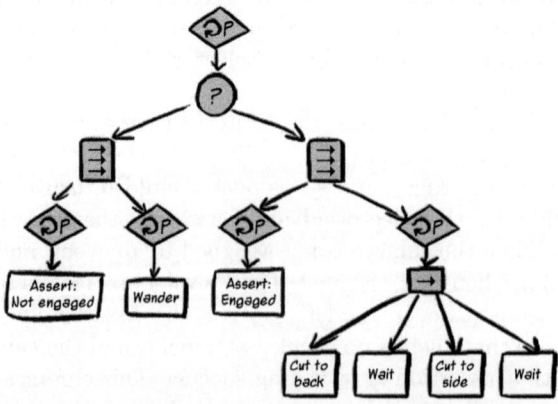

Fig. 4. This figure outlines a simple editing rule: the cameras currently only cut back and forth between two shots: a tracking shot from behind the target, and a stationary shot that pans with the target. This is a diagram of the behavior tree that the cameras are implementing.

what kind of situation we are in. The Selector in the right branch of the tree is the "Cinematographer Node", since it plays the role of cinematographer: deciding what kinds of shots to use based on the current situation.

Figure 4 illustrates a simple editing rule. The cameras currently cut back and forth between two shots: a tracking shot from behind the target, and a stationary shot that pans with the target. The camera has two branches for whether it's currently engaged with an event or not. When the camera is engaged, it enters a shot idiom. In this case, there's only one idiom: cut to a tracking shot behind the target, wait a certain amount of time, cut to a stationary side shot, wait, and repeat (until no longer engaged). This formulation is the foundation for enforcing the cinematography principles discussed above.

4.1 Smart Event Representation

"Smart Events" store the behavioral responses and parameter information inside the event [24]. These events update parameters in the Behavior Trees. This way a designer does not have to program every combination manually and can rely on the event to produce the correct shot. A "message board" updates global information as an event evolves and assigns the intelligent cameras to cover the events. A "blackboard" updates any local information for the behavior tree as the event evolves. Once a "smart event" occurs, it broadcasts to the "message board" and assigns an intelligent camera which is not currently engaged with an event. If all the cameras are assigned, the "message board" looks at the event priority and ShotDuration variables. Our formulation extends the parameters found in Stocker et al. [24] such as "Type", "Position", "Start Time", etc. for the event. Our formulation adds relevant information for the camera such as:

- **ShotIdiom(behavior names)** - set of possible behaviors for the camera
- **CameraIDs(IDs)** - ids of intelligent cameras assigned to event
- **Priority(p)** - the importance of the event
- **Participants(IDs)**- list of actors/objects camera should track
- **Position(x,y,z)** - position of the camera
- **Rotation(rx,ry,rz)** - rotation of the camera
- **Zoom(level)** - zoom level
- **DepthOfField(level)** - depth of field
- **FocusPoint(x,y,z)** - focus point, if different then center point
- **Style(type)** - behavior style of the camera
- **FollowDistance(dist)** - follow distance
- **FollowHeight(height)** - follow height
- **ShotDuration(time)** - how long the shot will be held
- **Cuttingspeed(speed)** - how fast cuts take place
- **LastCutPosition(x,y,z, rx,ry,rz)** - for the cameras

5 Results

Figure 5 shows a screenshot of one of our test environments featuring 3 intelligent cameras in our GUI. The cameras are color-coded across the top so that the user can easily match the physical cameras to their displays. The far left camera is the "master track" display for the final output color-coded in yellow. The main GUI window can switch among any intelligent camera, the master track, or a user-controlled 3D view. The user-control view allows for a "director" mode, where camera properties can be overridden and views selected, to achieve a novel playback. This is especially useful for making video playbacks of a player's gameplay for posterity. Normally, the intelligent cameras and smart events automatically create the master track with no additional user intervention. The system automatically assigns the intelligent camera and shot idiom behavior based on information from the "smart event". This mode is very useful during real-time gameplay.

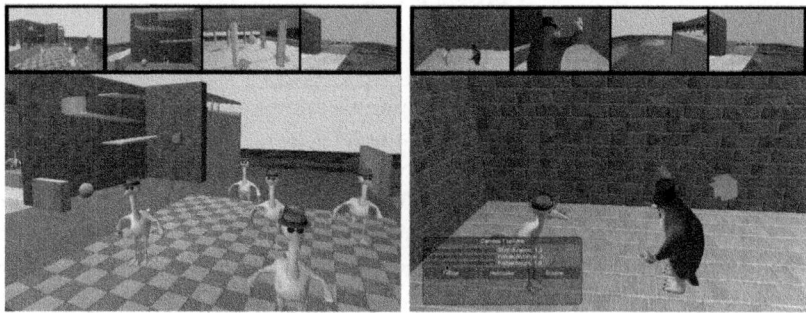

Fig. 5. The figure shows the director GUI. The main window features a user-controlled camera. The yellow window across the top is the "master track" window. The other windows (red, green, blue) are color-coded intelligent cameras. The image on the left is an example of our system shooting various events in a crowd. On the right, we demonstrate a simple dialogue scene when a penguin walks into a pub.

In Figure 5 on the left, the red camera is filming a ball rolling down several slopes (it is currently shooting an establishing shot of the ball with relation to the slopes), while the green camera is following a ball through a complex environment (it is currently shooting a tracking shot behind the ball). The master track is set to display the perspective of the main (user-controlled) camera. The blue camera is not engaged, so it randomly scans the environment until another "smart event" occurs. Figure 5 (on the right) depicts a dialogue scene between a penguin and stork. The red camera is engaged with the event and currently shooting an over-the-shoulder shot within the dialogue idiom. The green and blue cameras are not engaged and currently shooting establishing context shots.

Figure 6 shows a screenshot of a second test environment tracking balls rolling down various slopes. When a ball start rolling it, triggers a "smart event" and assigns a camera to start tracking the motion. The red camera's options are displayed, where the user can adjust certain settings, or change the "genre" of the camera: setting it to "Bourne/24" mode will cause it to shake and cut often. Shot duration sets the length of each shot before an edit occurs (when the shot duration is set to 0, either by the event or user, the camera never cuts from the event until it is fully completed). The camera keeps the ball visible through the best path it can calculate when following the ball through the obstacles.

Fig. 6. The figure shows the application of our intelligent camera system in a second virtual world featuring multiple rolling balls and difficult obstacles. The camera follows various shot idioms, while keeping the ball visible. The settings for the red camera are displayed in the left image. Users may use the GUI to compose playbacks of gameplay.

Fig. 7. This figure demonstrates how multiple intelligent cameras are assigned to the scene (highlighted by red circles) to handle the "conversation event" that is unfolding. A director may also assign cameras to enhance the visual experience.

Figure 7 shows a close-up of a "follow" idiom where the event is assigning intelligent cameras to cover the event as the user controls the penguin. These cameras are highlighted in red. Here, the camera is pulled back to "establish" the shot, providing information about the environment. As the shot sequence progresses, the camera draws closer when the player engages another agent. We have tested our scene with multiple events and multiple cameras without producing any lag in gameplay. Our test environments and user interactions use the Unity Game engine, however any game engine would work.

6 Conclusions

In this paper, we have presented a novel intelligent camera system using behavior trees and smart events. Our system automatically positions, pans, tilts, zooms, and tracks the camera to film events. Our system is very modular and dynamically reacts to "smart events" that occur in the scene in real-time. Our intelligent cameras take advantage of the modular abstraction behavior trees provide. This allows a game designer the ability to quickly create new shot idioms, and efficiently reuse the components to create more complex actions. Using "smart events" provides the necessary parameters to our cameras, and greatly simplifies having to program every possible event manually. This generalizes our approach since the designer does not have to plan out the camera in a game and can instead focus on the game's style and narrative. The intelligent camera will react to the event automatically and film it appropriately. This provides a high-quality visual experience to the player, thereby turning the game into the visual experience of a movie. We provide a user interface to allow a director or user to create their own videos. This feature may be used in a variety of ways in the future. A user could edit his own visual appearance for the game, or construct very strong playback videos of his game highlights to post online. The advantage here is that the camera can record the event BEFORE the great play, save, accomplishment, etc. is actually achieved. In the future, we hope to add more advanced shooting techniques to the system. Parameterizing and implementing camera blur, saturation, color, and contrast effects would all enhance the visual appearance. We also hope to improve the occlusion detection by applying "Director Volumes" and other complex visibility algorithms or directed paths.

References

1. Amerson, D., Shaun, K., Young, R.M.: Real-time cinematic camera control for interactive narratives. In: Proceedings of the 2005 ACM SIGCHI International Conference on Advances in Computer Entertainment Technology, ACE 2005, pp. 369–369. ACM, New York (2005), http://doi.acm.org/10.1145/1178477.1178552
2. Arijon, D.: Grammar of the Film Language. Communication Arts Books, Hastings House Publishers (1976)
3. Bares, W., McDermott, S., Boudreaux, C., Thainimit, S.: Virtual 3d camera composition from frame constraints. In: Proceedings of the Eighth ACM International Conference on Multimedia, MULTIMEDIA 2000, pp. 177–186. ACM, New York (2000), http://doi.acm.org/10.1145/354384.354463
4. Bares, W.H., Grégoire, J.P., Lester, J.C.: Realtime constraint-based cinematography for complex interactive 3d worlds. In: Proceedings of the Fifteenth National/Tenth Conference on Artificial Intelligence/Innovative Applications of Artificial Intelligence, AAAI 1998/IAAI 1998, pp. 1101–1106. American Association for Artificial Intelligence, Menlo Park (1998),
http://portal.acm.org/citation.cfm?id=295240.296260
5. Hecker, C., McHugh, L., Dyckho, M.A.,, M.: Three approaches to Halo-style behavior tree ai. In: Game Developers Conference (2007)
6. Christianson, D.B., Anderson, S.E., He, L.w., Salesin, D.H., Weld, D.S., Cohen, M.F.: Declarative camera control for automatic cinematography. In: Proceedings of the Thirteenth National Conference on Artificial Intelligence, AAAI 1996, vol. 1, pp. 148–155. AAAI Press (1996),
http://portal.acm.org/citation.cfm?id=1892875.1892897
7. Christie, M., Machap, R., Normand, J.-M., Olivier, P., Pickering, J.H.: Virtual Camera Planning: A Survey. In: Butz, A., Fisher, B., Krüger, A., Olivier, P. (eds.) SG 2005. LNCS, vol. 3638, pp. 40–52. Springer, Heidelberg (2005)
8. Christie, M., Olivier, P.: Camera control in computer graphics: models, techniques and applications. In: ACM SIGGRAPH ASIA 2009 Courses, SIGGRAPH ASIA 2009, pp. 3:1–3:197. ACM, New York (2009),
http://doi.acm.org/10.1145/1665817.1665820

9. Drucker, S.M., Galyean, T.A., Zeltzer, D.: Cinema: a system for procedural camera movements. In: Proceedings of the 1992 Symposium on Interactive 3D Graphics, I3D 1992, pp. 67–70. ACM, New York (1992), http://doi.acm.org/10.1145/147156.147166
10. Drucker, S.M., Zeltzer, D.: Camdroid: a system for implementing intelligent camera control. In: Proceedings of the 1995 Symposium on Interactive 3D Graphics, I3D 1995, pp. 139–144. ACM, New York (1995), http://doi.acm.org/10.1145/199404.199428
11. Elson, D.K., Riedl, M.O.: A lightweight intelligent virtual cinematography system for machinima production. In: AIIDE, pp. 8–13 (2007)
12. Friedman, D., Feldman, Y.A.: Automated cinematic reasoning about camera behavior. Expert Syst. Appl. 30, 694–704 (2006), http://dx.doi.org/10.1016/j.eswa.2005.07.027
13. Friedman, D.A., Feldman, Y.A.: Knowledge-based cinematography and its applications. In: ECAI, pp. 256–262 (2004)
14. Halper, N., Helbing, R., Strothotte, T.: A camera engine for computer games: Managing the trade-off between constraint satisfaction and frame coherence. Computer Graphics Forum 20(3), 174–183 (2001)
15. He, L.w., Cohen, M.F., Salesin, D.H.: The virtual cinematographer: a paradigm for automatic real-time camera control and directing. In: Proceedings of the 23rd Annual Conference on Computer Graphics and Interactive Techniques, SIGGRAPH 1996, pp. 217–224. ACM, New York (1996), http://doi.acm.org/10.1145/237170.237259
16. Isla, D.: Handling complexity in the Halo 2 ai. In: Game Developers Conference, p. 12 (2005)
17. Isla, D.: Halo 3 - building a better battle. In: Game Developers Conference (2008)
18. Jhala, A.: Cinematic Discourse Generation. Ph.D. thesis, North Carolina State University (2009)
19. Li, T.-Y., Cheng, C.-C.: Real-Time Camera Planning for Navigation in Virtual Environments. In: Butz, A., Fisher, B., Krüger, A., Olivier, P., Christie, M. (eds.) SG 2008. LNCS, vol. 5166, pp. 118–129. Springer, Heidelberg (2008)
20. Lino, C., Christie, M., Lamarche, F., Schofield, G., Olivier, P.: A real-time cinematography system for interactive 3d environments. In: Proceedings of the 2010 ACM SIGGRAPH/Eurographics Symposium on Computer Animation, SCA 2010, pp. 139–148. Eurographics Association, Aire-la-Ville (2010), http://portal.acm.org/citation.cfm?id=1921427.1921449
21. Lukas, C.: Directing for Film and Television. Anchor Press / Doubleday (1985)
22. Oskam, T., Sumner, R.W., Thuerey, N., Gross, M.: Visibility transition planning for dynamic camera control. In: Proceedings of the 2009 ACM SIGGRAPH/Eurographics Symposium on Computer Animation, SCA 2009, pp. 55–65. ACM, New York (2009), http://doi.acm.org/10.1145/1599470.1599478
23. Pereira, F., Gelatti, G., Raupp Musse, S.: Intelligent virtual environment and camera control in behavioural simulation. In: Proceedings of XV Brazilian Symposium on Computer Graphics and Image Processing, pp. 365–372 (2002)
24. Stocker, C., Sun, L., Huang, P., Qin, W., Allbeck, J.M., Badler, N.I.: Smart Events and Primed Agents. In: Safonova, A. (ed.) IVA 2010. LNCS, vol. 6356, pp. 15–27. Springer, Heidelberg (2010), http://portal.acm.org/citation.cfm?id=1889075.1889078
25. Young, R.M.: Story and discourse: A bipartite model of narrative generation in virtual worlds. Interaction Studies (2006)

A Decision Theoretic Approach to Motion Saliency in Computer Animations

Sami Arpa, Abdullah Bulbul, and Tolga Capin

Bilkent University, Computer Engineering Department,
Faculty of Engineering, 06800 Ankara, Turkey
{arpa,bulbul,tcapin}@cs.bilkent.edu.tr

Abstract. We describe a model to calculate saliency of objects due to their motions. In a decision-theoretic fashion, perceptually significant objects inside a scene are detected. The work is based on psychological studies and findings on motion perception. By considering motion cues and attributes, we define six motion states. For each object in a scene, an individual saliency value is calculated considering its current motion state and the inhibition of return principle. Furthermore, a global saliency value is considered for each object by covering their relationships with each other and equivalence of their saliency value. The position of the object with highest attention value is predicted as a possible gaze point for each frame in the animation. We conducted several eye-tracking experiments to practically observe the motion-attention related principles in psychology literature. We also performed some final user studies to evaluate our model and its effectiveness.

Keywords: saliency, motion, computer animation, perception.

1 Introduction

The impact of psychology and neuroscience disciplines to mature the techniques developed in computer graphics has increased through newly discovered biological facts. In psychological science, the sensitivity of human perception to motion is still a contemporary research issue. The fact that motion attracts attention is a former claim. New arguments focus on the attributes of motion. Recent developments in neurobiological science have helped to discover the reaction of brain to visual stimuli in very low detail. Recently, as opposed to the previous beliefs, it has been experimented that motion per se does not attract attention, but some of its attributes do [1].

We use neurobiological facts on motion and the hints provided by motion-related psychophysical experiments to develop a metric calculating the saliency of the objects due to their motion in computer graphics scenes. The model estimates the relative saliencies of multiple objects with different movements.

To evaluate our model, we performed a user study in which the observers' reactions to objects having high and low saliencies are analyzed. The results of this experiment verify that the proposed metric correctly identifies the objects with high motion saliency.

This paper presents a model to determine the perceptually significant objects in animated video and/or game scenes based on the motions of the objects. Instant decisions provided by the model could simplify interactive target decision and enable controlling the difficulty level of games in a perceptual manner.

The rest of the paper is organized as follows: In Section 2, a review of previous studies in computer graphics utilizing the principles related to motion perception and the psychological principles that affected our model are presented. Section 3 presents our model and the details of the user studies are given in Section 4 before concluding the paper in the last section.

2 Related Work

The related work for motion saliency could be divided into two parts as the usage of motion perception in Computer Graphics and the psychological studies related to the effect of motion on visual attention.

Computer Graphics. Saliency could be seen as the bottom-up stimulus driven part of the visual attention mechanism in which task dependent attention does not have a role. Recently, saliency computation has gained more interest in computer graphics. One of the earliest attempts to compute saliency of 2D images was described by Itti et al. [8]. A widely known saliency computation framework that works on 3D mesh models was proposed by Lee et al. [11] which computes saliency according to the surface curvature properties of the meshes. Both of these models compute saliency based on the center-surround mechanism of human visual attention. Compared to these more general saliency computation frameworks, there are less works on motion based saliency computation.

The saliency computation framework proposed by Bulbul et al. [4] calculates motion saliency in a center-surround fashion and combines it with geometric and appearance based saliencies to generate an overall saliency map. The motion saliency computation in this work is based on the idea that the regions having a distinct motion compared to their surroundings become more salient. Halit and Capin [6] proposed a metric to calculate the motion saliency for motion-capture sequences. In this work, the motion capture data is treated as a motion curve and the most salient parts of these curves are extracted as the keyframes of the animation.

Peters and Itti [13] observed the gaze points on interactive video games and concluded that motion and flicker are the best predictors of the attended location while playing video games. Their heuristic for predicting motion-based saliency (as for other channels like color-based and orientation-based) works on 2D images and it is also based on the center-surround machanism.

Visual sensitivity to moving objects is another aspect of motion perception that is utilized in computer graphics. Kelly [9] and Daly [5] studied to measure the spatio-temporal sensitivity and fit computational models according to their observations. Yee et al. [17] built on these studies and used the spatio-temporal sensitivity to generate error tolerance maps to accelerate rendering.

Psychological Literature. Andersen's research [2] elaborated low level processing of motion cues in visual system by showing specific roles of Where system in the brain, which is a part of visual cortex processing motion [12]. Spatial awareness based on motion cues and its hierarchical processing have been investigated in this study by analyzing different receptor cells having varied roles in Where system.

In spatial domain, visual system is tend to group stimuli by considering their similarity and proximity as introduced in Gestalt principles. It is shown that visual system searches similarities also in temporal domain and can group stimuli by considering their parallel motions [10]. A bunch of moving dots with the same direction and speed could be perceived as a moving surface with this organization.

Along with color, depth, and illumination; central-surround organization is also applied to motion processing in visual system. The neurons processing motion have a double-opponent organization for direction selectivity [2].

Visual motion may be referred as salient since it has temporal frequency. On the other hand, recent studies in cognitive science and neuroscience have shown that motion by itself does not attract attention. Phases of motion have different degrees of influence on attention. Hence, each phase of motion should be analyzed independently.

Abrams and Christ [1] experimented different states of motion to observe the most salient one. They indicated that the onset of motion captures attention significantly compared to other states. Immediately after motion onset, the response to stimulus slows with the effect of inhibition of return and attentional sensitivity to that stimulus is lost.

Singletons, having different motion than others within stimuli, capture attention in a bottom-up, stimulus driven control. If there is a target of search, only feature singletons attract attention. If it is not the target, observers' attention is not taken. However, abrupt visual onsets capture attention even if they are not the target [16].

Other than motion onset, the experiments in the work of Hillstrom and Yantis [7] showed that the appearance of new objects captures attention significantly compared to other motion cues.

3 Approach

By considering psychological literature given in the previous section, we describe a model to compare attention values of objects in terms of motion. Initially, we consider the motion attributes to discriminate different states of an object's motion. Following six states form the essence of a motion cycle (Fig. 1):

Static: No change of location.
Object Appearance: Appearance of an object which was not previously present on the screen.
Motion Onset: The start of motion (static to dynamic).
Motion Offset: The end of motion (dynamic to static).

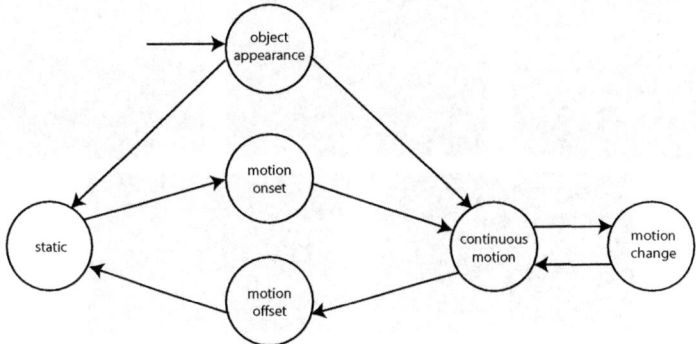

Fig. 1. Motion cycle of an object in an animation. Perceptually distinct phases are indicated as six states. Object appearance is the initial state for each object.

Continuous Motion: The state of keeping the motion with the same velocity.
Motion Change: Change in the direction or speed of a motion.

3.1 Pre-experiment

We performed an eye-tracker based pre-experiment to observe the relations between the defined states and the attentively attractive objects.

In the experiment, subjects were asked to watch the animations including movements of five balls within a 3D room. Eight different animations were used (Fig. 2). In each of them, different motion states and the observers' reactions to them are analyzed. We used an SMI Red Eye Tracker to observe and analyze gaze points of subjects during the animations. Eight voluntary graduate students who have normal or corrected to normal vision participated in the experiments. The subjects were not told about the purpose of the experiments and each of them watched eight different animations.

Experiment cases. The cases used in the pre-experiment are as follows:

- Case 1: Motion onset and motion offset are tested. Five initially static objects start to move in sequence with at least 3 seconds intervals. At the end, forty seconds later, all objects stop again in sequence with at least 3 seconds intervals.
- Case 2: Motion onset and motion offset are tested for shorter intervals. All objects start to move in sequence with 0.3 seconds intervals and stop the same way.
- Case 3: Object appearance is tested. Some objects starts to move and one object abruptly appears. There is an interval of five seconds between the latest motion onset and the object appearance.
- Case 4: Object appearance, motion onset, and motion change are tested. One object starts to move, one object appears, and another moving object changes its direction at the same time.

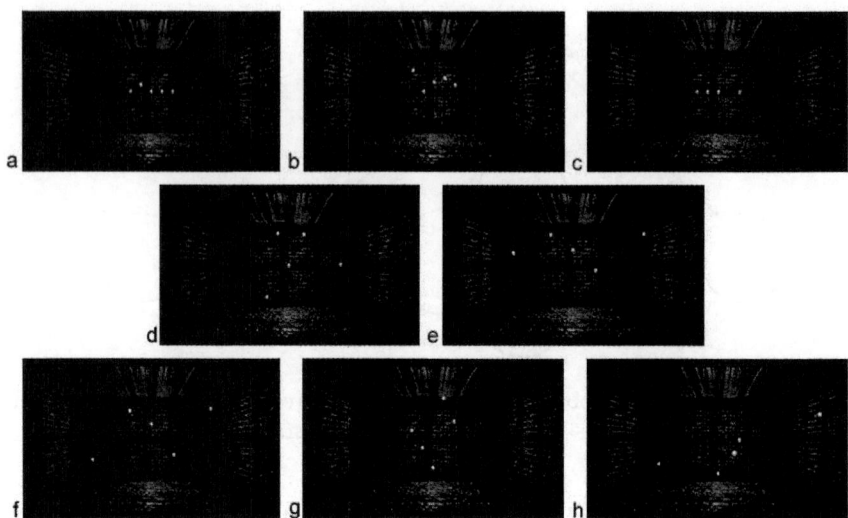

Fig. 2. Screenshots from the eight pre-experiment animations. **a:** Motion onset and offset are tested. **b:** Motion onset and offset are tested for shorter intervals. **c:** Object appearance is tested. **d:** Object appearance, motion onset, and motion change are tested. **e:** Object appearance, motion onset, and motion change are tested in larger spatial domain. **f:** Object appearance, motion onset, and motion change are tested in sequential order. **g:** Velocity difference is tested. **h:** States are tested altogether.

- Case 5: Object appearance, motion onset, and motion change are tested in larger spatial domain. Only difference from the forth case is that the objects are placed further points on the screen.
- Case 6: Object appearance, motion onset, and motion change are tested in sequential order. This time, three states do not occur at the same time, but in sequential order with intervals of 3 seconds.
- Case 7: Velocity difference is tested. Each object starts to move at the same time and the same direction with different velocities.
- Case 8: States are tested altogether.

Observations. The observations according to the pre-experiment results can be expressed as follows:

Motion onset, motion change, and *object appearance* states strongly attract attention. In the first case (Fig. 2-a), five object onsets were performed and among eight subjects, five subjects looked at all off the motion onsets. Each of the other three subjects missed only one motion onset and the missed objects were different for each of them. The gaze of all subjects was captured by the appearance of the object in the third animation (Fig. 2-c). In the cases four and five, none of the three objects with three different state sets dominate over the others (Fig. 2-d,e); indicating that *motion onset, motion change,* and *object appearance* states do not suppress each other. However, *motion offset, continuous motion,* and *static* states could be suppressed by any of the other three states.

Continuous motion and *motion offset* states capture attention merely over static state. The gazes of the subjects were rarely transferred to the objects with a motion offset event. However, when we asked the subjects, they have informed us that they were aware of all motion offsets but they did not move their gazes to see them. We can conclude that, in most cases, subjects perceive motion offsets in their peripheral view and their attention is not captured by these events.

None of the objects in *static state* captures attention while others are in different states in all of the experiments.

An important observation is that, if the time interval between two state transitions (not for the same object) is smaller than 0.3 seconds, the one which is later set was not captured by the subjects. In case two (Fig. 2-b), for instance, where all objects start to move in sequential order with 0.3 seconds intervals, none of motion onsets truly captured attention of the subjects. This is an expected behavior since following the first event, human attentional mechanism remains on this location in the first 0.3 seconds, causing new events to be discarded [15]. After this very short period, inhibition of return (IOR) mechanism slows the response to the current focus of attention enabling previously unattended objects to be attended. This decay time for the state is 0.9 seconds. After 0.9 seconds, the effect of state disappears [14] (Fig. 2-b,d,e,f).

Gaze is transferred to the closest object upon multiple events attracting attention. In the final case (Fig. 2-h), we observed that if more than one motion change, object appearance, motion onset, or motion change appears at the same moment, subjects gazes are commonly transferred to the closest object to the current gaze point.

Lastly, if more than one object have the same state with the same speed and the same direction of motion, they are recognized as a single object according to the Gestalt principles introduced in the previous section. In the case eight, subjects did not check each object separately in that moments, instead they looked at a point in the middle of this object group having the same motion direction and speed.

3.2 Overview

The overview of the proposed model is shown in Figure 3 and it contains two main parts. In the first part, individual motion saliencies of the objects are calculated. In the second part, the relations among the object are examined and final focus of attention is decided.

3.3 Individual Motion Saliency

Based on the observations from the pre-experiments and findings from the literature in psychology, we build an individual motion saliency model. The proposed model calculates instant saliency values for each object in an animation. Once the motion state of an object is detected, its saliency value is calculated as a time dependent variable.

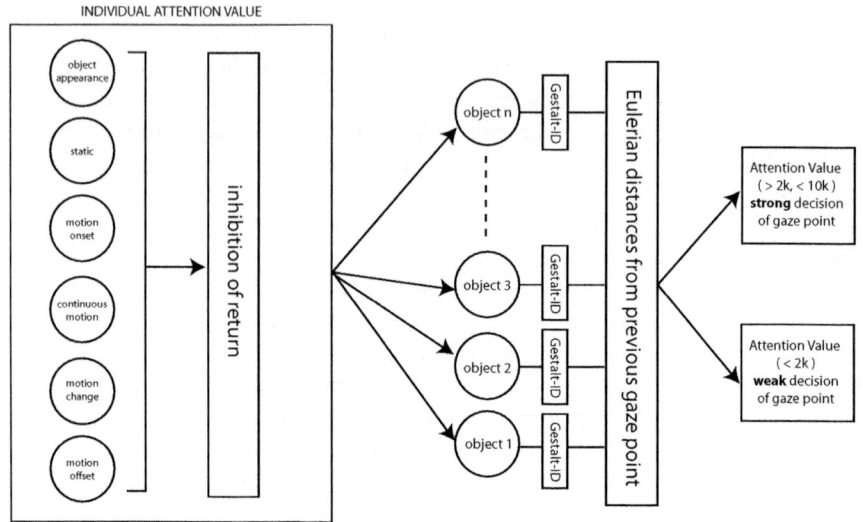

Fig. 3. Overview of the proposed model

We define an initial saliency value for each motion state according to the dominancy among the states (Fig. 4). These initial values are the peak saliencies and decays in time. Although these constants do not reflect an exact proportional dominancy result of the states among each other, they are used to make a correct decision with respect to their attentional dominancy. The initial saliency values for three most dominant states motion onset, motion change and object appearance are assigned as $10k$ while they are $2k$ for motion offset and continuous motion. For static state, it is $1k$. Usage of k as a coefficient enables converting the calculated saliencies for each object to probabilities defining the chance of getting the observers' gazes.

For each visible object, calculated individual saliency values change between $1k$ and $10k$ according to the formulas shown in Table 1 where t stands for the elapsed time after a state is initialized. Obviously, the saliency value for invisible objects is zero.

Saliency of an object in the static state is always $1k$, because we observed it never captures attention among other states. Also, saliency value is permanently $2k$ for continuous motion since a moving object may get attention anytime if nothing interesting, e.g. states of all other objects are static, happens on the screen and subject is not performing a target search [16]. Likewise, motion offset could get attention over static or continuous motion. However, it is under decay with the effect of IOR until the state becomes static.

Motion onset changes to continuous motion state; therefore, its value decays to $2k$ with IOR. It is exactly the same for motion change state. Hence, during inhibition of return ($0.3\text{sec} < t < 0.9\text{sec}$) [5] [6], attention value decays linearly from

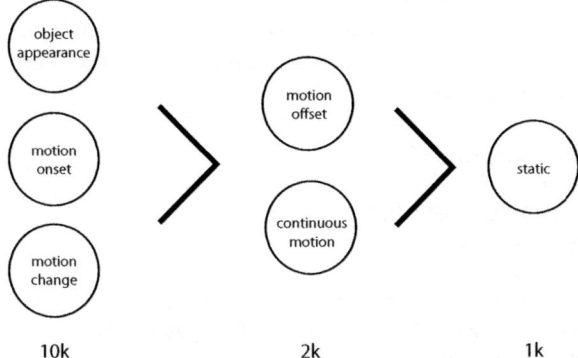

Fig. 4. Attentional dominancy of motion states over each other. Object appearance, motion onset and motion change are the most dominant states capturing attention. Motion offset and continuous motion is slightly more dominant over just static state.

Table 1. Individual Attention Values

States	$t \leq 300ms$	$300ms < t < 900ms$	$900ms \leq t$
STATIC	1k	1k	1k
ONSET	10k	$10k(1.25 - 7t/6)$	2k
OFFSET	2k	$10k(1.25 - 5t/6)$	1k
CONTINUOUS	2k	2k	2k
CHANGE	10k	$10k(1.25 - 7t/6)$	2k
APPEARANCE	10k	$10k(1.3 - 4t/3)$	1k

10k to 2k as shown on Table 1. Differently, object appearance decays to 1k because its state may become static. Similarly, motion offset decays linearly from its peak value 2k to 1k, since its following state is static.

Inhibition of return is not applied to any of the states if the elapsed time on a state is smaller than 300ms. As we mentioned earlier, during this time other state changes are not captured by subjects in the experiments.

This model provides calculating individual motion saliency values of each object in real time. However, it is still not sufficient to decide the focus of attention without examining the relationships of the objects among each other.

3.4 Global Attention Value

So far we have shown a model to calculate individual attention values of the objects. On the other hand, our visual system does not interpret objects in the scene individually. It tries to represent any stimulus in the simplest way. As Gestalt psychologists concluded that all similar objects in our vision are grouped and perceived as a simple object [3], we included a Gestalt organization into our model. Each object has a *Gestalt ID*. The objects having identical motion direction and speed are labeled with the same Gestalt ID. The pseudocode for this procedure is as follows.

```
SetGestaltIDs(objects[]){
  curGestalt = 1;
  for i = 1 to NUMBEROFOBJECTS
    gestaltSet = false;
    for j = 1 to i-1
      if objects[j].velocity equals to objects[i].velocity
        objects[i].gestaltID = objects[j].gestaltID;
        gestaltSet = true;
        break;
    if gestaltSet is false
      objects[i].gestaltID = curGestalt;
      curGestalt++;
}
```

All objects with the same Gestalt ID obtain the highest individual saliency among this group. In the pre-experiments, we clearly observed that subjects' gaze circulates around not one object if the objects have the same speed and direction with some other objects.

Another problem that is not solved by the individual saliency model is the case of equivalence. If more than one object with different Gestald IDs have the same highest individual attention value, which object will be chosen as the possible gaze point is not addressed. An observation we made during pre-experiments suggest a solution to this problem. If more than one states were set at the same time, subjects commonly looked at the closest object to the previous gaze point. Therefore, we included an attribute to our model to consider Eulerian distance of each object from previous decision of gaze point. It is calculated as the pixelwise Eulerian distance from the previously decided focus of attention in the screen.

Finally, if there are multiple Gestalt groups with the highest calculated saliency, the closest one to the previously decided focus of attention is selected as the current focus of attention.

4 Experiment

Experiment Design. We have performed a formal user study to validate our model. In the experiment, subjects have looked at a 22" LCD display where twenty spheres animate for two minutes in a 3D room (Fig. 5). For each half-second of animation, a random object changes its motion state to another random state. The subjects' task is pressing a button when the color of a sphere becomes the target color which is shown to the subjects during the experiment. Interval time for two color change is at least three seconds. In order to avoid color or shape related bias, all spheres have the same size and randomly selected colors having close luminances. The reason for selecting different colors for each sphere is to decrease the pop-out effect for the spheres that change color. During an animation, we have three cases of color changes. The first case is the color change of highly salient spheres, which are chosen with strong decisions of our model. In second case, among spheres having the lowest saliencies, the most distant spheres to the previously calculated gaze points are chosen. In third case, we choose the sphere in a fully random fashion. All cases are shown to the users in a mixed manner multiple times.

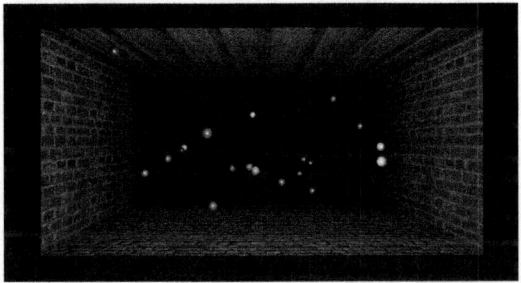

Fig. 5. Sample screenshot from the experiment

16 voluntary graduate or undergraduate level students (4 females, 12 males) whose average age is 23.75 attended to our experiment. All subjects have normal or corrected to normal vision and they are not informed about the purpose of the experiment. The experiment is introduced to the subjects as a game. In the game, to get a higher score, they should press the button as soon as possible when an object changes its color to the target color. Before starting the experiment, each subject performed a trial case to learn how to play the game.

Experiment Results. The results of the experiment can be seen in Fig. 6. We expect the response times to color changes of salient spheres to be shorter since they are expected to occur on the focus of attention. As expected, observers responded to color changes of salient spheres in a shorter time compared to those appeared on lowly salient spheres and randomly selected spheres. The differences for both cases are statistically significant ($p < 0.05$) according to the applied paired t-test.

5 Conclusion and Future Work

For motion saliency in computer animations we analyzed psychological findings on the subject by conducting an eye-tracking experiment and developed a decision theoretic approach to momentarily determine perceptually significant objects. Our observations from the experiment show that each phase of the motion has a different impact on perception. To that end, we defined six motion states and assigned attention values to them by considering their dominance. Individual attention values are determined for each object by considering their

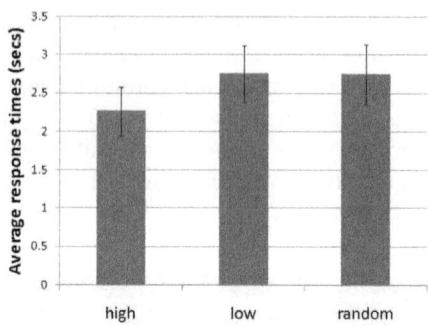

Fig. 6. The results of the experiment. Error bars show the 95% confidence intervals.

current state and elapsed time after a state initialization to include the impact of IOR. We elaborated our model by including the relationships of the objects on the scene with each other using Gestalt principles. Overall model makes decisions for the most salient object and its position is predicted as the gaze point. We carried-out a final experiment to evaluate the effectiveness of decisions our model make.

One of the limitations of our approach is the consideration of only bottom-up and stimulus-driven attention like most of other saliency works. Our final experiment had promising results although it included a simple task for users to search. On the other hand, more complex tasks could remove the effect of motion saliency. The model should be evaluated with further experiments and improved by the impact of new task-dependent cases. Furthermore, motion saliency and other object based saliency methods considering object material and shape should be compared. In our model we only consider saliency caused by motion. Dominancy of other saliency parameters on motion saliency is not evaluated in this paper.

Acknowledgments. We thank Funda Yildirim, Sukru Torun, and Bengu Kevinc for their help during our study. Also, we are grateful to all subjects attended to our experiment. This work is supported by the Scientific and Technical Research Council of Turkey (TUBITAK, Project number: 110E029).

References

1. Abrams, R.A., Christ, S.E.: Motion onset captures attention. Psychological Science 14, 427–432 (2003)
2. Andersen, R.A.: Neural mechanisms of visual motion perception in primates. Neuron 26, 776–788 (1997)
3. Arnheim, R.: Art and Visual Perception, pp. 50–60. University of California Press (1954)
4. Bulbul, A., Koca, C., Capin, T., Güdükbay, U.: Saliency for animated meshes with material properties. In: Proceedings of the 7th Symposium on Applied Perception in Graphics and Visualization (APGV 2010), pp. 81–88. ACM, New York (2010)

5. Daly, S.: Engineering observations from spatiovelocity and spatiotemporal visual Models. In: Proc. SPIE, vol. 3299, pp. 180–191 (1998)
6. Halit, C., Capin, T.: Multiscale motion saliency for keyframe extraction from motion capture sequences. Computer Animation and Virtual Worlds 22(1), 3–14 (2011)
7. Hillstrom, A.P., Yantis, S.: Visual motion and attentional capture. Perception - Psychophysics 55(4), 399–411 (1994)
8. Itti, L., Koch, C., Niebur, E.: A model of saliency-based visual attention for rapid scene analysis. IEEE Transactions on Pattern Analysis and Machine Intelligence 20(11), 1254–1259 (1998)
9. Kelly, D.H.: Motion and vision II. Stabilized spatio-temporal threshold surface. J. Opti. Soci. Ameri. 69(10), 1340–1349 (1979)
10. Koffka, K.: Principles of Gestalt psychology, pp. 106–177. Harcourt Brace, New York (1935)
11. Lee, C.H., Varshney, A., Jacobs, D.W.: Mesh saliency. In: ACM SIGGRAPH 2005, pp. 659–666. ACM, New York (2005)
12. Livingstone, M.: Vision and Art: The Biology of Seeing. ABRAMS, 46–67 (2002)
13. Peters, R.J., Itti, L.: Computational mechanisms for gaze direction in interactive visual environments. In: Proceedings of the 2006 Symposium on Eye Tracking Research & Applications (ETRA 2006), pp. 27–32. ACM, New York (2006)
14. Posner, M., Cohen, Y.: Components of visual orienting. In: Attention and Performance X, pp. 531–556 (1984)
15. Torriente, I., Valdes-Sosa, M., Ramirez, D., Bobes, M.: Vision evoked potentials related to motion onset are modulated by attention. Visual Research 39, 4122–4139 (1999)
16. Yantis, S., Hillstrom, A.P.: Stimulus driven attentional capture: Evidence from equiluminant visual objects. Journal of Experimental Psychology: Human Perception and Performance 20, 95–107 (1994)
17. Yee, H., Pattanaik, S., Greenberg, D.P.: Spatiotemporal sensitivity and visual attention for efficient rendering of dynamic environments. ACM Transactions on Graphics 20(1), 39–65 (2001)

Many-Core Architecture Oriented Parallel Algorithm Design for Computer Animation

Yong Cao

Department of Computer Science, Virginia Tech
yongcao@vt.edu

Abstract. Many-core architecture has become an emerging and widely adopted platform for parallel computing. Computer animation researches can harness this advance in high performance computing with better understanding of the architecture and careful consideration of several important parallel algorithm design issues, such as computation-to-core mapping, load balancing and algorithm design paradigms. In this paper, we use a set of algorithms in computer animation as the examples to illustrate these issues, and provide possible solutions for handling them. We have shown in our previous research projects that the proposed solutions can greatly enhance the performance of the parallel algorithms.

1 Introduction

The research of parallel computing has a long history and certainly is not new to the computer animation community. However, because of restricted access and lack of tools, computer animation researchers are reluctant to use supercomputers, on which most of parallel computing research focuses in the past few decades. In recent years, especially after the emergence of multi-core CPUs and many-core graphics processing units (GPUs), the situation has been changed. The computational power of a desktop machine is equivalent to the top supercomputers from ten years ago. Provided with these commoditized and easily accessible desktop supercomputers, all research fields in computer science are now embracing new opportunities for significant performance increase for their applications. At the same time, however, we also face a tremendous research challenge: *How to redesign all of our existing sequential algorithms towards a massive parallel architecture?*

Computer animation researchers, as part of the computer graphics community, may be ahead of some other research fields in terms of experiencing parallel algorithm design on GPUs, since GPUs were originally developed to enhance the performance of computer graphics applications. For example, the canonical smooth skinning algorithm for character animation has a standard GPU implementation using Vertex Shaders, and has been widely used in video games. However, after the release of the general proposal computing architecture for GPUs around 2006 (NVIDIA's GeForce 8 series), shader programming suddenly lost advantages for parallel algorithm design for general purpose animation algorithms. People have also realized that the traditional parallel programming models for shared memory systems should not be directly applied towards this emerging many-core architecture. Instead, a set of parallel algorithm design issues, such as problem decomposition and load balancing, should be addressed during the algorithm design process for the computer animation algorithms.

In this paper, I first describe some key features of the current many-core parallel computing architecture, and elaborate on the trend of development for such architecture in the near future. Some important parallel algorithm design issues will then be discussed using some well-known animation algorithms as the examples. I, then, provide a set of solutions as the results of my recent work to address these design issues. At the end, the paper is concluded with some suggestions on the new research frontiers for parallel algorithm design in computer animation.

2 Parallel Computing on Many-Core Architecture

The idea of parallel computing and concurrent execution appeared during the 50's of the last century. The parallel computing research, especially on supercomputers, boomed in 70's and 80's. Many different parallel architectures were introduced, parallel algorithm design strategies were explored, and parallel algorithm analysis models were developed. However, many research areas, including computer animation, did not invest much into the parallel computing and algorithm design research, because the supercomputer resources were limited, and for their applications, a fast single processor are sufficient in most research cases. People were satisfied with the rate of the growth in computational power of CPUs stated in the Moores Law. A nearly doubled performance of the algorithm without any major revision of the code was a comfortable situation of most of applications.

During an interview in 2005, Gordon Moore stated that the law cannot last forever. Intel also gave a prediction that end will come soon due to quantum tunneling, which will flatten the increase rate of the density of transistors on an IC chip. Since then, there is a sudden change in the strategies for CPU development: no more clock speed increases, but more processing cores on a chip. The free lunch of automatic performance increase of an application is over. For any application, if the performance needs significant improvement, a major revision of the source code is necessary to transfer the algorithm from sequential execution to parallel execution.

The development of GPUs is ahead of such trend in CPUs, because, as a coprocessor for graphics processing, GPUs have already adopted a massive parallel architecture. However, before the appearance of general purpose GPUs, the application areas were very limited because the architecture can only be accessed by graphics programming libraries and, more importantly, GPUs were strictly designed for a small set of data-parallel algorithms.

The renaissance of GPU computing started with the release of NVIDIA's GeForce 8 series GPUs and general programming framework, CUDA. The researchers outside of the computer graphics community soon realized that the commoditized GPUs can be an significant accelerator for certainly data-parallel algorithms, and the parallel implementation of these algorithms is trivial when using C-language based CUDA programming framework. Many data parallel applications, such as image processing and physics-based simulation, have reported a 50X or more than 100X of performance speedup on GPUs. On the other hand, researchers also found that some other non-data-parallel algorithms, such as quick-sort, cannot achieve a large performance gain with a direct algorithm mapping towards GPUs. Sometimes, such algorithms will result a slow-down in performance on GPUs.

In the rest of this section, I first present some key features of the current generation many-core architectures. Then, I point out several important parallel algorithm design issues for such architecture.

2.1 Many-Core Architecture

The concept of many-core is derived from multi-core architecture in CPU hardware design. There is no standard definition for many-core architecture. A commonly accepted description of many-core is its comparison against multi-core: *the number of processing cores on the same IC chip is too large that a multi-core technologies will fail to efficient deliver instructions and data to all the cores.* Therefore, the processing cores of a many-core system are normally designed as a much simplified version of the cores in multi-core systems. There is no support for advanced processing controls, such as branch prediction, instruction pre-fetching, and micro-instruction pipelining.

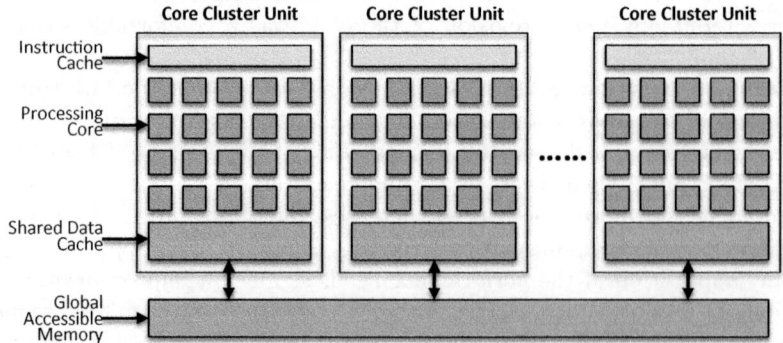

Fig. 1. A high-level overview of a many-core parallel architecture

To manage a large number of cores in a many-core system, the cores are grouped together into higher level cluster units (called as stream multiprocessors in NVIDIA GPUs), as shown in Figure 1, so that the complexity for controlling these cores can be simplified. The control inside each cluster unit is as simple as the control of a vector processor: pure data parallel processing. There is normally only one instruction fetching unit for each cluster unit, and all the cores inside a cluster unit concurrently execute the same instruction on different data. For diverged branching instructions between the cores inside a cluster unit (e.g. core 1 takes one branch, core 2 takes another), the execution will simply be sequentialized.

The complex management of the parallel execution are not focused on the core level, but on the cluster unit level, where asynchronized communication and task-parallel execution are supported. Such high-level control is essential for developing efficient parallel algorithms, because overlapped computation between processing cores can be managed.

Many-core system uses a shared memory architecture for communication between processing cores. A shared data cache inside a cluster unit is used for the communications between the cores inside a cluster unit. A global accessible memory, normally a slower DDR memory, is used for communication between the cores on different cluster units. Since both shared data cache and global memory can be accessed concurrently, some parallel access designs are normally applied to the memory hardware. Such memory architecture design normally favors a large memory bandwidth, but not a short latency.

2.2 Algorithm Design Issues for Many-Core Architecture

Due to the architecture design of the many-core architecture, especially the parallel memory access hardware, a certain type of algorithms, data parallel algorithms, execute much faster than the others. The common characteristics of a data-parallel algorithm include SIMD execution, little data dependency, and few branches. It is often reported that a large performance speedup can be achieved when porting a data-parallel algorithm from a single-core computing architecture to a many-core parallel architecture.

In computer animation, we have some algorithms express the features of data-parallel computation. For example, video-based tracking and image processing algorithms are widely used character animation. In one of our early projects [11], as shown in Figure 2, we analyzed a parallel video-based character tracking algorithm, called *Vector Coherence Mapping* (VCM), and implemented towards NVIDIA GPUs using CUDA programming framework. VCM includes three major processing steps: interest point extraction, normal correlation map (NCM) computation, and VCM computation. The operations used in these steps are mostly data parallel algorithms, such as image convolution, sub-image correlation, and image accumulation. By accelerating these operations on GPUs, we had an over 40 times of performance speedup compared against a CPU implementation.

However, data-parallel algorithms only represent a small portion of the algorithms used in computer animation. It has been shown that, without careful algorithm design and optimization, the many-core implementation of task parallel algorithms, such as quick-sort, does not guaranty a large performance increase on GPUs [7,15]. Intel also pointed out that, only applying standard optimization strategies on GPUs can only get an average of 2.5X speedup compared with the implementations on a Intel's CPU [13].

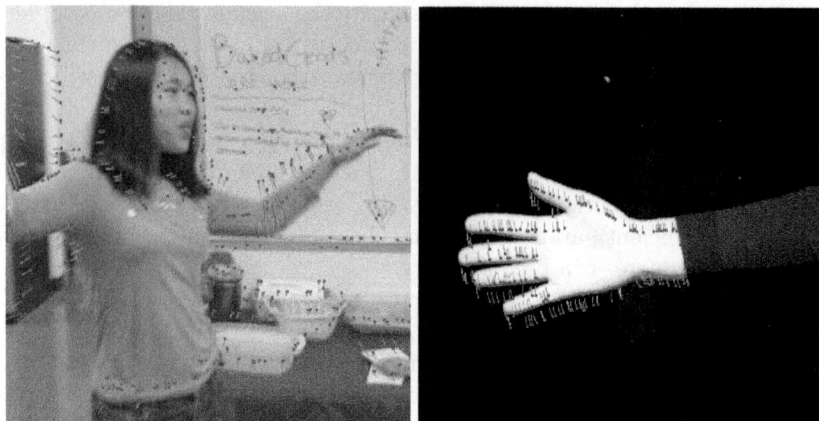

Fig. 2. The processing results of the GPU-accelerated motion tracking algorithm, VCM. Left: Girl dancing with camera zooming in. Right: Hand moving up.

Designing an algorithm towards many-core architecture is not a simple Implementation and porting work. The process involves the consideration of many different parallel computing issues. Often, the newly developed parallel algorithm is a complete transformation of its sequential counterpart. For computer animation research, there are a few important parallel algorithm design issues, as listed below, need to be considered carefully when a sequential algorithm is optimized on a many-core architecture.

1. *Problem decomposition and resource utilization.*
2. *Load balancing.*
3. *Algorithm design paradigm.*

In the next three sections, I will discuss these issues in detailed by using some example algorithms in computer animation.

3 Problem Decomposition and Resource Utilization

The concurrent execution of different tasks among all available computational resources is the key issue in parallel computing. If the resources, especially the processing cores, are under-utilized, the performance loss will occur. In parallel algorithm design, the issue is normally addressed by problem decomposition. In general, if a processing architecture has N cores, the problem should be decomposed into more than N (often multiple of N) sub-tasks. Each processing core is assigned with at least one sub-task, and no core is left idle.

In some scenarios, the size of problem is dynamically changing and unpredictable. Therefore, a static problem decomposition scheme can not optimize the final number of sub-tasks for better resource utilization.

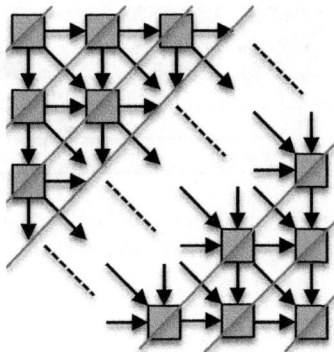

Fig. 3. The data dependency graph for an example dynamic programming algorithm. The diagonal lines in orange indicate the sweeping frontier for each computation step. All the nodes along these sweeping diagonal lines can be executed in parallel.

For example, as being used in a motion graph algorithm [2,3], dynamic programming usually features a "slow-start" initial processing phase. In Figure 3, we illustrate the data dependencies for all the computation of an example dynamic programming algorithm. Because the dependency, the concurrent computation can only occur among the sub-tasks among the diagonal lines, starting at the top-left corner. We can sweep the computation diagonally from top-left to bottom right, each time executing the sub-tasks along a sweeping line in parallel. It is obvious that, the concurrently executed sub-tasks will increase until reaching the half-way point of the whole computation, and will decrease after. This is a typical slow-start and slow-end problem. The question is how to increase the resource utilization rate at the beginning and the end of the computation, where only very few sub-tasks are available for N cores to finish.

The solution to the resource under-utilization problem is to apply a dynamic problem decomposition scheme based on the problem size. It is also call adaptive computation-to-core mapping. The main idea is to adjust the granularity of the problem decomposition in an adaptive fashion: when more processing cores are available (resource under-utilization), the sub-tasks can be decomposed into even smaller tasks so that the total number of sub-tasks for parallel execution is increased and all the cores will be utilized. However, we also do not want to create too many sub-tasks because of the high management cost.

Some other widely used algorithms in computer animation also expressed a slow-start or slow-end feature, such as breadth-first graph search and multi-resolution analysis. Adaptive computation-to-core mapping can be directly used in these algorithms. In one of our previous work for parallel temporal data mining [6], we have developed a hybrid solution to incorporate two different computation-to-core mapping schemes, and got a result of 263% performance increase when compared with a standard many-core implementation.

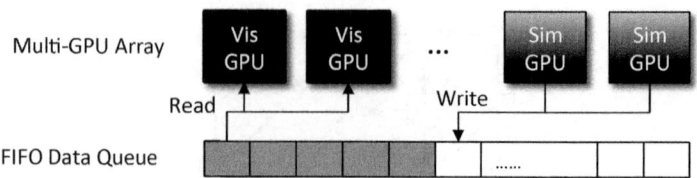

Fig. 4. A distributed task scheduling framework for balancing the workload between visualization and simulation on a multi-GPU architecture

4 Load Balancing

In some data-parallel algorithms and most task-parallel algorithms, such as animation or simulation Level Of Detail (LOD), the concurrently executed sub-tasks have different workload. Some sub-tasks can finish much earlier than the others. It can cause a significant performance loss because a processing core for executing a early completed sub-task has to wait until all other cores finish their tasks before continuing with the next task.

In many-core architecture, load-balancing problem can result in significant performance loss. The main cause of workload imbalance is due to the branching statements in the algorithm, which many-core architecture can not handle efficiently. If a branching statement causes a diverged execution between two cores in a core cluster unit, as shown in Figure 1, the execution of all diverged instructions has to be sequentialized, because a core cluster unit only has one instruction dispatch unit. In addition, if one branch takes much long to finish than another, non-balanced workload will cause further performance loss. For example, in agent-based crowd simulation algorithms, all agents are simulated concurrently. But there are some types of agents, such as leader agents, can take much heavier workload than the others.

Load balancing problem has been well studied in parallel computing research before many-core parallel architecture. The common strategies to resolve the problem, as listed below, can also be applied to many-core architecture.

1. Divide the subtasks into smaller ones to eliminate significant workload difference.
2. Group subtasks according to the workload, and assign the subtasks with similar amount of workload to the same core cluster unit.
3. Apply a distributed task scheduler for each processing core, so that after the completion of one subtask, it can immediately fetch the next subtask from a task pool.

The first two solutions are based on the static analysis of the algorithm. The last one, which is a run-time solution and more general than first two, is a very challenging solution one for many-core architectures. Distributed task control is commonly used strategy in supercomputers for task scheduling, where each processing unit coordinates with a global task pool to schedule its own

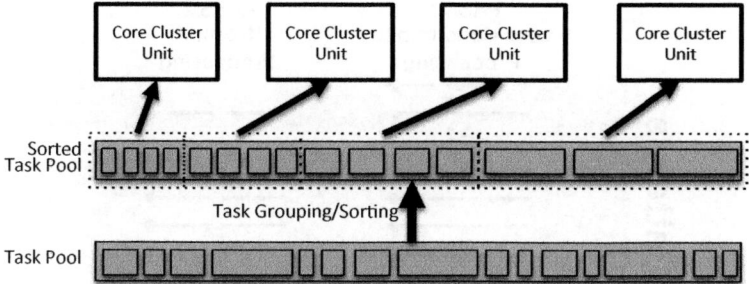

Fig. 5. A revised distributed task scheduling framework for many-core architectures, where the tasks in the task-pool are sorted first. The tasks with similar workload are submitted to core cluster unit for parallel execution.

execution of tasks. The strategy is an efficient solution for balancing the workload between core cluster units, and multiple many-core devices. For example, in one of our previous work [10], as shown in Figure 4, we used a data queue as the central task pool to schedule and balance the computation on multiple GPUs. A simulation task is assigned to a GPU when there is an empty slot in the queue. A visualization task reads the data queue and is assigned to a GPU to visualize the simulation result. The task scheduling criteria is based on the status of the data queue and performance history.

However, within a core cluster unit, such strategy will results in more divergent branching instructions, causing the sequentialized execution in the unit. To circumvent the problem in many-core architecture, the distributed task scheduler should be combined with subtask grouping methods to reduce divergent branching and load imbalance inside a core cluster unit. Since task scheduling inside a core cluster unit does not provide any meaningful performance gain, the sub-tasks with similar workload and the same instructions are sorted and grouped together before submitted to the same core cluster unit, as shown in Figure 5.

5 Algorithm Design Paradigm

It is a creative process to brainstorm new ideas for parallelize existing sequential algorithms. It is even more challenging to design entirely new parallel algorithms for certain problems. Such process should be guided by a set of design paradigms which are used to shape the mind of the design. For example, in traditional sequential algorithm design, when a search-based problem is presented, we instantly refer to some solution templates, such as divide-and-conquer, depth first search, and generic algorithms. Such design paradigms greatly simplify the process of algorithm design, and also enables the parallel implementation of some algorithm libraries, including Standard Template Library (STL).

In parallel algorithm design, there are some well-known design paradigms, such as Map-Reduce [8], which has been widely adopted in many-core algorithm

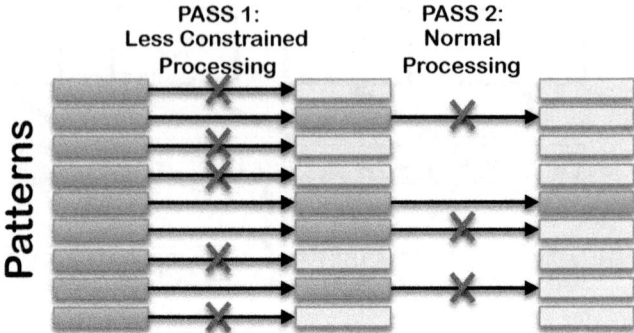

Fig. 6. An example of deferred computing: Pattern Elimination. In the first pass, most of the none-qualified patterns are eliminated by a less constrained and simple process. In the second pass, much less patterns needs to be processed by a complex elimination step.

design [16,4,9]. Since many-core system is an emerging architecture, we are expecting more parallel design paradigms being developed for this architecture.

In one of our previous work [14,5], we developed a very efficient parallel processing paradigm, which can be used in many computer animation algorithms. The paradigm, called *deferred computing*, divides the overall copmutation into several stages. The first several stages are for data preparation or analysis, and can be significantly accelerated in many-core architecture. The major computation of the problem is deferred to the last stage. By using the results from the preparation and analysis stages, the computation of the last stage can be far more efficient than before. In such deferred computing scheme, the overall computation for the problem is often larger than the original algorithm. However, due to the execution time saved at the last stage, the overall performance is actually increased.

To give an example, let us consider a problem to eliminate none-qualified patterns from a large array of candidate patterns [5]. Since the qualifying process for each pattern is the same for all candidate patterns, we can simply parallelize the processing of each pattern on each core. However, the qualifying process is very complex. The execution of the process on each core is not very efficient, due to some memory accessing constraints and the branching instructions in the process. We divide the qualifying processing into two passes, as shown in Figure 6. The first pass uses simplified constrains to process the patterns in parallel, where most of the memory constraints and branching instructions are removed in this pass. We found that the first pass can eliminate more than 90% of none-qualified patterns with its less constrained process, and can be executed much efficiently on many-core architectures. The second pass operates on the undetermined patterns from the first pass using a normal qualifying process. Since the left-over patterns for the second pass is very few and the first pass is very efficient, the overall performance of the two-pass elimination approach can be more than two times faster than the original one-pass algorithm.

6 Future Development Directions

Many-core architecture is currently in a rapid development era. Many vendors are proposing and releasing new many-core based products. GPU venders, including NVIDIA and ATI, are aiming at more processing cores and complex control logic to enable task-parallel processing. For example, NVIDIA's recent GPU architecture, code name "Fermi", starts to support up to 16 different kernel functions in a GPU simultaneously. Such feature allows the programmers to parallelize different instructions among the core cluster units.

Another important advance in many-core architecture has been proposed by CPU venders, including both Intel and AMD. In their recent release, Intel's Sandy Bridge CPUs [12] and AMD's Fusion APUs [1] both focus on a tightly integrated heterogeneous system, where a multi-core CPU, a many-core GPU and the memory controls (or L1 cache) are put on the same IC chip. Such design significantly reduces the communication overhead between the CPU and GPU, which was a large performance bottleneck for the most GPU-based parallel computing applications.

The advance also casts a spotlight on a already popular research direction for high performance computing, hybrid computing, where computational tasks are co-scheduled among a heterogeneous computing architecture. In hybrid computing, problems are analyzed and decomposed into sub-tasks based on their computational profiles. The sub-tasks suitable for data parallel processing are assigned to the GPU, and the sub-tasks suitable for task parallel processing are assigned to the CPU. Some central and distributed control is applied to synchronize the processing among these sub-tasks and computational resources. With a much improved architecture for inter-communication between CPUs and GPUs, hybrid computing research is embracing a booming period.

In computer animation researches, it is often that we have a very complex system including a variety of algorithms, which express totally different computational profiles. Therefore, the ability of concurrently executing these algorithms on their desired devices in a heterogeneous architecture will bring a significant performance gain. However, in my opinion, we are still in the stone-age for hybrid computing for computer animation applications. We need to focus on the algorithm design issues towards many-core architecture and hybrid computing.

7 Conclusion

Computer animation, like the other application areas in computer science, is facing the new era of parallel computing. With the rapid development of many-core architectures, such as GPUs, the research in parallel algorithm design for computer animation has already fallen behind. Given that almost every computer has adopted a parallel processing architecture, there is no coming back to the world of sequential algorithm design. In this paper, we have discussed several important parallel computing design issues for many-core architectures, including resource utilization, load balancing and algorithm design paradigms.

In my previous research, I have shown that careful consideration of these issues can greatly enhance the performance of the parallel algorithms.

Parallel algorithm design is not only for the scholars in the area of computing theory or high performance computing. It is also important for computer animation community to evaluate the algorithms in our applications, to analyze the time complexity of a proposed algorithm, and to discuss the scalability issues for a parallel implementation. We need to develop a set of software frameworks to facilitate the parallel implementation of computer animation applications based on such effort. We will be able to handle much larger scale problems and significantly increase the performance of the computer animation applications.

References

1. AMD: Fusion family of apus,
   http://sites.amd.com/us/fusion/apu/Pages/fusion.aspx
2. Arikan, O., Forsyth, D.A.: Interactive motion generation from examples. ACM Trans. Graph. 21(3), 483–490 (2002)
3. Arikan, O., Forsyth, D.A., O'Brien, J.F.: Motion synthesis from annotations. In: ACM SIGGRAPH 2003 Papers, SIGGRAPH 2003, pp. 402–408. ACM, New York (2003), http://doi.acm.org/10.1145/1201775.882284
4. Bakkum, P., Skadron, K.: Accelerating sql database operations on a gpu with cuda. In: Proceedings of the 3rd Workshop on General-Purpose Computation on Graphics Processing Units, GPGPU 2010, pp. 94–103. ACM, New York (2010), http://doi.acm.org/10.1145/1735688.1735706
5. Cao, Y., Patnaik, D., Ponce, S., Archuleta, J., Butler, P., chun Feng, W., Ramakrishnan, N.: Towards chip-on-chip neuroscience: Fast mining of frequent episodes using graphics processors. Tech. rep., arXiv.org (2009)
6. Cao, Y., Patnaik, D., Ponce, S., Archuleta, J., Butler, P., chun Feng, W., Ramakrishnan, N.: Towards chip-on-chip neuroscience: Fast mining of neuronal spike streams using graphics hardware. In: CF 2010: Proceedings of the 7th ACM International Conference on Computing Frontiers, May 17 - 19, pp. 1–10, No. 978-1-4503-0044-5. ACM, Bertinoro (2010)
7. Cederman, D., Tsigas, P.: Gpu-quicksort: A practical quicksort algorithm for graphics processors. J. Exp. Algorithmics 14, 4:1.4–4:1.24 (2010), http://doi.acm.org/10.1145/1498698.1564500
8. Dean, J., Ghemawat, S.: Mapreduce: simplified data processing on large clusters. Commun. ACM 51, 107–113 (2008), http://doi.acm.org/10.1145/1327452.1327492
9. Fang, W., He, B., Luo, Q., Govindaraju, N.K.: Mars: Accelerating mapreduce with graphics processors. IEEE Trans. Parallel Distrib. Syst. 22, 608–620 (2011), http://dx.doi.org/10.1109/TPDS.2010.158
10. Hagan, R., Cao, Y.: Multi-gpu load balancing for in-situ visualization. In: The 2011 International Conference on Parallel and Distributed Processing Techniques and Applications (to appear in, 2011)
11. Huang, J., Ponce, S., Park, S.I., Cao, Y., Quek, F.: Gpu-accelerated computation for robust motion tracking using the cuda framework. In: VIE 2008 - The 5th IET Visual Information Engineering 2008 Conference, July 29 - August 1, pp. 437–442 (2008)

12. Intel: Sandy bridge architecture,
    http://www.intel.com/content/www/us/en/processors/core/core-i5-processor.html
13. Lee, V.W., Kim, C., Chhugani, J., Deisher, M., Kim, D., Nguyen, A.D., Satish, N., Smelyanskiy, M., Chennupaty, S., Hammarlund, P., Singhal, R., Dubey, P.: Debunking the 100x gpu vs. cpu myth: an evaluation of throughput computing on cpu and gpu. In: Proceedings of the 37th Annual International Symposium on Computer Architecture, ISCA 2010, pp. 451–460. ACM, New York (2010), http://doi.acm.org/10.1145/1815961.1816021
14. Patnaik, D., Ponce, S.P., Cao, Y., Ramakrishnan, N.: Accelerator-oriented algorithm transformation for temporal data mining, pp. 93–100. IEEE Computer Society, Los Alamitos (2009)
15. Sengupta, S., Harris, M., Zhang, Y., Owens, J.D.: Scan primitives for gpu computing. In: Proceedings of the 22nd ACM SIGGRAPH/EUROGRAPHICS Symposium on Graphics Hardware, GH 2007, pp. 97–106. Eurographics Association, Aire-la-Ville (2007), http://dl.acm.org/citation.cfm?id=1280094.1280110
16. Stuart, J.A., Chen, C.K., Ma, K.L., Owens, J.D.: Multi-gpu volume rendering using mapreduce. In: Proceedings of the 19th ACM International Symposium on High Performance Distributed Computing, HPDC 2010, pp. 841–848. ACM, New York (2010), http://doi.acm.org/10.1145/1851476.1851597

Twisting, Tearing and Flicking Effects in String Animations

Witawat Rungjiratananon[1], Yoshihiro Kanamori[2], Napaporn Metaaphanon[3], Yosuke Bando[4], Bing-Yu Chen[5], and Tomoyuki Nishita[1]

[1] The University of Tokyo
[2] University of Tsukuba
[3] Square Enix
[4] TOSHIBA Corporation
[5] National Taiwan University

Abstract. String-like objects in our daily lives including shoelaces, threads and rubber cords exhibit interesting behaviors such as twisting, tearing and bouncing back when pulled and released. In this paper, we present a method that enables these behaviors in traditional string simulation methods that explicitly represent a string by particles and segments. We offer the following three contributions. First, we introduce a method for handling twisting effects with both uniform and non-uniform torsional rigidities. Second, we propose a method for estimating the tension acting in inextensible objects in order to reproduce tearing and flicking (bouncing back); whereas the tension for an *extensible* object can be easily computed via its stretched length, the length of an *inextensible* object is maintained constant in general, and thus we need a novel approach. Third, we introduce an optimized grid-based collision detection for an efficient computation of collisions. We demonstrate that our method allows visually plausible animations of string-like objects made of various materials and is a fast framework for interactive applications such as games.

1 Introduction

String-like deformable objects play an important role to represent hair strands, threads, elastic rods, cables and ropes in computer graphics. For realistic animations of such objects, we have to reproduce their interesting behaviors such as bending, stretching, twisting, tearing and flicking when pulled and released, according to their material properties. For example, threads are made of yarn that is barely stretched but easy to tear. An elastic rod made of rubber can be twisted and flicked but hard to break. A cable that has non-uniform density distribution within its cross-section or a partially braided rope such as fourragère has a non-uniform torsional rigidity. In the rest of this paper, we refer to such string-like objects as *strings*.

To simulate a string, several traditional methods can be used such as mass-spring systems [13,15], rigid multi-body serial chains [7], geometric approaches

[12,14] and elastic energy-based models [3,17,2]. However, all behaviors (twisting, tearing and flicking) of a string are not introduced together in a single framework by these methods.

Handling of inextensible strings, such as threads and cables, poses another technical challenge. To prevent inextensible strings from excessive elongation, many length-constraint schemes called *strain limiting* have been developed. With strain limiting, however, the tearing simulation becomes difficult; whereas an *extensible* string will break when its length or strain reaches a certain breaking point, we cannot see when an *inextensible* string will tear based on the constrained length. Moreover, beside the fact that an inextensible string is not elongated by their own weight, under a large applied force such as a large pulling force, the string should be elongated according to its material property. However, the strain limiting causes the material property unrelated to the applied force.

In this paper, we present a method that can handle twisting, tearing and flicking of strings in real-time. Our method is a simple pseudo-physically-based model which is easy to implement, yet visually plausible results can still be achieved. Our method is applicable to traditional simulation methods that explicitly represent a string by particles and segments. Our implementation is based on *Chain Shape Matching* (CSM) [14], which is a simplified version of the more versatile deformation method, *Lattice Shape Matching* (LSM) [12], since CSM inherits and enhances several advantages of LSM (e.g. CSM is fast, easy to implement and numerically stable). Specifically, we offer the following three contributions:

1. We introduce a simple method for twisting effects by adding twisting angles into each segment in a string which can handle both uniform and non-uniform torsional rigidities (Sec. 4).
2. We propose a method for estimating the tension for tearing and flicking effects in an inextensible string whose actual stress and strain values are constrained from the strain limiting (Sec. 5).
3. We introduce a collision searching scheme for efficient collision handling using a grid-based data structure which has a less number of neighbors to be searched compared to typical searching schemes. (Sec. 6).

2 Related Work

Simulation of Twisting Strings: Many researches on the twisting effect in string simulation introduced various models for solving the Cosserat and Kirchhoff energy equations. Bertails *et al.* [3] introduced a mechanical model called *super helices* for simulating human hair based on the Kirchhoff theory. However, handling collision responses is not straightforward due to the implicit representation of hair strands. Spillmann and Teschner [17] explicitly represented the centerline of an elastic string and used the finite element method (FEM) to solve the Cosserat energy equation. Recently, Bergou *et al.* [2] introduced a discrete model for simulating elastic strings based on the Kirchhoff theory. However, the twisting angles are computed using quasi-static assumption, thus the twisting of non-uniform torsional rigidity along the string is not addressed. There are

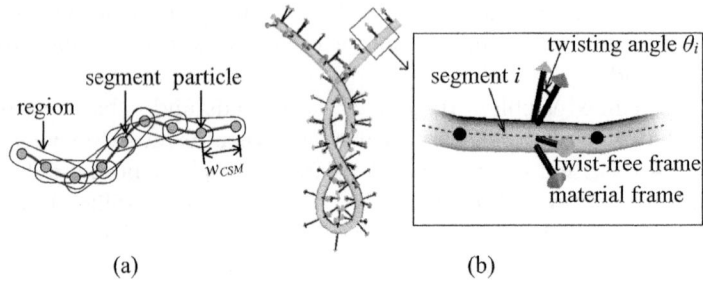

Fig. 1. Our string model. (a) Multiple overlapping chain region in CSM. (b) A twisting angle of a segment of an elastic string is an angle between a twist-free frame and a material frame.

also several works on pseudo-physical models that can capture the twisting effect without solving the energy equations. Hadap [7] introduced a model for capturing the torsion effect by integrating a torsion spring into each joint of rigid links. However, strings cannot be stretched and collision handling is not straightforward, because motion is propagated from top to bottom in one single pass (not affect backward). Selle *et al.* [15] represented a hair strand by a chain of tetrahedrons of springs and captured the torsion effect by introducing appropriate altitude springs. However, the configuration of springs is complex, auxiliary particles are required along a string.

Strain Limiting for Inextensible Strings: In order to handle inextensible objects simulated by deformation models, a variety of methods for stretch resistance have been continuously proposed; from Provot's iterative post-processing edge constraint [11], to a more recent constraint method based on impulse [5]. Some alternative ways of stabilizing stiff simulation were also proposed [1,10,6]. These methods, and many of their sequels, have a common goal to limit the maximal strain to a certain threshold. Accordingly, these kinds of methods are problematic in case of excessive stretch or when rupture should occur. Metaaphanon *et al.* [9] proposed a method to deal with cloth tearing using a mass-spring model. However, it tears cloth by checking lengths of springs; when and where yarns of cloth are cut were not directly related to user-applied external forces and cloth material properties, but dependent on how the method constrains the springs.

3 Chain Shape Matching (CSM)

Before describing the details of our algorithms, this section first briefly introduces *Chain Shape Matching* (CSM) [14], the basis model used in this paper. In CSM, a string is represented as a chain of particles connected by segments (see Fig. 1 (a)). The particles are grouped into multiple overlapping *chain regions* with the *region half-width* $w_{CSM} \in \{1, 2, 3, \ldots\}$. The chain region half-width corresponds to the stiffness of the string. The particles are independently moved by external

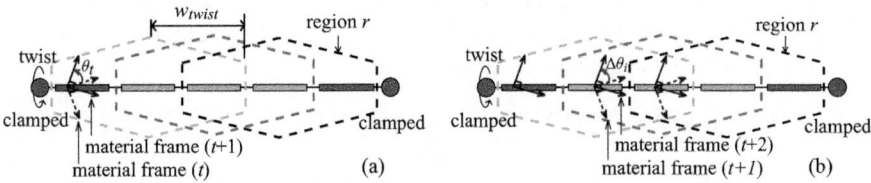

Fig. 2. (a) An elastic string clamped at both ends is twisted at one end with a twisting angle θ_t. (b) The increment of the twisting angle is propagated to next segments.

forces, and then an optimal rigid transformation (i.e., rotation and translation) of each region is computed. The rigidly-transformed positions of the particles are called *goal positions*. The goal position of each particle is weighed in the overlapping regions by *particle per-region mass*. Finally, each particle is updated toward the goal position.

4 Twisting Effects

Based on CSM, a string in our model is represented as a chain of $(n+1)$ particles connected by n segments (Fig. 1 (a)). A segment $i \in \{1, 2, \ldots, n\}$ has a twisting angle θ_i tracking how much the segment is twisted. The twisting angle can be represented as an angle between a *twist-free frame* (*bishop frame*) and a *material frame* (Fig. 1 (b)). In the initial state, we specify an initial angle θ_i^0 of each segment i according to the shape of the string. The twisting angle is assigned for each segment, not for each particle, to avoid the ambiguity.

The behavior of twisting can be clearly observed when a string clamped at both ends is twisted at one end. Therefore, we use this scenario for our explanation (Fig. 2). When we twist one clamped end with an angle θ_t, the angle θ_i of the segment is increased. The increment of the twisting angle of the segment is propagated to the next segments in order to minimize the elastic energy. We compute a goal twisting angle for each segment, similarly to finding a goal position for each particle in shape matching.

First, we group the segments into multiple overlapping chain regions with the region half-width $w_{twist} \in \{1, 2, 3, \ldots\}$ which affects the propagation speed of twisting angles in the string; the larger the w_{twist} is, the faster the change of twisting angles is propagated. The size of each region in a string can be varied for handling non-uniform torsional rigidity. The twisting angle increment $\Delta\theta_k^{region}$ of each region k is computed by averaging the $\Delta\theta_j = \theta_j - \theta_j^0$ weighted by mass m_j for the set of segments within the region S_k:

$$\Delta\theta_k^{region} = \frac{\sum_{j \in S_k}(\theta_j - \theta_j^0)m_j}{\sum_{j \in S_k} m_j}. \qquad (1)$$

Then, θ_i of each segment i is updated with the twisting angle increment $\Delta\theta_i^{segment}$. The goal twisting angle increment $\Delta\theta_i^{segment}$ is calculated by summing the $\Delta\theta_k^{region}$ of each region k that segment i belongs to:

$$\Delta\theta_i^{segment} = \sum_{k \in \Re} \Delta\theta_k^{region}, \qquad (2)$$

$$\theta_i \leftarrow \theta_i + \Delta\theta_i^{segment}, \qquad (3)$$

where $\Re$ is a set of regions that segment i belongs to. The twisting force $\mathbf{f}_i^{twist}$ can be treated as an external force to particle i and derived from elastic energy equation [2] as follows:

$$\mathbf{f}_i^{twist} = \frac{\beta}{L}(\theta_{i+1} - 2\theta_i + \theta_{i-1})(\frac{-\kappa\mathbf{b}_{i+1} - \kappa\mathbf{b}_{i-1}}{2l}), \qquad (4)$$

$$\kappa\mathbf{b}_i = 2\frac{\mathbf{e}_{i-1} \times \mathbf{e}_i}{|\mathbf{e}_{i-1}||\mathbf{e}_i| + \mathbf{e}_{i-1} \cdot \mathbf{e}_i}, \qquad (5)$$

where $\kappa\mathbf{b}_i$ is the curvature binormal, $\mathbf{e}_i$ is the segment vector, l is the length of the segment, β is the twisting stiffness of the string and L is the total length of the string.

5 Tearing and Flicking Effects

This section briefly reviews the material science of a string, and then describes *strain limiting*, a technique to constrain the length of an inextensible object. Finally, we describe the way to estimate the tension in an inextensible string in order to handle tearing and flicking.

5.1 Stress and Strain

In material science, the strength and elongation of a string is associated with its stress-strain curve [4]. The stress σ of a string is the average force per unit area of a cross-section surface:

$$\sigma = \frac{\|\mathbf{F}_n\|}{A}, \qquad (6)$$

where A is the cross-sectional area and $\mathbf{F}_n$ is the normal force. The total force acts on the cross-section surface in the surface normal direction. The strain ε of a string is expressed as the ratio of the elongation ΔL to the initial length L_0 of the string:

$$\varepsilon = \frac{\Delta L}{L_0} = \frac{L - L_0}{L_0}, \qquad (7)$$

where L is the current length of the string.

Along the curve, the material exhibits elastic behaviors until the *yield point*; prior to the yield point the material will return to its original shape if the applied

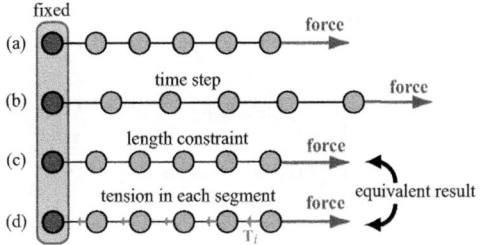

Fig. 3. A simple example of the tension computation. From (a) to (c), an ordinary length-constrained string simulation is performed. The tensions make the particles move from their unconstrained positions to the constrained positions in (d), yielding an equivalent result for (c).

force is removed. The slope of this elastic region is the *Young's modulus* $E = \sigma/\varepsilon$. Once the yield point is passed, the material becomes plastic; some fractions of the deformation will be permanent and non-reversible. As deformation continues, the material will break when the stress or strain reaches the *rupture point*.

The stress-strain curve can be derived via a strength testing of a material sample stored as a data set of the experimental result. However, the stress-strain curve of most materials in the elasticity state is linear with the Young's modulus as its slope. Therefore, the part of the curve from the origin to the yield point can be stored as a constant value. Still, the data set is required for the curve in the plasticity state. In our implementation, we simply approximate the curve by a line with a constant slope that fits the curve best. As a result, our implementation uses two constant values to represent the stress-strain curve in elasticity and plasticity states together with two constants for yield point and rupture point.

5.2 Strain Limiting

To prevent segments from stretching excessively, position constraints are imposed so that the length of each segment i does not exceed a certain threshold L_i^{max}. Since correcting the length of one segment may change the length of other segments, iterative adjustment is required. Each constraint is solved independently one after the other as done in [10].

5.3 Tension Estimation

As previously stated, due to the constraint on lengths unrelated to applied forces, actual stress and strain values cannot be directly computed from the simulation result. Here we propose a novel approach to estimate the actual stress and strain values for inextensible strings.

The actual stress and strain values can be computed by estimating the *tensions* in the string. To derive the tensions, we also consider the particle positions

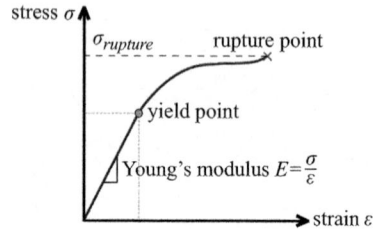

Fig. 4. Typical stress-strain curve of a string

computed *without* strain limiting. We model the *tension* $\mathbf{T}_i$ of a segment i as a stiff force that makes its particles i and $i+1$ at both ends move from their unconstrained positions $\mathbf{x}'_i$ and $\mathbf{x}'_{i+1}$ (Fig. 3 (b)) to the constrained positions $\mathbf{x}_i$ and $\mathbf{x}_{i+1}$ (Fig. 3 (c)). In our implementation, we compute the tension as follows:

$$\mathbf{T}_i = k_{stiff}(\|\mathbf{x}'_{i+1} - \mathbf{x}'_i\| - \|\mathbf{x}_{i+1} - \mathbf{x}_i\|)\mathbf{t}_i, \qquad (8)$$

where k_{stiff} is a coefficient and $\mathbf{t}_i$ is an unit vector from particle i to $i+1$. The tension derived this way is used to reproduce tearing and flicking as well as plastic behaviors of a string, as described in Sec. 5.4.

5.4 Tearing and Flicking a String

For tearing computation, we assign a rupture point or a stress threshold $\sigma_{rupture}$ for each segment. If segment's stress exceeds its stress threshold, the segment will be broken. The applied stress σ_i can be computed from tension $\mathbf{T}_i$ in each segment using Eq. (6) with $\mathbf{F}_n = \mathbf{T}_i$.

Similarly, we can handle the behavior of flicking using the tension. When an inextensible string is pulled and released or torn apart, the applied stress is vanished but the strain of the segment from the elongated length still remains. The bouncing back force can be computed from an internal stress translated from the strain by referencing the stress-strain curve (Fig. 4). However, the elongated length is computed from the tension, i.e., we can directly use the tension as the bouncing back force. Note that, without this technique, the string will just fall down quietly by the gravity force because the elongated length is very small.

As can be seen in the stress-strain curve (Fig. 4), a real string is lengthened according to the stress in the elasticity and plasticity states prior to the rupture point. Therefore, the maximum length L_i^{max} of each segment used in strain limiting (Sec. 5.2) should be updated accordingly (otherwise the string does not elongate). For this, we look up strain ε_i corresponding to applied stress σ_i from the stress-strain curve, and use it to compute the appropriate value of L_i^{max} using Eq. (7), $L_i^{max} = \varepsilon_i L_0 + L_0$. In the elasticity state, the strain ε_i of a string becomes zero when applied forces are removed. However, when its strain exceeds the yield point (plasticity state), ε_i is still the same as the last time the forces are applied. Our method also modifies the radius of a segment in order to preserve the volume of the segment when stretched.

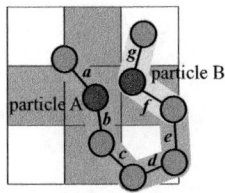

Fig. 5. A 2D example of our optimized searching scheme. When doing a collision detection between particles A and B, segment collision tests between ag, af, bg and bf capsules are tested.

6 Collision Handling

In this section, we introduce an optimized searching scheme for collision detection of strings. Previous works often use techniques based on bounding volume hierarchy (BVH) [16, 18, 15] for collision detection of strings. Apart from BVH, space partitioning using a grid-based data structure is a simple and efficient technique for collision detection of strings which have a large number of self-collisions. Specifically, we treat the segments as capsules and search for capsule collision pairs. For neighbor searches, we use a uniform grid of voxels. The number of voxels to be searched is 27 ($= 3 \times 3 \times 3$) in a naïve approach. For better performance, we found that it suffices to search for colliding segments in only seven neighboring voxels (top, bottom, left, right, front, back and center voxels) under the following three specifications.

- Specifying the voxel size equal to or larger than segment length l
- Storing indices of particles in each voxel
- Searching for capsule collision pairs from two adjacent segments of each particle in the seven neighboring voxels

For a better understanding, we describe using an example in 2D (five neighboring cells). The idea can be generalized to the 3D case in a straightforward manner. In Fig. 5, particles A and B are neighbors. Our method does the segment collision test between their two adjacent segments, i.e., pairs of segments ag, af, bg and bf. If two segments have an intersection, there is definitely a pair of particles at their both ends in the seven neighboring voxels that the intersection can be searched, even the intersection of segments is outside the seven neighboring cells. This could be easily proved, if one writes all possible cases in 2D with five neighboring cells (center, up, down, left and right).

The closest points of a pair of colliding segments i and j are indicated by fractions $s \in [0, 1]$ and $t \in [0, 1]$, respectively. In order to move the colliding segments to the non-intersection positions, we compute a displacement vector between the closest points. Then, we move the both-end particles of each segment corresponding to the fractions s and t similar to [18].

Moving a colliding segment may make the string discontinuous, and thus we repeat shape matching until particle positions converge. Conversely, shape

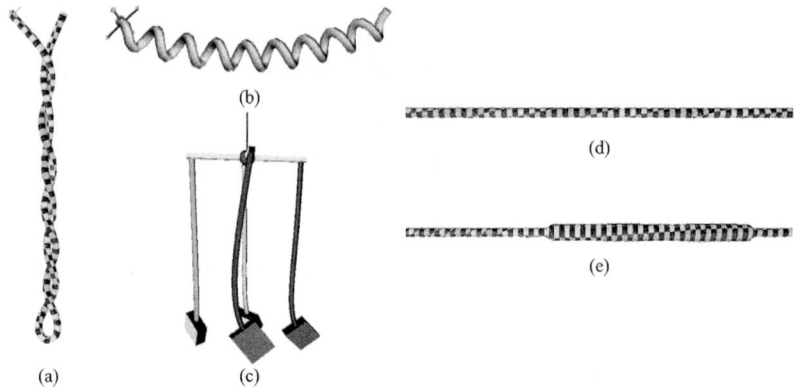

Fig. 6. Our simulation results of twisting effects. (a) The twisting effect of a string clamped at both ends. The string is gradually twisted on the left end and finally twisted to form a loop. (b) A twisted string that forms a spiral shape like a telephone cord. (c) An application for a hanging mobile in wind forces. (d) A string with uniform torsional rigidity. (e) A string with non-uniform torsional rigidity.

matching may cause a collision again. As a result, iterations are required for both shape matching and collision constraints. To lessen the iterations, we temporarily make the masses of colliding particles heavier so that shape matching barely moves the particles. In our experiments, by making the colliding particles three times heavier, only one iteration suffices.

7 Results

Our implementation was written in C++ with OpenGL. All experiments were conducted on a desktop PC with an Intel Core i7 3.20GHz CPU and 6GB RAM.

Fig. 6 shows the results of our twisting simulation. The twisting of strings can reproduce phenomena such as an instability of bending and twisting called *buckling* which makes a string to form a spiral shape (Fig. 6 (a) and (b)). An application for a hanging mobile is also presented. In Fig. 6 (c), objects at the tips of strings are rotated by wind forces and the strings are twisted. With twisting effects, the strings twist back to the rest state, making the objects rolling back and forth. Fig. 6d and Fig. 6e show the twisting of strings with uniform and non-uniform torsional rigidities, respectively. The twisting angles in the string with non-uniform torsional rigidity are distributed more equally in the larger cross-section. Fig. 7 shows the tearing simulation results with the variation of rupture thresholds. The rupture threshold is assigned to all segments in the string. However, that kind of completely uniform strength is impossible in real string. Our method randomly alters the rupture threshold in each segment with the range of variation up to 0.01%. Please see the supplemental video for more variation tests. Animation sequences of flicking are shown in Fig. 8. Without flicking,

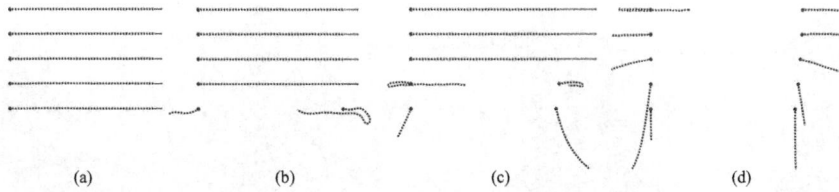

(a) (b) (c) (d)

Fig. 7. Tearing simulation results of five strings with rupture thresholds. Rupture thresholds of strings are varying, increasing from bottom to top. The rupture threshold in each segment of the string is randomly altered with the range of variation up to 0.01%. As expected, the bottommost string, which had the lowest rupture threshold, was torn first at the weakest point as animation sequences from (a) to (d).

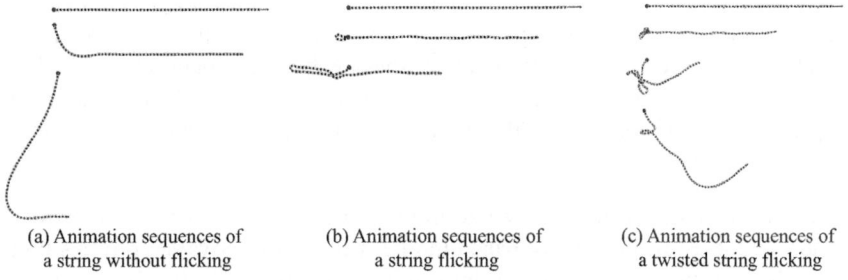

(a) Animation sequences of a string without flicking

(b) Animation sequences of a string flicking

(c) Animation sequences of a twisted string flicking

Fig. 8. Flicking animation sequences of strings from top to bottom

Table 1. The computational time in milliseconds of each process in one time step. The time step in our implementation is 0.01 second.

No. of segments	Time integration	CSM (Sec. 3)	Twisting comp. (Sec. 4)	Tension est. (Sec. 5)	Collision handling (Sec. 6)	Total time
100	0.011	0.086	0.098	0.221	1.31	1.73
150	0.022	0.168	0.184	0.424	1.36	2.16
200	0.029	0.221	0.237	0.564	1.37	2.42
746	0.128	0.501	0.739	1.67	3.13	6.17

the string in Fig. 8 (a) falls naturally when an applied force is removed. The string in Fig. 8 (b) bounces back by the tensions when the applied force is removed. When the twisted string in Fig. 8 (c) is pulled and released, the twisting effect also occurs. Fig. 9 shows simulation results of a destruction of a hanging bridge. Wooden boards (rigid bodies) are tied with strings (ropes in this case) to build the bridge. The ropes are gradually torn apart from collisions of the wooden boards and incoming crates which cause high tensions in the ropes. We used particle-based simulation method [8] for rigid body simulation in our implementation. The video of our results can be found in the following link: http://nis-lab.is.s.u-tokyo.ac.jp/~witawat/rod/stringAnimation.mov

Fig. 9. Animation sequences of a hanging bridge colliding with incoming crates

The breakdown computational time in each process for strings with a different numbers of particles is shown in Table 1. The strings in Fig. 6 (a), (b) and (c) consist of 100, 100 and 200 segments respectively, while each string in Fig. 7 and 8 has 150 segments. The number of segments in Fig. 9 is 746 segments. The computational time of the result in Fig. 9 is measured excluding the time for rigid body simulation.

Limitations: Our method has some limitations. As previously mentioned, our method is not a full physically-based model, thus, more advance physics behaviors such as spring-twisting pendulum and anisotropic bending in [2] are hard to generate. The rapid motion of strings could cause the strings to pass through each other or themselves. However, the problem did not occur in our experiments. In case of rapid motion, continuous collision detection should be considered.

8 Conclusion and Future Work

We have introduced a simple model for simulating twisting, tearing and flicking of strings, which is fast, easy to implement and applicable to traditional simulation models. We have demonstrated that our method can handle twisting effects of strings with both uniform and non-uniform torsional rigidities. Using our method, the tension in an inextensible string can be estimated for generating tearing and flicking effects. A variation in the quality of strings can be achieved. Whilst our method is not physically-based, it can successfully reproduce the interesting behaviors of strings that would greatly enrich the realism of interactive applications such as games.

The collision between segments is treated as a collision between rigid segments. We would like to improve the collision detection algorithm to handle the collisions between deformable segments. We also would like to improve an overall performance with a GPU implementation.

Acknowledgement. We gratefully thank the anonymous reviewers for helpful comments. This work was supported by Grant-in-Aid for JSPS Fellows (22·4748).

References

1. Baraff, D., Witkin, A.: Large steps in cloth simulation. In: ACM SIGGRAPH 1998 Conference Proceedings, pp. 43–54 (1998)
2. Bergou, M., Wardetzky, M., Robinson, S., Audoly, B., Grinspun, E.: Discrete elastic rods. ACM Transactions on Graphics 27(3), 63:1–63:12 (2008); (SIGGRAPH 2008 Conference Proceedings)
3. Bertails, F., Audoly, B., Cani, M.-P., Querleux, B., Leroy, F., Lévêque, J.-L.: Super-helices for predicting the dynamics of natural hair. ACM Transactions on Graphics 25(3), 1180–1187 (2006); (SIGGRAPH 2006 Conference Proceedings)
4. Bhuvenesh, C.G., Rajesh, D.A., David, M.H. (eds.): Textile sizing. CRC Press (2004)
5. Diziol, R., Bender, J., Bayer, D.: Volume conserving simulation of deformable bodies. In: Eurographics 2009 Short Papers, pp. 37–40 (2009)
6. Goldenthal, R., Harmon, D., Fattal, R., Bercovier, M., Grinspun, E.: Efficient simulation of inextensible cloth. ACM Transactions on Graphics 26(3), 49:1–49:8 (2007); (SIGGRAPH 2007 Conference Proceedings)
7. Hadap, S.: Oriented strands: dynamics of stiff multi-body system. In: Proceedings of the 2006 ACM SIGGRAPH/Eurographics Symposium on Computer Animation, pp. 91–100 (2006)
8. Harada, T.: Real-time rigid body simulation on GPUs. In: GPU Gems 3, ch. 29, pp. 123–148 (2007)
9. Metaaphanon, N., Bando, Y., Chen, B.Y., Nishita, T.: Simulation of tearing cloth with frayed edges. Computer Graphics Forum 28(7), 1837–1844 (2009); (Pacific Graphics 2009 Conference Proceedings)
10. Müller, M., Heidelberger, B., Hennix, M., Ratcliff, J.: Position based dynamics. Journal of Visual Communication and Image Representation 18(2), 109–118 (2007)
11. Provot, X.: Deformation constraints in a mass-spring model to describe rigid cloth behavior. In: Graphics Interface 1995 Conference Proceedings, pp. 147–154 (1995)
12. Rivers, A.R., James, D.L.: FastLSM: fast lattice shape matching for robust real-time deformation. ACM Transactions on Graphics 26(3), 82:1–82:6 (2007) (SIGGRAPH 2007 Conference Proceedings)
13. Rosenblum, R.E., Carlson, W.E., Tripp, E.: Simulating the structure and dynamics of human hair: Modeling, rendering and animation. The Journal of Visualization and Computer Animation 2(4), 141–148 (1991)
14. Rungjiratananon, W., Kanamori, Y., Nishita, T.: Chain shape matching for simulating complex hairstyles. Computer Graphics Forum 29(8), 2438–2446 (2010)
15. Selle, A., Lentine, M., Fedkiw, R.: A mass spring model for hair simulation. ACM Transactions on Graphics 27(3), 64:1–64:11 (2008); (SIGGRAPH 2008 Conference Proceedings)
16. Sobottka, G., Weber, A.: Efficient bounding volume hierarchies for hair simulation. In: Proceedings of the 2nd Workshop on Virtual Reality Interactions and Physical Simulations, pp. 1–10 (2005)
17. Spillmann, J., Teschner, M.: CORDE: Cosserat rod elements for the dynamic simulation of one-dimensional elastic objects. In: Proceedings of the 2007 ACM SIGGRAPH/Eurographics Symposium on Computer Animation, pp. 63–72 (2007)
18. Spillmann, J., Teschner, M.: An adaptive contact model for the robust simulation of knots. Computer Graphics Forum 27(2), 497–506 (2008); (Eurographics 2008 Conference Proceedings)

Adaptive Grid Refinement Using View-Dependent Octree for Grid-Based Smoke Simulation

Rinchai Bunlutangtum and Pizzanu Kanongchaiyos

Chulalongkorn University, Bangkok, Thailand
rinchai.b@student.chula.ac.th, pizzanu@cp.eng.chula.ac.th

Abstract. Computational cost is one of the major problems in animating smoke. Recently, adaptive grid refinement using octree structure has been proposed, which is a successful method for reducing the computational cost of a detail-preserving fluid simulation. Although octree grid is optimized for details, viewing is not addressed. Smoke distant from the viewing screen which usually has less visual attention and is unnecessary for high-detail simulation can be optimized for speed. However, applying such view-dependent optimization to the octree grid directly may cause animation artifacts and loss in natural fluid behaviours. This paper, we present a method for view-dependent adaptive grid refinement, extending the traditional octree grid by considering the viewing frustum, as well as variation in fluid quantities as criteria for grid refinement. In our method, refinement conditions with adaptive thresholds are proposed to optimize the grid for both view and details. Additionally, our method preserves visual details and fluid behaviours which allows high-detail smoke animations in relatively less amount of computational cost consumption, especially when applied for large scale simulations.

Keywords: Simulation of Natural Environments, Physics-based Animation, Fluid Dynamics, Adaptive Refinement.

1 Introduction

Physically-based fluid simulation is a widely used technique for animating smoke, fire and other fluid phenomena. It generates physically realistic results and stunning effects which are impossible for the artist to animate manually frame by frame. Unfortunately, physically-based simulation usually comes with high computational cost as a trade-off. For graphics and realism, the main focus is on generating plausible visual effects rather than accuracy. Since computational resources especially in terms of time and memory usage are limited, a challenging topic is how to minimize the computational cost, while still being able to obtain as highly detailed animations as possible.

Grid-based fluid simulation is a widespread used method for physically-based smoke animations. [9,17,7,18] use fixed uniform grid for smoke animations. Since smoke animations are becoming more and more demand in the special effects industry, animating on fixed uniform grid in a larger domain, or refinement for higher detail is not scalable, because of its high computational cost consumption. To address this, several adaptive grid refinement techniques were introduced to optimize the simulation. [13] and [16] replace the traditional fixed uniform grid with an adaptive non-uniform grid, using an octree structure. Adaptive grid refinement using an octree structure has been successful in optimizing the simulation. The grid is subdivided only in some specific areas that require higher detail and are merged to save computational cost when details are no longer necessary. Later,[1] implements the octree grid on graphics hardware, which utilizes high performance parallel computing. These adaptive grid techniques allow the capturing of small visual details while takes lower computational cost compared to the earlier fixed uniform grid.

Small-scale details can be neglected in some regions such as hidden or distant smoke as they usually have less visual attention, [2] proposed a method that is optimized for view by using a view-dependent grid. Instead of being constructed on Cartesian coordinates as usual, the grids are constructed on the transformed polar coordinate that is most fit for view. With a view-dependent grid, fluid details gradually decrease proportionally as the distance from the camera increases, thus providing constant screen-space detail across the simulation domain. However, unlike octree grid, the view-dependent grid is subdivided uniformly on transformed coordinates, thus, grid size is fixed and not adaptive for detail optimization.

The octree grid is optimized for details whereas the view-dependent grid is optimized for view. Optimizing the grid for both viewing and details by applying view-dependent optimization to octree grid directly is straightforward but unfortunately, might cause undesired simulation artifacts or ineffective optimized grid. Thus a proper handling method along with user adjustable parameters is preferred. This paper, we present a method for view-dependent adaptive grid refinement on octree grid that minimizes unnecessary computational cost while still preserving any small visual details and their natural behaviours. In our method, we propose adaptive thresholds that are view-dependent and proportional to the distance ratio with respect to the viewing frustum. These thresholds weight the subdivision and merging conditions in order to preserve details that are usually lost when optimizing the grid. Our method optimizes the grid for both viewing and details. Furthermore, it preserves small-scale fluid details while consuming a lower amount of computational cost compared to the simulation using either a traditional fixed uniform grid or an octree grid without view-dependent optimization.

2 Related Work

Grid-based fluid simulation was first introduced in computer graphics by [9] but because their model uses an explicit integration scheme, their simulations are only stable if the time step is chosen small enough, therefore, simulation is relatively slow. [17] proposed an unconditionally stable simulation by using

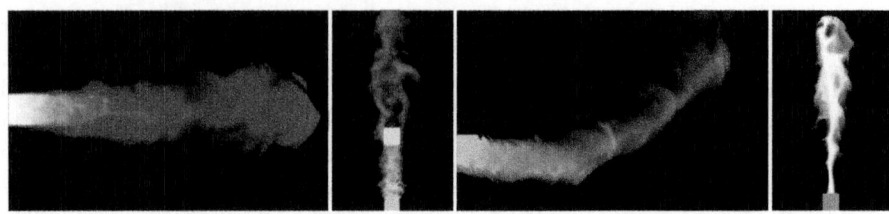

Fig. 1. Four different scenes of smoke simulation using octree grid with our view-dependent adaptive grid refinement. With our method, not only details are preserved but simulation also consumes lower computational cost with less of artefacts.

semi-Lagrangian advection scheme with implicit solvers. However, numerical dissipation was severe in this method. [7] introduced a vorticity confinement term to model the small scale rolling features characteristic of smoke to compensate the numerical dissipation caused by the implicit model. The methods have been extended to other fluid phenomena such as fire [14], explosion [8], viscoelastic materials [10] and bubbles [19]. These previous works can be categorized as fixed uniform grid as the grid are subdivided uniformly and their position are fixed entire simulation domain.

To animate fluid in a larger domain or to obtain higher details, [4,3] introduced adaptive mesh refinement (AMR) for compressible flows while [15] presented an adaptive mesh method using an octree. In computer graphics, the octree data structure has been proposed for adaptive grid refinement by [13] and asymmetric octree by [16], which results in detail optimization while [2] proposed a method that is optimized for view by using view-dependent grid, decreasing fluid details as distance from the camera increases, thus providing constant screen-space detail across the simulation. However, contrary to the adaptive grid using octree, view-dependent grid is subdivided uniformly, thus, lacking detail optimization.

Another recent grid refinement technique is Adaptive grid using tetrahedral meshes [12,5,6]. Tetrahedral meshes are easily to conform to complex boundaries and their size can be adjusted to optimize the simulation. However, simulation is more complicated for free surfaces and moving obstacles. Simulation also needs a specific scheme to prevent volume loss or artificial damping.

One of the main problems with octree grids is their dynamic and irregular structure, which is contrary to the design of graphics hardware. [1] present a problem decomposition for parallel processing that takes advantage of the graphics hardware while reducing expensive hierarchy traversals on non-uniform and adaptive octree grids.

3 Proposed Method

The idea to optimize the grid for both viewing and details is that cells should be divided for higher resolution if they are too close to the camera or their neighbouring cells are relatively different to each others. On the other hand,

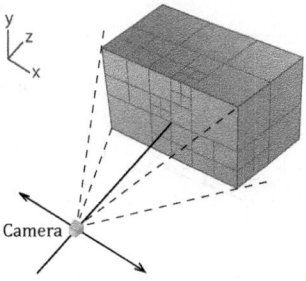

Fig. 2. Illustration of view-dependent octree grid

cells should be merged for lower resolution if their distances to the camera are too far for any fine details to be visualized or the variation of fluid quantities among neighbouring cell are no longer significant. However, not only does the distance from camera affect the grid refinement, but the dimensions of viewing frustum and its perspective are also important parameters that should be properly weighted with the refinement conditions in order to achieve an effective detail-preserved optimization.

Basically, refinement conditions are used to determine whether to perform subdivision or merging by comparing variation in fluid quantities with arbitrary constants, called refinement thresholds. To further optimize the grid for both viewing and detail, we propose a *view-dependent weighting factor* as a factor to weight these refinement thresholds. Thus, in this manner, the thresholds are adaptive and directly proportional to the viewing frustum. Thresholds with view-dependent weighting are called *adaptive thresholds* and the refinement with conditions compose of these thresholds is called *view-dependent adaptive grid refinement*. Detail of our method is described in the following subsections.

3.1 Octree Structure

We have constructed an adaptive grid with octree structure as illustrated in figure 2. A hierarchical grid with subdivision of 2^3 is employed to ensure transversal smoothness, whereas higher hierarchical subdivision e.g. 4^3 may cause visual artifact due to rapid changing in grid size during subdivision and merging. The velocity vectors are stored at the center of each cell as stated in [17], differing from the traditional MAC grid [11] which stores velocity at the cell faces, because memory usage for storing velocity at cell nodes is less than that for storing at cell faces, and it is also straightforward to implement. Pressure, density, temperature and other fluid quantities are stored at cell nodes as well (Figure 3).

3.2 Measuring Fluid Variation

[16] determine fluid variation by measuring variation in density. However, we found that measuring variation in velocity also yields a relevant result which can

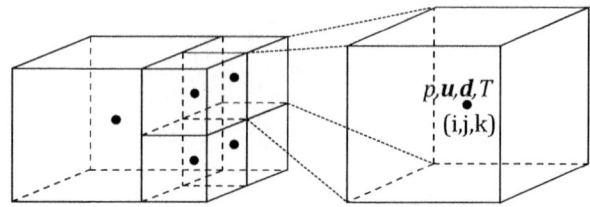

Fig. 3. Structure of octree grid where fluid quantities are stored at cell nodes

be used for inferring variation of other quantities as well. This is because density is always advected (carried) by velocity fields; thus, measuring velocity itself is reasonable. Moreover, by measuring variation of velocity, Laplacian terms shown in Equation 1 do not need to be computed, as they can be directly obtained from the diffusion step during solving Navier-Stokes equations (Section 4). Our equation for measuring variation in velocity is as follows:

$$C(x,y,z) = max(|\nabla_x^2 u|, |\nabla_y^2 v|, |\nabla_z^2 w|) \qquad (1)$$

Equation 1 measures the variation of velocity, where u, v, w denote scalar components of velocity vector: $\mathbf{u} = (u, v, w)$. ∇_x^2 is a Laplacian on x direction: $\nabla_x^2 u = \partial^2 u / \partial x^2$. ∇_y^2 and ∇_z^2 are defined likewise.

3.3 View-Dependent Weighting Factor

Any viewing parameters that affect the grid refinement are gathered and rewritten as a mathematical relation called *view-dependent weighting factor*, as a factor to weight the refinement thresholds.

Suppose that we are observing an arbitrary object within a rectilinear perspective view. If we move the camera constant speed away from the object then the observed size of that object is decreased hyperbolically. In addition, if we increase object's actual size and move the camera away accordingly then the observed size should be preserved as constant. We have inherited this relation for constructing a view-dependent weighting factor as the grid's resolution over distance should be coarsened away in a proportion that the observed grid resolution still remains constant.

Let Ψ represent a view-dependent weighting factor and r and R represent the Euclidean distances measured from camera to arbitrary cell's node and from camera to front clipping plane respectively (see Figure 4). Ψ should then be proportional to r. Moreover, Ψ should be affected by dimensions of the viewing frustum and its perspective. For instance, Ψ should be greater if r is large with respect to R or the viewing frustum has high perspective. The view-dependent weighting factor is:

$$\Psi = \alpha \left(\frac{r-R}{R} \right) \qquad (2)$$

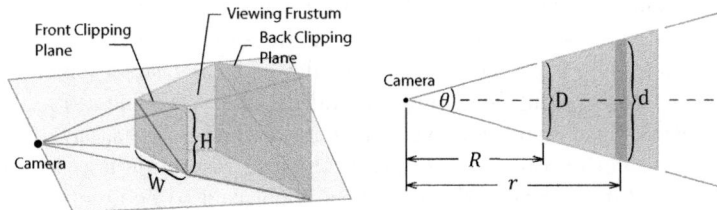

Fig. 4. Viewing frustum shown in three-dimensions (left) and its diagonal cross-section (right), where shading areas are the visible volume

Basically, Ψ is factored by distance ratio: r/R. However, we want the Ψ to be affected only further than the front clipping plane, not the origin; thus, we offset the ratio by R, which yields a distance ratio: $(r - R)/R$. α is a camera's perspective ratio defined as follow.

$$\alpha = \frac{D}{2R} = \tan(\frac{\theta}{2}) \tag{3}$$

Equation 3 refers to the viewing frustum (figure 4). D is a diagonal length of front clipping plane: $D = \sqrt{H^2 + W^2}$, where H and W are height and weight of front clipping plane respectively. R is a Euclidean distance from camera to the center of front clipping plane, θ is the camera's field of view (abbreviated as FOV, also called angle of view) measured diagonally.

3.4 Adaptive Thresholds

Grid refinement is performed by means of refinement conditions, i.e., merging condition and subdivision condition. In general, refinement conditions comparing fluid variation with constant thresholds are used. To further perform the view-dependent adaptive grid refinement, we propose refinement conditions incorporated with *adaptive thresholds* as stated below.

$$T^* = T(\tau\Psi + 1)\phi = T\left(\tau\alpha\left(\frac{r-R}{R}\right) + 1\right)\left(\frac{res_{grid}}{res_{image}}\right) \tag{4}$$

T^* is an adaptive threshold for arbitrary viewing frustum at distance r and FOV θ, where Ψ is the view-dependent weighting factor and τ is a view-dependent coefficient, specifying the weight that the view should affect the grid refinement. T is a refinement threshold specified on a front clipping plane of a viewing frustum at arbitrary FOV θ, obtained by $T = \alpha T_{90°}$, where $T_{90°}$ is a refinement threshold at $FOV = 90°$ and α is a camera's perspective ratio.

Altering the FOV might affect the grid resolution. For instance, narrow FOV (zooming) makes small details get larger hence, grid resolution must be coarsened to allow finer details. To preserve overall details whether FOV is changed, we factor a refinement threshold with a view-dependent weighting term: $(\tau\Psi + 1)$.

Image resolution, which is simply a pixel count per unit length of screen, is another factor that should be considered. If we lower the image resolution but keep everything else fixed, the grid can be allowed to be coarser (since details are negligible in a low-resolution image). To address this, we define a *resolution ratio* (ϕ) as a ratio of grid resolution over image resolution: $\phi = res_{grid}/res_{image}$. For example, a resolution ratio of two means the grid resolution is twice finer than the image resolution. Since grid resolution is no need to be greater than image resolution thus T^* should be higher to allow coarser grid.

3.5 Refinement Conditions

We have constructed refinement conditions for view-dependent adaptive grid refinement, defined as follows.

$$C(x,y,z) > T_s^* = T_s(\tau\Psi + 1)\phi \qquad (5)$$

$$C(x,y,z) < T_m^* = T_m(\tau\Psi + 1)\phi \qquad (6)$$

Equation 5 and 6 are refinement conditions for subdivision and merging respectively. $C(x, y, z)$ is the measuring of fluid variation while on the right hand side of these equations are adaptive thresholds inherited from equation 4 where T_s^* and T_m^* are for subdivision and merging respectively.

Refinement conditions categorize each cell in to one of these stages i.e., subdivision, merging and idle stage. If equation 5 is satisfied then the subdivision stage is assigned. If equation 6 is satisfied then the merging stage is assigned. Otherwise, if neither equation 5 nor equation 6 is satisfied then the idle stage is assigned therefore, no refinement is performed.

In Figure 5, we have illustrated the relation between variation $C(x, y, z)$ and distance r with several parameter adjustments. (a) and (b) show the comparison between using cameras with different FOVs. The perspective of camera, which is specified by FOV, corresponds to the steepness of slope which indicates the tendency of merging and division. A result of using a wider FOV is a greater view-dependent level of detail. As a consequence, grid resolution tends to be coarsened faster as the distance from the camera increases. In addition to a wider FOV, T_s^* and T_m^* are shifted upward to allow coarser grid resolution as details usually get smaller in wide-angle view. The result of using narrow FOV is inversion. Furthermore, if an infinitesimal value of FOV ($\alpha \approx 0$) is applied then the refinement results as no view-dependent optimization since the view-dependent terms are neglected and left only the constant terms T_s and T_m. The view-dependent terms are also neglected when the camera is placed at infinity ($R \approx \infty$), or the view-dependent coefficient is set to zero ($\tau = 0$).

The sensitivity of stage transitions (between subdivision, merging and idle) correspond to the differential value of the adaptive threshold T_s^* and T_m^*, which can be adjusted by altering T_s and T_m. In figure 5, (c) T_s^* is close to T_m^* which results in a narrow idle stage area; hence, it is sensitive to stage transition, whereas (d) T_s^* is much different to T_m^* therefore, it is tolerant to stage transition. As stage transitions consume computational cost, assigning inappropriate thresholds may

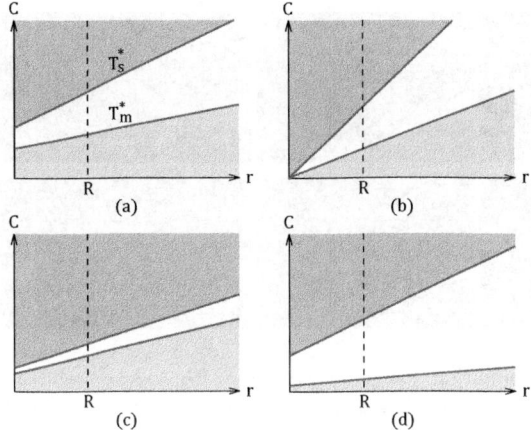

Fig. 5. Graphical plots of each stages i.e., subdivision (dark grey area), merging (light grey area), idle (white area) which are separated by T_s^* (upper lines) and T_m^* (lower lines) over variation $C(x, y, z)$ and distance r using narrow FOV camera (a), wide FOV camera (b), small (c) and large (d) of difference between T_s and T_m.

result in an excessive overhead due to frequent merging and subdivision or otherwise result in an inefficient optimization; thus, thresholds must be carefully selected. Moreover, to prevent excessive refinement overhead, grid size should be gradually adapted at each time step, which can be done by performing only one operation (i.e., subdivision, merging, or idle) per cell each iteration. This reduces recursive subdivision and merging overhead and also prevents rapid changing in cell size that might cause animation artifacts.

4 Smoke Simulation

After applying the refinement method, the grid is well optimized and ready for the simulation step. We solve the Navier Stokes equations that describe fluid flow and its behaviours with a stable scheme proposed by [17] and [7], then we follow a discretization scheme proposed by [13] to solve the Poisson equations on the octree grid, which is adaptive and has non-uniform structure.

5 Results and Discussion

In order to evaluate our refinement method, we have constructed and compared results of three different simulations i.e., an octree grid with view-dependent optimization, an octree grid without view-dependent optimization, and a fixed uniform grid. Results are compared by measuring both computational cost and animation quality. Computational cost is compared by measuring number of

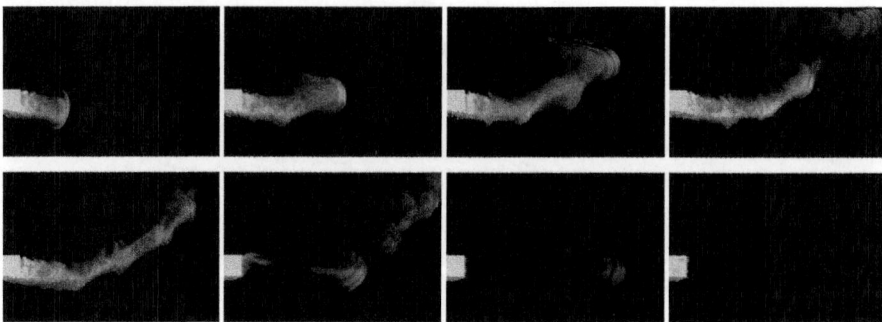

Fig. 6. Smoke animation using octree grid with view-dependent adaptive grid refinement. Simulated with view-dependent coefficient $\tau = 1$, initial grid resolution of $32 \times 20 \times 12$ and maximum grid resolution of $128 \times 80 \times 48$.

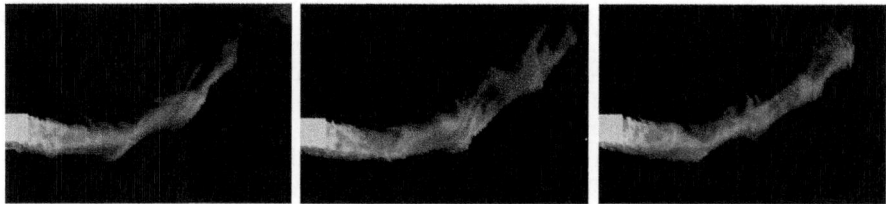

Fig. 7. Snapshots comparing visual results of using fixed uniform grid (left), octree grid without view-dependent refinement (center) and octree grid with view-dependent refinement (right). Detail loss by our method is unnoticeable at $\tau = 1$.

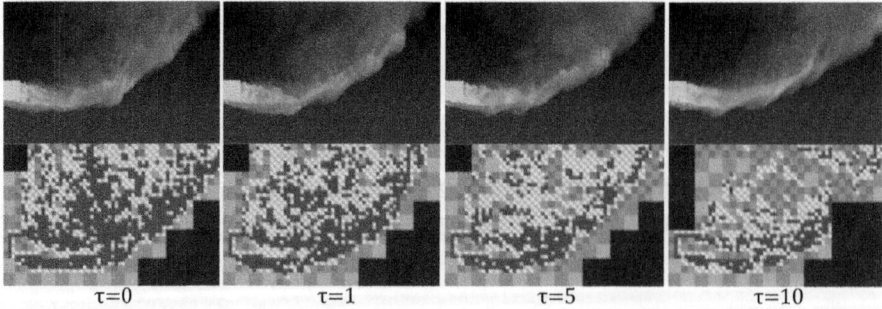

Fig. 8. Snapshots comparing the effect of view-dependent refinement by varying view-dependent coefficient τ. Visual results (above) showing preserved details and their corresponding cut away view (below) showing current grid size in range of color i.e., red is fine grid, blue is coarse grid. In this simulation, $\tau = 1$ is an optimal weighting value between speed and detail, $\tau = 5$ is a maximum practical value that detail loss still unnoticeable and with $\tau = 10$, simulation suffers from visible detail loss i.e., smooth flow and no small swirl effect.

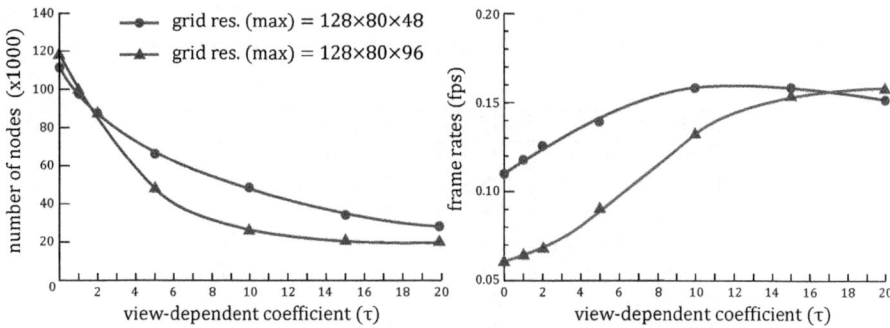

Fig. 9. Right: Number of cell nodes on various view-dependent coefficient. Left: The relation between frame rates and view-dependent coefficients. Incrementing the view-dependent coefficient decreases the number of nodes, which speed up the simulation.

frames per second while animation quality is compared using visual results. All experiments reported in this paper were performed on a machine with dual core CPU 2.40 GHz and 2 GB of RAM.

We have constructed a simulation domain as illustrated in figure 2 where the camera is placed on the z-axis facing toward the domain, and its visual angle is fixed at 90 degrees. We have applied two sets of grid resolution in our experiment. In the first set, an initial resolution of $32 \times 20 \times 12$ is applied to the octree grid with a specified maximum resolution of 128 x 80 x 48 while for the fixed uniform grid, the resolution is always fixed at 128 x 80 x 48. In the second set, we double only the domain depth in order to evaluate the efficiency of view-dependent optimization on different domain sizes. According to the results shown in Figure 9, simulation gains speed by applying our method. Moreover, the method efficiency is largely depends on fluid-to-camera distant (r), larger domains which usually contains a lot of distant smoke are more effective for optimization; hence, speed-up is significant in larger domains.

We have demonstrated the effect of the view-dependent adaptive grid refinement by varying only the view-dependent coefficient τ. Visual results are shown in Figure 8 and their corresponding computational cost are shown in Figure 9 and Table 1. The results show that applying a greater view-dependent coefficient reduces the number of cells in the domain which result in lower computational cost consumption. The simulation achieves a higher frame rate but detail loss is relatively greater. On the other hand, if a lower view-dependent coefficient is applied, more details are preserved but with higher computation cost as a trade-off. Furthermore, if the view-dependent coefficient is zero then view-dependent optimization is discarded. Grid refinement with a view-dependent coefficient of 1 is an optimal weighting between details and computational cost, since grid resolution is coarsened with an exact proportion to the frustum perspective. However, in our experiment, a view-dependent coefficient can be assigned up to 5 before detail loss becomes noticeable. This is because foreground smoke which usually has higher detail occludes others with lower detail behind.

Table 1. Result comparison of multiple view-dependent coefficients (τ) on two sets of different grid sizes. Speed-up is compared relative to records noted with asterisk(*) each set.

Grid type	Grid res. (max)	τ	fps	speed-up
Fixed uniform	128 × 80 × 48	-	.111	-
Adaptive octree*	128 × 80 × 48	0	.110	-
Adaptive octree	128 × 80 × 48	1	.118	7.28 %
Adaptive octree	128 × 80 × 48	2	.125	14.10 %
Adaptive octree	128 × 80 × 48	5	.139	26.57 %
Adaptive octree	128 × 80 × 48	10	.158	44.13 %
Fixed uniform	128 × 80 × 96	-	.052	-
Adaptive octree*	128 × 80 × 96	0	.061	-
Adaptive octree	128 × 80 × 96	1	.064	6.03%
Adaptive octree	128 × 80 × 96	2	.068	11.77%
Adaptive octree	128 × 80 × 96	5	.091	49.14%
Adaptive octree	128 × 80 × 96	10	.133	118.67%

6 Conclusion

We have presented a view-dependent adaptive grid refinement for simulating smoke on an octree structure. The refinement conditions with adaptive thresholds are constructed incorporating viewing information. Our proposed method has successfully optimized the grid for both viewing and details. Computational cost is minimized while visual details and fluid behaviours are still preserved. The method also yields a significant difference speed-up when applied to larger domains or those with greater perspective. Additionally, our method is adjustable to flexibly match user requirements i.e., higher view-dependent coefficient to gain speed, or lower view-dependent coefficient to preserve details.

Nevertheless, there are additional issues that are not yet addressed in this current implementation. First, we have not addressed invisible areas such as smoke behind obstacles or dense smoke. The invisible areas do not have to contain fine details; therefore, can reduce unnecessary processing time. Changing the camera viewpoint is another issue. As refinement is associated with the viewing position and the frustum, rapidly changing the view e.g., translation, rotation or even zooming might cause discontinuity artifacts and detail loss; therefore, view can be changed with a limited speed relative to the simulation frame rate.

Acknowledgements. This research was partially funded by the TRF-Master Research Grants (MAG) MRG-WI535E005, Yodia Multimedia Co.,Ltd and was in part supported by the CUCP Academic Excellence Scholarship from Department of Computer Engineering, Chulalongkorn University.

References

1. Ament, M., Straßer, W.: Dynamic Grid Refinement for Fluid Simulations on Parallel Graphics Architectures. In: Proc. Eurographics Symposium on Parallel Graphics and Visualization, pp. 9–15 (2009)
2. Barran, B.: View dependent fluid dynamics. M.S. thesis, Texas A&M University (2006)
3. Berger, M., Colella, P.: Local adaptive mesh refinement for shock hydrodynamics. Journal of Computational Physics, 64–84 (1989)
4. Berger, M., Oliger, J.: Adaptive mesh refinement for hyperbolic partial differential equations. Journal of Computational Physics, 484–512 (1984)
5. Chentanez, N., Feldman, B.E., Labelle, F., Brien, J.F.O., Shewchuk, J.R.: Liquid Simulation on Lattice-Based Tetrahedral Meshes Eurographics Association, pp. 219–228 (2007)
6. Elcott, S., Tong, Y., Kanso, E., Schröder, P., Desbrun, M.: Stable, circulation-preserving, simplicial fluids. In: ACM SIGGRAPH ASIA 2008, pp. 1–11 (2008)
7. Fedkiw, R., Stam, J., Jensen, H.: Visual simulation of smoke. In: Proc. Computer Graphics and Interactive Techniques, pp. 15–22 (2001)
8. Feldman, B.E., O'Brien, J.F., Arikan, O.: Animating suspended particle explosions. ACM Transactions on Graphics 22(3), 708 (2003)
9. Foster, N.: Realistic Animation of Liquids. Graphical Models and Image Processing 58(5), 471–483 (1996)
10. Goktekin, T.G., Bargteil, A.W., O'Brien, J.F.: A method for animating viscoelastic fluids. ACM Transactions on Graphics 23(3), 463 (2004)
11. Harlow, F.H., Welch, J.E.: Numerical Calculation of Time-Dependent Viscous Incompressible Flow of Fluid with Free Surface. Physics of Fluids 8(12), 2182 (1965)
12. Klingner, B.M., Feldman, B.E., Chentanez, N., O'Brien, J.F.: Fluid animation with dynamic meshes. In: ACM SIGGRAPH 2006 Papers, pp. 820 (2006)
13. Losasso, F., Gibou, F., Fedkiw, R.: Simulating water and smoke with an octree data structure. ACM Transactions on Graphics 23(3), 457 (2004)
14. Nealen, A.: Physically Based Simulation and Animation of Gaseous Phenomena in a Periodic Domain. I Can (2001)
15. Popinet, S.: Gerris: a tree-based adaptive solver for the incompressible Euler equations in complex geometries. Journal of Computational Physics 190(2), 572–600 (2003)
16. Shi, L., Yu, Y.: Visual smoke simulation with adaptive octree refinement. In: Proc. Computer Graphics and Imaging, 1319 (2004); Stam, J.: Stable fluids. In: Proceedings of the 26th Annual Conference on Computer Graphics and Interactive Techniques. ACM Press/Addison-Wesley Publishing Co., 121128 (1999)
17. Stam, J.: Stable fluids. In: Proc. Computer Graphics and Interactive Techniques, pp. 121–128. ACM Press/Addison-Wesley Publishing Co. (1999)
18. Stam, J.: Real-time fluid dynamics for games. In: Proc. Game Developer Conference, vol. 18 (2003)
19. Zheng, W., Yong, J.-H., Paul, J.-C.: Simulation of bubbles. Graphical Models 71(6), 229–239 (2009)

A Simple Method for Real-Time Metal Shell Simulation

Zhi Dong, Shiqiu Liu, Yuntao Ou, and Yunxin Zheng

School of Software of Engineering, South China University of Technology
{scut.zhidong,shiqiu1105}@gmail.com

Abstract. Realistic animation and rendering of the metal shell is an important aspect for movies, video games and other simulators. Usually this is handled by FEM method, which requires extremely high computational cost due to solving the stiffness matrix. We now propose a trick that could smartly avoid the large scale computation required by FEM, and could still generate visually convincing images of metal shell. We do so by first partitioning the shell into k rigid sub-shells that evolve independently during impact, before using a simple spring-mass model is applied between each adjacent vertex to retain continuity of the shell. This technique could produce realistically looking deformed rigid shells in real-time and can easily be integrated in any game engine and physics engine.

Keywords: Real-Time Simulation, Game Development, Physics Engine.

1 Introduction

Rendering of the metal shell plays an important role in games. Such as when rendering deformed vehicle shell, deformed bridge, traffic accident or simply metal simulation. The discussion of this phenomenon is mainly in the field of mechanics of materials. Early research focused on metal forming and metal cutting, for example [2] used finite element method (FEM) to simulate metal forming,[4] simulated metal cutting. Later, researches with more practical value started to take place, typically the research of vehicle collision[19].However, all these methods were based on FEM, which makes them impossible to be applied to any interactive system like games, because the required computational expanse of FEM is significantly high. We introduce a simple method to render metal shell, whose computational cost is much less than FEM solution. Our method consists of three steps:

1) Partitioning the shell into a number of sub-shells using K-Means.

2) Treating each sub-shell as a rigid-body and classic rigid-body solver can be applied to solve its movement.

3) Applying an elastic force calculated with spring-mass model to all the adjacent vertices in the shell to maintain continuity.

In the end of this paper we have shown the simulation result and analyzed the performance of our method, to demonstrate that it can produce visually convincing result and can be used in real-time.

2 Related Work

FEM was first initiated in Mechanics of Materials, and it has been applied to computer animation for a long while.

O'Brien et al. [7] and [8] presented a method based on FEM to simulate brittle and ductile fracture in connection with elasto-plastic materials, in which they used tetrahedral meshes combined with linear basis functions and Green's strain tensor. And the resulting equations were solved explicitly and integrated explicitly. The method produced realistic looking results, but it cannot be used for real-time purpose. In order to tackle the non-real-time performance of FEM, the boundary element method (BEM) was designed. BEM is an interesting alternative to FEM because all computations are done on the surface of the elastic body, not in its interior volume. The most common method in BEM is the spring-mass method, which was first used in computer graphics for facial modeling [10] [14] [18]. Not before long, dynamic models were used to simulate skin, fat and muscle[1] [4] [17]. The locomotion of creatures like snakes, worms and fish [5] [13]was also handled with spring-mass model. In these systems, spring rest-lengths vary over time to simulate muscle actuation. In previous researches, [6] mentioned the malleable metal deformation. That paper mainly focuses on fracture simulation; moreover, it proposed a solution to simulate plastic deformation, which had been successfully applied to the simulation of clay. Similar to our research, that solution has real-time performance, but it is not designed to simulate metallic material and its supported number of vertices is fairly small.

Numerous real-time techniques exist for handling deformations and fracture. The most related work to us is [11]. [9] proposed an advancing method for deformation in game environment, but it does not focus on deformation of malleable metal.

Based on the previous works, we have proposed a new method to simulate deformation of metal shell. Our method is not as accurate as FEM, but it is easy to implement and to be integrated in games while can still produce nice images of deformed metal shell.

3 Mesh Segmentation

In order to simulate deformation of metal shell, we first decompose the shell into a number of sub-shells. Here, we choose the method proposed in [12] to handle this task. The reason we chose this method is that it can finely decompose the shell in a way that triangle faces sharing the same plane are considered closer to each other and are more likely to be partitioned into the same sub-shell. Therefore, the simulated shell will be more likely to bend in area where the curvature is high. The methodology is stated clear in [12].Here we briefly summarize the gist below.

Given S, a polyhedral shell with n vertices, the goal is to decompose S into k disjoint sub-shell $S_1 - S_k$ whose union gives S.

It assumed that distant faces, both in terms of physical distance and in terms of angular distance, are less likely to be in the same sub-shells than faces which are close together. We therefore define the distance between two faces F_1 and F_2 as follows. If F_1 and F_2 are adjacent, then:

$$Distance(F_1, F_2) = (1-\delta)(1-\cos^2(\alpha)) + \delta Phys\_Dist(F_1, F_2) \quad (1)$$

The first term of the distance definition represents the angular distance, where α is the dihedral angle between the faces. Note that the expression. $(1-\cos^2(\alpha))$ reaches its maximum at $\pi/2$ and its minimum at 0 (or π). Thus, the faces share the same plane(or close to the same plane) are considered closer to each other and are more likely to belong to the same sub-shells. The second term represents the physical distance. It is the sum of the distances between the centers of mass of the two faces and the midpoint of their common edge. Here we set δ as 0.5.

The main idea of the method is to iteratively improve the decomposition quality by transferring faces from one sub-shell to another. This is very much similar to the concept of the K-means clustering algorithm. The algorithm can be divided into four steps: preprocessing, selecting the initial representatives of the sub-shells, determining the decomposition, and reselecting the representatives.

1. *Preprocessing*: In the preprocessing step the distances between all the adjacent faces are computed. It is evident that the number of sub-shells in the final decomposition should be at least the number of disconnected components.

2. *Electing the initial representatives of the sub-shells*: Each sub-shell is represented by one of its faces. In theory, the first representatives of the sub-shells could be chosen randomly.In practice, however, there are also several reasons for smartly choosing these representatives. First, this method converges to local minima, which makes the initial decomposition essential for the final quality of the decomposition. Second, good initial representatives mean that the algorithm will only need a small number of iteration to converge. The following is how we choose our initial representatives. Initially, one representative is chosen for each disconnected sub-shell. It is the face having the minimal distance between its center of mass and the center of mass of its component. Selecting is completed if the number of required sub-shells is less or equal to the number of representatives . Otherwise, the model should be partitioned further. It calculates, for each representative, the minimum distances to all the faces (e.g., using Dijkstra's algorithm). A new representative is added so as to maximize the average distance to all the existing representatives on the same connected component. New representatives are added one by one, until the required number of representatives (i.e., sub-shells) is reached. In case the user specifies that the system should automatically determine the number of sub-shells, or the value of K if we think of this method as K-Mean, new representatives are added as long as their distance from any existing representative is larger than a predefined distance, which is pre-defined. The number of required sub-shells can affect the fineness and computational cost of simulation. In practice, the number of sub-shells should be between 100-128, which is enough to achieve realistic-looking result with low computational cost.

3. *Determining the decomposition*: For each face, the distances to all the representatives within its connected component are calculated. Each face is

assigned to the sub-shells that have the closest representatives. This procedure produces a decomposition of the given model.

4. *Re-electing the representatives*: The final goal of the algorithm is to minimize the function

$$F = \sum_p \sum_{f \in sub-shell(p)} Dist_{fp} \quad (2)$$

Where $Dist_{fp}$ is the shortest distance from a sub-shells representative p to a face f belonging to the sub-shells which p represents. Therefore, $\sum_p \sum_{f \in sub-shell(p)} Dist_{fp}$ is the sum on the shortest distances of all the faces to their sub-shells' representatives. In order to converge to a solution, new sub-shells representatives are being elected. This is achieved by minimizing the sum of the shortest distances from each representative to the faces which belong to the relevant sub-shells. In other words, for each sub-shells a new representative p_{new} is elected as the face (belonging to the sub-shells) that optimizes the function min $_p \sum_f Dist_{fp}$.In practice,an alternative is to choose as a new representative the face whose center of mass is closest to the center of mass of the sub-shells, as was done in the initialization step. Obviously, the complexity and performance of the latter one is much better. Moreover, our experiments have shown that the decompositions produced by this technique are usually better. If any sub-shells had its representative changed in Step 4, the algorithm goes back to Step 3. An example is given in the figure below.

Fig. 1. The left picture is the original mesh of a car, and the right is the mesh model which is segmented with different colors denoting different sub-shells.

Now our shell is partitioned into sub-shells, we can now solve the movement of each sub-shell as a rigid-body.

4 Collision Detection and Response

The first phase of interacting with rigid body is collision detection. Here we use AABB bounding volume tree [15], whose leaf nodes denote sub-shells. When collision detection is performed from the root down to leaves, the GJK algorithm [16] can be applied to solve the narrow phase detection between rigid-bodies and sub-shells.

After collision detection, we get a series of contact points. To handle these contacts and compute impulses, we adopt penalty function which was initially proposed by [3].The most intuitive method to handle collisions is with springs, which means when a collision is detected, a spring is temporarily inserted between the points of closest gap (or deepest interpenetration) of the two colliding objects. The spring law is usually K/d, or some other functional form that goes to infinity as the separation d of the two objects approaches 0 (or the interpenetration depth approaches some small value). K is a spring constant controlling the stiffness of the spring. The spring force is applied equally and in opposite directions to the two colliding objects. The direction of the force is such as to push the two objects apart (or to reduce their depth of interpenetration). Our particular implementation handles variable elasticity by making a distinction between collisions where the objects are approaching each other and collisions where the objects are moving apart from each other. The two spring constants will be related by $K_{recede} = \varepsilon K_{approach}$ where ε is between 0 and 1.

Here we narrow our scope to metal shell. In previous researches, the metal shell's coefficient of restitution is known as a constant (as is often done, especially in games). The relationship between the coefficient of restitution (COR) and ε is written below:

$$COR = \sqrt{\varepsilon} \qquad (3)$$

The coefficient of restitution of different materials is listed in the chart below.

Table 1. Coefficient of restitution of different metal materials

Material	COR
Steel	0.2
Aluminum	0.15
Copper	0.1

The spring method is easily understandable and easy to implement. It is one of the most efficient ways to handle collision response in games.

Since we have already partitioned the shell into sub-shells, we now compute the force each sub-shell is suffering using the method described above.

5 Deformation Simulation

In order to achieve realistic looking result, we have analyzed the feature of deformed metal shell. There are primarily two features. The first one is that the dent direction when hit by an impulse is the same with the impulse direction. The second one is that creases are likely to appear in area close to the contact point. One of the most important defects of FEM is that it requires calculating the inverse of high order matrix when updating the stiffness matrix, which makes it unpractical for real-time usage. Our approach of doing this is to treat each sub-shell, which we get from step one, as a rigid-body. And since it's cheap to solve the rigid-body movement, the method could be applied to real-time simulation. Moreover, since each sub-shell evolve independently during impact, adjacent sub-shells are possible to suffer from different movements (translation and rotation), which naturally gives us illusion of crease. Therefore this method can effectively approximate second feature of deformed metal shell.

Each sub-shell has its own angular displacement $\mathbf{d_a}$ which is the rotation caused by collision, and linear displacement $\mathbf{d_l}$ representing translation(Shown in Fig. 2). The displacement of a sub-shell could be calculated as

$$\mathbf{d_l} = \frac{\sum \mathbf{f}}{S} \qquad (4)$$

$$\mathbf{d_a} = \mathbf{K_{xyz}} \frac{\sum \mathbf{r} \times \mathbf{p}}{S} \qquad (5)$$

In the formulations above $\mathbf{K_{xyz}}$ is a 3x3 matrix similar to inertia matrix, representing the stiffness distribution in x, y, z direction. S denotes the stiffness of the material. The symbol r represents the vector difference between contact point and mass center of sub-shells.

Here, we treat the stiffness as proportional to the mass of vertices. In accordance with linear translation, stiffness distribution $\mathbf{K_{xyz}}$ is equal to the inverse of inertia tensor of each sub-shell. It uses a simple approximation that the higher mass yields higher stiffness. Technical correctness could be more easily

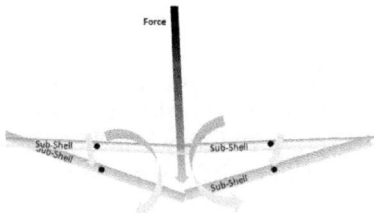

Fig. 2. The transparent sub-shells have not been displaced. The grey arrows denote the translation and rotation of sub-shells.

evaluated by comparing the proposed method directly to real picture. From the Fig. 3 we can tell the visual effect of our simulation is convincing already, but two major artifacts still remain. The first is that creases are way too steep, almost like fractures (evident in the front window in Fig. 3.), while in the real world the crease is much smoother. And secondly, the deformation is a local effect, which means distant areas from the colliding point do not suffer from any deformation. Those artifacts jeopardize the realism of the result of our method. The reason for those artifacts is we neglected the interaction between sub-shells, treating them as rigid-bodies, in previous steps. In order to eliminate this artifact, we are introducing the spring-mass model in the next section.

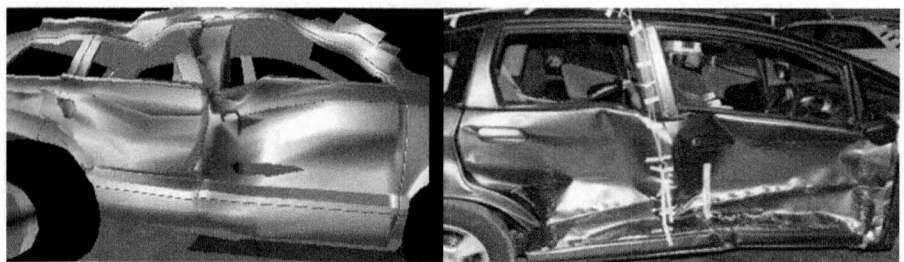

Fig. 3. Left: metal deformed without applying the spring-mass model. Right: Car collision in real world.

6 Globalize the Deformation with Spring-Mass Model

During the previous step, all the deformations are local effect, which do not take the interaction among sub-shells into account. We take into account all vertices on the metal shell using spring-mass model. Please note that this model is different from what we have proposed in Section 4.

We connect each pair of the adjacent vertices in the mesh with a spring. Springs are commonly modeled as being linearly elastic; the force acting on mass i, generated by a spring connecting i and j together is

$$\mathbf{f}_i = \mathbf{k}_s (\,|\mathbf{x}_{ij}| - \mathbf{l}_{ij}) \frac{\mathbf{x}_{ij}}{|\mathbf{x}_{ij}|} \qquad (6)$$

Where $\mathbf{x}_{ij}$ is the vector difference between the two masses' position of two adjacent vertices. $\mathbf{k}_s$ is the spring's stiffness and $\mathbf{l}_{ij}$ is its rest length. $\mathbf{l}_{ij}$ will be changed in the process of deformation, usually is set as the distance between vertex i and vertex j in the previous frame. Therefore when there is no collision, the distance between all vertices remain still, and the spring-mass model does not have any effect on the simulation result.

When applying spring-mass model to simulating metal shell deformation, some modifications need to be done to prevent deformation being too severe. To all the metal material there is a deformation threshold, higher than which fracture will occur. Since our method does not simulate fracture, we add a constraint to keep the stretching between any two vertices under that threshold. The movement of $\mathbf{x}_i$ in t+1 time step can be expressed by the following formulations when huge deformation occurs.

$$\mathbf{x}_i^{t+1} = \mathbf{x}_i^t + \lambda (\mathbf{x}_i^t - \mathbf{x}_j^t) \qquad (7)$$

Where $\mathbf{x}_i$ is linked with $\mathbf{x}_j$ by one spring, and λ is the threshold representing the range of spring stretching. When the stretching length is higher than λ we use Eq. 7 to calculate the displacement. Otherwise, we use Eq. 6 to calculate the displacement.

The figures below demonstrate the difference between simulation with and without the constraint of spring-mass model. From Fig. 4 we can clearly tell

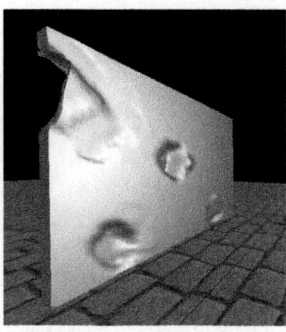 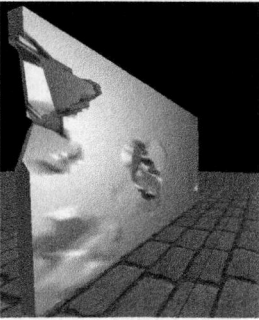

Fig. 4. Left: a metal shell is deformed with spring-mass model applied. Right: deformed without applying the spring-mass model.

that after applying spring-mass model, collision not only yield deformation in local area, but also affect distant area, and the crease is much smoother.

7 Result

In this section we provide two examples to show the result of our method, and to prove it can produce realistic looking images of the metal shell in real-time.

The first example is a car deformed by hitting walls. The rigid body motion is solved by Bullet 2.75.The deformation is not physically accurate, but is already visually convincing enough. This shows that our method could be applied to rendering vehicles in games. The number of vertices of the car is 14658, coefficients of restitution is 0.2 numbers of triangles are 26232, mass being 1K kg. The result is shown in Fig. 5 and in our accompanying video[1].

We can evaluate the technical correctness of our method by comparing with FEM solution. Two identical cars crash the wall, one is computed with our method and other is computed with FEM. We have plotted the one dimension curve of two bonnet's midline computed by our method and FEM. The result is shown in Fig. 6. The x axis indicates the distance to the leftmost of bonnet and the y axis indicates the height of vertices to the ground. The curve shows that height of bonnets caused by wrap is in nearly 80% close. The second example is balls hitting on a metal shell. The metal shell consists of 11144 vertices, 19200 triangles, with friction coefficient being 0.4. 128 sub-shells were generated. We shoot balls to the metal shell to deform the metal shell. The mass of each ball is 100kg, the result is shown in Fig. 7.

In this example, we use the number of colliding points during collision to measure the efficiency. In the diagram (Fig. 8) the x-axis is the number of colliding points during one collision, y-axis means the time cost per frame. The extra computational cost is rotation and translation of colliding sub-shells, which is linearly increased and fairly small, when compared with the cost of collision detection and spring mass model. Run-time evaluation can be done with colliding

---

[1] Accompanying video at www.youtube.com/watch?v=_1aoyEAXpwA

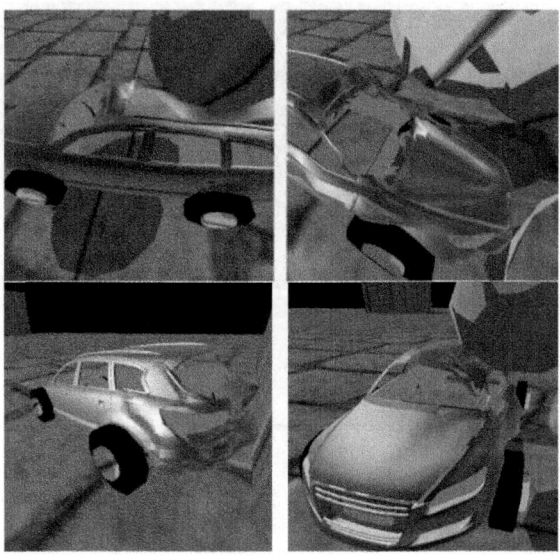

Fig. 5. A car is deformed by impact from walls and balls

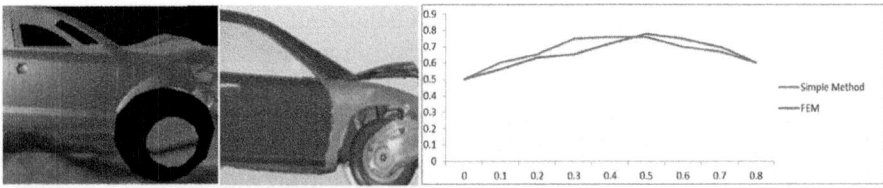

Fig. 6. The left picture is front part of car collision simulated by our method, the middle picture is the result computed by FEM, and the right picture is 1D curve comparison of two method

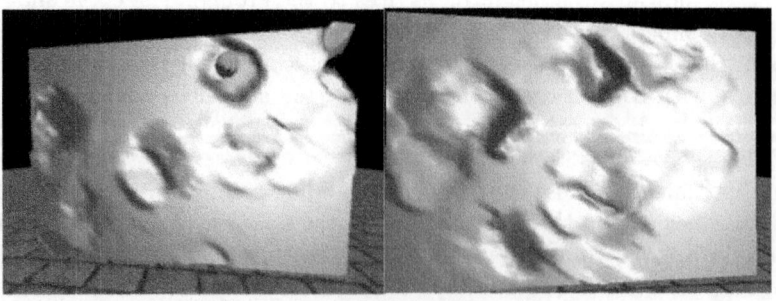

Fig. 7. Shooting balls to the metal shell

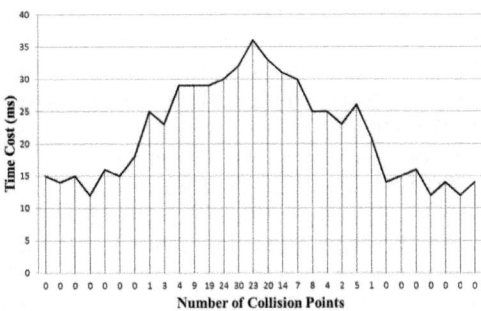

Fig. 8. Run time analysis

points taken into consideration. From Fig. 8, the time cost grows steadily when colliding points increased steeply. Our method can be used in real-time (24 frame per second) when the number of vertices does not exceeded 26500.

8 Conclusion

In this paper we have described a simple method to simulate metal deformation. The most important feature of this method is it's easy to understand and implement and it avoids solving the higher order matrixes smartly. In the meantime, the approximated result is still visually convincing enough to be integrated in games.

This method first uses K-Mean algorithm partition the entire metal shell into a number of sub-shells, during which vertices on different planes are considered further away from each other than vertices sharing the same plane.

In the second step, we compute the movement of each sub-shell as rigid-body. We adopt the classic penalty method to handle collision response. In this step, each sub-shell is displaced without any interaction with other sub-shell, therefore deformation we get in this step is local and discontinuity might occur.

In the final step, a spring-mass model is applied between all of the adjacent vertices to globalize the deformation, and to retain the continuity of the metal shell.

Acknowledgement. This work was supported by China University Student Scientific and Technological Innovation Projects (091056156) sponsored by Ministry of Education of the People's Republic of China. The authors would like to thank Professor Jie Yang for the support of mathematic theory.

References

1. Chadwick, J.E., Haumann, D.R., Parent, R.E.: Layered construction for deformable animated characters. In: Proc. of SIGGRAPH 1989, New York, NY, USA, pp. 243–252 (1989)
2. Fernandes, J.L.M., Martins, P.A.F.: All-hexahedral remeshing for the finite element analysis of metal forming processes. J. Finite Elements in Analysis and Design 43(8), 666–679 (2007)

3. Moore., M., Wilhelms, J.: Collision detection and response for computer animation. In: Proc. of SIGGRAPH 1988, New York, NY, USA, pp. 289–298 (1988)
4. Mamalis, A.G., Horvah, M., Branis, A.S., Manolakos, D.E.: Finite element simulation of chip formation in orthogonal metal cutting. J. Materials Processing Technology 110(1), 19–27 (2001)
5. Miller, G.S.P.: The motion dynamics of snakes and worms. In: Proc. of SIGGRAPH 1988, New York, NY, USA, pp. 169–173 (1988)
6. Mller, M., McMillan, L., Dorsey, J., Jagnow, R.: Real-time simulation of deformation and fracture of stiff materials. In: Proceedings of the Eurographic Workshop on Computer Animation and Simulation, New York, NY, USA, pp. 113–124 (2011)
7. O'Brien, J.F., Bargteil, A.W., Hodgins, J.K.: Graphical modeling and animation of ductile fracture. In: Proc. of SIGGRAPH 2002, New York, NY, USA, pp. 291–294 (2002)
8. O'Brien, J.F., Hodgins, J.K.: Graphical modeling and animation of brittle fracture. In: Proc. of SIGGRAPH 1999, New York, NY, USA, pp. 137–146 (1999)
9. Parker, R.G., O'Brien, J.F.: Real-time deformation and fracture in a game environment. In: Proc. of the 2009 ACM SIGGRAPH/Eurographics Symposium on Computer Animation (SCA 2009), New York, NY, USA, pp. 165–175 (2009)
10. Platt, S.M., Badler, N.I.: Animating facial expressions. In: Proc. of SIGGRAPH 1981, New York, NY, USA, pp. 245–252 (1981)
11. Rodrigues, T., Pires, R., Dias, J.M.S.: D4MD: deformation system for a vehicle simulation game. In: Advances in Computer Entertainment Technology, pp. 330–333 (2005)
12. Shlafman, S., Tal, A., Katz, S.: Metamorphosis of polyhedral surfaces using decomposition. Eurographics Proceedings (CGF) 22(3), 219–228 (2002)
13. Tu, X., Terzopoulos, D.: Artificial fishes: physics, locomotion, perception, behavior. In: Proc. of SIGGRAPH 1994, New York, NY, USA, pp. 43–50 (1994)
14. Terzopoulos, D., Waters, K.: Physically-based facial modeling, analysis, and animation. J. Journal of Visualization and Computer Animation 12, 73–80 (1990)
15. Van Den Bergen, G.: Efficient collision detection of complex deformable models using AABB trees. J. Graph. Tools 2(4), 1–13 (1998)
16. Van Den Bergen, G.: A fast and robust GJK implementation for collision detection of convex objects. J. Graph. Tools 4(2), 7–25 (1999)
17. Waters, K.: A muscle model for animation three dimensional facial expression. In: Proc. of SIGGRAPH 1987, New York, NY, USA, pp. 17–24 (1987)
18. Waters, K., Terzopoulos, D.: Modelling and animating faces using scanned data. J. Visualization and Computer Animation 2(4), 123–128 (1990)
19. Yun, Z.X., Long, J.X., Guo, Q.W., Zhi, G.Y.: Vehicle crash accident reconstruction based on the analysis 3D deformation of the auto-body. J. Advances in Engineering Software 39(6), 459–465 (2008)

LocoTest: Deploying and Evaluating Physics-Based Locomotion on Multiple Simulation Platforms

Stevie Giovanni and KangKang Yin

National University of Singapore
{stevie,kkyin}@comp.nus.edu.sg

Abstract. In the pursuit of pushing active character control into games, we have deployed a generalized physics-based locomotion control scheme to multiple simulation platforms, including ODE, PhysX, Bullet, and Vortex. We first overview the main characteristics of these physics engines. Then we illustrate the major steps of integrating active character controllers with physics SDKs, together with necessary implementation details. We also evaluate and compare the performance of the locomotion control on different simulation platforms. Note that our work only represents an initial attempt at doing such evaluation, and additional refinement of the methodology and results can still be expected. We release our code online to encourage more follow-up works, as well as more interactions between the research community and the game development community.

Keywords: physics-based animation, simulation, locomotion, motion control.

1 Introduction

Developing biped locomotion controllers has been a long-time research interest in the Robotics community [3]. In the Computer Animation community, Hodgins and her colleagues [12,7] started the many efforts on locomotion control of simulated characters. Among these efforts, the simplest class of locomotion control methods employs real-time feedback laws for robust balance recovery [12,7,14,9,4]. Optimization-based control methods, on the other hand, are more mathematically involved, but can incorporate more motion objectives automatically [10,8]. Recently, data-driven approaches have become quite common, where motion capture trajectories are referenced to further improve the naturalness of simulated motions [14,10,9]. For a more complete review, We refer the interested readers to the recent state-of-the-art report on character animation using simulated physics [6].

With so many locomotion control methods available now in academia, we cannot help but wonder: Can these methods work beyond their specific dynamics formulations or chosen physics engines? If they do generalize well across different physics engines, to what degree does the selection of a particular engine affect the stability and performance of the character control? What components are involved in porting a control scheme onto different simulation platforms? And how difficult would they be?

We show in this paper that it is relatively easy to deploy one type of locomotion control scheme [4] to multiple simulation platforms. Furthermore, the choice of simulation engines is not crucial, if the controller itself is sufficiently general and robust. We hope our work can encourage more researchers to demonstrate their character control schemes on publicly-available physics engines, for easy benchmarking and comparison.

From the perspective of game development, an observation is that passive object dynamics and Ragdoll simulation are very common features in action games today; yet the adoption of active character control is rare. As a result, simulation engines are tested extensively for their ability to simulate the motion of passive objects, such as an object knocking down a brick wall; while as far as we know, there is no test on physics engines for their ability to simulate active objects. We hope our work can help increase the awareness of game and engine developers, who usually work on one designated platform with tight schedule and budget constraints, that it is now the time to push more active character control into games and physics engines.

The locomotion control scheme we choose for deployment is the generalized biped walking control method of Coros et al. [4]. This scheme produces simple yet robust walking controllers that do not require captured reference motions, and generalize well across gait parameters, character proportions, motion styles, and walking skills. Moreover, the authors released their code online as a Google project named cartwheel-3d(http:://code.google.com/p/cartwheel-3d/). cartwheel-3d is built on top of an open-source dynamics engine ODE (Open Dynamics Engine), which is commonly used in the animation research community for its superior constraint accuracy. We further choose two simulation engines that are more popular in the game development community: PhysX and Bullet. PhysX is supported by NVIDIA and currently dominates the market share among the released game titles. Bullet is open source and has great overall performance. Other popular game physics engines today include Havok and Newton. Due to the space limit, we will not discuss these engines further. The biomechanics and robotics communities, however, are often skeptical of simulation results in the graphics literature because of the use of physics simulators that are also associated with games. Therefore, we choose a fourth engine Vortex to test the locomotion controllers. Vortex is currently the leading dynamics platform in the mechanical engineering and robotics industries. Its simulation tools have been widely used in virtual prototyping and testing, virtual training, mission rehearsal, as well as in serious games.

We will first give an overview of the chosen simulation platforms in Section 2. We then discuss the key steps in integrating character control and simulation with physics SDKs in Section 3. The implementation details are further discussed in Section 4. Readers who are not interested in these details can safely bypass Section 4 and jump directly to the evaluation Section 5. We concentrate only on implementation and performance issues pertinent to the porting of locomotion controllers. For evaluation and comparison of other aspects of physics engines, such as constraint stability or collision detection accuracy, we refer the interested readers to [1], where a series of simple tasks with passive objects and constraints are performed and compared.

2 Simulation Platforms Overview

ODE (Open Dynamics Engine) is an open source library for simulating rigid body dynamics and collisions [13]. The library is mostly written in C++, and provides both C

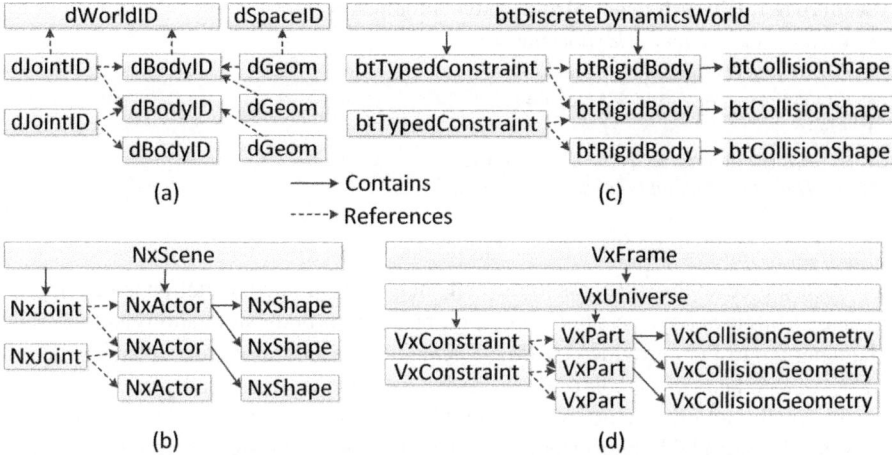

Fig. 1. Partial architecture diagrams relevant to active rigid character control and simulation of four physics SDKs: (a) ODE (b) PhysX (c) Bullet (d) Vortex

and C++ interface. All classes and functions are prefixed with "*d*". ODE uses fixed-time stepping. The latest ODE version 0.11.1 was released in October 2009, and currently ODE's development seems to be suspended.

The NVIDIA PhysX supports rigid and soft body dynamics, collision detection, fluids, particles, vehicle and character controllers [11]. The SDK has a C++ programming interface, and all classes are prefixed with "*Nx*". Fixed and variable time steps are possible. PhysX also provides GPU acceleration for fluids, clothes, and soft bodies, with a CUDA implementation. The latest PhysX SDK V3.0 was released in June 2011, which is a major rewrite of the PhysX SDK. Our code based on V2.8.4 does not work directly on V3.0.

Bullet provides rigid body and soft body dynamics, collision detection, and vehicle and character controllers [5]. It is open source and free for commercial use on many platforms including PLAYSTATION 3, XBox360, Wii, PC, Linux, Mac OSX and iPhone. Bullet is implemented in C++ and all classes are prefixed with "*bt*". It supports both variable and fixed time steps. The latest version of Bullet is 2.78 released in April 2011, which we use in our code.

The CMLabs Vortex supports rigid body dynamics, collision detection, fluids, particles, cables and vehicles [2]. It is a C++ toolkit and all classes are prefixed with "*Vx*". Vortex allows arbitrary changes to the structure of the simulated system in between steps, without any need to reconfigure or restart the simulation. It also integrates with graphics toolkits such as OpenSceneGraph (OSG) and Vega Prime. Fixed and variable time steps are possible. Our code is implemented on Vortex 5.0.1, and the latest release was in August 2011 version 5.0.2.

Fig. 1 shows partial architecture diagrams of the four engines. Relevant classes will be referred to in the following sections. From a programmer's perspective, PhysX and Vortex provide better documentation than ODE and Bullet. Although ODE and Bullet

Pseudocode 1. Character control and simulation pipeline

1: *Create a simulation world;* //Section 4.1
2: *Create objects;* //Section 4.2 and 4.4
3: *Create joints;* //Section 4.3 and 4.4
4: *Loop:*
5:     *Apply control and accumulate forces;*
6:     *Detect contact and collisions;*//Section 4.5
7:     *Timestep;*

are open source so direct access to the code helps where documentation is lacking. All dynamics engines provide sample code on basic rigid body simulation. Note that the character controllers provided by PhysX and Bullet do not use "real" physics, but are rather descendants of customized and dedicated code in traditional games to move a player. Such controllers employ heuristic kinematics and quasi-physics to achieve the illusion of controllable and responsive characters. Pure physics-based character controllers are still challenging to construct in games today, and this paper taps the tip of the iceberg by deploying a truly physical locomotion control scheme on various simulation platforms.

3 Character Control and Simulation Pipeline

We deploy the generalized biped walking controller of Coros et al. [4], who released an implementation in C++ on top of ODE. The simulation pipeline for active rigid character control is listed in Pseudocode 1. To switch dynamics engines, each step needs to be mapped to SDK-specific code. We explain Line 5 and Line 7 in this section, and defer all other implementation details to Section 4.

Line 5 of Pseudocode 1 basically is where the controller computes active control torques and accumulates external forces for each rigid link of the character. Then these torques and forces are passed to the physics engine. We refer interested readers to the paper [4] and our source code for details of the control algorithm. Line 7 of Pseudocode 1 steps the dynamics system forward in time for a small time step: constrained equations of motion are solved and kinematic quantities are integrated. Here the major difference of the four engines is whether they separate collision detection and timestepping into two parts. ODE separates them into two distinct steps as shown in Line 6 and 7; while PhysX, Bullet, and Vortex integrate collision detection into their timestepping so Line 6 should really be merged into Line 7 for these three platforms.

ODE provides two timestepping functions: *dWorldStep* and *dWorldQuickStep*. The first one uses the Dantzig algorithm to solve the LCP (Linear Complementarity Problem) formulation of the constrained equations of motion, while *dWorldQuickStep* uses the iterative PGS (Projected Gauss Seidel) method which sacrifices accuracy for speed. Both methods use a fixed user-defined time step. Hereafter we use ODEquick to refer to simulations on ODE using the iterative solver. The PGS method is also used in PhysX and Bullet, and the users can specify the maximum number of iterations allowed. Vortex provides both a standard and an iterative LCP solver, just like ODE. We only test its standard solver *kConstraintSolverStd* in this work. PhysX, Bullet, and Vortex can

Table 1. ODE decouples the simulation world into a dynamics world and a collision space. Thus it takes two commands to step the system forward. While PhysX, Bullet, and Vortex unify the two concepts and integrate collision detection into the timestepping.

	ODE	PhysX	Bullet	Vortex
simulation world	world space	scene	world	frame
timestepping function	dSpaceCollide(...) dWorldStep(...)	->simulate(...)	->stepSimulation(...)	->step()

advance fixed time steps as well as variable time steps during timestepping. For ease of comparison, we always use fixed time steps for all four engines in all our experiments.

4 Implementation Details

This section details the major procedures in supporting character control using different SDKs: managing a simulation world; instantiating rigid bodies and joints; and handling contacts and collisions. Commonalities and differences between ODE, PhysX, Bullet, and Vortex are summarized and contrasted. We also illustrate with pseudocode and snippets where necessary.

4.1 Simulation World

A simulation *world* is the virtual counterpart of the physical world that hosts the virtual objects and constraints governed by physics laws in dynamics engines. The control component of cartwheel-3d maintains a world of its own too, containing a copy of all the objects and constraints being simulated. Deploying the control on a new physics engine is thus equivalent to mapping between the SDK's world and the controller's world, as well as passing data between them.

The initialization of the simulation *world* involves specification of: dynamic properties of the world such as gravity; collision properties such as maximum number of contacts and maximum penetration depth allowed; and default contact materials such as coefficient of restitution and friction. ODE decouples the concept of the simulation world into a dynamics world which handles rigid body dynamics and a collision space which handles collision detection, as shown in Table 1. In PhysX, Bullet, and Vortex, however, one world handles both dynamics and collision. The world detects collisions inside the timestepping function shown in Table 1.

One point worth noting is the great flexibility and modularity of Bullet. Many parts of the Bullet world, including the world itself, can be switched to different implementations. We use the default dynamics world *btDiscreteDynamicsWorld*, for which we choose the default broadphase and narrowphase collision detection implementation and the default constraint solver *btSequentialImpulseConstraintSolver*. It is also interesting to note that Bullet actually contains the ODE quickstep solver, due to the open source nature of both engines, so that the users can switch the solvers easily if they so choose.

Table 2. Dynamic, geometric, and static objects have different names in different SDKs. We refer them as bodies, shapes, and static shapes in our discussion.

	body (dynamic object)	shape (geometric object)	static shape (static object)
ODE	*body*	*geom*	*geom* (not attached to a body)
PhysX	*actor*	*shape*	*actor* (with no dynamic properties)
Bullet	*rigidBody*	*collisionShape*	*collisionObject*
Vortex	*part*	*collisionGeometry*	*part* (frozen by users after creation)

4.2 Objects

Objects within the simulation world can be classified into three categories: the first type carries the kinematic and dynamic properties including position, velocity, and mass and inertia; the second type specifies the geometric properties, or shape, of an object. Hereafter we refer to the first type as bodies, and the second type as shapes. Shapes are usually attached to bodies for collision detection, and one body may be associated with one or more collision shapes. Common collision primitives include box, sphere, capsule, and plane. Advanced collision shapes such as height field, convex hull, and triangle mesh are also supported by these four engines. There is a third kind of objects that we call static shapes, which represent static objects such as ground which usually do not move and are only needed for collision detection. Static shapes do not attach to bodies and do not posses time-varying kinematic quantities. Table 2 lists the names of these types of objects in different physics SDKs.

In ODE there is a special type of *geom* called *space*, which can contain other *geoms* and *spaces*. The collision world in ODE is in fact a *space*. In PhysX, a body is called an *actor*. Actors with specified dynamic properties, such as mass and inertia, are dynamic; otherwise they are static. Similarly, a body in Vortex, called a *part*, can be either static or dynamic. A *part* is dynamic by default after creation, but users can freeze it as a static object. ODE, PhysX, and Vortex all support multiple compound collision shapes attached to a single body. But in Bullet, each body or static shape can only have one collision shape attached. Also Bullet does not support relative transformation between collision shapes and the bodies they attach to. Therefore collision shapes in Bullet posses identical position and orientation as the bodies they are associated with. To achieve more sophisticated collision shapes with various initial configuration in Bullet, users can first define a compound shape to store all the needed component shapes, and then encapsulate different relative transformations into the child shapes.

4.3 Joints

Joints are constraints that limit the relative movements of two otherwise independent bodies. We classify the types of joints by counting how many rotational and translational Degrees of Freedom (DoFs) a joint permits. Table 3 lists the common joint types supported by the four SDKs. Again the same type of joint may be named differently on different platforms.

All the engines support a large set of common joint types. PhysX and Bullet also provide a special kind of six-DoF freedom joint. Each DoF of a freedom joint can

Table 3. Common joint types supported by the four simulation engines. We classify the types of joints by counting how many rotational and translational DoFs a joint permits. For example, 1R1T means 1 rotational DoF and 1 translational DoF.

#DoFs	0	1R	2R	3R	1T	1R1T	6
ODE	fixed	hinge	universal	ball-and-socket	slider	piston	
PhysX	fixed	revolute		spherical	prismatic	cylindrical	freedom
Bullet		hinge	universal	point2point	slider		freedom
Vortex	RPRO	hinge	universal	ball-and-socket	prismatic	cylindrical	

```
NxD6JointDesc d6Desc;
d6Desc.xMotion = NX_D6JOINT_MOTION_LOCKED;
d6Desc.yMotion = NX_D6JOINT_MOTION_LOCKED;
d6Desc.zMotion = NX_D6JOINT_MOTION_LOCKED;
d6Desc.twistMotion = NX_D6JOINT_MOTION_FREE;
d6Desc.swing1Motion = NX_D6JOINT_MOTION_FREE;
d6Desc.swing2Motion = NX_D6JOINT_MOTION_LOCKED;
NxD6Joint * d6Joint=(NxD6Joint*)gScene->createJoint(d6Desc);
```

Snippet 1. Constructing a universal joint using a freedom joint in PhysX

be locked or unlocked independently, to model almost any type of joints. Snippet 1 illustrates how to construct a universal joint from a freedom joint in PhysX. In addition to the listed joint types, PhysX also implements distance joint, point in plane joint, point on line joint, and Pulley Joint. Bullet provides an additional cone twist constraint which is a special point to point constraint that adds cone and twist axis limits. Vortex supports even more types of constraints, such as the Angular2Position3, CarWheel, and Winch constraint. The zero-DoF joint RPRO can also be relaxed to model a six-DoF joint. Moreover, Vortex supports velocity constraints such as the ScrewJoint, Differential, and GearRatio constraints. In our case of walking control, however, the basic rotational joints of one to three DoFs are already sufficient.

To achieve desired joint behavior, correctly setting up the various joint parameters is the key. For instance, most rotational joints are modeled by an anchor point and up to two rotational axes. A third axis is computed implicitly as a cross product of the two defined axes. These axes form the right-handed local coordinate frame, as well as help define joint limits. In PhysX however, except for the 6DoF freedom joint, all other joints adopt a left-handed local coordinate frame. Understanding the joint local frame is crucial when using the built-in Proportional Derivative (PD) controllers to power or motorize certain joints, where users can specify the desired joint angles and velocities.

Specifying joint angle limits is usually straightforward except for ball-and-socket joints, for which only PhysX supports the specification of the local rotational axes. In PhysX and Bullet, however, limits can be specified for a twist-and-swing decomposition of the angular freedoms of 6-DoF freedom joints. We thus create ball-and-socket joints from freedom joints when using these two SDKs. In ODE and Vortex, we circumvent this problem by attaching an additional angular motor constraint to the two bodies that a

```
dJointID j = dJointCreateBall(worldID, 0); //create ball-and-socket joint
dJointAttach(j, parentBody, childBody);//attach to bodies
...//set joint parameters;
dJointID aMotor = dJointCreateAMotor(worldID, 0); //create angular motor
dJointAttach(aMotor, parentBody, childBody);//attach to bodies
...//set amotor parameters;
dJointSetAMotorAxis (j,0,rel,x,y,z);//set motor axis 0
dJointSetAMotorAxis (j,2,rel,x,y,z);//set motor axis 2
//set joint limits for swing angle 1
dJointSetAMotorParam(aMotor, dParamLoStop, minSwingAngle1);
dJointSetAMotorParam(aMotor, dParamHiStop, maxSwingAngle1);
...//set joint limits for swing angle 2 and twist angle
```

Snippet 2. Angular motors help specify joint limits for a ball-and-socket joint in ODE

```
NxRevoluteJointDesc revoluteDesc; //joint descriptor
revoluteDesc.actor[0] = actor1; //attach actors constrained by the joint
revoluteDesc.actor[1] = actor2;
revoluteDesc.setGlobalAnchor(NxVec3(p.x,p.y,p.z)); //set the anchor point
revoluteDesc.setGlobalAxis(NxVec3(a.x,a.y,a.z)); //set the rotation axis
//create the joint
NxRevoluteJoint * revoluteJoint =
(NxRevoluteJoint *) gScene->createJoint(revoluteDesc);
```

Snippet 3. Revolute joint setup in PhysX

ball-and-socket joint constrains, and then specifying limits for the angular motor along its three motor axes as shown in Snippet 2.

Lastly, ODE provides users contact joints for handling collisions. Contact joints prevent two bodies from penetrating one another by only allowing the bodies to have an "outgoing" velocity in the direction of the contact normal. We will discuss this further in Section 4.5 where we look at collision handling mechanisms of the four simulation platforms.

4.4 Creating Objects and Joints

Another difference of the four physics SDKs is the way objects and joints are created. In PhysX every object has a descriptor, which is used to specify all the arguments of an object before its creation. Snippet 3 shows a sample on how to create a revolute joint in PhysX. ODE, on the other hand, allows users to specify parameters for objects after their creation. Snippet 4 shows the code for creating the same revolute joint (although called hinge joint) in ODE. Bullet adopts yet another approach by providing object-creating functions with long lists of arguments. Snippet 5 illustrates this point. Vortex supplies two types of procedures, one with many arguments as in Bullet; and the other with less arguments during creation, but users need to specify additional parameters later on as in ODE.

These examples also show that different physics engines add objects into the simulation world in different ways. PhysX starts with a scene (i.e., the simulation world)

```
dJointID j = dJointCreateHinge(worldID, jointGroup); //create the joint
dJointAttach(j,body1,body2); //attach bodies constrained by the joint
dJointSetHingeAnchor(j, p.x, p.y, p.z); //set the anchor point
dJointSetHingeAxis(j, a.x, a.y, a.z); //set the rotation axis
```

Snippet 4. Hinge joint setup in ODE

```
//create the constraint with all necessary parameters
btTypedConstraint * constraint =
  new btHingeConstraint(object_a,object_b,pivot_in_a,pivot_in_b,...);
//add the joint into the world
world->addConstraint(constraint,bool disableCollision=true);
```

Snippet 5. Hinge constraint setup in Bullet

as the main object. Every other object is created using one of the creation methods of the scene with corresponding descriptors as arguments. In ODE users first apply for an object ID from the world, and then create the object with detailed specifications. In Bullet and Vortex, users add objects to the world after their creation.

4.5 Collision Detection and Processing

All four simulation platforms supply built-in collision detection engines. PhysX, Bullet and Vortex are generally acknowledged for providing more powerful and robust collision systems, such as stable convex hull collision detection and warmstart of contact constraints. From the point of view of walking control of a single character with rigid links, however, the basic ODE collision detection is already sufficient. The major difference of these platforms is how they activate the collision detection module. PhysX, Bullet, and Vortex provide fully automatic collision detection and seamless integration with the dynamics solver. Users only need to define collision shapes, and then all the collision constraints are generated implicitly and desired collision behavior will automatically happen. In ODE, however, users have to call the broad phase collision detection manually before timestepping, as shown in Table 1. In addition, users need to supply a callback function to further invoke the narrow phase collision detection, as shown in Snippet 6. Lastly, users must explicitly create contact joints from detected collisions for the dynamics solver to take into account the collisions, as shown in the for loop of Snippet 6.

4.6 Collision Filtering

The most effective way that users can influence the simulation performance is by filtering unnecessary collision detections. There are several mechanisms to filter collisions, as listed in Tabel 4.

ODE provides built-in support to filter collisions between different groups

Table 4. Collision filtering mechanisms

	object pairs	group pairs	bit mask	callback
ODE		✓	✓ 32-bit	must
PhysX	✓	✓	✓ 128-bit	optional
Bullet			✓ 32-bit	optional
Vortex	✓	✓		optional

```
void collisionCallBack(dGeomID shape1,dGeomID shape2,...)
{
    //filter collision
    ......
    //call the narrow phase collision detection function
    //cps records contact position, normal, penetration depth etc.
    num = dCollide(shape1,shape2,max,&(cps[0].geom),sizeof(dContact))

    //generate contact joint for each detected collision
    for(int i=0;i<num;i++)
    {
        //define the material parameters for the collision in cps
        ......
        //create a contact joint based on the collision point cps
        dJointID c=dJointCreateContact(worldID,contactGroupID,&cps[i]);
        //assign feedback variable for collision postprocessing
        dJointSetFeedback(c,&(jointFeedback[i]));
    }
}
```

Snippet 6. ODE narrow phase collision detection callback function

of shapes during the broad phase collision detection. Each *geom* also has a 32-bit "category" and 32-bit "collide" bitfield to bypass collision testing between shapes in different categories. As explained earlier, users have to define a collision callback function for ODE to incorporate contact and collision constraints into the dynamics. Inside this callback, users have complete freedom to further filter out collisions between shapes. In the context of character control, collisions between joined limbs, such as the upper arm and the lower arm, should be ignored.

In PhysX, collisions between pairs of jointed bodies are disabled by default. Moreover, users can change the collision detection behavior between an arbitrary pair of shapes or actor groups by setting related flags. Different from the 32-bit bit mask mechanism in ODE and Bullet, users are able to specify a 128-bit group mask for each shape in PhysX. This mask is further combined with user specified constants and operators to generate a boolean value indicating if contacts should be generated for a pair of shapes.

Bullet does not have built-in support to filter collisions between a given pair of shapes or groups. It does have a bitwise filter mechanism similar to that of ODE that can be used to tailor collision detection between shapes and groups. In Vortex, users can disable collision detection between pairs of objects, assemblies of objects, and groups of objects (identified by IDs), either through the appropriate container classes or through an intersect filter class.

Users can also define customized callback functions for total control over the collision or intersect filtering mechanism, in PhysX, Bullet, and Vortex, just like in ODE. The difference is that callback functions are optional except for ODE. It is worth noting that mask-based collision selection happens a lot further up the tool chain than the callbacks do, so collision masks are preferred to callbacks if they are sufficient for your purpose. PhysX and Vortex can also automatically detect inactive dynamic bodies,

Table 5. Motion deviation analysis. The simulated motion on ODE serves as the baseline. ODEquick uses the iterative LCP solver rather than the slower Dantzig algorithm. We investigate nine walking controllers: inplace walk, normal walk, happy walk, cartoony sneak, chicken walk, drunken walk, jump walk, snake walk, and wire walk.

	walk style	inplace	normal	happy	sneak	chicken	drunken	jump	snake	wire
control	desired speed	0.0	1.0	2.0	1.5	2.5	0.5	1.0	3.0	-1.0
parameter	cycle duration	0.6	0.6	0.5	0.6	0.5	0.6	0.5	0.5	0.6
	step width	0.12	0.12	0.1	0.14	0.12	0.2	0.15	0.13	0.1
motion	ODEquick-ODE	2.3e-4	1.6e-4	2.8e-4	9.5e-4	1.0e-3	1.6e-3	7.9e-4	6.6e-4	9.1e-4
distance	PhysX-ODE	5.5e-2	1.9e-2	9.6e-2	8.3e-1	8.4e-2	5.6e-2	9.6e-2	7.3e-2	1.5e-1
	Bullet-ODE	1.7e-2	1.2e-2	1.5e-2	5.9e-2	1.3e-2	1.7e-2	2.9e-2	1.5e-2	1.4e-2
	Vortex-ODE	1.8e-3	3.5e-3	7.1e-3	2.7e-2	6.4e-3	1.9e-3	6.1e-3	1.1e-2	3.7e-3

bodies that do not move for a period of time, and put them into sleep until external forces wake them up. Sleeping bodies are not detected for collision or simulated to save time.

4.7 Collision Postprocessing

Postprocessing of contact and collision forces is needed when the locomotion controller wishes to regulate the Ground Reaction Forces(GRFs) between the character and the ground, to calculate GRF-based feedback controls, or simply to monitor or visualize the GRFs. Collision postprocessing should be done after the timestepping, when the contact and collision forces or impulses have been resolved by the constrained dynamics solver.

Postprocessing contacts in ODE involves reading back the contact information from the *jointFeedback* array initialized on the last line of Snippet 6. Bullet initializes a collision dispatcher during the creation of the simulation world, and from the dispatcher the contact information can be obtained for postprocessing. In PhysX, users subclass *NxUserContactReport* and register an instanced object of this class during the initialization of the simulation world. Then *onContactNotify(...)* of the object receives the contact information for each pair of shapes or actors that has requested contact notification through proper flag setting. Similar to PhysX, Vortex users can subclass *VxIntersectSubscriber* to access contact events before or after timestepping. However, if users just need to read back the contacts after the dynamics has stepped forward, a simpler way is to access *VxDynamicsContact* via a pointer of *VxUniverse*.

5 Performance Evaluation and Comparison

We test nine controllers walking in various styles provided by the original cartwheel-3d online distribution. For common simulation parameters we use the cartwheel-3d defaults on all platforms, e.g., a ground friction of 0.8; a fixed time step of $0.5ms$ etc. Since each controller can walk the character successfully with a range of parameter settings, such as the desired walking speed, duration of one walk cycle, and width of the steps, we manually choose one point in the control parameter space as listed in Table 5. Then we measure the distance between the motion simulated on each engine

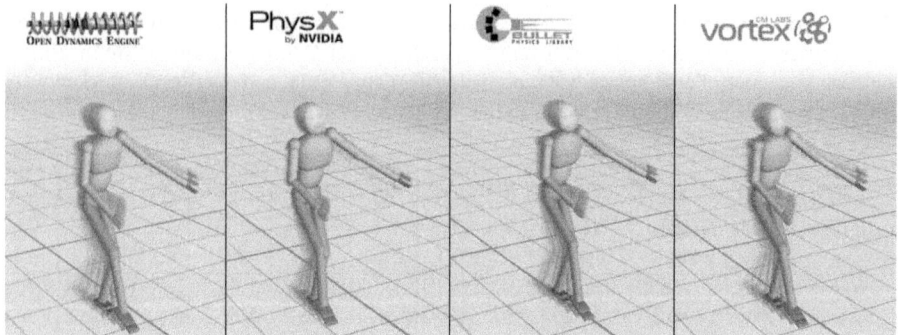

Fig. 2. Screen captures at the same instants of time of the happy walk, simulated on top of four physics engines: ODE, PhysX, Bullet, and Vortex (from left to right)

and that on ODE. That is, we use the motion simulated on ODE as the baseline. The distance $d(m,\tilde{m})$ between two simulated motions m and $\tilde{m}$ is defined as follows:

$$d(m,\tilde{m}) = \frac{\sum\limits_{k=1}^{n}\sum\limits_{i=1}^{l}\|\mathbf{p}_k^i - \tilde{\mathbf{p}}_k^i\|}{nlh} \quad (1)$$

where n is the number of frames in $\tilde{m}$ and l is the number of links of the character. We record ten cycles of a simulated walk at $30Hz$ as m and $\tilde{m}$, starting from the fifth cycle when the walk has converged onto its limit cycle. Then m is time aligned with $\tilde{m}$ and resampled to n frames for comparison. $\mathbf{p}_k^i$ is the center of mass location of each limb in the character root frame. h is the height of the character for normalization.

Perceptually the limit cycles of the simulated walks from all nine controllers are quite similar, although there are cases the step length or width is noticeably different. We encourage the readers to check the accompanying demo video yourself. The difference of the beginning start-up cycles is also notable. In fact, due to the initial difference, some characters walk diagonally rather than on the default straight line. Quantitatively, the simulations on ODE and Vortex resemble more, and their averaged limb position difference never exceeds 3% of the character height. Usually the simulations from PhysX differ more. Fig. 2 shows a side-by-side comparison of the same frames of the happy walk simulated on each platform.

We test the stability and robustness of the normal walk controller on each engine with respect to the size of the simulation time step. The original cartwheel-3d uses a default simulation time step of $0.5ms$ on top of ODE. We further search for three time steps as shown in Table 6. bound1 is the largest time step before the simulation becomes unstable; bound2 is the largest time step before the simulated character falls; and bound3 is the largest time step before the distance between the simulated motion from the default motion simulated at the default time step becomes larger than 0.1. Note that in PhysX the character falls using a time step larger than $0.9ms$, when the motion distance is 0.06. We can see that simulations in PhysX and Bullet are much more stable at large time steps than in ODE and Vortex, but they do not differ much in terms of the stability of the walking controller once the simulation moves into the stable region.

Table 6. Stability analysis with respect to the size of the time step in ms

Engine	bound1	bound2	bound3
ODE	18	1.6	1.0
ODEquick	18	1.4	1.0
PhysX	150	0.9	–
Bullet	100	1.3	1.0
Vortex	35	1.6	1.2

Table 7. Stability analysis of the normal walk with respect to external push

Engine	$d(m_{8/9}, m_{10/11})$	$d(m_{8/9}, m_{14/15})$
ODE	0.185	0.036
ODEquick	0.196	0.037
PhysX	0.172	0.006
Bullet	0.174	0.014
Vortex	0.157	0.002

Table 8. Average wall clock time of one simulation step in milliseconds using the default simulation time step $0.5ms$. Timing measured on a Dell Precision Workstation T5500 with Intel Xeon X5680 3.33GHz CPU (6 cores) and 8GB RAM. Multithreading tests with PhysX and Vortex may not be valid due to unknown issues with thread scheduling.

Engine	1 character	10 characters	100 characters	100 characters with 6 threads
ODE	0.099	0.96	9.9	×
ODE-quick	0.064	0.61	6.6	×
PhysX	0.300	1.57	14.2	11.6
Bullet	0.107	0.96	11.0	–
Vortex	0.120	1.60	17.4	12.4

We also test the robustness of the normal walk controller on each engine with respect to external perturbations. The character gets pushed by a planar force of $(250, 150)N$ backward and sideways for $200ms$ at the onset of the tenth cycle m_{10}. Using the motion from the eighth and ninth cycles, denoted as $m_{8/9}$, as the baseline motion, we then compare how much $m_{10/11}$ and $m_{14/15}$ differ from the baseline $m_{8/9}$. Table 7 shows that the motion error caused by the external push diminishes quickly, and the character eventually goes back to the original limit cycle. Note here we only measure the distance between the feet positions, as the controller uses a foot placement strategy to regain balance so the upper body postures do not differ too much after the perturbation.

The computational cost for simulating 10 characters is roughly distributed as follows: 2% on rendering; 18% on control; 65% on simulation including collision detection and constraint solving (except ODEQuick which is faster). Table 8 shows the average timing of one simulation step using the default time step $0.5ms$, for one character, ten characters, and a hundred characters. We see a near linear degradation of the performance, probably mainly because our characters all walk independently. We also tried simulating multiple characters with GPU acceleration turned on in PhysX, but we did not observe any performance gain with our NVIDIA graphics card GeForce GTX 570. This is because rigid body collisions are still processed by the CPU in the PhysX version we use. Furthermore, we tested the multithreading capability of PhysX and Vortex. Unfortunately our tests with 6 threads on our 6-core machine did not show significant speedup either. This contradicts with released tests from PhysX and Vortex. In diagnosing this problem, we found that only two of our six cores are active no matter how many threads we specify for the engine. This may be caused by the Python interface or wrapper used in our software, or unknown issues in the interaction between the Windows thread scheduler and Python. Bullet also provides multithreading and GPU acceleration, which we have not tested due to lack of documentation.

6 Conclusion

We have deployed the generalized locomotion controller in cartwheel-3d to multiple simulation platforms with ease. Our code is released online at http://animation.comp.nus.edu.sg/locotest.html. The porting part of this project was completed within four weeks by a first year graduate student who had no experience in simulation and control but had basic knowledge on computer animation. The original controllers can immediately walk the character successfully after porting, although in slightly different styles. The robustness of the controllers in multiple styles stays across different platforms. Our experience suggests that it is plausible and straightforward to integrate the chosen locomotion controller into game physics today.

We would like to emphasize that our results are specific to the type of controller being tested [4], and its specific implementation in cartwheel-3d. This implementation controls the walking style through explicit PD torques at every simulation time step. The advantages of such an implementation include: computing the control at each time step is cheap and easy; porting the controller to off-the-shelf physics engines is straightforward; and the simulated character exhibits natural compliance when pushed. The disadvantage is that the simulation has to take smaller time steps, compared to other methods which integrate the equations of motion directly into each control time step. However, all our tested engines provide built-in joint PD controls, some of which use implicit methods to achieve better stability at larger time steps. We plan to explore such stable PD controllers in the near future.

Our performance analysis mainly serves to test the plausibility of deploying the walking control to multiple simulation platforms, and is not for accurately comparing the performance of the physics engines themselves. Different engines have different parameter settings that can trade off among robustness, accuracy, and speed. We use default settings of these parameters on all platforms, which may favor different aspect of the performance depending on the preference of the specific engine. We believe more interactions between the academia and the game industry are needed to achieve better active character control for games and game engines today. Hopefully our effort in this work can serve as a solid starting point.

Acknowledgements. We wish to thank Michiel van de Panne and Stelian Coros for providing helpful suggestions on an early draft of this paper; and Daniel Holz from CMLabs for verifying our implementation details and multithreading test for Vortex.

References

1. Boeing, A., Braunl, T.: Evaluation of real-time physics simulation systems. In: GRAPHITE 2007 Proceedings of the 5th International Conference on Computer Graphics and Interactive Techniques in Australia and Southeast Asia (2007)
2. CMLabs Simulations, I.: Vortex 5.0.1 vx developer guide (2011)

3. Collins, S., Ruina, A., Tedrake, R., Wisse, M.: Efficient bipedal robots based on passive-dynamic walkers. Science 307(5712), 1082–1085 (2005)
4. Coros, S., Beaudoin, P., van de Panne, M.: Generalized biped walking control. ACM Transctions on Graphics 29(4), Article 130 (2010)
5. Coumans, E.: Bullet 2.76 physics sdk manual (2010)
6. Geijtenbeek, T., Pronost, N., Egges, A., Overmars, M.H.: Interactive character animation using simulated physics. In: Eurographics - State of the Art Reports (2011)
7. Hodgins, J.K., Wooten, W.L., Brogan, D.C., O'Brien, J.F.: Animating human athletics. In: Proceedings of SIGGRAPH 1995, pp. 71–78 (1995)
8. de Lasa, M., Mordatch, I., Hertzmann, A.: Feature-based locomotion controllers. ACM Transctions on Graphics 29(4), Article 131 (2010)
9. Lee, Y., Kim, S., Lee, J.: Data-driven biped control. ACM Transctions on Graphics 29(4), Article 129 (2010)
10. Muico, U., Lee, Y., Popović, J., Popović, Z.: Contact-aware nonlinear control of dynamic characters. ACM Transactions on Graphics 28(3), Article 81 (2009)
11. NVIDIA: Physx sdk 2.8 documentation (2008)
12. Raibert, M.H., Hodgins, J.K.: Animation of dynamic legged locomotion. ACM SIGGRAPH Computer Graphics 25(4), 349–358 (1991)
13. Smith, R.: Open dynamics engine v0.5 user guide (2006)
14. Yin, K., Loken, K., van de Panne, M.: Simbicon: Simple biped locomotion control. ACM Transactions on Graphics 26(3), Article 105 (2007)

Parametric Control of Captured Mesh Sequences for Real-Time Animation

Dan Casas, Margara Tejera, Jean-Yves Guillemaut, and Adrian Hilton

University of Surrey, GU2 7XH Guildford, United Kingdom

Abstract. In this paper we introduce an approach to high-level parameterisation of captured mesh sequences of actor performance for real-time interactive animation control. High-level parametric control is achieved by non-linear blending between multiple mesh sequences exhibiting variation in a particular movement. For example walking speed is parameterised by blending fast and slow walk sequences. A hybrid non-linear mesh sequence blending approach is introduced to approximate the natural deformation of non-linear interpolation techniques whilst maintaining the real-time performance of linear mesh blending. Quantitative results show that the hybrid approach gives an accurate real-time approximation of offline non-linear deformation. Results are presented for single and multi-dimensional parametric control of walking (speed/direction), jumping (heigh/distance) and reaching (height) from captured mesh sequences. This approach allows continuous real-time control of high-level parameters such as speed and direction whilst maintaining the natural surface dynamics of captured movement.

Keywords: computer animation, 3D video, performance based animation, surface motion capture.

1 Introduction

Advances in 3D actor performance capture from multiple view video [9,32,26] have achieved detailed reconstruction and rendering of natural surface dynamics as mesh sequences. These approaches allow replay of the captured performance with free-view point rendering for compositing of performance in post-production whilst maintaining photo-realism. Captured sequences have subsequently been exploited for retargeting surface motion to other characters [1] and analysis of cloth motion to simulate novel animations through manipulation of skeletal motion and simulation of secondary cloth movement [28].

Animation from 3D performance capture has been achieved by concatenation of segments of multiple captured mesh sequences based on a manually defined transitions [27]. Automatic transition graph construction and path optimisation has been introduced [13] allowing offline key-frame animation. The level of movement control in these approaches is limited to transition between the capture movement sequences. Recent work [36] has exploited skeletal tracking of mesh sequences to allow increased manipulation of the captured movement with a skeletal rig, together with photorealistic rendering by indexing a corresponding video database. In these approaches reuse of captured mesh sequences is limited to offline animation control.

This paper presents a framework for real-time interactive animation with continuous movement control using mesh sequences of captured actor performance. Two contributions are presented to achieve interactive animation: alignment of multiple mesh sequences of an actor performing different motions into a temporally consistent mesh structure; and high-level parameterisation of captured mesh sequences. A shape similarity tree representing the shortest non-rigid mesh deformation path is introduced for alignment of frames from multiple captured sequences. This representation enables robust non-rigid alignment of multiple sequences allowing resampling with a consistent mesh structure and vertex correspondence. Techniques are introduced for parameterisation of aligned mesh sequences with intuitive high-level parameters such as speed and direction. Parameterisation is achieved by non-linear interpolation between multiple mesh sequences of related motions. This approach is analogous to previous techniques for parameterisation of skeletal motion capture [22]. A hybrid non-linear mesh sequence interpolation approach is proposed to achieve real-time performance with accurate approximation of non-linear mesh deformation. Results on captured mesh sequences of actor performance demonstrate the potential of this approach for interactive character animation with continuous high-level parametric movement control and natural surface deformation.

2 Related Work

3D video capture and reconstruction: Kanade et al. [15] pioneered the reconstruction of 3D mesh sequences of human performance for free-viewpoint replay with the Virtualized Reality^{TM} system using a $5m$ dome with 51 cameras. Multiple view video reconstruction results in an unstructured mesh sequence with an independent mesh at each frame. Advances in performance capture from video have enabled reconstruction of mesh sequences for human performance capturing the detailed deformation of clothing and hair [9,26,32,38]. These approaches achieve a free-viewpoint rendering quality comparable to the captured video but are limited to performance replay. A critical step for editing and reuse 3D video data is the temporal alignment of captured mesh sequences to obtain a consistent mesh structure with surface correspondence over time. A number of approaches have been proposed for temporal alignment of mesh sequences based on sequential frame-to-frame surface tracking. These can be categorised into two methodologies: model-based approaches which align a prior model of the surface with successive frames [7,9,32]; and surface-tracking or scene flow approaches which do not assume prior knowledge of the surface structure [6,31,33]. Sequential alignment approaches have three inherent limitations: accumulation of errors in frame-to-frame alignment resulting in drift in correspondence over time; gross-errors for large non-rigid deformations which occur with rapid movements requiring manual correction; and sequential approaches are limited to alignment across single sequences. Recently, non-sequential alignment approaches [12,5] have been introduced to overcome these limitations, allowing the construction of temporally coherent 3D video sequences from multiple view performance capture database, as used in this work.

Reuse and editing of 3D video data: The lack of temporal coherence in the mesh sequence has prohibited the development of simple methods for manipulation. Animation from databases of mesh sequences of actor performance has been demonstrated by concatenating segments of captured sequences [13,27], which is analogous to previous example-based approaches to concatenative synthesis used for 2D video [3,23,10]. Recently, example-based approaches through resampling video sequences have been extended to body motion [36,10] allowing offline animation via key-frame or skeletal motion. In [36], model-based skeletal tracking was used to re-sample segments from a database of video sequences based on pose allowing photorealisistic rendering with skeletal control. These approaches preserve the realism of the captured sequences in rendering but are limited to replay segments of the captured motion examples and do not allow the flexibility of conventional animation.

Reuse and editing of skeletal data: Since the introduction of marker-based technologies for skeletal performance capture to the entertainment industry in the early 90's a range of techniques to support editing and reuse have been developed. Space-time editing techniques [11,18,21] provide powerful tools for interactive motion editing via key-frame manipulation. [4] introduced parametric motion control by interpolating pairs of skeletal motions. Parametric motion synthesis was extended to blending multiple examples to create a parameterised skeletal motion space [34,22,17,20]. This allows continuous interactive motion control through high-level parameters such as velocity for walking or hand position for reaching. This paper introduces analogous parametrisation for 3D video mesh sequences to allow interactive animation control.

3 Performance Capture

Actor performance is captured in a controlled studio environment using a multiple camera system for synchronised video acquisition [9,26,32]. Shape reconstruction is performed on a frame-by-frame basis using a multiple view silhouette and stereo approach building on state-of-the-art graph-cut optimisation techniques [24]. This results in a unstructured mesh sequences with both the vertex connectivity and geometry changing from frame-to-frame.

To construct a character model for animation control we require a set of temporally aligned mesh sequences for multiple motions with the same mesh structure at each frame across all sequences. Extending previous research in non-sequential alignment [12,5], we introduce a mesh sequence alignment approach to recover the non-rigid surface motion and represent all frames with a consistent structure, as illustrated in Figure 1(b-e). Alignment across multiple unstructured

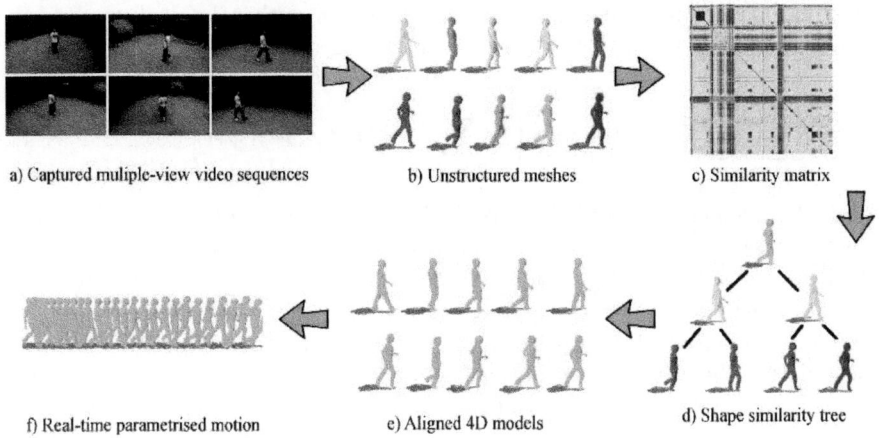

Fig. 1. Overview

mesh sequences is performed by constructing an intermediate *shape similarity tree*. This represents the shortest non-rigid surface motion path required to align each frame. The shape similarity tree allows frames from different mesh sequences to be aligned based on a measure of surface shape and motion similarity. The representation also ensures robust alignment of mesh sequences in the presence of large non-rigid deformations due to fast motion where sequential frame-to-frame surface tracking approaches may fail. The shape similarity tree is used to recover the non-rigid surface motion and obtain a consistent mesh structure for all sequences.

3.1 Shape Similarity Tree

To construct the shape similarity tree we require a measure of similarity $s(M_i(t_u), M_j(t_v))$ between pairs of meshes which can be evaluated without prior knowledge of the mesh correspondence. A number of similarity measures for mesh sequences taking into account both shape and motion have been investigated [30,14]. In this work we utilise the temporally filtered volumetric shape histogram [14] as a measure of shape and non-rigid motion similarity which has been shown to give good performance on reconstructed mesh sequences of people. Evaluation of shape similarity between mesh reconstructions for all frames across all sequences results in a similarity matrix as illustrated in Figure 1(c), where blue indicates high similarity and red low similarity.

Shape similarity is used to construct a tree representing the shortest non-rigid surface motion path required to align all meshes $\{M_i(t_u)\}_{u=1}^{N_i}$ from multiple captured mesh sequences. Initially a complete graph Ω is constructed with nodes for all meshes $M_i(t_u)$ in all sequences $i = [1, N]$ and edges $e_{i_u j_v} = e(M_i(t_u), M_j(t_v))$ connecting all nodes. Edges $e_{i_u j_v}$ are weighted according to the similarity measure $s(M_i(t_u), M_j(t_v))$. The shape similarity tree T_{sst} minimising the total non-rigid surface motion required for alignment can then be evaluated as the minimum spanning tree (MST) of the complete graph Ω.

$$T_{sst} = \arg\min_{T \in \Omega} \left(\sum_{(i,j,u,v) \in T} s(M_i(t_u), M_j(t_v)) \right) \quad (1)$$

Parallel implementation of Prim's MST algorithm requires $O(n \log n)$ time where n is the number of graph nodes [8]. This is prohibitively expensive for the graph Ω which typically has $10^3 - 10^5$ nodes. In practice as can be observed from the similarity matrix, Figure 1(c), many mesh pairs have a low similarity and are therefore not suitable for pairwise alignment. To reduce the computational cost in constructing the shape similarity tree we prune edges in the graph Ω according to a minimum similarity threshold s_{min}. A suitable similarity threshold can be calculated automatically from the similarity matrix as the minimum of the maximum similarity for each row in the matrix. Setting the threshold in this way ensures that all frames have at least one tree connection within the threshold. Computation time for a 1500 node graph takes $< 2s$ on a single CPU[1].

3.2 Mesh Sequence Alignment

The shape similarity tree T_{sst} defines the shortest path of non-rigid surface motion required to align the mesh for every frame across all sequence. Starting from the root node M_{root} we align meshes along the branches of the tree using a pairwise non-rigid alignment.

Non-rigid pairwise mesh alignment uses a coarse-to-fine approach combining geometric and photometric matching in a Laplacian mesh deformation framework [25]. This builds on recent work using Laplacian mesh deformation for sequential frame-to-frame alignment over mesh sequences [9,6]. Here we use both photometric SIFT features [19] and geometric rigid patch matching [6] to establish correspondence between pairs of meshes. The combination of geometric and photometric features increases reliability of matching by ensuring that there is a distribution of correspondences across the surface. Alignment is performed starting from a coarse sampling (30 patches) which allows large deformations and recursively doubling the number of patches in successive iterations to obtain an accurate match to the surface. Since estimated feature correspondences are likely to be subject to matching errors we use an energy based formulation to introduce feature matches as soft constraints on the Laplacian deformation framework as proposed in [25]:

$$\bar{x} = \arg\min_{x} \|Lx - \delta(x_0)\|^2 + \|W_c(x - x_c)\|^2 \quad (2)$$

L is the mesh Laplacian, $\delta(x_0)$ are the mesh differential coordinates for the source mesh with vertex positions x_0. x is a vector of mesh vertex positions used to solve for $Lx = \delta$. x_c are soft constraints on vertex locations given by

---

[1] All paper timings are single threaded on an Intel Q6600 2.4GHz CPU.

the feature correspondence with a diagonal weight matrix W_c. A tetrahedral Laplacian system [9] is used based on the discrete tetrahedron gradient operator G [2] with $L = G^T D G$, where D is a diagonal matrix of tetrahedral volumes. Equation 2 solves for the non-rigid deformation which minimises the change in shape whilst approximating the feature correspondence constraints.

Pairwise non-rigid alignment across the branches of the shape similarity tree T_{sst} results in known correspondence between the root mesh M_{root} and all other meshes $M_i(t_u)$. This correspondence allows every mesh to be resampled with the structure of the root mesh giving a consistent connectivity for all frames over all captured mesh sequences.

4 Mesh Sequence Parametrisation

Interactive animation from temporally aligned mesh sequences requires the combination of multiple captured sequences to allow continuous real-time control of movement with intuitive high-level parameters such as speed and direction for walking or height and distance for jumping. Methods for parameterisation of skeletal motion capture have previously been introduced [17,22,20] which allow continuous high-level movement control by linear interpolation of joint angles. Blending of meshes based on linear interpolation of vertex position is computationally efficient but may result in unrealistic deformation or mesh collapse if there are significant differences in shape. Non-linear blending of meshes produces superior deformation [16,25,29,37] but commonly requires least-squares solution of a system of equations which is prohibitive for real-time interaction. In this paper we introduce a hybrid solution which approximates the non-linear deformation whilst maintaing real-time performance. This allows high-level parameterisation for interactive movement control by blending of multiple mesh sequences.

Three steps are required to achieve high-level parametric control from mesh sequences: time-warping to align the mesh sequences; non-linear mesh blending of the time-warped sequences; and mapping from low level blending weights to high-level parameters (speed, direction, etc.). In this section we focus on real-time non-linear mesh blending which is the novel contribution of this work. As in previous work on skeletal motion parameterisation we assume that individual mesh sequences $M_i(t)$ are temporally aligned by a continuous time-warp function $t = f(t_u)$ [4,35] which aligns corresponding poses prior to blending such that $t \in [0, 1]$ for all sequences.

4.1 Real-Time Non-linear Mesh Sequence Blending

In this work we introduce a real-time approach to mesh blending which exploits offline pre-computation of non-linear deformation for a small set of intermediate parameter values. Differences between the linear and non-linear mesh deformation are pre-computed and used to correct errors in linear deformation. This approach approximates the non-linear to within a user-specified tolerance whilst allowing real-time computation with a similar cost to linear blending. The price paid is a modest increase in memory required to store intermediate non-linear mesh displacements for blending.

Given a set of N temporally aligned mesh sequences $\mathbf{M} = \{M_i(t)\}_{i=1}^{N}$ of the same or similar motions (e.g. walk and run) we want to compute a blended mesh deformation according to a set of weights $\mathbf{w} = \{w_i\}_{i=1}^{N}$: $M_{NL}(t, \mathbf{w}) = b(\mathbf{M}, \mathbf{w})$ where $b()$ is a non-linear blend function which interpolates the rotation and change in shape independently for each element on the mesh according to the weights $\mathbf{w}$ and performs a least-squares solution to obtain the resulting mesh $M_{NL}(t, \mathbf{w})$. This non-linear operation can be performed offline using existing approaches [16,25,29,37], throughout this work we employ a volumetric Laplacian deformation framework based on Equation 2.

Linear vertex blending gives an approximate mesh $M_L(t, \mathbf{w})$ as a weighted sum of vertex positions: $M_L(t) = \frac{1}{\sum w_i} \sum w_i M_i(t)$, where $w_i M_i(t)$ denotes the product of the mesh vertex positions $X_i(t)$ by weight w_i. Given the non-linear mesh deformation $M_{NL}(t, \mathbf{w})$ and linear approximation $M_L(t, \mathbf{w})$ we can evaluate a displacement field: $D_{NL}(t, \mathbf{w}) = M_{NL}(t, \mathbf{w}) - M_L(t, \mathbf{w})$. The exact non-linear deformation for blend weights $\mathbf{w}$ can then be recovered by linear interpolation together with a non-linear correction: $M_{NL}(t, \mathbf{w}) = M_L(t, \mathbf{w}) + D_{NL}(t, \mathbf{w})$. An advantage of storing the displacement field D_{NL} is that for blending between mesh sequences of similar motions linear blending gives a reasonable approximation for large parts of the surface $D_{NL} \approx 0$ allowing efficient compression whilst accurately reproducing regions of significant non-linear deformation.

To accurately approximate the non-linear deformation for blending a set of N source meshes $\mathbf{M}$ with arbitrary weights $\mathbf{w}$ we pre-compute the non-linear displacement field $D_{NL}(t, \mathbf{w}_j)$ at a discrete set of intermediate weight values $\mathbf{w}_j$ to give an additional set of N_{NL} reference meshes for interpolation: $M_j(t, \mathbf{w}_j) = (M_L(t, \mathbf{w}_j) + D_{NL}(t, \mathbf{w}_j))$. Real-time online interpolation is then performed using a linear vertex blending with the non-linear correction:

$$M(t, \mathbf{w}) = \sum_{j=1}^{N+N_{NL}} g(\mathbf{w}, \mathbf{w}_j)(M_L(t, \mathbf{w}_j) + D_{NL}(t, \mathbf{w}_j)) \qquad (3)$$

where $g(\mathbf{w}, \mathbf{w}_j)$ is a weight function giving a linear blend of the nearest reference meshes and zero for all other meshes. Equation 3 gives an exact solution at the original and non-linear interpolated reference meshes, and an approximate interpolation of the nearest reference meshes elsewhere. A recursive bisection of the weight space $\mathbf{w}$ is performed to evaluate a set of non-linearly interpolated source meshes such that for all $\mathbf{w}$ the approximation error $(M_{NL}(t, \mathbf{w}) - M(t, \mathbf{w})) < \epsilon$. Typically for interpolation of mesh sequences representing related motions only a single subdivision is required.

This approach allows accurate approximation of non-linear mesh deformation whilst maintaining the computational performance of linear blending to allow real-time interactive animation. Figure 2(a,b) presents comparison errors for linear interpolation (top) and hybrid non-linear interpolation (2nd/3rd rows) with respect to the exact non-linear interpolation (bottom). This shows that the proposed real-time hybrid non-linear mesh blending approach achieves accurate approximation even with a single intermediate non-linear displacement map (2nd row) whereas linear blending results in large errors (top). Table 1 presents quantitative results for error and CPU time.

a) Result of blending two poses of a street dancer using linear (top row), hybrid with one and three reference meshes (2nd/3rd row) and non-linear (bottom row). Top row shows that linear blending results in large errors (red) for the left leg which are corrected with the hybrid approach.

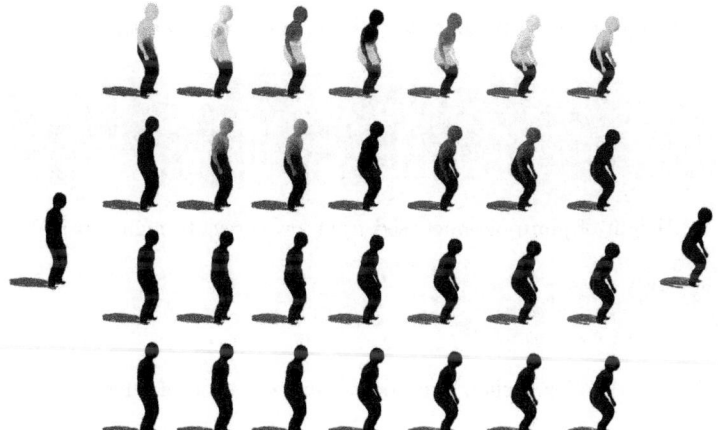

b) Result of blending two equivalent poses of the low jump (left) and high jump (right) sequences. 2nd and 3rd rows show that our proposed hybrid approach, with one and three references meshes respectively, gives an approximation to the non-linear blending whilst the top row shows large errors with linear blending.

Fig. 2. Comparison of linear, non-linear and hybrid mesh blending. Heat-maps show error vs. non-linear blending from dark-blue (zero) to red (maximum).

Table 1. Maximum vertex displacement error with respect to non-linear blending as a percentage of model size for in meshes in Figure 2

Sequence	#vertices	Method	Max. Error	Time
a) Street dancer	5580	Linear	14.38 %	0.008 sec / frame
		Hybrid 1 reference	3.67 %	0.015 sec / frame
		Hybrid 3 references	1.60 %	0.017 sec / frame
		Non-linear	0.00 %	0.749 sec / frame
b) Jumping pose	3000	Linear	9.14 %	0.004 sec / frame
		Hybrid 1 reference	1.34 %	0.014 sec / frame
		Hybrid 3 references	0.93 %	0.016 sec / frame
		Non-linear	0.00 %	0.789 sec / frame

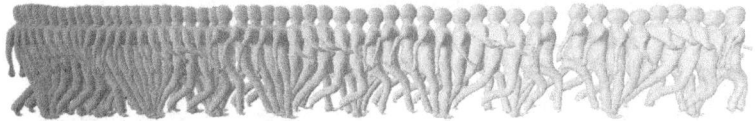

(a) Walk-to-run speed parametrisation, from walk (green) to run (yellow)

(b) Length of jump parametrised from short (red) to long (orange)

(c) Height of jump parametrised from low (grey) to high (purple)

(d) walk (green) to jog (yellow) motion parameterisation of a female character

Fig. 3. Examples of parameterised motions between two motion sequences with continuous parameter variation (every 5th frame)

4.2 High-Level Parametric Control

High-level parametric control is achieved by learning a mapping function $h(\mathbf{w})$ between the blend weights and user specified motion parameters $\mathbf{p}$. As in skeletal motion blending the blend weights do not provide an intuitive parameterisation of the motion. We therefore learn a mapping $\mathbf{w} = h^{-1}(\mathbf{p})$ from the user-specified

Fig. 4. Meshes showing the path interactively travelled by the user. Four original motions (walk, jog, 90° left/right turn) allow full control of both speed and direction.

parameter to the corresponding blend weights required to generate the desired motion. Motion parameters **p** are high-level user specified controls for a particular class of motions such as speed and direction for walk or run, and height and distance for a jump. The inverse mapping function $h^{-1}()$ from parameters to weights can be constructed by a discrete sampling of the weight space **w** and evaluation of the corresponding motion parameters **p** [17].

5 Results

Datasets used in this work are reconstructed from multiple view video capture of actor performance with 8HD cameras equally spaced in a circle and capture volume $5m^2 \times 2m$. Reconstruction is performed using multi-view stereo followed by temporal alignment of all frames to have a consistent mesh structure. Throughout this work we use a single intermediate mesh for hybrid non-linear interpolation which gives a very close approximation, as shown in Figure 2.

Figure 3 shows parameterised motion spaces for walking and jumping constructed from pairs of mesh sequences. Figure 4 presents a multi-parameter character animation constructed from four mesh sequences with walking speed and direction control, in which our hybrid blending method with 1 reference runs at 0.020 $secs/frame$ using 4 input sequences and 3 blending weights, with a maximum displacement error of 0.73% with respect to the non-linear approach. Rendered meshes are coloured to show the parameter change. The supplementary video[2] shows the real-time interactive animation control. These results show that the proposed mesh sequence blending approach using the hybrid non-linear deformation achieves a natural transition between the captured motions.

6 Conclusions

A system for real-time interactive character animation from multiple camera capture has been presented. The approach is based on a database of temporally

---

[2] http://vimeo.com/28291052

aligned mesh sequence reconstructions of an actor performing multiple motions. Extending previous research, a shape similarity tree has been used to allow non-sequential alignment of a database of captured sequences into a consistent mesh structure with temporal correspondence. Real-time continuous high-level parametric motion control is achieved by blending multiple mesh sequences of related motions. This allows interactive control of a 3D video character, analogous to previous research with skeletal motion capture [22,34]. A hybrid mesh blending approach has been introduced, which combines the realistic deformations achieved with non-linear blending [16,25,29,37] with the fast performance of linear blending. Results for a single CPU based implementation of the parametric control demonstrate a frame-rate $> 50Hz$ for a mesh resolution of 3000 vertices. Further research will investigate transitions between parametric motions, which would increase the range of parametrised motions in our final scenario. The incorporation of photorealism in the final render will also be investigated.

References

1. Baran, I., Vlasic, D., Grinspun, E., Popović, J.: Semantic deformation transfer. In: Proceedings of ACM SIGGRAPH (2009)
2. Botsch, M., Sorkine, O.: On linear variational surface deformation methods. IEEE TVCG 14(1), 213–230 (2008)
3. Bregler, C., Covell, M., Slaney, M.: Video rewrite: Driving visual speech with audio. In: Proceedings of ACM SIGGRAPH, pp. 1–8 (1997)
4. Brundelin, A., Williams, L.: Motion signal processing. In: Proceedings of ACM SIGGRAPH, pp. 97–104 (1995)
5. Budd, C., Huang, P., Hilton, A.: Hierarchical shape matching for temporally consistent 3d video. In: Proc. International Conference on 3D Imaging, Modeling, Processing, Visualization and Transmission (3DIMPVT 2011), Hangzhou, China (May 2011)
6. Cagniart, C., Boyer, E., Ilic, S.: Free-Form Mesh Tracking: a Patch-Based Approach. In: Conference on Computer Vision and Pattern Recognition, CVPR (2010)
7. Carranza, J., Theobalt, C., Magnor, M., Seidel, H.P.: Free-viewpoint video of human actors. In: Proceedings of ACM SIGGRAPH, pp. 565–577 (2003)
8. Chong, K., Han, Y., Lam, T.: Concurrent threads and optimal parallel minimum spanning trees algorithm. J.ACM 48(2), 297–323 (2001)
9. de Aguiar, E., Stoll, C., Theobalt, C., Ahmed, N., Seidel, H.P., Thrun, S.: Performance Capture from Sparse Multi-view Video. ACM SIGGRAPH 27(3) (2008)
10. Flagg, M., Nakazawa, A., Zhang, Q., Kang, S.B., Ryu, Y., Essa, I., Rehg, J.: Human Video Textures. In: ACM Symposium on Interactive 3D Graphics (2009)
11. Gleicher, M.: Motion Editing with Spacetime Constraints. In: ACM Symposium on Interactive 3D Graphics (1997)
12. Huang, P., Budd, C., Hilton, A.: Global temporal registration of multiple non-rigid surface sequences. In: CVPR (2011)
13. Huang, P., Hilton, A., Starck, J.: Human Motion Synthesis from 3D Video. In: IEEE Int.Conf. on Computer Vision and Pattern Recognition, CVPR (2009)
14. Huang, P., Hilton, A., Starck, J.: Shape similarity for 3d video sequences of people. International Journal of Computer Vision 89, 362–381 (2010)
15. Kanade, T., Rander, P.: Virtualized reality: Constructing virtual worlds from real scenes. IEEE MultiMedia 4(2), 34–47 (1997)

16. Kircher, S., Garland, M.: Free-Form Motion Processing. ACM Transactions on Graphics 27(2), 1–13 (2008)
17. Kovar, L., Gleicher, M.: Automated extraction and parameterization of motions in large date sets. In: Proceedings of ACM SIGGRAPH, vol. 23(3), pp. 559–568 (2004)
18. Lee, J., Shin, S.: A Hierarchical Approach to Interactive Motion Editing for Human-Like Figures. In: Proceedings of ACM SIGGRAPH, pp. 39–48 (1999)
19. Lowe, D.: Distinctive image features for scale invariant keypoints. Int. J. of Computer Vision 60(2), 91–110 (2004)
20. Mukai, T., Kuriyama, S.: Geostatistical Motion Interpolation. In: Proceedings of ACM SIGGRAPH (2005)
21. Popović, Z., Witkin, A.: Physically Based Motion Transformation. In: Proceedings of ACM SIGGRAPH (1999)
22. Rose, C., Cohen, M., Bodenheimer, B.: Verbs and adverbs: multidimensional motion interpolation. IEEE Computer Graphics and Applications 18(5), 32–40 (1998)
23. Schodl, A., Szeliski, R., amd Salesin, D., Essa, I.: Video textures. In: Proceedings of ACM SIGGRAPH, pp. 489–498 (2000)
24. Seitz, S., Curless, B., Diebel, J., Scharstein, D., Szeliski, R.: A Comparison and Evaluation of Multi-View Stereo Reconstruction Algorithms. In: Conference on Computer Vision and Pattern Recognition (CVPR), pp. 519–528 (2006)
25. Sorkine, O.: Differential Representations for Mesh Processing. Computer Graphics Forum 25(4) (2006)
26. Starck, J., Hilton, A.: Surface capture for performance based animation. IEEE Computer Graphics and Applications 27(3), 21–31 (2007)
27. Starck, J., Miller, G., Hilton, A.: Video-Based Character Animation. In: ACM SIGGRAPH/Eurographics Symposium on Computer Animation. pp. 49—58 (2005)
28. Stoll, C., Gall, J., de Aguiar, E., Thrun, S., Theobalt, C.: Video-based Reconstruction of Animatable Human Characters. In: ACM SIGGRAPH ASIA (2010)
29. Sumner, R., Popović, J.: Deformation Transfer for Triangle Meshes. In: Proceedings of ACM SIGGRAPH (2004)
30. Tung, T., Matsuyama, T.: Dynamic Surface Matching by Geodesic Mapping for Animation Transfer. In: Conference on Computer Vision and Pattern Recognition, CVPR (2010)
31. Vedula, S., Baker, S., Rander, P., Collins, R., Kanade, T.: Three-Dimensional Scene Flow 27(3) (2005)
32. Vlasic, D., Baran, I., Matusik, W., Popović, J.: Articulated mesh animation from multi-view silhouettes. In: Proceedings of ACM SIGGRAPH (2008)
33. Wand, M., Adams, B., Ovsianikov, M., Berner, A., Bokeloh, M., Jenke, P., Guibas, L., Seidel, H.P., Schilling, A.: Efficient Reconstruction of Non-rigid Shape and Motion from Real-Time 3D Scanner Data. ACM Trans.Graphics 28(2) (2009)
34. Wiley, D., Hahn, J.: Interpolation synthesis for articulated figure motion. In: IEEE Virtual Reality International Symposium, pp. 157–160 (1997)
35. Witkin, A., Popović, Z.: Motion Warping. In: Proceedings of ACM SIGGRAPH (1995)
36. Xu, F., Liu, Y., Stoll, C., Tompkin, J., Bharaj, G., Dai, Q., Seidel, H.P., Kautz, J., Theobalt, C.: Video-based Characters - Creating New Human Performances from a Multi-view Video Database. In: Proceedings of ACM SIGGRAPH (2011)
37. Xu, W., Zhou, K., Yu, Y., Peng, Q., Guo, B.: Gradient domain editing of deforming mesh sequences. Proceedings of ACM SIGGRAPH 26(3) (2007)
38. Zitnick, C., Kang, S., Uyttendaele, M., Winder, S., Szeliski, R.: High-quality video view interpolation using a layered representation, pp. 600–608 (2004)

Real-Time Interactive Character Animation by Parallelization of Genetic Algorithms

Min Zou

Academy of Mathematics and Systems Science, Graduate University of Chinese
Academy of Sciences, Chinese Academy of Sciences, Beijing 100190, China
zoumin@amss.ac.cn

Abstract. We present an online algorithm for interactive character animation in realtime. Interactive character animation is to select a sequence of actions that perform well. Each action sequence is evaluated by the sum of discounted costs over a finite horizon. A large number of action sequences are evaluated simultaneously by parallelization of genetic algorithms on GPU. Benefiting from the power of parallel computing on modern GPU, our method produces high quality animations in realtime.

Keywords: Data Driven Animation, Human Animation, Genetic Algorithm.

1 Introduction

Realistic and interactive character animation is an important problem in computer games and virtual environments. In the past decade, motion graph based methods have been a common approach to this problem. The efficiency of graph traversing is the primary bottleneck of this approach. More recently, reinforcement learning techniques have been employed to construct character controllers. However, reinforcement learning cannot handle environments that haven't been experienced. Also, reinforcement learning is bedeviled by the curse of dimensionality. Hence, realtime online computing techniques are urgent for a wide range of applications.

Fig. 1. Obstacle Avoidance. The character is running forward according to the player's input. It automatically detects obstacles in front and chooses actions to avoid them.

Two main hurdles in interactive character animation are the large computation effort and the realtime restriction. Character animation requires a large amount of computation to find a string of motion clips that can be pieced together naturally. Meanwhile, applications such as video games are sensitive to computation time, so all computation tasks must be finished in realtime.

In this paper, we employ parallel computing techniques to cope with these hurdles. Each action sequence is evaluated by the sum of discounted costs over a finite horizon. The genetic algorithm is selected to address our problem because we look for fast parallel evaluation methods and genetic algorithms are ideal for parallelization [16]. We implement our algorithm on CUDA [15] which is a parallel computing architecture on GPU. Benefiting from the power of modern GPU, high quality animations can be generated in real-time. As no precomputing is needed, our algorithm is applicable to a wide range of applications.

Our algorithm extracts similar motion clips automatically from the input motion data. These similar motion clips are parameterized so they can be represented by low dimensional variables such as turning angle and walking speed. Unlike the optimal controllers that evaluate each action in an infinite horizon, our controller selects each action based on its performance over a finite horizon. Theoretical analysis and experiments show high quality animations can be produced by short horizon planning.

Contributions. The introduction of parallel computing techniques to character animation is our main contribution. Our approach shows that short horizon planning will produce high quality animations. This enables us to construct efficient character controllers on GPU. Other contributions of this paper include an automatic method for extracting similar action clips.

2 Related Work

Data-driven character animation has been extensively explored in the past decade as it is an effective way to generate new animations based on motion capture examples. Early works [2,7,11] proposed a new data structure called *motion graph* to organize motion data. Plausible transition points are identified as nodes and short motion clips are edges in *motion graph*. High quality animations can be synthesized by carrying on various search methods on motion graph such as branch-bound [11] and randomized search methods [2]. However, these methods are too slow for interactive avatar control as graph traversing is time consuming.

In the following years, motion graph was strengthened and augmented in several aspects. First, the connectivity was strengthened by building fully connected subgraphs between similar motion clips [13,19], by adding intermediate poses interpolated from similar motion clips [23] or by caching good blending samples [9]. Second, parameterization was applied to similar motion clips [3,19]. Third, interpolation was added to gain precise control [4,17].

Benefiting from previous techniques, high quality fast motion planning and interactive character animation became possible. Reinforcement learning has been used to solve the interactive character animation problems in many works

[6,8,10,12,21,22]. Lee [6]computed the control policy by value iteration. Ikemoto [8] estimated the optimal controller using reinforcement learning. Treuille [21] approximated the value function by a linear combination of basis functions. McCann [12] added a simple model of player behavior to reinforcement learning. Lo [10] used a tree-based regression algorithm for reinforcement learning. Lee [22] generated connecting controllers that aggregate independent ones. Other precomputing techniques such as precomputed search tree proposed by Lau [5] also appeared. The main drawback of these precomputing techniques is that they cannot adapt policies to new environments different from the training ones. On the contrary, our algorithm doesn't suffer from this problem as it makes decisions online. Also, neither training nor storing policies is needed in our approach.

Genetic algorithms have been used to solve many computer animation problems. Ngo [14] employed the genetic algorithm to compute solutions to space time constraints problems for simple 2D skeletal creatures. Sims [20] generated creatures that can evolve their morphologies with the help of genetic programming. Because the genetic algorithm is ideal for parallelization [16] and we look for fast parallel evaluation methods on GPU, it is employed to address our problem.

3 Motion Clips Extraction

Our approach has two main components: the automatic extraction of short motion clips that can be pieced together naturally and the selection of action sequences. We describe how to extract motion clips in this section.

Suppose $M = \{p_i | 0 \leq i < N\}$ is the input motion, where p_i is the ith pose. At first, we measure the the distance between each pair of poses p_i and p_j by the distance function $d(p_i, p_j)$ described by Kovar [11]. As $d(p_i, p_j)$ takes the neighboring poses of p_i and p_j into consideration, if $d(p_i, p_j)$ is small enough then motion clips ending with p_i will naturally transit to clips starting with p_j, and vice versa. Let $S_i = \{p_j | d(p_i, p_j) < \tau\}$, where τ is the predefined threshold, be the set of poses similar to p_i. Motion clips starting and ending with poses in the same S_i are extracted as they can be sewed together seamlessly. For example, p_6 and p_{10} are very similar to p_1 in Figure 2, so $S_1 = \{p_1, p_6, p_{10}\}$. Then motion clips $m_1 = \{p_1, p_2, \ldots, p_6\}, m_2 = \{p_6, p_7, \ldots, p_{10}\}, m_3 = \{p_1, p_2, \ldots, p_{10}\}$ are extracted. In practice, only clips between 20 and 30 frames are extracted.

There are N groups of motion clips for a input motion of length N. Let G_i be the ith group. The quality of G_i is measured by the size of the parameter area expanded by motions in G_i. For example, to select the group expanding the largest turning angle, we first sort motion clips in the same group by the turning angle. And then each motion group is ranked based on the following equation:

$$Score(G) = \sum_{1}^{|G|-1} f(\alpha_i, \alpha_{i+1}) \quad (1)$$

where

$$f(\alpha_i, \alpha_{i+1}) = \begin{cases} \alpha_{i+1} - \alpha_i, & \text{if } \alpha_{i+1} - \alpha_i < \epsilon; \\ 0, & \text{else.} \end{cases} \quad (2)$$

α_i is the turning angle of the ith motion clip. $\epsilon = 5°$ in our experiments. Equation 2 means turning angles of neighboring motion clips should be close enough. The group of motion clips having the largest score, that is expanding the largest parameter area, is selected as our final motion clips.

Fig. 2. Motion Clips Extraction. Poses in the first row are samples of the input motion. Since p_1, p_6, p_{10} are similar, short motion clips $m_1 = \{p_i | 1 \leq i \leq 6\}$ (the second row), $m_2 = \{p_i | 6 \leq i \leq 10\}$ (the third row) and $m_3 = \{p_i | 1 \leq i \leq 10\}$ are extracted.

4 Controller Construction

We construct the controller in this section. The controller selects fine *actions* based on the character's current *state*. The *state* includes the character's position, direction and the trajectory of current motion clip. Each *action* is a motion clip along with its parameterization.

$$s = <m_s, \alpha, x, z, l_s>$$
$$a = <m_a, d_\alpha, d_x, d_z, l_a>$$

m_s and m_a are motion clips. x, z, α are the character's position and direction. d_α is the turning angle of m_a, (d_x, d_z) is the relative position of the end frame in m_a. l_s and l_a are trajectories. For simple motions such as walking and running, the trajectory is approximated by a short line segment. For special motions such as jumping and crawling, we store the trajectories of these motions directly. The character's new state s' is updated from the old state s as follows:

$$\begin{aligned} m'_s &= m_a \\ x' &= x + \cos\theta d_x - \sin\theta d_z \\ z' &= z + \sin\theta d_x + \cos\theta d_z \\ \theta' &= \theta + d_\theta \\ l'_s &= l_a \end{aligned} \quad (3)$$

For convenience, Equation 3 is abbreviated as $s' = s \oplus a$.

4.1 Problem Formulation

A high quality controller responds to player's input quickly and transits between motion clips smoothly. It also plans animations ahead and detects collisions efficiently. These considerations are described separately and unified in the final formulation.

Agile Responses. A special variable s_g is used to represent the *goal state* indicated by player's input. The cost is assigned according to the distance between current state and the *goal state*. For example, we take the angle deviation as the distance to the *goal state* in the navigation task.

$$c_g(s, s_g) = \min\{|\theta_s - \theta_{s_g}|, 2\pi - |\theta_s - \theta_{s_g}|\} \tag{4}$$

θ_s is the character's current direction and θ_{s_g} is the direction of the *goal state*.

Natural Transitions. The transition cost $c_t(s_i, s_{i+1})$ is proportional to the distance between the last frame of s_i and the first frame of s_{i+1}.

Collision Detection. The environment is abstracted as an height map and stored as a quadtree in a piece of consecutive memory on the GPU memory. Each sample point on the trajectory is used to perform collision detection with the quadtree. Let e be the environment. The collision function is defined as:

$$c_c(s, e) = \begin{cases} 1, \text{ if collision happens;} \\ 0, \text{ else.} \end{cases} \tag{5}$$

As long as we know the trajectories of obstacles, we can pre-compute their positions and store them on the GPU side. In such way, we can control characters in the environment with moving obstacles.

Put above considerations together, the immediate cost of a state is:

$$cost(s_i) = \zeta_g c_g(s_i, s_g) + \zeta_t c_t(s_{i-1}, s_i) + \zeta_c c_c(s_i, e) \tag{6}$$

where $\zeta_g, \zeta_t, \zeta_c$ are scaling factors.

Planning. The difficulty of character animation is that not only the current state but its influence on the next one should be taken into consideration. Interactive character animation is to find a sequence of actions that have minimal cost in the long run:

$$\begin{aligned} \min_{\{a_t\}} & \sum_{t=1}^{\infty} \gamma^t cost(s_t) \\ \text{s.t.} \quad & s_t = s_{t-1} \oplus a_t \\ & a_t \in A \end{aligned} \tag{7}$$

The cost value of s_t is discounted by γ^t to model the uncertainty of future states in the dynamic environment and to promise the convergence of the objective function. s_0 is the character's current state. We simplify the objective function in Equation 7 by just keeping the first T items:

$$\min_{\{a_t\}} \sum_{t=1}^{T} \gamma^t cost(s_t) \tag{8}$$

T is called the planning length. Equation 8 means each action is evaluated over a finite horizon. For $0 \leq \gamma < 1$, the infinite sum C_∞ will converge, so it can be approximated by the sum of the first T items C_T with careful selection of T. Once C_T is close to C_∞ the actions selected by Equation 7 and Equation 8 will be similar. A brief analysis of the accuracy is given in the next section.

4.2 Approximation Accuracy

The approximation accuracy of Equation 8 is measured by the ratio r between C_T and C_∞:

$$r = \frac{\sum_{t=1}^{T} \gamma^t cost(s_t)}{\sum_{t=1}^{\infty} \gamma^t cost(s_t)}$$

$$= \frac{\sum_{t=1}^{T} \gamma^t cost(s_t)}{\sum_{t=1}^{T} \gamma^t cost(s_t) + \sum_{t=T+1}^{\infty} \gamma^t cost(s_t)}$$

$$= \frac{1}{1 + \gamma^T \frac{\sum_{t=T+1}^{\infty} \gamma^{t-T} cost(s_t)}{\sum_{t=1}^{T} \gamma^t cost(s_t)}}$$

Let $\rho = \frac{\sum_{t=T+1}^{\infty} \gamma^{t-T} cost(s_t)}{\sum_{t=1}^{T} \gamma^t cost(s_t)}$, then $r = \frac{1}{1+\rho\gamma^T}$.

We assume the first T costs are not smaller than latter ones:

$$\min_i cost(s_i) \geq c \geq \max_j cost(s_j) \qquad (9)$$

where $0 \leq i \leq T$ and $j > T$. c is any value satisfying above equation. Although this hypothesis is not strict for general character animation, it does make sense for interactive character animation. For example, if we tell the character to turn around, the first several costs are larger than latter ones because the character's direction is opposed to the desired one at first but similar to the goal direction after several steps. Likewise, the first several costs of avoiding obstacles are larger because once the character has walked around the obstacle the cost drops a lot. Under this hypothesis, we have

$$\rho = \frac{\sum_{t=T+1}^{\infty} \gamma^{t-T} \frac{cost(s_t)}{c}}{\sum_{t=1}^{T} \gamma^t \frac{cost(s_t)}{c}}$$

$$\leq \frac{\sum_{t=T+1}^{\infty} \gamma^{t-T}}{\sum_{t=1}^{T} \gamma^t}$$

$$= \frac{1}{1-\gamma^T}$$

Now, $r \geq \frac{1}{1+\frac{\gamma^T}{1-\gamma^T}}$

The approximation accuracy depends on both T and γ. T depends on the number of actions required to complete certain tasks. γ depends on the lengths of motion clips. Short motion clips require larger γ than long motion clips do. The approximation accuracies using different planning lengths and discount factors are shown in Figure 3.

Figure 3 shows approximation accuracies grow fast as T increases. When $T = 16$ approximation accuracies are over 80% for discount factors less than 0.9 and over 90% for discount factors less than 0.85.

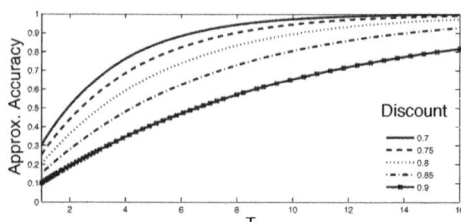

Fig. 3. Approximation accuracy. T is the planning length. Approximation accuracies of different discount factors are plotted in different types of lines.

4.3 Parallelization of Genetic Algorithms

We use the genetic algorithm to evaluate a large amount of action sequences and try to find the best sequence that minimizes Equation 8. The parallelization of the genetic algorithm is implemented on CUDA. We detail the parallelization of the genetic algorithm in this section.

Initialization. Each sequence of actions to be evaluated is encoded as a chromosome. The whole population is a large set of sequences of actions. Each chromosome in the first generation is initialized by picking up T motion clips randomly from the database.

Evaluation. Beginning with character's current state s_0, subsequent states are updated from previous ones. They are measured by the cost function shown in Equation 6. This procedure is summarized in Algorithm 1.

Selection. In each thread, we randomly select H individuals from the whole population and just keep the best one in the matting pool.

Crossover and Mutation. The single cross point is chosen randomly. Parents exchange sub-sequences after the cross point. The single mutation point is also decided randomly. The motion clip at the mutation point will be replaced by another one picked up randomly from the database.

Parallelization on CUDA. There are 5 kernels[1] implemented on CUDA: *Init_Population*, *Evaluation*, *Crossover*, *Mutation* and *Selection*. They are responsible for different operations in the genetic algorithm. Each kernel is executed on a single grid[2] with K blocks and each block has K threads. The population size is $K \times K$ so each thread is responsible for a single individual. The population and the fitness values are stored in the global memory.

---

[1] A global function that executes on the GPU device is typically called a kernel [18].
[2] A collection of threads is called a block and a collection of blocks is called a grid [18].

```
Input: a_0,a_1,...,a_{T-1},s_0,s_g,e
Output: cost
cost ← 0;
γ ← 1;
s_{bkp} ← s_0;
for i = 1 to T do
    s ← s_{i-1} ⊕ a_{i-1};
    cost ← cost + γ * (ζ_t C_t(s_{bkp}, s) + ζ_g C_g(s, s_g)) + ζ_c C_c(s_i, e);
    γ ← γ * DISCOUNT;
    s_{bkp} ← s;
end
return cost;
```

Algorithm 1. Fitness Function. This algorithm evaluates a sequence of actions $\{a_i\}$. s_0 is the character's current state and s_g is the goal state. e is the environment. $DISCOUNT$ is the discount factor.

5 Experiments

Three experiments are used to produce the results[3]. The first one shows the relation between the planning length T and the animation quality. The second one shows the efficiency of our algorithm. The last one shows our algorithm can incorporate special actions easily.

The motion data is downloaded from the CMU Motion Capture Database [1]. 1,181 frames of running and jumping motions are selected to construct the database. 100 motion clips are extracted. The frequency of these data is 30fps. Geforce GTX 460 and CUDA 3.2 are used for the parallel computing. The population size is 4096; cross ratio is 0.6; mutation ratio is 0.1; discount factor is 0.8; $\zeta_t = 1, \zeta_g = 50, \zeta_c = 1000$.

The scene in the first experiment contains a character that is running forward and a large obstacle in front of it. Animations of different qualities are generated by altering the planning length. Each T from 1 to 16 is tested 1,000 times. Figure 4 shows some example scenes and Figure 5 shows average costs and average computation times using different T.

When $T = 2$, the character crosses the obstacle, see Figure 4. This is because the character cannot detect the obstacle until it is close up to the obstacle. Although the collision is avoided when $T = 4$ as the character detects the obstacle in time, the animation is unnatural because the character cannot plan to avoid the obstacle until the obstacle is very close. When $T = 6, 8$, natural animations are generated as the character detects the obstacle far away. High quality animations are generated at $T = 10$. The second row of Figure 4 shows further increase of T improves the animation quality little.

Average costs in Figure 5 show the relation between the planning length and the animation quality numerically. Costs are high when $T = 1, 2, 3$ because of collisions. Collisions are avoided when $T \geq 4$ so the cost drops drastically. After

---
[3] Video clips can be found in http://www.zoumin.org/projects/avatar_control/

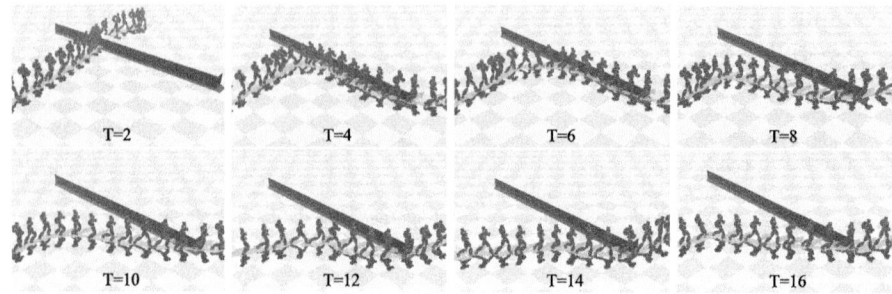

Fig. 4. The character is running forward according to the player's input. A large obstacle is placed in front to test the character's reactions under different planning lengths which are annotated in each picture respectively. ⇒ is the player's input and ⇒ is the character's current direction.

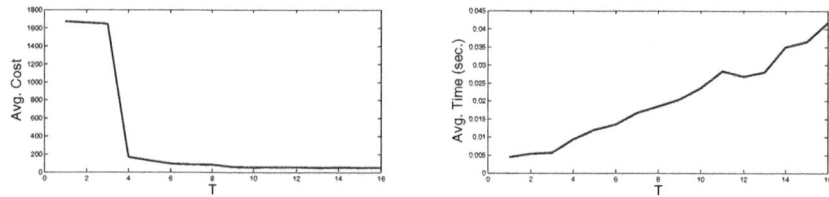

Fig. 5. Left: The average costs under each planning length. The x axis is the planning length and the y axis is the cost. Right: The average computation times(in seconds) under each planning length. The y axis is the computation time.

Fig. 6. Jump Over Obstacles. 50 cylinders are generated randomly as obstacles in this scene.

T is increased to 10, the average cost is low as natural animations are generated. Further increase of planning length improves little. The numerical results are consistent with animations shown in Figure 4. Average computation times in Figure 5 show the animations are generated in realtime. This experiment shows a short planning length will help the character avoid obstacles and a little longer planning length will create natural animations.

To demonstrate the efficiency of our algorithm under complex environments, we navigate the character in an environment with 50 randomly generated obstacles. Figure 1 is the screen-shot of this task. ⇒ is player's input direction and ➡ is the character's current direction. Figure 1 shows the character goes through the scene smoothly and avoids the obstacles several steps ahead. $T = 10$. The computation time is 0.028.

Our algorithm incorporates special actions by modifying the fitness function accordingly. Figure 6 shows the character is navigated in a scene with 50 randomly generated cylindrical obstacles. When low obstacles appear in front, the character will jump over them. $T = 10$. The average computation time is 0.025.

6 Discussion and Future Work

In this paper, we have presented a realtime approach for interactive character animation. Each action sequence is evaluated by the sum of discounted costs in a finite horizon. The genetic algorithm is adopted to evaluate action sequences in parallel on GPU. The approximation accuracy of the finite sum is analyzed. Experiments show our algorithm gains high control quality in realtime.

Our method is a 'tradeoff' between local and global search methods. Our algorithm approaches the quality of global search methods at the cost of computation time close to local search methods. As an approximation algorithm, it cannot guarantee optimal solutions. However, the planned sequence of actions guarantee high quality animations. The relations between local search, our method and global search are:

$$Quality : local\ search \ll our\ method < global\ search$$
$$Speed : global\ search \ll our\ method < local\ search$$

Compared with reinforcement learning methods used in character animation, neither off-line training nor pre-computed policies is needed in our method. Also, it doesn't matter whether current environment has been experienced. On the contrary, the control policies obtained by the reinforcement learning methods [6, 8, 10, 12, 21, 22] cannot be applied to environments different from the training ones. Moreover, reinforcement learning suffers from the curse of dimensionality: the number of parameters to be learned grows exponentially as the dimension of the state variable increases. Although techniques such as function approximation [21] have been applied to mitigate this problem, dimensionality issue still constrains reinforcement learning methods to relative simple environments. On the other hand, the merits of reinforcement learning are also obvious: it guarantees fast speed and optimal control policy once the precomputing phase is finished. As reinforcement learning makes optimal choices, we used it as the ground truth to analyze our controller in the navigation task. Figure 7 shows the average cost of both controllers. The performance of our controller is close to the optimal one in most cases. We believe reinforcement learning is ideal for low dimensional environments while our method is more suitable for tasks that actions must be evaluated online in realtime.

The main drawback of our approach is that it is difficult to gain precise motion control. This problem also troubles other approaches using motion clips as

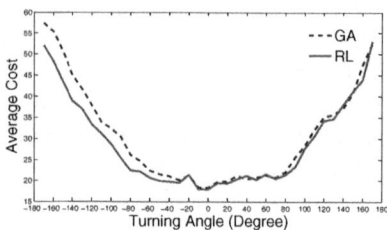

Fig. 7. Average costs of different methods. x axis is the input turning angle and y axis is the average cost of instruction. The dash line shows average costs of our method under different inputs. The solid line shows that of the reinforcement learning method.

underlying motion model. The blending techniques described in [10] may alleviate this problem but cannot eliminate it. For example, the character cannot respond to the input until current motion clip is running out. The number of motion clips has great influences on the performance of our algorithm as it determines the size of search space. Classifying motion clips into groups will relax this problem. Parameter selection is another important issue in our approach. Experiments show less than 16 planning steps can produce very high quality animations for obstacle avoidance tasks. The computation time is the main concern when choosing population size. Other parameters as well as the codes used to produce experiment results are not optimized. However, CUDA C codes need optimizations especially to achieve high performance. The performance of our algorithm should improve a lot after optimizing both parameters and codes.

Our future work includes applying our method to generate adversarial two-player games such as boxing and martial art. This can be achieved by adapting min-max algorithm into the fitness function. A further step may incorporate our algorithm into the multi-agent games.

Acknowledgments. The author would like to thank Professor SongMao Zhang for her help during the preparation of this paper.

References

1. CMU Graphics Lab Motion Capture Database (2011), http://mocap.cs.cmu.edu
2. Arikan, O., Forsyth, D.A.: Interactive motion generation from examples. ACM Transactions on Graphics 21(3), 483–490 (2002)
3. Heck, R., Gleicher, M.: Parametric motion graphs, p. 136. ACM (2007)
4. Kovar, L., Gleicher, M.: Flexible automatic motion blending with registration curves, p. 224. Eurographics Association (2003)
5. Lau, M., Kuffner, J.J.: Precomputed search trees: Planning for interactive goal-driven animation. pp. 299–308. Eurographics Association (2006)
6. Lee, J., Lee, K.H.: Precomputing avatar behavior from human motion data, pp. 79–87. Eurographics Association (2004)
7. Lee, J., Chai, J., Reitsma, P.S.A.: Interactive control of avatars animated with human motion data. ACM Transactions on Graphics 21(3), 491–500 (2002)

8. Leslie Ikemoto, O.A., Forsyth, D.: Learning to move autonomously in a hostile world, p. 46. ACM (2005)
9. Leslie Ikemoto, O.A., Forsyth, D.: Quick transitions with cached multi-way blends, p. 151. ACM (2007)
10. Lo, W.Y., Zwicker, M.: Real-time planning for parameterized human motion, pp. 29–38. Eurographics Association (2008)
11. Lucas Kovar, M.G., Pighin, F.: Motion graphs (2002)
12. McCann, J., Pollard, N.: Responsive characters from motion fragments, p. 6. ACM (2007)
13. Gleicher, M., Shin, H.J., Kovar, L., Jepsen, A.: Snap-together motion: assembling run-time animations, pp. 181–188. ACM (2003)
14. Ngo, J.T., Marks, J.: Spacetime constraints revisited (1993)
15. NVIDIA: Cuda (2011)
16. Ramnik Arora, R.T., Deb, K.: Parallelization of binary and real-coded genetic algorithms on gpu using cuda, pp. 1–8. IEEE (2010)
17. Safonova, A., Hodgins, J.K.: Construction and optimal search of interpolated motion graphs, p. 106. ACM (2007)
18. Sanders, J., Kandrot, E.: CUDA by example: an introduction to general-purpose GPU programming (2010)
19. Shin, H.J., Oh, H.S.: Fat graphs: constructing an interactive character with continuous controls, p. 298. Eurographics Association (2006)
20. Sims, K.: Evolving virtual creatures (1994)
21. Treuille, A., Lee, Y., Popović, Z.: Near-optimal character animation with continuous control, p. 7. ACM (2007)
22. Yongjoon Lee, S.J.L., Popović, Z.: Compact character controllers. ACM Transactions on Graphics (TOG) 28(5), 1–8 (2009)
23. Zhao, L., Safonova, A.: Achieving good connectivity in motion graphs, pp. 127–136. Eurographics Association (2008)

Improved Benchmarking for Steering Algorithms

Mubbasir Kapadia[1,2], Matthew Wang[1],
Glenn Reinman[1], and Petros Faloutsos[1,3]

[1] University of California, Los Angeles
[2] University of Pennsylvania
[3] York University

Abstract. The statistical analysis of multi-agent simulations requires a definitive set of benchmarks that represent the wide spectrum of challenging scenarios that agents encounter in dynamic environments, and a scoring method to objectively quantify the performance of a steering algorithm for a particular scenario. In this paper, we first recognize several limitations in prior evaluation methods. Next, we define a measure of *normalized effort* that penalizes deviation from desired speed, optimal paths, and collisions in a single metric. Finally, we propose a new set of benchmark categories that capture the different situations that agents encounter in dynamic environments and identify truly challenging scenarios for each category. We use our method to objectively evaluate and compare three state of the art steering approaches and one baseline reactive approach. Our proposed scoring mechanism can be used (a) to evaluate a single algorithm on a single scenario, (b) to compare the performance of an algorithm over different benchmarks, and (c) to compare different steering algorithms.

1 Introduction

Goal driven autonomous agents are used to populate dynamic virtual worlds in a wide variety of applications ranging from urban simulations, movies, games, and education. A large variety of approaches have been proposed to address the problems of steering and navigation in dynamic environments. However, evaluating the performance of steering techniques is still a fundamental open problem.

Crowd simulations are evaluated using one of the following methods: (a) manual inspection, (b) comparison to real-world data, or (c) statistical analysis. In this work, we focus on the use of computational methods and statistical tools to analyze, evaluate, and test crowd simulations. The statistical analysis of multi-agent simulations requires a definitive set of benchmarks that represent the wide spectrum of challenging scenarios that agents encounter in dynamic environments, and a scoring method to objectively quantify the performance of a steering algorithm for a particular scenario.

Prior work has proposed a rich set of application-specific benchmarks and metrics to evaluate and analyze crowd simulations. The test cases are usually limited to a small set of manually designed test cases, and ad hoc, scenario-dependent criteria. The work of [7] uses *presence* as a metric for crowd evaluation. The number of collisions and a measure of effort are often used as quantities that need to be minimized by steering algorithms [8, 2]. The work in [3] uses the "rate of people exiting a room" to analyze evacuation simulations. Many other approaches simply rely on visual fidelity and a subjective evaluation of the simulation. The work in [4] provides users with the flexibility of defining derived metrics in order to specify and detect custom behaviors in multi-agent simulations.

SteerBench [10] is the first work to propose a comprehensive set of manually defined benchmarks and a scoring method to objectively compare different steering algorithms in an application independent manner. However, it suffers from limitations that need to be addressed in order to provide a standard method of evaluating current and future steering approaches. The work in [6] performs random sampling in the space of obstacle and agent configurations to generate a very large set of *representative scenarios* that represent all the possible configurations an agent is likely to encounter while steering in dynamic environments. In addition, it defines three metrics: (1) success, (2) normalized time, and (3) normalized path length in order to objectively evaluate steering algorithms. These metrics can be used to measure coverage, quality, and failure for steering algorithms in the representative scenario space.

In this paper, we first evaluate and analyze three state of the art steering algorithms and one baseline reactive approach using SteerBench. The three steering algorithms are: (a) a local field based approach that performs steering and implicit space-time planning [5], (2) a hybrid method that combines reaction, prediction, and planning for steering and navigation [9], and (3) a method based on reciprocal velocity obstacles for collision avoidance [1]. From our first hand experience with SteerBench, we identify important limitations and open questions that need to be addressed (Section 2). Second, we propose a measure of effort that can be used to effectively measure the performance of a steering algorithm for a particular scenario (Section 3). Our scoring measure penalizes sub-optimal paths, deviations from the desired speed of an agent, and collisions in a single metric without the need of arbitrarily combining metrics with different units. In addition, we propose a measure of *optimal effort*. By normalizing the score with respect to an optimal, our scores have meaning on their own. They can therefore be used to compare the performance of an algorithm across different scenarios, as well as to compare different algorithms on the same scenario. Third, we propose an improved set of benchmark categories, and procedurally generate a large number of scenarios for each category in order to identify a definitive set of *challenging scenarios* that agents encounter in dynamic environments (Section 4). Finally, Section 5 presents a rigorous evaluation of three steering algorithms using the improved benchmarks and metrics, and Section 6 concludes the paper.

2 Experience with SteerBench

SteerBench [10] provides a benchmark suite of 38 scenarios (56 test cases) which are used to challenge a steering algorithm in the following broad categories: (1) simple validation scenarios, (2) basic agent-agent interactions, (3) agents interacting in presence of obstacles, (4) group interactions, and (5) large scale scenarios.

In addition, it proposes the following primary metrics to evaluate the efficiency of a steering algorithm: (1) number of collisions, (2) total time, and (3) total energy. A weighted sum of the three metrics is used to compute a *score* which can serve as a comparative measure for different steering algorithms. We use SteerBench to evaluate and compare four steering techniques: (1) EGOCENTRIC [5], (2) PPR [9], (3) RVO [1], and (4) one baseline reactive approach. The SteerBench scores of these four algorithms are provided in Table 1. The average time per agent in reaching goal (seconds) and total energy spent per agent ($kg \cdot m^2/s^2$) for EGOCENTRIC is also provided for reference. In this section, we describe our experience with using SteerBench and identify some limitations and open questions that need to be addressed. Please note that these limitations are not due to *bugs* but are fundamental shortcomings in the method of evaluation.

Observations. The four algorithms, including the reactive approach, can successfully solve 36 out of the 38 scenarios provided in SteerBench. We observe little or no difference in the scores of all four algorithms on the simple scenarios and basic agent interactions. The values of the scores range from 100 to 500 depending on the length and difficulty of the scenario. This only allows us to compare the performance of different steering algorithms on the same scenario and prevents the score from being considered on its own or across different scenarios.

The Oncoming-groups is a challenging scenario that results in different behaviors from the three approaches. We notice that EGOCENTRIC results in group formations where the the two oncoming groups of agents stick together and smoothly maneuver around the other group, taking a longer but collision-free trajectory. In PPR and REACTIVE, the agents do not deviate from their optimal trajectories and resort to reactively avoid oncoming threats. However, the resulting scores of these approaches is not much different and does not capture these emergent and vastly different behaviors.

The Overtake scenarios were designed to test the ability of an agent to pass an agent from behind while in a narrow passage. We observe that the scores for all 4 algorithms are approximately the same. However, However, visual inspection of the simulation shows that PPR and REACTIVE did not demonstrate an overtaking behavior. The Surprise scenarios challenge agents to suddenly react to crossing threats in narrow corridoors. However, the effect of the interesting interaction between agents on the overall score is diluted due to the length of the scenario. Finally, the scenarios with $3-4$ agents interacting with one another all have approximately the same score. Agent interactions can be vastly different depending on the initial conditions and manually designing a few scenarios to test interactions between agents is not sufficient.

We identify the following limitations from our first hand experience with SteerBench:

- The evaluation of the steering algorithm is limited to the 56 hand designed test cases that are provided with SteerBench which cannot capture the entire spectrum of scenarios that an agent may encounter while steering in dynamic environments and are prone to the problem of overfitting.

Table 1. Evaluation Results using SteerBench – Lower score is better. Numbers in () is the average number of collisions per agent.

Test Case	Time	Energy	Egocentric	RVO	PPR	Reactive
Simple-3	5.75	112.0	117.76	114.41	118.77	117.87
Simple-obstacle-2	14.2	253.13	267.33	265.67	268.23	268.23
Curves	21.5	363.85	385.35	431.22	385.5	385.5
Crossing-6	22.2	277.8	298.32	298.94	295.25	295.25
Oncoming-obstacle	16.83	267.87	284.7	289.64(0.5)	284.1	276.75
Oncoming-groups	41.72	598.87	640.5	643.83	637.53	638.75
Fan-out	32.25	519.98	552.24	549.48	551.3	551.3
Cut-across-2	33.57	505.9	539.49	546.82	537.1	536.9
Surprise-2	25.7	353.84	429.54(1)	401.56	407.15	406.62
Overtake-obstacle	16.9	279.27	296.17	300.28	291.23	297.6
4-way-confusion-2	15.26	253.4	268.67	267.0	269.13	265.63
Double-squeeze	22.63	308.43	331.05	371.3(1)	354.6(0.5)	379.5(1)
Doorway-two-way	–	–	Fail	331.38	Fail	Fail
Wall-squeeze	–	–	Fail	Fail	434.43(2)	Fail

- Often, the most interesting portion of a scenario is the interaction between agents and obstacles which is only a small portion of the scenario. The analysis of the entire scenario thus reduces the effect of the *interaction of interest* on the cumulative score.
- The metrics are scenario dependent, i.e., the scores produced by SteerBench vary greatly over different scenarios. This is because the metrics are computed in a time dependent manner. As a result, scenarios that take longer to complete have larger scores. As a result, it is only meaningful to compare the scores of two simulations for a test case. However, it is impossible to evaluate the efficiency of steering algorithms independently for one scenario over different scenarios.
- There exists no definition of ground truth or optimality for the scenarios. The notion of a perfect score for a particular scenario would provide a strong basis for comparison and help better identify the areas of a particular algorithm that needs improvement.
- The scores are only intended to serve as a basis for comparison between two algorithms and have no meaning on an absolute scale.
- The weights used to sum three primary metrics also did not have any intuitive meaning.

Hence, there exists no definitive set of benchmarks that represent the wide variety of challenging scenarios that agents encounter in complex virtual worlds. Also, we need metrics that can measure the performance of an algorithm in a time and scenario independent fashion. This greatly limits the objective evaluation and comparison of different steering and navigation techniques.

3 Metrics for Evaluation

In this section, we propose a bio-mechanically inspired measure of effort to objectively score the performance of a steering algorithm on a particular scenario. We also calculate the optimal value of effort required to solve a scenario which allows us to normalize our score. Our proposed scoring mechanism can be used (a) to evaluate a single algorithm on a single scenario, (b) to compare the performance of an algorithm across different benchmarks, and (c) to compare different steering algorithms.

The work in [12] describes that steering agents should obey two principles while navigating in dynamic environments: (1) they should minimize the distance traveled in reaching their destination, and (2) they should attempt to move at their preferred speed. A collision-free trajectory is a fundamental requirement that must also be met. A simple effort function that measures the distance travelled by an agent to reach the goal does not address the influence of speed. Similarly, a metric that only measures the time to reach the goal will result in the agents walking at their maximum speed rather than at their preferred speed, expending more energy than necessary.

The Principle of Least Effort states that an organism will maintain on average the least possible work expenditure rate as estimated by itself. When applied to steering, it means that agents will naturally choose a path to their goal which they expect will require the least amount of *effort*. Biomechanics research has quantified the energy expended by a walking human as a function of the subject's instantaneous velocity [13]. The effort, $E_m^a(s)$ of an agent a as the metabolic energy expended while walking along a path for a given scenario s is computed as follows:

$$E_m^a(s) = m \int_{t=0}^{t=T} e_s + e_w |\mathbf{v}|^2 dt. \qquad (1)$$

Here, m is the mass of an agent, T is the total time of the simulation, and e_s, e_w are per agent constants. For an average human, $e_s = 2.23 \frac{J}{Kg \cdot s}$ and $e_w = 1.26 \frac{J \cdot s}{Kg \cdot m^2}$.

Collision Effort. We introduce an effort penalty, $E_c^a(s)$ for collisions. For every second that an agent, a is in a state of collision, this penalty is a function of the penetration of the collision.

$$E_c^a(s) = m \int_{t=0}^{t=T} e_c c_p(t) dt, \qquad (2)$$

where $e_c = 10 \frac{J}{Kg \cdot m \cdot s}$ is a penalty constant for collisions. The collision penetration function, $c_p(t)$ estimates the current penetration depth of the collision if the agent is colliding with another agent at that point of time.

Optimal Effort. The optimal effort for an agent a in a scenario s is defined as the energy consumed in taking the optimal route to the target while traveling at the average walking speed $= \sqrt{\frac{e_s}{e_w}} = 1.33 m/s$. Let L_{opt} be the optimal length for an agent a to reach the target. The optimal effort, $E^a_{opt}(s)$ for an agent a is calculated as follows:

$$E^a_{opt}(s) = 2mL_{opt}\sqrt{e_s e_w}. \qquad (3)$$

The derivation of Equation 3 can be found here [2]. We calculate L_{opt} as the length along the optimal trajectory (found using A*) for an agent to reach its goal, taking into account only static obstacles.

Normalized Effort. The normalized effort for a particular agent a in a scenario s is defined as the ratio of the optimal effort in reaching a target to the actual effort taken, accounting for collisions. It is calculated as follows:

$$E^a_r(s) = \frac{E^a_{opt}(s)}{E^a_m(s) + E^a_c(s)} \qquad (4)$$

The normalized effort for all agents for a given scenario is calculated as follows:

$$E_r(s) = \frac{\sum_{a=1}^{a=N} E^a_r(s)}{N} \qquad (5)$$

where N is the number of agents in the scenario. The value of $E_r(s)$ ranges from 0 to 1 with a higher value indicating better performance for a given scenario. A *perfect* steering algorithm would have $E_r(s) = 1$.

Average Quality. The average quality of a steering algorithm over a set of scenarios is computed as the average value of $E_r(s)$ for all scenarios.

4 Benchmarks for Evaluation

Based on the work in [6], we define a scenario as one possible configuration of agents and obstacles. A large number of scenarios can be generated by randomly sampling agent and obstacle configurations. However, in the majority of cases, it is of particular interest to define scenarios which capture challenging interactions between agents. Trivial scenarios where agents need not perform any steering to reach their destination (i.e. agents never interact with one another) are generally not going to provide a meaningful comparison. To ensure agent interactions, we place a constraint on scenario generation such that all agents must interact (i.e. their optimal paths must cross in space and time). The resulting scenarios generated focus on more *interesting interactions* between agents, and therefore avoid diluting evauation scores in our methodology by measuring trivial steering simulations where agents do not interact. We also provide the flexibility place additional user-defined constraints on the generated scenario in order to meet certain criteria in order to define specific categories of scenarios.

We define a set of benchmark categories that uniquely capture the different *challenges* that steering and navigating agents encounter in dynamic worlds. These benchmark categories are described below.

- **Single Agent Navigation.** These scenarios have one agent with a fixed initial and desired position. We randomly sample obstacle configurations in order to evaluate the navigation capabilities of an algorithm. Figure 1(a) illustrates an example scenario generated for this category.
- **Agent Interactions.** These scenarios represent different configurations of oncoming as well crossing agents (Figure 1(b)-(c)). Agents are randomly positioned at the boundary with goals at the opposite end of the environment to ensure that all agents will arrive at the center of the environment at approximately the same time, thus forcing an interaction. An obstacle is randomly positioned in the center to pose an additional challenge. The number of agents is varied from $2 - 10$.
- **Narrow Passages.** These scenarios challenge oncoming agents to travel in narrow passages that are just big enough to allow two agents to pass through (Figure 1(d)). The number of agents is varied from $2 - 4$.
- **Narrow Crossings.** These scenarios capture combinations of oncoming and crossing interactions between agents in narrow corridors (Figure 1(e)-(f)).
- **Oncoming Groups.** The scenarios in this category represent interactions between oncoming groups of agents (Figure 1(g)-(h)). Agents are randomly positioned on two opposing sides of the environment forming two oncoming groups. Different obstacle configurations may also be randomly positioned in the center of the environment to pose as an additional challenge. The number of agents in the group is varied from $2 - 5$.
- **Crossing Groups.** These scenarios represent interactions between crossing groups of agents (Figure 1(i)-(j)). Agents are randomly positioned in 2 adjacent groups which interact in the center of the environment. Obstacles may also be randomly positioned in the center of the environment. The number of agents in each group is varied from $2 - 5$.
- **Group Confusion.** This category captures interactions between 4 groups of agents that arrive at the center of the environment from opposite sides (Figure 1(k)-(l)). The number of agents in each group is varied from $2 - 4$.

We randomly generate 10,000 scenario samples for each of the benchmark categories and and calculate the mean of the average quality of the three steering algorithms [5, 9, 1]. Figure 2 illustrates the average quality distribution for the benchmark categories described above. We identify the 100 scenarios with the lowest quality scores as the failure set for each benchmark category. These are highlighted in blue in Figure 2. The next 900 scenarios (highlighted in red) with lowest quality measures are identified as challenging scenarios for the respective benchmark category. The average quality thresholds for the failure set and the challenging scenarios are given in Table 2.

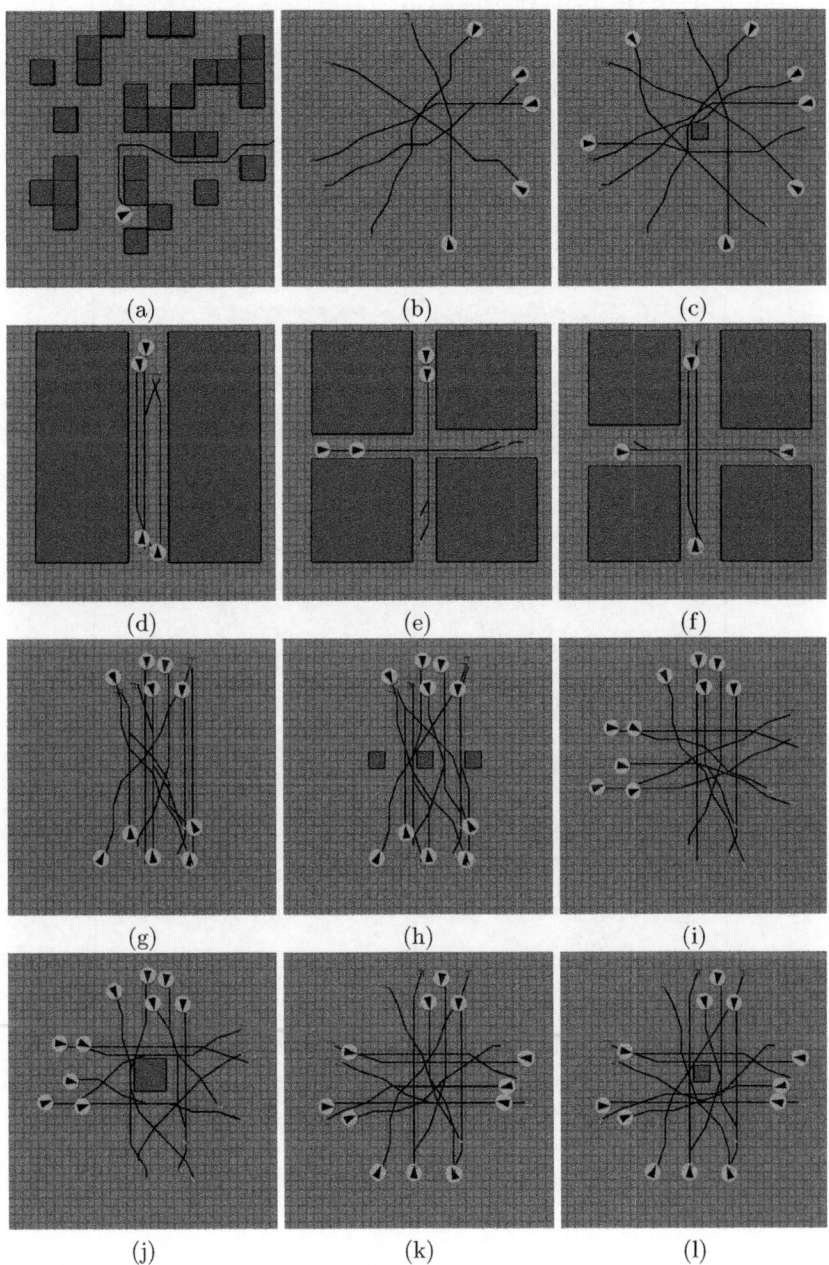

Fig. 1. Randomly generated scenarios for each of the benchmark categories

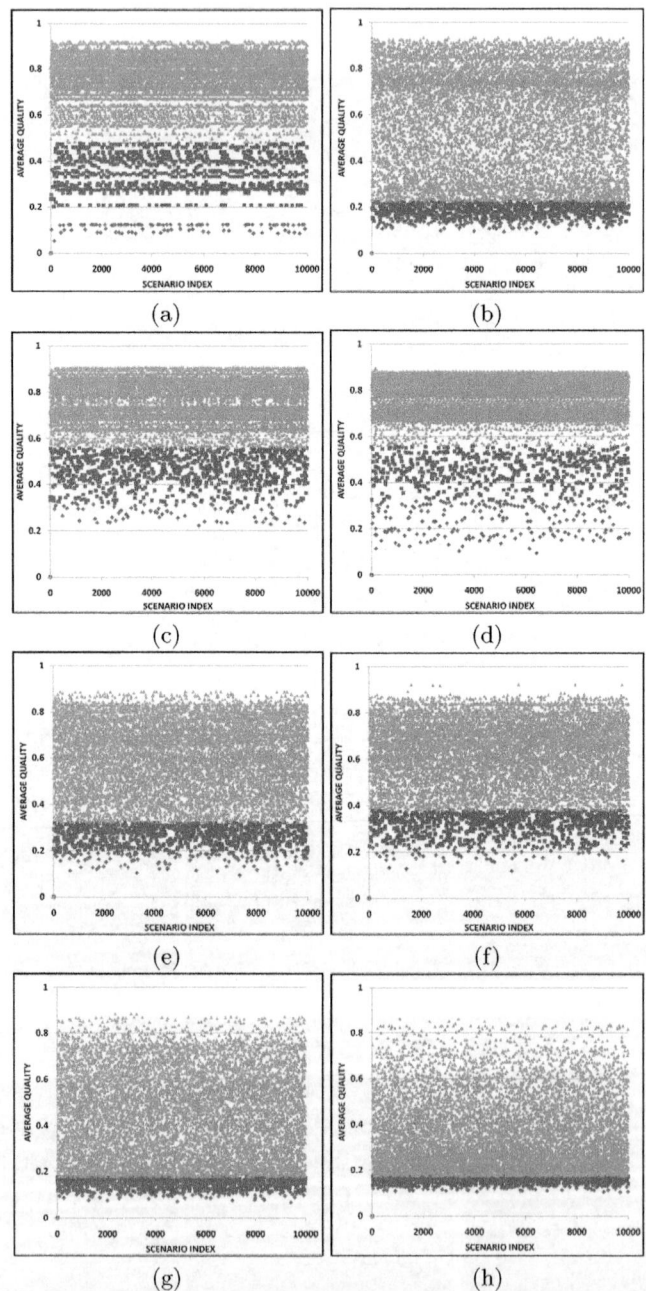

Fig. 2. Mean of average quality of EGOCENTRIC,PPR,RVO for the following benchmark categories. (a) Single agent navigation. (b) Agent interactions with obstacles. (c) Narrow passages. (d) Narrow crossings. (e) Oncoming groups. (f) Crossing groups. (g) Group confusion. (h) Group confusion with obstacles. The blue, red, and green points highlight the failure set, challenging scenarios, and the remaining scenarios respectively.

Table 2. The average quality thresholds used to identify the failure set and the challenging scenarios for each benchmark category. In Figure 2, the scenarios which fall below are the failure threshold are highlighted in blue while the challenging scenarios are highlighted in red.

Benchmark Category	Failure Threshold	Challenge Threshold
Single Agent Navigation	0.125	0.481
Agent Interactions	0.212	0.303
Agent Interactions Obstacle	0.136	0.225
Narrow Passages	0.322	0.566
Narrow Crossings	0.245	0.631
Oncoming Groups	0.192	0.322
Oncoming Groups Obstacle	0.115	0.176
Crossing Groups	0.222	0.380
Crossing Groups Obstacle	0.149	0.258
Group Confusion	0.112	0.177
Group Confusion Obstacle	0.132	0.175

5 Results

In this section, we evaluate EGOCENTRIC, PPR, RVO and REACTIVE using the proposed metrics and benchmark categories described in Section 3 and Section 4. Table 3 provides the average quality measures of the four steering algorithms for the aforementioned benchmark categories. The FAIL quality measure describes the quality of the algorithm for the scenarios in the failure set. The CHALLENGE quality measures describes the quality measure of the algorithm on the challenging scenarios. Finally, the ALL quality measure describes the quality of the algorithm on the remaining sampled scenarios.

Observations. The Single Agent Navigation benchmarks are primarily used to test the planning abilities of the algorithms. We observe that the three standard algorithms have similar quality measures while REACTIVE performs particularly poorly as it constantly steers towards a local target that is chosen by casting a ray towards the goal. In contrast, the quality measures of REACTIVE are comparable to PPR for the benchmarks involving agent interactions, as these scenarios challenge the reactive behavior of agents to avoid other dynamic threats. The Narrow Passages and Narrow Crossing are particularly challenging benchmarks as it challenges the ability of the steering agents to predictively avoid oncoming and crossing threats and prevent possible deadlock situations. A large percentage of the energy calculation in these two benchmark categories was due to collisions where agents were simply unable to predictively avoid oncoming and crossing threats and simply resorted to colliding with other agents. For all the Group Interactions benchmarks, we observe that PPR and REACTIVE both have similar quality measures. This is because PPR turns off predictions in the presence of crowds (more than 4 agents) and resorts to purely reactive behavior which is reflected in the scores. EGOCENTRIC outperforms the other algorithms

Table 3. Average Quality of EGOCENTRIC, RVO, PPR, and REACTIVE on all benchmark categories: (1) FAIL: Failure Set (100 most difficult scenarios generated for that category). (2) CHALLENGE: Challenging Scenarios (1000 most difficult scenarios generated for that category, excluding the failure set). (3) ALL: The remaining 9000 scenarios that were generated.

Benchmark Category	Quality	Egocentric	RVO	PPR	Reactive
Single Agent Navigation	FAIL	0.102	0.154	0.113	0.0076
	CHALLENGE	0.321	0.385	0.334	0.121
	ALL	0.691	0.776	0.715	0.543
Agent Interactions	FAIL	0.204	0.210	0.203	0.198
	CHALLENGE	0.271	0.267	0.260	0.257
	ALL	0.653	0.643	0.641	0.645
Agent Interactions Obstacle	FAIL	0.132	0.142	0.121	0.113
	CHALLENGE	0.191	0.193	0.183	0.178
	ALL	0.601	0.613	0.564	0.546
Narrow Passages	FAIL	0.302	0.256	0.278	0.132
	CHALLENGE	0.476	0.432	0.452	0.332
	ALL	0.744	0.732	0.734	0.687
Narrow Crossings	FAIL	0.182	0.174	0.178	0.123
	CHALLENGE	0.465	0.452	0.445	0.343
	ALL	0.781	0.755	0.742	0.698
Oncoming Groups	FAIL	0.182	0.171	0.161	0.157
	CHALLENGE	0.312	0.286	0.255	0.253
	ALL	0.656	0.617	0.572	0.567
Oncoming Groups Obstacle	FAIL	0.133	0.127	0.103	0.097
	CHALLENGE	0.189	0.165	0.145	0.138
	ALL	0.465	0.426	0.392	0.390
Crossing Groups	FAIL	0.221	0.209	0.193	0.192
	CHALLENGE	0.348	0.327	0.305	0.301
	ALL	0.667	0.643	0.603	0.612
Crossing Groups Obstacle	FAIL	0.156	0.143	0.134	0.134
	CHALLENGE	0.245	0.223	0.204	0.210
	ALL	0.534	0.509	0.481	0.491
Group Confusion	FAIL	0.125	0.123	0.101	0.091
	CHALLENGE	0.167	0.156	0.145	0.143
	ALL	0.512	0.476	0.428	0.412
Group Confusion Obstacle	FAIL	0.142	0.134	0.121	0.115
	CHALLENGE	0.175	0.167	0.154	0.144
	ALL	0.412	0.387	0.341	0.324

in the group interactions due to the emergence of group behavior where nearby located agents tend to stick together while handling other agent groups.

6 Conclusion

In this paper, we propose a set of benchmark categories to capture different situations that steering agents encounter in dynamic environments and a measure of *normalized effort* that penalizes deviation from desired speed, optimal paths, and collisions in a single metric. We use our method to objectively evaluate and compare three state of the art steering approaches and one baseline reactive approach. Our proposed scoring mechanism can be analyzed on its own, can be used to compare the performance of an algorithm over different benchmarks, and also be used to compare different steering algorithms. For future work, we would like to analyse the performance of steering approaches based on principles of energy minimization [2] and approaches that use more complex locomotion models [11]. We would also like to to compute metrics for real crowds to serve as *ground truth* for the benchmarks.

Acknowledgements. Intel supported this research through a visual-computing grant and the donation of a 32-core Emerald Ridge system with Xeon X7560 processors. We thank Randi Rost and Scott Buck from Intel for their support.

References

1. van den Berg, J., Lin, M.C., Manocha, D.: Reciprocal velocity obstacles for real-time multi-agent navigation. In: Proceedings of ICRA, pp. 1928–1935. IEEE (2008)
2. Guy, S.J., Chhugani, J., Curtis, S., Dubey, P., Lin, M., Manocha, D.: Pledestrians: a least-effort approach to crowd simulation. In: SCA, pp. 119–128 (2010)
3. Helbing, D., Farkas, I., Vicsek, T.: Simulating dynamical features of escape panic. Nature 407, 487 (2000)
4. Kapadia, M., Singh, S., Allen, B., Reinman, G., Faloutsos, P.: Steerbug: an interactive framework for specifying and detecting steering behaviors. In: SCA 2009, pp. 209–216. ACM (2009)
5. Kapadia, M., Singh, S., Hewlett, W., Faloutsos, P.: Egocentric affordance fields in pedestrian steering. In: I3D 2009, pp. 215–223. ACM (2009)
6. Kapadia, M., Wang, M., Singh, S., Reinman, G., Faloutsos, P.: Scenario space: Characterizing coverage, quality, and failure of steering algorithms. In: SCA (2011)
7. Pelechano, N., Stocker, C., Allbeck, J., Badler, N.: Being a part of the crowd: towards validating vr crowds using presence. In: AAMAS, pp. 136–142 (2008)
8. Shao, W., Terzopoulos, D.: Autonomous pedestrians. In: SCA. ACM (2005)
9. Singh, S., Kapadia, M., Hewlett, W., Faloutsos, P.: A modular framework for adaptive agent-based steering. In: I3D 2011. ACM (2011)
10. Singh, S., Kapadia, M., Naik, M., Reinman, G., Faloutsos, P.: SteerBench: A Steering Framework for Evaluating Steering Behaviors. In: CAVW (2009)
11. Singh, S., Kapadia, M., Reinman, G., Faloutsos, P.: Footstep navigation for dynamic crowds. In: CAVW (2011)
12. Still, K.G.: Crowd Dynamics. Ph.D. thesis, United Kingdon (2000)
13. Whittle, M.: Gait analysis: An introduction (1996)

When a Couple Goes Together: Walk along Steering

Markéta Popelová, Michal Bída, Cyril Brom, Jakub Gemrot, and Jakub Tomek

Charles University in Prague, Faculty of Mathematics and Physics,
Malostranské nám. 2/25, Prague, Czech Republic

Abstract. Steering techniques are widely used for navigation of single agents or crowds and flocks. Steerings also have the potential to coordinate movement of human-like agents in very small groups so that the resulting behavior appears socially believable, but this dimension is less explored. Here, we present one such "social" steering, the Walk Along steering for navigating a couple of agents to reach a certain place together. The results of a believability study with 26 human subjects who compared the new steering to the known Leader Following steering in eight different scenarios suggest the superiority of the Walk Along steering in social situations.

1 Introduction

Various types of entities can move in applications featuring 3D virtual reality, ranging from inanimate objects, such as rockets and vehicles, to virtual animals and humans. For controlling bodily movement of animate entities, called intelligent virtual agents (IVAs) henceforth, a three-layer architecture can be employed to a great advantage [15]. The top-layer, responsible for high-level action selection and searching for a path in a large environment using global information, a kind of map, is usually supplemented by a middle layer, which refines the high-level path employing a reactive approach that takes local information into account. The lowest layer, a physical/animation engine, is then responsible for actual locomotion.

A favorite reactive mechanism used to implement the middle layer is steering techniques (steerings) of Craig Reynolds. His first techniques served to steer large groups of virtual birds, herds and fish [14]. Later, these techniques were extended for general virtual agents [15]. Even though these techniques are simple, they can be used to steer large groups of agents and the resulting behavior looks naturally. At the same time, these techniques are deterministic, which helps with debugging, and computationally inexpensive. For these qualities, Reynolds' steerings and their derivations are useful in various applications: crowd simulations, safety modeling, traffic planning, computer games, films, educational applications etc.

Steerings may serve well for navigating single agents or agents in a crowd or a flock. Especially steerings for avoiding collisions with other IVAs or static obstacles are researched a lot, e.g., [4, 5, 6], or steerings for crowd/flock behavior, e.g., [2, 8].

However, steerings can also be used for other purposes than for purely mechanistic navigation: they can help a designer to express relations between agents, their personality or mood and other social traits. Even though some steerings are used for controlling human-like IVAs in intrinsically social situations, such as Seek, Flee, and

Leader Following, the social dimension of steerings has not been explored much. To our knowledge, only few works explored this line of research: the authors of [9, 10, 11] investigated group conversation dynamics and human territorial behavior during social interactions, and the authors of [7, 12] researched behavior of small groups.

We are interested in this second way of using the steering approach: for social expressions of human-like IVAs. One of main motivations is the usage of steerings in our educational micro-game Cinema Date [1]. The game features two virtual teenagers dating on their way to the cinema. The player influences the course of the date by shaping behavior of one of the characters with a particular game goal.

In this paper, we present one result from this ground – a new steering named Walk Along (WA), which we designed and implemented. The goal of this steering is to steer two virtual agents who go to a certain place together. Ideally, the agents should go side by side. It may happen that the IVAs would need to avoid static and dynamic obstacles on their way, pass narrow corridors consecutively etc. However as they return to free space, they should walk side by side again. Also, it may happen that one of the IVAs will get stuck or delayed along their way (e.g., that it stops and watches a shop-window, lets a car go by, etc.). The second IVA should notice this situation and wait for the first IVA or return for it.

In general, the WA steering is supposed to navigate agents in open spaces, not inside small enclosed rooms. At the same time, its main purpose is to create single pairs of people, not crowds composed of pairs of people (although such usage could also be possible). To create a perfect impression of two friends going together to a certain place, it would be necessary to use appropriate animations expressing what they are talking about, their mood, emotions and other social behavior. These issues are out of scope of this paper (but see [1]).

A possible solution of the walk along assignment is the steering Leader Following (LF) by Reynolds [15], extended for following the leader at a certain position – next to the leader in our case. One of the two walking IVAs would be the leader and the other would follow it on its side. This solution has certain disadvantages. In the basic form of that steering, the leader does not wait for its follower(s). For instance, if a follower gets stuck, the leader keeps going to its target, which is not a very plausible behavior (unless the leader is angry at the follower). In the WA steering, both agents have the same role and give the impression of more balanced relationship.

In our evaluation with human subjects, we compare the WA steering to the modified LF in eight different scenarios with the intention to demonstrate possibilities and limitations of the new steering. For the purposes of the evaluation, we also implemented six other steerings which may be combined together and with the WA. These steerings are based on the Reynolds' seminal work [15].

The paper proceeds as follows: general architecture and six implemented steerings are briefly described in Section 2. The Walk Along steering is detailed in Section 3. Section 4 describes the evaluation results and Section 5 concludes.

2 General Architecture and Implemented Steering Behaviors

We implemented the three-layer architecture for controlling motion of IVAs designed by Reynolds [15]. It is composed of an *action selection* layer, a *steering* layer and a *locomotion* layer. At the action selection layer, it is decided which steerings are active and how they are parameterized. The steering layer computes the velocity of a steered agent in the next tick (the time in our simulation is discrete). The locomotion layer moves the agent according to the given velocity.

Every steering has the following information: the current location and velocity of the agent, and locations and velocities of all other visible agents (in 180° range). Inanimate obstacles are detected by five rays: one front ray, two short lateral and two long front-lateral rays (note that we tested the WA steering also with an agent with seven and nine rays). The result of computation of each steering in one tick is a single force vector. By combining all steering force vectors with the velocity vector from the previous tick, a new velocity vector is computed and passed to the locomotion layer.

As a means of combining the force vectors of the steerings, we chose a weighted average of all nonzero steering vectors (with the previous velocity vector). The weight of the previous velocity vector can influence smoothness vs. prompt reactions ratio (the higher the weight is, the smoother the motion is, but reactions may be slower).

In our application, we have implemented the following six steerings: Target Approaching, Obstacle Avoidance, Path Following, Leader Following, Wall Following, and People Avoidance. The first five are based on [15] while the last one uses a similar approach as in [5]. The LF steering allows for setting the agent's relative position to the leader, which is our innovation to Reyonolds' version of this steering. All steerings are detailed in [13]. The seventh steering, detailed in Section 3, is Walk Along. We have used UnrealEngine2Runtime as a 3D engine, our own 0.25 km^2 large virtual city as a virtual environment, and the Pogamut platform for developing AI of the virtual characters [3].

3 Walk along Steering Behavior

The goal of the Walk Along steering is to steer an agent in such a way that it will, together with another agent (a *partner*), reach a certain place. Both of them should walk alongside each other keeping a certain distance between them. They should be capable of catching up with their partner or slowing down so that their partner will reach them sooner, if necessary. As opposed to the Leader Following steering, no agent is in the leading position and both know their target.

The steering has six parameters:

1. *Partner* – the agent, with whom the steered agent should walk along to the target.
2. *Target* – the target location.
3. *Distance* – the ideal distance between partners. They will keep it if the environment does not make it impossible.
4. *Force Scale* – a scaling constant; scales the magnitude of the resulting force vector to units that can be interpreted in the given virtual environment (cm_{UE2R}, m_{UE2R},...).
5. *Give way* – a boolean parameter which helps to make sure that partners do not get too close to one another. It solves situations where one of the agents is between the other agent and the target location.
6. *Wait for Partner* – a boolean parameter with which a steered agent that is much closer to the target location than the partner waits for the partner instead of going towards it and then returning back together with it. This influences only certain kinds of topological arrangements of partners and their target.

The WA steering steers only one of the agents and does not need to communicate with the other agent except of knowing the joint target, and the position and the velocity vector of the partner. To achieve the right behavior, both partners have to be steered by the steering Walk Along with the same or similar parameters.

The resulting force of the steering has three components: a_T (attractive force to the target), a_p (attractive force to the partner) and r_p (repulsive force from the partner). The first handles reaching the target place and the other two keep correct distance between partners. At every moment, either a_p or r_p is zero. We now explain how these force components are calculated, starting with introducing the naming conventions.

The *Target* parameter is just one location and both partners can not stand on this location together. Therefore each partner will have its own location: T_m (my target) and T_p (the partner's target).

Figure 1 shows an outline of the situation: T stands for the *Target* parameter, L_m is the location between the partners, and *axis* is the straight line going through L_m and T. The locations T_m and T_p lie on the straight line going through T that is perpendicular to *axis*. The distance between T_m and T is the same as the distance between T_p and T and equals the half of the parameter *Distance*. T_m is the location nearer to the steered agent and T_p is the other location. We will further need three distances: d_p is the current distance between partners, D_p is the distance between the partner and its target T_p, and D_m is the distance between the steered agent and its target T_m.

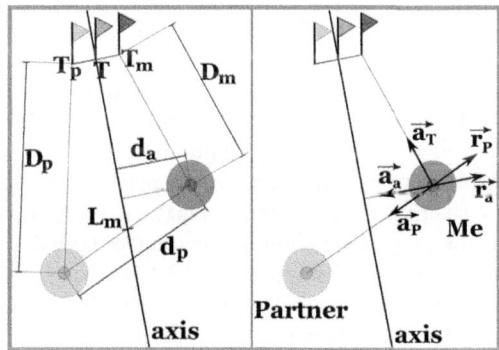

Fig. 1. A drawing of partners, their targets, distances (left) and forces (right) of the Walk Along steering for the darker agent

The first component of the resulting steering force is the vector a_T, the attractive force to the target. Its direction is from the location of the steered agent to the T_m location. Its magnitude is determined by the equation:

$$F \cdot 2^{\min(1.5, \ D_m - D_p)} + c, \qquad (1)$$

where F is the value of *Force Scale*, and c is a small positive constant iff $D_m > D_p$, or 0 otherwise. The purpose of c is to increase the agent's speed when it is farther from the target than its partner (c is approximately $F \cdot 1/7$ in our implementation). Note that when the agents walk next to each other ($D_m = D_p$), a_T equals F. When they are not in a pair, the magnitude of a_T for the farther agent increases at least by $F+c$ but it is truncated at the upper bound $F \cdot 2^{1.5}+c$ (which corresponds to the maximal agent's speed; the value 1.5 can be changed when a different maximal speed is needed). At the same time, the magnitude decreases for the nearer agent to zero, which means that the agent will go increasingly slower (with increasingly higher distance between the agents). The lower speed of the nearer agent and the higher speed of the farther agent allow the farther one to catch up with the nearer one.

The other two components of the resulting steering force (a_p and r_p) are calculated according to the value of d_p, the actual distance between the partners. The direction of a_p, the attractive force to the partner, is from the location of the steered agent to its partner, and magnitude of a_p is determined by the equation:

$$F \cdot \frac{\max(0, d_p - D)}{D}, \qquad (2)$$

where D is the value of the parameter *Distance* and the other parameters are as above. The higher the actual distance between the agents is, the higher the attractive force is. When the actual distance is the same as *Distance* or lower, the a_p's magnitude is zero.

The vector r_p leads to the steered agent away from its partner and the vector's magnitude is determined by the equation:

$$F \cdot \frac{\max(0, D - d_p)}{D}, \qquad (3)$$

where the parameters are as above. This vector is nonzero *iff* the actual distance between the partners is lower than *Distance*. The lower the actual distance is, the higher the repulsive force is. Note the maximal magnitude of r_p equals to F.

Eventually all three steering components, a_T, a_p and r_p, are combined. If the magnitude of the resulting steering force exceeds a maximal value, it is truncated. Because the a_p component is the only one without its own upper bound, its contribution to the resulting steering force can be substantial relative to the other two components. This becomes useful when the IVAs are far apart from each other.

Due to these three force components, the partners are able to walk smoothly together to the target. If they are far apart from each other at the beginning of the simulation, they run to each other at first. Subsequently, they go to the target and try to keep the right distance between each other. If one of them gets stuck, the other slows down (if the first is not too far away), or returns back to the first one (if the first one is far away). If they get close to the target, the steering (in our implementation) returns the requirement for stopping the agent and if no other steering returns a nonzero force, the agent stops.

3.1 Advanced Walk along Behavior   The *Give Way* Parameter

The WA steering behavior described so far has one problem. When the agents are approaching each other, it may happen that they both end up at or very close to *axis*. Now, it will take some time until both partners form a pair perpendicular to *axis*, even if they have enough space around them. The reason is that r_p and a_T forces of the partner farther from the target have nearly opposite direction and they may nearly cancel each other out. Therefore, the farther partner slows down not to get too close to the agent closer to the target. However, the farther agent should have sped up to get next to its partner to form a pair. At the same time, the repulsive force of the agent closer to the target has the same direction as this agent's attractive force to the target. Therefore, the closer agent speeds up, but it should have slowed down.

The parameter *Give Way* solves this problem. Instead of detecting that partners are too close to each other, the steering uses d_a, the distance from *axis*. Instead of the force component r_p, we now use the force component r_a, the repulsive force from the *axis* (see Figure 1). The magnitude of the r_a force is determined by the equation:

$$F \cdot \frac{\max(0, D - 2 \cdot d_a)}{D}, \qquad (4)$$

where F and D are as above. If d_a is higher than half of *Distance*, the force r_a is 0. Otherwise, the lower the actual distance is, the higher the repulsive force r_a is. When the partners form a couple staying perpendicular to *axis*, r_a equals to r_p from the basic WA variant. Otherwise, each partner moves to its side (away from *axis*) making a way for the second partner. Thus, both can get next to each other.

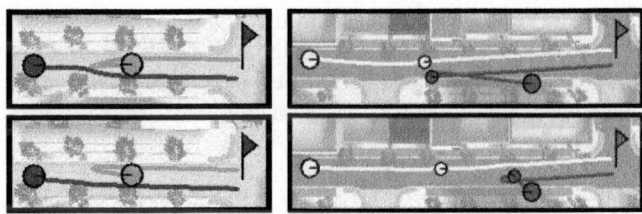

Fig. 2. The steering Walk Along without (top left) and with (bottom left) the parameter *Give Way*, and the WA steering without (top right) and with (bottom right) the parameter *Wait For Partner*. The heading of the agents is denoted by a short line, the flags denote the targets.

Figure 2 compares the same situation without (top left) and with (bottom left) the parameter *Give Way*. On the left top figure, the agents get too close to each other and it lasts too long until they form a pair staying perpendicular to *axis*. On the left bottom figure, they give way to each other and quickly get next to each other.

3.2 Advanced Walk along Behavior — The *Wait for Partner* Parameter

The steering Walk Along offers yet other functionality by means of the *Wait for Partner* parameter. It becomes useful in situations where one partner (Partner A) is approximately between the second partner (Partner B) and their target, and Partner B is quite far away. The basic steering behavior or the behavior with the *Give Way* parameter switched on steers Partner A to run to Partner B. When they meet, they continue together to the target, which means that Partner A, after a while of walking together with partner B, returns back to where it already was. This behavior may be natural in certain situations, e.g., when two young lovers run to each other to be with each other as soon as possible. However, the person closer to the target would often simply wait for the other person so that it does not have to walk the same route twice. With the parameter *Wait for Partner* switched on, Partner A is steered to wait until Partner B comes to it and only then they continue together to the target location.

We operationally define above described situation by two conditions: Firstly, the current distance between partners is higher than the *Distance* parameter. Secondly, the difference between D_p and D_m is higher than triple of *Distance* (the exact multiple can be changed). If both conditions are satisfied, the following calculation is used:

1. If d_a, the actual distance from *axis*, is higher than half of *Distance*, the sum of a_p and a_a forces is used instead of the force component a_p. The force a_a is the attractive force to *axis* and its magnitude is determined by the equation:

$$F \cdot \frac{d_a}{D}, \qquad (5)$$

where the parameters are as above. The farther the steered agent is from the axis, the higher this force component is, which attracts the agent to *axis* and the partner.
2. If d_a is lower than or equal to *Distance*, the steering returns the requirement for stopping the steered agent and turning it to the partner.

Figure 2 compares a same situation with the *Wait for Partner* parameter switched off (top right) and on (bottom right). On the top, the agents run directly to each other. On the bottom, the darker agent just gets closer to the lighter one and waits there until the lighter one comes. Subsequently, they both continue together to the target.

4 Evaluation

We have tested the six steerings mentioned in Section 2 and the WA steering described in Section 3 in several dozen of scenarios in [13]. Moreover, to demonstrate usefulness of the WA steering, we have designed a formal evaluation study. Recall that the WA task can be also addressed by the extended Leader Following steering, where the follower walks next to the leader. The purpose of this study was to compare believability of the two solutions.

4.1 Method

We designed 8 different scenarios, which can be solved by both steerings. All scenarios have following common features: a) two virtual characters (friends) go together to the same place, b) they know about each other from the beginning and c) both of them know about the target place from the beginning. In some of the scenarios, characters meet at first and then continue together to the target.

We created videos[1] of the eight scenarios. Each video had two variants demonstrating how the LF or WA steering, respectively, solves the scenario. One scenario had

---

[1] All steering videos we have created and used are publicly available at:
http://artemis.ms.mff.cuni.cz/emohawk/
doku.php?id=emohawk_steering_videos.

four variants (see below). Twenty-six human subjects (20 males, 6 females, average age = 27, all except of four having a high previous experience with 3D VR applications) had to judge believability of every scenario using a six point Likert scale and add verbal comments on the believability of the videos. In particular, the subjects were introduced every scenario, stressing the point that the IVAs knew each other and should have walked along to the target, and should have judged to what extent the motion of IVAs appears believable (from 5 – "totally unbelievable" – to 0 – "this cannot be improved further"). The subjects were also asked to focus on the IVAs' trajectories, speed, heading, distance towards each other and pauses in movement, but not at the quality of animations. The order in which the two (four) variants of every scenario were showed to a viewer was randomized. The viewers did not know which steering was used in which variant. The scenarios are depicted on Figure 3 and listed below. Note that the last three were inspired by SteerBench [16].

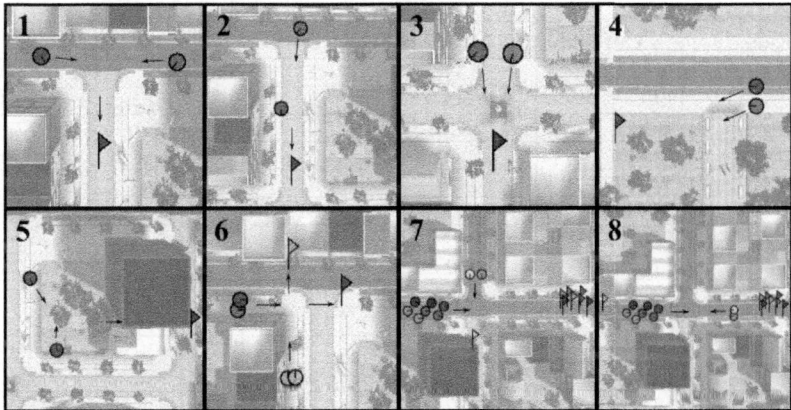

Fig. 3. The eight tested scenarios. The circles denote the starting locations of agents, the flags denote their targets, and arrows indicate direction of the agents' trajectories

1. Two friends meet at a crossway and continue together on the street.
2. Two friends meet on a street and continue together on the street. This scenario had four variants: WA with the *Wait for Partner* parameter switched (i) on and (ii) off, and LF where the leader is (i) the agent nearer to the target and (ii) the agent farer from the target.
3. Two friends walk together on the street and avoid an obstacle (a spherical statue).
4. Two friends walk together in a park and one of them suddenly stops. In the tested scenario, he gets stuck in front of a low bench, which is intentionally so low that agent's rays do not detect it. The viewers were instructed to imagine, that the stuck agent, e.g., laces its shoes, and judge the believability of the other agent's behavior.
5. Two friends meet in a park and walk together through a passage to a street.
6. Two friends go on a pavement along a building. A different pair of friends goes from the other side of the building and both pairs meet at the corner of the building. The pairs see each other at the very last moment. They should avoid all collisions and continue in the previous direction.

7. Two friends have to avoid collisions with the crossing group of people.
8. Two friends have to avoid collisions with the oncoming group of people.

4.2 Results

The scores of every two variants were compared using a paired T-test since the data were not grossly non-normal. For the second scenario, we compared the two WA variants against each other, and the better WA variant (i.e., with the lower mean of score) to the better LF steering variant. The results are showed in Table 1.

Table 1. Results of the Walk Along steering evaluation. The scores are scaled to 0 (the best) – 1 (the worst). The effect sizes were calculated using classical Cohen's d, where the classification is negligible (<0.2), small (<0.5), medium (<0.8), and large (over 0.8). In scenario 2, LF ii scored worse than LF i, thus, we used the latter for the comparison.

Scenario	Variant	Mean	STD	P-value	Cohen's d
1	WA	0.33	0.25	0.088	0.48
	LF	0.45	0.26	+	small
2	WA i	0.25	0.21	0.0022	0.73
	WA ii	0.42	0.25	**	medium
2	WA i	0.25	0.21	< 0.001	1.10
	LF i	0.52	0.32	***	large
3	WA	0.15	0.21	0.2	0.28
	LF	0.22	0.23	-	small
4	WA	0.42	0.27	0.0032	0.91
	LF	0.68	0.31	**	large
5	WA	0.20	0.20	< 0.001	1.66
	LF	0.58	0.25	***	large
6	WA	0.12	0.14	< 0.001	4.57
	LF	0.85	0.18	***	large
7	WA	0.53	0.30	0.95	-0.01
	LF	0.52	0.30	-	negligible
8	WA	0.20	0.28	0.32	0.25
	LF	0.27	0.27	-	small

We see that in the scenarios 2, 4, 5, and 6 the WA solution significantly outperformed the LF solution, and in the scenario 1, the difference is not significant but there is a clear trend favoring the WA steering. Arguably, concerning scenarios 1, 2, 4, and 5, this is because the partners wait on each other, or a partner basically reflects the existence of the other agent (see the supplementary videos). Additionally, concerning 5 and 6, the ignorance of the follower by the leader in the LF approach leads to severely limiting the movement possibilities of the follower.

On the other hand, there are no significant differences in scenarios 3, 7, and 8. This could be caused by the social aspects of the WA steering (waiting on the partner, reflecting its existence) not being important for solving situations 3, 7 and 8.

In general, the scores of both steerings suggest that the steerings are not perfect for most of the situations. Thus, the subjects' comments on the believability limitations are important. We now list the most recurring complaints for both steerings:

1. When the agent nearer to the target waits for the farther partner, or goes towards it, this nearer agent then rotates in the unnatural direction when the partner arrives and they both continue to the target. In particular, it rotates from the partner instead of to the partner. (Scenarios 2 and 4 – see the supplementary video).
2. Some respondents said that it is unnatural that the agents run to each other at first, but later they just walk. Few respondents noted that it could look naturally if the characters represented a pair of lovers who had not seen each other for a long time. But then they would have to walk very close to each other. (Scenarios 1, 2 and 5.)
3. It would look nice, if the agents stopped for a while and exchanged greetings etc. when they met. (Scenarios 1, 2 and 5.)
4. Partners could both go around an obstacle from the same side. (Scenario 3.)
5. Partners could both go around a group of other characters from the same side. (Scenario 8).
6. In scenario 2, when the parameter *Wait for Partner* is switched on, the waiting agent waits almost until its partner comes to it but it makes several steps to the partner just shortly before this moment and then it turns and continues with the partner. Some respondents emphasized this feature as a very natural detail whereas others regarded it more natural to wait until the partner comes.

4.3 Discussion and Possible Improvements

In general, the results demonstrated that the WA steering is useful. However, further improvements would add to its believability. Possible improvements can be divided intro three groups: a) at the level of the WA steering, b) at the action selection layer during combining the force vectors of individual steerings, c) by implementing a new steering. Concerning Group (a), we have already made three improvements[1] based on the results of our evaluation. In particular, we fixed:

- Unnatural direction of turning (Point 1 above). Briefly, we added yet another force vector to the vectors a_p, a_a, r_p, r_a, and a_t (the solution can not be detailed here due to the space constraints).
- Running towards each other (Point 2 above). We added a parameter for truncating the maximal velocity. Consequently, the partners do not run to each other, even if they are far away from each other.
- Waiting until the partner comes (Point 6 above). We implemented optional behavior for the *Wait for Partner* parameter that the agent waits until its partner really comes to it and then it just turns in place and continues with the partner.

Points 3, 4 and 5 belong to Group (b). In our opinion, these issues can be solved relatively easily at the action selection layer. In general, at this layer, additional behavior may be implemented by changing the WA steering parameters in runtime. For instance, various social relations between the partners may be expressed by setting *Distance* and *Wait for Partner* parameters (switching *Wait for Partner* on may be suitable for general use, but it may be better to switch it off for small children or a pair in love). Another possibility is combining WA with a different steering, for instance, for walking in a pair along a street on a pavement.

WA is currently able to steer a pair of agents. A future extension could include the ability to steer small groups of three or four people. Finally, note that the described WA steering is intended for open spaces. For closed space with narrow corridors and many obstacles, more changes of the WA steering, or even a new steering, would be necessary, which represents the Group (c).

5 Conclusion

In this paper, we have presented the Walk Along steering, which steers a pair of agents to reach a certain place together, ideally walking alongside each other. The steering is used to control their movement, not their animations. We have conducted an evaluation of believability of the WA steering and compared it to an extended version of the Leader Following steering. The evaluation has shown that the WA steering is useful and may lead to more believable behavior than the extended LF steering. In particular, the WA outperforms (in terms of believability) the LF solution in situations where a social behavior is expected by a human observer and/or the LF approach limits the movement possibilities of the follower. On the other hand, there are negligible or small differences between the solutions in situations in which the social aspects of the WA steering are not important. We have also already solved the most problematic issues related to the WA about which the respondents complained.

Our method keeps the advantage of Reynolds' steerings: it is simple and computationally inexpensive. In our opinion, the WA steering may be used in applications where a pair of virtual agents walking together to a common target is needed, such as computer games, educational applications or human crowd simulation, where pairs of virtual agents could contribute to natural impression of the crowd. Finally, the WA steering shows that steerings may not only control low-level navigation, but they may also be used to express social relations between agents.

Acknowledgments. This research was partially supported by project P103/10/1287 (GACR), by a student grant GA UK No. 0449/2010/A-INF/MFF, by SVV project number 263 314 and the research project MSM0021620838 of the Ministry of Education of the Czech Republic.

References

1. Bída, M., Brom, C., Popelová, M.: To Date or Not to Date? A Minimalist Affect-Modulated Control Architecture for Dating Virtual Characters. In: Vilhjálmsson, H.H., Kopp, S., Marsella, S., Thórisson, K.R. (eds.) IVA 2011. LNCS, vol. 6895, pp. 419–425. Springer, Heidelberg (2011) (accepted, to appear)
2. Ho, C.S., Nguyen, Q.H., Ong, Y.-S., Chen, X.: Autonomous Multi-agents in Flexible Flock Formation. In: Boulic, R., Chrysanthou, Y., Komura, T. (eds.) MIG 2010. LNCS, vol. 6459, pp. 375–385. Springer, Heidelberg (2010)
3. Gemrot, J., Kadlec, R., Bída, M., Burkert, O., Příbil, R., Havlíček, J., Zemčák, L., Šimlovič, J., Vansa, R., Štolba, M., Plch, T., Brom, C.: Pogamut 3 Can Assist Developers in Building AI (Not Only) for Their Videogame Agents. In: Dignum, F., Bradshaw, J., Silverman, B., van Doesburg, W. (eds.) Agents for Games and Simulations. LNCS, vol. 5920, pp. 1–15. Springer, Heidelberg (2009), http://pogamut.cuni.cz (6.7.2011)

4. Guy, S.J., Lin, M.C., Manocha, D.: Modeling collision avoidance behavior for virtual humans. In: Proceedings of the 9th International Conference on Autonomous Agents and Multiagent Systems: Richland: International Foundation for Autonomous Agents and Multiagent Systems, vol. 2, pp. 575–582 (2010)
5. Karamouzas, I., Heil, P., van Beek, P., Overmars, M.H.: A Predictive Collision Avoidance Model for Pedestrian Simulation. In: Egges, A., Geraerts, R., Overmars, M. (eds.) MIG 2009. LNCS, vol. 5884, pp. 41–52. Springer, Heidelberg (2009)
6. Karamouzas, I., Overmars, M.: A Velocity-Based Approach for Simulating Human Collision Avoidance. In: Safonova, A. (ed.) IVA 2010. LNCS, vol. 6356, pp. 180–186. Springer, Heidelberg (2010)
7. Karamouzas, I., Overmars, M.: Simulating the Local Behaviour of Small Pedestrian Groups. In: Proc. Of the 17th VRST, pp. 183–190 (2011)
8. Olfati-Saber, R.: Flocking for multi-agent dynamic systems: Algorithms and theory. IEEE Transactions on Automatic Control 51(3), 401–420 (2006)
9. Pedica, C., Vilhjálmsson, H.H.: Social Perception and Steering for Online Avatars. In: Prendinger, H., Lester, J.C., Ishizuka, M. (eds.) IVA 2008. LNCS (LNAI), vol. 5208, pp. 104–116. Springer, Heidelberg (2008)
10. Pedica, C., Vilhjálmsson, H.: Spontaneous Avatar Behavior for Human Territoriality. In: Ruttkay, Z., Kipp, M., Nijholt, A., Vilhjálmsson, H.H. (eds.) IVA 2009. LNCS (LNAI), vol. 5773, pp. 344–357. Springer, Heidelberg (2009)
11. Pedica, C., Högni Vilhjálmsson, H., Lárusdóttir, M.: Avatars in Conversation: The Importance of Simulating Territorial Behavior. In: Safonova, A. (ed.) IVA 2010. LNCS, vol. 6356, pp. 336–342. Springer, Heidelberg (2010)
12. Peters, C., Ennis, C.: Modeling Groups of Plausible Virtual Pedestrians. In: IEEE CGA, pp. 54–63 (2009)
13. Popelova, M.: Knihovna steering technik pro virtualni agenty. Bachelor thesis. Charles University in Prague. (2011) (in Czech), http://amis.mff.cuni.cz/emohawk/ (6.7.2011)
14. Reynolds, C.: Flocks, herds and schools: A distributed behavioral model. In: Proceedings of the 14th Conference on Computer Graphics and Interactive Techniques, pp. 25–34 (1987)
15. Reynolds, C.: Steering behaviors for autonomous characters. In: GDC, pp. 763–782 (1999)
16. Singh, S., Naik, M., Kapadia, M., Faloutsos, P., Reinman, G.: Watch Out! A Framework for Evaluating Steering Behaviors. In: Egges, A., Kamphuis, A., Overmars, M. (eds.) MIG 2008. LNCS, vol. 5277, pp. 200–209. Springer, Heidelberg (2008)

Parallel Ripple Search – Scalable and Efficient Pathfinding for Multi-core Architectures

Sandy Brand and Rafael Bidarra

Delft University of Technology
Mekelweg 4, 2628 CD Delft, Netherlands
sjrbrand@gmail.com, R.Bidarra@tudelft.nl
http://graphics.tudelft.nl

Abstract. Game developers are often faced with very demanding requirements on huge numbers of agents moving naturally through increasingly large and detailed virtual worlds. With the advent of multi-core architectures, new approaches to accelerate expensive pathfinding operations are worth being investigated. Traditional single-processor pathfinding strategies, such as A* and its derivatives, have been long praised for their flexibility. We implemented several parallel versions of such algorithms to analyze their intrinsic behavior, concluding that they either have a large overhead, yield far from optimal paths, do not scale up to many cores, or are cache unfriendly. In this paper we propose *Parallel Ripple Search*, a novel parallel pathfinding algorithm that largely solves these limitations. It utilizes a high-level graph to assign local search areas to CPU cores at 'equidistant' intervals. These cores then use A* flooding behavior to expand towards each other, yielding good 'guesstimate points' at border touch on. The process does not rely on expensive parallel programming synchronization locks, but instead relies on the opportunistic use of node collisions among cooperating cores, exploiting the multi-core's shared memory architecture. As a result, all cores effectively run at full speed until enough waypoints are found. We show that this approach is a fast, practical and scalable solution, and that it flexibly handles dynamic obstacles in a natural way.

1 Introduction and Previous Work

As virtual game worlds grow increasingly larger, pathfinding has once again come into the spotlight. The basic motivation for this is that, being a computationally expensive but indispensable component in many games, any performance gains here will typically bring about noticeable improvements. In this line, more attention is currently being paid to re-designing pathfinding algorithms, so that they better suit current multi-core architectures.

Classic pathfinding algorithms such as *A** and its many derivatives, have been long praised by game developers for their flexibility and completeness. A* is a best-first search strategy that relies on a cost computing function $f(n) = g(n) + h(n)$ for providing rough cost estimations of a path running through a node n of a search graph (see [10]). Function $g(n)$ represents the currently known cost for reaching node n from the start node S, and heuristic estimation function $h(n)$ is often implemented by using a cheap 'guesstimate' of the remaining travel distance, such as a Manhattan or Euclidean distance, between node n and the goal node G. This heuristic function effectively controls how A* floods its search space. Moreover, $h(n)$ results in optimal paths as long as it remains 'admissible', i.e. it never overestimates the true cost for an actual path between node n and the goal node G.

The A* algorithm utilizes the $f(n)$ function to maintain a sorted *Open* list of most promising search candidates while it iterates through the search space, which is also its most computationally expensive component. For each iteration, the algorithm will remove the most promising candidate and place on the list all its not yet visited neighbors. If a neighbor node was already in the *Open* list, A* will perform a crucial 'correction step': it determines if a cheaper path was possible through the candidate node and, if so, modifies its entry accordingly in the *Open* list.

As the flood boundary grows, the algorithm takes increasingly more time to find each successive node that forms the desired path. Empirically, the node which is halfway down the resulting path is closed at roughly a third of the total time taken to find the complete path. This sorting component has also proven a road-block for parallelization attempts because it institutes a data dependency that would generate a lot of communication overhead on distributed processing architectures. Many past attempts have already been made to eliminate this need for sorting on single processor architectures such as *Iterative Deepening A** (or IDA* for short) (see [9]), but have not resulted in easier distributed processing schemes.

A late addition to the family of A* derivatives, which we used extensively in this research, is called *Fringe Search* (FS); see [2]. Fringe Search avoids the need for a sorted candidate list by simply keeping track of all nodes at its search boundary (or 'fringe') and opening those that are less expensive than a certain threshold value, which is iteratively incremented. Although this now forces the algorithm to scan through a large unsorted *Now* list from begin to end, it gains its speed-up by making the actual visitations extremely cheap. Each node that has an $f(n)$ value higher than the threshold value will simply be moved to a '*Later*' list. Each new iteration starts by simply swapping the *Now* and *Later* lists, and the node/list manipulations themselves can be implemented very effectively using simple pointer logic.

Recent path finder parallelization attempts (see [3] and [6]) have mainly focused on translating A* variants into shaders, so that they can run on GPUs or similar Vector Processors. These schemes benefit from either taking work-load off the main CPU, or by running pathfinders for a large amount of agents in parallel. Although such approaches have been very successful, these also have the drawback that they take up precious resources that one would rather devote solely to rendering graphics. Also, from a practical point of view, a game-play programmer will have to take extensive measures to apply such pathfinding approaches without serious disruptions of the rendering pipeline. For multi-core architectures, specifically, the world simulation and rendering logic are often running in separate threads that are uniquely assigned to specific cores.

A more traditional approach has been to parallelize A* and related algorithms, and make them more suitable for distributed computing on CPU clusters and grids (see [7], [8] and [12]). Although these attempts have demonstrated beneficial advantages, they also require more 'exotic' hardware and software approaches such as MPI (Message Passing Interface) which are highly uncommon on virtually any gaming hardware platform up to this date. For practical purposes, these approaches are thus unsuitable and have currently no real relevance in the game development industry.

In conclusion, there is a definite need for simple and portable variants of the A* algorithm that successfully and efficiently exploit today's multi-core architectures. This paper first describes and compares a number of parallel pathfinding implementations, focusing on the efficiency of their multi-core use. They all rely on the underlying hardware to implicitly perform the necessary synchronizations, without any blocking. We then introduce a novel algorithm called *Parallel Ripple Search*, that can easily scale with the number of available CPU cores. It requires no special libraries or hardware interfacing, nor any special synchronization primitives.

2 Parallel Pathfinding Implementations

In this section we describe our investigation on a number of parallelized variants of A* and Fringe Search, in order to study how they perform on multi-core architectures. Please refer to [5] for a detailed discussion of each algorithm, including its pseudo-code. This study gave us significant insight on how to effectively utilize the computing potential of these architectures for pathfinding purposes.

2.1 PBS: Parallel Bidirectional Search

The most obvious strategy to use *two* CPU cores for pathfinding is to have them start at each path extremity, search towards each other and let them 'meet halfway'; hence the name *Parallel Bidirectional Search* (PBS). As the main strategy of A* is to keep opening the most promising node, we can consider all nodes at the boundary of the flood area 'most' optimal (although this is not always strictly true). Whenever we hit a node flooded by an opposite core, we can immediately complete the path using the alternate core's pathfinding meta data. There is no need for expensive mutexes; both cores can just check a shared 'break flag' in main memory to see if they should stop because the other core found a collision or gave up.

An example path found using PBS is shown in Figure 1. On the left, we see that a collision was detected somewhere halfway, when both cores have done, in parallel, virtually the same amount of work. Connecting the two 'half-paths' together yields a path that is only slightly more expensive than the most optimal path. Most discrepancies relative to A* are not erroneous when taking the flow of the full path into account, but rather the result of a different bias because of the reversed search direction. The insignificant loss of optimality is due to the fact that PBS stops the search just a bit too soon, when it detects a collision. Often, the area around the collision node does not get fully flooded, so potentially there might be cheaper nodes in this area, which will no longer be discovered. However, this deviation is generally very low given a fairly uniform travel cost between neighboring nodes.

We can, therefore, conclude that, strictly speaking, PBS is no longer optimal, but it is still complete, *i.e.* it will find a path if it exists. In worst-case scenarios where no collision occurs, PBS is basically reduced to a normal A* search.

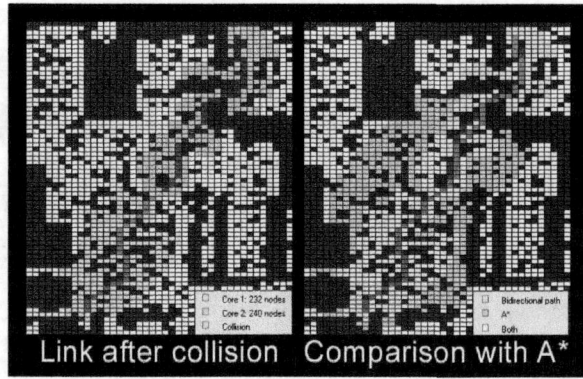

Fig. 1. (Left) Using PBS, two cores flood towards each other until a collision is detected. The full path is then constructed by linking both 'halves' together at the collision node. (Right) PBS path overlaid with the optimal A* path, whereby the red cells denote path deviations. Clearly, much less nodes are flooded by PBS than by A*.

2.2 DFS: Distributed Fringe Search

Our second attempt towards parallelization speed-up was to use the Fringe Search's *Now* and *Later* lists to literally distribute 'work' among multiple CPU cores. As mentioned above, during each pass through the *Now* list, Fringe Search performs some very simple tests in order to determine if new nodes should be processed. This processing mostly involves adding new nodes to the *Later* list. The main idea behind the new algorithm we came to call *Distributed Fringe Search* (DFS), is thus to distribute the *Now* List over all available cores, have them process their share, merge the individual *Later* lists, swap this with *Now*, and start all over again. A nice feature of Fringe Search is that the *Now* and *Later* lists do not need any sorting, thus distributing them is very easy. Also, each core can compute the smallest $f(n)$ value it has found locally, so that the master core can collect them and only needs to do a few comparisons to determine the cost threshold that should be used next for all cores.

The main advantage of DFS is that it can utilize more cores effectively, being no longer limited to two cores as PBS. Although this is a great strength, it is also its Achilles' heel. By distributing nodes 'arbitrarily' over multiple cores, we have lost the ability to perform the 'correction step' as a normal A* and/or Fringe Search implementation would do. This means that it is no longer guaranteed that DFS will find the cheapest path, i.e. DFS is not optimal, as we can clearly see in Figure 2.

Another drawback of DFS is that it is also no longer possible to keep track of the 'parent-child' relation of nodes during flooding, although this information is needed to reconstruct the resulting path. The solution, therefore, is to use a shared buffer in which all cores write to signal flooded nodes to each other, and then a separate 'private' buffer for reach core to store $g(n)$ values to evade race-conditions. The final path can then be correctly reconstructed by starting at the goal node G and then searching our way back to the start node S by repeatedly traversing towards the neighboring node with the lowest $g(n)$ value found in any of the private buffers. Although this sounds discouraging, it is, in practice, not critical; we found surprisingly

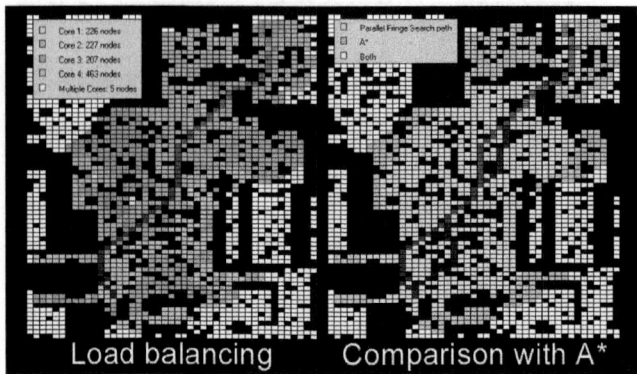

Fig. 2. (Left) The load-balance achieved by DFS. (Right) With the loss of the corrective property, DFS ends up with less than optimal paths. Note that the deviations with the optimal A* path are also just a matter of different bias, the actual additional path cost was only roughly 2%.

few cases of 'over-flooding' (nodes tagged 'Multiple Cores', in Figure 2, left). Mostly, nodes only have a single $g(n)$ computed for them, so no expensive floating-point comparisons are needed to find the lowest one.

The overall load-balance seems fairly good (see Figure 2, left), although we have noticed that there is always one core that seems to be doing most of the work. That core has often flooded most of the areas in which the final path was found, suggesting that this is likely due to the A* heuristic function: this function is designed to pull the search towards the goal node and, as long as this goes on 'unhindered', it will always favor nodes for that particular core. The other cores will often be searching through 'branches' elsewhere that later on turn out to be dead-ends.

Conceptually, the DFS approach sounds promising because it allows us to distribute the workload quite naturally over all available cores. In practice, however, the results obtained are less spectacular. After some profiling, it turned out that a significant amount of time is still wasted on cores waiting for each other, suggesting that the load balancing is still far from optimal.

2.3 PHS: Parallel Hierarchic Search

Another attractive way to utilize multi-core architectures is to have each core find small segments of the total path. Small searches whereby the segment's goal node is relatively close to its start node are significantly faster because far less nodes will become flooded. In order to do this, however, we need to guess where some *way-points* will be located in the search space so that, as it were, we can 'connect the dots' between them. This can only be properly done if we employ a high-level graph representation of the actual graph to search through. With this high-level graph we can roughly guess how the full path will traverse the search space and obtain way-points from it; hence the name *Parallel Hierarchic Search* (PHS).

There are many techniques to obtain such high-level graphs, ranging from manually adding way-points to automated schemes such as 'Probabilistic Roadmap Method'; see [1], [2] and [11]. For our PHS implementation, we created a grid randomization

Parallel Ripple Search – Scalable and Efficient Pathfinding for Multi-core Architectures

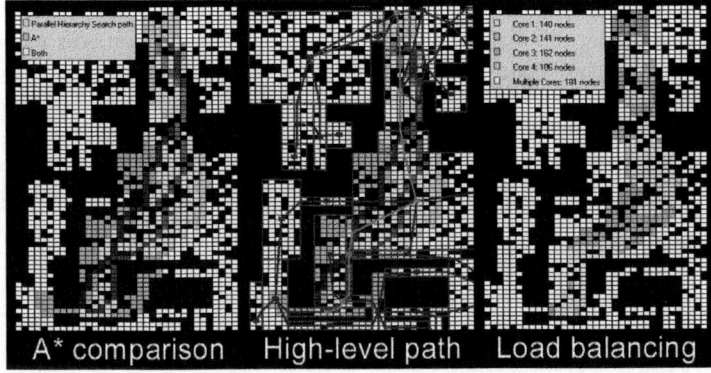

Fig. 3. A path generated by the PHS algorithm. (Left) Substantially less nodes have been flooded than with classic A*, but the resulting path is not as optimal and smooth. (Middle) The high-level graph and path used to form the resulting path. (Right) The flooding progress per core.

algorithm with a top-down approach, which generates 'chambers' that are linked with smaller corridors, which are then filled with randomly placed obstacles. This enabled us to easily generate lots of correct high-level hierarchies so that we could run large test batches.

Each node in the high-level graph is linked to a corresponding anchor node in the actual graph that needs to be searched. The first step in the PHS algorithm is to find a path through the high-level graph and then finding sub-paths connecting the consecutive anchor nodes. Doing this will, however, never result in an immediately natural looking path because the anchor nodes might be needlessly off course. So a 'beautification' step is applied by constructing new way-points halfway at the found path segments (by just picking the middle node of the path-segments sequence of solution nodes). The idea behind this is that it will help us find 'short-cuts' between the high-level way-point anchor nodes. We found that just a single beautification iteration already yields quite acceptable results.

Parallelizing the algorithm is basically a matter of having the master core generate the way-points, and then letting all the cores try to construct the path segments. To enable the cores to gain access to the path segments information buffer, we are forced to employ a more expensive 'critical section' which is provided by the operating system. This will allow safe access to selecting a path segment and returning a pointer to found path segment solutions (cores are not allowed to clear these solutions until all processing has been completed, so that the master core can safely access them). We can give each core its own copy of the graph so that there will be no cache collisions during the searches themselves.

Figure 3 shows an example of a path generated using the PHS algorithm. We can clearly see that PHS only floods nodes in the near vicinity of the final path and does not fan out into a 'leaf' shaped flood space as A* would do. The algorithm was about 1.6 times faster than a classic A* approach, but this came with a penalty: the resulting path has a noticeably higher cost, and has a less 'smooth' appearance. In the middle of the figure we can see that the high-level path is distanced quite far away from the optimal path, as could be expected. Finally, on the right we see that the load balancing is fairly acceptable. A lot of nodes have been flooded by multiple cores, but this is again due to the second phase smoothing. Because cores will process new path segments when they are done with the previous one, we will see some nodes being flooded by different cores in different phases.

In general, the results obtained with PHS are rather divergent. In some cases we can obtain very good speed-ups, and in other cases we do not. The overall path quality leaves a lot to be desired; often the paths will stray quite a bit from the optimal path, further contributing to increase the search duration.

3 Algorithm Evaluation and Comparison

In all preceding experiments, no special attempts have been made to 'optimize' the parallel algorithms, other than those dictated by common sense. Moreover, they all use established basic libraries, such as the C++ Standard Template Library (STL), expressly chosen for their stability rather than for their performance.

We obtained our measurements from a total of 2000 samples, by finding 100 random paths in 20 random maps. For each sample, we measured the time taken to find a path between 2 randomly selected nodes from a 400 by 400 8-way connected uniform grid, internally represented by a directed graph. An Euclidean distance was used as A* search heuristic. Each sample was repeated 5 times for each algorithm so that cache content would 'stabilize'. The best result of all the taken samples was then taken as the ultimate measurement result. All threads and processes were running on highest priorities. All samples have been taken on a 2.4 GHz Intel Core2 Quad CPU running Windows XP Pro SP2.

Because Fringe Search plays such a prevalent role in our experiments, wherever possible we have used this algorithm as an A* alternative. Therefore, Fringe Search has also been included in all measurements so that we can clearly tell if the speed-up is due to the parallelization, and not just the fact that Fringe Search was used instead of a classic A* implementation.

The measurement results are shown in Figure 4. For very short paths the results are mixed, which probably means that the parallelization overhead is too high compared to the amount of work that has to be done. As the path length increases, the parallelized algorithms start to outperform the classic A* implementation extensively. Still, PHS is the 'main loser', as it has the worst overall performance, probably due to requiring a mutex and 'beautification' iteration. It has also by far the worst path cost overhead, ranging from 20% up to 45%. For DFS, we can conclude that it is only worthwhile on longer paths; otherwise, the normal Fringe Search implementation still (slightly) outperforms it. It is apparently only for the longer paths that cores manage to get work done without interfering too much with each other's caches, which makes sense because the flooded areas will be much larger and further spaced apart. DFS can yield up to 2,2 speed-up relative to a classic A* implementation. As expected, its qualitative output is hampered by the fact that DFS has lost its corrective property in a far more significant degree than that of PBS: it has up to 4% additional path cost. For PBS, the loss of its corrective property is only accumulated near the area of the collision node, which is generally very small. This clearly makes PBS a winner on all fronts: up to an impressive speed-up of 6,7 relative to A*, while generating paths that, on average, are less than 1% more expensive than the optimal A* path.

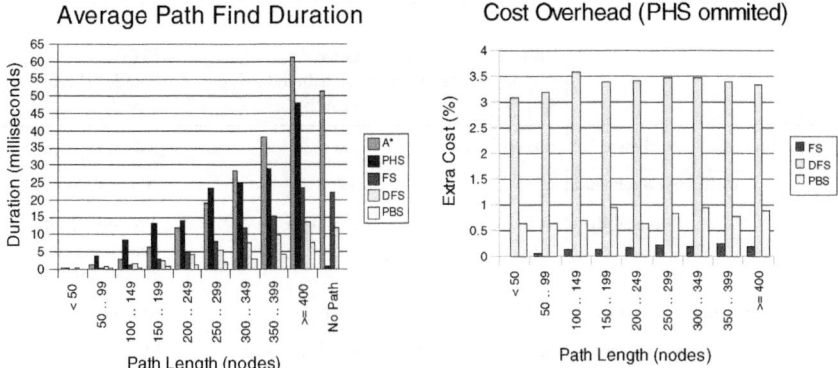

Fig. 4. (Left) Overview of average pathfinding duration. Note how PBS can outperform a classic A* implementation almost 7 times. (Right) Overview of average path cost overhead, relative to the length of the optimal path found by classic A*. (PHS results are omitted, as they can raise up to 45%).

The analysis of all these results is summarized in Table 1. We conclude that:

1. Cache penalties have by far the largest impact on these algorithms' performance on multi-core architectures. The longer we can prevent cores to flood nodes in each other's areas, the better the performance will be. PBS clearly does this best because both cores start their search at the maximum possible distance apart from each other.
2. High-level graphs tend to 'malform' paths interpolated from them, and require quite some 'post-processing' to smoothen them out.
3. High-level paths can seriously thwart the path finder when dynamic obstacles are in the way.

4 PRS: Parallel Ripple Search

In this section, we present a novel algorithm called *Parallel Ripple Search* (PRS), which capitalizes on the results of the experiments above, in order to combine the strengths of all those algorithms while minimizing their weaknesses.

4.1 Algorithm

Parallel Ripple Search requires a high-level graph to guess where the final path will be located in the search space, and uses it to position the cores at roughly equidistant way-points. However, in contrast to PHS, the cores will now find path segments by doing a normal A*-like flood towards their nearest neighbors instead. Like ripples in a pond, at some point their flood boundaries will overlap and we can use these collisions to link the path-segments together into the full path.

The high potential of PRS is that when we find enough collisions, we can 'short-circuit' and find connecting paths through previously flooded areas (for which we know that a path must exist). There is a good chance that these areas might still be

Table 1. Summary of strengths and weaknesses of the 3 parallel pathfinding implementations

	PBS: Parallel Bidirectional Search	DFS: Distributed Fringe Search	PHS: Parallel Hierarchy Search
Speed increase over classic A*	2,5 – 6,7	1,6 – 2,2	1,2 – 1,6
Path cost overhead	< 1%	3% – 4%	20% – 45%
Scalability	Bad: 2 cores only	2 or more	2 or more (but potentially much more effective than DFS)
Extra memory required	Low	High	Medium
Load-balancing	Very easy: both cores always run at full speed	Hard, so we are always bound by the slowest CPU core	Medium, the quality of the high-level graph will automatically improve this
Cache 'friendliness'	Very friendly	Very unfriendly	Fairly friendly
Implementation	Very easy and intuitive	More involved, needs many more synchronization moments, requires special techniques to optimize	Fairly easy (closer to 'classic' parallelization).
Other	Any A* variant can be used	–	Requires high-level graph

(partially) lingering in a core's cache, so that accesses can be fast. This algorithm is also able to deal with dynamic obstacles a lot better than PHS could. If way-points turn out to be (partially) blocked, then this will just mean that adjacent ripples will not collide (not now, at least). So although it might take longer before a collision occurs with a ripple located further away, we will no longer run the risk of pulling the path in weird directions. Another advantage of this new approach is that we can utilize many more cores; basically one for each segment of the high-level path, thus overcoming the main restriction of PBS.

The cores that flood from the start node S and goal node G process what we could call the 'essential' ripples: we call them the *essential* cores, as opposed to all other *non-essential* cores. In a worst-case scenario whereby none of the non-essential ripples ever collide with the essential ones, PRS will basically have degraded to a parallel bidirectional search (PBS), which was shown to perform very well.

The entire algorithm is roughly described by the following steps:

- Find a high-level path P between start node S and goal node G.
- Two cores are assigned to the way-points at both ends (S and G) of path P.
- Depending on the number of edges in path P we try to assign other cores at fairly equidistant way-points, these cores will form the 'non-essential ripples'.
- Phase 1: All cores start flooding the search space until enough collisions have been found to form a complete path:

- Essential cores search towards each other's local start node (basically like PBS).
- The remaining non-essential cores search towards the local start nodes of their direct neighbors.
- The master core will examine all the reports from the cores and determines which cores need to generate their path segments between which collision nodes. Note that some cores might have become superfluous, or may need to be linked in a non-sequential order (it can happen!)
- Phase 2: All relevant cores construct their local paths and report these back to the master core.
- The master core assembles the final path.
- All cores perform a final clean-up.

During phase 1, the essential cores basically perform a normal Fringe Search towards the way-points of their neighbor cores. Their searches start, of course, at either start node S or goal node G, and not at the start or goal way-points of the high-level path. The search will continue until either a path can be constructed, or until there are no more nodes available which means we have to give up. Collisions with the 'non-essential' cores are analyzed to determine if a full path can be constructed, but they will not stop the cores. With some luck, we might be able to by-pass some non-essential cores, or maybe link up directly with the other essential core itself.

The 'non-essential' cores use a slightly different heuristic for cost estimation function. This function is initially biased to flood towards the local start nodes of the adjacent cores:

$$h(n) = min(Estimate(LocalS_{i-1}, n), Estimate(LocalS_{i+1}, n))$$

Estimate() is a cost estimation function, such as the Euclidean distance. As soon as a first collision with a direct neighbor has been detected, we switch to a normal heuristic that will only flood in the opposite direction, towards the other neighbor's local start node. Once we have collided with that one as well, but determined that a full-path is not yet constructed, we just keep flooding with the original heuristic function again. This will make the flood boundary expand in all directions again which in turn might find other collisions that prove to be more beneficial. Only when a non-essential core runs out of nodes will it abort the search. This event does not explicitly have to be reported back to the master core in any way, it might just mean that our initial guess using the high-level path was 'wrong', and that the non-essential core started its search in an area that became isolated due to dynamic obstacles.

Once enough collisions have been detected and the master core has determined which cores will take part in the full path we can start phase 2. During this phase it is up to the corresponding cores to construct their local sections of the final full path. Synchronization between cores can all be done using spin-locks to ensure that there is no unintentional operating system overhead. Now, for essential cores it is very easy to construct their local path segments. As discussed earlier, the A* algorithm keeps track of a 'parent node' for each node that it floods in order to link back towards its original start node. We thus only need to look-up the collision node and follow the parent links back to what will either be the original start node S or goal node G.

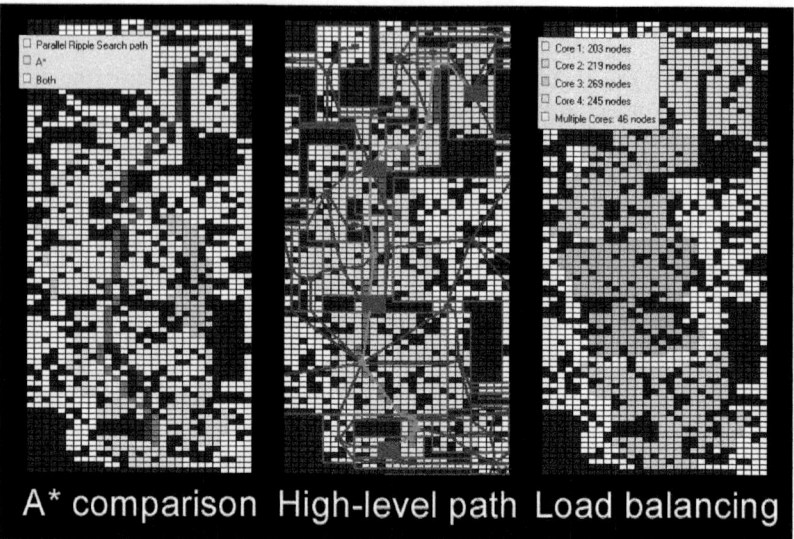

Fig. 5. Path generated with the PRS algorithm. (Left) comparison with the classic A*. (Middle) The high-level path used, and the way-points used to start off the non-essential cores. (Right) Each core has flooded roughly the same amount of nodes. The yellow nodes indicated collisions.

For non-essential cores we need to employ a different approach. We cannot use the parent links because these will always lead us back to the local start node at the location of the corresponding high-level path anchor node. As discussed previously for PHS, we need a smoothing phase in an attempt to 'iron out' the potential outlier that is the high-level path node itself. Especially if dynamic obstacles blocked our way, we need to make sure that the high-level path will not pull the resulting path way off course. For this, we do a new pathfinding session in order to find a suitable path between the two collision nodes that will ultimately 'bridge the gap' between the neighbors of the core. We can, however, significantly speed up this process by simply limiting the flood area to nodes that have been flooded before. This information is often directly available via 'visited flags' in the nodes themselves and thus the only extra cost is the pathfinding session itself. Note that, because the flood areas will ideally be relatively small, a large amount of data will already be in the core's cache, thus making such re-visits a very fast process. Once all local path segments have been obtained, the master core simply needs to copy them into a single buffer, making sure that no duplicate entries from the collision nodes are copied.

The overall implementation time of PRS was significantly longer compared to PBS, but not as long as that of DFS, provided that we already have the means for generating high-level paths. PRS requires more synchronization moments, and we do need to keep track on how to safely access memory without having race conditions causing real problems. The cores always share one memory pool in which they will write their unique core IDs for each node they flood. In this way, other cores can detect when they trod on each other toes and handle collisions. If we limit the size of the IDs to a single byte we can be sure enough that writing them is 'atomic' and the

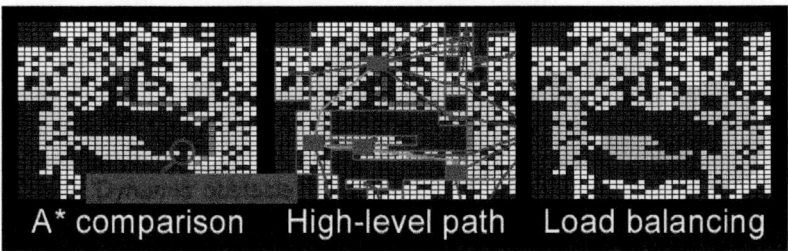

Fig. 6. Example of how the PRS algorithm still manages to bypass unexpected obstacles on the high-level path (middle). In this case, two cores did not manage to collide with each other (right) and thus only the other cores contributed to the resulting path. A comparison with the classic A* implementation (left) shows that both paths were virtually identical.

chance on race conditions is actually very small. And even then, if this does happen, the cores are bound to detect the collision during their next iterations as they further flood into each others 'body mass'.

Figure 5 shows an example of a path obtained with the PRS algorithm, 60% faster than a classic A*. The differences between both paths are small, mainly due to the fact that the high-level path has managed to make a very good 'guess'. PRS is also more robust and can much better handle unexpected obstacles on the high-level path, as shown in Figure 6. The quality of the paths is in general good, although they are still influenced by the orientation of the high-level path.

4.2 Performance

We have repeated for PRS the experimental measurements described in Section 3. As PBS was clearly the best alternative so far, we will limit the discussion here to Fringe Search, PBS and PRS in order to keep a clear overview.

From Figure 7 we conclude that PBS is still a very strong candidate on short to medium path lengths. Above roughly 200 nodes, PRS finally starts to capitalize on the fact that it can utilize more than two cores, at which the speed-up factor is in the range 2,5–10 compared to classic A*. Up to that point, PRS has too much overhead and/or cannot utilize all its cores when not enough way-points are found in the high-level graph. Regarding path quality, we can see that PRS generates paths that are on average about 4% more expensive. This deviation is partially due to the fact that the algorithm relies on the collisions to be favorable (which is, of course, not always the case), and also on the Fringe Search threshold relaxation, an 'artificial increment' in the FS's $f(n)$ threshold for opening new nodes, so that it expands faster outwards; see [4]. Also, in contrast to classic A*, we do not explicitly search for better nodes around collision nodes. The cost overhead for PBS is very low, less than 1% on average, which makes it an excellent alternative for short to medium length paths. The fact that PRS seems to have a 'constant' overhead factor indicates that, although the algorithm is 'probabilistic' in nature, it is still able to make good enough 'guesses' on a consistent basis. This is directly linked to the quality of the high-level graphs, which is therefore an essential component of any successful PRS implementation.

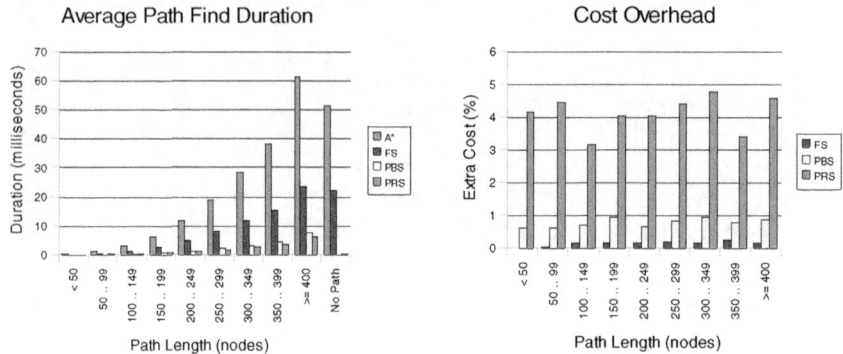

Fig. 7. (Left) Comparison of average pathfinding duration. (Right) Comparison of average cost overhead. The cost overhead remains fairly constant for all variants.

5 Conclusion and Future Work

We have implemented a number of parallel pathfinding algorithms in order to investigate their behavior and performance in multi-core architectures. We concluded that all these algorithms exhibit one or more weaknesses, for example, they either have a large overhead, yield far from optimal paths, do not easily scale up to many cores, or are cache unfriendly. The latter was found to be crucial, as currently available multi-core CPUs have good cache look-ahead prediction, as long as shared pages do not get written into too often. In other words, data separation is key to efficient pathfinding for these architectures.

In this paper we proposed *Parallel Ripple Search* (PRS), a novel parallel pathfinding algorithm that largely solves the above limitations. Basically, the algorithm employs (i) two 'essential cores' to flood at the path extremities (like Parallel Bidirectional Search does), and (ii) all other available 'non-essential cores' to flood local search areas, starting at 'equidistant' intervals on a high-level path. These cores then use A* flooding behavior to expand towards each other, yielding good 'guesstimate points' at border touch on. As a result, all cores effectively run at full speed until enough waypoints have been found.

Like most other parallel algorithms, PRS sacrifices some path quality for speed: it runs roughly 2,5 up to 10 times faster than a classic A* implementation, with only an average minor penalty of 4% in path cost. This inevitable loss of optimality justifies the use of the Fringe Search variant, which is instrumental to further improve performance by means of its threshold relaxation: not only is more work done in parallel, it also expands flood boundaries faster, resulting in earlier collisions.

The PRS algorithm does not rely on any expensive parallel programming synchronization locks or mutexes, but instead relies on the opportunistic use of node collisions among cooperating cores, exploiting the multi-core's shared memory architecture. As a result, PRS is easily portable to different platforms that provide Symmetric Multiprocessing architectures and/or embedded systems that do not provide concurrent programming primitives other than threads.

Future research should focus on, at least, two directions. First, it would be worthwhile improving the quality of the high-level path, enabling PRS to make better guesstimates on where the non-essential cores should best start flooding from. Second, new performance gains should be achieved by further reducing cache collisions between cores, e.g. by re-arranging the memory location of nodes to better reflect their real-world topology.

In short, the PRS algorithm (i) is a fast and practical pathfinding solution for large and complex maps, (ii) it flexibly handles dynamic obstacle in a natural way, and (iii) it guarantees good scalability facing the increasing amount of cores of present day hardware.

References

1. Amato, N.: Randomized Motion Planning. Texas, USA (2004),
   http://parasol.tamu.edu/~amato/Courses/padova04/lectures/L8.prms.pdf
2. Björnsson, Y., Enzenberger, M., Holte, R., Schaeffer, J.: Fringe Search: Beating A* at Pathfinding on Game Maps. In: Proceedings of IEEE Symposium on Computational Intelligence and Games, Essex, pp. 125–132 (2005),
   http://www.cs.ualberta.ca/~games/pathfind/publications/cig2005.pdf
3. Bleiweiss, A.: GPU Accelerated Pathfinding. In: Proceedings of Eurographics 2008 (2008)
4. Botea, A., Muller, M., Schaeffer, J.: Near Optimal Hierarchical Path-Finding (HPA*). Department of Computing Science, University of Alberta (2006)
5. Brand, S.: Efficient obstacle avoidance using autonomously generated navigation meshes. MSc Thesis, Delft University of Technology, The Netherlands (2009)
6. Buluç, A., Gilbert, J.R., Budak, C.: Solving Path Problems on the GPU. Parallel Computing (2009), doi:10.0106/j.parco.2009.12.002
7. Cohen, D., Dallas, M.: Implementation of Parallel Path Finding in a Shared Memory Architecture. Department of Computer Science Rensselaer Polytechnic Institute, Troy, NY (2010), http://www.cs.rpi.edu/~dallam/Parallel.pdf
8. Cvetanovic, Z., Nofsinger, C.: Parallel Astar Search on Message-Passing Architectures. System Sciences. In: Proceedings of the Twenty-Third Annual Hawaii Conference, vol. 1, pp. 92–90 (1990)
9. Patel, A.J. (2004) Variations of A*. Amit's Game Programming Site,
   http://www.dc.fi.udc.es/lidia/mariano/demos/amits/
   theory.stanford.edu/~amitp/gameprogramming/variations.html
10. Sniedovich, M.: Dijkstra's Algorithm. The University of Melbourne, Australia,
    http://www.ms.unimelb.edu.au/~moshe/620-261/dijkstra/dijkstra.html
11. Nohra, J., Champandard, A.J.: The Secrets of Parallel Pathfinding on Modern Computer Hardware. In: Intel Software Network, Intel Corp. (2010)
12. Sturtevant, N.R., Geisberger, R.: A Comparison of High-Level Approaches for Speeding Up Pathfinding. In: Proceedings of the Conference on Artificial Intelligence and Interactive Digital Entertainment, AIIDE 2010 (2010)

Hybrid Path Planning for Massive Crowd Simulation on the GPU

Aljosha Demeulemeester, Charles-Frederik Hollemeersch, Pieter Mees, Bart Pieters,
Peter Lambert, and Rik Van de Walle

Ghent University - IBBT,
Department of Electronics and Information Systems, Multimedia Lab,
Gaston Crommenlaan 8 bus 201, B-9050 Ledeberg-Ghent, Belgium
aljosha.demeulemeester@ugent.be,
http://multimedialab.elis.ugent.be/

Abstract. In modern day games, it is often desirable to have many agents navigating intelligently through detailed environments. However, intelligent navigation remains a computationally expensive and complicated problem. In the past, the continuum crowds algorithm demonstrated the value of using a dynamic potential field to guide many agents to a common goal location. However this algorithm is prohibitively resource intensive for real time applications using large and detailed virtual worlds. In this paper, we propose a novel hybrid system that first uses a coarse A* path finding step. This helps to eliminate unnecessary work during the potential field generation by excluding areas of the world from the potential field calculation. Additionally, we show how an optimized potential field solver can be implemented on the GPU using the concepts of persistent threads and inter-block communication. Results show that our system achieves considerable speedups compared to existing path planning systems and that up to 100,000 agents can be simulated and rendered in real time on a mainstream GPU.

Keywords: Crowd Simulation, Path planning, GPU Acceleration, Real-time.

1 Introduction

Computer game technology has evolved significantly with the advent of modern programmable graphics hardware. The new capabilities offered by this hardware allow the size and detail of the worlds to increase. Also, more characters can be drawn on the screen. However, the systems responsible for the animation and control of these characters have not seen an equal evolution. While multi-core processors can offer increased throughput for character control, path finding and animation systems have become the bottleneck when increasing the character count in modern game applications. Besides running the simulation, an additional bottleneck is transferring all the agent state information to the graphics processing unit (GPU) for rendering. While graphics cards have large on board bandwidth, the PCI Express bus has significantly less bandwidth.

Recently, several General-Purpose GPU (GPGPU) APIs have been released that allow running non-graphics code on the massively parallel architecture of the GPU. Examples are NVIDIA Compute Unified Device Architecture (CUDA),[1] Khronos' OpenCL,

---
[1] "http://developer.nvidia.com/category/zone/cuda-zone"

and Microsoft's DirectX 11 compute shader platforms. These general-purpose computing platforms allow direct access to the graphics processor, without the need for extensively rewriting the algorithms in terms of graphics primitives such as textures and triangles. This enables many new applications to run on the GPU. Offloading the simulation from the CPU to the GPU looks promising because each agent's path and behavior can be calculated (almost) independently from the other agents. This maps well to the GPU's processor paradigm. Also, by calculating and storing the state of the agents on the GPU, we can avoid the need to copy this data from main memory to video memory every rendered frame.

In this paper we present the CrowdE framework which addresses the issues that arise when simulating large groups of agents on massive parallel processing systems such as the modern graphics processors. The proposed hybrid system runs entirely on the GPU and targets real-time, interactive 3D applications. Because the GPU is also used for rendering, the agent simulation step is seriously constrained in time (in the order of milliseconds). Figure 1 shows a screenshot of our application[2] that demonstrates the simulation and rendering of 100,000 agents, achieving on average 24 frames per second. The renderer also uses a CUDA accelerated virtual texturing system as described in [7]. To summarize, the CrowdE system is designed with the following requirements in mind. The system should:

- support the movement, animation and rendering of large groups (more than 75,000 individuals) of agents in real time,
- support efficient path planning in large environments without compromising on detail in these environments,
- limit the amount of data transferred between the GPU and the CPU,
- offer visually plausible results. This means the paths don't need to be globally optimal but agents should not fail to reach their destination or display unrealistic behavior,
- allow dynamically setting the goal location of an individual agent or a group of agents.

The paper is structured as follows: Section 2 provides an overview of related work. Section 3 presents our hybrid path planning system and its advantages. Section 4 presents the details of our GPU-based implementation. Section 5 presents our performance results followed by Section 6 that presents our conclusions.

2 Related Work

Path planning, essential to the simulation of crowds, can be very taxing, even on modern computer hardware. The navigation process usually consists of two separate stages. First, the global path towards the goal position is calculated based on the information of the game world, while taking obstacles into account. Second, collisions with other moving obstacles (local avoidance) in the virtual environment are avoided while following

---

[2] A video of the demo can be found on:
"http://multimedialab.elis.ugent.be/demonstrations."

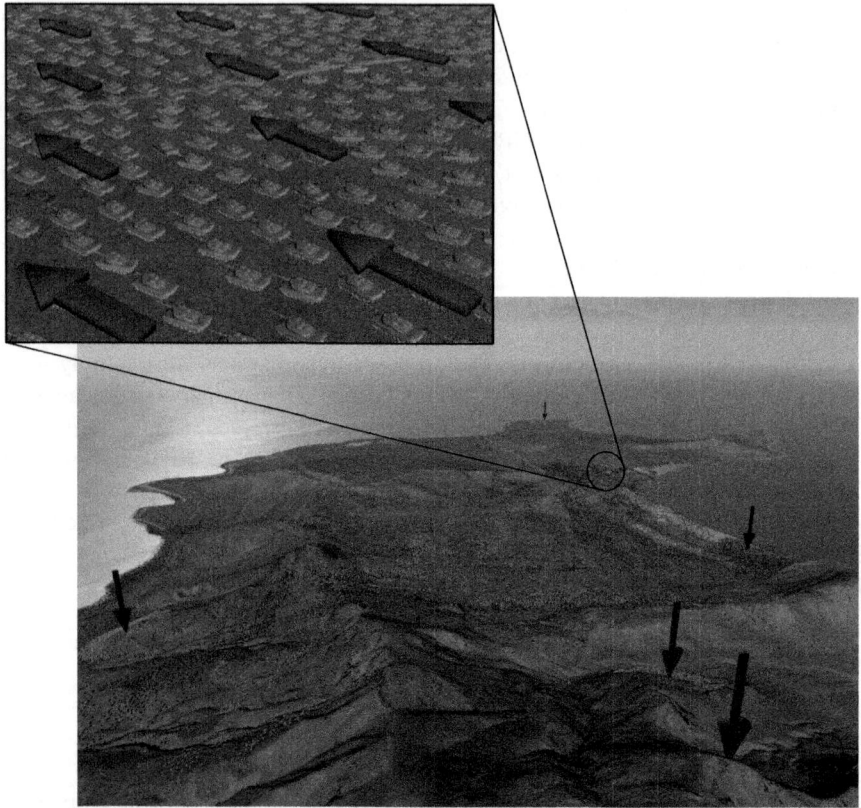

Fig. 1. Screenshot of our demo application simulating 100,000 agents (tanks) in real time with 8 different goal locations (downward arrows) using 512x256 flow fields for the global path planning

this path. Every simulation step, the combination of navigation algorithms determines a direction to follow for every agent. An additional physics system is then used to constrain the agent movements and speeds.

In modern computer games, the virtual world is typically represented by a sparse graph data structure. A node in this graph represents a location in the world. Each edge represents a viable path between two nodes and contains a value describing the cost for an agent to travel between those nodes. This cost is calculated based on the features of the virtual world (e.g., terrain type, terrain slope, crowd density, etc.) and describes the length (i.e., travel time or travel distance) of the path. The graph can either be set up by manually placing waypoints and edges or be automatically generated by some algorithm that analyses the world's structure.

Global path finding then consists of a search over this navigation graph from a start to a goal node, leading to a path with the minimum cost. A common problem is that agents can only safely move along the generated path. Straying too far off this path could no longer guarantee that agents won't get stuck at dead ends in the environment. This leads to aesthetically unpleasing results, especially when large groups of agents are involved and when few nodes are used to represent the world.

More advanced path planning techniques can be used to generate smooth and divergent paths between two points. Navigation graphs [11] define a navigation flow between two nodes with a set of varied paths. The Corridor Map Method [5] defines traversable corridors in the world and uses pseudo forces to guide an agent through these corridors resulting in a smooth and visually appealing path. A small random force is applied to give divergent results. The Continuum Crowds algorithm proposed by Treuille et al. [13] takes a different approach by viewing motion as a particle energy minimization. The whole environment is subdivided in small cells with an associated cost function, describing the travel time to move from one cell to a neighboring location. A potential field solver then transforms this cost function to a potential field that describes the total travel cost from every location to a goal region. The gradient (flow field) of this potential field indicates the optimal travel direction for the shortest path to the goal. The flow field technique scales well with the number of agents because it is computed spatially, instead of per-agent. Also, this approach unifies global path planning and local collision avoidance into one framework by adding a dynamic cost to the cost function based on the agent density in a world cell. The model results in emergent behavior (e.g., lane and vortex forming) which have been observed in real crowds. The downside of this method is that it requires a lot of calculations to update the flow field. Morini et al. [10] propose a hybrid technique that uses the continuum crowds algorithm in regions of high interest (e.g., the view frustrum) while using a combination of a navigation graph and local avoidance outside these regions. This allows simulating larger worlds while preserving the benefits of the potential field approach in key areas. However, agents can be governed by different rule sets depending on their location.

As described in Section 1, use of the GPU to run the path planning could potentially allow simulating many more agents in real time. However, adapting existing algorithms to be efficiently executed by this processor type can be challenging. The possibility of evaluating the A* algorithm on the GPU was investigated by Bleiweiss [2]. Although A* is inherently an irregular and divergent algorithm, a significant performance increase was reported by the authors when calculating many paths concurrently. Although a high throughput of calculated paths can be attained, the total execution time and memory cost is prohibitively high for a real-time application. Shopf et al. [12] describe how the continuum crowds algorithm can be executed on the GPU. This allows for a significant increase in the resolution of the potential field. This field is used only for the global navigation (including crowd avoidance). An additional local avoidance algorithm is used because the resolution of the potential field (hence also the resolution of the flow field) is still not adequate for the size of the world. The limited density (i.e., a potential field cell covers a relatively large world region) of the potential field prohibits correctly navigating around complex constructions such as U-shaped fences and walls because the global path finding grid does not have adequate resolution to represent these obstacles. This can also not easily be handled by a local avoidance technique.

In this work we present a hybrid technique that uses a coarse A* path finding step that selects a region of interest (ROI) for the potential field calculation. This region covers an area from all start positions of the agents to the goal location(s). Usually, only a limited area of the world is selected allowing us to use denser flow fields. This enables simulating thousands of agents in real time in larger and more complex virtual environments. All agents are guided by the flow field to their goal, aided by a local avoidance algorithm described by Fiorini and Shillert [4]. Additionally, an optimization to the Shopf et al. potential field generator is proposed. The entire simulation is executed on the GPU, similar to the work proposed in Shopf et al.

3 Overview of the Proposed System

When agents travel to a common goal location, the followed paths usually only cover a small part of the world. This is especially the case when their start locations lie in close proximity to each other. To guarantee an optimal global path with the continuum crowds technique, a potential field needs to be calculated for the entire world.

We propose a hybrid technique that limits the area for which to generate a potential field by first using a coarse A*-based solver to determine a ROI for the actual path planning step. This differs from most hybrid techniques by only using flow fields for the global path planning instead of using this technique locally or for only part of the global path (e.g., as described by Morini et al.). Using our hybrid system, the followed paths in the ROI are globally near-optimal. All agents in the worlds are governed by the same flow field technique for their global navigation. As shown in Section 4, the simplicity of this approach enables an efficient execution on the GPU.

The offline phase of our hybrid system consists of generating a sparse graph that resembles the world with very few nodes (see Section 3.1). The online phase of the global path planning (when allocating a new target location to a group of agents) is visualized in Figure 2 and consists of the following steps:

- find the nearest graph node for every agent's start position,
- find the path from every graph node to the goal node using A*,
- generate a ROI mask around the found A* paths,
- generate the potential field in that ROI,
- generate the flow field from the created potential field.

Similar to the technique described by Treuille et al., values from a crowd density field and an average agent velocity field are used in the cost function for the potential field generation. This allows us to easily incorporate crowd avoidance and results in lane formation. The flow fields are periodically updated to reflect changes in the crowd density and speed fields. Additionally, we use a local avoidance technique based on velocity objects comparable to the one described in Shopf et al.

3.1 Constructing the Graph

As input for the A* algorithm we need a graph representing traversable paths in the world. This graph is generated offline and stored together with the environment geometry. The actual generation of this graph is not the focus of this paper. We use a regular 2D grid of nodes with connections between every node and its eight neighbors but our system can handle any graph layout. However, to limit the time for the A* path finding step, the amount of nodes should be kept small (i.e., less than 512 in our implementation, see Section 4.1).

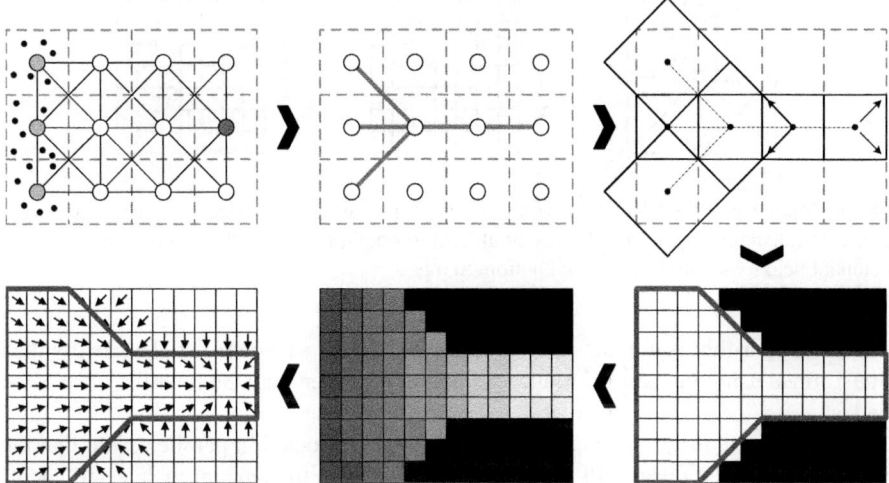

Fig. 2. Overview of the hybrid system. In order of the flow: (1) graph node selection, (2) concurrent A* path finding, (3) edge expansion to a ROI, (4) ROI mask generation, (5) potential field generation, and (6) flow field generation.

The costs assigned to the graph edges are calculated using the continuum crowds algorithm. An edge is expanded into a cost calculation area as shown in Figure 3. Then, to attain the minimal cost to traverse from the top to the bottom row of cells, all bottom row potential cells are designated as goal cells (with zero potential) and the potential field is calculated. After this calculation, the top row cell with the lowest potential contains the cost of the optimal path from the top to the bottom row in the calculation area. Although the real cost for an agent crossing the area depends on its entry and exit points of that area, this value gives a good indication of the real cost and is thus used as the edge cost.

3.2 Determining the Region of Interest

When a new target is assigned to a group of agents, the ROI will have to be determined. In our system the region of interest is represented as a two-dimensional grid containing boolean values (i.e., our mask). The grid is relatively low resolution and determines for every 16x16 block of potential field cells whether it should be subsequently considered by the potential field solver.

The first step in determining the ROI is selecting the list of start nodes for the A* solver. For every agent assigned to the new target, the nearest node is determined by iterating over all the nodes and calculating the distance to these nodes. Because this is performed in parallel on the GPU (one thread per agent), no optimizations based on the knowledge of the graph layout are needed. The first step in Figure 2 conceptually shows the function of the start node selection algorithm. The nodes marked in light grey are the nearest nodes to the agents (represented by the black dots). The output of the

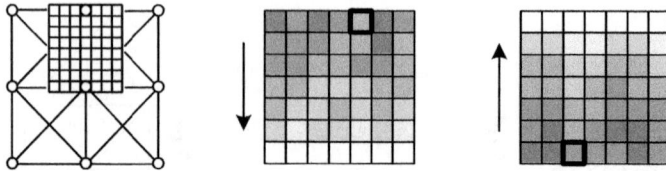

Fig. 3. Graph edge cost calculation with a potential field around the edge. Left: edge expansion to a cost calculation area. Middle: potential field to obtain the cost from top to bottom. Right: potential field to obtain the cost from bottom to top.

selection algorithm is a node state (i.e., selected or not selected) list. This list is then transformed using the parallel reduce primitive [6] to generate the final list of selected nodes.

For all selected start nodes an A* search is then executed in parallel. Note that the amount of selected nodes will usually be a lot less than the amount of selected agents (See step 1 in Figure 2). We will describe our GPU-based implementation in more detail in Section 4. The output of the A* algorithm is a list of graph edges that lead from every start node to the destination nodes (see step 2 in Figure 2). Since all start nodes lead to a common set of destination nodes it is likely there will be some edges which will be used by more than one path. However, we currently do not optimize this list further since, as we will show in Section 5, the ROI mask generation is currently not the bottleneck of our system.

To generate the ROI on the GPU, this list of edges is then fed as a list of line primitives to the Direct3D graphics pipeline. The input lines are processed using a geometry shader that draws a quad for every edge (see step 3 in Figure 2). The size of the generated quads is currently a constant based on the spacing of the graph nodes ensuring that the entire world is covered when expanding all edges. These quads are then subsequently rasterized and rendered using a trivial pixel shader which simply outputs a boolean value for all rendered pixels (see step 4 in Figure 2). This way a mask that marks the blocks that will be considered by the potential solver is efficiently generated in GPU memory by using the hardware rasterizer.

3.3 Potential Field Solver

Our potential solver uses the *Fast Iterative Method* algorithm described by Jeong et al. [8]. This is a solver variant that is suited for parallel execution by dividing the entire potential field in smaller blocks of potential cells. Each block can be processed independently. However, potential values need to be exchanged at the block borders to ensure correctness. Therefore, calculating the potentials inside a block is an iterative process that optimally should halt when all blocks are converged, i.e., changes to the potentials inside a block are below a threshold value. In our system, a block is marked as active when it is inside the ROI and not fully converged. Step 5 in Figure 2 shows a potential field calculated inside the ROI. Note that the resolution of the potential field should be sixteen times larger (in both dimensions) than the ROI mask generated in step 4 (not shown for clarity). Thus, a potential cell in the figure is in reality a block of potential cells.

After the potential field solver has completed, the gradients along the potential field are calculated resulting in a flow field that contains the direction of the optimal path to the nearest goal location for every cell inside the ROI. In Section 4 we will describe how we mapped this algorithm to the CUDA architecture.

Note that our two-stage algorithm no longer guarantees to find the optimal path. For example, if an optimal path between two nodes follows a highly curved shape the path may effectively lie outside the region marked by our ROI. However in practice we never encountered this problem and paths are always (visually) optimal. Also note that strategically adding nodes to the graph (during an offline preprocessing step) could minimize the difference between an optimal path in the selected ROI and the true optimal path found when evaluating a flow field for the entire world.

4 GPU Implementation

All navigation algorithms used in the hybrid system (i.e., graph start node selection, A* path finding, flow field calculation, local avoidance, and basic physics) are performed by the GPU using the NVIDIA CUDA platform.

4.1 A* Implementation

To implement the A* path finding algorithm on the GPU, we first store the A* graph as a set of 1D textures. This ensures cached reads even on older generations of CUDA hardware. For every selected start node (i.e., path to calculate, see Section 3.2) a set of local variables is then allocated. Most notable are the list of active and visited nodes maintained by the A* algorithm. We currently statically allocate these lists to be N elements, where N is the number of nodes in the map. This requires a total of $O(NT)$ memory, where T is the number of paths to calculate concurrently. Note that the required amount of memory is usually much lower than the cost of storing the potential fields in our system because we only use a small amount of nodes. The rest of our implementation is highly optimized and uses similar techniques as described by Bleiweiss [2].

4.2 Potential Field Solver

Shopf et al.[12] proposes solving the potential field by simply executing a kernel[3] a fixed number of times without checking the convergence of the individual blocks. However, this sometimes leads to unnecessary work on blocks which have already converged. An additional problem is that since there are no global synchronization primitives on the current generation of GPUs, the kernel has to be invoked many times which adds an additional overhead. These invocations are needed because only the state of

---

[3] A kernel in the CUDA terminology is a GPU program that is executed N times in parallel by N different CUDA threads.

the current block is known in the kernel. There is no information on the states of other blocks. This external state information is needed to exchange the potentials at the block borders and to stop iterating the block when all blocks have converged.

The problem of multiple kernel invocations could be solved by trying to implement a global barrier synchronization mechanism [3]. However we solve the problem by using a more fine grained approach using a work queue. This avoids two problems with global barrier synchronization. First, multiprocessors only have to spin when the queue is empty and second, processors only call threadfence[4] when they have finished a block avoiding the slowdowns reported by Feng et al. [3] when many threads try to call threadfence at once.

Our solution allows us to incorporate the ROI into the solver as well as stopping the solver as soon as the solution has converged for a given area. Our solver handles every active block in the active list described in Section 3.2 as a separate CUDA block. Blocks consist of bundles of 16×16 CUDA threads, where each thread is responsible for an individual potential grid cell. Since all the cells within a block need to access the values of the neighboring cells we store the cell values in shared memory. Because the individual threads read adjacent memory addresses in groups of 16 threads to fetch the neighbor values, shared memory bank conflicts are avoided.

Our queue-based solver uses persistent threads [1]. This involves launching a number of threads corresponding to the amount of CUDA cores to optimally use all the hardware available on the GPU. Also, a queue is used to allow the threads to work together on solving the problem. When dealing with unpredictable workloads, this facilitates using the full capacity of the GPU and helps to reduce the number of kernel launches. A single kernel invocation suffices to solve the flow field.

5 Results

In this section we will analyze the performance of our system and compare it to previous work. All our results were generated with an Intel Q6600 processor, 2 GiB of system memory, and an NVIDIA Geforce GTS 250 video board with 1 GiB of video memory.

We first discuss the results of our A* implementation. Table 1 presents our results for different numbers of nodes in the graph. These results are generated by doing a parallel path search from all nodes to one destination node. Thus, in every test, the amount of paths to calculate concurrently equals the amount of nodes in the graph. This represents the worst case scenario that all nodes are selected as start nodes. Note that besides the amounts of paths to calculate, due to the nature of the test, the node count also determines the average path length which also influences the execution time. The results show that the length of the execution time is sufficiently small to use parallel A* in an interactive application that periodically needs the GPU for other purposes (e.g., rendering, local avoidance, physics, etc.). In our system, we experienced 20 milliseconds as the upper bound to prevent visually noticeable stalls during the execution. This translates to an upper bound of 512 nodes in the graph.

---

[4] The CUDA threadfence function stalls the calling CUDA threads until their global memory and shared memory writes are visible to all other threads.

Table 1. Absolute execution times (ms) and memory footprint (MiB) for the A* kernel

Graph node count	64	128	256	512	1024
Execution time (ms)	2.2	4.2	9.4	20.8	73.9
Memory (MiB)	0.13	0.5	2.0	8.01	32.02

Table 2. Absolute execution times (ms) for the flow field solver

Flow field resolution	128x128	256x256	512x512	1024x1024	2048x2048
Straightforward	5.7	26.2	157.0	898.3	2,664.4
Without convergence test	2.4	19.2	120.8	649.0	2,303.1
Persistent threads	3.0	8.9	59.6	289.4	502.1

In practice, our hybrid system requires very few nodes for the A* navigation since it is only used as a coarse ROI selection method. This number is usually too small to optimally use the parallel computing power of current GPUs and limits the performance increase when compared with a CPU implementation. However, by running all the steps in our system on the GPU, no costly copies are necessary between the host and video memory. The second row in Table 1 shows the amount of video memory needed by the system we described in Section 4.1 during the A* execution. Although parallel A* uses memory very inefficiently, due to the low amount of graph nodes, memory usage is not an issue in practice.

We now analyze the performance of our persistent thread-based flow field solver. Table 2 compares our persistent system with a straightforward implementation of the flow field solver. We also included our implementation of the approach used by Shopf et al. [12] where a fixed number of iterations is executed without a convergence test. When comparing our persistent thread implementation against our non-persistent implementation we observe a twofold speedup for a 256×256 flow field. Shopf et al. report an execution time of 20 ms for a 256×256 field. In comparison, our implementation needs 8.89 ms for a similar field.

Finally, we analyze how our hybrid system compares with the traditional method of solving the full flow field. To measure the results of the A* and mask generation in our hybrid system, we measure the worst case situation. This is the situation where all the nodes in the world are selected, i.e., they have agents nearby who need to navigate to the destination. To measure the performance of the flow field solver we average the execution times of the tiled flow field solver using the four masks shown in Figure 4. Table 3 then shows the execution times comparing the flow field without a hybrid system compared with the hybrid system (i.e., this includes the A* pass, the mask generation and the flow field calculation). When using flow fields with limited resolution, we notice that the additional overhead of the A* path finding step results in an increase in the total execution time. Starting from flow fields with 256×256 cells, the time saved avoiding unnecessary work outweighs the overhead of the ROI calculation. This proves the validity of our approach.

Table 3. Absolute execution times (ms) comparing the hybrid system with a flow fields only system

Flow field resolution	128x128	256x256	512x512	1024x1024	2048x2048
A* graph nodes	64	128	256	512	1024
Persistent threads	3.0	8.9	59.6	289.4	502.1
Hybrid system	4.3	9.5	24.3	99.1	239.0

Fig. 4. The masks used for the test results in Table 3

6 Conclusions

In this paper we have shown how we can accelerate the simulation of large crowds in detailed environments by using a hybrid approach. Our path planning and agent management is done entirely on the GPU, resulting in a system that scales up to 100,000 agents on a mainstream graphics card. Our hybrid approach based on a coarse A* phase followed by a detailed flow field solution performs up to four times faster than solving a flow field for the entire world while still resulting in visually optimal agent paths.

Besides our hybrid approach we also presented an optimized flow field solver. This solver using persistent threads offers a fast solution to the flow field problem without compromising on solution quality as is the case when using a fixed amount of iterations.

Our hybrid system eliminates unnecessary work when calculating a flow field. However, in our current implementation the memory usage of a potential field and a flow field is not optimized. The next generation of our system should support a compact potential field and flow field storage format that introduces a minimal overhead in the simulation kernels.

Section 3.1 describes how we assign the costs to the graph edges based on a potential field calculated around every edge. Although our tests showed believable trajectories for all agents, the current method does not ensure that the optimal path for every agent lies inside the ROI. Careful positioning of the graph nodes could minimize the impact of our coarse A* step. Also, the size of the calculated flow field around every node or the size of the graph edge expansion area can impact the final agent paths. We aim to investigate this in the future.

Acknowledgments. The research activities that have been described in this paper were funded by Ghent University, the Interdisciplinary Institute for Broadband Technology (IBBT), the Institute for the Promotion of Innovation by Science and Technology in Flanders (IWT), the Fund for Scientific Research-Flanders (FWOFlanders), the Belgian Federal Science Policy Office (BFSPO), and the European Union.

References

1. Aila, T., Laine, S.: Understanding the efficiency of ray traversal on GPUs. In: Proceedings of the Conference on High Performance Graphics, HPG 2009, pp. 145–149. ACM, New York (2009)
2. Bleiweiss, A.: GPU accelerated pathfinding. In: Proceedings of the 23rd ACM SIGGRAPH/EUROGRAPHICS Symposium on Graphics Hardware, GH 2008, pp. 65–74. Eurographics Association, Aire-la-Ville (2008)
3. Feng, W., Xiao, S.: To GPU synchronize or not GPU synchronize? In: Proceedings of 2010 IEEE International Symposium on Circuits and Systems (ISCAS), May 30 - June 2, pp. 3801–3804 (2010)
4. Fiorini, P., Shillert, Z.: Motion planning in dynamic environments using velocity obstacles. International Journal of Robotics Research 17, 760–772 (1998)
5. Geraerts, R., Overmars, M.H.: The corridor map method: a general framework for real-time high-quality path planning: Research articles. Comput. Animat. Virtual Worlds 18, 107–119 (2007)
6. Harris, M., Sengupta, S., Owens, J.D.: Parallel prefix sum (scan) with CUDA. In: GPU Gems 3, pp. 851–876. Addison-Wesley Professional (2007)
7. Hollemeersch, C.F., Pieters, B., Lambert, P., Van de Walle, R.: Accelerating virtual texturing using CUDA. In: GPU Pro: Advanced Rendering Techniques, vol. 1, pp. 623–641. AK Peters (2010)
8. Jeong, W., Whitaker, R.T.: A fast eikonal equation solver for parallel systems. In: SIAM Conference on Computational Science and Engineering 2007, Technical Sketches (2007)
9. Karamouzas, I., Geraerts, R., Overmars, M.: Indicative routes for path planning and crowd simulation. In: Proceedings of the 4th International Conference on Foundations of Digital Games, FDG 2009, pp. 113–120. ACM, New York (2009)
10. Morini, F., Yersin, B., Maym, J., Thalmann, D.: Real-time scalable motion planning for crowds. In: Proceedings of the 2007 International Conference on Cyberworlds, pp. 144–151. IEEE Computer Society, Washington, DC (2007)
11. Pettré, J., Ciechomski, P.d.H., Maïm, J., Yersin, B., Laumond, J.P., Thalmann, D.: Real-time navigating crowds: scalable simulation and rendering: Research articles. Comput. Animat. Virtual Worlds 17, 445–455 (2006)
12. Shopf, J., Barczak, J., Oat, C., Tatarchuk, N.: March of the froblins: simulation and rendering massive crowds of intelligent and detailed creatures on GPU. In: ACM SIGGRAPH 2008 Classes, SIGGRAPH 2008, pp. 52–101. ACM, New York (2008)
13. Treuille, A., Cooper, S., Popović, Z.: Continuum crowds. In: SIGGRAPH 2006: ACM SIGGRAPH 2006 Papers, pp. 1160–1168. ACM, New York (2006)

Space-Time Planning in Dynamic Environments with Unknown Evolution

Thomas Lopez[1], Fabrice Lamarche[2], and Tsai-Yen Li[3]

[1] MimeTIC Lab, IRISA / INSA Rennes, France
[2] MimeTIC Lab, IRISA / University of Rennes 1, France
[3] IM Lab, National Chengchi University, Taipei, Taiwan, R.O.C.
{thomas.lopez,fabrice.lamarche}@irisa.fr,
li@nccu.edu.tw

Abstract. Numerous path planning solutions have been proposed to solve the navigation problem in static environments, potentially populated with dynamic obstacles. However, in dynamic environments, moving objects can be used to reach new locations. In this paper, we propose an online planning algorithm for dynamically changing environments with unknown evolution. This method focuses on accessibility and on the use of objects movements to reach a given target. Among other examples, we will show that this algorithm is able to find a path through moving platforms to reach a target located on a surface that is never directly accessible. We will also show that the proposed representation enables several kind of adaptations such as avoiding moving obstacles or adapting the character postures to environmental constraints.

Keywords: Path Planning, Dynamic Environments, Autonomous Characters, Accessibility.

1 Introduction

In the last decades, path planning has been widely studied and numerous solutions for static environments, eventually populated of dynamic obstacles, have been proposed. Our method addresses a new kind of path planning problem by focusing on a virtual character navigating in dynamically changing environments where the evolution of the topology is not known a priori. Moreover, dynamic objects are not only considered as obstacles but also as navigable parts of the environment that can be used to access new locations such as a plank acting as a bridge and connecting two disconnected regions. Using the character capabilities, our method builds a dual representation of objects which identifies the impact of objects in terms of accessibility and obstruction. This representation is used to characterize and track topological modifications while considering the temporal aspect. Two disconnected regions of the environment can thus be linked thanks to a moving elevator even though no explicit or static path exists between them. We will refer to this situation as the *elevator problem*. We will show that our solution is able to solve such complex cases in real time by generating collision-free paths and adapting the character's postures among dynamic obstacles whose movements are not known a priori. This property makes our algorithm suitable for interactive applications where an external user or a script may act on the environment at runtime. Such an approach is useful in several application fields including video games where non-player characters are evolving in dynamic environments where changes are not always known a priori.

In the following, we first introduce the related works. We then describe the precomputation steps associated to the character representation and the dual representation of the dynamic objects. The next section focuses on the use of those representations to plan a path and adapt postures of a virtual character evolving in a dynamic environment. Finally, we show and analyze some results.

2 Related Work

Path planning has been widely studied in robotics where spatial reasoning provides robots with the critical functionality of autonomy of navigation [13,15]. Given a character, its navigation capabilities and a description of the environment, the purpose is to plan a collision-free path for the character between two specific locations. The general formulation of this problem relies on the exploration of the configuration space (C-space). This C-space is defined as a N-dimensional space for which each of the N axis represents a degree of freedom (DOF) of the character. The C-space is generally divided in C-free, containing valid configurations, and C-obstacle, containing obstructed ones. Thus, planning a collision-free path for a character is equivalent to finding a path in C-free that links two specific configurations. The basic planning problem focuses on finding a valid path in a static environment. Proposed methods mostly fall into two categories: cell decomposition and roadmaps. The cell decomposition methods are either approximate, representing a subset of C-free with cells of predefined shapes [10,21], or exact, representing C-free using trapezoidal decomposition, Delaunay triangulations and variants [7,12]. Probabilistic methods, such as PRMs [9,3] or RRTs [11], explore C-free by computing a roadmap in which nodes are non-colliding configurations randomly sampled over C-free and edges are collision-free paths linking two nodes. Most of the methods generally consider navigation in a connected environment. However, few methods focused on static but disconnected environments [3,17,20].

The need of planning paths in dynamically changing environments arises in many application fields. Most of the proposed methods focus on avoiding dynamic obstacles. On the one hand, some methods considered that obstacles movements are known and use this knowledge to guide and speed-up the path planning [14,4]. On the other hand, fast replanning techniques are used when an obstacle is detected along the planned trajectory [1,24]. Various reactive methods based on PRMs [1] or RRTs [6] have been proposed. This kind of methods validates precomputed edges of the PRMs during planning to take dynamic changes into account [8]. Velocity obstacles and extensions [2] propose a reactive approach which updates the agent speed to generate trajectories avoiding collisions with dynamic obstacles. Finally, methods based on rapidly computed generalized Voronoï diagram have also been proposed [5,22].

To our knowledge, the first method handling space-time planning in a dynamic and disconnected environment has been recently proposed by Levine et al. [16]. The singularity of both our and their methods is that moving platforms are no longer considered as obstacles but also as navigable regions used during navigation. However, their method is based on the strong hypothesis that the objects movements have known trajectories. This involves that the future evolutions of the environment are always known and thus that accessibilities between objects can be precomputed. Based on this hypothesis they compute their path using a trial-and-error solver, trying different motion controllers until a correct motion to adopt along the path is found.

Our method handles space-time planning in a dynamically changing environment with no a priori knowledge on the topology evolution. By observing this evolution at runtime, our algorithm characterize and track topological relations over time. Based on this information, our method is able to compute in real time paths among moving and disconnected surfaces while avoiding dynamic obstacles and adapting the character's postures to environmental constraints.

3 Characters and Objects Representations

Our path planning problem considers a non-flying character evolving in a dynamic environment composed of non-deformable objects. We make no assumption on the spatio-temporal evolution of the environment that we only assume to be observable. To propose a solution compatible with interactive applications the character representation is simplified using bounding volumes, which reduce the number of DOF of the problem. Those volumes are used to extract a dual representation of the objects which characterizes the topological impact of an object and enables to rapidly identify accessibility and obstructions.

3.1 The Character and Its Navigation Capabilities

We consider a character with navigation capabilities mainly constrained on the floor. In order to speed-up path planning and uncouple it from the animation process, we represent our character using bounding volumes [14,2,17] that reduce the number of DOF. For each navigation capability i, we define a cylinder C_i, centered on the character's root, which bounds its geometry when playing the motion M_i. Jump motions are particular as a character could get hurt when it jumps down or might not be able to reach a high location. To model this, the jump motion is labeled with a maximum vertical impulse speed, a maximum horizontal impulse speed and a maximum vertical landing speed. Finally, we assume that our character follows a ballistic trajectory when jumping.

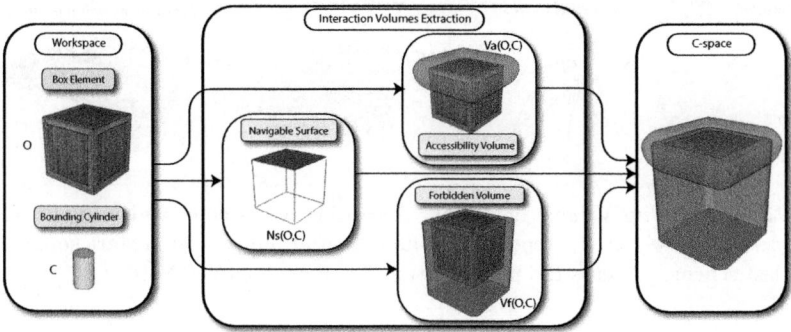

Fig. 1. *Interaction Volumes*: given an original geometry O and a cylinder C bounding a considered motion capability, we compute three *Interaction Volumes*: the *Navigable Surface* $Ns(O,C)$, the Accessibility Volume $Va(O,C)$, and the *Forbidden Volume* $Vf(O,C)$. On the right, the dual representation of O which is inserted in the C-space.

3.2 Augmenting Geometry with Interaction Volumes

Definition of the Interaction Volumes. From the character's point of view, a geometric object impacts on the local topology in three different ways. It can obstruct a region, present navigable areas or create an access to other surfaces. Obstruction, navigability and accessibility properties rely on the character's navigation capabilities. Regarding those capabilities, we extract a dual representation of objects, called the *Interaction Volumes*, which characterizes feasible, colliding and reachable configurations of the C-space. Once navigable areas of an object have been identified, we associate to each surface a precomputed roadmap.

Given the cylinder bounding a navigation capability of our character, a configuration in this C-space represents the position of the character's root located at the bottom center of the cylinder. In the following, we assume that the (X,Y) axes represent the horizontal plane and that the Z-axis is the height axis of the environment. Considering an object O and a cylinder C_m bounding the navigation capability m, we define three types of *Interaction Volumes*(see Fig. 1): the *Forbidden Volume*, the *Navigable Surface* and the *Accessibility Volume*.

Forbidden Volume, denoted $V_f(O, C_m)$, represents the set of configurations where the character collides with the object O. This volume is obtained by extruding the object's shape along the Z-axis using the height of the cylinder C_m. This shape is then extended along the (X,Y)-axes using the cylinder's radius.

Navigable Surface, denoted $Ns(O, C_m)$, represents the surface where the character can stand. We use an interval of navigable slopes associated to m to determine whether or not a character is able to stand on the considered surface. $Ns(O, C_m)$ is computed by grouping all triangles of the object's mesh with navigable slopes minus configurations lying in $V_f(O, C_m)$.

Accessibility Volumes denoted $V_a(O, C_m)$, contains all configurations reachable from $Ns(O, C_m)$ when jumping. First, the maximum reachable height is used to extrude $Ns(O, C_m)$ along the height axis. Second, given the jump mo-

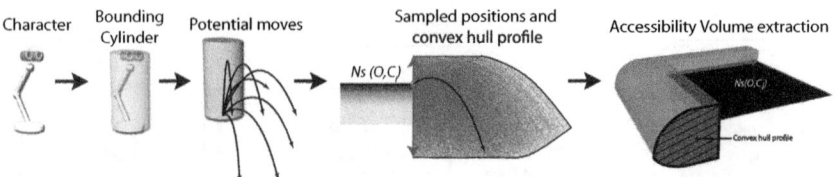

Fig. 2. *Accessibility Volume* definition : regarding a character and its jumping capability, we extract a profile representing its potential jumps from a start configuration. The last scheme presents the profile extraction along edges of $Ns(O,C)$.

tion characteristics, we compute an Accessibility Profile (see Fig. 2) by randomly sampling the set of admissible jumping trajectories and computing the convex hull shape of the sampled trajectories. This profile is then extruded along the borders of the $Ns(O, C_m)$ to finalize $V_a(O, C_m)$.

Local roadmap generation. Since the global structure of $Ns(O, C)$ does not change, a local roadmap is precomputed on each surface. Different methods have been proposed in the literature to build a roadmap. We chose the well-known Probabilistic RoadMaps method (PRM) to create local roadmaps [9]. We thus randomly sample configurations in $\bigcup_m Ns(O, C_m)$ and annotate each sampled configuration c with the set of motion capabilities that are valid i.e. $\{m | C \in Ns(O, C_m)\}$. Each sample is then connected to its k-nearest neighbors iff the configurations share at least one common motion capability m and that a linear path lying in $Ns(O, C_m)$ exists.

3.3 Properties of the Representation

The *Interaction Volumes* represent the impact of objects on their local environment's topology. Identifying a topological relation between two objects in the workspace is thus equivalent to detecting an intersection between their respective *Interaction Volumes* in the C-space. Given two objects (O_i, O_j) and a motion capability m, accessibility and obstruction relations are defined as follow:

- **Accessibility:** $A(O_i, O_j, C_m)$, holds when $V_a(O_i, C_m) \cap Ns(O_j, C_m) \neq \emptyset$ and characterizes an access from O_i to O_j with the motion capability m. This relation is not a bijection as the character may have more difficulties to climb on objects than to go down (see Fig. 2).
- **Obstruction:** $O(O_i, O_j, C_m)$, holds when $V_f(O_i, C_m) \cap V_a(O_j, C_m) \neq \emptyset$, i.e., O_i obstructs some navigable parts of O_j for the given capability m.

The identification of those relations coupled with local roadmaps allow us to locate the topological impact of the detected relations at runtime. Thus, an accessibility relation results in a connection between two distinct roadmaps while an obstruction invalidates some parts of the roadmap. Obstruction relations have an impact on obstacle avoidance but also on posture adaptation as an obstruction might, for instance, force the character to adopt a crouching capability to

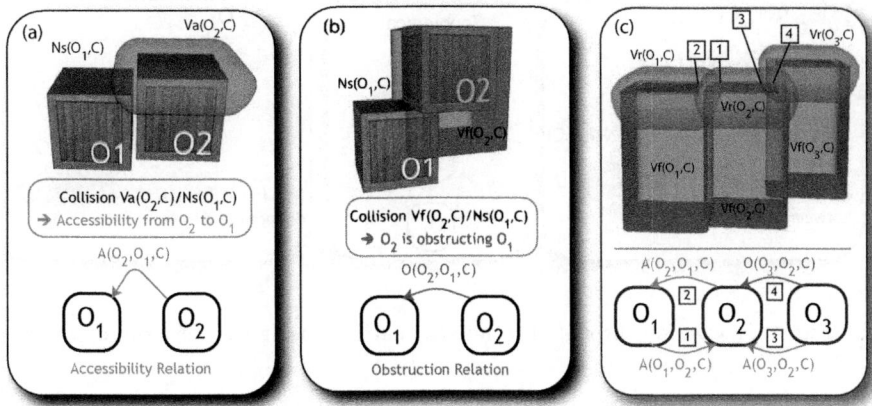

Fig. 3. *Topological Graph* construction. Characterization of an accessibility (a), and of an obstruction (b). Example of a more complex situation (c) with 4 detected relations.

navigate along its path. The identification of topological relations is reduced to a collision detection between *Interaction Volumes* and the path validation to a simple ray casting between the local path and the relevant *Forbidden Volumes*. Those properties are intensively used in our algorithm.

4 Finding a Path in a Dynamic Environment

In dynamic environments, the topology evolves and moving objects act as obstacles, bridges or elevators for instance. Topology relations need to be tracked in order to consider them during navigation. We now present how the *Interaction Volumes* representation is used to track topology modifications while taking time into account to avoid moving obstacles but also detect moving platforms linking disconnected surfaces. Our two level path planner is then presented. The first level computes a path between *Navigable Surfaces* at the topological level, while the second level plans a local path on each *Navigable Surface*.

4.1 Tracking Topology Modifications

In order to track the topology over time, we introduce the *Topological Graph*. This directed graph aims at building a global representation of the environment's topology by representing each object as a node and each topological relation as a link between the concerned objects (see Fig.3). As the character has no a priori knowledge on the environment's evolution, this graph allows it to build its own representation of the environment by observing the evolution of topological relations over time. As described previously, detected collisions between *Interaction Volumes* allows us to identify topological relations existing at a given time. Thanks to the 3-dimensionality of the *Interaction Volumes*, those collisions are detected using a tuned collision detection (CD) algorithm [23]. Every time

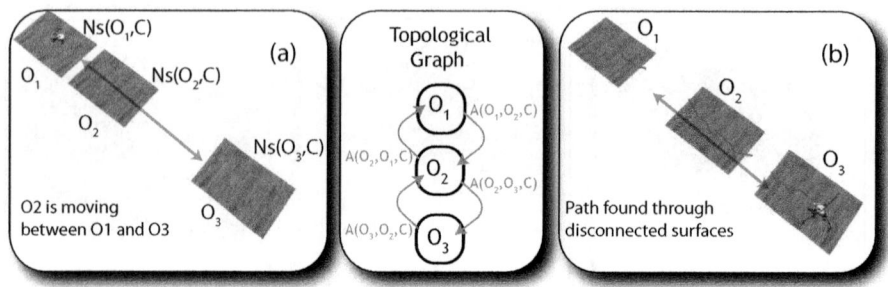

Fig. 4. Navigation through disconnected surfaces using the *Topological Graph*

a relation is detected by the CD, the corresponding edge is added or updated in the *Topological Graph*. Edges are labeled with the number of times the relation was valid, the mean validity and non-validity times of the relation and the mean relative speed of the objects. The mean validity time of the relation and the mean relative speed of the objects give an estimate of the relation's stability. The sum of mean validity and non-validity times gives an estimate of its periodicity. Finally, the number of times the relation was valid allows the *Topological Graph* to automatically identify and characterize periodic and punctual relations between objects. The *Topological Graph* thus contains statistical information about validity and stability of topological relations. This is crucial as we use this information to characterize relations over time. Thanks to the coupling with the CD algorithm, the *Topological Graph* is an anytime representation of the topology. Moreover, the temporal information on relations enables to automatically represent periodical relations in space and time (see Fig. 4).

Nevertheless, this graph is a coarse representation of the global topology as it only identifies relations between pairs of objects. Regarding the definition of accessibility, an object O_j is reachable from O_i with a jump capability C_m iff $V_a(O_i, C_m) \cap N_s(O_j, C_m) \neq \emptyset$. To refine this relation and avoid potential collisions with *Forbidden Volumes*, we randomly sample a set of jumps from O_i to O_j. First, a target configuration c_t is selected from the local roadmap (PRM) associated to O_j. Second, its nearest source configuration c_s belonging to the local roadmap associated to $N_s(O_i, C_m)$ is also selected. Finally, a random configuration c_r is sampled such as it vertically projects on the segment (c_s, c_t) and its Z-coordinate is greater than the maximum Z coordinate of c_s and c_t. Given the configurations c_s, c_r and c_t, the second order polynomial corresponding to the unique ballistic trajectory passing through those three configurations is computed (see Fig. 5(a)). The obtained jump is validated iff the impulse and landing speeds satisfy the constraints associated to the jumping capability C_m and the trajectory does not collide with a *Forbidden Volume* (see Fig. 5(b)). Each validated jump is then stored in the corresponding accessibility edge of the *Topological Graph*. To amortize the cost of the sampling phase, a sampling budget is allocated at each time step. This budget is then distributed among the currently valid accessibility relations.

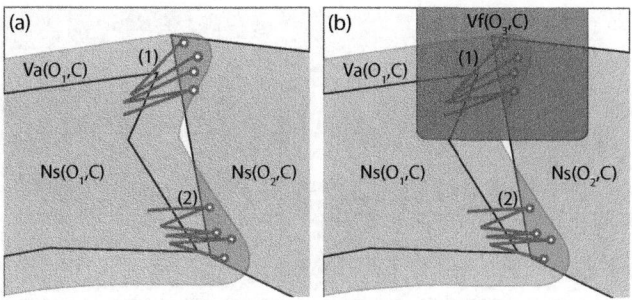

Fig. 5. Reachability from O_1 to O_2 (top view). Several valid configurations are sampled in $Va(O_1,C) \cap Ns(O_2,C)$ and linked to the O_1's roadmap (a). Then relevant *Forbidden Volumes*, here $Vf(O_3,C)$, are retrieved from the *Topological Graph* and obstructed jumps are filtered (b), such as links from the region (1).

4.2 A Two-Level Path Planner

In order to find a path in the environment, we designed a two-level path planner. This planner first selects *Navigable Surfaces* on the way, using the *Topological Graph* and the temporal information. Then local paths are computed on each surface using the associated local roadmaps.

In order to identify *Navigable Surfaces* on the way, we first filter the *Topological Graph*. Thus, we discard obstruction relations as well as unfeasible accessibility for which a feasible jump has not been identified. For safety reasons, we also invalidate accessibility relations for which either the mean relative speed of the objects exceeds a given threshold or the mean validity time is lower than a time threshold. To compute the global path, we run a Dijkstra algorithm on this filtered view of the *Topological Graph*. Costs associated to the accessibility relations are set to their periodicity (sum of the mean validity and non-validity time) for dynamic relations and to an ϵ-value for stable relations (relations which are always valid). This cost function thus tends to favor paths through stable links and minimizing the waiting time. The global path planner finally provides a sequence of *Navigable Surfaces* that must be crossed in order to reach the goal.

Then, the local path planner has to generate local paths on each roadmap associated to the identified *Navigable Surface* while handling obstacle avoidance and posture adaptation. To compute this path in the local PRM, we use a multi-target A* algorithm that starts from the current configuration of the character and finds a path to the nearest target configuration. The target can be either the global target or the source of a jump to access the next *Navigable Surface*. An edge is valid if at least one motion capability m associated to the edge does not collide with local *Forbidden Volumes* and if m is compatible with the motion capability used to reach this edge. Edges validity is checked during planning in the space-time domain. In this domain, we anticipate objects positions using a linear extrapolation of their current movements over time [1]. As the evolution is not known a priori, we limit the impact of the extrapolation error by setting

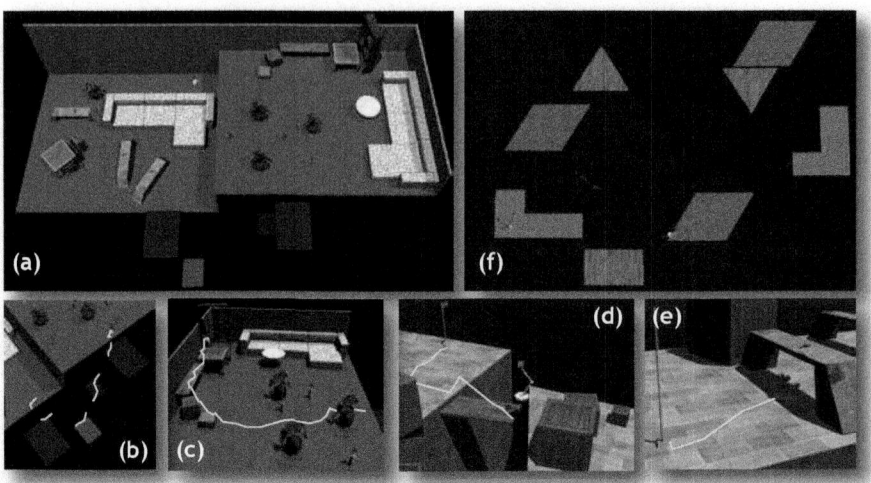

Fig. 6. We present our environments: the living room (a) and the disconnected environment (f). Some results are show such as: navigation between disconnected and moving surfaces (b), the dynamic obstacle avoidance(c), posture adaptation regarding the motion capabilities (d) and the environmental constraints (e).

a maximum extrapolation time. If the time needed to reach the currently explored configuration is greater than this limit, the object is assumed to be static. Once the path is computed, the character follows it. If a new potential collision is detected during navigation, a replanning is executed. When a local target is reached, the character waits to access the next surface. Using the jump properties, the jump decision is taken by extrapolating the position of the targeted surface and nearby obstacles. If the landing area lies on the targeted surface and the trajectory does not collide with obstacles, the character jumps. The local planning is repeated on each identified surface until the final target is reached.

Based on the *Topological Graph* and on the analysis of temporal information, our two-level planner solves complex planning problems such as detecting a sequence of moving platforms disconnected in space and time that must be crossed to reach a given goal. The search space is also reduced for the local planner which only plans paths and adapts postures on relevant *Navigable Surfaces*.

5 Results

In our test cases, the character uses three navigation capabilities: sliding on the ground while (1) standing or (2) crouching and (3) jumping. The jumping capability allows the character to reach disconnected areas of the workspace. The heights of the bounding cylinders are set to 50 cm for capabilities (1) and (3), 20 cm for capability (2). The radius of those cylinders is set to 20 cm for capability (1) and (3), 30 cm for capability (2). When using the jumping capability, our

Table 1. Benchmarks

Environment Name	Collision Detection	Topological Graph update	average Path Planning time	Obstruction Tests (%path planning)
Disconnected Env	0,75 ms	0,24 ms	6,22 ms	-
Living-room	14,12 ms	6,46 ms	93,98 ms	67,77 %

character is able to jump with maximum vertical and horizontal impulse speeds of $2 m.s^{-1}$ and we limit the landing speed to $3 m.s^{-1}$. We evaluated our method using different dynamic environments. A demo video presenting our results is available online[1].

Disconnected environment. This environment is composed of disconnected and moving platforms (see Fig. 6(f)). By jumping from platform to platform when connections are identified, the character is able to reach every parts of the environment. This example shows how temporal information is used to detect paths in space and time even though the *Navigation Surfaces* are not directly connected. There is no obstacles in the environment.

Living room. This environment, presented in Fig. 6(a), demonstrates the various properties of our method. It is composed of numerous complex objects: tables, chairs, sofas, shelves, plants... Those objects all act as obstacles or navigation surfaces and some can constraint the character's postures. The environment is highly constrained leaving only a few room for navigation. Moreover, *flying books* are used as elevators to connect the two floors together. This environment focuses on connections between distinct surfaces, path obstructions replanning and posture adaptation during navigation.

Benchmarks have been realized on an Intel Core i7, CPU X920, 2GHz. We used Bullets Physics CD library to identify *Interaction Volumes* collisions. Our implementation is currently mono-threaded. Our benchmarks results are presented in Table 1. This table summarizes average times of: the CD between *Interaction Volumes*, the *Topological Graph* update and the connections computation between *Navigable Surfaces*, and the path planning process. The last column presents the percentage of time spent in testing the validity of roadmap edges during the path planning step. Results presented in Table 1 show that our algorithm performs topology detection and processes path planning requests at interactive frame rates in our testing environments.

Our algorithm first continuously tracks the collisions between *Interaction Volumes* to identify the evolution of the topology. This process performances are directly correlated with the CD library that is used. The time spent in the graph update is negligible but Table 1 shows that the use of numerous objects with complex geometries (such as the living room) decreases algorithm performances. In order to reduce the time spent in the collision detection, simplified versions of original meshes (called collision meshes) are often used in real time physical

---

[1] http://www.irisa.fr/bunraku/GENS/tlopez/video/MIG2011video/MIG2011video.html

simulations. We could extend those methods to simplify the shapes of the *Interaction Volumes*. Second, we defined a dynamic path planner which is able to provide temporal trajectories through disconnected surfaces while avoiding predicted collisions. However, the local path planner is the most time consuming process as it needs to test the validity of trajectories regarding the future obstacle locations. The validity tests represent around 70% of the computation time. Whenever an unexpected obstacle appears on the character's trajectory, a new local path planning request is emitted. To increase performances and avoid redundant computations, a D* algorithm could be used.

6 Conclusion and Future Work

In this paper, we presented our approach to online path planning in dynamic environments with unknown evolution. The originality of our approach is that dynamic objects are not only obstacles but can also be used to navigate and reach previously unreachable locations. The characterization offered by *Interaction Volumes* makes possible to track the evolution of the environment's topology. The analysis of this evolution is then used to solve complex planning problems such as finding a path between regions disconnected in space and time. Moreover, the same representation is used to adapt postures to environmental constraints and locally plan collision-free paths avoiding dynamic obstacles. Finally, contrary to Levine et al. approach [16], our method does not require a prior knowledge on the evolution of the world but builds its knowledge at runtime by observing the environment's evolution to propose a real time path planner.

The collision detection algorithm, used for topology tracking and local path planning, is a major bottleneck. However, some recent work focusing either on collision detection parallelization on CPU/GPU [18] or on GPU-based planning algorithms [19] are promising for scaling our algorithm to very complex environments. Another aspect is that the character may sometimes miss the targeted surface and fall down due to an extrapolation error, if the targeted object has chaotic movements for instance. This can be viewed as a limitation of our technique or as something realistic, since the same case can arise in a real situation.

Future work will focus on scalability studies of the method. We are interested in path planning of different characters with individual motion capabilities in the same environment at the same time. Finally, we intend to increase the dynamic and the unpredictability of the environment by considering navigation in physical worlds with physical objects and destructible structures as it can be seen in numerous video games.

References

1. Van den Berg, J., Ferguson, D., Kuffner, J.: Anytime path planning and replanning in dynamic environments. In: Proc. IEEE ICRA (2006)
2. Van den Berg, J., Lin, M., Manocha, D.: Reciprocal velocity obstacles for real-time multi-agent navigation. In: Proc. IEEE ICRA (2008)

3. Choi, M.G., Lee, J., Shin, S.Y.: Planning biped locomotion using motion capture data and probabilistic roadmaps. ACM Transactions on Graphics 22(2) (2003)
4. Gayle, R., Sud, A., Lin, M., Manocha, D.: Reactive deformation roadmaps: motion planning of multiple robots in dynamic environments. In: IEEE IROS (2007)
5. Hoff III, K.E., Keyser, J., Lin, M., Manocha, D., Culver, T.: Fast computation of generalized voronoi diagrams using graphics hardware. Computer Graphics 33 (1999)
6. Jaillet, L., Simeon, T.: A prm-based motion planner for dynamically changing environments. In: IEEE International Conf. IROS (2004)
7. Kallmann, M., Bieri, H., Thalmann, D.: Fully dynamic constrained delaunay triangulations. Geometric Modelling for Scientific Visualization (2003)
8. Kallmann, M., Matarić, M.: Motion planning using dynamic roadmaps. In: Proc. of the International Conference on Robotics and Automation (2004)
9. Kavraki, L., Svestka, P., Latombe, J.C., Overmars, M.: Probabilistic roadmaps for path planning in high-dimensional configuration spaces (1994)
10. Kuffner, J.J.: Goal-Directed Navigation for Animated Characters Using Real-Time Path Planning and Control. In: Magnenat-Thalmann, N., Thalmann, D. (eds.) CAPTECH 1998. LNCS (LNAI), vol. 1537, pp. 171–186. Springer, Heidelberg (1998)
11. Kuffner, J.J., LaValle, S.M.: Rrt-connect: An efficient approach to single-query path planning. In: IEEE Int. Conf. on Robotics and Automation (2000)
12. Lamarche, F.: Topoplan: a topological path planner for real time human navigation under floor and ceiling constraints. Computer Graphics Forum (2)
13. Latombe, J.C.: Robot Motion Planning. Kluwer Academic Publishers (1991)
14. Lau, M., Kuffner, J.: Behavior planning for character animation. In: Proc. of Symposium on Computer Animation (2005)
15. LaValle, S.M.: Planning Algorithms. Cambridge University Press (2006)
16. Levine, S., Lee, Y., Koltun, V., Popović, Z.: Space-time planning with parameterized locomotion controllers. Transactions on Graphics (TOG) 30(3) (2011)
17. Li, T.Y., Huang, P.Z.: Planning humanoid motions with striding ability in a virtual environment. In: Int. Conf. on Robotics and Automation (2004)
18. Pabst, S., Koch, A., Straßer, W.: Fast and scalable cpu/gpu collision detection for rigid and deformable surfaces. Computer Graphics Forum 29 (2010)
19. Pan, J., Lauterbach, C., Manocha, D.: g-planner: Real-time motion planning and global navigation using gpus. In: AAAI Conference on Artificial Intelligence (2010)
20. Safonova, A., Hodgins, J.K.: Construction and optimal search of interpolated motions graphs. ACM Transactions on Graphics 26(3) (2007)
21. Shiller, Z., Yamane, K., Nakamura, Y.: Planning motion patterns of human figures using a multi-layered grid and the dynamics filter. In: IEEE ICRA (2001)
22. Sud, A., Gayle, R., Andersen, E., Guy, S., Lin, M., Manocha, D.: Real-time navigation of independent agents using adaptive roadmaps. In: Symposium on Virtual Reality Software and Technology (2007)
23. Teschner, M., Kimmerle, S., Heidelberger, B., Zachmann, G., Raghupathi, L., Fuhrmann, A., Cani, M., Faure, F., Magnenat-Thalmann, N., Strasser, W., et al.: Collision detection for deformable objects. In: CGF, vol. 24 (2005)
24. Zucker, M., Kuffner, J., Branicky, M.: Multipartite rrts for rapid replanning in dynamic environments. In: IEEE ICRA (2007)

Automatic Generation of Suboptimal NavMeshes

Ramon Oliva and Nuria Pelechano

Universitat Politècnica de Catalunya, Barcelona, Spain
ramon.oliva.martinez@gmail.com, npelechano@lsi.upc.edu

Abstract. Most current games perform navigation in virtual environments through A* for path finding combined with a local movement algorithm. Navigation Meshes are the most popular approach to combine path finding with local movement. This paper presents a new Automatic Navigation Mesh Generator (ANavMG) that subdivides any polygon representing the environment, with or without holes, into a suboptimal number of convex cells where local movement algorithms can be applied without deadlocks. We introduce the concept of convex relaxation to further reduce the number of cells depending on the flexibility of the local movement algorithm. Finally we show results of the ANavMG and its application to a multi player game.

Keywords: Navigation meshes, Convex decomposition, Crowd navigation.

1 Introduction

Navigation meshes (NavMeshes) are commonly used to represent the walkable geometry within a virtual environment. Path finding can then be performed on a graph which abstracts away the geometry details, by representing each walkable area as a cell and the crossing segments between cells, as the portals of the graph.

When creating these NavMeshes we have two main restrictions: the first one given by the path finding algorithm which implies reducing the number of cells so that the path finding algorithm will find a suitable route as fast as possible, while the second one is given by the local movement algorithm and it implies having convex cells so that agents can move in a straight line between any two points of the cell.

In many cases, game designers need to create these navigation meshes by hand, which is extremely time consuming and can introduce errors which may either leave areas of the walkable space not accessible to the Non Player Character (NPC), get the NPCs stuck in concave regions, or create paths that do not look natural.

In this paper we introduce a new approach to automatically obtain NavMeshes for a given environment. For clarity, we will explain the algorithm for the case of 2D environments, where the input polygon representing the environment can be seen as the floor plan, and the holes represent static obstacles. This implies that we are not currently handling environments consisting of several levels with staircases, ramps, etc., but we will explain how the method could be easily extended to 3D.

The main contribution of this paper is an algorithm that takes as an input any 2D simple polygon (i.e. no self-intersections) with or without holes, and automatically splits it into a suboptimal subdivision of convex polygons that are highly suited to path finding by avoiding the presence of both degenerated polygons and almost all ill-conditioned polygons. We also introduce the concept of convex relaxation to achieve smaller navigation meshes based on the flexibility of the local movement algorithm being used for obstacle avoidance.

There is a trade-off when generating the NavMesh between having the minimum number of cells possible, so that path finding can run as fast as possible, and having portals that best guarantee natural traversals when applying local movement. Therefore the overall goals of our navigation mesh generator are:

1) To achieve as few cells as possible
2) To achieve portals as short as possible (since it introduces less inaccuracies when setting attractors to drive the natural movement of the agents).
3) To avoid cells with interior angles close to zero, since it complicates the local movements and leads to agents being physically in more than two cells simultaneously. (For the rest of the paper, we shall define an ill-conditioned polygon as a polygon with interior angles close to zero.)

In this paper we are not concerned about the time complexity of our algorithm, since it can be executed during pre-processing, and given that it only deals with static geometry, no further changes need to be made at run time. Dynamic obstacles and other agents are avoided through local movement techniques based on Reynolds' steering behaviors [13].

Once the subdivision is created, we automatically generate the cell and portal graph (CPG) representing the environment, where cells are the convex polygons resulting from the subdivision, and portals are the segments created to subdivide the original polygon into convex cells.

We finally present an example of a multi player game where path finding is carried out through A* over the generated NavMesh and movement within cells and dynamic obstacle avoidance are performed through steering behaviors. The physical library *Bullet* [2] has been integrated for several purposes including: speed up of the local movement simulation, guarantee non overlapping between agents, and keeping track of agents' within each cell to quickly update their mental maps in cases where agents are accidentally pushed through portals. Section 4 shows results of our ANavMG as well as multi agent navigation in a game application.

2 Related Work

The concept of *Navigation Mesh* was introduced by Snook in his paper *Simplified 3D Movement and Pathfinding Using Navigation Meshes* [14]. He also proposed some ideas to acquire a good *NavMesh* based on polygon triangulation, but the method does not consider the creation of ill-conditioned cells that could introduce problems when local movement methods are applied.

In most games navigation meshes are used to perform path finding. The navigation mesh is then represented through a Cell and Portal Graph (CPG), where the cells correspond to convex walkable areas, and the portals correspond to the segments that are shared by adjacent cells and that can be used for crossing between those cells [11].

Navigation has also been performed through roadmaps [7], Voronoi diagrams [15] or hierarchical representation of informed environments [10]. Many techniques have been introduced for local movement within convex cells [1][11][13]. Lerner et. al. [8] presented an algorithm to automatically generate a CPG for visibility that worked both for interiors and exterior scenarios but, since the goal of their algorithm was visibility, their method generates cells that are not guaranteed to be convex. Haumount, et. al. [1] introduced an algorithm for generating CPG of interiors based on a voxelization followed by a watershed.

Hertel and Mehlhorn [5] presented a non optimal partition by diagonals, which works only for polygons without holes. The algorithm first triangulates the polygon and then removes inessential diagonals. Partitions based on diagonals are commonly used in location problems where they need to keep the total number of vertices of the polygon. But when doing a partition for navigation, it is not strictly necessary to maintain the number of vertices, and thus new vertices can be created if they result in a better partition (meaning less cells or portals that lead to more natural looking movement of the agents).

Kallman proposes an automatic triangular *NavMesh* generation method [1] based on Delaunay's triangulation, so it generates the lowest possible number of degenerated triangles. Using a triangular *NavMesh* is a good first approach because it guarantees that every cell created is convex, so a character can move in a straight line from any pair of points inside the cell. In addition, geometric operations over triangles are very efficient. The main drawback is that many unnecessary cells are created, increasing the time for calculating a path between two given cells, which can be specially problematic in videogames where we need a real-time response.

Although in many cases the *NavMesh* is created by hand, some Game Engines and third parties programs offer the functionality of an automatically generated navigation mesh for a given virtual map, but they generate a great number of ill-conditioned cells or are map-type-specific. For example, Valve [17] uses a *NavMesh* generator based on subdividing the virtual map by quadrilaters. This method creates a non-optimal convex decomposition and is not really extensible to maps with arbitrary geometry.

Unreal Engine [16] has its own *NavMesh* generator, but it generates a great number of ill-conditioned convex polygons that can affect the application of local movement methods and the quality of generated paths. Recast [12] is actually the open-source *NavMesh* generator most used on popular games such as Bulletstorm, but we have detected that unnecessary cells are created that could easily be merged together, decreasing the final number of cells.

3 The Automatic Navigation Mesh Generator (ANavMG)

There are two possibilities when subdividing a polygon into convex cells. The first one consists of subdividing by adding diagonals, which are edges between pairs of vertices in the original geometry. The second one consists of using segments which are edges between a vertex of the geometry and a new point created on the boundary of the original geometry. The algorithm presented in this paper carries out a partition based on segments, and thus we are not limited by the position of the vertices in the original geometry.

3.1 Previous Concepts

The approach followed by our algorithm consists of subdividing the input polygon by first detecting which are the notches (concave vertices, i.e. interior angle larger than π) that appear in the polygon and then splitting them by creating portals so that for each original notch in the geometry, we will split it into two new angles that are both convex (i.e. interior angle smaller than π). In this way, we guarantee that if all the notches in the original polygon are split into convex angles we will obtain a partition consisting only of convex cells.

In order to ensure that we only require one new segment in the geometry to split the notch into two convex angles, we define the area or interest, I_i of a notch v_i given by two edges of the geometry, $e_{i-1,i}$ and $e_{i,i+1}$ as the resulting interior area of prolonging $e_{i-1,i}$ and $e_{i,i+1}$ as we indicate in figure 1 (left), where $e_{i-1,i}$ is the edge that joins v_{i-1} with v_i.

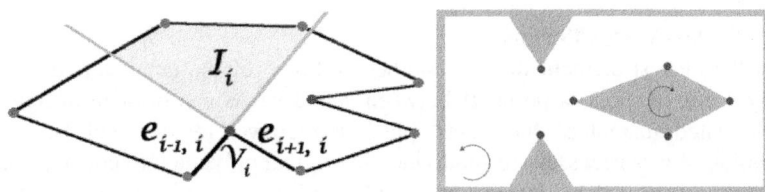

Fig. 1. On the left, we show the interest area, I_i of a notch v_i. Green vertices are convex, and blue vertices are notches that need to be split. On the right, we show a simple example of an input given to the algorithm, with the order of the vertices implying polygon (*in white*) or holes (*in grey*).

The floor plan of the virtual environment where we want our characters to navigate is given as a simple polygon, and the vertices are given in counter-clockwise order. Any obstacle within the virtual environment will be given as a polygon with its vertices in clockwise order. Obstacles can be seen as holes in the main polygon that represents the entire map (figure 1, right).

The input geometry consists of a polygon P enclosing other polygons $H_1, ..., H_m$, where all holes are simple empty polygons. Let δP be the boundary of the polygon P, and δH_i the boundary hole δH_i. We assume that the following conditions apply:

$$\begin{aligned} &1)\quad \delta P \cap \delta H_i = \emptyset, \quad \forall i = 1,...,h \\ &2)\quad H_i \cap H_j = \emptyset, \quad \forall i \neq i \end{aligned} \qquad (1)$$

The first step of the algorithm consists of determining which vertices are notches. This step is performed through an orientation test based on calculating the signed area of the triangle defined by three consecutive vertices, v_i, v_{i+1}, v_{l+2}:

$$A(v_i v_{i+1} v_{i+2}) = \frac{1}{2} \begin{vmatrix} \overline{v_i v_{i+1}}_{,x} & \overline{v_{i+1} v_{i+2}}_{,x} \\ \overline{v_i v_{i+1}}_{,y} & \overline{v_{i+1} v_{i+2}}_{,y} \end{vmatrix} \qquad (2)$$

If the area $A(v_i, v_{i+1}, v_{l+2})$ is positive, it means that vertex v_{i+2} is on the left hand side of edge $e_{i,i+1}$ given by the previous vertices v_i, and v_{i+1}. If it is negative, it means that

v_{i+2} is on the right hand side of edge $e_{i,i+1}$. So for the main polygon which is given in counter-clockwise order, if the area is negative it means that v_{i+1} is a notch and thus needs to be split, whereas for the holes, given in clockwise order, we will also find a notch when the area is negative. We will introduce all notches of the geometry in a vertex list $\mathcal{V}$ to be treated in order. This step has cost $O(n)$ where n is the total number of vertices of the geometry.

3.2 Creating Portals

For each v_i in $\mathcal{V}$, the algorithm looks for the closest element in the geometry that falls within its area of interest I_i to create a portal with it. This has cost $O(n \cdot r)$, where n=*number of vertices*, and r=*number of notches*. Elements can be other vertices, edges of the original geometry, or portals. Depending on the element being selected, we classify three types of portals: vertex-vertex, vertex-edge, vertex-portal. Each of these cases needs to be treated differently.

3.2.1 Vertex-Vertex Portals
When the closest element to v_i is another vertex v_j of the geometry, the algorithm simply needs to create a portal p_i between v_i and v_j. As can be seen in figure 2, the portal created guarantees that v_i gets split in two convex regions, and thus no further processing of v_i is necessary to subdivide the original polygon into convex cells. If the other vertex v_j was also contained in $\mathcal{V}$ (which means that it is also a notch), then the algorithm also checks whether by creating portal p_i, v_j gets split in two convex angles. This will happen exclusively when v_i falls within I_j as we can see in the example shown in figure 2.

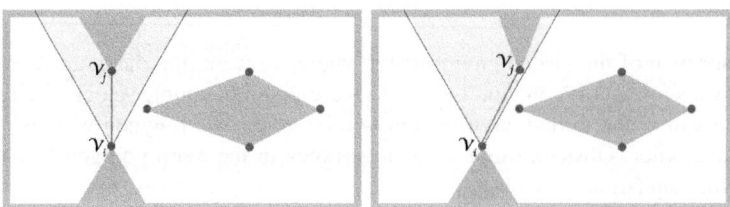

Fig. 2. Vertex-Vertex portal creation. On left, v_i also falls within I_j, so it can be removed from $\mathcal{V}$, on the right, v_i does not fall within I_j and since it is a notch it still needs to be split.

3.2.2 Vertex-Edge Portals
When the closest element to v_i is an edge $e_{j,j+1}$ of the geometry, the algorithm needs to create a portal p_i between v_i and a point q in the segment $e_{j,j+1}$. Since we want portals to be as short as possible, we first consider the closest point within the segment, which is calculated as the projection of v_i over $e_{j,j+1}$, so in this case $q=(proj_e\ v_i)$.

If q falls within I_i then a new portals is created and the algorithm proceeds with the next notch in $\mathcal{V}$ (see figure 3, left), but it could be possible that even though the edge $e_{j,j+1}$ is the closest element to v_i, we could have its projection falling outside $e_{j,j+1}$ or outside the interest area, I_i, and thus the portal between those two points would not be enough to split v_i in two convex angles (see figure 3 center and right).

Therefore if the projection is not a good candidate to create a unique portal, the algorithm considers four new candidates:

- the two end vertices of $e_{j,j+1}$, v_j and v_{j+1} (see figure 3, center).
- the two intersection points q_l and q_r (if they exist) where q_l is the intersection between the closest edge $e_{j,j+1}$, and the result of extending the segment $e_{i-1,i}$ (segment on the left of v_i), and q_r is the intersection between $e_{j,j+1}$, and the result of extending the segment $e_{i,i+1}$ (segment on the right of v_i) (see figure 3, right). There is a chance that depending on the orientation of each segment, none of those intersections exist, and therefore only the ends of segment $e_{j,j+1}$ are considered.

Among the four possible vertices mentioned above, the algorithm selects the closest one that falls within I_i and a new portal is created between v_i and the selected vertex.

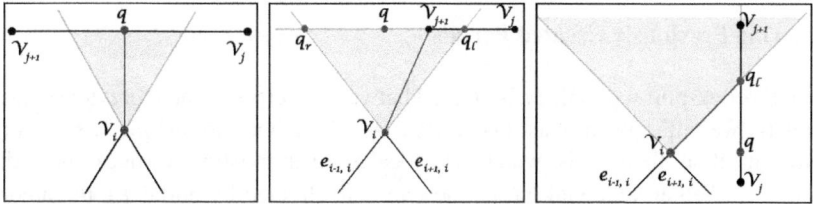

Fig. 3. Vertex-Edge portal. Candidate point q being the projection *(left)*, candidates being the end points of segment v_{j+1} *(center)*, and candidate points being the intersections *(right)*.

In figure 3 we can see the three different types of portals created in the category of vertex-edge portal. As we can see the cases on the left (projection) and the right (intersection points) are the only cases where new vertices are added into the geometry. These vertices can never be notches, therefore the algorithm does not need to do any further processing with them.

3.2.3 Vertex-Portal Portals

In the case where the closest element to v_i in the geometry is a previously created portal, the treatment when creating portals differs from the vertex-edge portal since we do not want to have intersecting portals (or T-shapes), which would be the case for calculating a projection or intersection over an existing portal.

Therefore we assume that when the closest element is a portal p_k, we will need to create a new portal p_i with either end vertex of segment p_k. The algorithm selects the closest vertex that falls within I_i (figure 4, left and center). But since only vertices that fall within I_i can guarantee that v_i will get split into two convex areas, if none of the end vertices of p_k satisfy that requirement (figure 4, right), then the algorithm needs to create two portals instead of one. The new portals will be p_i which joins v_i with the left end of p_k and p_{i+1} which joins v_i with the right end of p_k. Notice that given the type of geometry we are dealing with, the interior angle between p_i and p_{i+1} will always be smaller than π, and therefore we guarantee that when adding these two portals, v_i will get split in three convex regions.

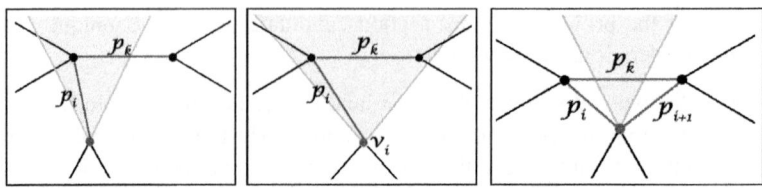

Fig. 4. Vertex-Portal portal. Only one end of p_k falls within I_i *(left)*, both ends of p_k fall within I_i *(center)*, and none of the ends of p_k fall within I_i *(right)*.

This case of portal creation is the only one that may require two new portals instead of just one per notch, but in most cases when creating these portals we will be able to remove the original portal p_k, and thus we are on average creating one portal per notch.

Removing Previously Created Portals

When a vertex-portal portal, p_i, is created between a vertex v_j and a previously created portal p_k, we will have at least one vertex, v_i, where both portals meet, since portals always meet at their ends which are located over existing vertices. In order to determine whether we could merge the two cells divided by portal p_k, the algorihtm checks whether p_k is still a necessary portal, since it is possible that by adding p_i to vertex v_j, this vertex already gets split in two convex regions, and thus there is no need to have two portals splitting one vertex.

To be able to remove portal p_k it is necessary to check whether both the left and right vertices of the portal need p_k not to be a notch. This step is performed by calculating the interior angle between the two neighouring segments of portal p_k at each end vertex (which can be edges of the geometry or other portals) and testing for convexity. If they both pass the convexity test, then we can remove p_k, and thus merge two convex cells into one larger convex cell (see figure 5).

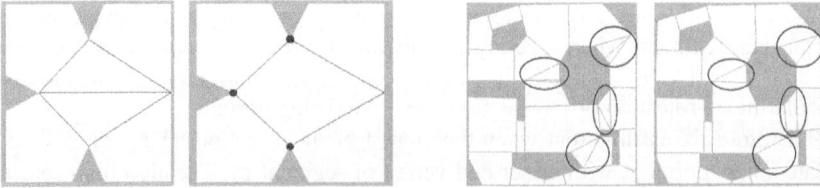

Fig. 5. Removal of previously created portal, p_k when creating a new set of portals p_i and p_{i+1} *(left)*, or several cases of just one new portal being created *(right)*

3.3 Convexity Relaxation

A vertex is defined to be convex, if its internal angle is smaller or equal than π, otherwise it is a notch. This is the mathematical definition of convexity but, in some applications such as the creation of navigation meshes, it may not be necessary to consider such a strict definition. As described previously in this paper, most navigation meshes consist of a set of convex cells with portals representing the traversal segments between them. Movement within a convex cell and between cells is driven by some local movement algorithm which can usually deal relatively easily with small concavities through obstacle avoidance behavior which also applies to static geometry (such as walls). Therefore, depending on the local movement algorithm being implemented, we can relax the definition of convexity by allowing a certain threshold τ. Relaxing the definition of convexity results in a smaller number of portals since more cells can be merged together into τ-convex cells, where τ is the threshold given by the local movement algorithm. We provide the following definitions:

Def: a vertex v_i is said to have τ-convexity if its internal angle is smaller than $\pi + \tau$.

Relaxing convexity affects not only the classification of vertices into notches, but also the definition of the area of interest of a node.

Def: an area of interest I_i is said to have τ-convexity if its internal angle is $\alpha_i + \tau$, where α_i is the original internal angle of I_i before applying convexity relaxation.

In order to avoid obtaining degenerate or non-simple polygons, it is necessary to refine the definition of the threshold per vertex, so that we ensure that the best candidate for any given vertex v_i, will never be laying over the same edge as v_i, or causing an intersection with the boundary of the original polygon. This is achieved by limiting $\alpha + \tau$ to always be smaller than π. And this leads us to the next definition:

Def: a polygon P is said to have been split into τ-*convexity* cells, when all its vertices have at most τ-*convexity*.

The effect of increasing the internal angle of the I_i with the threshold τ, implies a larger area to look for candidates, which not only reduces the total number of cells, but also implies a reduction in the number of ill-conditioned polygons (see figure 6).

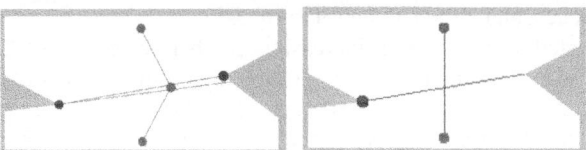

Fig. 6. On the left a cell created with strict convexity, on the right the same scenario but applying the concept of convexity relaxation

3.4 Discussion on the Navigation Mesh Created

Considering a polygon P with r notches, let the optimal number of convex cells, O be within the following bounds:

$$\left\lceil \frac{r}{2} \right\rceil + 1 \leq O \leq 2r + 1 \tag{3}$$

Since at most two diagonals are essential for any notch [5] then any subdivision without inessential diagonals is within four times of the minimum subdivision (which gives us the upper bound). This holds even for polygons with holes, as proved in [4]. The lower bound is given by the best case scenario where we only need one portal to join pairs of notches.

In the case of subdivision based on diagonals, there may be more than one edge created per concave vertex, since it is possible that no vertex of the geometry fall within the area of interest. If we create an edge outside this area, we will split the current concave vertex into two regions, one convex and one concave, therefore, we will still need additional edges to guarantee that all the final regions are convex.

Since our algorithm is not limited to diagonals, it only needs one new edge per concave vertex, which indicates that our number of cells will be of $O(r)$. This indicates that our method is always going to give a subdivision with fewer cells than any solution based exclusively on diagonals. In fact as we will see in the results section, our algorithm provides a subdivision of less than r cells.

4 Results and Future Work

The method presented in this paper generates navigation meshes that can successfully be used for path finding and driving local movement between cells. The subdivision meshes generated in all cases contain a number of cells lower than the number of notches in the geometry. Since calculating the optimal subdivision mesh for a convex polygon with holes is NP-hard, we consider that any algorithm that can guarantee a maximum number of cells equal to the number of notches can be considered a good suboptimal subdivision.

Another advantage of our method is that we obtain NavMeshes without degenerated polygons, and almost no ill-conditioned polygons. Therefore our NavMeshes can be used with any local movement technique guaranteeing natural looking movement of the characters.

Even though the time complexity of our method was not the main concern, the ANavMG can generate NavMeshes with a temporal cost of $O(r \cdot n)$, where r is the number of notches, and n the number of vertices.

We have tested scenarios with increasing numbers of obstacles (see table 1), and the results show that for the first version of the algorithm (strict convexity rule and no elimination of old portals as new ones are generated) we achieve a ratio on average of 0.8 cells per notch. When applying the optimization of previous portal removal explained in section 3.2.3, we achieve an improvement of 10%, with the new ratio being 0.71 cells per notch. Finally the contribution based on convexity relaxation (section 3.3), achieves a ratio of 0.67 cells per notch on average, which implies an improvement of around 20% with τ-convexity=5°.

As the number of vertices in the geometry increases, we observe that the ratio of cells/notches drops, since there are more chances of a vertex-vertex portal splitting simultaneously two notches, and thus reducing the number of portals per notch needed towards 0.5. We have tested scenarios of up to 136 vertices, with 106 being notches, and we believe that the average ratios calculated would be reduced even further as we test larger scenarios.

Figure 7 shows an example of a NavMesh obtained with ANavMG. (The following video *http://www.lsi.upc.edu/~npelechano/videos/MIG2011_NavMesh.avi* shows the result generated step by step as well as its associated CPG.

Table 1. Results from 8 scenarios with increasing number of notches. For each version of the algorithm we have calculated the number of resulting cells, and the ratio cells/notches.

Geom.	#Notches	#cells original	ratio c/r	#cells Portal removal	ratio c/r	#cells Conv. relaxation	ratio c/r
1	15	15	1.00	12	0.80	12	0.80
2	22	21	0.95	17	0.77	16	0.73
3	32	27	0.84	22	0.69	21	0.66
4	43	34	0.79	30	0.70	29	0.67
5	55	39	0.71	38	0.69	35	0.64
6	68	46	0.68	46	0.68	42	0.62
7	93	63	0.68	63	0.66	58	0.62
8	106	73	0.69	72	0.68	62	0.58
Average			0.8		0.71		0.67

Game Application: Capture the Flag

Our ANavMG generator has been successfully integrated into *Ninja Flag*, a tactical multiplayer online game, inspired by the famous outdoor sport called *Capture The Flag*, that we have developed.

To determine how a character moves from one cell to another and to describe its behavior inside a convex cell, we use several steering behaviors [13]. Attractors are set based on the agents' projection over the portals, as they move within a cell. This avoids agents sharing the same attraction points when crossing and leads to natural looking movement.

Overlapping is solved by integrating the physical library *Bullet* [1]. To keep track of characters within a cell at all times, we employ *Bullet's GhostObjects*, which are special physic bodies that do not interact with the rest of the standard physics bodies of the simulation, but they track an updated list of the objects they are in contact with.

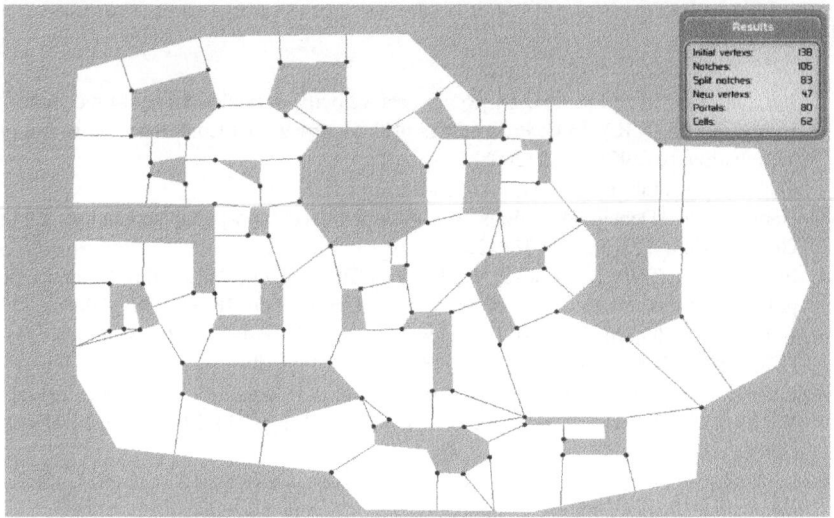

Fig. 7. Example of a NavMesh with 106 notches and 62 cells. Green lines represent portals.

5 Conclusions and Future Work

The ANavMG provides an automatic convex cells subdivision for any simple polygon with our without holes. The polygons can represent the floor plan of a given environment, with holes representing static objects such as walls. Although the current work has been tested with environments consisting of only one level, it could be expanded by considering each different level individually, and then creating cells for ramps, stairs, etc. connecting two levels following the same idea.

We have introduced a novel algorithm which focuses on the idea of sequentially splitting notches into convex areas instead of being limited to some preliminary triangle subdivision. Since our approach is based on subdividing the original polygons with segments, instead of diagonals, we achieve on average a smaller number of convex cells in the environment than previous work in the literature based on diagonals.

In this paper we have also included the concept of convexity relaxation, based on the fact that small concavities in the environment can be easily overcome with most local movement algorithms, and thus we state that for navigation meshes it is not strictly necessary to be limited to interior vertices smaller than π. We have experimentally observed that a τ-convexity of 5° is a conservative value which works well in all the tested scenarios, however in the future we would like to further explore this idea, so that the τ-convexity can be automatically calculated, and moreover, dependent not only on the interior angle of the vertex, but also on other factors such as the length of the adjacent edges, or the type of vertices at either end of the adjacent edges. Adjusting the τ-convexity per vertex, will allow us to have even larger values for the threshold τ which will lead to an even smaller number of cells generated.

Acknowledgments. We would like to acknowledge the Spanish Ministry grant TIN2010-20590-C02-01.

References

1. Berg, J., Lin, M., Manocha, D.: Reciprocal velocity obstacles for real-time multi-agent navigation. In: ICRA 2008: Proceedings of the International Conference on Robotics and Automation, pp. 1928–1935 (2008)
2. Bullet Physics Library, http://bulletphysics.org
3. Haumont, D., Debeir, O., Sillion, F.: Volumetric cell-and-portal generation. Computer Graphics Forum 22(3), 303–312 (2003)
4. Fernandez, J., Toth, B., Canovas, L., Pelegrin, B.: A practical algorithm for decomposing polygonal domains into convex polygons by diagonals. TOP 16, 367–387 (2008)
5. Hertel, S., Mehlhorn, K.: Fast Triangulation of Simple Polygons. In: Karpinski, M. (ed.) FCT 1983. LNCS, vol. 158, pp. 207–218. Springer, Heidelberg (1983)
6. Kallmann, M.: Navigation Queries from Triangular Meshes. In: Boulic, R., Chrysanthou, Y., Komura, T. (eds.) MIG 2010. LNCS, vol. 6459, pp. 230–241. Springer, Heidelberg (2010)
7. Lamarche, F.: TopoPlan: a topological path planner for real time human navigation under floor and ceiling constraints. Computer Graphics Forum 28(2), 649–658 (2009)

8. Lerner, A., Chrysanthou, Y., Cohen-Or, D.: Efficient Cells-and-portals Partitioning. Computer Animation and Virtual Worlds 17(1), 21–40 (2006)
9. Lien, J.-M., Amato, N.M.: Approximate convex decomposition of polygons. In: ACM Symposium on Computational Geometry, vol. 35(1-2), pp. 100–123 (2006)
10. Mekni, M.: Hierarchical path planning for situated agents in informed virtual geographic environments. In: Proc. of the 3rd International ICST Conference on Simulation Tools and Techniques, pp. 1–10 (2010)
11. Pelechano, N., Allbeck, J.M., Badler, N.I.: Controlling individual agents in high-density crowd simulation. In: Proc. of the ACM SIGGRAPH/Eurographics Symposium on Computer Animation, pp. 99–108 (2007)
12. Recast Toolkit, http://code.google.com/p/recastnavigation
13. Reynolds, C.W.: Steering Behaviors For Autonomous Characters. In: Game Developers Conference, San Jose, pp. 763–782 (1999)
14. Snook, G.: Simplified 3D Movement and Pathfinding Using Navigation Meshes, Game Programming Gems, Ed. Mark DeLoura, Charles River Media (2000)
15. Sud, A., Andersen, E., Curtis, S., Lin, M.C., Manocha, D.: Real-time path planning in dynamic virtual environments using multiagent navigation graphs. IEEE Transactions on Visualization and Computer Graphics 14, 526–538 (2008)
16. Unreal Engine's NavMesh Generation Method,
http://udn.epicgames.com/Three/NavigationMeshReference.html
17. Valve's NavMesh Generation Method,
http://developer.valvesoftware.com/wiki/Navigation_Meshes

Roadmap-Based Level Clearing of Buildings

Samuel Rodriguez and Nancy M. Amato*

Parasol Lab, Dept. Computer Science and Engineering, Texas A&M University
sor8786@neo.tamu.edu, amato@tamu.edu

Abstract. In this paper we describe a roadmap-based approach for a multi-agent search strategy to clear a building or multi-story environment. This approach utilizes an encoding of the environment in the form of a graph (roadmap) that is used to encode feasible paths through the environment. The roadmap is partitioned into regions, e.g., one per level, and we design region-based search strategies to cover and clear the environment. We can provide certain guarantees within this roadmap-based framework on coverage and the number of agents needed. Our approach can handle complex and realistic environments where many approaches are restricted to simple 2D environments.

1 Introduction

Searching an environment is a problem that has been extensively studied and has application in games, virtual reality, computational geometry, and robotics. In this problem, the searching agents have requirements of either clearing an environment or searching as much or as quickly as possible. This can be a highly cooperative scenario which may involve many agents working together to achieve their goal. Target scenarios include searching for adversarial agents, guarding an environment and search and rescue to find people in distress or discover dangerous areas. The target environments of interest often include simple one level environments, but in games and virtual reality, environments often include terrains and multi-level structures. Our approach is not only applicable to 2D planar environments but can be used for multiple level environments.

The encoding of this problem has been done in a number of ways. Many approaches simplify the environmental representation to be able to provide more complete solutions. For example, graph-based approaches to the pursuit-evasion game often limit the agents to moving on the nodes and edges [19]. Geometric approaches limit the types of environments that can be handled as they are often 2D, polygonal environments [9]. Visibility restrictions on agents are one of the main limiting factors [10,8]. While providing a means for developing a more complete solution, these assumptions limit the scope of the problem and

---

* This research supported in part by NSF awards CRI-0551685, CCF-0833199, CCF-0830753, IIS-096053, IIS-0917266 by THECB NHARP award 000512-0097-2009, by Chevron, IBM, Intel, Oracle/Sun and by Award KUS-C1-016-04, made by King Abdullah University of Science and Technology (KAUST).

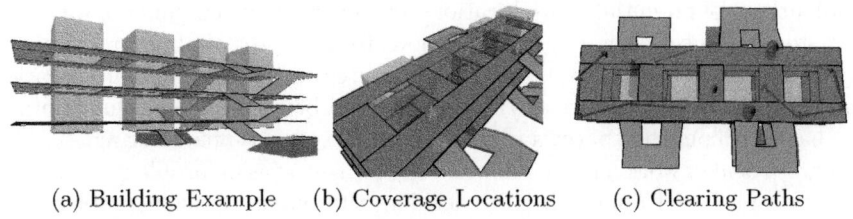

(a) Building Example (b) Coverage Locations (c) Clearing Paths

Fig. 1. (a) A building example with four levels and multiple passages between each level. (b) Agents clearing a level by using coverage locations. (c) Clearing paths generated for top-level given agent visibility restrictions.

consequently the applicability of the techniques to more complex scenarios. Extending to scenarios where 3D visibility is considered is essential for handling more complex problems.

In our previous work [21,20], we proposed our overall approach to pursuit-evasion in complex 3D environments which included basic heuristic search, pursuit and evasion behaviors. In [20], we also presented a tracking algorithm which was applicable to 3D structured environments that would allow agents to track other agents that have left an agent's view.

In this paper, we develop specialized search strategies for building environments with multiple levels. Within our search strategies we partition the environment into regions (levels) and apply ideas which have been applied in simple 2D environments to each region. In this way we can handle complex 3D environments and offer some guarantees given the underlying roadmap. This approach is also tunable so that the searching agents can function with varying levels of intelligence. As will be shown in the results, the quality of the underlying roadmap and agent capabilities can affect how well the agents clear/cover each level. Also, depending on the difficulty a game designer might desire a scenario to be, our approach can give insight into the coverage that can be attained given the number of agents available.

2 Related Work

In this section, we describe work that is relevant to the problem that we consider. This problem is similar to the art gallery problem and the pursuit evasion problem. Our extension to 3D building-like structures differentiates our approach from others that have been proposed.

An overview of the art gallery problem is presented in [18] which includes solutions, bounds and variants. In the most basic form of this problem, the goal is to cover a simple polygon with as few guards as possible. The polygon is considered covered if every point in the polygon lies within the visibility range of one of the guards. A discussion of the 3D version of the same problem (guarding a polyhedron) is included. An experimental approach to finding guard locations is presented in [2] where the goal is to heuristically find guard locations. A candidate set of potential guard locations are generated in a number of ways. The next step is the selection of guard locations from the set of all guard locations. In our approach, we use a similar greedy strategy for selecting guard locations from the selections of nodes at the current level being searched. Our approach also has to account for pathways between levels to guarantee clearing.

A great deal of work has been done on the pursuit-evasion problem. A classical, purely graph-based approach [19] considers the pursuit-evasion problem on a graph in which agents can only move on edges between nodes and where the pursuer can capture the evader by occupying the same graph node. Another classic approach for polygonal environments is described in [9]. There has also been work in finding exact bounds on the number of pursuers needed in 2D environments [17]. A frontier approach is described in [23] based on exploring undiscovered portions of the environment.

Roadmap-based pursuit-evasion is described in [11] where the pursuer and evader both share a roadmap, navigate solely on the graph, and play different versions of the pursuit-evasion game. The versions of these games include determining if the pursuer can eventually collide with the evader and if collision can occur within some predefined amount of time.

In [3,4], the benefits of integrating roadmap-based path planning techniques with flocking techniques were explored. A variety of group behaviors, including exploring and covering, were simulated utilizing a roadmap. This work was done in strictly 2D environments.

Our roadmap-based approach to 3D pursuit-evasion problems was first proposed in [21]. The work focused on different types of 3D problems that could be studied using a roadmap-based framework which included terrains, multi-level environments, in crowds of agents and for actual robots. The work did not include in depth analysis on guaranteed searching behaviors or requirements necessary to find a target in an environment.

Many forms of the pursuit-evasion problem have been considered. A graph-based approach to the pursuit-evasion problem is given in [16] where agents use either blocking or sweeping actions by teams of robots to detect all intruders in unknown 2D environments. One form of the problem [14] involves a team of agents with the goal of maximizing the average number of targets that are observed by at least one of the team members. Large teams of robots have been considered to detect intruders with communication allowed between agents within some range and with no map of the environment [15]. Other forms of collaboration between searching agents have been considered where agents utilize frontier information [6] with communication to switch between roles [7].

An agent's visibility plays an important role in what the agents detect in the environment and what kinds of environments can be handled. The problem of restricting or limiting the amount of visibility is considered in [10] with the field of view being variable in [8]. In [5] a team of agents with limited sensory abilities attempt to capture a single evading agent using sweep formations. The problem of pursuit-evasion on height maps, which restrict agent visibility is described in [13].

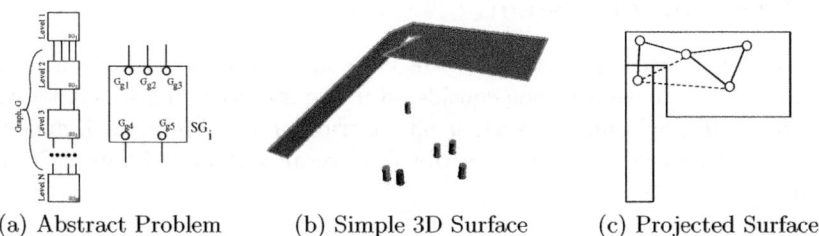

Fig. 2. (a) An abstraction of the problem is given showing a complete graph, G, with the subgraphs labeled $SG_{1..N}$. Each level in our building construction can be decomposed to subgraphs, with exits defining connections between other levels. (b) An example 3D surface with a long ramp leading up to the main level. (c) The surface projected to 2D. Also shown are sample configurations with valid and invalid connections.

3 Problem Definition

The search strategy presented here is for clearing a building-like environment which consists of multiple levels with stairwells between levels. The goal is to develop search strategies that can guarantee a clearing of the environment. A geometric covering of the environment would ensure that when agents are stationed at guard locations, the environment would be completely covered (i.e. each point defined by the surface at that level would lie within an agent's view radius). A clearing of the environment is similar to coverage, however, agents that are clearing only have to guarantee that portions of the environment that have been cleared do not become recontaminated.

While we do not guarantee that the geometric model of the environment is covered, we provide guarantees within our roadmap-based framework. We can guarantee that, given a set of agents, a certain percentage of the roadmap (which represents the environment) is covered at each level. We can also provide the maximum number of agents needed to cover or clear each level of the environment. The overall behavior is a clearing of the environment from one end of the environment to the other (bottom-up or top-down).

3.1 Environment Encoding

The building-like environments studied here are composed of levels, stairwells and exits. Each level represents a floor which the agents should try to cover. Adjacent levels are connected by stairwells. Input to the problem includes connections between levels and stairwells. Exits for a level are where stairwells connect to the level. We use the exits to define areas of the graph that must be guarded in order to guarantee a clearing. Graph algorithms could be used to find these portions of the graph automatically. A map of this type of environment has a structure like the graph shown in Figure 2(a). The subgraphs are shown, labeled SG_i, which represent valid movements at level i.

4 Overview of System

Our roadmap-based approach allows us to handle many classical problems along with many that have not been considered in the literature. This includes agents moving in 3D environments such as on a terrain, in multi-level environments or in areas with crowds. Here we describe our overall system and approach to this problem.

4.1 Approach

Overall, our approach uses a real-time simulation which consists of the movement of agents (utilizing the roadmap), complex pursuit/evasion/search strategies, and interesting agent interactions with both the environment and other agents. We have designed and implemented a simulation infrastructure for storing and manipulating agents, behaviors, the environment, groupings, and relationships between groups. The focus of this paper is on a search strategies within our framework.

Agents have the ability to have different parameters. This affects their knowledge of the environment, behavior, movement through the environment, and interactions. In the search strategy we consider here, the main parameter affecting the result is the agent's view radius. This parameter determines the distance at which points in the environments are visible.

The behaviors of agents determine how they react throughout the simulation. In our framework, agents have either individual or group-based behaviors. While an agent performing an individual behavior, operates mainly independently, a group behavior often deals with more complex coordination. The level clearing behavior that is described in this paper is a group-based behavior requiring coordination where a leader agent computes guard and coverage locations and other agents in the same search group use those goals when finding paths.

Visibility is mainly affected by two factors. The first is obstacles and surfaces which can block visibility in the environment. The second parameter, mentioned earlier, is an agent's view radius. For simplicity, we assume an agent has a full circular view angle although in our simulation we have the ability to restrict this angle. We also have the ability in our simulation to have visibility be further restricted by considering that agents may block one another's view in the environment.

4.2 Roadmaps

The roadmap is an encoding of the environment that gives agents insight into potential paths through the environment. The complex environment is reduced to this abstract representation through a two stage process. The first stage is a series of sampling valid configurations in the environment which is followed by a connection phase where samples are connected and valid edges are kept if they do not collide with the environment. Standard sampling techniques [12,1,22] can be used in the portion of the environment dictated by the plane and obstacles in the plane.

When agents also operate on surfaces, this sampling process consists of randomly selecting configurations that are on the surface, projected to the 2D plane, and then obtaining the height component by finding where the projected point belongs on the surface. On a surface, valid connections are made between samples on the same surface which have a straight line connecting them which is completely inside the projected surface. This allows agents to navigate on the surface. An example surface and its projection to a 2D surface is shown in Figure 2(b,c).

5 Level Clear Algorithms

Our level clearing algorithm is an intuitive approach to handle complex three-dimensional environments within our roadmap-based approach. It can be described as a process where agents iteratively attempt to clear adjacent levels of the environment until reaching the last level. This clearing process is done by guarding the stairwells between levels, which prevents recontamination from portions of the environment that have not been cleared. The first step is to generate a roadmap based on the environment. The roadmap is then partitioned into sub-graphs, as in Figure 2(a), based on the input configuration of the environment and exits and stairwells that exist. The partitioning is something that could be automated with more advanced graph-based techniques; we leave this for future work. The agents then search the environment from one level to the next until each level has been cleared. We describe two strategies for clearing of each level. The first strategy involves selecting coverage locations from the roadmap with the goal of covering the entire roadmap at a given level. The second strategy involves building clearing paths between portions of the roadmap that are cleared to uncleared areas until the roadmap (at that level) is fully cleared. The agents plan their paths to goal locations dictated by each strategy and traverse their path reaching the final goal. Once all agents are at the goal locations, the environment at that level is considered covered (to some extent) and the process can continue at the next level.

5.1 Strategy 1: Guard and Coverage Locations

The process of generating coverage locations for a given level, i, is shown in Algorithm 1. In this process, $nodes_i$ in the input roadmap at level i are first selected. Each exit at level i is considered a guard location G_{g_i}. These exits are located near stairwells and would prevent a target agent from entering or leaving the current level without being detected. These locations are shown in Figure 2(a) and correspond to input and output of the underlying subgraph at level i, SG_i. In our current problem formulation, these exit locations are input configurations.

The remaining problem is to cover level i as much as possible with the given agents. We achieve this using a greedy algorithm based on the roadmap nodes that were generated at level i. The nodes, $nodes_i$, which are covered by guard locations G_{g_i} are marked as cleared. Coverage locations, G_{c_i}, for level i are generated in a greedy manner such that the next node added to G_{c_i} is the node that will maximize coverage among all the remaining uncleared nodes in $nodes_i$. This is a process similar to what was presented in [2]. The number of agents needed to guarantee a covering of level i is $G_{g_i} + G_{c_i}$.

Overall, the maximum number of agents needed to guarantee a clearing of an environment is given by: $\max_{i \in env} \{G_{g_i} + G_{c_i}\}$ where i represents each level to clear and G_{g_i} are guard locations at each level and G_{c_i} are the coverage locations selected.

An interesting aspect to this solution is that the ordering of the returned coverage locations affects the amount of coverage. Often, the total number of searching agents needed may be much more than the number of agents available. In these cases, we can report the portion of each environment that would be covered based on the coverage value returned by the number of agents available. These agents would also attempt to maximize coverage by going to coverage locations in the order that they were selected based on the greedy algorithm presented in Algorithm 1.

Algorithm 1. Generate Coverage Locations

Input: environment env, roadmap $rdmp$, current level searching i
1: $nodes_i \leftarrow rdmp.\text{nodesAtLevel}(i)$
2: $G_{g_i} \leftarrow env.\text{ExitsAtLevel}(i)$
3: $markNodesCleared(nodes_i, G_{g_i})$
4: $G_{c_i} \leftarrow \emptyset$
5: **while** existNodesUncleared($nodes_i$) **do**
6:     $N_j \leftarrow$ uncleared node $\in nodes_i$ with max coverage
7:     $G_{c_i}\mathrel{+}= N_j$
8:     markNodesCleared($nodes_i, N_j$)
9: **end while**
10: **return** $\{ G_{g_i} + G_{c_i} \}$

5.2 Strategy 2: Guard Locations and Clearing Paths

The basic idea of this strategy is similiar to Strategy 1. However, when using clearing paths, agents can clear entire areas using the underlying encoding of the roadmap and cooperation between other agents. As in Algorithm 1, guard locations are generated initially and the nodes covered are marked as clear. The main difference is that instead of selecting the node that maximizes the coverage, the clearing path selected is one that maximizes the path traveled through the level as a way of maximizing the area covered by the next clearing path added. Due to space limitations, we only give an overview of how clearing paths are generated in our framework.

Clearing paths are started on the frontier of the area that is already covered (i.e. from nodes that are not already cleared). A clearing path, CP, keeps track of the nodes that are initially covered, N_{init}, and nodes that are currently covered,

N_{cur}. As a clearing path is built up we consider the set of potential moves to be the nodes that are outgoing from N_{cur} which are not in N_{cur} or N_{init}. A move is considered valid if moving to that node leaves the nodes leading to the previous outgoing nodes covered. In this way we can ensure clearing paths are built up which prevent their N_{cur} from becoming contaminated. We build the paths up from all frontier nodes and continue until no more valid moves exist. We use a greedy strategy to select the path that maximizes the area covered. We continue to build clearing paths until all nodes on a level are cleared.

5.3 Pathway Assignments

The process of pathway assignment is critical when attempting to guarantee that contamination of a covered region does not occur. As a simple example, a guard agent at a guard location on level i whose group of agents is progressing to level $i+1$ might naturally be the guard of the exit associated with the stairwell connecting level i and $i+1$. This may not happen if an agent is present whose pathway is shorter to the guard location at level $i+1$. In the assignment process, all agents have pathways generated from their current location to one of the goal locations generated for the next level. The goal locations are then assigned by the leader agent based on the path distance. This is an iterative process where the shortest path is selected from all the pathways. Once an agent and goal location pair has been selected, its associated pathways are removed from the full pathway list as are the pathways that are associated with the goal location assigned. In this way, we guaranteed that an agent guarding a stairwell at level i leading to another level $i+1$ is selected to guard the exit at level $i+1$.

5.4 Dependence on Mapping

The main aspects of this approach, generating coverage locations, generating clearing paths, and pathway assignments, have an inherent dependence on the roadmap. When attempting a full coverage, we assume that the roadmap gives a good coverage of the environment. One way we attempt to ensure this is by preventing samples or configurations from being generated too close to one another. In this way, the nodes representing the free space in the environment are spread out. The assignment of pathways also assumes that valid pathways exist between guard locations, through stairwells, between levels. We ensure that the roadmap is generated in such a way that these pathways do exist although it is a known limitation to our approach. Due to the inherent dependence on the roadmap, our searching agents can be made more or less intelligent based on the quality of the mapping. This will be shown in the results. Agents that have a better mapping will have a better chance of fully clearing an environment whereas agents with a simpler mapping may miss portions of the environment. This may in fact be useful in games when trying to have varying capabilities of adversarial agents.

6 Experimental Results

We present results in two simulated building-like environments, shown in Figures 1(a) and 3. Each of these environments consists of multiple levels with stairwells connecting adjacent levels. In these problems, stairwells do not exist between non-adjacent levels. We present results in the form of the average number of agents that would be needed to cover each level of the environment given the visibility constraints by varying the view radius (VR) distances. The number of agents needed to clear the environment would be the maximum needed over each of the individual floors (which is based on the roadmaps generated). Results are generated using roadmaps that adequately cover the environment, which includes valid pathways between open areas, hallways and exits. The effect of agent view radius restrictions is not taken into account during the roadmap construction phase. Results presented are averaged over ten trial runs, unless specified otherwise. Animations and additional results can be found on our webpage: http://parasol.tamu.edu/groups/amatogroup/research/flock/.

6.1 4 Floor, 5 Hallways

This environment, shown in Figure 1(a), consists of four levels. The first level consists of an open area with stairwells leading to the second level. The second level and each subsequent level is divided by four obstacles, creating five hallways off the main two hallways. The upper levels are connected by two stairways between the levels. The environment dimensions are 230 units ×140 units. We tested our search algorithm with a number of agent view radius capabilities (10, 30, 60, 120 and 240 units); results are shown in Table 1. Results are omitted for view radius capabilities of 240 units since they match those for agents with a view radius of 120 units. The maximum number of searchers needed to clear each level is shown.

As the view radius increases, the number of agents needed to cover each level decreases. In fact, once the view radius gets large enough, the average number of agents necessary to cover an environment levels off. In this environment, this happened when the view radius was at 120 and 240 units, requiring the same number of agents at each level. For a view radius of 60 units and higher, the upper levels all require the same number of searchers. This corresponds to guard agents blocking off the exits and hallways and agents required for guarding the hallways.

The coverage of the environment can be analyzed as coverage locations are added. The coverage gradually increases until complete coverage is achieved. Given N agents available to cover and clear an environment, the first N coverage locations would be used as goals to maximize coverage. If coverage were only required to a certain level, our approach could give insight into the number of agents necessary to achieve this coverage. For example, if only 98 percent coverage were required then only 6 agents would be needed as goal locations 7 and 8 would be unnecessary for the first three levels.

Table 1. Search results showing number of agents needed in 4 Floor, 5 Hallway environment

	Strategy 1 Coverage Locations				Strategy 2 Clearing Paths			
Level	1	2	3	4	1	2	3	4
VR: 10 - Avg. number of searchers needed to clear	41	50	49	50	23	30	31	27
VR: 30 - Avg. number of searchers needed to clear	16	11	12	12	12	7	7	6
VR: 60 - Avg. number of searchers needed to clear	8	8	8	6	5	8	7	5
VR: 120 - Avg. number of searchers needed to clear	4	8	8	6	4	7	7	4

Table 2. Search results in 3 Level Office Building

	Strategy 1 Coverage Locations			Strategy 2 Clearing Paths		
Level	1	2	3	1	2	3
VR: 30 - Avg. number of searchers needed to clear	68	41	41	39	27	26
VR: 60 - Avg. number of searchers needed to clear	39	26	26	23	16	16
VR: 300 - Avg. number of searchers needed to clear	34	22	22	19	13	13

The number of agents needed when generating clearing paths in this environment is much fewer than are needed when trying to cover each level with agents. This is because the agents can build off the areas that are previous covered to expand the area they clear while preventing contamination of that region. In fact, when agents have smaller view radius values using the clearing paths strategy requires far fewer agents to clear the levels.

6.2 3 Floor Office Building

The second environment we performed experiments in is shown in Figure 3. This environment is much more complex than the previous one. It consists of three levels, with many rooms on each level with walls obstructing the view between rooms and hallways. There are three stairwells between the first and second floor and two between the second and third floor. This environment has dimensions of 355 units × 275 units. We tested our search algorithms with a number of agent view radius capabilities (30, 60, and 300 units); results are shown in Table 2. The first floor has 900 samples to cover the inside and outer portions of the building while floor 2 and 3 have 250 samples to cover. This minimal sampling is good enough to have expected pathways through the environment. As before, for each view radius tested, the average number of searchers needed per level is shown.

When agents are equipped with a view radius of 300 units they have the ability to see across almost the entire environment. This results in much fewer searchers needed to guarantee a clearing of the roadmap. The first level generally requires more searchers because the open space around the building is also considered

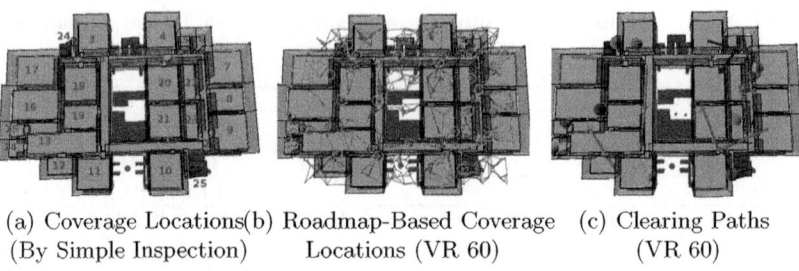

(a) Coverage Locations (By Simple Inspection) (b) Roadmap-Based Coverage Locations (VR 60) (c) Clearing Paths (VR 60)

Fig. 3. Office Example

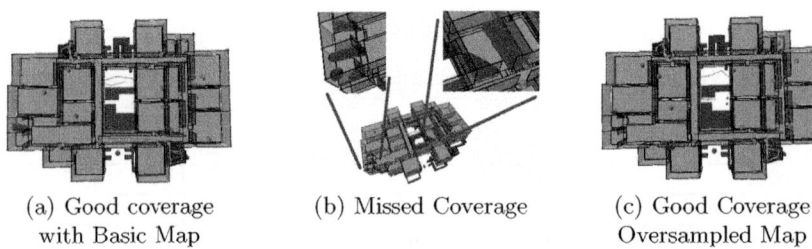

(a) Good coverage with Basic Map (b) Missed Coverage (c) Good Coverage Oversampled Map

Fig. 4. Coverage examples of 3D office example. Goal locations shown in green. Missed samples (out of 100,000 samples) shown in red for third floor.

area to cover in the problem. When agents have a view radius of only 30 units, the number of searchers needed to cover the roadmap is nearly twice the number needed when the view radius is 300 units.

The number of agents needed to cover the roadmap with a view radius of 60 units is similar to when they have a view radius of 300. Although we do not have the ability to compute the optimal geometric coverage locations, we look at the number of locations needed to guarantee coverage on the third floor of this environment. By simple inspection, the number of coverage locations needed is shown in Figure 3(a) when an infinite view radius is used. These locations correspond to two searchers for the main four hallways (Locations 1 and 2), one for each main room (Locations 3–23) and two to guard the exits (Locations 24 and 25). These locations would guarantee a geometric coverage of the third level (with guarding of the exits). With a view radius of 60 units, an example of locations that are generated is shown in Figure 3(b). For the most part, the locations shown correspond to those in Figure 3(a) although one room (corresponding to Location 19) is not guaranteed to be covered. The underlying roadmap was covered though.

Our approach results in fewer agents needed when the view radius is set to 300 units. This is because while the roadmap may be covered, the geometric representation of the environment is not guaranteed to be covered. An example of both good and missed coverage locations is shown in Figure 4. In this example, we generated 100,000 random samples on the third level of the environment. Samples that were not covered by the coverage locations are drawn in red. These locations are generally in the corner of rooms, however cases can occur where a room seems to be covered based on the roadmap nodes covering that room which may leave a large portion of the room uncovered (Figure 4(b)). If more complete coverage is desired, a more densely sampled map can be generated as in Figure 4(c).

We are able to use clearing paths in this complex environment to clear each level. It can be seen in Table 2 that fewer agents are needed when using the clearing paths strategy. This is true at each level of the environment but especially when the agents have the more limited view radius (VR 30) where at the first level close to 30 fewer agents are needed to clear the level. An example of the clearing paths generated can be seen in Figure 3(c).

7 Conclusion

In this paper we describe a level search algorithm to clear a building. This problem is inspired by art gallery and pursuit-evasion problems. Our heuristic approach offers guarantees within our roadmap-based approach. This is an extension to existing approaches however we have the ability to solve problems in complex environments. These 3D environments have received less attention but are as important to solve as simple, single level environments. This approach is tunable to allow for different levels of difficulty to be supported.

References

1. Amato, N.M., Bayazit, O.B., Dale, L.K., Jones, C.V., Vallejo, D.: OBPRM: An obstacle-based PRM for 3D workspaces. In: Robotics: The Algorithmic Perspective, pp. 155–168. A.K. Peters, Natick (1998); Proc. Third Workshop on Algorithmic Foundations of Robotics (WAFR), Houston, TX (1998)
2. Amit, Y., Mitchell, J.S.B., Packer, E.: Locating guards for visibility coverage of polygons. In: Proceedings of the Workshop on Algorithm Engineering and Experiments, ALENEX (2007)
3. Bayazit, O., Lien, J.M., Amato, N.M.: Better group behaviors in complex environments using global roadmaps. In: Artif. Life, pp. 362–370 (December 2002)
4. Bayazit, O., Lien, J., Amato, N.M.: Roadmap-based flocking for complex environments. In: Proc. Pacific Graphics, pp. 104–113 (October 2002)
5. Bopardikar, S., Bullo, F., Hespanha, J.: Cooperative pursuit with sensing limitations. In: American Control Conference (ACC), pp. 935–953 (July 2007)
6. Burgard, W., Moors, M., Fox, D., Simmons, R., Thrun, S.: Collaborative multi-robot exploration. In: Proc. IEEE Int. Conf. Robot. Autom (ICRA), pp. 476–481 (2000)
7. Durham, J.W., Franchi, A., Bullo, F.: Distributed pursuit-evasion with limited-visibility sensors via frontier-based exploration. In: Proc. IEEE Int. Conf. Robot. Autom. (ICRA), pp. 3562–3568 (2010)
8. Gerkey, B.P., Thrun, S., Gordon, G.: Visibility-based pursuit-evasion with limited field of view. Int. J. Robot. Res. 25(4), 299–315 (2006)
9. Guibas, L.J., claude Latombe, J., Lavalle, S.M., Lin, D., Motwani, R.: Visibility-based pursuit-evasion in a polygonal environment. International Journal of Computational Geometry and Applications, 17–30 (1997)

10. Isler, V., Kannan, S., Khanna, S.: Randomized pursuit-evasion with limited visibility. In: Proc. ACM-SIAM Symposium on Discrete Algorithms, pp. 1060–1069 (2004)
11. Isler, V., Sun, D., Sastry, S.: Roadmap based pursuit-evasion and collision avoidance. In: Proc. Robotics: Sci. Sys., RSS (2005)
12. Kavraki, L.E., Švestka, P., Latombe, J.C., Overmars, M.H.: Probabilistic roadmaps for path planning in high-dimensional configuration spaces. IEEE Trans. Robot. Automat. 12(4), 566–580 (1996)
13. Kolling, A., Kleiner, A., Lewis, M., Sycara, K.: Solving pursuit-evasion problems on height maps. In: IEEE International Conference on Robotics and Automation (ICRA 2010) Workshop: Search and Pursuit/Evasion in the Physical World: Efficiency, Scalability, and Guarantees (2010)
14. Kolling, A., Carpin, S.: Cooperative observation of multiple moving targets: an algorithm and its formalization. Int. J. Rob. Res. 26, 935–953 (2007)
15. Kolling, A., Carpin, S.: Multi robot pursuit evasion without maps. In: Proc. IEEE Int. Conf. Robot. Autom (ICRA), pp. 3045–3051 (May 2010)
16. Kolling, A., Carpin, S.: Pursuit-evasion on trees by robot teams. Trans. Rob. 26(1), 32–47 (2010)
17. Lavalle, S.M., Lin, D., Guibas, L.J., Claude Latombe, J., Motwani, R.: Finding an unpredictable target in a workspace with obstacles. In: Proc. IEEE Int. Conf. Robot. Autom. (ICRA), pp. 737–742 (1997)
18. O'Rourke, J.: Art Gallery Theorems and Algorithms. Oxford University Press, New York (1987)
19. Parsons, T.D.: Pursuit-evasion in a graph. In: Theory and Applications of Graphs. Lecture Notes in Mathematics, vol. 642, pp. 426–441. Springer, Heidelberg (1978)
20. Rodriguez, S., Denny, J., Mahadevan, A., Vu, J., Burgos, J., Zourntos, T., Amato, N.M.: Roadmap-based pursuit-evasion in 3d environments. Transactions on Edutainment (to appear, 2011)
21. Rodriguez, S., Denny, J., Zourntos, T., Amato, N.M.: Toward Simulating Realistic Pursuit-Evasion Using a Roadmap-Based Approach. In: Boulic, R., Chrysanthou, Y., Komura, T. (eds.) MIG 2010. LNCS, vol. 6459, pp. 82–93. Springer, Heidelberg (2010)
22. Wilmarth, S.A., Amato, N.M., Stiller, P.F.: MAPRM: A probabilistic roadmap planner with sampling on the medial axis of the free space. In: Proc. IEEE Int. Conf. Robot. Autom. (ICRA), vol. 2, pp. 1024–1031 (1999)
23. Yamauchi, B.: Frontier-based exploration using multiple robots. In: International Conference on Autonomous Agents (Agents 1998), pp. 47–53 (1998)

From Geometry to Spatial Reasoning : Automatic Structuring of 3D Virtual Environments

Carl-Johan Jorgensen and Fabrice Lamarche

Université de Rennes 1
IRISA, UMR CNRS 6074
Université Européenne de Bretagne
carl-johan.jorgensen@etudiant.univ-rennes1.fr,
flamarch@irisa.fr

Abstract. In this paper, we address the problem of automatically creating a meaningful spatial representation of 3D virtual environments, suitable for spatial reasoning. We propose a spatial analysis technique that distinguishes indoor, outdoor and covered parts of the environment. It also separates buildings into floors linked by stairs and represent floors as rooms linked by doorsteps. On this basis, we compute a natural hierarchical representation of the environment. We also demonstrate that this representation can be used to handle multi-criterion queries relating to spatial reasoning including zone selection and path planning.

Keywords: spatial analysis, spatial reasoning, path planning.

1 Introduction

Many application fields such as video games, virtual reality or virtual training, tends to immerse the user in virtual environments automatically crowded with autonomous virtual humans. In order to improve the user's experience, these humanoids must show realistic behaviors. One of the most important behaviors is the ability to navigate inside a virtual environment as this skill is continuously used. Human navigation is influenced by the nature of the environment [1,2] and eventually by external factors. For instance, if a pedestrian wants to go from home to the nearest bakery in a rainy day, he may want to follow a covered path. However, he will not walk through his neighbors' houses under the pretext it is the shortest and better-covered path. To reproduce such a behavior, a virtual human should be aware of buildings locations and be able to plan paths that make a compromise between the travelled distance and the use of covered zones. This kind of information should be available when using informed virtual environments. However, most of 3D environments are modeled with modelers that do not provide an information system. In such a case, manually adding information to the geometry can be a long and tedious process.

In this article, we propose an original method that aims at automatically extracting a meaningful representation from 3D environments. This method relies on a spatial analysis process that distinguishes indoor, outdoor and covered environments. It also identifies buildings and their internal structure. Floors linked by stairs are identified and floors are represented as rooms connected through doorsteps. We show how this representation can be used to handle zone selection and multi-criteria path planning in order to enhance the quality and credibility of generated paths. In the next section, we present related work. Then, the spatial analysis and spatial reasoning processes are explained and discussed in the result section.

2 Related Work

To populate a virtual environment, modelling the navigation behaviour is crucial. This behaviour relies on the ability of planning a path inside a complex environment which itself relies on an adequate representation of the environment structure. Path planning and environment representation have been widely studied in robotics where navigation is a necessary task to achieve [3]. In this field, two main techniques can be distinguished: the roadmap and the cell decomposition approaches.

The roadmap approach captures the connectivity of the free space thanks to sets of standardized paths [4,5,6]. This kind of approach focuses on creating a data structure enabling path planning but does not explicitly model the borders of obstacles which is a prerequisite of our approach. The cell decomposition approach represents the free space with a set of cells. Those decomposition approaches can be either approximate or exact. Approximate cell decompositions uses predefined cells shapes (uniform grids, quad trees, circles) whose union is strictly included in the free space [7,8]. Exact cell decompositions exactly cover the free space. Among other techniques [3], Constrained Delaunay Triangulations (CDT) have been used in last ten years to compute an exact cell decomposition of virtual environments [9,10] and has been slightly modified to identify bottlenecks (most constrained part of the environment) [11]. Its good properties in terms of navigation queries [12] and path finding [13] have been demonstrated.

Based on constrained Delaunay triangulations, several techniques have been proposed to produce a hierarchical abstraction of the environment topology. The main idea is to qualify cells or sets of cells (regions) given the number of accesses (dead ends, corridors, crossings) [11,14]. On this basis and eventually on the basis of the geometric shape of the identified regions, a topological abstraction is automatically computed and mainly used to increase path planning performances. Such a kind of abstraction is based on the geometric properties of the identified regions but does not rely on standard notions such as indoor / outdoor locations or rooms, corridors, floors or stairs for instance.

To handle more complex cases and increase the realism of simulations, the notion of informed environment has been introduced. The idea is to associate a data structure to regions of the environment. This data structure stores information dedicated to the behaviour [7]. This approach has been used to model populated cities [1] and to propose semantic abstractions of a city structure [15].

More recently, this approach has been used in [16] to propose a hierarchical decomposition of multilayered environments taking into account notions of floors and stairs for instance. It has also been used in the field of geographic information systems to provide an informed and hierarchical representation of virtual geographic environments that is used to speed up and enhance the quality of computed paths [17]. One main aspect of informed environments is the fact that they need to be modelled with specific tools or manually informed on the basis of the original geometry.

The aim of our approach is to automatically generate a meaningful and hierarchical representation of virtual environments that is suitable for path planning and more generally for spatial reasoning. It relies on an analysis of the 3D environment structure to automatically generate an abstraction of the environment including notions such as indoor / outdoor locations, identification of floors and stairs in indoor environments and a topological decomposition including notions of rooms and corridors that relate to the real nature of the environment. In those terms, it generates an augmented representation that is closer to the notion of informed environment than previously proposed approaches in the field of automated environment analysis.

3 Spatial Analysis of Geometric Environments

In our everyday life, we unconsciously differentiate buildings and outdoor environments. Inside buildings, we identify floors, stairs, rooms or corridors for instance. The aim of the proposed method is to automatically create a representation that includes those concepts. To do so, we analyze a 3D environment geometry in which all furniture has been removed. We start by computing a spatial subdivision of this geometry which is well suited for spatial analysis. Then, this spatial subdivision is analyzed to compute zones that can be identified (indoor, outdoor, rooms, stairs...). Once this analysis is achieved, a hierarchical representation, grouping rooms into floors, floors linked by stairs into buildings is computed.

3.1 Prismatic Subdivision and Low Level Topology

The prismatic subdivision has been introduced in [18] to analyze the structure of 3D environments provided has a set of 3D triangles. Its aim is to organize a set of 3D polygons in order to capture ground connectivity and identify floor and ceiling constraints. It represents the environment by a set of vertical 3D prisms dividing the input database into layers of 3D triangular cells. The figure 1 depicts the computation process, for more details we invite the reader to read [18]. The figure 2 shows the prismatic subdivision of a simple environment that will be used in the following to demonstrate the results of our spatial analysis.

Based on this spatial subdivision, with respect to some characters characteristics (minimum navigable height, maximal navigable slope and maximum surmountable height), a low level topological graph is constructed. Each node

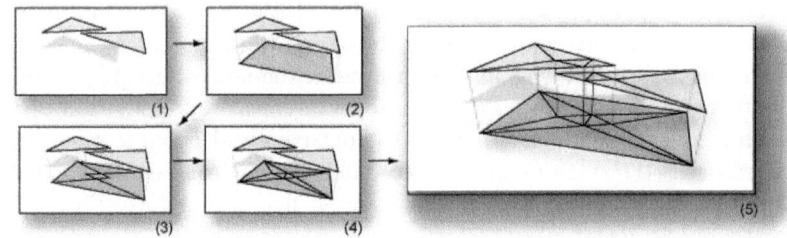

Fig. 1. Prismatic subdivision computation

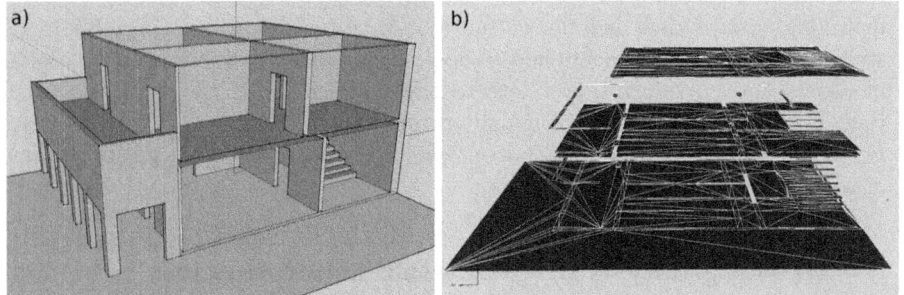

Fig. 2. a) A simple example environment (wall and ceiling masked for more visibility) b) Its prismatic decomposition as generated by TopoPlan [18]

of this graph is a navigable 3D triangular cell (in terms of minimum navigable height and maximum navigable slope) of the subdivision and each edge is an accessibility relation between cells. An edge is created between two nodes if the cells are located into adjacent prisms and if the height difference between those cells is lesser than the maximum step height. Edges are tagged *continuous* if the height difference is lesser than a given threshold or *step* otherwise. The prismatic spatial subdivision and its associated low level topological graph constitute the input of our spatial analysis algorithm which is described in the following section.

On the basis of the low level topological graph, the 3D triangular cells of the spatial subdivision can have three type of borders: *step*, *obstacle* and *surmountable*. By extension, borders of zones (groups of connected cells) can be classified into those three categories.

3.2 Meaningful Zones Computation

The prismatic spatial subdivision and its associated low level topological graph constitute the input of our spatial analysis algorithm. Based on those data structure, we propose a four step algorithm which aims at (1) differentiating interior and exterior zones, (2) extracting floors and stairs and (3) decomposing floors into rooms and doorsteps.

Covered and uncovered regions. The first step of our algorithm identifies covered and uncovered regions of the environment. This step uses the prismatic spatial subdivision to tag 3D triangular cells as *covered* if the cell is surmounted by another cell belonging to the same prism and *uncovered* otherwise. Based on this process, two set of zones (group of mutually accessible cells) are extracted: $\mathcal{Z}_c$, the set of covered zones and $\mathcal{Z}_u$, the set of uncovered zones. The result of this decomposition on our example environment is depicted Fig. 3(a).

Floors and stair steps. The second step consists of dividing each zone of $\mathcal{Z}_c \cup \mathcal{Z}_u$ at any *step* border. Those step borders are identified with the low level topological graph computed in the previous section. This produces two new sets of zones : $\mathcal{Z}'_c$ and $\mathcal{Z}'_u$. In covered zones, this process extracts floors and stair steps. In uncovered zones, this process can differentiate roads and sidewalks for instance. Zones mainly having *step* borders are tagged *step*. The figure 3(b) depicts the result of this process on our example environment.

Topological maps. For each zone of $\mathcal{Z}'_c \cup \mathcal{Z}'_u$, we compute a topological map. This map is computed using the 2D spatial subdivision technique presented in [11]. A constrained Delaunay triangulation is computed on the projection onto the XY plane of the zones borders. This triangulation keeps the nature of the zone borders namely *obstacle* or *step* border. This Delaunay triangulation is then modified by computing the bottlenecks [11] and triangles are merged into convex polygons if all bottlenecks remains present as a border of convex polygons. Keeping the identified bottlenecks is important as they are likely to identify doorsteps borders. The result of this processing applied to our example is depicted in Figure 3(c).

Room decomposition. Each covered zone identified as a *floor* is assumed to be an interior zone belonging to a house or a building. A building floor or house floor is composed of rooms and corridors separated by doorsteps. To achieve room decomposition, we thus need to identify doorsteps. To identify those doorsteps, we define a 'door likelihood' function that is computed for each convex cell c of the topological map. Let $S(c)$ be the surface of cell c, $H(c)$ be the average ceiling height of cell c, $N(c)$ be the set of neighboring cells, $B(c)$ be the set of *free* borders of cell c and $L(s)$ be the length of border s. The 'door likelihood' function is computed thanks to three criteria:

- $C_1(c) = \frac{\sum_{c' \in N(c)} (S(c'))}{S(c)}$. A door is a small zone between bigger ones.
- $C_2(c) = \sum_{c' \in N(c)} (\| H(c') - H(c) \|)$. A door's ceiling is often lower than the one of surrounding rooms.
- $C_3(c) = \frac{1}{\sum_{b \in B(c)} (L(b))}$. A door is bordered with narrow bottlenecks.

On the basis of those three criteria, the 'door likelihood' function (DL) is defined as follow: $DL(c) = C_1(c) * (1 + C_2(c)) * C_3(c)$. This function tends to return low values for cells belonging to rooms and high values for cells defining doorsteps. To separate doors and rooms, we compute the mean value of the DL function applied to each cell of the topological map. Cells having a DL value greater than the mean value are tagged *door*, other ones are tagged *room*. The figure 4 shows

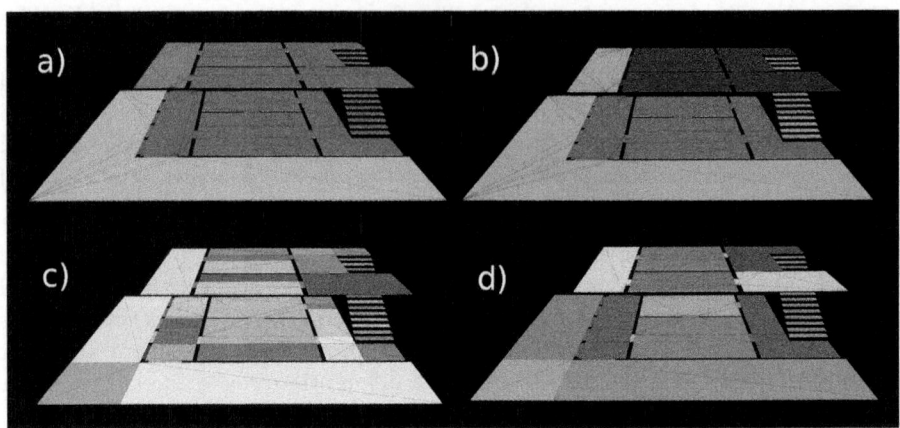

Fig. 3. Decomposition steps : a) buildings decomposition, b) floors decomposition, c) convex cells decomposition d) rooms decomposition

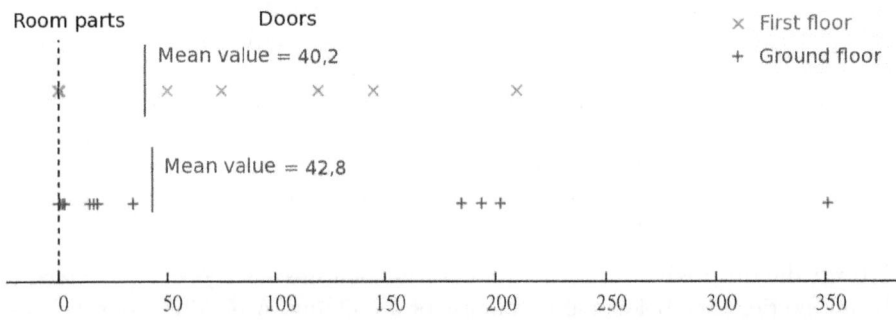

Fig. 4. Repartition of door likelihood values for covered convex zones

the values computed for the two floors of our house example and the resulting environment decomposition is depicted in figure 3(d).

3.3 Informed Hierarchical Topological Graph

In the previous section we described our environment analysis and tagging. Based on this analysis, a set of topological maps has been extracted and cells of those topological maps are tagged in several ways: covered, uncovered, room, door and step. On this basis, we create an informed hierarchical topological graph. Nodes of this graph are cells of the topological maps or group of cells. Edges represent accessibility between cells or zones. The hierarchy associated to the graph contains four levels leading to a natural description of the environment structure:

- The level four contains all cells of the topological maps (nodes) and their accessibility relations (edges).
- The level three groups mutually accessible cells having the same tags and belonging to the same topological map. Therefore, in this level, each step of a stair, each room, each doorstep is identified by a unique node. At this level, we are also able to distinguish covered exterior zone and indoor environments. A room is retagged *covered exterior* if its borders are mainly tagged *surmountable* or *step* and if it is mainly connected to uncovered zones. More generally, at this level, a set of rules can be defined and used to better qualify zones' nature. For instance, a rule can be used to qualify a corridor as a room surrounded by at least three doors.
- The level two groups steps into stairs, rooms and doors into floors.
- The level one groups floors and stairs into buildings, uncovered zones into exterior zones and covered exterior zones.

We can observe that levels three, two and one lead to a natural representation of an environment. It automatically provides a meaningful representation that (1) distinguishes indoor and outdoor environments, (2) decomposes building into floors linked by stairs, (3) each floor being itself decomposed into room linked by doorsteps. as we will see in the next section, this representation can be used for enhancing path planning quality. For instance, we can plan paths favoring the navigation in outdoor environments, while avoiding entering building if not needed. The hierarchical representation can also be used to enhance path planning performances by identifying high level paths that can be refined when needed.

4 Multi-criteria Path Planning

Navigation is subject to multiple constraints of various importances. For instance, one would want to minimize a path length while avoiding entering an unknown building and favoring navigation in covered regions if it is raining. A path corresponding to such a request is a compromise between several heterogeneous criteria. In this section, we propose a multi-critera path planning algorithm that makes intensive use of our environment representation. This algorithm uses a zone matching function that evaluates the adequacy of a zone given a multi-criteria request.

4.1 Zone Matching

In many cases, finding a zone or a set of zones that exactly satisfy all criteria included in a request is not possible. Therefore, the first step toward multi-criteria path planning is to evaluate the distance between a request which characterize an ideal zone and a zone extracted from the environment. Criteria used in the request can be of different nature: maximizing a given value, favoring zones having some given properties. To evaluate the satisfaction of a criterion, we use several kinds of functions that returns values in $[0;1]$ interval, 0 meaning the criterion is not satisfied and 1 meaning the criterion is satisfied:

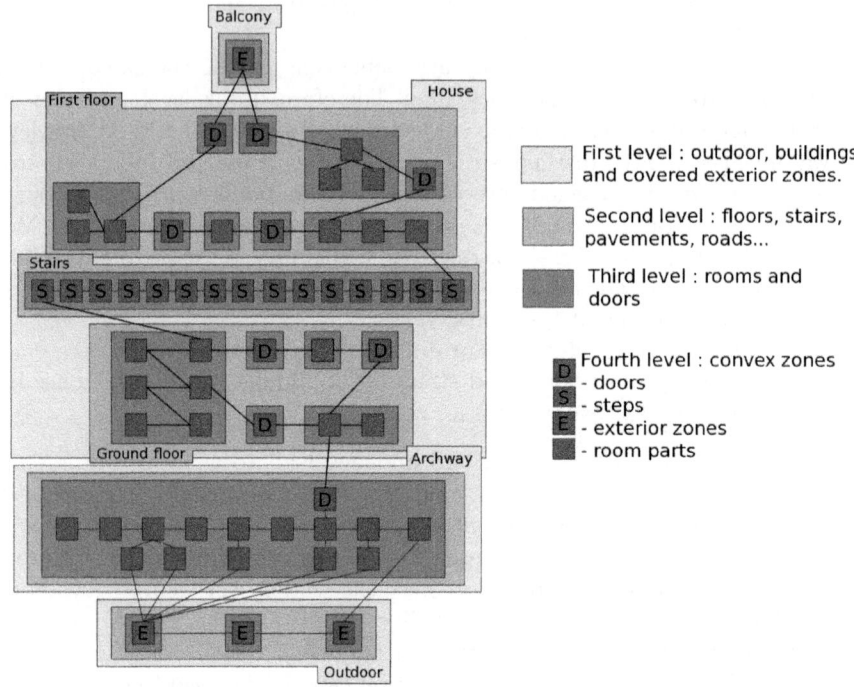

Fig. 5. Picturing of generated topological graph for our example environment

- For criteria relating to zones' nature (covered, does not belongs to a building for instance) we use a step function returning 1 if the criterion is satisfied and 0 otherwise (Cf. Fig. 6(a)).
- For a criteria concerning comparison between numerical values (zone's surface should be over 9 square meters for instance) we also use a step function (Cf. Fig. 6(b)).
- For criteria concerning values that should be minimized or maximized (ceiling height should be the highest possible) we use a linear function which is normalized using the maximum possible value in the current environment (Cf. Fig. 6(c)).
- For criteria concerning values that should be closed to a given value (zone's surface should be around 12 square meters) we use a gaussian-shaped function returning a maximum of 1 for the wished value (Cf. Fig. 6(d)).

In our system, a request is a conjunction of criteria. To take into account the importance of a given criterion, a weight w_c is associated to each criterion c. Given that the valuation of criterion c on a zone z is evaluated by the function $V_c(z)$, we define a function $D(z, R)$ giving the distance between the considered zone and the ideal zone described by the request R as follow:

$$D(z, R) = \sum_{c \in R}((1 - V_c(z)) * w_c)$$

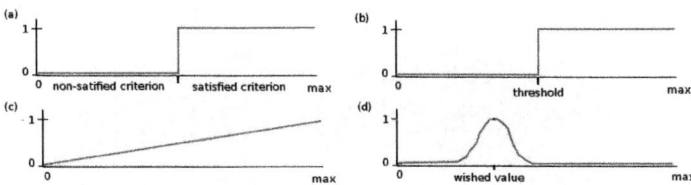

Fig. 6. Normalizing functions for a) criteria on zones nature, b) numeric values to compare to a threshold, c) numeric value to maximise, d) wished value to get near of

This function returns a value in interval $[0; \sum_{c \in R} w_c]$, 0 being the value associated to a zone perfectly satisfying the request. This function can be used for several requests purposes. For instance, it can be used to select a set of zones that maximize similarities with the ideal zone described by the request. For instance, one could want to select the nearest covered zone in order to avoid rain. Moreover, as we will see in the next section, it can be used during a path planning process to bias generated paths.

4.2 Multi-criteria Path Planning

The aim of our path planning process is to find a path going through zones that tend to match a multi-criteria request. In the previous section, we explained how we defined a distance function $D(z, R)$ evaluating the distance between the ideal zone described by the request R and the currently explored zone z. This distance function is used in a cost function that evaluates the cost of a path. Let $C(P, R, I_d)$ be the function evaluating the cost of path P in function of planning request R and giving importance $I_d \in [1; \infty]$ to the path length criterion. Let $L(P, z)$ be the length of the path P traversing the zone z. The function $C(P, R, I_d)$ is defined as follow:

$$C(P, R, I_d) = \sum_{z \in P} (L(z, P) * (I_d + D(z, R)))$$

In this function, the length of the path going through a zone z is multiplied by the sum of two factors: I_d and D(z,R). As D(z,R) is minimal for zones matching request R, paths traversing zones that match request R are encouraged. On the other hand, the I_d factor tends to select shortest paths for high values or paths matching request R for small values.

To plan a path inside our virtual environment, we use a Dijkstra algorithm. This algorithm is ran on the level four of our informed hierarchical topological graph and $C(P, R, I_d)$ is used to evaluate the cost of going through a cell z of the topological maps. Currently, as we have no hypothesis on the requests nature, the algorithm does not use the hierarchical representation to increase path planning performances but only to increase the quality of generated paths.

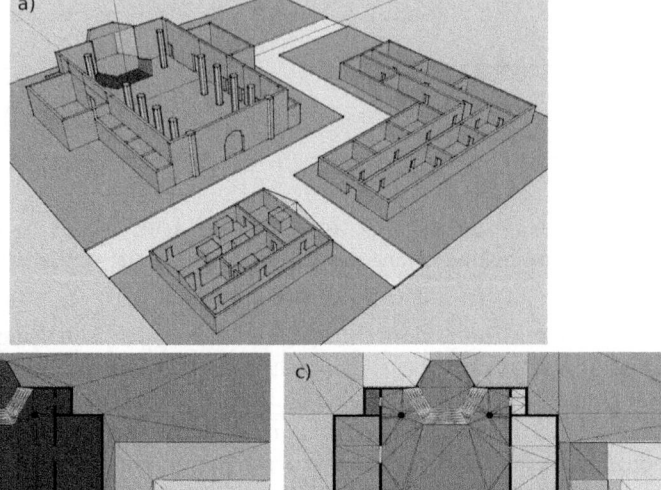
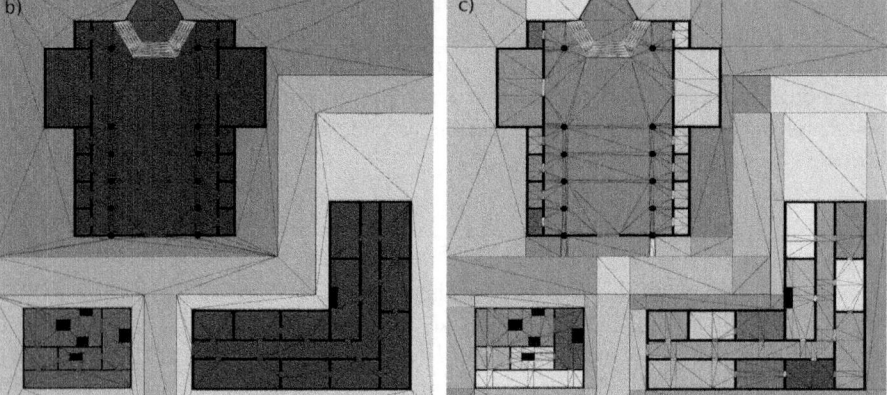

Fig. 7. a) A more complex example environment (roofs masked for better visibility) b) Its computed floor decomposition c) its computed room decomposition

5 Results

We tested our spatial analysis technique on a complex example depicted Fig. 7(a). The environment contains a road with sidewalks, a church and two houses. The church has heterogeneous rooms size and doorstep dimensions. It also contains pillars in the body of the church and unusual stairs leading to the pulpit. The building on the right of the figure contains a long and narrow corridor exhibiting numerous bottlenecks. The house on the left contains doorsteps of different width and height as well as a step roof and obstacles in some rooms. As presented in Fig. 7(b) and (c), buildings have been identified as well as stairs, doorsteps and rooms. This demonstrates the robustness of our technique which has been able to identify all relevant information despite potential interferences induced by obstacles, pillars or irregular doorsteps width and height.

To test path planning and related queries, we set up an environment with covered and uncovered exterior zones. This environment, depicted in Fig. 8, is used to test the behavior of our algorithm in the rainy day example. The planning

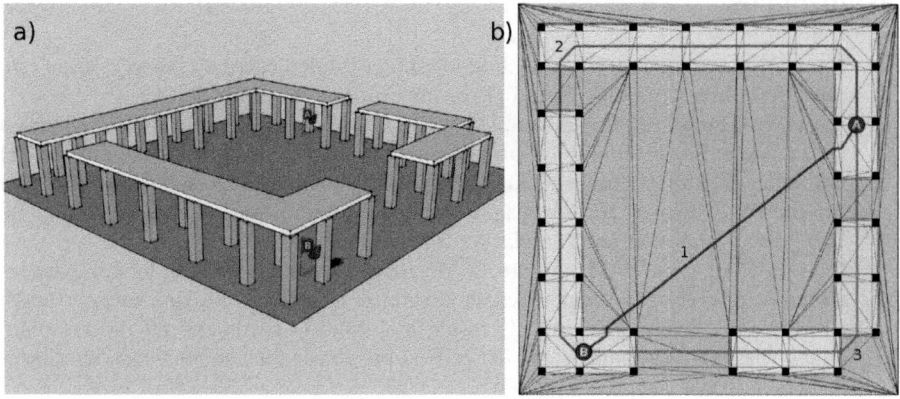

Fig. 8. Environment used for spatial reasoning test and path calculated in it out of three different requests

request is set up by giving a constraint on navigating in covered zones (to avoid the rain) and changing weights associated to the covered and path length criteria. Computed paths are presented Fig. 8(b). Path 1 has been generated by giving a weight of 1 to the covered criterion and a weight of 2 to the path length. As expected, the shortest path is used. Path 2 has been generated by giving a weight of 2 to the covered criterion and 1 to the distance. In such a case, our character uses the longest path but this path minimizes the exposition to rain. Finally, path 3 has been generated by giving an equal value of 1 to the covered criterion and the path length. Our character navigates mostly in covered zones and is also exposed to rain. This example demonstrate that our algorithm can help characters to exhibit more natural behaviors by taking into account the environment nature.

6 Conclusion

We proposed an original method extracting an abstract, meaningful and hierarchical representation out of a 3D geometric environment. Our technique uses a spatial analysis algorithm that automatically detects the real structure (in terms of rooms, doorsteps, floors, stairs...) of the environment described by a 3D database. We showed that this structuring can be used to increase path planning quality and credibility through the use of multi-criteria requests. Our spatial analysis can be extended by adding specific rules to enhance the tagging process by taking into account some architectural standards for instance. However, we believe that an automatic process cannot deduce all information. For instance, the function of a room (kitchen, bedroom...) cannot be determined without analyzing its associated furniture. Nevertheless, if more precise information is needed, our method could be used to assist manual tagging by pre-identifying specific zones and thus decreasing the effort needed to manually inform virtual environments.

References

1. Thomas, G., Donikian, S.: Modeling virtual cities dedicated to behavioral animation. Computer Graphics Forum (Proc. of Eurographics) 19 (2000)
2. Turner, A., Doxa, M., O'Sullivan, D., Penn, A.: From isovists to visibility graphs: a methodology for the analysis of architectural space. Planning and Design 28 (2001)
3. Latombe, J.: Robot motion planning. Kluwer Academic Publishers, Boston (1991)
4. Arikan, O., Chenney, S., Forsyth, D.A.: Efficient multi-agent path planning. In: Computer Animation and Simulation 2001 (2001)
5. Bayazit, O.B., Lien, J.-M., Amato, N.M.: Roadmap-based flocking for complex environments. In: Pacific Conference on Computer Graphics and Applications (2002)
6. Geraerts, R., Overmars, M.H.: Creating high-quality roadmaps for motion planning in virtual environments. In: IEEE/RSJ International Conference on Intelligent Robots and Systems, IROS (2006)
7. Shao, W., Terzopoulos, D.: Environmental modeling for autonomous virtual pedestrians. In: Digital Human Modeling for Design and Engineering Symposium (2005)
8. Pettre, J., Laumond, J.P., Thalmann, D.: A navigation graph for real-time crowd animation on multilayered and uneven terrain. In: V-Crowds (2006)
9. Kallmann, M., Bieri, H., Thalmann, D.: Fully dynamic constrained delaunay triangulations. Geometric Modelling for Scientific Visualization (2003)
10. Mekni, M.: Hierarchical path planning for situated agents in informed virtual geographic environments. In: 3rd International Conference on simulation Tools and Techniques, SIMUTools (2010)
11. Lamarche, F., Donikian, S.: Crowd of virtual humans: a new approach for real time navigation in complex and structured environments. Computer Graphics Forum (Proc. of Eurographics) 23(3) (2004)
12. Kallmann, M.: Navigation Queries from Triangular Meshes. In: Boulic, R., Chrysanthou, Y., Komura, T. (eds.) MIG 2010. LNCS, vol. 6459, pp. 230–241. Springer, Heidelberg (2010)
13. Demyen, D., Buro, M.: Efficient triangulation-based pathfinding. In: National Conference on Artificial Intelligence - AAAI (2006)
14. Paris, S., Donikian, S., Bonvalet, N.: Environmental abstraction and path planning techniques for realistic crowd simulation. In: Computer Agents and Social Agents (2006)
15. Farenc, N., Boulic, R., Thalmann, D.: Informed environement dedicated to the simulation of virtual humans in urban context. Computer Graphics Forum (Proc. of Eurographics) 18 (1999)
16. Jiang, H., Xu, W., Mao, T., Li, C., Xia, S., Wang, Z.: A semantic environment model for crowd simulation in multilayered complex environment. In: the 16th ACM Symposium on Virtual Reality Software and Technology (2009)
17. Mekni, M.: Automated Generation of Geometrically-Precise and Semantically-Informed Virtual Geographic Environments Populated with Spatially-Reasoning Agents. PhD thesis, Université Laval (2010)
18. Lamarche, F.: Topoplan: a topological path planner for real time human navigation under floor and ceiling constraints. Computer Graphics Forum 28(2) (2009)

Reconstructing Motion Capture Data for Human Crowd Study

Samuel Lemercier[1], Mathieu Moreau[2], Mehdi Moussaïd[2], Guy Theraulaz[2], Stéphane Donikian[1,3], and Julien Pettré[1]

[1] INRIA Rennes - Bretagne Atlantique
Campus de Beaulieu, 35042 Rennes, France
[2] CRCA, CNRS, 31062 Toulouse Cedex 9, France
[3] Golaem
samuel.lemercier@inria.fr

Abstract. Reconstruction is a key step of the motion capture process. The quality of motion data first results from the quality of raw data. However, it also depends on the motion reconstruction step, especially when raw data suffer markers losses or noise due, for example, to challenging conditions of capture. Labeling is a final and crucial data reconstruction step that enables practical use of motion data (e.g., analysis). The lower the data quality, the more time consuming and tedious the labeling step, because human intervention cannot be avoided: he has to manually indicate markers label each time a loss of the marker in time occurs. In the context of crowd study, we faced such situation when we performed experiments on the locomotion of groups of people. Data reconstruction poses several problems such as markers labeling, interpolation and mean position computation. While Vicon IQ software has difficulties to automatically label markers for the crowd experiment we carried out, we propose a specific method to label our data and estimate participants mean positions with incomplete data.

1 Introduction

Optoelectronic motion capture systems are among the most precise tools to track human movements. For this reason, we used motion capture techniques on small crowds of pedestrians for the purpose of experimental studies. More precisely, we captured up to 28 volunteers walking along a circular lane delimited by walls as illustrated in Figure 1 (Right). They were tracked with a 12-camera Vicon System placed all around the observation area. However, raw motion data often suffer some occlusion as each marker has to be viewed from 2 or 3 cameras to be located in 3D which led to incomplete data.

Indeed, participants concealed their markers each other when passing beside a camera. Markers also got hidden by walls. The number of cameras was limited and the experimental area was large: some parts were covered by only two cameras which is a strict minimum to enable capture. We obtained incomplete data, particularly with high density trials (approximately 33% of data loss when

Fig. 1. Left: Picture of the experimental system (empty). Right: Picture taken during the experiment with participants walking along a circular path delimited by a wall.

the 28 participants were walking along the inner wall). Moreover, due to the number of subjects, we were not able to use whole-body sets of markers to track each participant; that would have brought the total number of markers to more than 1000 markers in the trials with 28 participants, which would not have been possible to track. Consequently, we used of a limited set of 4 markers that did not enable the existing automatic reconstruction technique (provided with motion capture system) to correctly work on our dataset. This resulted in a very long manual labeling treatment and we opted for developing our own labeling technique with the aim of saving working time.

In this paper, our first objective is to automatically reconstruct the raw motion data we obtained from our experiments. We faced several difficulties: the temporary loss of some markers, the complete loss of some markers in time during the trial, the temporary loss of all the markers belonging to one participant, but also the presence of *ghost markers* (noise interpreted as markers by the system). Our second goal is to estimate the global position of each participant with a robust method given the reduced set of markers and the loss of data. Our contribution is an automatic method to meet these objectives. Details are provided in Section 3.

2 Related Work

We acquired our data using the VICON MX-40 motion capture system. Data Reconstruction with Vicon IQ software is based on a skeleton model of the tracked subject which defines the segments that connect the markers. The software is then able to detect when a segment appears and can automatically label the markers. This automatic process perfectly works when data quality is high enough and information sufficient to avoid ambiguities. In the case of our experiments, as all the subjects were only wearing four markers, the system was not able to differentiate subjects' skeletons and markers and this technique failed.

Our data also showed loss of markers due to occlusion. Different methods for filling markers occlusions have already been proposed. Li et al. [7] classify them into several categories: spline and linear interpolations (only used for short period occlusions), skeleton-based [5], dimensionality reduction and latent variables [11], database backed [1], Kalman filters [4], dynamical systems [2,7]. However, our problem differs in two main points. First, our markers have not been labeled yet and we are not able to find a marker once it has disappeared. Second we do not try to retrieve articular trajectories from a whole-body set of markers but attempt to estimate the global position of each participant from a reduced set of markers.

The objective of carrying out experimentations on pedestrian crowds are to study pedestrian behavior, enable the elaboration of pedestrian behavioral models, calibrate and validate these models by comparing real and simulated data [8]. The interest of using such a system is to acquire more precise data and to be able to track a pedestrian not only in a local area but in the whole observation system. Previously, several observations had already been carried out for crowd studies. Some natural observations have been made by Yamori [12] who placed a camera above a large pedestrian crosswalk. Experimental observations have also been processed to study pedestrian behavior at bottlenecks [6,9] or for more general situations [3]. However none of these experiments used an optoelectronic motion capture system to track pedestrians but only optic cameras. We here expect to obtain a more accurate dataset with the constraint to face challenging conditions for motion capture.

3 A Method for Automatic Labeling and Reconstruction of Crowd Motion Data

The objective of our method is to estimate the global position and motion of all the participants tracked during experiments from a soup of partial unlabeled markers trajectories. As previously said, the main difficulty is the quantity of data loss which can reach more than a third in the worst cases. Participants were wearing four markers: one on the head (called H), one on the left shoulder (called L), and two on the right shoulder (called R for the one the more on the right and N for the other one) to know their orientation, which still resulted in tracking up to 112 markers when 28 participants were captured.

From Motion Capture software, we obtain markers trajectories in a Cartesian system of coordinates which are rarely continuously tracked during a whole record. The software is not able to recognize a marker when it reappears after being lost: a "new marker" is then created which multiplies the final total number of markers and trajectories. Merging together these portions of trajectories is required to estimate continuous motion along a whole record. Two reasons explain markers occlusion: some observed areas were not well-covered by our camera system, and participants concealed their markers each other when passing beside a camera. Thereby, data quality decreases when participant density increases. We elaborated a method which is composed of the following steps:

- Alignment of motion data with the horizontal plane,
- Markers labeling,
- Estimation of pedestrian position.

3.1 Global Motion Data Transformation

We are mainly interested in the horizontal component of motion data. Before performing motion capture, the capture coordinate system is defined by tracking the so-called L-Frame the geometry of which is known to the system. Because our experimental area is large in comparison to this frame, a drift is observed: motion is not contained into a horizontal plane. To solve this question we transform motion data to align the floor as defined by the frame and the horizontal plane. We perform a multivariate linear regression of motion data to estimate the mean plane of motion. We assume this plane is aligned with the actual floor. We compute the angle formed by the vertical axis and the normal to the floor, and globally rotate data by this angle. Once this step done, motion data can be projected to the horizontal plane without biasing data by artificially introducing deformations. Next step however still consider vertical motion coordinate to automatically label markers.

3.2 Markers Labeling

The objective of this step is to regroup the markers by participant and then label each of them. From raw data, the position **Z** of a marker i at time t is described as follows:

$$\mathbf{Z}_i(t) = [x_i(t)\ y_i(t)\ z_i(t)] \qquad (1)$$

As participants walk on a circular lane, we consider that their distance to the center of the system is approximately the same and constant in time. Thus, we switch into a polar system of coordinates which center is the center of the system. The position of a marker i at time t is now described as follows:

$$\mathbf{Z}_i^{cyl}(t) = [\theta_i(t)\ r_i(t)\ z_i(t)] \qquad (2)$$

θ coordinate of markers' trajectory with respect to time is plotted in Figure 2. Note that discontinuity is due some marker occlusion and reappearance with reinitialized value $\theta \in [0, 2\pi]$. Plots show motion data of various qualities.

Removing ghost-markers. As well as markers occlusion problem, we observe ghost-markers, i.e. markers that are recognized by the system while they are not present. Two kinds of ghost-markers can appear: residual ones which last during a long period of time but which are very few, and temporary ones which only last a little time. We remove markers trajectories which last less than one second. This removes most of the ghost-markers and cleans the data without removing much information.

Grouping markers by participants. The goal of this step is to group markers trajectories together when they belong to a same participant. This is detected by their proximity along θ coordinate during all the time they are both detected. The distance between two markers i_1 and i_2 is defined (in m) as

$$\mathbf{d}_{i_1,i_2} = r * |\theta_{i_1} - \theta_{i_2}| \qquad (3)$$

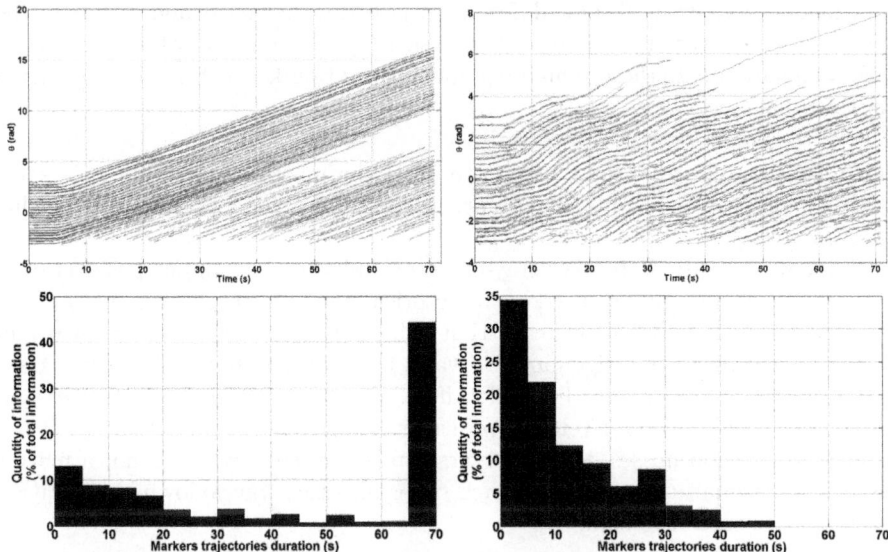

Fig. 2. Top: Markers positions along θ axis as a function of time for 2 trials with 24 pedestrians (Left: trial with good tracking conditions. Right: trial with bad tracking conditions). One can observe that many markers occlusions happen but some markers are tracked during all along the trial with no loss. Bottom: Repartition of information by markers trajectories duration for the same trials. Most of the information is contained in long (resp. short) markers trajectories on the left (resp. right) plot.

with r the mean radius of both markers. Markers should be grouped if and only if belonging to the same participant. Ambiguities occur in the noisiest parts of motion data. We apply two conservative rules to decide on markers grouping. Markers i_1 and i_2 are grouped if:

- the mean distance $\overline{\mathbf{d}_{i_1,i_2}}$ between markers during the period of time they are both detected is below $1.3 * 10^{-1} m$.
- th maximum distance $\mathbf{d}_{i_1,i_2}^{max}$ between markers is below $3.3 * 10^{-1} m$.

At the end of this step, participants' trajectory is described by the ones of a group of markers. The number of markers ranges from 1 up to 4 depending on occlusions. But in most challenging conditions, a complete loss of markers belonging to a same participant is observed. The trajectory of a participant can be described as a succession of separated pieces of group of markers. However, they are not labeled as belonging to the same participant. Thus, these pieces need to be merged and regrouped.

Matching trajectories. We merge some pieces of trajectories that do not overlap in time by using a linear extrapolation method, in time, on θ axis. We only make short-time ($< 2sec$) extrapolations to avoid risks of ambiguities.

Finally, there are still some different trajectories that must match, due to the fact that they overlap in time or do not satisfy the conditions of extrapolation. We manually merge these remaining trajectories thanks to their visual position in time on θ coordinate.

Labeling markers. Next task is to label the markers belonging to a same participant. Figure 3 (Top) shows markers positions along r (Left) and z (Right) coordinates.

First we identify H marker trajectories thanks to their upper position on z axis. Then we identify left-marker trajectories thanks to their position on r axis (This position is higher if the pedestrian walks in the anti-trigonometric way and lower if he walks in the trigonometric way). It is easier to detect L markers once head-markers have already been identified. Finally we identify N marker and R marker thanks to their relative positions on the r axis. Note that when too much information misses, these markers can be inverted, which is not a matter since they are actually close one each other and that the following estimation step palliate such inversion.

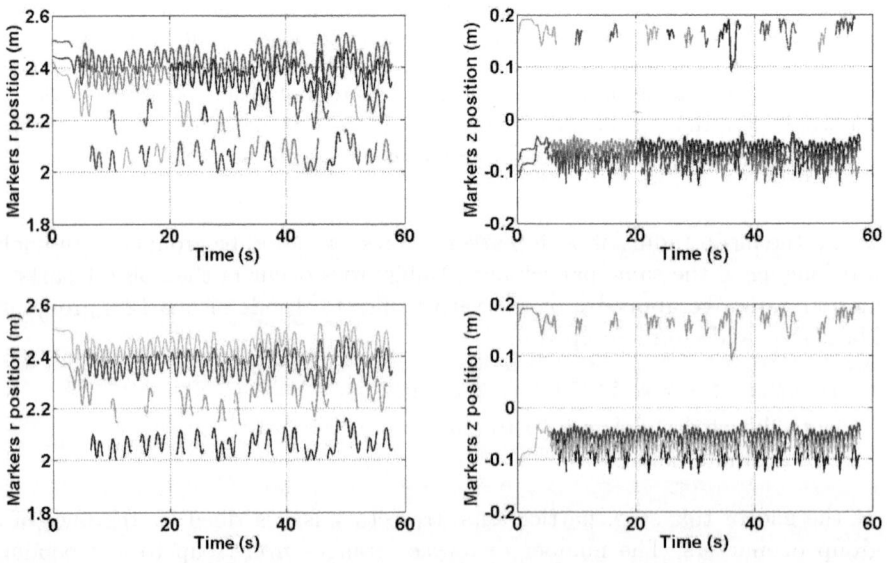

Fig. 3. Top: Unlabeled markers positions on r (Left) and z (Right) axes. Bottom: Identified markers positions on r (Left) and z (Right) axes. H, L, R and N marker are clearly observable.

3.3 Estimation of Participant Position

We aim at estimating the participant position $\mathbf{X}(t)$ at each time t whatever the number of markers describing the motion, and even if no data is available at this time. The method is based on the following hypothesis: a group of markers belonging to a same participant follows the motion of a solid in translation and rotation. Under this hypothesis, the position of a $i-$marker Z_i^*

$$Z_i^*(t) = \mathbf{X}(t) + \mathbf{R}_z(\alpha(t)).\mathbf{L}_i \tag{4}$$

where $\mathbf{X}(t)$ is the pedestrian position at time t, $\alpha(t)$ is the pedestrian orientation angle i.e. the direction in which it is moving, $\mathbf{R}_z(\alpha)$ is the rotation matrix around z axis with a given angle α and $\mathbf{L}_i$ is the vector from the pedestrian position to the $i-$marker. We call the $\mathbf{L}_i$ rigid skeleton of the pedestrian. Pedestrian position, orientation and skeleton are the model's parameters and should be evaluated through the markers positions measurements $\mathbf{Z}_i(t)$. We choose to explicitly estimate $\mathbf{L}_i$ and α to obtain a well-posed linear (easy to solve) problem for finding the pedestrian position.

Estimation of L_i. The skeleton is calculated in three steps:

- centering of measurements $\mathbf{Z}'_i = \mathbf{Z}_i - \frac{1}{4}\sum_{j=H,R,L,N} \mathbf{Z}_j$, where the subscripts H, R, L, N refer to the markers names given above.
- rotation of the $\mathbf{Z}'_i$ to align $(\mathbf{Z}'_L - \mathbf{Z}'_N) \times (\mathbf{Z}'_R - \mathbf{Z}'_N)$ on the y axis.
- the skeleton points $\mathbf{L}_L$, $\mathbf{L}_R$, $\mathbf{L}_H$ and $\mathbf{L}_N$ are respectively the median points of the rotated $\mathbf{Z}'_L$, $\mathbf{Z}'_R$, $\mathbf{Z}'_H$, $\mathbf{Z}'_N$.

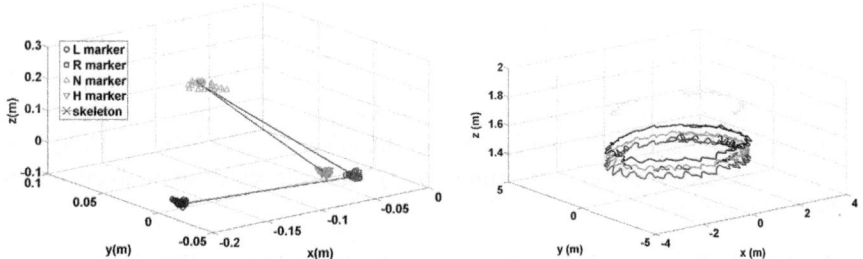

Fig. 4. Left: Example of an evaluated pedestrian skeleton using four markers. Right: A reconstructed pedestrian position over time obtained from its H, L, R and N markers. Only 5% of the markers positions are drawn for representation purpose.

An example of a pedestrian skeleton is shown in Figure 4 (Left). If the markers of one pedestrian are never visible all together at the same time, we use a mean skeleton over the other pedestrians.

Assumptions on the skeleton motion. During a given time interval T, the pedestrian position coordinates time-evolution can be approximated by a polynomial function:

$$\mathbf{X}(t+t') = \sum_{k=1}^{3}\sum_{j=1}^{N_k} U_{j+k(N_k-1)} t'^{(j-1)} \mathbf{e}_k \text{ with } t' \in \left[-\frac{T}{2}, \frac{T}{2}\right] \tag{5}$$

where N_k are the polynomial degrees in the different k-directions (i.e. x, y, and z), U_j its coefficients and $\mathbf{e}_k$ the corresponding unit vectors. This equation is a truncated Taylor series of $\mathbf{X}(t)$ around t, where $(U_{1+k(N_k-1)})_{k=1..3}$ is the position X at time t so that the approximation is only valid for small duration T. Introducing this expression into eq. 4 and using the explicit approximations for the skeleton $\mathbf{L}_i$ and orientation $\alpha(t)$ leads to a linear set of equations in term of U_j.

Estimation of participant orientation. It is assumed that the participants follow a rotational motion. Thus, their orientation is simply given by the direction of θ axis according to their positions. An orientation is associated to each measurement $\mathbf{Z}_i$, then $\alpha(t)$ is evaluated by a linear fitting of this orientation, assuming a constant velocity during the duration T.

Numerical resolution. We use a standard linear least square method to evaluate the U_j coefficients. The number of unknown parameters values is $\sum_{k=1}^{3} N_k$ and the number of equations is three times the number of measurements during the time interval T, which is denoted by $N_T(t)$. Several precautions must be taken in the choice of T. First, from a numerical point of view, to solve the set of equations and prevent numerical instabilities, the duration T must be small enough to ensure the validity of equation 5 and large enough to ensure that the problem is overdetermined. Second, it is well known that a least square fitting procedure could give inaccurate results in case of unbalanced data, i.e. when all available data are on the same side of the point of interest.

To circumvent such limitations, we choose an initial value of T: $T_0 = 8.33 * 10^{-3}s$, i.e. the frame rate at which the data were recorded. If all the data are on the same side or $N_T < 10 * max_{k=1..3}(N_k)$, we increment the value of T by T_0.

Sharp variations in $T(t)$ could results in sharp variation in the estimation of the pedestrian position. To avoid such a problem and ensure $\mathbf{X}(t)$ continuity, we detect the jump in $T(t)$ and overestimate $T(t)$ before or after the jump depending on the variation sign.

Interpolation using neighbors. When all the markers of one participant are occluded for a long period of time (> 2 sec), previous approximation can cause major difference between estimated and real positions. In such cases, we use the fact that participants are walking in lane and prefer to use the positions of the participant neighbors (previous and next) to interpolate his position on θ coordinate. We define the ratio $R(t)$ as:

$$R(t) = \frac{\theta_i(t) - \theta_{i+1}(t)}{\theta_{i-1}(t) - \theta_{i+1}(t)} \tag{6}$$

When $t \in [t_s, t_e]$ the time gap where no data is available for the considered participant, we linearly interpolate $R(t)$ as follows:

$$\widetilde{R}(t) = R(t_s) + (R(t_e) - R(t_s)) * \frac{t - t_s}{t_e - t_s} \tag{7}$$

Thus we get participant θ position:

$$\theta_i(t) = \theta_{i+1}(t) + R(t) * (\theta_{i-1}(t) - \theta_{i+1}(t)) \tag{8}$$

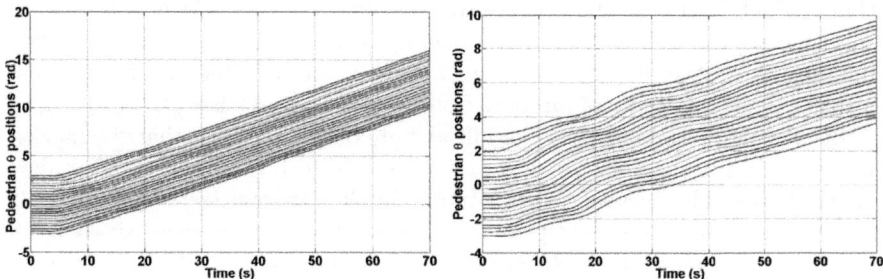

Fig. 5. Plot of resulting pedestrians trajectories corresponding to the ones of Fig 2

4 Results and Evaluation

4.1 Validation of the Pedestrian Position Estimation

To validate the method presented in section 3.3, the algorithm is applied to trials with best tracking conditions. We use an experimental record with 16 pedestrians walking in lane around a two meters radius circle. For 3 of these 16 participants, measurements of the four markers are fully available (i.e., at each time step). For these 3 participants, we compare the reconstructed position to the mean of the four markers instantaneous positions. Each trajectory of approximately 54 seconds consists in 6427 3-dimensional positions for each of the four markers. Reconstructions and evaluations are performed for all discrete time values. The method validation is performed on the accuracy of position reconstruction and on the robustness to the lack of measurements.

Comparison of results to mean positions of markers. With the following numerical parameters : $T_0 = 0.1s$, $N_1 = 2$, $N_2 = 2$, $N_3 = 1$, the mean distance between positions obtained by the reconstruction method and the mean markers one is $1.4 * 10^{-3}m$ and the maximum distance is $2 * 10^{-2}m$. The new method gives results similar to the one of the mean marker method in fully-available markers position cases. Different parameters could not significantly improve this margin which is attributed to the skeleton evaluation step, errors being of the same order of magnitude. Numerical tests (not presented here) show that this error level is reached for a large range of parameters N_k and T_0, for example, with ($N_k \in [2, 20]$ and $T_0 = 0.1$ s) or ($N_k \in [4, 10]$ and $T_0 = 0.1$ s). This robustness to numerical parameters is attributed to the dynamical procedure for the T fitting duration computation which links T to T_0 and N_k. We use the parameter values listed above in the following subsection to make the parameter fitting as local as possible to improve the robustness to errors on markers position.

Robustness to marker loss. The robustness of the position estimation method to marker loss is investigated. To mimic markers loss, we work from high quality data again and remove some measurements using the following two states Markov chain model describing the discrete time-evolution of the marker visibility: state 1 : the marker is visible and state 0 the marker is invisible. The probability of jumping from state 0 to state 1 is dt/τ, with τ the life-time of a marker disappearing. The probability of jumping from state 1 to state 0 is $a\, dt/((1-a)\tau)$, with a the proportion time of loss. The initial state of this model is that the marker is visible with a probability of $1-a$ and corresponds to the mean steady solution of the model. The accuracy of this model in the range of tested parameter has been checked (results are not presented here). This model is successively applied to the measurements of each marker of the three fully available participants' trajectories. The degraded data are then processed by the reconstruction algorithm and compared to the mean marker method with fully-available markers data which are used as a reference to evaluate the method. Twenty replicates of the three trajectories are performed to compute mean error of the reconstruction method.

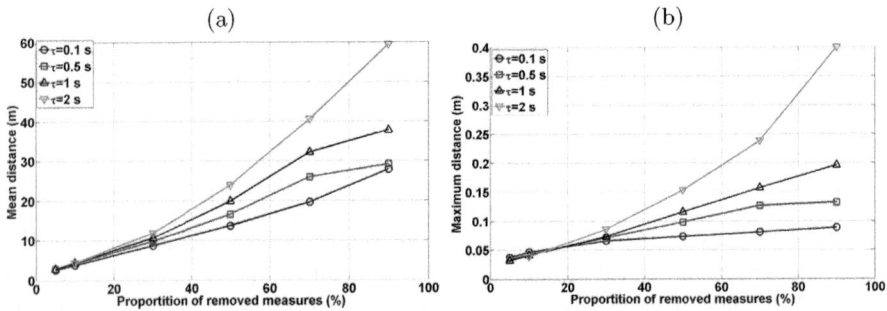

Fig. 6. Evolution of the distance between reconstructed positions and the reference method with the proportion of removed measurements for different disappearing life time τ. (a) Mean values and (b) maximal values.

Figure 6 shows the evolution of the distance between the position reconstructed using data with removed data and the reference position for different a and τ parameters: from 5% to 90% data removed during a duration from 0.1 s to 2 consecutive seconds. As expected, the distance error increases with increasing of the lack of data and with the time that a marker stay continuously invisible but its means remain lower than $6*10^{-2}m$ (Fig. 6a). Such a mean error level is smaller than a human's width (approximately $5.50*10^{-1}m$ [10]) and validates the algorithm to accurately track the participants. We should notice that the maximal distance error is larger than $3*10^{-1}m$ for $(a>0.7)\&(\tau \geq 2s)$, so that this reconstruction is problematic at some time or under specific conditions. When the reconstruction is performed on such cases, an additional attention must be provided to access the validity of the participant trajectory evaluation. This error estimation versus the quality of the measures helps us to a priori determine whether the collected data are sufficient or too bad to be analyzed.

4.2 Evaluation of the Overall Method

As we have trials of different quality, we evaluate our method as follows:

- From the trial with good tracking conditions presented in Figure 2, we randomly remove information in a way to have both the same quantity of missing information and the same distribution of markers lengths than on the trial with bad tracking conditions.
- We run our method on this new trial.
- We compare its resulting participants trajectories with the ones obtained with the original trial.

We observe a mean difference of position on θ coordinate of $1.13 * 10^{-2} rad$ ($std = 7.30 * 10^{-3} rad$, $max = 5.02 * 10^{-2} rad$) which is very low and superimposes the original trajectories. A higher mean difference is observed on r coordinate: $6.73 * 10^{-2} m$ ($std = 6.78 * 10^{-2} m$, $max = 4.93 * 10^{-1} m$). We do not re-generate oscillations due to pedestrian stepping activity as we are not mainly interested in this study but more on longitudinal observations.

5 Discussion and Conclusion

We proposed a method that computes a human mean position from motion capture raw data. This method is composed of four steps: markers grouping, markers labeling, computation of participant skeleton and estimation of participant position. From capture with 30% missing information, we obtained continuous estimations of positions.

The main assumption in the position estimation method is the rigidity of marker skeleton motion, i.e. the distance between markers of a subject remains constant. Removing this assumption will result to a problem formulation on the form of a non-linear optimization problem which is known to be difficult to numerically handle. However, restricting our attention to cases where the definition of a rigid skeleton is valid, the position estimation method can be generalized to any planar motion by only changing the evaluation of the participant orientation. This can easily be achieved by expressing α in terms of instantaneous velocities or of a vector relying markers direction. Finally, the labeling method can be easily extended to any 1-D crowd study.

In the context of crowd study, kinematic capture is important for modeling and evaluation purpose but difficult due to acquisition conditions. Our data are intended to be available for crowd study and we detail their reconstruction process.

Acknowledgments. This work has been funded by French research agency ANR via PEDIGREE project ANR-08-SYSC-015. We also thank the M2S laboratory members, University of Rennes2, who helped us a lot in the preparation and execution of the experimental studies.

References

1. Chai, J., Hodgins, J.K.: Performance animation from low-dimensional control signals. ACM Trans. Graph. 24, 686–696 (2005)
2. Courty, N., Cuzol, A.: Conditional stochastic simulation for character animation. Computer Animation and Virtual Worlds 21, 443–452 (2010)
3. Daamen, W., Hoogendoorn, S.P.: Qualitative results from pedestrian laboratory experiments. In: Pedestrian and Evacuation Dynamics (2003)
4. Dorfmller-Ulhaas, K.: Robust optical user motion tracking using a kalman filter. Tech. rep., Universittsbibliothek der Universitt Augsburg (2003)
5. Herda, L., Fua, P., Plänkers, R., Boulic, R., Thalmann, D.: Skeleton-based motion capture for robust reconstruction of human motion. Comp. Animation, 77 (2000)
6. Kretz, T., Grnebohm, A., Schreckenberg, M.: Experimental study of pedestrian flow through a bottleneck. Journal of Statistical Mechanics: Theory and Experiment, 10014 (2006)
7. Li, L., McCann, J., Pollard, N., Faloutsos, C.: Bolero: a principled technique for including bone length constraints in motion capture occlusion filling. In: Proceedings of ACM SIGGRAPH/Eurographics Symposium on Computer Animation (2010)
8. Pettré, J., Ondřej, J., Olivier, A.H., Cretual, A., Donikian, S.: Experiment-based modeling, simulation and validation of interactions between virtual walkers. In: Proceedings of ACM SIGGRAPH/Eurographics Symposium on Computer Animation (2009)
9. Seyfried, A., Passon, O., Steffen, B., Boltes, M., Rupprecht, T., Klingsch, W.: New insights into pedestrian flow through bottlenecks. Transportation Science 43, 395–406 (2009)
10. Still, G.: Crowd dynamics. Ph.D. thesis, University of Warwick, UK (2000)
11. Taylor, G.W., Hinton, G.E., Roweis, S.: Modeling human motion using binary latent variables. In: Advances in Neural Information Processing Systems (2006)
12. Yamori, K.: Going with the flow: Micro-macro dynamics in the macrobehavioral patterns of pedestrian crowds. Psychological Review 105, 530–557 (1998)

A Quantitative Methodology to Evaluate Motion-Based Animation Techniques

Gutemberg Guerra-Filho, George Raphael, and Venkat Devarajan

University of Texas at Arlington,
Arlington, TX USA 76019
guerra@cse.uta.edu, george.thekkanathraphael@mavs.uta.edu, venkat@uta.edu

Abstract. We present a novel methodology to quantitatively evaluate the synthesized motion generated by a motion-based animation technique. Our quantitative evaluation methodology provides a measure of how well each algorithm synthesizes motion based on their rotational and translational similarities to the ground truth in a motion database. To demonstrate the effectiveness of our methodology, we focus on techniques that combine different motions into a single spliced action where individual motions are performed simultaneously. We implement three splicing algorithms to perform a comparison study based on our quantitative evaluation methodology. The splicing algorithms considered are spatial body alignment, segmentation-based, and naïve DOF replacement. The spatial body alignment adapts the spliced motion according to this joint correlation and, consequently, performs best under our evaluation methodology.

Keywords: quantitative evaluation, motion-based animation, motion splicing.

1 Introduction

In general, the correctness of an algorithm for motion synthesis or analysis is mostly assessed visually. This is very subjective in nature and does not provide a uniform method of evaluation. On the other hand, the performance of any algorithm can be quantitatively evaluated when they are tested with precise data providing sampling of all motion variations in a principled controlled fashion.

In this paper, we introduce a novel technique to quantitatively evaluate and compare synthesized motions against actual captured motions. Our quantitative evaluation methodology provides a measure of how well each algorithm synthesizes motion based on their rotational and translational similarities to the ground truth in a motion database. Initially, the synthesize motion is time-aligned to the ground truth motion. The time-displacement for each DOF is used to produce a normalized spliced motion. This normalized motion is compared to the ground truth motion by computing a similarity distance based on translational and rotational data at three orders of derivatives.

In our evaluation methodology, the input data for the evaluated techniques and the corresponding ground truth output data is obtained from the Human

Motion Database (HMD) [3]. To validate our quantitative evaluation methodology, we perform a comparison study focused on motion splicing techniques. Motion splicing techniques combine different actions into a single motion where the individual actions are performed simultaneously. For example, given an action where the subject jumps and an action where the subject reaches, a splicing method combines the jump action with the reach action to generate a single whole-body motion where the subject simultaneously jumps and reaches (see Fig. 1).

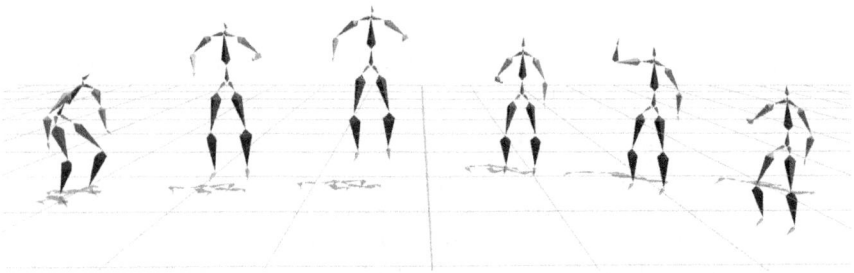

Fig. 1. A spliced motion for the Jump and Reach actions

The main contributions of this paper are: (1) a novel quantitative evaluation methodology for motion-based animation techniques which enables the precise assessment of these methods and (2) a comparison of three significant motion splicing methods to validate our comparison methodology. This is the first time a quantitative evaluation is performed on motion-based techniques. We will make this methodology and the human motion database available to the research community to further promote progress in this field. In this sense, this methodology and the associated data will serve as an objective criteria for measuring this progress and for providing better guidance for future research efforts.

The rest of this paper contains details of the quantitative evaluation methodology, the splicing techniques used to validate our evaluation methodology, and the application of our quantitative evaluation methodology to compare their results. Section 2 discusses preliminary work on synthesized motion evaluation. Section 3 introduces our quantitative evaluation methodology. Section 4 reviews the three methods selected to apply our quantitative evaluation methodology. Section 5 presents the experimental results obtained by performing our quantitative evaluation in the splicing algorithms. Our conclusions are discussed in Section 6.

2 Related Work

The motion-based animation field concerns the synthesis of motion from existing real motion data captured previously using motion capture technology. Recently, there is significant progress in this area addressing several problems such as motion retargetting [2,11], motion generalization [14,16,12], motion transitioning [1,9], and motion splicing [4,7,13]. However, in this paper, we are concerned specifically with the quantitative evaluation of such methods.

Kwon et al. [10] used footprint pattern to validate locomotion. Kim et al. [8] analyzed the beat pattern in a motion to segment a motion and validate the data. Safonova et al. [15] showed how to analyze the physical correctness of interpolated motion. Jang et al. [7] examined the static balance of generated motion to test its physical validity. These methods basically use indirect criteria based on the geometry of the motion (*i.e.*, location of footsteps), on the frequency of the motion (*i.e.*, beat pattern), or on its physical feasibility. However, none of these methods directly compare the synthesized motion to the ground truth. In our methodology, we take advantage of a data benchmark for several motion-based animation problems, the Human Motion Database, where we have access to sets of input motion with the corresponding ground truth motion. This allows the direct comparison between the synthesized motion and the correct motion.

Ikemoto et al. [6] used Support Vector Machines (SVM) to validate synthesized motion. The synthesized data is compared against a large set of training motion data, only to verify whether the synthesized motion can be classified as a natural motion. In this context, a natural motion concerns any motion aesthetically similar to how a real human would perform the same motion. Therefore, the output of this SVM technique is only related to how natural the synthesized motion is in a general sense. The response of the SVM methodology is not specific to the particular motion being evaluated. For example, an algorithm could synthesize a natural walk motion as a jump forward motion and still be validated by this method.

3 Quantitative Evaluation Methodology

The quantitative evaluation methodology is a three-stage process: time-alignment, motion normalization, and motion distance computation. During the first stage of the evaluation, each degree of freedom of the ground truth motion (M_G) is independently time-aligned to the respective degree of freedom of the synthesized motion (M_S). In the second stage of the evaluation, the aligned frames are used to compute a time-normalized version (M'_S) of the synthesize motion. In the third stage, the motion distance $D(M_G, M'_S)$ for all aligned frames between ground truth and normalized motion is computed for rotational data (joint angle, angular velocity, and angular acceleration) and translational data (joint position, linear velocity, linear acceleration). Next, each step is explained in detail.

3.1 Time-Alignment

Initially, we perform the time-alignment between motion M_G during a given period of time ranging from frame t_G^0 to frame t_G^1 and motion M_S during a given period of time ranging from frame t_S^0 to frame t_S^1. For each DOF j in the skeleton

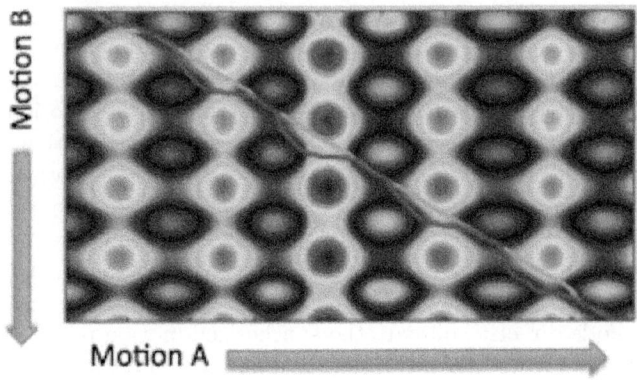

Fig. 2. The 2D matching space for an alignment path

model, we use Dynamic Time Warping (DTW) [9] to find the time displacement function $\Delta_j = DTW(M_G^j(t_G^0, ..., t_G^1), M_S^j(t_S^0, ..., t_S^1))$, where $M_X^j(t)$ is the value assumed by DOF j at frame t in motion M_X. DTW finds the optimal matching displacement between M_G^j and M_S^j such that $M_G^j(t)$ corresponds to $M_S^j(t + \Delta_j(t))$. Note that M_G is the reference motion and DTW only uses rotational data for the matching.

3.2 Naïve Degree of Freedom Replacement

The time-displacement function Δ_j corresponds to an alignment path in the 2D matching space $W = [t_G^0, t_G^1] \times [t_S^0, t_S^1]$ (see Fig. 2). A discrete point (t, t') in the matching space W represents the possible matching between frame t of M_G^j and frame t' of M_S^j. DTW assumes an alignment path is monotonic and, consequently, for a point (t, t') in an alignment path, the next point in the path is either $(t+1, t'+1)$, $(t+1, t')$, or $(t, t'+1)$ which is associated with a diagonal step, a horizontal step, or a vertical step, respectively. Note that a horizontal step matches two frames of M_G^j to a single frame of M_S^j. While computing the best alignment path using DTW, we introduce a penalty function p_h on the number n_h of consecutive horizontal steps and a penalty function p_v on the number n_v of consecutive vertical steps. This way, the recursive path cost function $C(t, t')$ representing the matching cost between $M_G^j(t_G^0, ..., t)$ and $M_S^j(t_S^0, ..., t')$ is defined as

$$C(t, t') = c(t, t') + \min\{C_d, C_h, C_v\},$$

where

$$c(t, t') = |M_G^j(t) - M_S^j(t')|,$$
$$C_d = C(t-1, t'-1),$$
$$C_h = C(t-1, t') + p_h(n_h(t-1, t') + 1),$$
$$C_v = C(t, t'-1) + p_v(n_v(t, t'-1) + 1).$$

We define $p_y(x)$ as $\frac{\epsilon * x}{\kappa - x}$ for $y = \{h, v\}$, where ϵ is a constant error factor to penalize for consecutive horizontal or vertical steps, and κ is the maximum number of allowed horizontal or vertical steps. The number $n_h(t, t')$ of consecutive horizontal steps and the number $n_v(t, t')$ of consecutive vertical steps are computed recursively as:

$$n_h(t, t') = \begin{cases} n_h(t-1, t') + 1 & \text{if } C(t, t') = c(t, t') + C_h \\ 0 & \text{otherwise} \end{cases}$$

$$n_v(t, t') = \begin{cases} n_v(t, t'-1) + 1 & \text{if } C(t, t') = c(t, t') + C_v \\ 0 & \text{otherwise} \end{cases}$$

The alignment path that corresponds to the displacement function Δ_j is obtained by backtracking the computed path cost C starting at $C(t_G^1, t_S^1)$. At each discrete point (t, t'), $\Delta_j(t) = t' - t$ and the previous point in the path is the point $(t^*, t^{*\prime})$ such that $C(t^*, t^{*\prime}) = \min\{C(t-1, t'-1), C(t-1, t'), C(t, t'-1)\}$.

3.3 Motion Normalization

Once the time displacement function is found for all DOFs, we can generate the time-normalized motion M_S' from the spliced motion M_S such that every frame of M_S' is aligned to the corresponding frame of the ground truth motion M_G. We generate the normalized motion using the time displacement functions Δ_j computed for each DOF j in the time-alignment step. For every DOF j, a frame t of the ground truth corresponds to a frame t' of the spliced motion such that $t' = t + \Delta_j(t)$. Hence, the normalized spliced motion $M_S^{j'}(t)$ at frame t is obtained from the corresponding frame t' of the spliced motion $M_S^j(t')$: $M_S^{j'}(t) = M_S^j(t + \Delta_j(t))$. Note that the normalized motion has the same length of the ground truth motion to allow a one-to-one matching of frames.

The time-normalization is necessary to avoid artifacts in the evaluation due to arbitrary coordination of different joints. For example, a synthesized motion splicing a clap action and a walk action could be coordinated in such a way that the clapping happens exactly when the left foot is landing in front. However, the ground truth was captured in such a way that the subject claps when the right foot lands. In this case, if time-normalization is not performed, any measure will result in a large distance between the synthesized motion and the ground truth. On the other hand, if the synthesized motion is time-normalized to the ground truth, we will compare a normalized motion which is aligned to the ground truth and, consequently, avoid such artifacts in the evaluation. For each joint angle, the time-normalization mostly corrects for a constant offset between the synthesized motion and the ground truth motion. Therefore, the time-normalization consists of a time shift that alters the synthesized motion only minimally in terms of angular velocity and angular acceleration of the joint angle functions.

3.4 Motion Distance Computation

Once the time-alignment is found for each DOF, the metric $D(M_G, M'_S)$ between two motions M_G and M'_S is defined as:

$$D(M_G, M'_S) = \frac{\sum_{t=t_G^0}^{t_G^1} \sum_{j=1}^{d} |M_G^j(t) - M_S^{j'}(t)|}{t_G^1 - t_G^0},$$

where d is the number of DOFs (joint angles or 3D coordinates of joint points). This metric considers rotational data (joint angles) for the 0th order derivative (position). We consider a total of six different versions of this metric with all combinations between two different motion representations (rotational data and translational data) and three derivative orders (position, velocity, and acceleration). After generating the normalized motion M'_S, we may compute the translational data (3D Cartesian coordinates for all joints) for each frame. Given the rotational data and translational data for motion M_G and for normalized motion M_S, we then compute the first and the second order derivatives.

For example, lets consider translational data and the first derivative (velocity). First, we compute the time-alignment, second we perform the motion warping, third we compute the translational data for both M_G and M_S, then we find the linear velocity and finally, we compute the distance for all the frames between t_G^0 and t_G^1. For translational data, we use Euclidean distance instead of calculating the absolute difference between values. For a pose associated with a particular frame t, the distance is the sum of the Euclidean distances between the corresponding joints in the two different motions. In order to avoid the need for spatial alignment (translation and rotation), we set the first six degrees of freedom associated with global position and global orientation to be zeroes.

4 Motion Splicing Validation

In this section, we describe the three splicing techniques considered for comparison using our quantitative evaluation methodology: spatial body alignment [4], segmentation-based algorithm [7], and naïve DOF replacement [13]. We selected these techniques because they are among the most significant and novel methods of motion splicing. The spatial body alignment method considers the correlation between joints. The segmentation-based algorithm is based on the kinetic parameters and accounts for balance in the spliced motion. The naïve DOF replacement is a method capable of splicing any pair of motions.

Spatial body alignment splices whole-body motion from two different actions performed while in locomotion. A temporal alignment is performed between the two motions using only the lower limbs and a path with least resistance for frame replacement is determined. A spatial alignment between the matched upper frames of both the motions is performed and a spliced motion is generated. The segmentation-based algorithm consists of segmenting the motion based on the overall body kinetic energy. A new spliced motion is synthesized by replacing similar partial motions associated with segments, where a partial motion is the motion of a connected component of the skeleton. The naïve DOF replacement of joints transfers some joint angle values associated with one joint from one motion to the corresponding joint in the spliced motion. Hence, the exact same motion associated with this joint in one motion is replicated on the spliced motion. As a part of our comparative study, we implemented these three motion splicing techniques. Thus we provide additional detail on each of these methods.

4.1 Spatial Body Alignment

Heck et al. [4] presented a simple and efficient technique for splicing together the upper body action of one motion and the lower body locomotion of another motion in a manner that preserves the fidelity of the original source motions. The approach was fundamentally based on the idea that interactive applications often divide character control to motion and locomotion while preserving the correlation between them.

The splicing algorithm works as follows. Suppose we have motion A and motion B with possibly the same locomotion performed by the lower body and different actions performed by the upper body. The algorithm decouples the upper body motion from the lower body motion of both motion A and motion B to create four individual motion sets: A_{Lower}, A_{Upper}, B_{Lower}, and B_{Upper}. Then the algorithm uses dynamic time warping [9] to find the best match between the lower body motions A_{Lower} and B_{Lower}. Once the time-alignment has been found using the lower body point cloud (x, y, and z global location of the lower body joints in the Cartesian coordinate system), the upper body motions A_{Upper} and B_{Upper} are matched according to the time-alignment obtained from the lower body motions. The spatial alignment translates and rotates the upper body of motion B to match that of the motion A.

Using the pelvis as the pivotal point between the upper body and lower body, the algorithm finds the best orientation for pelvis of the spliced motion using Horn's method [5]. Finally, in order to maintain the posture of the character in the spliced motion similar to the original action (B_{Upper}), the pelvis is tweaked again to best match the shoulder alignment of the spliced motion to the shoulder alignment of motion B. The best orientation is computed using shoulders, spine, pelvis, and the hips.

4.2 Segmentation-Based Algorithm

In the segmentation-based algorithm [7], the motion is divided into partial motions involving fewer DOFs. Each partial motion corresponds to a connected component of the skeleton. Partial motions from different segments are spliced together to generate a complete motion. Segmentation, principal component analysis, and clustering techniques are used to find the best matches between base partial motions used to enable the combination of different partial motions. Realism and physical plausibility of the combined motions are verified using the Support Vector Machines approach [6]. The key advantage of this technique is the reduction in database requirements and instantaneous generation of motion. This splicing technique allows any group of joints in one motion to be replaced with a similar set of joints from the other motion. Since the segmentation and clustering is based on the kinetic parameters, the spliced motion would closely follow the kinetic nature of the base motion to maintain the balance of the body.

4.3 Naïve Degree of Freedom Replacement

Naïve DOF replacement [13] is the technique for generating motions by replacement of any particular joint or groups of joints from one motion with that from another motion. Naïve DOF replacement has been widely used in the animation industry. Many motion-splicing algorithms incorporate additional blocks to naïve DOF replacement method, that would either find matching clusters or automatically check for physical plausibility of the synthesized motion.

Let M_A be a walking motion and M_B be a waving motion, the joint angles of the right arm in the motion M_A can be replaced by the joint angles of the right arm in motion M_B to create a spliced motion M_S that resembles a motion where the character walks and waves.

5 Experimental Results

The quality of the synthesized motion is one of the most important features of any motion-based animation technique. Unfortunately, there is no standard method to quantitatively measure motion quality. We propose a novel quantitative evaluation methodology where the motion synthesized using various techniques is compared to ground truth motion data. This is the first time such a quantitative evaluation approach has been presented. Our method uses one to one comparison between the synthesized data and the ground truth. For the purpose of comparison, we used ground truth data from the Human Motion Database [3] constructed by acquiring real motion from volunteer subjects using optical motion capture.

5.1 Human Motion Database

The Human Motion Database (HMD) [3] contains real motion information from human subjects for different phenomena associated with several aspects of human movement such as a praxicon (a lexicon of human actions), a cross-validation set, generalization, transitioning, co-articulation, splicing, and interactions. This database is primarily focused on assisting motion-based animation techniques concerning training and testing data for several problems. The set of motions in the motion splicing dataset includes actions being performed individually and in combination with other action. For example, a splicing motion set contains a motion where a subject waves while standing (first individual motion), a motion where the subject drinks water while standing (second individual motion), and a third

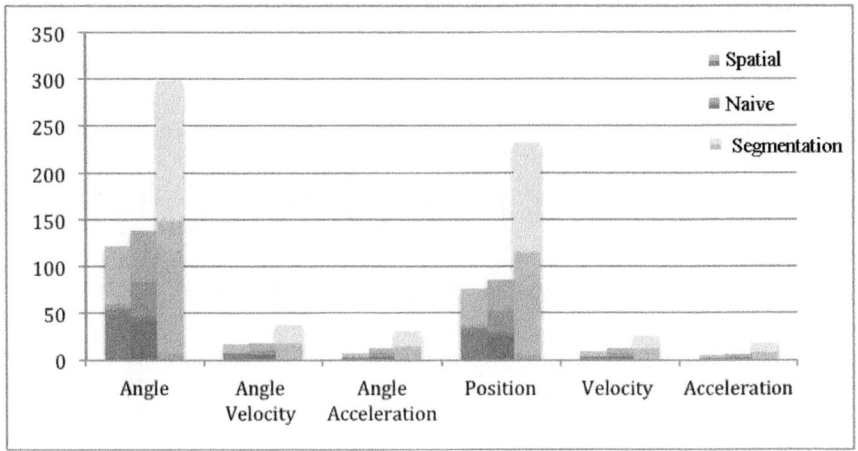

Fig. 3. Experimental results of our quantitative evaluation for motion splicing comparison

motion where the subject drinks and waves at the same time while standing (combination motion). Therefore, the input for a motion splicing algorithm is the motion capture data associated with the two individual motions to be spliced into a single synthesized motion where the subject performs both actions simultaneously. The output of the motion synthesis algorithm is compared to the ground truth motion data which consists of the combined motion in our database. The ground truth spliced motion data was captured from the same subject just after the individual motions. More specifically, just after we collected the two individual motions, we also captured the motion where the subject performs both individual actions at the same time. The Human Motion Database contains 38 splicing motion sets that consist of the simultaneous combination (*i.e.*, splicing) of two actions. The 38 captured combination motions served as the ground truth motion data in our comparison. The individual actions are used as the input for the three splicing techniques and the output-synthesized motions using these techniques are compared to the corresponding ground-truth motions.

5.2 Motion Splicing Evaluation

The experimental results of our quantitative evaluation are shown in Figure 3. Each bar in the graph represents the average error values of each motion splicing technique for all 38 motion sets. Note that the error distance $D(M_G, M'_S)$ for a particular motion set is normalized according to the time length of the ground truth: $t_G^1 - t_G^0$. However, the distance accumulates errors for all d DOFs. The blue bar shows the error obtained using the spatial body alignment method [4]. The error for the rotational data (angular position, angular velocity, and angular acceleration) and translational data (position, linear velocity, and linear acceleration) came out to be 122.18, 16.74, 7.57, 76.94, 9.53, 5.40, respectively.

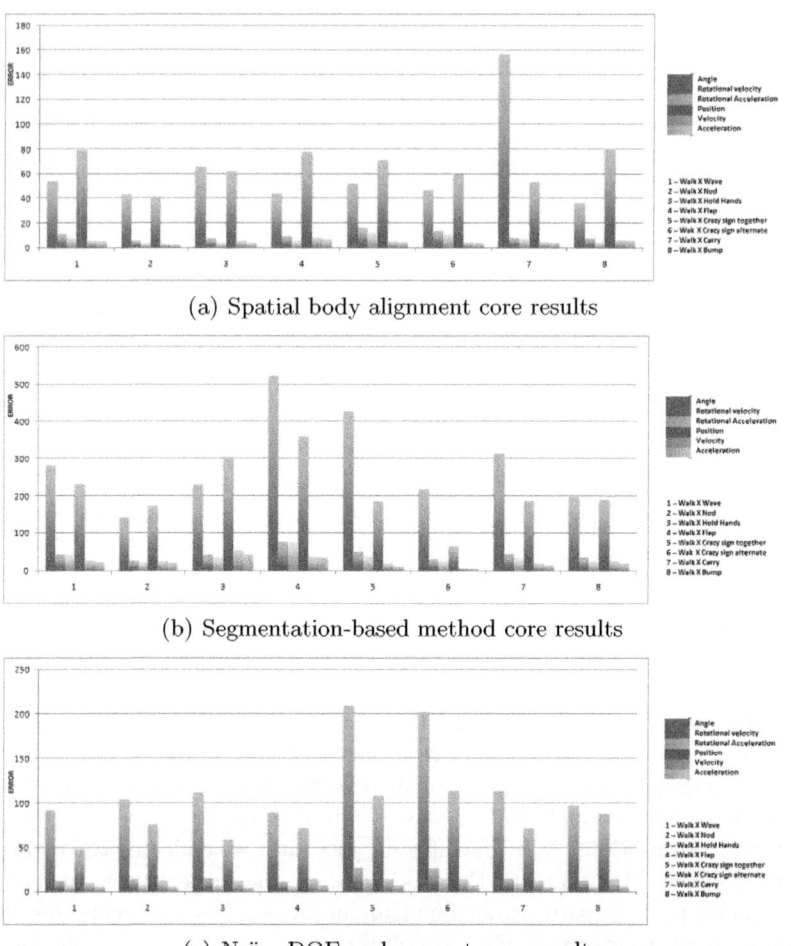

Fig. 4. Evaluation results for a core subset of spliced motions

The red bar corresponds to the naïve DOF replacement technique with rotational and translational values of 138.22, 17.72, 12.80, 85.96, 12.58, 5.58, respectively. The green bar represents the segmentation-based method [7] with the maximum error for translational and rotational data of 298.39, 37.57, 30.46, 232.48, 25.82, 18.02, respectively. For an absolute measure of quality, the ultimate goal of an algorithm is to achieve zero error for all motion distances. As a first quantitative evaluation of any motion-based animation algorithm, our results show that there is room for improvement in the state-of-the-art of motion splicing algorithms. However, the error values obtained by our evaluation are useful for the relative comparison between the different algorithms.

Our quantitative evaluation shows that the spatial body alignment method for splicing upper body action with locomotion is the best method for motion splicing. The reason for this might be that the spatial body alignment method accounts for the correlation of the body movement. In Fig. 4(a), we show the evaluation of the spatial body alignment method for a core subset of eight spliced motions: walk X wave, walk X nod, walk X hold hands, walk X flap, walk X crazy sign together, walk X crazy sign alternate, walk X carry, and walk X bump. These spliced actions were selected as core motions because they satisfy all the assumptions made by all considered algorithms. For example, spatial body alignment requires both individual motions to contain a locomotive action in the lower body.

On the other hand, the segmentation-based method is the worst because of the large jerkiness in the spliced motion. We are reasonably certain that this jerkiness is caused by the improper segmentation of the motion. The entire motion is segmented at local maximum and minimum of the total body kinetic energy, which divides a single action into multiple artificial parts. For example, the kick action is segmented into four different segments, since there are three minimum and two maximum values of velocity. When splicing this action on the other motion, if there were only two consecutive segments matching the segments in the kick, the action gets trimmed at undesirable frames creating jerkiness in the spliced motion. The results of the evaluation of the segmentation-based method for the core subset of actions are presented in Fig. 4(b).

Naïve DOF replacement is a technique that works better for splicing motions where the primary joints don't overlap. For example, in the case of an action where the person waves and an action where the person drinks using different hands, the naïve DOF replacement best splices these motions, as there are no additional constraints. However, in the case of an action, where the person jumps and kicks, this technique splices the motion, which looks unrealistic, as there are absolutely no parameters accounting for the balance and the comfort parameters in a motion. Fig. 4(c) shows the results obtained by this method.

6 Conclusion

This paper presents a novel way of quantitatively evaluating synthesized motion obtained using different motion-based animation techniques. This is the first time a quantitative evaluation is performed on a motion-based animation technique. The research effort in quantitatively evaluating synthesized motion has been non existent. Previously, synthesized motions have been validated either visually or using a set of training data rather than using the exact ground truth data.

In this paper, to demonstrate the effectiveness of our quantitative evaluation methodology, we implemented three significant splicing techniques and the motions generated using these methods were compared to the ground truth data in the Human Motion Database. The ground truth data consists of a diverse set of motions captured to test any splicing motion. Using 38 sets of motions in the ground truth data and the normalization technique mentioned earlier, quantitative motion evaluation now has an elegant solution. The results of our quantitative evaluation showed that the spatial body alignment method, in which the correlation of the joints is taken into account, provides the most realistic results. Segmenting a motion at local maximum and minimum of total kinetic energy can generate spliced motions with lesser similarity to the ground truth. Naïve DOF replacement is a good splicing technique, if the joints are carefully replaced. Implementing additional constraints can potentially improve this method.

References

1. Arikan, O., Forsyth, D.: Interactive motion generation from examples. ACM Transactions on Graphics 21(3), 483–490 (2002)
2. Gleicher, M.: Retargetting motion to new characters. In: Proceedings of ACM SIGGRAPH 1998, pp. 33–42 (1998)
3. Guerra-Filho, G., Biswas, A.: The human motion database: A cognitive and parametric sampling of human motion. In: Proceedings of IEEE International Conference on Automatic Face and Gesture Recognition (2011)
4. Heck, R., Kovar, L., Gleicher, M.: Splicing upper body actions with locomotion. Computer Graphics Forum 25(3), 459–466 (2006)
5. Horn, K.: Closed-form solution of absolute orientation using unit quaternions. Journal of the Optical Society of America A(4), 629–642 (1987)
6. Ikemoto, L., Forsyth, D.: Enriching a motion collection by transplanting limbs. In: Proceedings of ACM Siggraph/Eurographics Symposium on Computer Animation, pp. 99–108 (2004)
7. Jang, W., Lee, W., Lee, J.: Enriching a motion database by analogous combination of partial human motions. Proceedings of Visual Computing 24(4), 271–280 (2008)
8. Kim, T., Park, S., Shin, S.: Rhythmic-motion synthesis based on motion-beat analysis. In: Proceedings of ACM SIGGRAPH 2003, pp. 392–401 (2003)
9. Kovar, L., Gleicher, M., Pighin, F.: Motion graphs. ACM Transactions on Graphics 21(3), 473–482 (2002)
10. Kwon, T., Shin, S.: Motion modeling for on-line locomotion synthesis. In: Proceedings of ACM Siggraph/Eurographics Symposium on Computer Animation, pp. 29–39 (2005)
11. Lee, J., Shin, S.: Hierarchical approach to interactive motion editing for human-like figures. In: Proceedings of ACM SIGGRAPH 1999, pp. 39–48 (1999)
12. Lim, I., Thalmann, D.: Construction of animation models out of captured data. In: Proceedings of IEEE Int. Conf. on Multimedia and Expo., pp. 829–832 (2002)
13. Perlin, K.: Real time responsive animation with personality. IEEE Transactions on Visualization and Computer Graphics 1(1), 5–15 (1995)
14. Rose, C., Cohen, M., Bodenheimer, B.: Verbs and adverbs: multidimensional motion interpolation. IEEE Computer Graphics and Applications 18(5), 32–40 (1998)
15. Safonova, A., Hodgins, J., Pollard, N.: Synthesizing physically realistic human motion in low dimensional behavior-specific spaces. In: Proceedings of ACM Siggraph 2004, pp. 514–521 (2004)
16. Wiley, D., Hahn, J.: Interpolation synthesis of articulated figure motion. IEEE Computer Graphics and Applications 17(6), 39–45 (1997)

Parallelized Incomplete Poisson Preconditioner in Cloth Simulation

Costas Sideris[1], Mubbasir Kapadia[1,2], and Petros Faloutsos[1,3]

[1] University of California Los Angeles
[2] University of Pennsylvania
[3] York University

Abstract. Efficient cloth simulation is an important problem for interactive applications that involve virtual humans, such as computer games. A common aspect of many methods that have been developed to simulate cloth is a linear system of equations, which is commonly solved using conjugate gradient or multi-grid approaches. In this paper, we introduce to the computer gaming community a recently proposed preconditioner, the *incomplete Poisson* preconditioner (IPP), for conjugate gradient solvers. We show that IPP performs as well as the current state-of-the-art preconditioners, while being much more amenable to standard thread-level parallelism. We demonstrate our results on an 8-core Mac Pro and a 32-core Emerald Rigde system.

1 Introduction

Simulating flexible materials, such as cloth, is an important task for applications involving virtual humans such as computer games and visual effects. High quality offline simulations are achieved by using implicit methods for simulating cloth [20–22]. Real-time applications on the other hand use explicit or semi-explicit methods for cloth simulation in order to meet time constraints [5, 17]. Despite the decades of research on simulating flexible materials, the efficient simulation of cloth remains an important challenge for computer animation.

There exists a large amount of research that addresses algorithmic optimizations for speeding up implicit integration methods for simulating cloth. The use of preconditioners [4, 9, 13] have been shown to greatly reduce the number of iterations of the conjugate gradient method in an effort to achieve convergence. In this paper, we explore the use of a novel preconditioning scheme – *the incomplete poisson preconditioner* – that has not been used before in clothing simulation. Using a variety of standard benchmarks, we first demonstrate that this preconditioner is just as good, if not better than currently used methods. A major advantage of this method is that it is extremely easy to parallelize and can take advantage of the processing power available in current and next generation multi-core hardware. Current state of the art preconditioners [13] are not as suitable for parallelization and do not scale well with increase in computational resources. This paper makes the following contributions:

1. To our knowledge, we propose for the first time the use of the incomplete poisson preconditioner (IPP) for clothing simulation.
2. We compare the IPP to the most commonly used preconditioning methods in terms of efficiency, quality and ease of parallelization.
3. We demonstrate that a parallel implementation of the IPP achieves significant performance improvement on multi-core computers.
4. We demonstrate the scalability of the IPP on a state of the art 32-core compute server and show that it is ready for the next generation of hardware resources.

The rest of this document is organized as follows. Section 2 reviews related work. Section 3 presents an overview of the method we use for simulating cloth. We describe the Jacobi preconditioner, the Symmetric Successive over Relaxation, and the incomplete Cholesky preconditioner which are commonly used to accelerate convergence. In addition, we propose the use of the incomplete poisson preconditioner for cloth simulation. Section 4 compares the four preconditioning methods on four standard benchmarks and also demonstrates the effectiveness of parallelizing the incomplete poisson preconditioning scheme. Finally, Section 5 concludes with a discussion of future work.

2 Related Work

Early work by [20–22] has applied techniques from mechanical engineering and finite element communities to cloth simulation. Since then, there has been an extensive amount of work by different research groups [5, 7, 10, 23] that have addressed several aspects of simulating cloth. An extensive overview of cloth simulation techniques can be found in two survey papers [8, 16].

Preconditioners play a very important part in implicit cloth simulation as they can greatly speed up convergence of numerical methods. The work in [3] used a simple diagonal preconditioner for the modified preconditioned conjugate gradient method (MPCG). The work in [9] demonstrated 20% speedup by using a 3×3 block diagonal preconditioner. This work was extended in [4] by proposing an approximation of the filter matrix A of the MPCG. The work in [13] demonstrates the effectiveness of the incomplete Cholesky and Successive Symmetric over Relaxation (SSOR) preconditioning schemes by reducing the number of iterations by 20%.

Relation to Prior Work. In this paper, we first examine the fitness of three commonly used preconditioning schemes [3, 13] in comparison to the proposed incomplete poisson preconditioner. Our simulation method is similar to the implicit simulation method described in [2, 3]. We perform collision detection using distance fields [11]. Collision resolution is performed using the techniques described in [6] and [18].

3 Cloth Simulation Overview

There are many aspects to cloth simulation. A cloth simulator is required to solve a linear system of equations which is used to step the simulator forward by one time step. This system of equations is derived taking into account the specifics of the internal forces and their derivatives. Different soft and hard constraints are imposed on the simulation which must be met. Collision detection and resolution is another area of research that has many contributions. We refer the reader to excellent works in cloth simulation research [3, 12, 14, 15] for more information. In this paper, we focus on the methods of preconditioning that are used to accelerate the preconditioned conjugate gradient solver. Section 3.1 presents an overview of the preconditioned conjugate gradient solver and Section 3.2 describes the different methods of preconditioning for cloth simulation.

3.1 Preconditioned Conjugate Gradient Solver

An overview of the preconditioned conjugate gradient solver is shown in Algorithm 1. A detailed description of the algorithm can be found here [19]. The preconditioned conjugate gradient method takes as input the following: (a) a symmetric positive semi-definite matrix $\mathbf{A}$, (b) a symmetric positive definite preconditioning matrix $\mathbf{P}$ of the same dimension as $\mathbf{A}$, and (c) a vector $\mathbf{b}$. The algorithm iteratively solves the linear system of equations, $\mathbf{Ax} = \mathbf{b}$ and the iterations stop when $|\mathbf{b} - \mathbf{Ax}| < \epsilon|\mathbf{b}|$, where ϵ is a user-defined tolerance value. The preconditioning matrix $\mathbf{P}$, which must be easily invertible, speeds convergence to the extent that $\mathbf{P}^{-1}$ approximates $\mathbf{A}$.

3.2 Preconditioning Methods

We examine the performance of three commonly used preconditioning methods: (1) `diagonal`, (2) `symmetric successive over relaxation (SSOR)`, and (3) `incomplete cholesky` against the unconditioned conjugate gradient method. We also examine a new preconditioning scheme, the incomplete Poisson preconditioner, proposed by Ament et al.[1] for the Poisson problem. Their motivation was to find an easily parallelizable preconditioner for simulations on multi-gpu systems. To the best of our knowledge, this is the first time this preconditioning scheme has been applied to cloth simulation. The mathematical formulation of these preconditioners is as follows.

Diagonal (Jacobi) Preconditioner:

$$P = \text{diag}\{\mathbf{A}\}^{-1} \quad \text{or} \quad P_{i,i} = \frac{1}{A_{i,i}} \tag{1}$$

This simple preconditioning scheme approximates the inverse of a diagonal matrix. Although lacking in quality, it can be computed quickly and provides increase in performance in many cases. The computation of P^{-1} is relatively simple and this preconditioner can be subsequently applied using SpMV.

```
Procedure Preconditioned Conjugate Gradient Solver(A, x, b, P, ε)
Input: A: Left hand side of linear system of equations Ax = b.
Input: x: Input constraint.
Input: b: Right hand side of linear system of equations Ax = b.
Input: P: Preconditioner
Input: ε: Maximum tolerance
Output: x: Result.
// Initialization
r = b - Ax; // residual
d = P⁻¹ · r;
d_new = r · d;
while  i < MAX ∧ d_new > ε² do
    q = A · d;
    c = d · q; // curvature
    if c < 0 then
        return FAIL;
    else if c == 0 then
        break;
    end
    α = d_new/c;
    x = x + α · d;
    r = r - α · q;
    s = P⁻¹ · r;
    d_old = d_new;
    d_new = r · s;
    if d_new < 0 then
        break;
    end
    β = d_old/d_new;
    d = s + β · d;
    i = i + 1;
end
if d_new < 0 ∨ i == MAX then
    return FAIL;
else
    return SUCCESS;
end
```

Algorithm 1. Preconditioned Conjugate Gradient Solver

Incomplete Cholesky Preconditioner:

$$P = \left(LL^T\right)^{-1}, \tag{2}$$

where L is the Choleshy factorization defined as follows:

$$L_{i,i} = \sqrt{A_{i,i} - \sum_{k=1}^{i-1} L_{i,k}^2}, \tag{3}$$

$$L_{i,j} = \frac{1}{L_{i,i}}(A_{i,j} - \sum_{k=1}^{i-1} L_{i,k}L_{j,k}), \quad i > j, \tag{4}$$

with the additional constraint to keep the original sparsity pattern of A. The Incomplete Cholesky is derived from the Cholesky decomposition method. A symmetric positive-definite matrix can be decomposed into the product of a lower triangular matrix and its conjugate transpose. These triangular matrices can quickly be inverted in order to solve linear systems. In that sense, the Incomplete Cholesky preconditioner approximates the full inverse of A without incurring the cost of actually inverting it. It should be noted that P^{-1} is calculated using expensive forward and backward substitutions, which are inherent serial processes because of the triangular structures of L and L^T.

Incomplete Poisson Preconditioner:

$$P = HH^T \tag{5}$$

where

$$H = I - L\text{diag}\{A\}^{-1}. \tag{6}$$

and L is the strictly lower triangular matrix of A. This novel preconditioner has a simple structure and is kind of an approximate inverse. As a result, no substitutions are required and this preconditioner can be applied efficiently with SpMV and thread-level parallelism.

Symmetric Successive Over Relaxation:

$$P = (M1 * M2)^{-1}, \tag{7}$$

where

$$M1 = \frac{1}{\omega} * D + L, \tag{8}$$

$$M2 = \frac{1}{(2-\omega)} * (I + \omega * D^{-1} * U) \tag{9}$$

and L,U,D are the strictly lower triangular, the strictly upper triangular and the diagonal matrix of A respectively. Symmetric successive over-relaxation is a variant of the Gauss-Seidel method but with improved convergence speed. As with Incomplete Cholesky, a relatively expensive forward and backward substitution step occurs to calculate P^{-1}. It should also be noted that the choice of ω influences convergence. We use the following ω:

$$\omega = \frac{1}{max([1, max(L), max(U)])}. \tag{10}$$

4 Evaluation Results

In this section we compare the proposed incomplete poisson preconditioner to the most commonly used preconditioners. Section 4.1 describes the test cases we use for the comparison. Section 4.2 evaluates the fitness of each of the preconditioning methods and Section 4.3 provides the results of parallelizing the incomplete poisson preconditioner on next generation multi-core hardware. A visual comparison of using each of the preconditioners on the benchmarks can be seen in the accompanying video. All preconditioners seem to produce results of similar quality.

4.1 Benchmarks

We use four benchmarks for the purpose of exercising the preconditioners on a variety of challenging scenarios that are frequently encountered in simulating cloth. The three benchmarks are described below.

1. **Free Fall.** This is more of baseline case, where a piece of cloth falls under gravity and come to rest on a static sphere with no tangling (Figure 2(a)).
2. **Curtain.** This case extends the previous benchmark by including fixed point constraints (Figure 2(b)).
3. **Moving Collider.** Further extending the previous case, a cloth patch hung as a curtain interacts with a moving spherical collider (Figure 2(c)). This benchmark is used to test the behavior of the simulator in a dynamic environment.
4. **Tangling.** Tangling is one of the toughest cases for cloth simulators to handle because of the complexities introduced by the multiple self-collisions (Figure 2(d)). As far as the conjugate gradient solver is concerned, for tangled states the number of nonzeros (thus the stiffness) of the matrix $A(Ax = b)$ increases significantly. The increased matrix density can significantly affect performance.

4.2 Preconditioner Evaluation

We test the performance of the preconditioners by simulating 200 frames for each of the benchmarks described above. The parameters used for the cloth simulator are described in Table 1. The inter-particle forces were shear, bend and stretch. The evaluation results are illustrated in Figure 3. From the results, it is apparent that the Incomplete Poisson preconditioner performs on par with Incomplete Cholesky for cloth simulation. Table 2 demonstrates the performance results of all preconditioning schemes with increase in number of nodes on cloth patch. Here, we see that IPP scales well with increase in resolution of cloth patch, but the incomplete Chokesly preconditioner does not. The main advantage of this novel preconditioner is that it can be easily parallelized whereas Incomplete Cholesky is inherently a serial algorithm.

Table 1. Simulation Parameters

Simulation Parameter	Value
Grid resolution	50×50
Spring Constant	1000
Inter-particle distance	0.005
Damping Factor	2
Time step	0.01
Error Threshold	10^{-15}
Mass of particle	1

Table 2. Performance results (number of iterations and simulation time in seconds) for all preconditioning schemes with increase in number of nodes

#Nodes	Cholesky		Poisson		SSOR		Jacobi		None	
	#Iter	Time(s)	#Iter	Time(s)	#Iter	Time(s)	#Iter	Time (s)	#Iter	Time (s)
2500	10	0.079	11	0.032	11	0.035	18	0.062	13	0.028
3600	10	0.099	11	0.046	11	0.046	18	0.080	13	0.049
4900	10	0.160	11	0.054	11	0.064	18	0.090	13	0.058
6400	10	0.133	11	0.062	11	0.078	18	0.101	13	0.064
8100	9	0.150	11	0.076	11	0.096	18	0.121	13	0.083
10000	9	0.151	11	0.084	11	0.110	18	0.138	13	0.091
19600	9	0.241	11	0.157	11	0.217	18	0.241	13	0.182
30625	9	0.482	12	0.326	11	0.359	18	0.388	13	0.337
40000	9	1.649	12	0.396	11	0.490	18	0.567	14	0.542

4.3 Parallelization Results

In order to evaluate parallelization options for the Incomplete Poisson preconditioner, we implemented a parallel version using pthreads. This parallel version assigns to each thread an equal number of columns of the matrix as a workload. This number is calculated as $No.Columns / No.threads$. The input of the parallelization function is A and the output $P = HH^T$, where $H = I - L\text{diag}\{A\}^{-1}$. We tested for different numbers of threads and the times we report include construction of the threads as well as thread synchronization. Our tests were performed on an 8 core Mac Pro running OS X 10.6 with 12GBs of RAM(Figure 1(a)) and a 32 core Emerald Ridge server with Intel Xeon X7560 processors and 32GMBs of RAM running OpenSuse Linux 11.3 (Figure 1(b)). Both systems are hyper-threaded. To compute execution time we used system specific high resolution timers: `mach_absolute_time()` on OS X

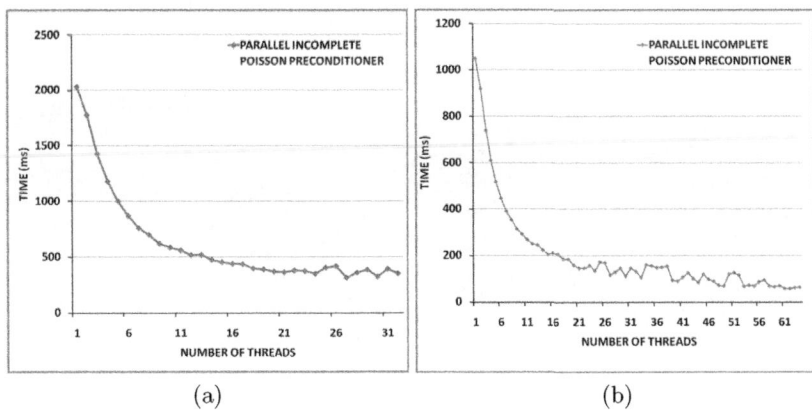

Fig. 1. Parallelization results on multi-core hardware. (a) 8 core machine. (b) 32 core machine.

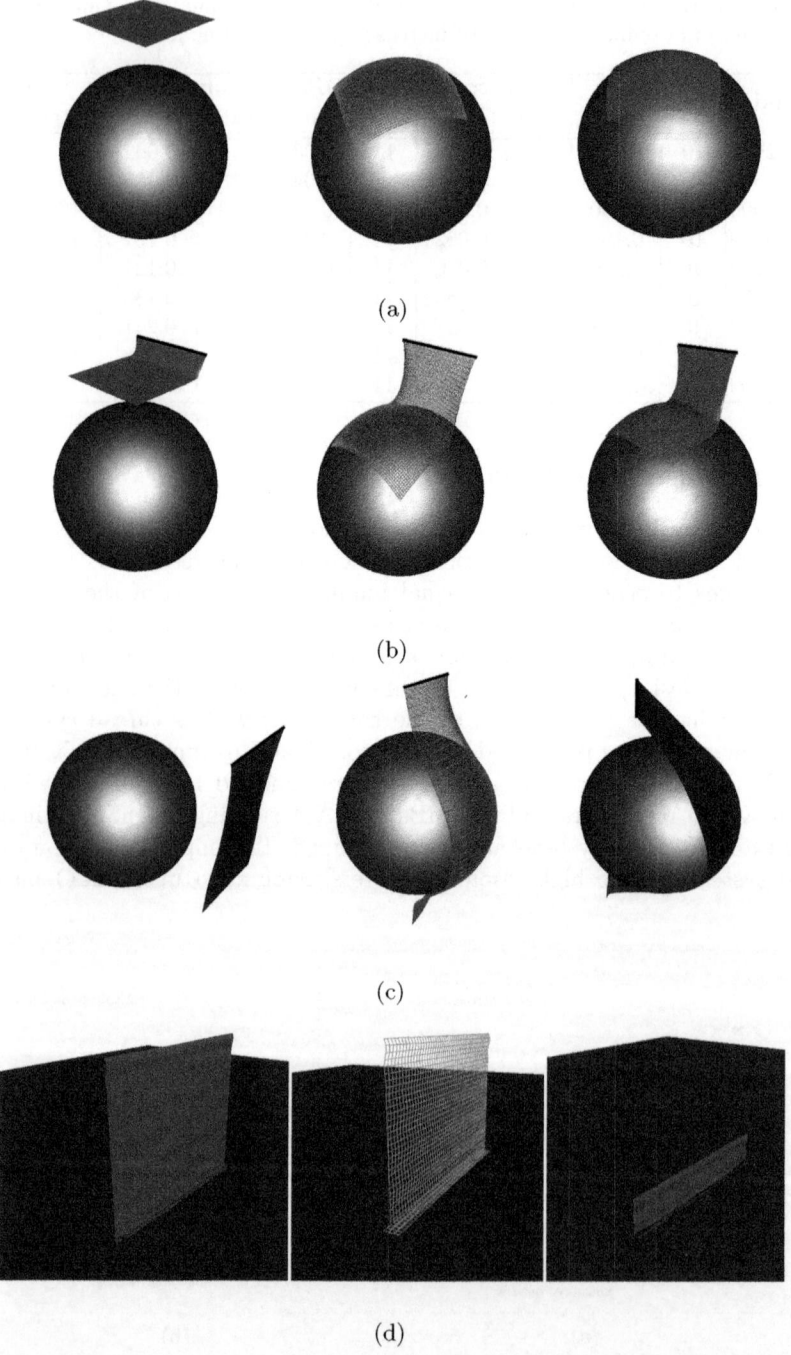

Fig. 2. Benchmark Scenes. (a) Cloth falling on a sphere. (b) Cloth hanging as a curtain colliding with sphere. (c) Cloth patch colliding with moving spherical object. (d)Tangling cloth. In the middle frames the red color indicates edges under stress.

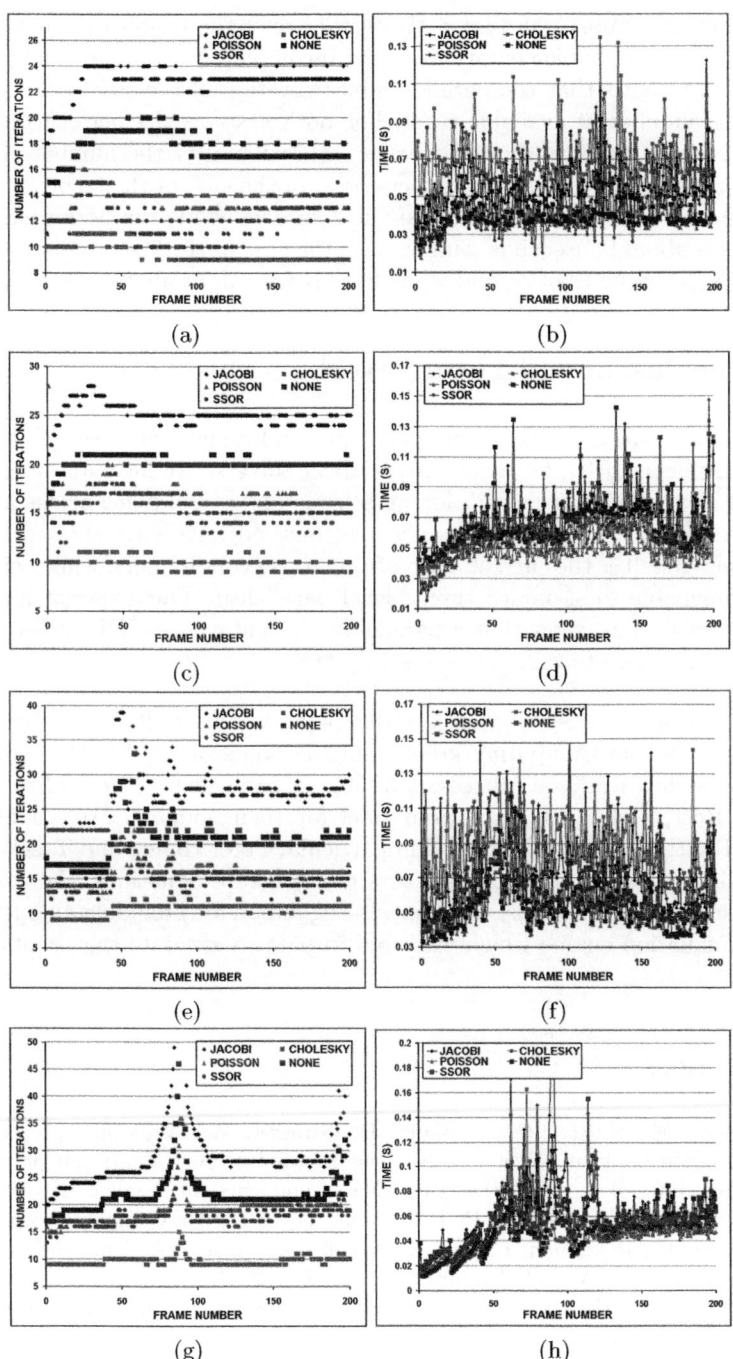

Fig. 3. Performance results of different preconditioning schemes on all benchmarks. (a),(b): Number of iterations and simulation time for Free fall benchmark. (c),(d): Curtain benchmark. (e),(f) Tangling benchmark. (g),(h) Moving collider benchmark.

and clock_gettime() on Linux. We further refer the reader to Ament et al [1] for GPU parallel implementations of the Incomplete Poisson preconditioner.

Figure 1 shows that the parallel implementation of the IPP scales very well with the number of available cores. For both systems the performance of the IPP increases significantly and reaches saturation after the number of threads equals the number of available hyper-cores. In the case of the 8-core system the performance of a single thread is about 2 seconds while the performance of 16 threads is about 0.5 seconds. Similarly, in the case of the 32-core system a single thread takes more than second while 64 threads run at about 0.06 seconds.

5 Conclusion and Future Work

We have presented a recently proposed preconditioner, the *incomplete Poisson* preconditioner (IPP), for conjugate gradient solvers. We have analyzed the fitness of the proposed preconditioning scheme on several benchmarks and compared its performance to commonly used methods. We have showed that IPP performs as well as the current state-of-the-art preconditioners, while being much more amenable to standard thread-level parallelism. Our experiments on two multi-core systems show that a parallel implementation of IPP scales very well with the number of available processing cores.

Acknowledgements. The work in this paper was partially supported by Intel through a Visual Computing grant, and the donation of the 32-core Emerald Ridge system with Xeon processors X7560. In particular we would like to thank Randi Rost, and Scott Buck from Intel for their support. We would like to thank Rhythm&Hues Studios and in particular Peter Huang and Tae-Yong Kim for their their support through grants and software donations. We would also like to extend our gratitude to Thanasis Vogiannou for providing an open source cloth simulation engine which was used in part to generate the results for this paper.

References

1. Ament, M., Knittel, G., Weiskopf, D., Strasser, W.: A parallel preconditioned conjugate gradient solver for the poisson problem on a multi-gpu platform. In: Proceedings of the 2010 18th Euromicro Conference on Parallel, Distributed and Network-based Processing, PDP 2010, pp. 583–592. IEEE Computer Society (2010)
2. Ascher, U., Boxerman, E.: On the modified conjugate gradient method in cloth simulation. The Visual Computer 19, 526–531 (2003)
3. Baraff, D., Witkin, A.: Large steps in cloth simulation. In: Proceedings of ACM SIGGRAPH, pp. 43–54 (1998)
4. Boxerman, E.: Speeding up cloth simulation. Ph.D. thesis, The University of British Columbian, BC, Canada (2003)
5. Breen, D.E., House, D.H., Wozny, M.J., Breen, D.E.: Predicting the drape of woven cloth using interacting particles (1994)

6. Bridson, R., Fedkiw, R., Anderson, J.: Robust treatment of collisions, contact and friction for cloth animation. In: ACM SIGGRAPH 2005 Courses, SIGGRAPH 2005. ACM, New York (2005)
7. Carignan, M., Yang, Y., Thalrnann, N.M., Thalrnanrp, D.: Dressing animated synthetic actors with complex deformable clothes. In: Computer Graphics (Proc. SIGGRAPH), pp. 99–104 (1992)
8. Choi, K., Ko, H.: Research problems in clothing simulation. Computer-Aided Design 37(6), 585–592 (2005)
9. Choi, K.J., Ko, H.S.: Stable but responsive cloth. In: Proceedings of ACM SIGGRAPH, pp. 604–611 (2002)
10. Eberhardt, B., Weber, A., Strasser, W.: A fast, flexible, particle-system model for cloth draping. IEEE Comput. Graph. Appl. 16, 52–59 (1996)
11. Fuhrmann, A., Sobottka, G., Grob, C.: Distance fields for rapid collision detection in physically based modeling. In: GRAPHICON (2003)
12. Goldenthal, R., Harmon, D., Fattal, R., Bercovier, M., Grinspun, E.: Efficient Simulation of Inextensible Cloth. SIGGRAPH (ACM Transactions on Graphics) 26(3) (2007)
13. Hauth, M., Etzmuss, O., Strasser, W.: Analysis of numerical methods for the simulation of deformable models. The Visual Computer 19, 581–600 (2003)
14. Müller, M.: Hierarchical position based dynamics. In: Proceedings of Virtual Reality Interactions and Physical Simulations (VRIPhys 2008), pp. 13–14 (2008)
15. Müller, M., Heidelberger, B., Hennix, M., Ratcliff, J.: Position based dynamics. J. Vis. Comun. Image Represent. 18, 109–118 (2007)
16. Nealen, A., Müller, M., Keiser, R., Boxerman, E., Carlson, M.: Physically based deformable models in computer graphics. Computer Graphics Forum 25, 809–836 (2006)
17. Okabe, H., Imaoka, H., Tomiha, T., Niwaya, H.: Three dimensional apparel cad system. In: Proceedings of the 19th Annual Conference on Computer Graphics and Interactive Techniques, SIGGRAPH 1992, pp. 105–110. ACM, New York (1992)
18. Selle, A., Su, J., Irving, G., Fedkiw, R.: Robust high-resolution cloth using parallelism, history-based collisions, and accurate friction. IEEE Transactions on Visualization and Computer Graphics 15, 339–350 (2009)
19. Shewchuk, J.R.: An introduction to the conjugate gradient method without the agonizing pain. Tech. rep. (1994)
20. Terzopoulos, D., Fleischer, K.: Deformable models. The Visual Computer 4(6), 306–331 (1988)
21. Terzopoulos, D., Fleischer, K.: Modeling inelastic deformation: Viscoelasticity, plasticity, fracture. Computer Graphics (Proc. SIGGRAPH 1988) 22(4), 269–278 (1988)
22. Terzopoulos, D., Platt, J., Barr, A., Fleischer, K.: Elastically deformable models. Computer Graphics (Proc. SIGGRAPH 1987) 21(4), 205–214 (1987)
23. Volino, P., Courchesne, M., Magnenat Thalmann, N.: Versatile and efficient techniques for simulating cloth and other deformable objects. In: Proceedings of ACM SIGGRAPH, pp. 137–144 (1995)

Walk This Way: A Lightweight, Data-Driven Walking Synthesis Algorithm

Sean Curtis, Ming Lin, and Dinesh Manocha

University of North Carolina at Chapel Hill,
Chapel Hill, NC, USA
{seanc,lin,dm}@cs.unc.edu
http://gamma.cs.unc.edu/Walking

Abstract. We present a novel, biomechanically-inspired, kinematic-based, example-driven walking synthesis model. Our model is ideally suited towards interactive applications such as games. It synthesizes motion interactively without *a priori* knowledge of the trajectory. The model is very efficient, producing foot-skate free, smooth motion over a large, continuous range of speeds and while turning, in as little as 5 μs. We've formulated our model so that an artist has extensive control over how the walking gait manifests itself at all speeds.

1 Introduction

Games define a unique problem space. Hard real-time constraints demand that the systems in the game be evaluated efficiently to provide interactive feedback to the player. Furthermore, the story-telling aspects of games require these efficient systems to be art-directable to support desired themes and styles. Data-driven motion synthesis (DDMS) has proven to be the most widely applied, in-game solution. Research in DDMS has produced increasingly sophisticated, generalized models, leading to higher fidelity motion. These approaches, while suitable for a few interactive characters, may still consume too many resources to be suited for gaming. Instead of generalized DDMS, we need to use a hybrid approach combining DDMS and a targeted targeted algorithm to satisfy the needs of games [1]. Artist-controlled sample motion is processed by intelligent algorithms which understand the specific domain of motion.

We present such a model for synthesizing walking motion. Our approach continuously transforms a single walking example consisting of two straight-line walking steps, without any *a priori* knowledge of the trajectory. The straight-line motion is transformed, on-the-fly, to support arbitrary speeds and turning motion. While the approach is based on biomechanical principles, the core of the model is a set of user-defined functions (defined in the same manner as keyframe function curves.) This gives artists control, not only over the example data, but over how that motion changes with respect to speed and turning.

Ultimately, our model seeks to solve the the locomotion synthesis problem subject to a unique set of constraints: minimal input to maximize the productivity of the artist (a single clip), minimum computation time to maximize its utility to a game engine (11 μs per skeleton, computed serially), while still producing foot-skate free motion over a continuous velocity space in response to a sequence of arbitrary velocities.

Organization. In Section 2, we briefly discuss related work. We define concepts related to walking and our model in Section 3. In Section 4 we discuss our model in three layers: steady-state walking, mid-stride acceleration, and turning. Finally, we illustrate and discuss the product of our model in Section 5.

2 Related Work

There has been extensive research in *dynamics-based* motion synthesis. Due to space limitations, we refer the readers to a survey [2] and limit our discussion to procedural, data-driven, and footstep-driven methods.

Procedural methods generate locomotion through functions based on underlying principles of biomechanics [3–7]. For each joint, these approaches define a unique parametric function mapping time and gait parameters directly to values of the degrees of freedom. However, it is difficult for these approaches to express distinctly organic traits such as: high-frequency phenomena, asymmetries, and personality. Our system shares some of the underlying biomechanical models of these procedural approaches, but rather than use them to synthesize motion *ex nihilo*, we use them to transfrom an input clip according to biomechanical principles to satisfy required walking speeds.

DDMS methods generate new motion from input motion. New motion is produced by concatenating existing clips or blending motion clips [8–10], or some combination. Motion graphs [11, 12] operate by creating a graph of motion clips and then perform a search to find a sequence of adjacent nodes that fit a desired trajectory. The clips themselves can be parametrically extended to encompass a space of motions [13, 14]. If the database contains human motion capture, the data encodes the subtle nuances and high-frequency phenomena inherent in human motion (e.g. small twitches or irregular motions.) However, in addition to requiring large databases, these systems operate at clip resolution. Each clip in the sequence is played from beginning to end; changes in the middle are not supported.

Treuille et al. [15] described an algorithm which uses a learned controller to transition between nodes in the motion graph and blend results to produce continuous motion. However, the approach may be unsuited to general application in games. Their motion synthesis is directly tied into their naviation algorithm; generating motion for an arbitrary trajectory planner may be problematic. Furthemore, the authors report that transitions in their motion graph take 100 ms to calculate and blending motion costs 40 μs. In contrast our approach requires only 11 μs to compute the configuration for a single skeleton.

Our model shares traits in common with Johansen [16]. His work uses "semi-procedural" methods to transform straight-line motion into turning. We use the same principle but use a different model for anticipating final foot position and effect the transformation differently. The biggest difference between Johansen's work and our own is that blended motion serves as the basis of his synthesized motion. The walking speeds he can generate is dependent on the speeds of the different input clips to his system. In contrast, we transform a single input clip for both turning and speed changes.

Footstep-driven walking synthesis takes as input a sequence of timed foot configurations. The foot configurations serve as constraints to motion synthesis. Van Basten et al. [17] presented an approach which uses a library of walking clips, segmented into steps, and selects the clip closest to the configuration of footprints, possibly performing motion warping if the source step motion deviates from the constraints. While these approaches can generate high quality motion, it assumes the problem of foot placement has already been solved. Footstep-driven motion synthesis cannot generate motion from a sequence of velocities (one of the most common inputs to locomotion synthesis in games.) Furthermore, the quality of the motion is still dependent on the size of the motion database.

There has also been recent research on editing the style of motion [18, 19]. Our transformation of the leg motion from forward-kinematic to inverse-kinematic is similar to that applied to the whole body in Neff and Kim [19]. They provide a very general system for applying arbitrary transformations to the entire skeleton and indirectly modify the torso based on correlations with wrist positions. This leads to a greater possible range of modification and expression. However, the generality comes at a cost (with a reported cost of 3.6 ms to update a single skeleton.) Furthermore, rather than their data-driven, linear correlations between wrist position and spine, we've exploited biomechanical knowledge to correlate gait parameters, e.g. stride length and ankle flexion.

3 Walking Gait

In this section, we briefly present key concepts and notation used in the balance of the paper. For more detail on human walking, we recommend [20] and [21].

The walking gait is a form locomotion in which at least one foot is always in contact with the ground and, at times, both are. Our system operates on the intervals defined by changes in contact (i.e. when a foot leaves or makes contact with the ground.) We define the beginning of a step when the new support foot makes contact with the ground at *initial contact* (IC). The swing foot lifts off the ground at *opposite toe off* (OT). The swing foot passes next to the support foot at *feet adjacent* (FA). Finally, the swing foot makes contact at *opposite contact* (OC) which is the IC event for the next step. We denote the times at which these events occur as T_{IC}, T_{OT}, T_{FA}, and T_{OC}, respectively The fraction of the gait in which both feet are in contact is called *double support time* (DS).

3.1 Gait Properties

A walking gait has many properties [21-23]. These properties define the gait and are exhibited at all speeds, albeit with varying values. We parameterize how six of these properties *change* as speed changes, i.e. "gait functions": stride frequency, double support time, foot flexion, vertical hip excursion (apex and nadir) and pelvic swivel. The first two are parameterized with respect to speed and the last four are parameterized with respect to stride length.

Together, stride frequency and double support time define the timing of a step. Stride frequency determines the overall duration of the step and DS time determines the amount of time the swing leg spends in contact with the ground.

Given stride frequency and speed, we can easily compute stride length. Foot flexion, vertical hip excursion, and pelvic swivel are all mechanical techniques which increase a biped's effective stride length and smooth the trajectory of the center of mass [21].

Biomechanical literature [21–23] suggests mathematical models for the naturally occuring relationships. Given "realistic" gait functions this transformation approach produces dynamically consistent motion. In games, however, not all characters walk with a strictly realistic gait. To support arbitrary artistic needs, we model these gait functions as user-editable Hermite curves. Thus, our approach applies equally well to a wide range of walking styles, from realistic to cartoon-like.

3.2 Motion and Motion Warping

We represent the configuration of a skeleton as a state vector, $\mathbf{X} \in \mathbb{R}^n$, where the skeleton has n degrees of freedom. Animation arises from varying this vector with respect to time, $\mathbf{X}(t)$. The time-varying data for each degree of freedom is a channel.

We use motion warping [24] to transform an input motion sample into new motion. Specifically, we use a global time warp function, $\tau(t)$, and warp the ith channel of the motion data, $X_i(t)$, with one of two types of warp functions:

- **Offset:** $X'_i(t) = X_i(t) + o(t)$. The original data is simply offset by a time-varying term, $o(t)$.
- **Scale:** $X'_i(t) = s(t) * X_i(t)$. The original data is scaled by a time-varying scale term, $s(t)$.

We model the warp functions with Hermite splines. Each function, $x(t)$, is defined by an ordered list of constraint tuples: $(t_i, x_i, \dot{x}_i)$, such that $t_i < t_{i+1}$. Section 4 provides the details on how specific warp functions are defined.

4 Gait Transformation

Our approach is based on two simple ideas. First, although human locomotion is a dynamically-complex phenomenon, humans solve it consistently and robustly. Second, the gait properties vary smoothly with speed, and these changes can be empirically observed and directly modeled. Thus a model based on human motion capture data can be transformed into valid walking motion by applying the empirically observed gait property models.

Our approach synthesizes new walking motion by transforming an input clip, based on a set of *gait functions*, the current velocity, and the figure's current configuration, **X**. We transform the motion in three stages. First we apply motion warping to individual channels in the input clip. Second, the root and swing foot are transformed from straight-line motion into turning motion. Finally, an IK-solver computes joint angles for the degrees of freedom in **X**.

4.1 Offline Processing

The *canonical clip*, $C(t)$, is the input motion data representing a walking motion with several properties. The motion consists of two footsteps, walking in a straight line along the z-axis. The motion is loopable (i.e. the first and last configurations are identical.) The motion begins at the IC event. And, finally, the joint angle representation of the hip, knee and ankle joints are replaced with an inverse-kinematic (IK) representation for foot position and orientation. Creating a clip with these properties is straightforward. The specific details are not within the scope of this discussion; it can be done algorithmically or by an artist. However, we present the details of the IK representation and solver in Section 4.5.

The input state vector for the canonical clip, $\mathbf{X} \in \mathbb{R}^{22}$, is defined as follows: $\mathbf{X} = \begin{bmatrix} \mathbf{Root} & \mathbf{Ankle_R} & \mathbf{Ankle_L} & \mathbf{Toes} \end{bmatrix}$, where $\mathbf{Root} \in \mathbb{R}^6$, including three degrees of rotation and translation, $\mathbf{Toes} \in \mathbb{R}^2$, a single rotational degree of freedom for each foot, and $\mathbf{Ankle_R}, \mathbf{Ankle_L} \in \mathbb{R}^7$ consisting of three dimensions of translation and rotation for each ankle joint and one *pole vector* value. The pole vector value is used to determine the direction the knee faces in solving the IK system (see 4.5.)

Although the canonical clip consists of two steps, each step is transformed individually. The balance of the paper will focus on a single step and eschew the descriptions of "left foot" and "right foot" in favor of "support foot" and "swing foot".

Not all of the channels in the canonical clip are warped. For example, our system does not change the side-to-side movement of the pelvis, so we do not warp the root's x-translation. Table 1 enumerates the five channels in $C(t)$ which have motion warping applied. The rotation of the support and swing feet are also transformed to faciliate turning (see Section 4.4.)

Table 1. The five warped channels from $C(t)$, the type of motion warp applied and the times of the constraints in each motion warp

Joint	Channel	Warp Function	Constraint Times
root	ty	Offset	$T_{IC}, T_{OC}, t_{MAX}, t_{MIN}$
root	tz	Offset	T_{IC}, T_{OC}
root	ry	Scale	T_{IC}, T_{OC}
swing foot	tx	Offset	T_{OT}, T_{OC}
swing foot	tz	Offset	T_{OT}, T_{OC}

The *gait functions*, F, are the set of six functions that parameterize the properties listed in Section 3.1. They relate speed and stride length to the various gait properties. They serve as the basis for defining the warp functions' constraints.

- $F_f(v)$ maps speed, v, to stride frequency.
- $F_{DS}(f)$ maps stride frequency to double-support time, DS.
- $F_{FF}(l)$ maps stride length, $l = v/F_f(v)$ to foot flexion, FF.
- $F_{PS}(l)$ maps stride length to pelvic swivel, PS.
- $F_{AP}(l)$ maps stride length to the apex of vertical hip excursion, AP.
- $F_{ND}(l)$ maps stride length to the nadir of vertical hip excursion, ND.

4.2 Steady-State Gait

The steady-state gait arises after maintaining a constant velocity for multiple steps. By definition, this motion is straight-line walking. The parameter values in the gait functions are fully realized in the steady-state gait.

We create the steady-state gait by evaluating the gait functions and using those results to define the specific constraint tuples for the warp functions. Table 2 shows the constraint values for each of the terms in the warp functions. The constraint definitions use the following variables:

L, the average stride length of C(t).
$l = v * F_v(v)$, the stride length for speed v.
$\Gamma = L - l$, the change in stride length.
β_W, the forward bias from the swing foot. Forward bias is the fraction of the distance in front of the back foot towards the front foot at which the pelvis lies. For the swing foot, this value is defined at T_{IC}.
β_P, the forward bias from the support foot, defined at T_{OC}.
$t_{\max}$, the time at which the pelvis is at its peak (usually shortly after T_{FA}.)
$t_{\min}$, the time at which the pelvis is at its nadir (usually shortly after T_{IC}.)

Table 2. Warp function constraints for steady-state gait. Constraint values marked with * are discussed in Sec. 4.2.

Channel	Warp Term	Constraints $(t_i, x_i, \dot{x}_i)$
time	$\tau(t)$	$(0, T_{IC}, *), (F_{DS}(F_f(v))/F_f(v), T_{OT}, *), (1/F_f(v), T_{OC}, *)$
root.tz	$o(t)$	$(T_{IC}, (\beta_W - 1)\Gamma, 0), (T_{OC}, \beta_P \Gamma, 0)$
root.ty	$o(t)$	$(T_{IC}, *, *), (t_{\max}, F_{AP}(l), 0), (t_{\min}, F_{ND}(l), 0), (T_{OC}, *, *)$
root.ry	$s(t)$	$(T_{IC}, F_{PS}(l), 0), (T_{OC}, F_{PS}(l), 0)$
swing.tx	$o(t)$	$(T_{OT}, 0, 0), (T_{OC}, 0, 0)$
swing.tz	$o(t)$	$(T_{OT}, 0, 0), (T_{OC}, \Gamma, 0)$

The temporal warp function, $\tau(t)$, changes duration to account for changes in stride frequency and changes the proportion of time spent in double support by moving the world time mapping for the T_{OT} event. The tangents of the curve are calculated to produce smooth, monotonically increasing interpolation between constraints. The root.ty channel's warp constraints are somewhat more elaborate. The bobbing is oscillatory. The time and value of the apex and nadir points of the oscillation define the behavior. To compute the offset and tangent values at T_{IC} and T_{OC}, we logically extend the peak and valley periodically according to the step duration and then infer the value at T_{IC} and T_{OC} from the cubic interpolation provided by the Hermite spline. Straight-line motion does not alter the warp function for the swing foot's x-translation (see Section 4.4.)

The rotation of the feet due to foot flexion is more complex. Both the support and swing foot's flexion changes with stride length (although the changes to the swing foot are more extreme.) We compute "flexion functions", W_{FF} and P_{FF}, for the swing and support foot, respectively. They are defined as Hermite splines with a set of constraint tuples but the values of the functions are applied quite differently.

Traditional motion warping operates on each channel independently. Rotation is a complex operation in which the various degrees of freedom are interrelated. Orientation for the feet is a "world" orientation and, as such, we cannot modify individual channels with predictable results. Changes in foot flexion change the foot's orientation around its *local* x-axis, regardless of the actual orientation of the foot in gait space. The value of the flexion function is interpreted as an amount to rotate the foot around its x-axis. Table 3 defines the foot flexion constraints in steady state.

Table 3. Foot flexion function constraints. The variable θ_X is the ratio of the support foot's flexion value in the data between T_X and T_{OT}. Similarly, ψ_X is the same for the swing foot.

Foot	Constraints $(t_i, x_i, \dot{x}_i)$
Support	$(T_{IC}, F_{FF}(l) * \theta_{IC}, 0)$, $(T_{OT}, 0, 0)$ $(T_{FA}, 0, 0)$, $(T_{OC}, F_{FF}(l) * \theta_{OT}, 0)$, $(T_{TO}, F_{FF}(l), 0)$
Swing	$(-T_{MS}, 0, 0)$, $(T_{IC}, F_{FF}(l) * \psi_{OC}, 0)$, $(T_{OT}, F_{FF}(l), 0)$, $(T_{OC}, F_{FF}(l) * \psi_{IC}, 0)$

4.3 Mid-stride Acceleration

In interactive applications, the trajectory a character follows, $\boldsymbol{P}(t)$, is generated dynamically, directly from user controls or in response to user decisions. At any given display frame, motion must be generated without knowing anything about the future trajectory. More particularly, a velocity change can occur at any point during the walking cycle.

The application maintains a logical position of the game character (usually the product of Euler integration.) The motion generated must adhere to this logical, or *ideal* position. Furthermore, the motion must remain physically plausible. Here we define plausibility with two crieteria. First, feet in contact with the ground cannot move. Second, the joint trajectories of the skeleton must maintain

C^1-continuity; we do not allow the current configuration to "pop" nor the rate of change of the configuration to change instantly. Our approach for accomodating mid-stride acceleration satisfies both requirements.

We require that our motion follows the ideal position faithfully. However, constraining the center of mass of the character to that point is unrealistic. When walking a straight line, a real human's center of mass oscillates around the ideal position derived by assuming constant average velocity. To account for this, each skeleton plans its motion such that the physical center of mass oscillates around the ideal position, but perfectly aligns every second step.

When the speed changes mid-stride from v_- to v_+, our system changes the warp functions so that the current configuration is preserved and the position of the center of mass aligns with the ideal position at the end of the step. This depends on determining how much time remains in the current step after the speed change.

We apply a heuristic to determine the remaining time of the step, t_R. If the current gait time is before T_{FA}, we assume that the skeleton can move from its current position, p_C, to a position consistent with the full stride length, p_v, inherent in the steady-state gait for v_+. The remaining time is the time required for the center of mass to travel this distance. If current gait time is after T_{FA} it's the world time the v_+ steady-state gait would take to get from t_C to T_{OC}.

$$t_R = \begin{cases} (p_v - p_C)/v_+ & \text{if } t_C < T_{FA} \\ \tau_+^{-1}(T_{OC}) - \tau_+^{-1}(t_C) & \text{if } t_C \geq T_{FA} \end{cases} \quad (1)$$

We define the new warp function, e.g. $o_+(t)$, in terms of the remaining time, the old warp functions, e.g. $o_-(t)$, and the gait functions. The new warp function constraints completely replace the previous set. Table 4 shows the constraints and uses the following values: τ_v is the temporal warp for the steady-state gait at speed v, τ_- is the temporal warp before the speed change, $\Delta t = \tau_-^{-1}(t_C) - \tau_v^{-1}(t_C)$, and l_+ is the expected stride length at T_{OC} (it may be different from the steady-state stride length.) Finally, to guarantee C^1 continuity in the joint trajectories, we introduce new constraints, consisting of the old warp function values and derivatives at the current time.

4.4 Turning

Our system can further transform the warped motion data to allow the character to turn as it travels, even exhibiting the subtle phenomenon of leaning into the turn.

Humans lean into turns for the same reason that an inverted pendulum would lean inwards while moving along a circular path, centripetal force. As the centipetal force diminishes, human paths straighten out and they stop leaning to the side. We model this using a critically-damped angular spring. We rotate the position of the root around the straight-line along which the motion is defined. Finally, we transform the line, rotating and displacing it, to achieve turning motion.

To compute the leaning, we define a spring with spring coefficient, k. We assume unit mass and require the system to be critically damped giving us the

Table 4. Transient warp function constraints. Constraints with parameter value T_X are only included if $t_C < T_X$.

Channel	Warp Term	Constraints $(t, x_i, \dot{x}_i)$
time	$\tau_+(t)$	$(\tau_v(t_C) + \Delta t, t_C, \dot{\tau}_v(t_C))$, $(\tau_v(T_{OT}) + \Delta t, T_{OT}, *)$, $(\tau_v^{-1}(t_{OC}), T_{OC}, *)$
root.tz	$o_+(t)$	$(t_C, o_-(t_C), \dot{o}_-(t_C))$ $(T_{OC}, p_v, 0)$
root.ty	$o_+(t)$	$(t_C, o_-(t_C), \dot{o}_-(t_C))$, $(t_{MIN}, F_{ND}(l_+), 0)$ $(T_{OC}, *, *)$
root.ry	$s_+(t)$	$(t_C, s_-(t_C), \dot{s}_-(t_C))$, $(T_{OC}, F_{PS}(l_+), 0)$
swing.tz	$o_+(t)$	$(t_C, o_-(t_C), \dot{o}_-(t_C))$, $(T_{OC}, l_+, 0)$

damping coefficient $c = 2\sqrt{k}$. At run time we compute the centripetal acceleration, $a_c = v * \omega = v_+ * \cos^{-1}(<\hat{v}_+, \hat{v}_->)/\Delta t$, where $\hat{v}_-$, $\hat{v}_+$, Δt are the direction of the old velocity, new velocity and the elapsed time, respectively. We then apply the force to the spring and integrate the state of the spring. The displacement of the spring, θ, is used to rotate the warped position of the root, $Root_w$ around the z-axis to produce the leaning root, $Root_l$

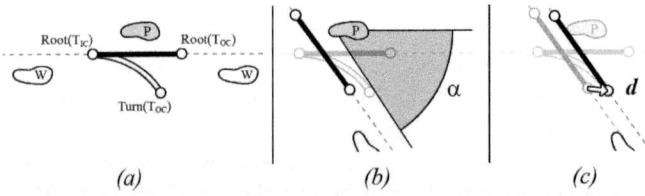

Fig. 1. Illustration of how straight-line motion is transformed to turning. The swing foot is marked W and the support with a P. (a) the initial relationship between straight (black line) and curved (white line) trajectories. (b) the straight-line space is rotated around the support foot α radians to point in the same direction as the final velocity. (c) the space is translated by d to so that the straight-line end point aligns with the ideal position.

To create the effect of turning motion, we apply a principle similar to that presented in [7]: we transform the space of the straight-line walk to align with the turning direction. Our solution is different in several respects: first, we do not rotate the full canonical clip. We only transform the root and the swing foot. Second, during double support we perform no transformation at all. Together, these two heuristics guarantee that feet in contact with the ground will not slide. The final position of the root and swing foot for $t_C > T_{OT}$ are given by:

$$Root_f(t) = Root_l * R_\alpha + \mathbf{d}, \qquad (2)$$
$$Swing_f(t) = Swing_w * R_\alpha + \mathbf{d}, \qquad (3)$$
$$SwingPV_f t = Swing.pv * R_\alpha + \mathbf{d}, \qquad (4)$$

where R_α is a matrix that performs a rotation of α radians around the y-axis. These turning parameters, α and $\boldsymbol{d}$, are encoded in three more warp-like functions: d_x, d_z and α. For each curve, the initial constraints are $\{(T_{OT}, 0, 0), (T_{OC}, 0, 0)\}$. When velocity direction changes mid-stride, we determine the parameter values at T_{OC} as outlined above and set a constraint at t_C to maintain continuity.

This turning action leads to a particular artifact. By the end of the motion, the support foot is no longer in line with the root and swing foot. This support foot becomes the next swing foot. To maintain continuity its inital position must take into account the misalignment. This is when the warp functions for swing.tx and swing.ry are used. At a step switch they are initialized to have constraints at T_{OT} and T_{OC}. The values at T_{OT} maintain the foot position and orientation from the previous step and at T_{OC} they are zeroed out.

4.5 Inverse Kinematics Solver

We operate on "world" positions and orientations of root and feet in our motion synthesis. We use a simple IK-solver to analytically solve for the joint trajectories. The legs act as a simple two-bone chain with three degrees of freedom at the hip and one at the knee. For a given positions of hip and foot, there are an infinite number of solutions. To resolve this ambiguity, we apply a pole-vector constraint to determine the orientation of the knee. The pole vector is a point in space approximately three body lengths in front of the figure. The time-varying position of this point is extracted from the original motion data. At the default speed, the IK-solver reproduces the canonical clip exactly. As stride length changes, the same pole vector value is used. This keeps the pattern of knee orientation consistent across all speeds.

5 Results and Analysis

Motion synthesis algorithms are best evaluated by viewing the motion they produce. We highlight the features of our algorithm in a video found at the given URL. We demonstrate the fidelity of the motion following arbitrary trajectories as well as real-time user input. We show the simplicity with which the gait functions can be modified and the impact that has on the personality of the motion. Finally, we show the scalability of our approach by synthesizing the motion for 800 characters in real-time.

5.1 Performance and Limitations

We have implemented our system in C++ and have run our experiments on an Intel i7 CPU at 2.65 GHz. Individual skeletons update in 11 μs. For the 800 characters, we updated skeletons in parallel (by simply applying an OpenMP for-loop to the skeleton updates) and were able to update all skeletons in less than 4 ms per frame, or 5 μs per skeleton, on average.

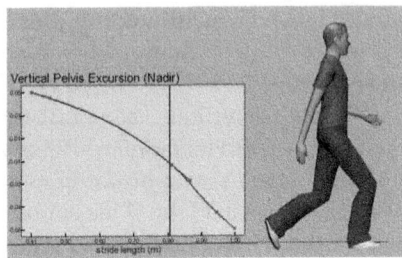 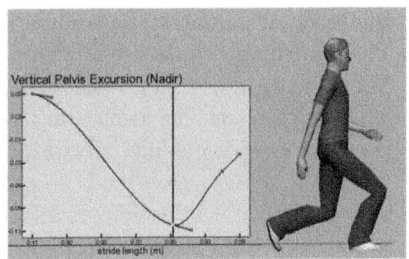

Fig. 2. For a fixed stride length, the vertical position of the pelvis at its nadir has been edited. The figure on the right shows a much lower pelvis in its gait.

Our model is specific to forward walking. Walking backwards or sideways are different gaits. For a more complete walking system, these other, less common gaits, would need to be modeled.

Our model follows the trajectory precisely. The quality of synthesized motion is dependent on the quality (an admittedly unknown quantity) of the trajectory. Furthermore, our system doesn't admit stopping. Depending on speed, a real human requires one or more steps to come to a rest. If the trajectory arbitrarily ends, we have no reasonable mechanism for instantaneously arresting motion.

6 Conclusion

We have presented a novel method for synthesizing walking motion. Our system is lightweight in both memory and computation and, as such, is well-suited to interactive applications with hundreds of characters. The motion is free from foot skating. The personality of the gait is defined by an input clip and the way the gait changes with speed is easily determined by an artist in an intuitive manner. Furthermore, motion is generated "on-the-fly" without latency from input, making our approach suitable for user-controlled avatars as well.

In the future, we will look into incorporating transitions between walking and standing as well as modelling other gaits. We'd also like to explore transformations to accomodate irregular surfaces, uneven terrain and other limitations on valid stepping areas.

Acknowledgments. This work was supported in part by ARO Contract W911NF-10-1-0506, NSF awards 0917040, 0904990 and 1000579, and RDECOM Contract WR91CRB-08-C-0137.

References

1. Gleicher, M.: More Motion Capture in Games — Can We Make Example-Based Approaches Scale? In: Egges, A., Kamphuis, A., Overmars, M. (eds.) MIG 2008. LNCS, vol. 5277, pp. 82–93. Springer, Heidelberg (2008)
2. Multon, F., France, L., Cani, M.-P., Debunne, G.: Computer Animation of Human Walking: a Survey. J. Vis. Comput. Animat. 1, 39–54 (1999)

3. Bruderlin, A., Calvert, T.W.: Goal-directed, dynamic animation of human walking. In: Proc. of ACM SIGGRAPH, pp. 233–242 (1989)
4. Bruderlin, A., Williams, L.: Motion signal processing. In: Proc. of ACM SIGGRAPH, pp. 97–104 (1995)
5. Boulic, R., Magnenat-Thalmann, N., Thalmann, D.: A global human walking model with real-time kinematic personification. The Visual Computer 6, 344–358 (1990)
6. Ko, H., Badler, N.I.: Straight Line Walking Animation Based on Kinematic Generalization that Preserves the Original Characteristics. In: Proceedings Graphics Interface, pp. 9–16 (1993)
7. Sun, H.C., Metaxas, D.N.: Automating gait generation. In: Proc. SIGGRAPH 2001, pp. 261–270 (2001)
8. Park, S.I., Shin, H.J., Kim, T.H., Shin, S.Y.: On-line motion blending for real-time locomotion generation: Research Articles. Comput. Animat. Virtual Worlds 3(4), 125–138 (2004)
9. Pelechano, N., Spanlang, B., Beacco, A.: Avatar Locomotion in Crowd Simulation. In: Proc. CASA (2011)
10. Menardais, S., Kulpa, R., Multon, F., Arnaldi, B.: Synchronization for dynamic blending of motions. In: Symposium on Computer Animation, pp. 325–336 (2004)
11. Kovar, L., Gleicher, M., Pighin, F.: Motion graphs. ACM Trans. Graph. 3, 473–482 (2002)
12. Gleicher, M.: Graph-based motion synthesis: an annotated bibliography. In: ACM SIGGRAPH 2008 Classes, pp. 1–11 (2008)
13. Heck, R., Gleicher, M.: Parametric Motion Graphs. In: Proc. I3D 2007 (2007)
14. Lau, M., Bar-Joseph, Z., Kuffner, J.: Modeling spatial and temporal variation in motion data. ACM Trans. Graph., 1–10 (2009)
15. Treuille, A., Lee, Y., Popović, Z.: Near-optimal Character Animation with Continuous Control. ACM Trans. Graph. 3 (2007)
16. Johansen, R.S.: Automated Semi-Procedural Animation for Character Locmotion. Aarhus University (2009)
17. van Basten, B.J.H., Stuvel, S.A., Egges, A.: A hybrid interpolation scheme for footprint-driven walking synthesis. Graphics Interface, 9–16 (2011)
18. Shapiro, A., Cao, Y., Faloutsos, Y.: Style Components. In: Proc. of Graphics Interfaces (2006)
19. Neff, M., Kim, Y.: Interactive Editing of Motion Style Using Drives and Correlations. In: ACM SIGGRAPH/Eurographics Symposium on Computer Animation (2009)
20. Whittle, M.W.: Gait Analysis: An Introduction. Elsevier (2007)
21. Inman, V.T., Ralston, H.J., Todd, F., Lieberman, J.C.: Human Walking. Williams & Wilkins (1981)
22. Dean, G.A.: An Analysis of the Energy Expenditure in Level and Grade Walking. Ergonomics 1, 31–47 (1965)
23. Murray, M.P.: Gait as a total pattern of movement. Am. J. Phys. Med. 1, 290–333 (1967)
24. Witkin, A., Popović, Z.: Motion Warping. In: Proc. SIGGRAPH, pp. 105–108 (1995)

Long Term Real Trajectory Reuse through Region Goal Satisfaction

Junghyun Ahn[1], Stéphane Gobron[1], Quentin Silvestre[1],
Horesh Ben Shitrit[1], Mirko Raca[1], Julien Pettré[2],
Daniel Thalmann[3], Pascal Fua[1], and Ronan Boulic[1]

[1] EPFL, Switzerland
[2] INRIA-Rennes, France
[3] NTU, Singapore

Abstract. This paper is motivated by the objective of improving the realism of real-time simulated crowds by reducing short term collision avoidance through long term anticipation of pedestrian trajectories. For this aim, we choose to reuse outdoor pedestrian trajectories obtained with non-invasive means. This initial step is achieved by analyzing the recordings of multiple synchronized video cameras. In a second off-line stage, we fit as long as possible trajectory segments within predefined paths made of a succession of region goals. The concept of region goal is exploited to enforce the principle of "sufficient satisfaction": it allows the pedestrians to relax the prescribed trajectory to the traversal of successive region goals. However, even if a fitted trajectory is modified due to collision avoidance, we are still able to make long-term trajectory anticipation and distribute the collision avoidance shift over a long distance.

Keywords: Motion trajectories, Collision handling.

1 Introduction

The present paper is motivated by two goals: first producing more plausible pedestrian crowds by reusing pedestrian trajectories captured with non invasive means, and second, relying on general principles of human behavior to minimize the computing cost when reusing as large as possible trajectory segments. We believe that a first step towards the ecological validity of the crowd motion is to capture pedestrian trajectories in an outdoor pedestrian area. Second, this material has to be obtained through a non-invasive means; for this reason we exploited multiple overlapping video cameras.

Instead of inferring a characterization of the captured pedestrian area, such as in term of a force field, we chose to completely decouple the measured trajectories from their initial context by searching how they could fit to a new spatial environment. Our objective is to assemble as fast as possible and adjust as little as possible large segments of real pedestrian trajectories to obtain a plausible variety of crowd motions. In particular we wish to reduce the occurrences of implausible short term collision avoidance by taking advantage of the short term future of the pedestrian paths. The adjustment to the trajectories are designed to be minimal owing to the interaction of two general principles of human behavior identified in Psychology [28,20,24] and already partly exploited in crowd simulation [10,2]. The principle of least efforts [28] states that people selects the action that require the least effort when given multiple choices to accomplish a task. It has been exploited in [10] to justify the choice of energy minimizing path (both movement and turning effort) when moving through a crowd. However Simon [20] pointed out that humans do not necessarily search for the optimal solution based on all the available solution because they lack the cognitive resources. They rather "satisfice", a term he coined by combining "satisfy" and "suffice", *i.e.* they reach good-enough solution through simplifying heuristics despite their occasional failing [24]. Within this frame of mind, we advocate for generalizing the concept of region goals introduced in [2] for steering an isolated pedestrian towards an oriented region goal. In the present case we intend to select real trajectories so that they fit in a succession of region goals and to adjust them through collision avoiding shifts that satisfy those region goals. One key advantage is the reduced cost of the adjustment step that allows to distribute the trajectory shift long before the potential collision occurrence.

The next section recalls the main background material mostly on crowd simulation. The human trajectory extraction is described in section three while section four presents the new approach for the reuse of long term trajectory segments and their on-line adjustment. Section five and six respectively shows some result and offer some directions for future work.

2 Related Works

The topic of crowd simulation has stimulated a large number of contributions. For this reason we focus in priority on those exploiting pre-existing real or synthesized trajectories or force fields. Brogan and Johnson [4] have built a walking path model from measurements from which they construct a heading chart ensuring trajectories with minimal radius of curvature towards a goal while avoiding static obstacles. By construction the chart is dedicated to the original environment and suited for the goals that were recorded. Chenney proposed to assemble flow tiles over the whole environment to guide pedestrians [5]; it has a clear interest for low cost background movement but it lacks the natural variety of human movements. Likewise [15] combines the attractive force field of a guiding trajectory with other standard force fields. These ideas are also developed in [17]. In [21] the proposed guiding flow is based on the concept of natural movement stating that humans have the tendency to follow their line of sight [8]. The work of Treuille *et al* offers an elegant solution based on a dynamic potential field for guiding groups of pedestrians with the same goals in large scale environments [22]. Reitsma and Pollard evaluate the suitability of an environment to a set of recorded movement organized as a motion graph [19]. In [13] an agent model is learned from recorded aerial view of group motion and is able to reproduce a wide range of behaviors; it is still limited by its computing cost. Similarly [6] exploits crowd video footage but here to extract time series of velocity fields that are later used to advect people along a time varying flow. An alternate approach is proposed in [14] in which local relative movements are identified from video and stored in a database. Then the database is searched on-line to derive short term movements from the closest found pattern. The computing cost of this type of approach is still high. Yersin *et al* have proposed the concept of Crowd patch that can be assembled on the fly to allow the travel through a potentially infinite inhabited virtual city [27]. Periodic trajectories running through multiple patch constitute the core element of this contribution. Multiple contributions have focused on the simulation of groups [12,11,25] but this is beyond the scope of the present paper as we don't address the constitution and the controlled deformation of groups.

Our own approach relies on the one described in [18] for the stage of general trajectory planning producing a set of variant paths for large group of pedestrians between two regions in a virtual environment. We differ in the way the variant paths are exploited to produce the individual pedestrian trajectories. Our contribution is to fit the longest possible real trajectory segment within the path variant and to adjust them on the fly by taking advantage of the three zones of interest proposed in [26].

3 Extracting Human Trajectories from a Real Scene

Extracting human trajectories in a crowded scene is an active domain in the vision community. There exist several methods for reliable tracking in long sequences [1,3]. Our multiple people tracking relies on pedestrians detections from multiple cameras [7], and multiple object tracking [1]. As the pedestrians detector requires multiple synchronized and calibrated cameras, we initialize our processing pipeline with calibrating the cameras using the Tsai calibration model [23]. Then, we subtract the background and the shadows from the video frames and feed only the binary foreground-background masks to the pedestrians detector. The pedestrians detector integrates the binary masks from all the cameras. The ground-plane is partitioned into grid cells. In each frame, the people detector estimates the probability of each grid cell to be occupied by a person [7]. Next, the tracking algorithm efficiently solves the detection association task by formulating it as a global optimization problem, which is solved using the K-Shortest Paths algorithm (KSP) [1]. Finally, we post-process the trajectories in order to obtain smooth and accurate trajectories. In the following subsections, we explain in great detail the different algorithms used in this work.

3.1 Background Subtraction and Shadows Removal

The background subtraction produces binary images, in which static parts are labeled differently than the dynamic ones. This technique is efficient, but it can be sensitive to differences in lighting conditions, colors of subjects similar to the background and shadows. For our system we used the EigenBackground algorithm [16], which models the background using eigenvalue decomposition of several reference images. It is capable of dealing with global illumination changes, but does not remove pedestrians shadows as they are dynamic as well.

Elimination of shadows in the footage was made additionally difficult due to low quality of our video sequences and lack of distinct colors in the clothing of the pedestrians present. This meant that we could not use different statistical properties of the surface which are usually used to detect shadows such as texture information. Our method uses the fact that the shadows are *(i)* darker variations of the background color and *(ii)* have a distinct shape usually spread in the horizontal direction, which is the main difference from the human shapes which are primarily oriented in the vertical direction. After simple background subtraction each pixel in the foreground can be classified into one of 8 labels based on which angular direction has the largest number of foreground pixels (the *dominant orientation*, Fig 1(c)). By specifying the expected dominant orientation of the shadows, we can substitute the appropriate pixels with the original background color (Fig 1(d)) or remove them from the foreground map used by the tracking algorithm (Fig 1(e)). Since this approach is possible due to consistency in the shadow direction, it needs to be refined to handle dynamically changing shadows or shadows with dominant penumbra component.

Fig. 1. Shadows removal process. (a) Original frame with shadows; (b) Foreground map after simple background subtraction; (c) Dominant orientations of each foreground pixel. Notice that the shadow areas have consistent classification compared to the rest of the human body; (d) Final video frame, with shadow pixels re-colored with background color; (e) Final foreground map.

3.2 Multiple Pedestrian Detection and Tracking

We adopt the multiview people detector of [7]. In each frame, the detector integrates the binary background-foreground information from different cameras with respect to their calibration, and estimates the positions of the pedestrians on the ground plane. The ground plane is partitioned into uniform, non-overlapping grid cells, typically with size of 25 by 25 (cm). The detector provides an estimation of the probability of each grid cell to be occupied by a person. Hence, it produces a Probability Occupancy Map (POM) [7]. We use the publicly available implementation of the algorithm[1].

---

[1] POM: http://cvlab.epfl.ch/software/pom

Given the person locations estimated by POM, we use the K-Shortest Path (KSP) tracker [1]. The KSP formulates the tracking task as a global optimization problem on a Directed Acyclic Graph (DAG), yielding a convex objective function. Its computational complexity is $O(k(m + n \log n))$, where m, n, and k are the number of graph nodes, edges, and trajectories. The algorithm is suitable for tracking people in large areas for a long time period. However, even though the KSP has a space complexity of $O(n)$, this turns out to consume a lot of memory resources. Using the publicly available version of the algorithm[2], we could only process 2000 frames. Therefore, we introduced a pruning mechanism for reducing the consumed memory. Using the POM results, we kept only the detections that were above a certain threshold $Thr1 = 0.75$, in addition to their spatio-temporal neighborhood. We defined the neighborhood as all the cells that are proximate less than $Thr2 = 12$ cells to a cell with a detection. Using this very low threshold we managed to keep the tracking performance high, and still to prune more than half of the graph's edges. Thus, we have the ability to process more than 6000 frames, in one batch.

3.3 Trajectory Rectification

As was mentioned in the previous subsection, positions of human trajectories have been extracted from 25 cm square grid cells. Because of this approximation, we couldn't avoid the problem of rough trajectories. Besides, other issues depicted in Fig 2 gave us the motivation to design rectification steps as follows:

1. Generate local and global confidences of all the frames and trajectories
   – **Local confidence:** defines reliability of a single frame in a trajectory
   – **Global confidence:** defines reliability of the entire trajectory
2. Remove low local confidence frames (issues #1 and #3 in Fig 2)
3. Remove low global confidence trajectories (issue #2)
4. Fill missed frames in each trajectory
5. **Smoothing** rough trajectories (issue #4)

Local confidence. Two different formulations have been defined for local confidence. One from distance measure and the other one from speed at a given frame (see upper and lower equation of Fig 2). We defined two different distance measures d_1 and d_2, which represents distance to the border of capture area and distance between two trajectory positions at the same frame, respectively. The speed (m/s) is defined by subtracting the current position to the previous frame. In the upper equation, $C_d(d)$, constant k, which defines the slope of the *logistic function*, was set to 3. In the lower equation of Fig 2, $C_s(s)$, constants $S1$ and $S2$ are respectively the average human walking speed 1.4 and the width of the *gaussian function* defined as 24.5 (full width at half maximum 3.5). We pruned frames to $C_d(d_1) < 0.55$ and $C_s(s) < 0.6$.

---

[2] KSP: http://cvlab.epfl.ch/software/ksp

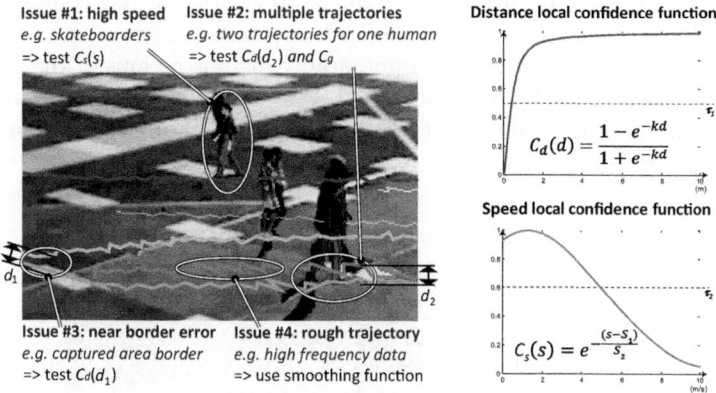

Fig. 2. Problems statement and their relation to local confidence equations. Bold red texts state problems of reconstruction and blue texts starting with "⇒" their solutions. On the right, shows two different local confidence equations with their pruning threshold (horizontal dashed line). Each equation's y-axis gives a value range [0,1], which represents the reliability of a reconstructed frame.

Global confidence. The global confidence, $C_g = (\sum_{k \in Tr} \rho_k)/|Tr|$, is a general measure that defines how high were the probabilities of the detections. It is based on the sum of detection probabilities ρ_k at each location k which belong to the trajectory Tr. This sum is normalized by the length of the trajectory $|Tr|$. By construction, the KSP algorithm provides trajectories with global confidence $C_g > 0.5$. During the rectification process, we solve the "issue #2" stated in Fig 2. We first check if two trajectory positions at a given frame is $C_l(d_2) < 0.5$, and remove one of them by comparing C_g of both trajectories.

Smoothing. Smooth filtering was exploited for the purpose of removing noisy effect on the trajectories. We applied different smoothing filters such as *Moving average*, *Savitzky-Golay*, and *Local Regression* with various span parameters from 0.1% to 5.0%. All filters were processed with 2nd degree polynomial smoothing. Among them, we found *Local Regression* with 0.5% had more similarity to the rough trajectories with low noisy effects.

4 Re-using Human Trajectories in a Virtual Scene

4.1 Generating Path from Given Trajectories

Environment setup with navigation graph. A typical trajectory capture session should result in a few hundreds trajectory segments with a wide variety of lengths. Each trajectory maintains the information of position, direction and speed of each frame. The first problem we want to address is to fit the longest possible trajectory segment within a set of region-to-region path variants pre-computed according to the approach described in [18]. The path variants are constructed from a navigation graph where nodes are (static) collision-free circular regions called vertices (Fig 3 left). Each path variant is defined by a set of successive vertices that link two potentially distant regions of the virtual environment (Fig 3 right). By construction, the path variants may share vertices in narrow parts of the scene, so it is also necessary to address dynamic collision detection as we show later.

Fig. 3. The Navigation graph [18] illustrated in this city scene (top view) guarantees that no collision with static elements of the environment can occur within the sampled circular regions (left); path variants are automatically built to link distant regions through a list of vertices (right)

Preprocessing path trajectory. The detailed process of determining a path trajectory is illustrated in Fig 4. The process is off-line and we have the guarantee that the match will succeed owing to a sufficient pool of short trajectory segments and to the relatively large size of the vertices. In order to ensure some variety of trajectory, we randomly initialize the candidate trajectory segment as follows: 1) random position of the starting position (P_1 in V_0) within the start vertex and 2) random orientation of the candidate segment start-to-end vector within the angular sector under which the target vertex (P_2 in V_{end}) is viewed. At the end of the matching process we apply a local smoothing, by bezier curve approximation, in the region linking successive segments.

4.2 Real-Time Collision Handling

The advantage of reusing known trajectories is the possibility to estimate collision long time ahead. Based on future trajectory information, we formulated a real-time collision avoidance algorithm illustrated in Fig 5. For the collision avoidance model we first define two circular shape areas as follows. The first circle represents a **colliding area** (inner circle) which represents average breast width of human, and second circle represents a **shift influencing area** (dashed circle) which represents an area where people feel threat of collision. We admit that the shape of shift influencing area is rather an elliptic or more complex shape [14] [9], however, in this paper we simplify our approach for real-time simulation, and to compensate this area simplification, we gave more weights to the collision threat coming from forward walking direction.

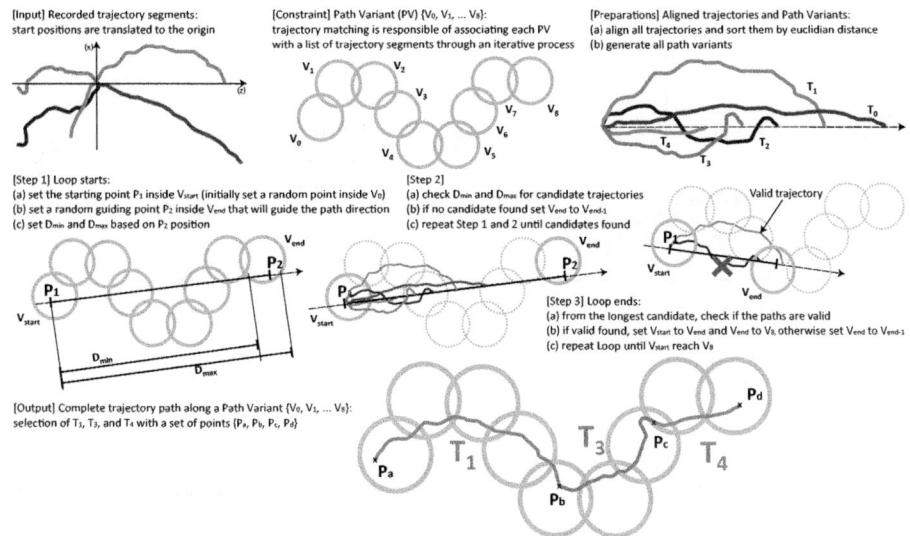

Fig. 4. A fully detailed process of trajectory path generation on a path variant

The proposed collision avoidance method has mainly two steps: generating 1) direction and 2) magnitude of trajectory shift. The detail of getting this instantaneous avoiding direction is as follows. At a given time t_0, a virtual character H_i checks its collision by looking up trajectory paths ahead. In the present implementation we sub-sampled future positions every N_f frames. We denote t_c as the time of a collision detected after time t_0, and t_f as the time after the collision such that t_f-t_c is equal to t_c-t_0. When H_i detects a collision at t_c, it analyzes the relative positions of all the other characters (H_{ij}) in the current View Frustum (VF). Here the relative positions $H_{ij}(t_0)$, $H_{ij}(t_c)$, and $H_{ij}(t_f)$ are the positions of H_{ij} in H_i local coordinate. For each character H_{ij} two line segments $l_{ij}(t_c)$ and $l_{ij}(t_f)$ are built (see Fig 5). Given these line segments, we are able to compute the **shift influence vectors** $\mathbf{v}_{ij}^s(t_c)$ as in Eq 1. First, we define a vector $\mathbf{v}_{ij}^l(t_c)$, which represents the minimum distance vector from $l_{ij}(t_c)$ to H_i. The vector $\mathbf{v}_{ij}^s(t_c)$ is generated by re-scaling $\mathbf{v}_{ij}^l(t_c)$ with the radius of the shift influencing area R_s. The vector $\mathbf{v}_{ij}^s(t_f)$ is calculated in a similar way by replacing t_c by t_f.

$$\mathbf{v}_{ij}^s(t_c) = \frac{R_s - |\mathbf{v}_{ij}^l(t_c)|}{|\mathbf{v}_{ij}^l(t_c)|} \mathbf{v}_{ij}^l(t_c) \qquad (1)$$

By accumulating all the shift influence vectors ($\sum_{j \in VF}(w_c \mathbf{v}_{ij}^s(t_c) + w_f \mathbf{v}_{ij}^s(t_f))$), we finally get a **trajectory shift vector** $\mathbf{v}_i(t_0)$, which guides H_i to avoid collision at time t_0. The weighting factors w_c and w_f are defined as 2/3 and 1/3.

Additional shift influence vectors. Besides these shift influence vectors, other factors were also considered for calculating the trajectory shift vector.

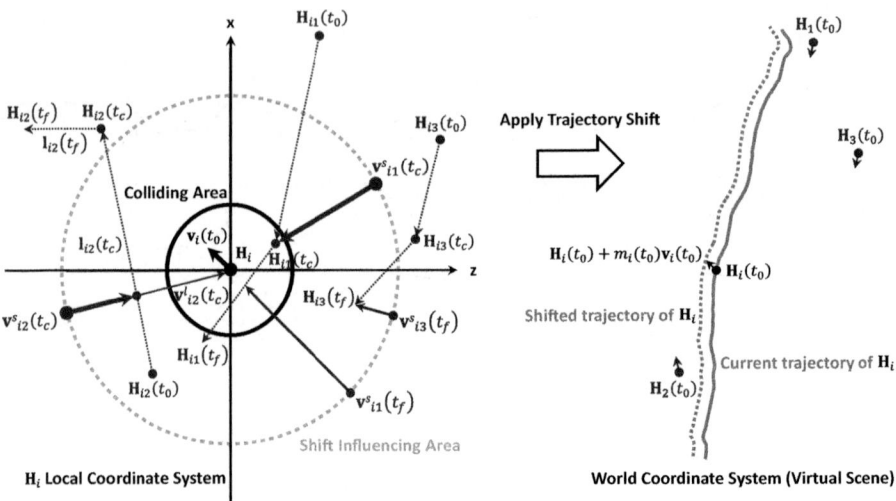

Fig. 5. The collision avoidance mechanism of character H_i; Left: the trajectory shift vector $\mathbf{v}_i(t_0)$; Right: shifting trajectory at run time

Each trajectory path may not surpass the limit of the current path variant's vertex. We check the magnitude of the sum of the shifting vectors accumulated from previous simulation loops, and apply an additional shift influence vector heading toward the original trajectory. Moreover, the case of ideal linear frontal collision without any other intruder is singular and fails to produce avoidance. To solve this problem, we give a weak left or right shift influence on forward walking direction. The trajectory shift vector $\mathbf{v}_i$ is *normalized* after adding all shift influence vectors.

Magnitude of trajectory shift vector. For a realistic collision avoiding movement, we formulated a magnitude m_i, which gives an instantaneous distance to deviate a path. For each simulation loop, if a character H_i detects a collision threat at time t_c, it analyzes the scaling factor $m_i(t_0)$ (see Eq 2), which will be multiplied by the given normalized vector $\mathbf{v}_i(t_0)$ for shifting H_i's trajectory. Eq 2 computes the instantaneous collision avoidance speed for the current time step. The durations $\Delta t_s(t_0)$ and Δt_v are respectively the current inverse of display rate at time t_0, and the inverse of captured video rate (constant $0.04sec.$). The distances R_c and $min(|\mathbf{v}_{ij}^l(t)|)$ are respectively the radius of collision area and the minimum distance among the different j. Finally, the parameter $f_c(t_0)$ is the number of frames left before collision at time t_0. A maximum magnitude has been also defined to reduce jerky motions.

$$m_i(t_0) = \frac{\Delta t_s(t_0)(R_c - min(|\mathbf{v}_{ij}^l(t_c)|))}{\Delta t_v f_c(t_0)} \qquad (2)$$

5 Results

From the video capture, we obtained 30,000 frames recorded at 25-fps. Among them, 10,000 frames have been selected as rough trajectories and 297 trajectories were generated by the reconstruction and rectification process. By the smoothing process, we applied optimal filtering methods and parameters to retain as much as we could from the original trajectory while reducing noisy effects.

Fig 6 illustrates the results of our approach. The city scene consists of 357 path variants over the entire walkable area. For each path variant, in average, around 135 successive *navigation graph vertices* are connected. A vertex is shared by a number of path variants which makes possible to generate lots of variant paths. In our result, one trajectory path was generated for each path variant. The size of preprocessed 357 trajectory paths was 161 MB in ASCII format.

Fig. 6. Top left: reconstructed and rectified real trajectories from video capture; Top right: real trajectory scene with free viewpoint; Bottom left: preprocessed trajectory paths; Bottom right: trajectory reused scene with collision avoidance (500 characters)

An experiment of simulation speed was conducted by varying the number of characters. We compared to a previous work [26] and the results show as in Table 1. The computing cost of our approach was slightly higher than the previous work. However, from the movie at http://iig.epfl.ch/movies, we could see that real trajectories can produce more plausible animations path. We also noticed that characters following real trajectories look more realistic with various speed and movement along a path. However, the collision avoidance was not considered. Our collision avoidance algorithm didn't work perfectly in a high density crowd scene. We think this problem can be solved by considering the speed variation on trajectory shifting.

Table 1. A display rate (fps) comparison between two different methods from the same camera view point (environment: NVidia GTX 460 1GB)

# of characters	250	500	1000	2000
Yersin et al [26]	60.0	27.7	14.7	7.7
Our approach	60.0	25.6	13.6	6.6

6 Conclusion

The methods presented in this paper cover the whole pipeline for automating non-invasive pedestrian trajectories processing and reuse in arbitrary scenes. Contributions encompass both the real trajectories recovery from multiple video cameras, for which large speedups have been obtained, and the trajectory reuse for long-term prediction and avoidance of collisions. We will proceed to extensive benchmarking to evaluate whether the simplified circular shape of the shift influence area is detrimental for the plausibility of the resulting crowd motion. More comparisons with prior approaches would be beneficial although none have adopted our reuse strategy for collision avoidance. Future work will also focus on the exploitation of this know-how in Augmented Reality to demonstrate the efficient editing of the original captured crowd (*e.g.* adding lifelike pedestrians or removing existing pedestrians).

Acknowledgements. This research has been funded by the Swiss National Science Foundation Synergia project AerialCrowds.

References

1. Berclaz, J., Fleuret, F., Türetken, E., Fua, P.: Multiple object tracking using k-shortest paths optimization. PAMI (February 2011)
2. Boulic, R.: Relaxed Steering Towards Oriented Region Goals. In: Egges, A., Kamphuis, A., Overmars, M. (eds.) MIG 2008. LNCS, vol. 5277, pp. 176–187. Springer, Heidelberg (2008)
3. Breitenstein, M.D., Reichlin, F., Leibe, B., Koller-Meier, E., Van Gool, L.: Online multiperson tracking-by-detection from a single, uncalibrated camera. IEEE Transactions on Pattern Analysis and Machine Intelligence 33, 1820–1833 (2011)
4. Brogan, D.C., Johnson, N.L.: Realistic human walking paths. In: CASA 2003, pp. 94–101 (2003)
5. Chenney, S.: Flow tiles. In: SCA 2004, pp. 233–242 (2004)
6. Courty, N., Corpetti, T.: Crowd motion capture. Computer Animation and Virtual Worlds 18, 361–370 (2007)
7. Fleuret, F., Berclaz, J., Lengagne, R., Fua, P.: Multi-camera people tracking with a probabilistic occupancy map. PAMI 30(2), 267–282 (2008)
8. Hillier, B., Penn, A., Hanson, J., Grajewski, T., Xu, J.: Natural movement: or, configuration and attraction in urban pedestrian movement. Environment and Planning B: Planning and Design 20(1), 29–66 (1993)
9. Kapadia, M., Singh, S., Hewlett, W., Faloutsos, P.: Egocentric affordance fields in pedestrian steering. In: I3D 2009, pp. 215–223. ACM (2009)

10. Karamouzas, I., Heil, P., van Beek, P., Overmars, M.H.: A Predictive Collision Avoidance Model for Pedestrian Simulation. In: Egges, A., Geraerts, R., Overmars, M. (eds.) MIG 2009. LNCS, vol. 5884, pp. 41–52. Springer, Heidelberg (2009)
11. Karamouzas, I., Overmars, M.: Simulating the local behaviour of small pedestrian groups. In: VRST 2010, pp. 183–190. ACM (2010)
12. Kwon, T., Lee, K.H., Lee, J., Takahashi, S.: Group motion editing. ACM Transactions on Graphics 27, 80:1–80:8 (2008)
13. Lee, K.H., Choi, M.G., Hong, Q., Lee, J.: Group behavior from video: a data-driven approach to crowd simulation. In: SCA 2007, pp. 109–118 (2007)
14. Lerner, A., Chrysanthou, Y., Lischinski, D.: Crowds by example. Computer Graphics Forum 26(3), 655–664 (2007)
15. Metoyer, R.A., Hodgins, J.K.: Reactive pedestrian path following from examples. In: CASA 2003. IEEE Computer Society (2003)
16. Oliver, N.M., Rosario, B., Pentland, A.P.: A bayesian computer vision system for modeling human interactions. PAMI 22(8), 831–843 (2000)
17. Park, M.J.: Guiding flows for controlling crowds. Vis. Comput. 26, 1383–1391 (2010)
18. Pettré, J.: Populate Your Game Scene. In: Egges, A., Kamphuis, A., Overmars, M. (eds.) MIG 2008. LNCS, vol. 5277, pp. 33–42. Springer, Heidelberg (2008)
19. Reitsma, P.S.A., Pollard, N.S.: Evaluating motion graphs for character animation. ACM Trans. Graph. 26 (October 2007)
20. Simon, H.A.: Rational choice and the structure of the environment. Psychological Review 63(2), 129–138 (1956)
21. Stylianou, S., Fyrillas, M.M., Chrysanthou, Y.: Scalable pedestrian simulation for virtual cities. In: VRST 2004, pp. 65–72. ACM (2004)
22. Treuille, A., Cooper, S., Popović, Z.: Continuum crowds. ACM Trans. Graph. 25, 1160–1168 (2006)
23. Tsai, R.Y.: A versatile cameras calibration technique for high accuracy 3d machine vision mtrology using off-the-shelf tv cameras and lenses. JRA 3(4), 323–344 (1987)
24. Tversky, A., Kahneman, D.: Judgment under uncertainty: Heuristics and biases. Science 185(4157), 1124–1131 (1974)
25. van den Akker, M., Geraerts, R., Hoogeveen, H., Prins, C.: Path planning for groups using column generation. In: Boulic, R., Chrysanthou, Y., Komura, T. (eds.) MIG 2010. LNCS, vol. 6459, pp. 94–105. Springer, Heidelberg (2010)
26. Yersin, B., Maïm, J., Morini, F., Thalmann, D.: Real-time crowd motion planning: Scalable avoidance and group behavior. Vis. Comput. 24, 859–870 (2008)
27. Yersin, B., Maïm, J., Pettré, J., Thalmann, D.: Crowd patches: populating large-scale virtual environments for real-time applications. In: I3D, pp. 207–214 (2009)
28. Zipf, G.: Human Behaviour and the Principle of Least-Effort. Addison-Wesley, Cambridge (1949)

Directional Constraint Enforcement for Fast Cloth Simulation

Oktar Ozgen and Marcelo Kallmann

University of California, Merced
Merced, CA, 95343, USA
{oozgen,mkallmann}@ucmerced.edu
http://graphics.ucmerced.edu

Abstract. We introduce a new method that greatly improves the iterative edge length constraint enforcement frequently used in real-time cloth simulation systems for preventing overstretching. Our method is based on the directional enforcement of constraints and on the simultaneous progressive scanning of the cloth edges, starting from fixed vertices and propagating on the direction of gravity. The proposed method successfully detects the meaningful springs to be corrected and ignores the ones that do not have any significance on the overall visual result. The proposed approach is simple and robust and is able to achieve realistic cloth simulations without overstretching, without causing any visual artifacts, and dramatically decreasing the computational cost of the constraint enforcement process.[1]

Keywords: Physically Based Simulation, Cloth Simulation, Constraint Enforcement.

1 Introduction

Cloth simulation is widely used in computer graphics and many systems are able to simulate in real time moderately complex cloth models. Among the several possible approaches for achieving deformable surfaces, particle-based systems remain the most popular model for achieving interactive, real-time results. One common undesired behavior in particle-based cloth models is the effect of overstretching, and specific geometric edge length enforcement procedures are commonly employed.

Iterative enforcement of constraints coupled with explicit integration methods is well suited for cloth simulation systems with modest particle numbers. This combination successfully avoids the requirement of solving systems of equations and therefore leads to computationally fast and visually satisfying simulations, suitable for computer games. Although research has been developed to the problem of constraint enforcement in general, the useful iterative geometric edge length enforcement method has not been improved since its introduction by Provot [15]. We present in this paper a new approach that greatly improves this method. Our method is simple to be implemented, robust, and

---
[1] Accompanying video at
http://graphics.ucmerced.edu/projects/11-mig-edgcorr/

is able to achieve realistic stiff cloth behavior without any visual artifacts and improving the computation time of the regular iterative constraint enforcement by up to 80%.

The proposed method is based on computing a meaningful one-pass ordering of edge corrections by considering the direction in which stretching occurs most. First, we experimentally determine the correction priorities over the different types of considered springs in order to minimize the stretch effect of the gravitational pull. Then, we employ corrections starting from all the fixed vertices in a given simulation and synchronously expanding towards the bottom of the cloth. We also limit the correction number of each vertex. By prioritizing the correction order of different types of springs and limiting the correction number of all vertices to a small number, our method successfully detects the important springs to be corrected and ignores the ones that do not have any significance on the overall visual result. Our final method is able to dramatically decrease the cost of the iterative constraint enforcement process and at the same time successfully eliminates undesired overstretching effects.

2 Related Work

Cloth simulation is a central topic in computer graphics and there is a rich literature available [5,4,15,8,21,3,10,6,19,18]. We focus our review on how constraint enforcement has been used in previous works.

A common approach for the iterative constraint enforcement procedure is proposed by Provot [15]. In this method, the cloth is scanned in an iterative way and all springs that are disturbed more than a given threshold in respect to their rest lengths are identified. These springs are then restored to their rest length by moving the two particles connected to a spring along the spring axis, bringing them closer if the spring is over stretched; or further away from each other if the spring is over compressed (see Fig. 1).

The result of the described procedure is that a stiffer cloth behavior is produced. Note however that not all springs can be perfectly corrected since one spring correction can alter a previously corrected spring. There are a number of additional limitations inherent to this kind of brute-force correction approach. One corrective iteration over the cloth does not always guarantee a visually satisfying result, and in addition, the cloth might exhibit an oscillatory behavior in several areas. To overcome these limitations, a common approach is to apply the corrective procedure several times until a visually satisfying result can be obtained. Obviously, increasing the number of constraint enforcement iterations will decrease the performance of the simulation and there is no reliable way to determine how many iterations would be necessary to achieve the desired results. In [15] it is mentioned that the order of correction of springs depends entirely on their used data structure and in cases where constraints are globally extending to the whole cloth object, the order of springs would probably have more importance and should be studied. This observation is the primary motivation for our proposed directional constraint enforcement method.

Aside from iterative approaches, it is also possible to address the problem by solving a system of non-linear constraint equations. Terzopoulos et al [19] used the Gauss-Seidel method to approximate the solution with a linear system of equations [19]. Another popular method is called the Reduced Coordinate Formulation. In this

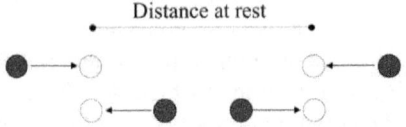

Fig. 1. Direction of correction for two particles connected by a spring

formulation, an unconstrained system with a given number of degrees of freedom is subject to a set of constraints that remove some of the degrees of freedom and parameterizes the rest; thus leading to generalized coordinates [11]. Lagrange multiplier formulations are also widely used and have the advantage of defining the velocity and other types of constraints which cannot be formulated using the Reduced Coordinates method [1,2].

Among these several approaches, our proposed method is most suitable for applications where speed of computation and simplicity of implementation are most important, such as in computer games and real-time simulations.

3 Cloth Model

The mesh structure of our cloth model is based on the scheme presented by [6]. The cloth is represented as a quadrilateral mesh of particles. Particles are connected to each other by massless springs. There are three types of spring elements, which are responsible for the stretch, shear and bend forces. The connectivity of the springs is described in the following way: a particle indexed by $p(i,j)$ is connected by stretch springs to its neighbor particles indexed by $p(i\pm 1, j), p(i, j\pm 1)$. The shear springs connect the particle to $p(i\pm 1, j\pm 1)$, and the bend springs connect the particle to $p(i\pm 2, j), p(i, j\pm 2)$ and $p(i\pm 2, j\pm 2)$.

3.1 Forces

The dynamics of the system is governed by Newton's second law of motion $\boldsymbol{F} = m\boldsymbol{a}$, where m is the mass and $\boldsymbol{a}$ is the acceleration of a particle. The acceleration is computed at every time step based on the total force $\boldsymbol{F}$ applied to the particle, and which accounts for all external and internal forces.

The gravitational force is given by $\boldsymbol{F}_g = m\boldsymbol{g}$ and it is the only external force in our system. The internal forces acting on a particle are the forces which originate from the stretch, bend and shear springs connected to each particle. The spring force $\boldsymbol{F}_s$ between two particles is given by Hooke's law:

$$\boldsymbol{F}_s = -k_s(|\boldsymbol{l}| - r)\frac{\boldsymbol{l}}{|\boldsymbol{l}|} \qquad (1)$$

where $\boldsymbol{l} = \boldsymbol{x}_i - \boldsymbol{x}_j$ is the difference between the positions of the two particles, r is the rest length of the spring and k_s is the linear spring constant.

3.2 Verlet Integration

Although it is possible to couple the constraint enforcement process with various integration methods, we use the verlet integration method in this work. The Verlet integration is a numerical method that originated from the field of molecular dynamics. Thanks to its simplicity, performance and stability, it has become popular for real-time cloth simulation, in particular in computer games.

The Verlet method stores the current and previous positions of each particle as the state of the system. The velocity is thus implicitly represented by positions. The position update step for each particle is computed with:

$$x_{t+1} = 2x_t - x_{t-1} + ah^2, \qquad (2)$$

where x_{t+1}, x_t and x_{t-1} are the positions of a particle at the next, current and previous timesteps, a is the current acceleration influencing the particle and h is the integration timestep. The acceleration influencing the particle is calculated based on the total force acting on it. The damping of the system might be fine-tuned by changing the constant multiplier (of value 2) in the equation. Decreasing the value to less than 2 will increase the damping; whereas increasing to more than 2 will decrease the damping.

Because the velocity is implicitly calculated, the method tends to stay stable even when relatively large timesteps are used. However, although the simulation remains fast and stable, the use of large timesteps will lead to overshooting of positions and result in a super-elastic cloth. Therefore, simulations relying on Verlet integration are often coupled with an iterative constraint enforcement process that attempts to restore the original distances between each pair of particles connected by a spring in the cloth model.

4 Directional Constraint Enforcement

Our directional constraint enforcement method achieves improved results with a meaningful traversal order of spring corrections. Our method minimizes the number of total corrections needed by preventing redundant repetition of corrections and avoiding the oscillation behavior that often results from a simple iterative constraint enforcement traversal.

Our method is based on the observation that the most stretched springs tend to be the ones on the regions most influenced by the contact forces in a given simulation scenario. Therefore, the most stretched regions on the surface of the cloth are expected to be the regions close to fixed vertices of the cloth, which are vertices that tend not to move relative to their respective colliding object. By defining a traversal order that first corrects the springs around the fixed vertices of the cloth, and expanding the corrections on the direction of the gravity, it is possible to ensure that corrections will be effective and without redundancy.

Our algorithm assumes that the cloth stretches under gravity and has a set of fixed vertices. These fixed vertices correspond to vertices that attach the cloth to a character's body, a flag to a flag pole or a table cloth to the table, etc. Since there may possibly be more than one fixed vertex to start the correction expansion, it is important to synchronize the corrections originating from different fixed vertices. Our experiments showed

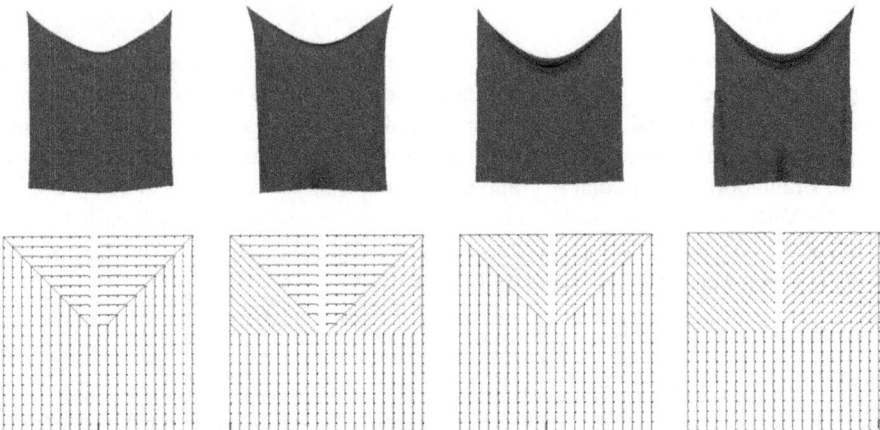

Fig. 2. Correction patterns and their respective deformation results obtained from choosing different correction orders among the different types of springs

that failing to synchronize the expansions are causing serious visual artifacts; and the simultaneous expansion remains an important aspect of the algorithm.

It is also crucial to analyze the overall visual look of the cloth according to the order chosen on the different types of springs. If we categorize the different types of springs along with their elongation directions, we can come up with three major categories: 1) stretch springs elongating towards left or right (horizontal stretch springs), 2) stretch springs elongating towards the bottom of the cloth (vertical stretch springs) and 3) shear springs elongating towards the bottom of the cloth. Note that we do not take into account springs elongating upwards, to make sure that the correction will be expanded towards the gravity direction.

It is not straightforward to determine which type of spring should be given correction priority over other types. We have experimented with different orderings for the three different types of springs, leading to six different combinations. Two of these combinations produced similar correction orders as others; so, we ended up having four different correction orders possible. The correction maps of these four different orderings and their associated deformation results are shown in Fig. 2. The experiment of switching among the different orderings to observe the resulting cloth postures can be found on the accompanying video of this paper. This experiment showed that the best-looking deformations are obtained with the following order of correction: 1) Horizontal stretch springs, 2) Vertical stretch springs, 3) Shear springs.

With the ordering for processing the different types of springs determined, an edge traversal process respecing this ordering can then be devised. Algorithm 1 summarizes our final edge correction ordering generation process. Details of the algorithm are given in the next paragraphs.

Algorithm 1 receives as input the set of fixed vertices V_f. At the beginning of the algorithm, we use an empty queue Q to maintain the synchronous order of correction expansions. When the algorithm terminates, list L will be filled with the right order of edges to be corrected during run time.

The overall algorithm proceeds as follows: first, all the fixed vertices are pushed into the expansion queue Q. Then, until there is no vertex left in the queue, the vertices are popped and expanded one by one. Procedure *Get Horizontal Stretch Springs* (v_s) returns the horizontal stretch springs connected to the vertex v_s. Similarly, *Get Vertical Stretch Springs* (v_s) returns the vertical stretch springs connected to the vertex v_s, and *Get Shear Springs* (v_s) returns the shear springs connected to the vertex v_s. Finally, procedure *Get Goal Vertex* (v_s, s) returns the vertex that is connected to the vertex v_s by the spring s.

Algorithm 1. Ordered Edge Correction

Compute_Correction_List (V_f)

1. $L \leftarrow null$
2. **for all** v such that $v \in V_f$ **do**
3. $Q.push(v)$
4. **end for**
5. **while** Q is not empty **do**
6. $v_S \leftarrow Q.pop()$
7. $S_h \leftarrow$ *Get Horizontal Stretch Springs* (v_s)
8.   **for all** s such that $s \in S_h$ **do**
9. $v_g \leftarrow$ *Get Goal Vertex* (v_s, s)
10.   *Expand* (L, v_s, v_g)
11.   **end for**
12. $S_v \leftarrow$ *Get Vertical Stretch Springs* (v_s)
13.   **for all** s such that $s \in V_s$ **do**
14. $v_g \leftarrow$ *Get Goal Vertex* (v_s, s)
15.   *Expand* (L, v_s, v_g)
16.   **end for**
17. $S_s \leftarrow$ *Get Shear Springs* (v_s)
18.   **for all** s such that $s \in S_s$ **do**
19. $v_g \leftarrow$ *Get Goal Vertex* (v_s, s)
20.   *Expand* (L, v_s, v_g)
21.   **end for**
22. **end while**
23. **return** L

For each vertex expanded we first find all the horizontal stretch springs connected to it. Then, we find the goal vertices that the vertex is connected to through these springs. Finally, we try to expand the correction map towards those vertices. When the *Expand* procedure is called, the expansion to the goal vertex is not guaranteed. The algorithm first checks how many times the goal vertex has been visited. If it already reached the visit limit number then we do not expand. If the visit limit is not reached yet, the algorithm expands to the goal vertex and adds the edge from the current vertex to the goal vertex to the ordered correction list L. The visit count of the goal vertex will be incremented and the goal vertex will be added to the expansion queue Q. These procedures will be repeated for vertical stretch springs and shear springs as well. The algorithm will stop when there is no vertex left in the queue. At the end of the algorithm, we will have the ordered correction list L completed.

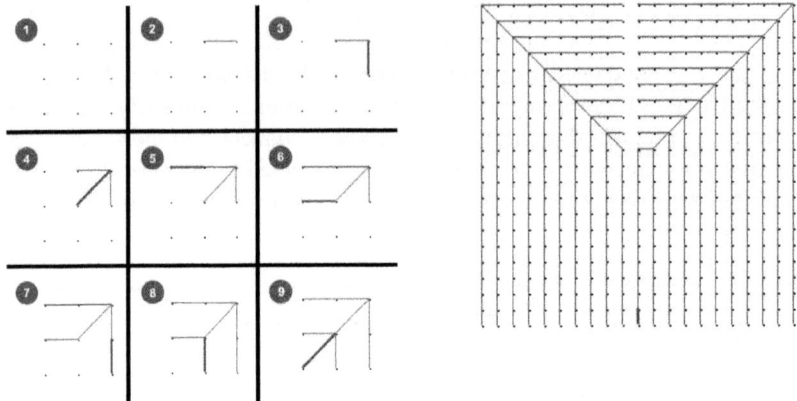

Fig. 3. Left: step-by-step order of correction starting from an upper right fixed vertex of the cloth. Right: correction map created for a cloth fixed from the two top corners.

List L is precomputed in advance for each set of fixed vertices to be considered during the real-time simulation. Then, after each integration step in the simulation, the iterative constraint enforcement step will traverse the edges in L, correcting only the position of the second vertices in each edge, satisfying the desired length of each edge. Example results obtained with the algorithm are shown in Figure 3.

4.1 Using Multiple Correction Maps

Our method relies on precomputed fixed orderings (encoded in list L) in order to maximize computation performance in real time. Since the set of fixed vertices may change during a simulation, the validity of the precomputed list L may be reduced depending on how irregular and unpredictable the deformation events are. We tested our method on various scenes such as a planar cloth interacting with a solid ball and a complex cloth model interacting with a women model performing a "catwalk". At both simple and complex scenarios, the obtained varied cloth-object collisions and cloth-cloth collisions did not seem to cause any significant degradation in the obtained quality of results.

It is also possible to precompute several correction maps to further increase the performance and the accuracy of the animation. Precomputed maps corresponding to different collision states that repeatedly occur in the animation can be used by switching between them according to events in the simulation. For example, in the animation of the walking character wearing a long skirt, the character's knees are interchangeably colliding with the skirt generating a visible event with impact on the edge correction list. Everytime a knee collides with the skirt, the colliding vertices are going to be corrected by the collision detection module; we can as well treat them as fixed vertices in additional correction lists. We have obtained improved results with three correction maps for the cases where 1) the knees do not touch the skirt, 2) only the right knee touches the skirt and 3) only the left knee touches the skirt. As shown in Figure 4, everytime we detect a knee collision (or obsence of collision) we switch to its corresponding correction

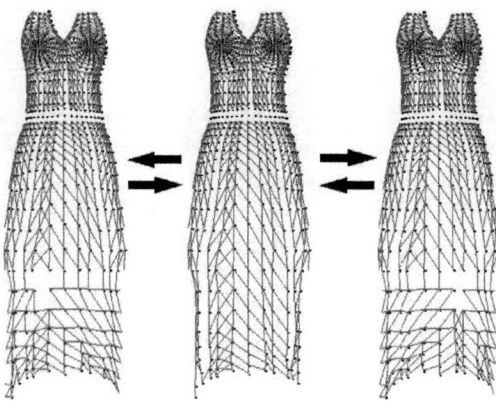

Fig. 4. Three alternating correction maps used for the long skirt simulation during walking: map with right knee collision (left), map with no knee collision (center), and map with left knee collision (right)

map. If the deformation is specific for one given walking animation, such events can be encoded in the time-parameterization of the animation, eliminating decisions based on collision detection events. The use of multiple correction maps is therefore suitable for simulations dependable on cyclic animations such as walking.

5 Results and Discussion

In order to test the applicability of our method to different cloth simulation scenarios we have tested our directional correction algorithm with clothes with different number of fixed vertices and at different places. Figure 5 shows the different correction maps produced for different initial sets of fixed vertices. Although the order of the corrections change, the number of springs to be corrected stays practically the same. The only exception is the scenario with the falling cloth on the table. In that scenario, a large circular set of fixed vertices is naturally marked as fixed, and the number of springs to be corrected is much less.

We have also tested our method on a more complex long skirt cloth model interacting with a walking character. Our method proved to be efficient and did not cause any undesired visual artifacts. Additional examples of edge correction orders obtained for the skirt cloth model are shown in Figure 6 and rendered results are shown in Figure 7.

Our correction methodology is dependent on the set of fixed vertices on the surface of the cloth. In most of the cloth simulation scenarios, such as hanging clothes, capes, flags, table clothes, or dressed characters, the set of fixed vertices stay the same during the whole animation. Therefore, in this cases the correction map would only be pre-computed once and in a very small amount of time. The precomputation time of the correction map is about 0.52 seconds for a cloth of 1681 particles on a 2.4 GHz Intel Core 2 Duo computer.

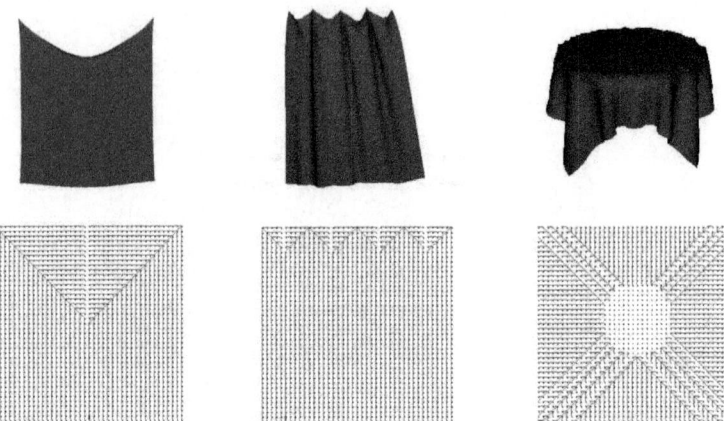

Fig. 5. The figure shows the correction maps generated by our algorithm and their associated cloth simulation scenarios

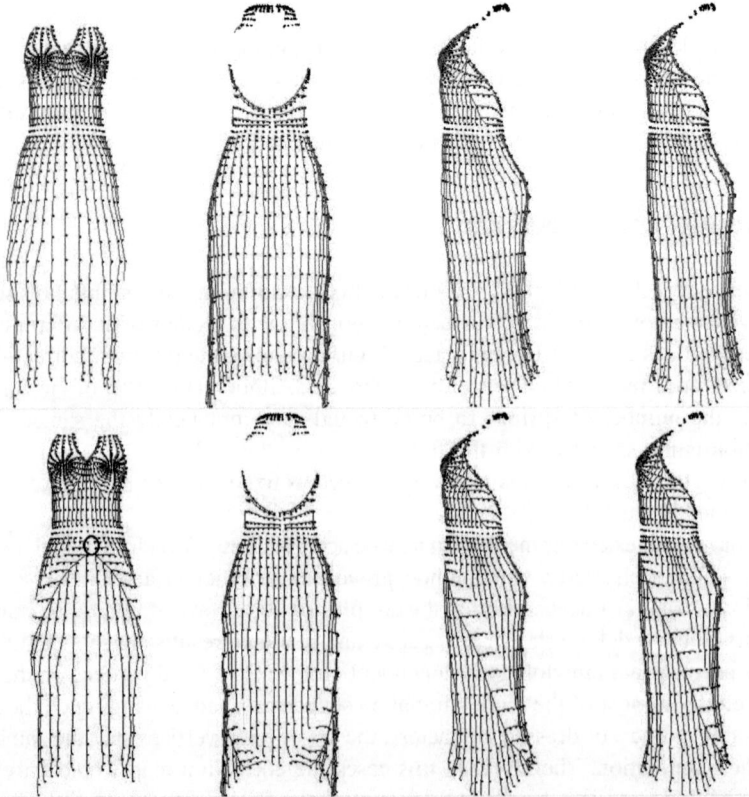

Fig. 6. Top row: Order of correction obtained with fixed vertices selected at the shoulder and belt regions. Bottom row: A small number of vertices (shown by the circle on the bottom-left image) is added to the set of fixed vertices. Notice how the new correction order obtained is different and how the correction map visually corresponds to the expected buckling of the cloth.

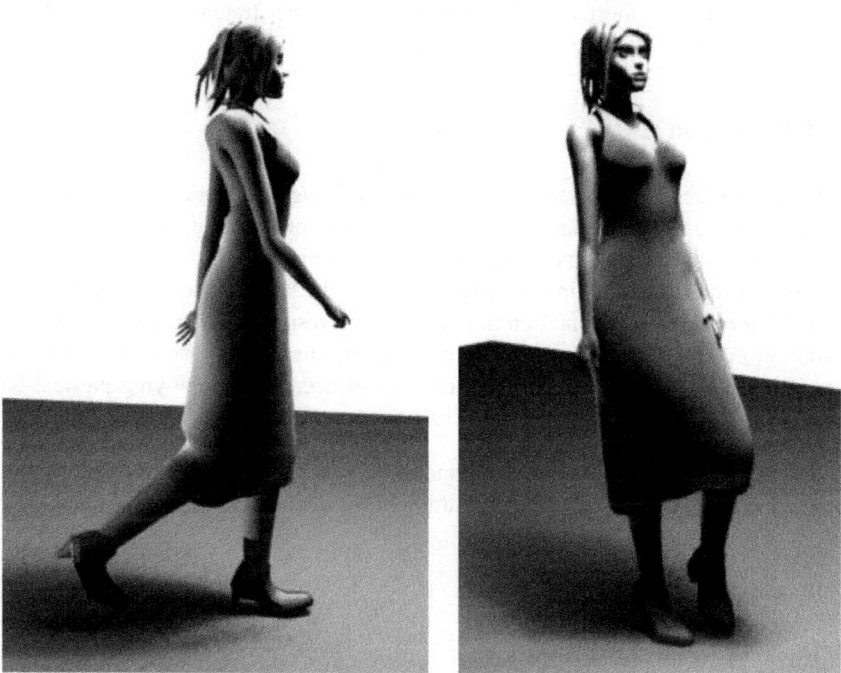

Fig. 7. Example of a long skirt that would significantly overstretch if no constraint enforcement is made. Our method eliminates the overstreching in an efficient manner.

In terms of visual quality our model achieves visually satisfying results from a single correction pass over the list of edges. This is a major improvement in respect to the original (non-ordered) constraint enforcement procedure that relies on several passes to achieve good results. One aditional important advantage of our method is that the directional correction completely eliminates the shaky cloth behavior that is frequently seen in multiple pass procedures.

5.1 Limitations

As previously stated, our correction methodology is dependent on how predictable the set of fixed vertices is. In cloth simulation scenarios where the set of fixed points change very frequently, our method would need to update the correction map after each significant change. In such situations an automatic procedure for detecting the validity of correction list L and triggering an ordering update everytime the set of fixed vertices significantly changes from the original set can be integrated in the simulation system. However, this would still maintain the negative effect of penalizing the overall performance of the simulation. On the other hand, if the change on the set of fixed vertices is not frequent, this will not represent a major slow down in the overall computation time.

We are also assuming that the cloth stretches under one single major constant external force (gravity). Although this assumption addresses the vast majority of cloth simulation scenarios, more complex situations where the stretch direction would be affected by multiple varying external forces have not been tested.

6 Conclusion

We have introduced a new methodology for determining an efficient and effective traversal order for the iterative edge length enforcement in cloth simulations. Our method is robust, simple to be implemented and is able to achieve realistic stiff cloth behavior without causing overstretching or visual artifacts (like shaky effects). Furthermore, our method improves the computation time by 80 % in respect to the regular iterative constraint enforcement procedure. We believe that our directional constraint enforcement approach will prove itself useful to a number of scenarios employing particle-based deformable models, and in particular in real-time applications such as computer games.

Acknowledgments. We would like to thank Robert Backman for the valuable help with the scene rendering and with the preparation of the accompanying video.

References

1. Baraff, D.: Linear-time dynamics using lagrange multipliers. In: Computer Graphcis Proceedings, Annual Conference Series, New York, NY, USA, pp. 137–146 (1996)
2. Baraff, D., Witkin, A.: Physically based modeling: Principles and practice. In: ACM SIGGRAPH 1997 Course Notes (1997)
3. Baraff, D., Witkin, A.: Large steps in cloth simulation. In: Proc. of SIGGRAPH 1998, New York, NY, USA, pp. 43–54 (1998)
4. Breen, D., House, D., Wozny, M.: Predicting the drape of woven cloth using interacting particles. In: Proc. of SIGGRAPH 1994, pp. 365–372. ACM, New York (1992)
5. Carignan, M., Yang, Y., Magenenat-Thalmann, N., Thalmann, D.: Dressing animated synthetic actors with complex deformable clothes. In: Proc. of SIGGRAPH 1992, pp. 99–104. ACM, New York (1992)
6. Choi, K., Ko, H.: Stable but responsive cloth. In: Proc. of SIGGRAPH 2002, pp. 604–611. ACM, New York (2002)
7. Desbrun, M., Schröder, P., Barr, A.: Interactive animation of structured deformable objects. In: Proc. of Graphics Interface, San Francisco, CA, USA, pp. 1–8 (1999)
8. Eberhardt, B., Weber, A., Strasser, W.: A fast, flexible, particle-system model for cloth draping. In: IEEE Computer Graphics and Applications 1996, pp. 52–59. IEEE (1996)
9. Hauth, M., Etzmuß, O., Straßer, W.: Analysis of numerical methods for the simulation of deformable models. The Visual Computer 19(7-8), 581–600 (2003)
10. House, D.H., Breen, D.E. (eds.): Cloth modeling and animation. A. K. Peters, Ltd., Natick (2000)
11. Isaacs, P.M., Cohen, M.F.: Controlling dynamic simulation with kinematic constraints, behavior functions and inverse dynamics. In: Computer Graphcis Proceedings, Annual Conference Series, New York, NY, USA, pp. 131–140 (1987)
12. Ling, L.: Aerodynamic effects. In: House, D.H., Breen, D.E. (eds.) Cloth Modeling and Animation, pp. 175–195. A. K. Peters, Ltd., Natick (2000)
13. Ling, L., Damodaran, M., Gay, R.K.L.: Aerodynamic force models for animating cloth motion in air flow. The Visual Computer 12(2), 84–104 (1996)

14. Müller, M., Schirm, S., Teschner, M., Heidelberger, B., Gross, M.: Interaction of fluids with deformable solids: Research articles. Computer Animation and Virtual Worlds 15(3-4), 159–171 (2004)
15. Provot, X.: Deformation constraints in a mass-spring model to describe rigid cloth behavior. In: Proc. of Graphics Interface 1995, New York, NY, USA, pp. 147–155 (1995)
16. Robinson-Mosher, A., Shinar, T., Gretarsson, J., Su, J., Fedkiw, R.: Two-way coupling of fluids to rigid and deformable solids and shells. ACM Transactions on Graphics (Proc. of SIGGRAPH 2008) 27(3), 1–9 (2008)
17. Selle, A., Su, J., Irving, G., Fedkiw, R.: Robust high-resolution cloth using parallelism, history-based collisions, and accurate friction. Transactions on Visualization and Computer Graphics 15(2) (2009)
18. Terzopoulos, D., Fleischer, K.: Deformable models. The Visual Computer 4(6), 306–331 (1988)
19. Terzopoulos, D., Platt, J., Barr, A., Fleischer, K.: Elastically deformable models. In: Proc. of SIGGRAPH 1987, pp. 205–214. ACM, New York (1987)
20. Tu, X., Terzopoulos, D.: Artificial fishes: physics, locomotion, perception, behavior. In: Proc. of SIGGRAPH 1994, pp. 43–50. ACM Press, New York (1994)
21. Volino, P., Courchesne, M., Thalmann, N.M.: Versatile and efficient techniques for simulating cloth and other deformable objects. In: Proc. of SIGGRAPH 1995, pp. 137–144. ACM, New York (1995)

A Comparison and Evaluation of Motion Indexing Techniques

Gutemberg Guerra-Filho and Harnish Bhatia

Department of Computer Science and Engineering,
University of Texas at Arlington,
Arlington, TX USA
guerra@cse.uta.edu, harnish.bhatia@mavs.uta.edu

Abstract. Motion indexing concerns efficient ways to identify and retrieve motions similar to a query motion from a large set of motions stored in a human motion database. In this paper, we perform the first quantitative evaluation and comparison of motion indexing techniques. We extend PCA-based algorithms for motion segmentation to address the motion indexing problem and perform a survey of the most significant motion indexing techniques in the literature. We implement five different techniques for motion indexing: two principal component analysis (PCA) based methods, a feature-based method, and two dynamic time warping (DTW) based methods. The indexing accuracy is evaluated for all techniques and a quantitative comparison among them is achieved. The two PCA-based techniques have the lowest number of false negatives but, at the same time, they have a large number of false positives (close to 90%). The feature-based and DTW quaternion-based techniques perform better than the PCA-based techniques. While the DTW-3D technique has a small number of false positives, the false negatives are also very few. The Dynamic Time Warping 3D-based technique performed best among all techniques when compared by false positives and false negatives metrics.

Keywords: motion indexing, quantitative evaluation, motion-based animation.

1 Introduction

Given a motion library, motion indexing consists of the recovery of motion data similar to a query motion for its reuse to generate novel motion according to the current status of a digital game (synthesis). The generation of new motion is achieved by motion-based animation techniques such as retargeting, generalization, transitioning, and splicing. More recently, motion indexing has also become essential to action recognition using 3D sensing (analysis). In the kinematic domain, human motion is represented as the evolution of a set of joint angles. Once kinematic motion (also known as motion capture data) is retrieved from video through whole body tracking (*e.g.*, kinetic), the action recognition problem in the visual domain is reduced to motion indexing in the human kinematic domain. This classification of human activity from video is an essential step in the interface of digital games.

Motion indexing concerns efficient ways to retrieve motions similar to a query motion from a large set of motions stored in a human motion database. Efficient indexing methods are necessary to retrieve logically related motions to be reused via motion editing techniques. Motion indexing involves the extraction of suitable motion sequences from a motion capture database according to some user-defined requirements. In some applications, a textual description or a query motion sequence (query-by-example) describes the content of the motion sequences to be retrieved.

Content-based retrieval compares different motions using the notion of similarity. Two motions are similar if they represent variations of the same action concerning the spatial and temporal domain. Given a motion segment as a query, motion indexing concerns the automatic location and extraction of motion segments such that these segments are logically similar to the query motion.

This problem is similar to time-series retrieval where a distance metric is used to search a database for sequences whose distance to the query is below a threshold value ε [6]. Initially, a low-dimensional representation is obtained for each time-series in the database. Examples of low-dimensional representations include a few coefficients of a Fourier transform [1] or a wavelet transform [5], the average values in adjacent windows [4], and bounding boxes [12]. A distance metric is defined over the low-dimensional representation to estimate the distance between time-series. The low-dimensional signals are stored in a spatial data structure such as an R-tree [8].

Kovar and Gleicher [9] identify numerically similar matches and these matches are submitted as new queries. This process iterates until no new matches are found. The motion data is preprocessed into a match web. The *match web* is a compact representation of all motion segments that would be considered similar according to a sufficiently large threshold value.

Arikan *et al.* [2] used Support Vector Machine (SVM) classifiers to annotate a motion database with a vocabulary of actions. Initially, a few examples are annotated manually. They consider the annotation process of each action separately. For a particular action, the annotated frames are divided into two groups: the frames that perform the action (group 1) and the frames that do not perform the action (group -1). The frames of a non-annotated motion are classified into either group using SVM.

Fu *et al.* [7] combined uniform scaling and dynamic time warping in time series querying. They address the problem of finding the best match to a query sequence for any rescaling in a given range. The best match is the sequence with the smallest distance from the query sequence according to a Dynamic Time Warping distance.

In this paper, we perform the first quantitative evaluation and comparison of motion indexing techniques. We extend PCA-based algorithms [3] for motion segmentation to address the motion indexing problem and perform a survey of the most significant motion indexing techniques in the literature. We implement five different techniques for motion indexing: two principal component analysis (PCA) based methods [3], a feature-based method [10], and two dynamic time warping (DTW) based methods [11]. The indexing accuracy is evaluated for all techniques and a quantitative comparison among them is achieved.

The main contributions of this paper consist of the extension of PCA-based techniques to solve the motion indexing problem, and the quantitative evaluation of representative motion indexing methods. These contributions have an impact in the efficient retrieval of motion data and in the action and gesture recognition problem when kinematic data is provided.

The rest of this paper is organized as follows. Section 2 describes the PCA-based methods. Section 3 presents the feature-based method. Section 4 introduces the DTW-based methods. Section 5 discusses the evaluation and comparison of five motion indexing methods. Section 6 has our final conclusions on these experiments.

2 PCA-Based Methods

Automatic motion segmentation decomposes a long sequence of motion into smaller subsequences based on statistical properties of the motion data that characterizes different behaviors. Barbic et al. [3] introduced two PCA-based techniques to segment long motion sequences into small motion clips with different activities. The first method uses PCA to segment the motion based on the change of intrinsic dimensionality. The second method uses probabilistic PCA to create a probabilistic distribution model of the model.

Principal Component Analysis reduces the dimensionality of high-dimensional data which represent a large number of related variables while preserving the most important variation of the data. PCA transforms the high-dimensional motion frame m_i into a motion m_i' in reduced space based on a number r of vectors $v_1, v_2, ..., v_r$ denoted as principal components. The first few r components retain the most variation of the original data such that $m_i' = \overline{m} + x_{i1}v_1 + x_{i2}v_2 + \cdots + x_{ir}v_r$, where $\overline{m}$ is the mean of the motion sequence (centroid of the 4J-dimensional trajectory), $x_{i1}, x_{i2}, ..., x_{ir}$, are the coefficients of the motion m_i when projected into a r-dimensional hyperplane (reduced space) whose axes are $v_1, v_2, ..., v_r$.

The motion is represented by rotations of joints using quaternions. Hence, the motion is a trajectory in a 4J-dimensional space, where J is the number of joints in the skeleton and each joint corresponds to a quaternion (a vector of length 4). Each frame m_i ($i = 1, ..., n$) in the motion M is a point in the 4J-dimensional space, where n is the number of frames in the motion. Therefore, the motion M is represented by a matrix Q of size $n \times 4J$ which contains the 4 quaternion values for all J joints and all n frames.

Before performing PCA on the motion M, the centroid $\overline{m}$ of the motion is subtracted from the matrix Q. Singular Value Decomposition (SVD) is applied to the matrix $Q' = Q - \overline{m}$ to obtain three matrices U, V, and Σ such that $Q' = U\Sigma V^T$, where U and V have orthogonal unit vectors as columns and Σ is a diagonal square matrix with decreasing non-negative eigenvalues σ_j in the diagonal. The first r columns of V are the basis vectors $v_1, v_2, ..., v_r$ of the r-dimensional hyperplane. These vectors are the principal components of motion M and the motion dimension is reduced from $4J$ to r.

The number r of dimensions is ideally determined as the lowest number that preserves the most information. Hence, we search for the smallest value of r such that a preserved information ratio E_r is greater than a particular threshold $\tau \in [0, 1]$. The ratio E_r relates to the amount of information in the original motion which is preserved when r dimensions are maintained and the remaining $4J-r$ dimensions are discarded. The preserved information ratio E_r is defined as: $E_r = \sum_{j=1}^{r} \sigma_j^2 \Big/ \sum_{j=1}^{4J} \sigma_j^2$.

Given an appropriate threshold τ ($\tau = 0.9$), the smallest value of r preserves the information necessary to discern one motion from another while introducing little change to the original motion.

2.1 PCA-Based Motion Segmentation

The PCA-based segmentation [3] is based on the local change of the intrinsic dimensionality of the motion. Similar and correlated motions have frames which are clustered around the mean of the motion sequence and, consequently, require fewer dimensions to represent the motion. As the motion transitions from one action to another, the number of dimensions required to minimize the loss of information (or projection error) increases. Hence, the change from one behavior to another increases the loss of information when the number of reduced dimensions is kept constant.

Initially, the PCA-based segmentation algorithm determines the value of r using the first k frames of the motion ($k = 240$). At each iteration, the algorithm performs PCA for the first i frames ($i \geq k$), where i increases by one at each iteration, and the projection error e_i is obtained using the fixed reduced dimension r. The projection error is defined as $e_i = \sum_{j=1}^{i} \left\| m_i - m_i' \right\|^2$, where $\| \ \|$ is the Euclidean norm.

Theoretically, the error e_i increases with a constant slope when a single simple motion is considered. In this case, the hyperplane representing the reduced space remains almost the same as new frames introduce little additional projection error. On the other hand, frames corresponding to a different action will introduce larger projection errors and the error e_i rises significantly faster. Hence, to detect change between distinct behaviors in the same motion sequence, the derivative of the projection error $d_i = e_i - e_{i-1}$ is used, where the value l guarantees enough gap between frames to avoid noise artifacts ($l = 60$).

The average and standard deviation of the error derivatives for all previous data points d_j, $j \leq i$, is found. If the current error derivative d_i is greater than α times the standard deviation from the average ($\alpha = 3$), a segment boundary is created at frame i and the algorithm is restarted with the remaining frames in the motion.

A second PCA-based segmentation algorithm uses the covariance matrix C obtained by the following equation: $C = \dfrac{V \tilde{\Sigma}^2 V^T}{n-1}$, where the matrix $\tilde{\Sigma}$ is a $4J \times 4J$ diagonal matrix obtained from Σ by replacing all discarded singular values with σ such that $\sigma^2 = \dfrac{\sum_{j=r+1}^{4J} \sigma_j^2}{4J - r}$.

Once the value of the mean motion $\overline{m}$ and the covariance matrix C are obtained, the likelihood of frames $k+1, \ldots, k+t$ is estimated using the Mahalonobis distance H:

$$H = \frac{1}{t} \sum_{i=k=1}^{k+t} (m_i - \overline{m})^T C^{-1} (m_i - \overline{m}).$$

The Mahalanobis distance decreases gradually and reaches a valley (local minimum) when the motion of a single simple motion is considered. On the other hand, when frames of a different behavior appear, there is an increase in the Mahalanobis distance. A subsequent decrease in H is achieved when the distribution accommodates to the new behavior. Hence, the creation of a segment boundary takes place at the peaks of the distance H when a valley is followed by a peak with a difference greater than some threshold $(H_{max} - H_{min})/10$, where H_{max} and H_{min} are the maximum and minimum possible values of H.

2.2 PCA-Based Motion Indexing

Here, we extend the PCA-based motion segmentation to address the motion indexing problem. Once a sequence of motion segments is obtained for two long motion sequences, the indexing of these two motions involves the indexing of their respective segments. Each segment is associated with the dimension r, the start frame, and the end frame. The indexing of two motion segments s_1 and s_2 consists in combining the two segments into a single segment s_{12} by concatenating s_2 into the end of s_1. After that, the preserved information ratio E_{r1} for the combined segment is found using the dimension r_1. Similarly, we obtain the combined segment s_{21} by concatenating s_1 into the end of s_2 and the ratio E_{r2}. The segment s_1 is similar to s_2 if $|E_{r1} - E_{r2}| < \varepsilon$ and E_{r1}, $E_{r2} > \tau$, where ε is a small constant.

3 Feature-Based Method

The feature-based technique [10] uses several qualitative features describing geometric relations between specific body parts (joints of the body or subsequences of poses). Each relational feature is Boolean and encodes spatial, velocity, and directional information. Theoretically, this binary encoding is invariant under spatial and temporal transformations which results in a robust similarity measure for the comparison of motion sequences.

Formally, a Boolean feature is equivalent to a function $F: \mathcal{R}^{3J} \to \{0, 1\}$ mapping the set of poses $\mathcal{R}^{3J}$ into the binary set $\{0, 1\}$. Different Boolean functions may be combined to form any Boolean expression using conjunction and disjunction. Given f Boolean functions for some $f \geq 1$, a combined function $F: \mathcal{R}^{3J} \to \{0, 1\}^f$ is obtained. The feature vector $F(m_i)$ of the pose $m_i \in \mathcal{R}^{3J}$ is the binary version of the pose m_i. The total number of different feature vectors for a feature function F is equal to 2^f.

A generic relational feature depends on a set of joints, $j_1, j_2, \ldots, j_s$, and on a threshold value or range θ, where s is the number of joints used in the feature. There are three basic types of feature functions based on a plane, an angle, and a velocity.

A plane-based feature $F_{plane}(j_1, j_2, j_3, j_4)$ uses a plane passing through the joints j_1, j_2, j_3. The feature has value 1 if the joint j_4 lies on the plane or in front of the plane, distance is greater than or equal to 0, and value 0 when the joint j_4 is behind the plane.

A bone is defined by two joints of the body and an angle is defined between two bones. Angle-based feature functions $F_{angle}(j_1, j_2, j_3, j_4)$ use an angle determined between bones specified by two pairs of joints (j_1, j_2) and (j_3, j_4). The function has value 1 if this angle is within the range θ. Otherwise, the function has value 0.

The velocity-based functions $F_{velocity}(j_1)$ compute the velocity of a joint j_1 for each frame by using a few previous frames and a few subsequent frames. The function takes the value 1 if the magnitude of the velocity is greater than the threshold, else the function assumes the value 0.

When applied to the motion sequence, a feature function produces a binary version of the motion. This document is a matrix of zeros and ones for all features and all frames. This binary sequence is segmented according to the binary values of feature vectors for consecutive frames. Given the feature function $F: \mathcal{R}^{3J} \to \{0, 1\}^f$, two poses m_i, $m_{i+1} \in \mathcal{R}^{3J}$ are F-equivalent if the corresponding feature vectors $F(m_i)$ and $F(m_{i+1})$ are the same. An F-run of motion M is defined as a subsequence of M consisting of consecutive F-equivalent poses. The maximal F-runs are denoted as F-segments of the motion M. Each of these segments corresponds to a unique feature vector. Hence, a document is a sequence of feature vectors referred to as the F-feature sequence of motion M.

To perform similarity checks on the binary motion, information retrieval based on inverted lists is used. Inverted lists are indexing data structures that map from a specific content to its locations in a document. For each feature vector $v \in \{0, 1\}^f$, an inverted list $L(v)$ is constructed. This list consists of all indices $k \in [0, m]$ such that $v = w_k$ in the feature sequence $w = (w_0, w_1, \ldots, w_m)$. An inverted index of a motion database Γ consists of the 2^f inverted lists $L(v)$ for all possible feature vectors v.

3.1 Feature-Based Motion Indexing

The feature-based motion indexing finds only exact matches of a motion. Two motion sequences are considered similar only if they correspond to the same feature sequence according to a given feature function. Formally, given the two feature sequences $w = (w_0, w_1, \ldots, w_m)$ and $v = (v_0, v_1, \ldots, v_n)$, an exact match is associated with an index $k \in [0, m]$ such that v is a subsequence of consecutive feature vectors in w starting at w_k. This exact match is denoted as the expression vkw. The set $H_\Gamma(v)$ of all exact matches in the motion database Γ is defined as $H_\Gamma(v) = \bigcap_{k=0}^{n}(L(v_k) - k)$.

The indexing algorithm initializes the intersection to $L^0 = L(v_0) + 1$. After the initialization, for each $k = 0, \ldots, n\text{-}1$, L^{k+1} is the intersection of L^k and $L(v_{k+1})$ incremented by 1: $L^{k+1} = (L^k \cap L(v_{k+1})) + 1$. Once L^n is found, the value $n+1$ is subtracted from the intersection set to adjust the inverted lists: $H_\Gamma(v) = L^n - (n+1)$.

4 DTW-Based Methods

Dynamic Time Warping finds an optimal warping function to correspond two time series [11]. The algorithm finds the warping function and the matching cost between the two time series. Formally, consider two sequences $(a_1, a_2, ..., a_n)$ and $(b_1, b_2, ..., b_m)$ of different length: $n \neq m$. The algorithm first finds the distances d_{ij} between all pairs (a_i, b_j) of elements in the two sequences. The matching cost matrix C is found by dynamic programming using the optimization criterion $c_{ij} = d_{ij} + \min(c_{i-1, j-1}, c_{i, j-1}, c_{i-1, j})$, where c_{ij} is the minimal cost between the subsequences $(a_1, a_2, ..., a_i)$ and $(b_1, b_2, ..., b_j)$. A warping function is obtained by finding the path in the matching cost matrix from the element c_{11} to element c_{nm} consisting of those elements c_{ij} which have contributed to the distance in c_{nm}.

We implemented two different distances for motion indexing based on DTW. The first distance function considers joint positions represented as a 3D point cloud. The second distance function considers joint rotations described as quaternions.

4.1 3D Point Cloud Based Distance

Each frame of a motion sequence may be represented as a cloud of 3D points where each point corresponds to a joint in the skeleton. The distance between two poses $\Gamma(i), \Gamma(j) \in \Re^{3J}$ is defined as

$$C^{3D}(\Gamma(i), \Gamma(j)) = \min_{\theta, x, z} \left(\sum_{k=1}^{J(2\rho+1)} w_k \| p_k - T_{\theta, x, z}(p_k') \| \right),$$

where ρ is the number of preceding and subsequent frames in the motion window used to compute the distance, $T_{\theta, x, z}$ is the transformation that rotates all 3D points about the y-axis by an angle θ and translates the resulting points by a vector $(x, 0, z)$, w_k is the weight associated with the 3D point p_k in the cloud corresponding to pose $\Gamma(i)$. In our experiments, the ρ is 12 and the weights w_k are all set to 1.0.

4.2 Quaternion Based Distance

If two poses are represented by joint rotations in terms of quaternions, the distance between two poses uses the inner product between single quaternions:

$$C^{Quat}(\Gamma(i), \Gamma(j)) = \sum_{b \in B} w_b * 2/\pi * \arccos|q_b \bullet q_b'|,$$

where $|q_b \bullet q_b'|$ is the absolute value of the inner product of quaternions q_b and q'_b, w_b is the weight associated with joint b, and B is the set of joints in the skeleton.

5 Evaluation and Comparison

The five motion indexing methods are implemented following closely the description of the original work. Any algorithm parameter is set to the value indicated by the respective authors as the most appropriate value according to their own design and experiments. Hence, we avoid experiments where these parameters vary in order to closely reproduce and quantitatively evaluate their original results.

To evaluate the accuracy of the five indexing methods, each method is tested on a data set of 150 motion sequences with a number of query motions. The motions were obtained from the CMU Motion Capture Database [13] and manually segmented to contain a single action per motion file. The segmented motion files contain motion performed by 43 different subjects and the files range from 200 frames (1.67 sec) to 5,400 frames (45 sec). Each query is performed on the whole dataset of 150 motions to find the matching motions among them. Manually annotated data for the 150 motion sequences was prepared. The annotation is helpful in comparing the result of the query on the test data set with the ground truth. The motion files are manually annotated with a label for the correct action being performed. Therefore, when an algorithm retrieves a particular motion file as a possible match for a query motion, we use this label to decide whether the retrieved motion is a correct match (i.e., the retrieved motion has the same label of the query motion).

The dataset of 150 motions contains various actions covering a large range of human activities. We selected a subset of query actions that cover a substantial part of the entire dataset. The selected motion queries are walk, jump, punch, sit, and pick up the box actions. Each of the five query actions corresponds to a number of actual queries (at least 10 query instances per query action) using motion files which are not in the 150-motion dataset. The dataset has 113 motions similar to at least one of the query actions, which represents more than 75% of the database. Among these 113 actions, there are 40 walk actions, 35 jump actions, 15 sit actions, 13 punch actions, and 10 pick up actions. The remaining 37 motions are different from all queries. Since the number of instances of each different motion in this remaining set of 37 motions is very little, these motions are not suitable as query motions (because the number of true positives is insignificant compared to the number of true negatives). However, these actions were kept in the overall dataset to provide diversity and true negatives for all queries. Each query motion has multiple correct matches in the dataset of 150 motions and, consequently, the retrieval of the sole best match is not appropriate. The goal of a motion indexing algorithm is to retrieve all correct matches.

For each query, the techniques are quantitatively evaluated according to the ratio of false positives and false negatives. The false positives ratio is the number of positive matches which do not correspond to a positive match in the manually annotated data divided by the total number of true positive matches. The false negatives ratio is the number of negative matches which do not correspond to negative matches in the manually annotated data divided by the total number of true negative matches.

The first PCA-based technique, PCA-SVD, segments the motion and then finds matching segments for the given motion. The results reveal that the number of false negatives is low (see Fig. 1a). On the other hand, the technique identifies many false positives (see Fig. 1b). The improper motion segmentation (inaccurate start and end boundary points) deteriorates the indexing accuracy.

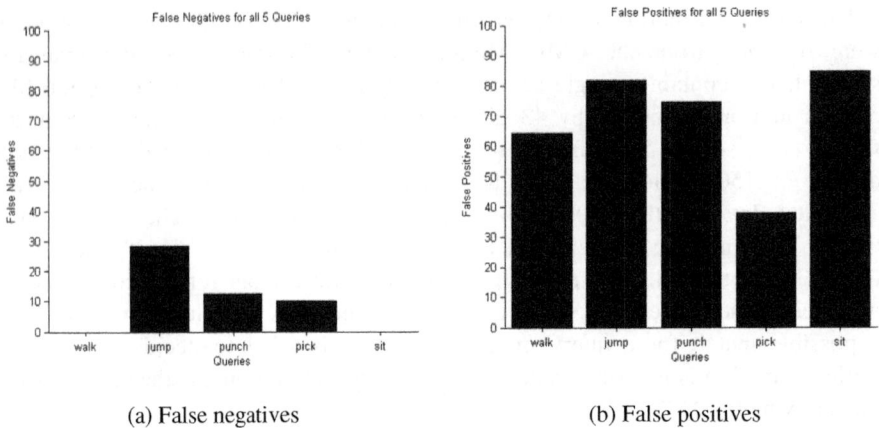

Fig. 1. Results for all 5 query motions on 150 motions for the PCA-SVD technique

The experimental results for the second PCA-based technique, PPCA, are also unsatisfactory. The number of false negatives is again reasonably low (see Fig. 2a). However, the segmentation creates a number of false segments. These small and false segments are responsible for a large number of false positives (see Fig. 2b).

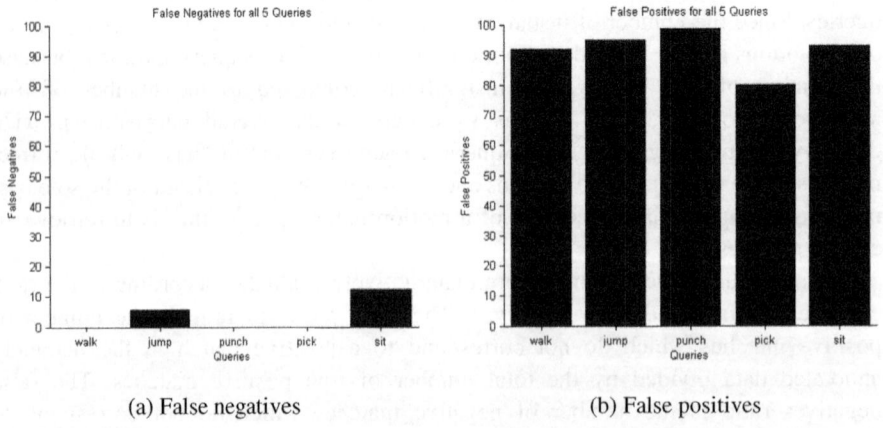

Fig. 2. Results for all 5 query motions on 150 motions for the PPCA technique

The feature-based technique finds only exact matches for each query sequence. The results are accurate but are constrained by the fact that the binary sequence of the query and the motion should be exactly the same. That reduces the number of matches and results in a large number of false negatives (see Fig. 3a). The number of false positives is also very low (see Fig. 3b).

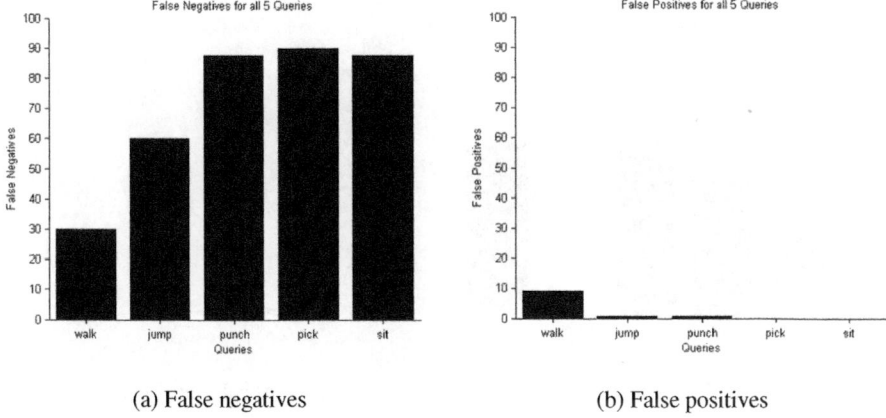

Fig. 3. Results for all 5 query motions on 150 motions for the feature-based technique

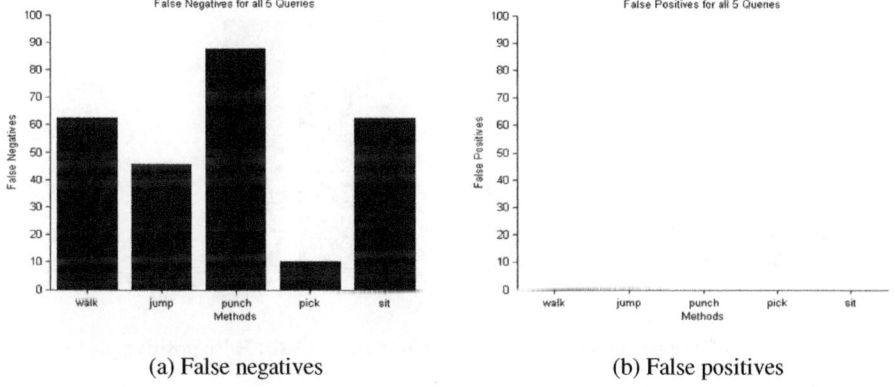

Fig. 4. Results for all 5 query motions on 150 motions for the DTW-Quat technique

Dynamic time warping finds the matching between the two motions based on the minimum cost warping function. DTW matching is affected by pattern differences in the motions. For example, if the query is an action describing a jump and the dataset motion is a hop, then DTW indexing algorithm will return a mismatch. Similarly, a fast walk or a walk with swinging arms gives a low matching score when compared to a normal walk. Hence, there are a large number of false negatives detected by the DTW-Quaternion technique (see Fig. 4a). The quaternion-based distance between two poses increases even if a small number of joints mismatch. The noticeable feature of this technique is that the number of false positives is zero because a very small difference in joint configurations is required for a match (see Fig. 4b).

Similar to the quaternion-based method, Dynamic Time Warping using 3D points performs better than PCA-based and feature-based techniques. The false negatives are few for all queries compared to the quaternion-based method because the latter is very

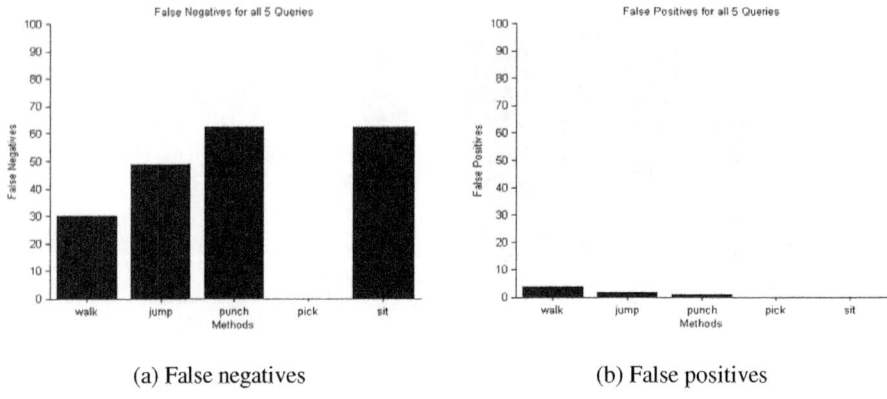

Fig. 5. Results for all 5 query motions on 150 motions for the DTW-3D technique

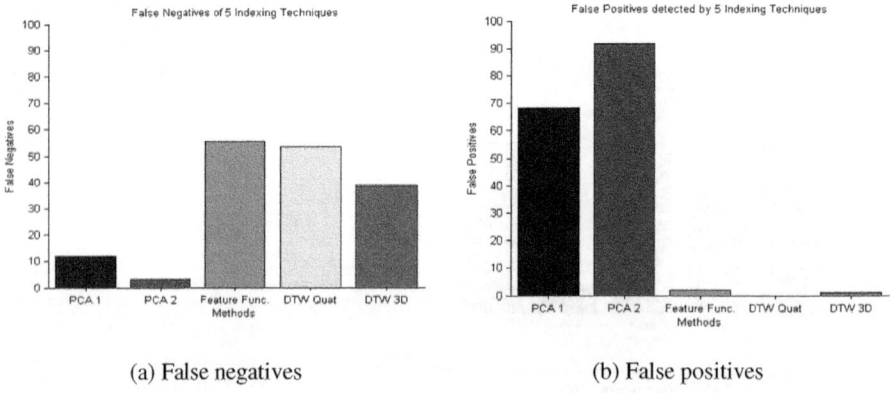

Fig. 6. Results for all 5 query motions on 150 motions for all techniques

sensitive to small differences in joint configurations (see Fig. 5a). For example, the pick up the box query gives 0% false negatives since all pick up box motions have the same absolute orientation and position. The number of false positives is also less than quaternion-based false positives (see Fig. 5b).

6 Conclusions

The two PCA-based techniques have the lowest number of false negatives but, at the same time, they have a large number of false positives (close to 90%). This shows that these two techniques incorrectly classify non-matches as matches very often. The feature-based and DTW quaternion-based techniques perform better than the PCA-based techniques. They have almost similar results with DTW-Quat performing a little better. DTW-3D has the best performance among all the techniques. Although the DTW-3D technique has a small number of false positives, the false negatives are also very few. Several methods of motion indexing were implemented and compared. Dynamic Time Warping 3D-based technique was found to perform the best among all techniques when compared by false positives and false negatives metrics.

We presented the first quantitative comparison between different motion indexing techniques. These techniques were selected from a small survey of representative motion indexing techniques. The PCA-based techniques, originally designed to solve the motion segmentation problem, was adapter to address the motion indexing problem in this paper. Our experimental results show the superior indexing accuracy of a DTW approach using 3D point clouds as motion representation. Although these results are not surprising, they are far from obvious.

Our evaluation of each method used a motion dataset with 150 actions and a large number of queries expanding a subset of 5 different actions which compose 75% of the dataset. This setup allowed a significant test of all techniques considering a large and diverse set of 150 actions.

References

1. Agrawal, R., Faloutsos, C., Swami, A.: Efficient similarity search in sequence databases. In: Int. Conf. on Foundations of Data Organization and Algorithms, pp. 69–84 (1993)
2. Arikan, O., Forsyth, D., O'Brien, J.: Motion synthesis from annotations. ACM Transactions on Graphics 22(3), 402–408 (2003)
3. Barbic, J., Safonova, A., Pan, J., Faloutsos, C., Hodgins, J., Pollard, N.: Segmenting motion capture data into distinct behaviors. In: Graphics Interface, pp. 185–194 (2004)
4. Chakrabarti, K., Keogh, E., Mehrotra, S., Pazzani, M.: Locally adaptive dimensionality reduction for indexing large time series databases. ACM Transactions on Database Systems 27(2), 188–228 (2002)
5. Chan, K., Fu, W.: Efficient time series matching by wavelets. In: IEEE Int. Conf. on Data Engineering, pp. 126–133 (1999)
6. Faloutsos, C., Ranganathan, M., Manopoulos, Y.: Fast subsequence matching in time-series databases. In: ACM SIGMOD Int. Conf. on Management of Data, pp. 419–429 (1994)
7. Fu, A., Keogh, E., Lau, L., Ratanamahatana, C., Wong, R.: Scaling and time warping in time series querying. The VLDB Journal 17(4), 899–921 (2008)
8. Guttman, A.: R-trees: A dynamic index structure for spatial searching. In: ACM SIGMOD Int. Conf. on Management of Data, pp. 47–57 (1984)
9. Kovar, L., Gleicher, M.: Automated extraction and parameterization of motions in large data sets. ACM Transactions on Graphics 23(3), 559–568 (2004)
10. Muller, M., Rader, T., Clausen, M.: Efficient content-based retrieval of motion capture data. ACM Transactions on Graphics 24(3), 677–685 (2005)
11. Muller, M.: Information Retrieval for Music and Motion. Springer, Heidelberg (2007)
12. Vlachos, M., Hadjieleftheriou, M., Gunopulos, D., Keogh, E.: Indexing multi-dimensional time-series with support for multiple distance measures. In: ACM SIGKDD Int. Conf. on Knowledge Discovery and Data mining, pp. 216–225 (2003)
13. CMU Motion Capture Database, http://mocap.cs.cmu.edu/

Detecting 3D Position and Orientation of a Wii Remote Using Webcams

Jerry van den Heuvel and Jacco Bikker

NHTV - University of Applied Sciences, Breda, The Netherlands
mail@jerhill.com, bikker.j@nhtv.nl

Abstract. In this paper we present a method to detect the three dimensional position and orientation of a Wii Remote with one or more emissive spheres attached to it, providing an input device that has six degrees of freedom. Unlike other systems, our system can focus in different directions surrounding the user, with a high precision, and at a low cost. We describe the way object-, motion- and orientation tracking is done, as well as the applicability of the final product. We further describe how to improve the noisy data that is retrieved from the sensors of the Wii Remote, how to smooth detected positions, and how to extrapolate position and orientation.

Keywords: Wii-Remote, PlayStation-Move, Webcam, Triangulation, Object Tracking, Position, Orientation.

1 Introduction

Interactive entertainment systems where the player's actual body is used as primary input to interact with games, like Nintendo's Wii with the Wiimote, Sony's PlayStation3 with the Move and recently Microsoft's Xbox360 with the Kinect, received considerable attention [12]. All these systems require the player to face one direction: towards the screen where the game is displayed on. For environments where the player needs to be able to look in different directions, e.g. a setup where the player is surrounded by multiple screens, these systems do not suffice. The Wii Remote for example needs the sensor bar to determine its absolute position and orientation [32]. The PlayStation Move is only able to keep track of its exact position if it is visible to the Playstation Eye [26].

In this paper, we present a system that is able to determine the transformation, i.e. the orientation and position of a user input device, with six degrees of freedom, in a CAVE-like environment [29]. To reduce the cost of the system, we use a combination off-the-shelf hardware. A Nintendo Wiimote (extended with the MotionPlus sensor) is used to determine yaw, pitch and roll of the device. Two light orbs from the Playstation Move controller are used together with a number of low-cost cameras to increase the accuracy of the yaw and pitch, and to determine the position of the input device. Using four cameras, the player can face in any direction inside a cubical room.

We describe how the data from the various sensors and the cameras is combined in a filtered and stable final transformation that can be used to control Virtual Reality and Augmented Reality applications.

2 Previous Work

Determining the orientation and position of an input device is not new. In his seminal 1968 paper, Sutherland describes both mechanical and ultrasonic (carrier phase) head-tracking systems [28].

Later, Raab et al. proposed a three-axis input device based on quasi-static magnetic-dipole fields [23], which was originally invented by Kuipers [17]. More recently, this technique was refined by Paperno et al. [22], who use a rotating magnetic dipole to determine azimuth, elevation and distance from the source to a sensor.

In terms of low-cost tracking of an input device in the context of a CAVE environment, Sharlin et al. propose a wireless feet tracker that can be assembled for under $200 US, and achieves an accuracy of 10cm at 20Hz [27]. This approach does not detect precise movement, nor does it determine orientation.

Foxlin et al. describe a tracking system based on an inertial navigation system aided by ultrasonic time-of-flight range measurements to a constellation of wireless transponder beacons [8]. They report accuracies better than 2mm. This was further improved to 1mm accuracy for in-cockpit augmented reality by Foxlin et al. [9], and is commercially available from InterSense [14].

Commercial optical solutions are available from several companies, e.g. the FlashPoint system by Image Guided Technologies [13], the laserBIRD2 system by Ascension technology [1], and the CODA Motion Capture System by B&L Engineering [3].

Digital cameras are used in motion-capture systems such as the HiRes 3D Motion Capture System by the Motion Analysis Corporation [15; 21] to track a relatively large number of targets, albeit at a relatively low rate because of the need for 2-D image processing.

In the context of object tracking in 2D images, many approaches have been described. For our system, we use the approach of Derhgawen [6], who describes color based object tracking using thresholds to remove redundant colors from the image.

The use of Wii Remotes for a 3D user interface has been previously described by Wingrave et al. [32], who describe how the Wii Remote can be used as a "spatially convenient device". They describe in detail how to determine the orientation and position of the Wii Remote and its applications.

3 In Theory

In this section, we describe how position and orientation is determined using the sensors in the Wii Remote and the Playstation Move system.

3.1 The Wii Remote and the Wii MotionPlus

The Wii Remote itself contains one internal motion sensor: an accelerometer, which reports acceleration in the device's x, y, and z directions, expressed in the unit of gravity g. The sensor bar, included with the Wii, is a box containing five IR-LEDs on each side (see Figure 1).

The Wii Remote detects up to four IR blobs [24], produced by any IR emitting source, using an infrared optical camera [5]. It then converts the tracked light blobs into 2D positions, along with their size in pixels, and sends this data to the Wii using a Bluetooth connection [32; 11].

The Wii MotionPlus is an extension for the Wii Remote and contains a gyroscope which detects the angular velocity about its x, y and z axis [32].

Combined, the data from these sensors is used to calculate the Wii Remote's precise position and orientation. Each individual Wii Remote collects its own data, which makes it possible to distinguish between different Wii Remotes.

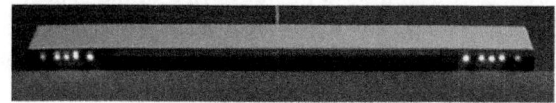

Fig. 1. Wii's sensor bar

Determining Position

When the Wii Remote is pointed at the sensor bar, the Wii Remote picks up two points, $P_L = (x_L, y_L)$ and $P_R = (x_R, y_R)$ from the LED arrays, using the relative sizes of the points on the optical sensor's image. The distance d from the Wii Remote to the sensor bar can be found by calculating the distance corresponding to the left and right points on the optical sensor's image (see Equation 1, where $diam_{LED}$ is the diameter of the actual LED marker from the sensor bar, $diam_{L,R}$ is the diameters of the points in the optical sensor's image, θ is the optical sensor's viewing angle, m is the distance between the LEDs on the right and left side of the sensor bar and w_{img} is the width of the image taken from the optical sensor).

$$d = \sqrt{d_L^2 + (m/2) - 2d_L(m/2)^2 cos(\phi)} \tag{1}$$

$$d_L = \frac{w_L/2}{\tan(\theta/2)}$$

$$d_R = \frac{w_R/2}{\tan(\theta/2)}$$

$$cos(\phi) = \frac{d_L^2 m^2 - 2d_R^2}{2md_L}$$

$$w_L = \frac{w_{img} \cdot diam_{LED}}{diam_L}$$

$$w_R = \frac{w_{img} \cdot diam_{LED}}{diam_R}$$

Determining Orientation

The same points the Wii Remote used to detect its position ($PL = (x_L, y_L)$ and $PR = (x_R, y_R)$ - IR blobs produced by the sensor bar) can be used to calculate theWii Remote's rotation about its y-axis relative to its neutral orientation where $z+$ is facing upwards. This rotation (*roll*) is calculated with respect to the Wii Remote's x-axis (Equation 2).

$$roll = \arccos\left(\vec{x} \cdot \frac{\vec{v}}{\|\vec{v}\|}\right) \qquad (2)$$
$$\vec{x} = (1,0)$$
$$\vec{v} = P_L - P_R$$

The accelerometer reports acceleration in the device's x, y, and z dimensions, expressed in the unit of gravity g. This reported acceleration vector is composed of the Wii Remote's actual acceleration a' and the Earth's gravity g, so obtaining the actual acceleration requires subtracting the gravity vector from the Wii Remote's reported acceleration a. Additionally, g is always oriented towards the Earth, so it is used to find a part of the Wii Remote's orientation (Equations 3 and 4).

$$pitch = \arccos\left(a_{gz}/a_{gy}\right) \qquad (3)$$

$$roll = \arccos\left(a_{gz}/a_{gx}\right) \qquad (4)$$

The accelerometers alone are not sufficient for calculating the yaw because the gravity vector aligns with the z-axis, meaning that it cannot be measured when theWii Remote rotates about its z-axis. Apart from that, the orientation can only be measured when there is no acceleration.

It is possible to combine the data retrieved from the gyroscopes of the Wii MotionPlus with the data retrieved from the accelerometer of the Wii Remote itself. This data however is noisy and needs to be filtered before it is useful.

In the context of VR/AR, the Kalman filter [16] is commonly used to reduce noise in the input signals [2; 18; 30; 31]. The Kalman filter is a set of mathematical equations that recursively estimate the state and error covariance of a signal, while minimizing the mean of the squared error covariance. We use the Kalman filter to reduce the noise of both sensors so the data of the gyroscopes can be merged with the data of the accelerometers. The absolute values of the accelerometer are used to get an estimate of the current orientation, and the relative values of the gyroscopes are used to improve this data and predict the orientation when there is acceleration.

3.2 PlayStation Move

The PlayStation Move motion controller contains three internal motion sensors: an accelerometer, a gyroscope and a terrestrial magnetic field sensor [11]. The terrestrial magnetic field sensor, also called magnetometer, resembles a compass and improves the detection of the device's motion and orientation. An external device called the PlayStation Eye, a 60 to 120Hz camera used to track the colored ball on top of the PlayStation Move, is needed to calculate the position of the device. The colored ball is also used to distinguish between different PlayStation Moves. Like theWii Remote, the PlayStation Move sends data via Bluetooth. At the time of writing, this data cannot be used on the PC.

Determining Position
The accelerometer and gyroscope of the PlayStation Move motion controller are used to get the relative position of the device. The PlayStation3, the PlayStation Eye and

the data received from the sensors are used to detect the precise movement and absolute position in 3D space of the PlayStation Move [26; 19]. The PlayStation Eye is used to track the glowing ball on top of the PlayStation Move where the position and the size of the ball, in camera space, are used to calculate the x, y and z position [20], with a precision of 1 millimeter in the x-axis and y-axis and a precision of 2 centimeters in the z-axis [19]. Detailed information about tracking algorithms and calculations has not been published by Sony, and so far, this information has not been reverse engineered.

Determining Orientation

As for the position, nothing is revealed yet. It is likely however that the data received from the motion sensors is used for this. The camera will not be able to tell the orientation of the glowing ball. Presumably, the magnetometer is used to determine the yaw of the device. The gyroscopes and accelerometer are more precise and accurate than the ones from the Wii Remote, and most probably used to calculate the pitch and roll.

3.3 Discussion

An important difference between the Wii Remote combined with MotionPlus and the PlayStation Move is the terrestrial magnetic field sensor which can be found in the PlayStation Move but is absent in the Wii Remote, with or without extension. This sensor is of great importance when determining the device's orientation, as it determines the absolute yaw of the device. Another difference is the fact that the Wii Remote is able to detect the position data itself while the PlayStation Move requires an external camera for this.

The Wii Remote currently is the best fit for our requirements: it is affordable and widely available, it is able to detect motion that can be used to deduct orientation and position and it provides convenient user input through buttons. Most important however is the fact that it is possible to connect the Wii Remote to any PC via Bluetooth. In theory, the PlayStation Move would be a better fit: it has the same capability and more accurate sensors to detect its motion and orientation. However, unfortunately there is no possibility to communicate with a PC, so it's not possible to control or receive data from this device.

To detect an object's position with six degrees of freedom, the above described methods are not enough. The Wii's method requires the user to point the Wii Remote at the sensor bar to be able to detect its position. The PlayStation Move on the other hand does not really need to be pointed at the PlayStation Eye, but the glowing ball needs to be visible to be able to track it. It thus still requires the user to keep the device in front of the camera. Combining both methods makes it possible to track an object from different angles. Using the PlayStation Move method to detect a colored object, in combination with theWii method of using triangulation to calculate the Wii Remote's position, creates new possibilities to determine the position of an object.

To detect the orientation of the object, the formulas provided earlier can be used (see Equations 2, 3 and 4). In case the calculated yaw will not be accurate enough it is considered to detect a second object's position that, together with the first object's position, can be used to determine the final yaw.

4 Implementation

In this section, we describe how our system determines the transform of the input device, which consists of a position and orientation. The position can be calculated using object tracking and triangulation. The orientation can be determined using the data from the sensors inside the Wiimote and object tracking. Our system performs object tracking using color based detection. The delay that is caused by object detection is reduced by using prediction.

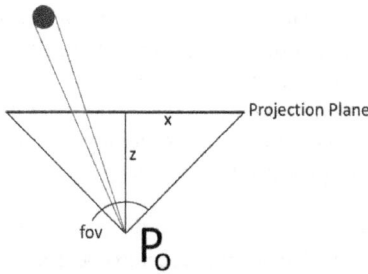

Fig. 2. Projection Explanation

4.1 Determining Position Using Triangulation

Using multiple cameras and triangulation allows us to detect the position of a single object.

To obtain a 3D position based on 2D images captured by the cameras, a minimum of two projected 2D positions is required. If only one camera is able to see the object, we can still approximate its position by calculating the distance from the sphere to the camera. Similar to the Playstation Move system, this distance can be determined using the size of the object. The actual size of the object relative to its size in the captured 2D image combined with the field of view allow us to estimate the distance of the object to the camera. However, when only a certain part of the object is visible, the smaller size on the captured image leads to a overestimation of the distance.

When the 2D position is found, a Z value is added to define the 3D position in camera space, where Z is the distance from a virtual point P_O to the plane the image is projected on (see Figure 2). The virtual point is calculated using the field of view of the webcam.

The 3D position is then used to construct a ray from the virtual point through this point. Once rays have been constructed and converted to world space, they are intersected, which yields a single position in world space, which is the position of the object.

4.2 Determining Orientation

Accelerometer

Values retrieved from the accelerometer are absolute acceleration values based on the gravitational force and can be converted to roll and pitch values ranging from -90 to 90 degrees (in the C++ libraries used to communicate with the Wii Remote [25]).

These values contain considerable noise. To use these values optimally, they need to be in a range of 360 degrees instead of 180, and the noise needs to be filtered to be usable.

Gyroscopes

The gyroscopes detect a relative angular velocity over all three axes. The values retrieved from this sensors are slightly inaccurate and contain some noise as well. This problem is reduced by careful calibration. To calibrate the gyroscopes, the Wii Remote needs to be hold still while the motion data gets recorded. The recorded values can then be used to estimate noise in motion measurements, which can be subtracted from subsequent detected motion values to even out the imprecision.

Another potential problem is the time dependence of velocity measurements. If the measured data is used by independent devices, these devices need to agree on time. When the application is running on a PC, this is not trivial to do. Apart from this, we need to take latency into consideration. This latency is caused by the actual data transfer, and the time required to process the data.

Combining Sensor Data

To combine the data retrieved from the accelerometers with the data retrieved from the gyroscopes, we use the Kalman Filter [16].

The data of the accelerometers is used to create an acceleration vector. This vector holds the pitch and roll of the device. As this only works when the device is not accelerating, the data of the gyroscopes is used to create a second direction vector for orientation of the device. This vector is calculated using the estimated orientation of the previous frame and the currently measured speed. The two vectors are used to determine the final orientation vector for the current frame, by combining them using a fixed factor, based on the reliability of the gyroscopes.

Adding a Second Light Orb

To improve on the relative orientation data a second glowing ball (*light-orb*) with a different color is added, to retrieve an absolute orientation. Both light-orbs are tracked by the cameras, determining their positions. These positions are then used to calculate a directional vector. From this directional vector a pitch and yaw angle is derived. For the roll the absolute, filtered value retrieved from the accelerometer is used, corrected by the gyroscopes.

4.3 Combining Position and Orientation

Smoothing Position

The accuracy of the detection of objects in images captured by the cameras is affected by the noise in the captured camera images. The noise results in inaccurate size estimates for the blobs, and this in turn affects the 2D position as well as the final 3D position. The user perceives this as random movements, even when the object is not moving.

To reduce these random movements, damping is applied to the detected 3D position. For damping, we use Equation 5. In this equation, P is the estimated position, Pprev is the previous position, Plast is the last known position and d is the damping factor. A small factor results in less damping, and an estimated position that is closer to the new position. A larger factor results in more damping, which causes the estimated position to be closer to the old position.

$$P = P_{prev} \times d + P_{last} \times (1-d) \qquad (5)$$

The damping factor is based on relative movement. If the movement is small, a lot of damping will be applied but when the movement is large, the damping factor will be small so only a little damping is applied. This results in smooth movement when the relative movement is small, while it is still possible to make fast movements without having a delay in the result, which would have been the case if a static damp factor was used.

By applying this smoothing to both light orbs, the orientation calculated using these is also smoother.

4.4 Object Tracking

To find an object in three dimensions using one or more cameras, the object must be detected in the captured 2D images. To be able to find an object, it needs to be recognizable and obvious, which explains the choice in the PlayStation Move system for an emissive colored ball. The ball shape is easily recongnized, as it is orientation independent. To make it detectable under most lighting conditions, the ball is made emissive and is able to change color. This way, the color of the ball can be chosen to contrast with the colors in the environment, which further improves detection [7].

Color-Based Object Detection

The easiest way to recognize an object in an image is by looking for its color, so it is best to have an object consisting of one solid color. Ideally, this color does not occur in the image, apart from the object that is to be detected. Different lighting should cause the object to change color. For this purpose, we created a custom version of the light orb, where we attach the glowing ball from the PlayStation Move to a Wiimote.

Camera Settings

Camera settings affect the precision of the color detection. Optimal settings reduce the need to filter. In Figure 3, it is clearly visible that the webcam filters out most of the unwanted environment.

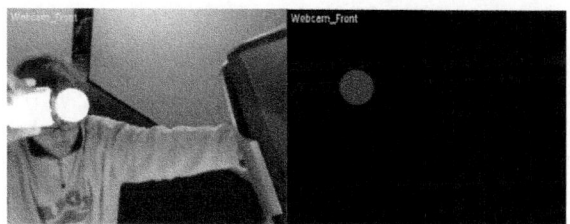

Fig. 3. Camera Settings – Left: Default, Right: Low Exposure

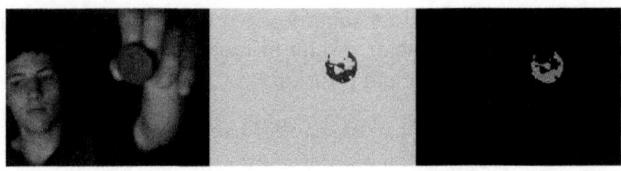

Fig. 4. Detecting a color in an image. Left: original; center: filtered color; right: color mask.

For color detection, we essentially filter out every other color in the image, until the only color that is left is the object color. This results in an image containing blobs where the colors matched (see Figure 4).

Nearby blobs are then combined. The result is used to determine the size and position of potential objects. Ideally, there should be only one object, which is generally the case if the color was picked well and the camera settings are correct. If we do however find more than a single object, we chose the largest blob.

Prediction

The rate at which the webcams provide images is independent from the update speed of the motion tracking system. When the system is updating at a higher high frame than the cameras, the detected position will lag behind which causes the motion to be delayed and possibly become choppy. In this case, we apply motion prediction to fill up the positions in the frames where there is no detected position available. Prediction is done by using the previous position and orientation combined with velocity to extrapolate position and orientation. Note that velocity is measured independently from the captured images, which allows us to use this quantity even if no images are available.

Velocity and angular velocity can both be retrieved in two ways, if we use the Wii Remote together with the light orbs.

The first option is to deduct them from the retrieved values of the Wii MotionPlus. Alternatively, we can calculate them using data from the previous frame. It is also possible to combine both approaches, which in practice gives the best result.

Our system uses prediction for all frames. This way, whenever a detection is available, the prediction and the detection are combined and averaged, and used as the final result for a frame. The averaging is needed to make the motion smoother, especially when the accuracy of the prediction was low. For frames in which there is no detection available, only the prediction is used.

5 Results

We performed our tests in a cubical area of $352 \times 352 \times 262 cm$ ($l \times w \times h$). In every upper corner a webcam is placed that is focused at the center of the area in horizontal direction and at a height of $125 cm$ from the ground in vertical direction. The range the orb can be detected in ranges from $20 cm$ to $200 cm$ in vertical direction (relative from the ground) and $-80 cm$ to $80 cm$ in horizontal direction (relative to the focus point of the cameras). The precision of the detection is averaged to $0.5 cm$ in any direction. The visible delay is approximately $500 ms$: position detection in our system is smooth, but when moving fast, the delay is clearly visible.

The orientation detection while using only one orb is also smooth, but the yaw tends to go out of sync when making wild movements. Adding a second orb solved this issue. After this modification, angular precision is $0:6deg$.

The total cost of the system is €185,- (see Table 1 for detailed information), excluding the projection screens and beamers.

Table 1. Test setup. Apart from these hardware components, we used 3rd party (C++) libraries to communication with the Wii Remote, for image processing and for multithreading.

Amount	Description	Cost (€)	Total (€)
4	30Hz webcam	15	60
2	Light orb (glowing ball from Playstation Move, and some custom hardware)	46	92
1	Wii Remote + Motion Plus extension	25	25
1	Bluetooth dongle	8	8

6 Conclusion and Future Work

We presented a system that combines Wii Remotes with methods used by the PlayStation Move system to determine the orientation and position in any direction surrounding the player. Our system uses two light emissive objects and a minimum of two webcams. The webcams are used to find the 3D position of the emissive objects.

Using a second emissive object allows us to accurately determine the direction of the device and deduct an absolute yaw and pitch. The Wii Remote allows us to to calculate the roll and determine the final orientation.

To improve the object detection speed, the current webcams could be replaced by webcams having a higher frame rate. This will reduce the number of frames for which we need to rely on prediction, resulting in more accurate and smooth results. Using higher resolution webcams could improve precision as well. This will particularly improve the detection of small movements.

The position and orientation prediction is currently partly done by extrapolation. This can be improved by using smarter algorithms that recognize movements.

For better object tracking the HSV color (instead of RGB) scheme could be used. This will improve the object detection in more challenging lighting conditions.

Acknowledgments. Jimmy van den Heuvel created the light orb (glowing ball tool). We used the WiiYourself!_1.15 [25] library to be able to communicate with the Wii Remote. OpenCV2.1.0 [4] library was used for processing captured images. Nils Deslé created the (multithreaded) job system.

References

1. ASCENSION. laserBIRD2 system (2011), http://www.ascensiontech.com
2. Azuma, R.T.: Predictive tracking for augmented reality. PhD thesis, Chapel Hill, NC, USA. UMI Order No. GAX95-38370 (1995)
3. The CODA system, http://www.bleng.com
4. Bradski, G.: Opencv2.1.0 (2010)
5. Castaneda, K.: Nintendo and pixart team up (2006)

6. Derhgawen, A.: Real-time color based object tracking (2007)
7. Fenlon, W.: How playstation move works (2010)
8. Foxlin, E., Harrington, M., Pfeifer, G.: Constellation: A wide-range wireless motiontracking system for augmented reality and virtual set applications (1998)
9. Foxlin, E., Altshuler, Y., Naimark, L., Harrington, M.: Flighttracker: A novel optical/inertial tracker for cockpit enhanced vision. In: Proceedings of the 3rd IEEE/ACM International Symposium on Mixed and Augmented Reality, ISMAR 2004, pp. 212–221. IEEE Computer Society, Washington, DC (2004)
10. Fraga, E.S.: Symmetric multiprocessing algorithm for conceptual process design (2000)
11. Greenwald, W.: Nintendo wii remote vs playstation move: How do they work? (2010)
12. Hruschack, P.J.: Wiimote vs. move vs. kinect: Comparing control schemes in the three-way battle for motion control (2010)
13. IGT. Flashpoint 5500 system (2011), http://www.imageguided.com
14. INTERSENSE. Intersense corporation (2011), http://www.isense.com
15. Kadaba, M.P., Stine, R.: Real-time movement analysis techniques and concepts for the new millennium in sports medicine (2000), http://www.motionanalysis.com
16. Kalman, R.: A new approach to linear filtering and prediction problems. Transactions of the ASME-Journal of Basic Engineering 82(series D), 35–45 (1960)
17. Kuipers, J.: Object tracking and orientation determination means, system and process. In: U.S. Patent 3 868 565 (1975)
18. Luinge, H.J., Veltink, P.H., Baten, C.T.M.: Estimating orientation with gyroscopes and accelerometers. Technol. Health Care 7, 455–459 (1999)
19. Mikhailov, A.: Playstation move tech interview (2010)
20. Miller, P.: Playstation move: everything you ever wanted to know (2010), http://www.engadget.com/2010/03/11/playstation-moveeverything-you-ever-wanted-to-know
21. MotionAnalysis, Hires 3d motion capture system. MotionAnalysis Corporation (2011)
22. Paperno, E., Sasada, I., Leonovich, E.: A new method for magnetic position and orientation tracking. IEEE Transactions on Magnetics 37, 1938–1940 (2001)
23. Raab, F.H., Blood, E.B., Steiner, T.O., Jones, H.R.: Magnetic position and orientation tracking system. IEEE Transactions on Aerospace and Electronic Systems AES 15, 709–718 (1979)
24. Sathrum, L.R.: Using a nintendo Wii remote to help navigate a robot (2010)
25. Saugnier, N.: WiiYourself! v1.15 (2010)
26. SCE. Playstation®move motion controller for playstation 3. Tech. rep. (2010)
27. Sharlin, E., Figueroa, P., Green, M., Watson, B.: A wireless, inexpensive optical tracker for the CAVE(tm). In: Proceedings of the IEEE Virtual Reality 2000 Conference, VR 2000, pp. 271–278. IEEE Computer Society, Washington, DC (2000)
28. Sutherland, I.E.: A head-mounted three dimensional display. In: Proceedings of the 1968 Fall Joint Computer Conference, vol. 33, pp. 757–764 (1968)
29. Defanti, T.A., Sandin, D.: A 'room' with a 'view'. In: IEEE Spectrum, pp. 30–33 (1993)
30. Welch, G.F.: History: The use of the kalman filter for human motion tracking in virtual reality. Presence: Teleoper. Virtual Environ. 18, 72–91 (2009)
31. Williamson, B.M.: Realnav: Exploring natural user interfaces for locomotion in video games (2010)
32. Wingrave, C.A., Williamson, B., Varcholik, P., Rose, J., Miller, A., Charnonneau, E., Bott, J.: Spatially convenient devices for 3D user interfaces (2010)

Author Index

Ahn, Junghyun 412
Allbeck, Jan M. 132
Amato, Nancy M. 340
André, Elisabeth 15
Arpa, Sami 168

Badler, Norman I. 144, 156
Bando, Yosuke 192
Bee, Nikolaus 15
Ben Shitrit, Horesh 412
Bhatia, Harnish 436
Bída, Michal 278
Bidarra, Rafael 290
Bikker, Jacco 448
Boulic, Ronan 412
Brand, Sandy 290
Brom, Cyril 278
Bulbul, Abdullah 168
Bunlutangtum, Rinchai 204

Cao, Yong 27, 180
Capin, Tolga 168
Casas, Dan 242
Chen, Bing-Yu 192
Chen, Je-Ren 51
Curtis, Sean 400

Damian, Ionut 15
Davison, Richard 63
Demeulemeester, Aljosha 304
Devarajan, Venkat 377
Dong, Zhi 216
Donikian, Stéphane 365

Egges, Arjan 74
Endrass, Birgit 15

Faloutsos, Petros 266, 389
Fua, Pascal 412

Garcia, Francisco M. 144
Geijtenbeek, Thomas 74
Gemrot, Jakub 278
Giovanni, Stevie 227
Gobron, Stéphane 412

Guerra-Filho, Gutemberg 377, 436
Guillemaut, Jean-Yves 242

Hasegawa, Shoichi 86
Hilton, Adrian 242
Hollemeersch, Charles-Frederik 304
Huber, Peter 15

Jones, Matthew 144
Jorgensen, Carl-Johan 353

Kallmann, Marcelo 39, 424
Kanamori, Yoshihiro 192
Kanongchaiyos, Pizzanu 204
Kapadia, Mubbasir 266, 389
Kenwright, Ben 63
Kider Jr., Joseph T. 156
Komura, Taku 110

Lamarche, Fabrice 316, 353
Lambert, Peter 304
Lemercier, Samuel 365
Li, Tsai-Yen 316
Li, Weizi 132
Lin, Ming 400
Liu, C. Karen 1
Liu, Shiqiu 216
Lopez, Thomas 316

Mahmudi, Mentar 39
Manocha, Dinesh 400
Markowitz, Daniel 156
Masaoka, Naoki 120
Mead, Robert 144
Mees, Pieter 304
Metaaphanon, Napaporn 192
Mitake, Hironori 86
Moreau, Mathieu 365
Morgan, Graham 63
Moussaïd, Mehdi 365

Nishita, Tomoyuki 192

Oliva, Ramon 328
Oshita, Masaki 120
Ou, Yuntao 216
Ozgen, Oktar 424

Author Index

Park, Seung In 27
Pelechano, Nuria 328
Peng, Chao 27
Pettré, Julien 365, 412
Pieters, Bart 304
Popelová, Markéta 278

Raca, Mirko 412
Raphael, George 377
Reinman, Glenn 266
Rodriguez, Samuel 340
Rungjiratananon, Witawat 192

Sato, Makoto 86
Shapiro, Ari 98
Shoulson, Alexander 144, 156
Sideris, Costas 389
Silvestre, Quentin 412
Steed, Anthony 51

Tejera, Margara 242
Thalmann, Daniel 412
Theraulaz, Guy 365
Tian, Jie 27
Tomek, Jakub 278

van den Heuvel, Jerry 448
Van de Walle, Rik 304
Vasilescu, Diana 74

Wang, He 110
Wang, Matthew 266

Yin, KangKang 227

Zheng, Yunxin 216
Zordan, Victor B. 1
Zou, Min 254

GPSR Compliance

The European Union's (EU) General Product Safety Regulation (GPSR) is a set of rules that requires consumer products to be safe and our obligations to ensure this.

If you have any concerns about our products, you can contact us on ProductSafety@springernature.com

In case Publisher is established outside the EU, the EU authorized representative is:

Springer Nature Customer Service Center GmbH
Europaplatz 3
69115 Heidelberg, Germany

Batch number: 09478804

Printed by Printforce, the Netherlands